Plight of Jammu and Kashmir

The Unknown Files

Plight of Jammu and Kashmir

The Unknown Files

Justice GD Sharma
(Retd Judge: J&K High Court)

Manas Publications
(We Convert Fighters into Writers)
New Delhi - 110 002 (INDIA)

Manas Publications
(We Convert Fighters into Writers)
(Publishers for Defence, IAS, IPS, IFS, IRS, Judges, Press etc)
4402/5-A, Ansari Road (Opp. HDFC Bank)
Darya Ganj, New Delhi-110 002 (INDIA)
Off.: ☎ **23260783, 23265523, Res. 23842660**
Fax: **011-23272766**
E-mail: **manaspublications@gmail.com**
manaspublications@yahoo.com
website: **www.manaspublications.in**

The author has decided to donate his royalty from the sale of this book to charity.

ISBN: 978-81-7049-500-0
₹ 1495.00

Designed at
Manas Publications

Printed in India at
Printways, Delhi and
published by Mrs Suman Lata for
Manas Publications, 4402/5-A, Ansari Road
(Opp. HDFC Bank)
Darya Ganj, New Delhi-110 002 (INDIA)

Dedicated

in the service of

my parents

Late Pt Ram Saran Sharma

and

Late Smt Ganga Devi Sharma

to the memory of

the victims of militancy who laid down their lives
for the defence of the country and to uphold
the secular credentials of the State of
Jammu and Kashmir

Contents

Preface

The idea of writing this book came about for the simple reason that by a stroke of luck I came across and remained closely associated with thousands of militants of all hues and shades including their mentors both locals, non-locals as well as foreigners for several years. Not only that, I also had the opportunity of going through the contents of confidential records seized by the government showing hidden involvement of some black sheep members of the civil society. Those underground and over ground supporters provided fuel to the ongoing proxy war waged by the militants in order to overthrow the duly established government and substitute it by establishing the so-called 'Nizam-e-Mustafa' (Muslim rule). J&K State was their first achievable object because it has dominant Muslim population. In early 1990s to some extent, they had achieved their target as Hindu and Sikh population had been driven away from the Kashmir Valley including a good number of members of the majority community who openly were found to have opposed either their ideology or movement. The cult of 'Jehad' survived as it got support from some bigoted politicians, bureaucrats, as well as from misguided government employees in large numbers representing every department of the State. My association to deal with the militants and their organizations goes back to the year of 1980 when after promotion as District and Sessions Judge, I was posted as First Additional District and Sessions Judge of Kashmir Division (including Ladakh). That court was also designated as Anti-Corruption Court-cum-Special Court to try the cases of anti-nationals under the Enemy Agents Ordinance of Samvat 2007 (AD 1950).

The very first time I dealt with a sensitive case, it left an indelible scar in my memory. The case related to the trial of the head of a most prominent and deadly militant organization for the commission of offences of murder and dacoity committed in a remote branch of the J&K Bank in the Kashmir Valley. At that time, the question which fell for consideration and determination on the plea raised by the Defence Counsel was regarding the bifurcation of the trial which already had been done by my predecessor as well as lodging the said head of the militant organization in a different jail of the country for security reasons. The defence lawyers had vehemently urged in the application moved before me that he should remain in Central Jail Srinagar along with other accused. After hearing both the sides of the case I passed the order in accordance with law. This order did not go down well with the then Housing Minister and his Deputy Minister who, as it appeared, sympathized with the militant organization. Their annoyance led them to unfairly cancel the allotment of my residential quarter without any notice to me and had it sealed when I was on leave. I protested in writing to the then Chief Minister Sheikh Abdullah as well as the then Acting Chief Justice Mufti Baha-ud-Din Farooqi but my protests fell on deaf ears.

While holding the court proceedings regarding militants' cases in the premises of Central Jail Srinagar, I came to know how anti-national under-trials were given preferential treatment over their counterparts of other cases.

The second memorable experience was while dealing with a ban of an administrative nature imposed upon eight militant organizations in 1990 by the then Hon'ble Governor Shri Jagmohan. After due exercise done by the Central Government on the basis of laid down criteria a scrutiny was done for the selection of the Chairman of newly created Special Tribunal constituted under the J&K Criminal Law Amendment Act of 1983. At that time, I was posted as Principal District and Sessions Judge Jammu and the responsibility fell upon my shoulders to do this national job which had not only national but international ramifications. From the record which had been seized by the intelligence agencies, I came to know how in a wayward and casual manner, the State of J&K was allowed to be governed by Dr Farooq Abdullah as Chief Minister. He had won the elections of 1982 by securing a majority of seats in the name of his political party National Conference by joining hands with Moulvi Farooq—head of a separatist organization of Kashmir Valley. This period provided a breeding ground for upbringing the subdued militancy and raising its ugly head. This rule of Dr Farooq Abdullah ended on March 7, 1986 when his brother-in-law GM Shah succeeded in toppling his government. GM Shah's rule ended on September 6, 1986. Unfortunately, Dr Farooq Abdullah later on entered into an unwritten accord with Congress when Rajiv Gandhi was the Prime Minister of India. Both the parties agreed to share the crumbs of power at the ratio of 60:40. The period of rule ended in 1990 when there was total chaos. As there had remained no opposition in the State Legislature there was no proper check on arbitrary, capricious and whimsical government actions. The notorious elections of 1987 held under the Government of Dr Farooq Abdullah had ignited heart-burning and spirit of revenge amongst some energetic young people who had participated in the Assembly elections but their entries were prevented by resorting to corrupt electoral practices. During this period the State administration had surrendered its remaining authority before the anti-nationals. It was found that the militants had coined a new fundamentalist theory to project Kashmir as a separate nation on the basis of 'Kashmiriat'. The seized record produced before me in the above said Tribunal was of very voluminous nature and it required judicial scrutiny. The heads of the prominent banned organizations had contested the ban affecting their organizations after hiring the services of top ranking local advocates. This was a historical event regarding the militancy which had brought gun culture in the State and I decided that for the knowledge of our progeny as well as for the information of the citizens of the country all these facts should be recorded in a book in a concise manner. At this stage the Quit Kashmir Movement which was started by Sheikh Abdullah in 1946 was also in my mind as the perusal of the seized record had made me wiser. There I had found that Sheikh Abdullah had used the words 'Plebiscite' and 'Jehad'. When Sheikh Abdullah was removed from power in 1953, he had formed 'Plebiscite Front', a political organization which was found to be a secessionist organization and was banned in the early 1970s. This ban had been judicially confirmed by the then Chief Justice of J&K High Court Hon'ble Murtaza Fazal Ali who was appointed Chairman of the Tribunal. That judicial verdict was also in my possession and I wanted to make it public in this book. It is a well-known saying, "History is no blind Goddess as it does not excuse blindness in others." History as has been revealed in this book would make it known to the public at large and they would judge Maharaja Hari Singh more fairly than the contemporary historians have done so far. My book has opened different avenues, different prospects and unfolded many myths. Mostly it contains the objective events besides my subjective satisfaction made on the basis of record.

This was a valuable record upon which I had recorded judicial verdicts and at that time had decided to get those decisions published in the form of a book in a summarized manner at a relevant time to rebut the theory from recorded history of Kashmir that Kashmir was never a separate nation but a part and parcel of the Indian subcontinent from the time immemorial, of course, having their separate culture, way of life, customs etc. This is not a special feature because all the remaining four regions of J&K State, i.e. Jammu,

Ladakh, Baltistan and Gilgit have separate individuality. When this Commission (under J&K Criminal Law Amendment Act of 1983) was wound up in 1992, I was appointed as member of the J&K Special Tribunal which is the highest judicial forum in the State to adjudicate on the decisions in appeals and revisions respectively rendered by revenue courts, local self-bodies created under civic laws and co-operative bodies etc, with additional duties as a senior member of the J&K State Advisory Board under the Chairmanship of late Justice IK Kotwal. The Board is a statutory judicial forum created under the J&K Public Safety Act. There, I got the opportunity of interacting directly with thousands of militants and acquired the knowledge as to how their impressionable minds had been polluted to perpetuate crimes against humanity by their mentors. Ninety per cent militants were found between the age limit ranging from teens, twenties, thirties and hardly a few were above the age of forty. My association with this Advisory Board continued up to 1995 when I was elevated as Judge of the J&K High Court. Thereafter, till my retirement in 2001, I remained mostly in Srinagar wing of the High Court and almost all the militancy related cases including habeas corpus petitions were usually listed in my assigned cause list.

In Kashmir Valley, I received maximum cooperation from the members of the Bar Association of Srinagar and they were always satisfied with my judicial work and conduct. Even after my retirement I had been visiting Srinagar Bar Association's office whenever there was an opportunity. I was showered warmth, love and affection and the same warm hospitality was extended to me while working as Chairman of the J&K Consumer Redressal Commission.

As a judge, I have personally dealt with cases of subversive nature, so some samples of judgments in a summary manner have been incorporated in this book. I have also tried to unfold how there is persistent discrimination with residents of Jammu and Ladakh regions in matters of employment, in allocation of funds meant for development annually received from the Central government. Constant endeavours to change the demographic composition of Jammu region are being made and lakhs of kanals of forest land and State land have been occupied mostly by the members belonging to the majority community in an organised but unauthorized manner. This game plan has been dealt with elaborately in this book. The causes of rampant spread of corruption have also been exposed. More importantly, political discrimination in the right of voting for the inhabitants of Jammu region has been dealt with in a detailed manner. It bleeds the heart of every patriotic Indian who believes in the doctrine of equality before law and no discrimination on the basis of religion, caste, place of birth and sex. Indian Constitution guarantees right to live in an honourable and dignified manner. The main cause for the spread of militancy is unbelievable incompetence, widespread corruption and passive connivance of State actors. The administrative machinery stood hijacked by the subversionists and their collaborators. Majority of the officials were active or passive supporters of those elements and the others were mortally afraid. Public interest in general and national interest in particular demand the publication of this book.

Mostly, I have recorded the facts in this book from my own experience and knowledge while dealing with militancy related cases and militants in large numbers in the capacity as a judge. The rest of the assertions have mostly been verified on the basis of references made from the books of different authors of eminence and few amongst them are Shri Jagmohan (hon'ble former Governor of J&K State and former Cabinet Minister of NDA Government). Dr Karan Singh has reproduced many of his experiences in his autobiography while discharging the duties as Regent of the State, as elected Head of the State (Sadar-i-Riyasat) and first-time Governor of the State. His period as head of the State related to the most difficult and turbulent history of the State. A topic regarding accession made by Maharaja Hari Singh dealt in its true perspective by Shri Prem Shankar Jha in his book *The Origins of a Dispute: Kashmir 1947* have also been referred to support my contention that Maharaja was not solely responsible for the creation of Kashmir dispute. Last but least I have also referred official communications by the last Prime Minister of the State Shri Mehr Chand Mahajan in his book *Looking Back*.

With my long judicial experience, ranging from 1965 up to 1980 as a Judicial Officer at the lower level of judiciary and from 1980 to mid-1995 as a member of the higher judicial service as District and Sessions Judge's cadre, I mostly remained posted in important districts of the State up to 1990 and thereafter as Chairman and member of different judicial tribunals. From 1995 up to 2001 as Judge of J&K High Court, I mostly remained in Kashmir wing of the High Court. Lastly, for 5 years period from 2006 to 2011 as President of the J&K Consumer Redressal Commission. I had ample opportunities to acquire sufficient knowledge regarding understanding mind-set. This I could do because I understand, speak to some extent, all the major dialects spoken in the State as well as Constitutionally recognized languages such as Dogri, Kashmiri, Urdu, Hindi, Punjabi, Gujarati and Sanskrit. With this gift of the gab I had a personal rapport with litigants, members of the legal fraternity as well as militants. I tried to rebuild on rickety and moth-eaten foundations of the supremacy of the rule of law to the possible limits with my limited intellect. During the heyday of militancy from 1990 to 1996 and thereafter with diminished effects, the administration of justice up to the districts level in the valley had come to a grinding halt giving way to the militants to establish Islamic Courts in the rural areas. They had chosen some of their ideologues from the members of the bar and religious clerics to man those courts where death sentences were awarded within hours according to their wishes. Decisions were given in matrimonial matters, civil and revenue disputes.

It is regrettable that Jammu and Kashmir problem has been allowed to assume a monstrous form for the humanity in the subcontinent of India and Pakistan. It has consumed lakhs of innocent human lives both civilian and paramilitary forces. The Central Government had been in the knowledge from the year 1952 that the case of a Plebiscite, ignorance, parochialism and religion would be exploited by the Anglo-American block by prompting Sheikh Abdullah. Had Sheikh Abdullah fulfilled the promises given by him to Maharaja Hari Singh and Pandit Jawaharlal Nehru and each of them had worked at tandem there would have been no Jammu and Kashmir problem. Instead of eliminating these forces of exploitation the infirmities in the governance were allowed to multiply and particularly after 1975 because after that period the governance permeated with politics of deception, exploitation, discrimination and corruption was allowed unchecked. We have failed to establish real democracy based on equitable justice and developing the State economically instead of allowing the pocketing of thousands of crores of rupees given by the Central Government by way of aid. This amount has gone in the pockets of a few thousand politicians, their relatives, chosen bureaucrats and their political henchmen.

I have arranged the topics in sequence with the purpose of exposing so-called Kashmir problem which in the real sense is a problem of the State of Jammu and Kashmir and has been erroneously thought to be limited to Kashmir. People of Kashmir region have their main problem of fear psychosis of losing their identity and discrimination by the Centre. The people of Jammu and Ladakh regions have their grievances with the ruling class of Kashmir Valley and Central Government. I may have been critical of few individuals on the basis of facts and truth as there was no other choice. The criticism is not personal. It is a criticism based on the object that the people of all the three regions of the State should get corruption-free efficient government with due equal participation.

G.D. SHARMA

Acknowledgements

I am deeply indebted to former Governors of Jammu and Kashmir State namely, Shri Girish Chandra Saxena, IPS (former Secretary, RAW) and Lt Gen SK Sinha with whom I have remained closely associated to uphold the Rule of Law in the State of Jammu and Kashmir in accordance with the mandates of Indian Constitution and the Constitution of Jammu and Kashmir State. They have all along encouraged me to get published my judicial verdicts in the form of a book. Equally, I am indebted to former Governor Shri Jagmohan who during his second short term as Governor of J&K State in the year 1990 had entrusted me with the most challenging job as a District and Sessions Judge to adjudicate upon the legal vires of the administrative ban at the touchstone of judicial anvil. Also, I am indebted to my friend Shri Arun (Director, J&K Study Centre) who provided me with some valuable records having a bearing on the subjects discussed in this book.

Special thanks are due to the cooperation which has been rendered by my wife Shrimati Kusum Sharma for her encouragement to devote sufficient time to follow my dream of writing this book. I would also like to mention the invaluable help rendered by my son Dr Pallav Sharma who spared sufficient time for typing the manuscript as well as sourced relevant material from internet. All my grandsons too have helped with the typing and I am grateful to them and each one from my loving family for their support and patience.

I would also like to thank Ms Dahlia Sen Oberoi, advocate of Delhi, who helped me in improving the final draft in consonance and in conformity with the provisions of copyrights and patent laws with her specialized knowledge.

At the end, I shall be failing in my duty in case my heartfelt gratitude is not extended to the publisher of this book for waiting patiently for the completion of the manuscript and helping in making my dream a reality.

Justice GD Sharma (Retd)

CHAPTER 1

Territory and Its People

The State is not only a territory of landmass but it is a territory inhabited by people professing different faiths, speaking different languages and dialects. In the 19th century because of historical developments Maharaja Gulab Singh brought this heterogeneous population of three regions—Jammu, Kashmir, Ladakh and frontier areas—under his rule and carved out the biggest State in area in the Indian history which existed at the time of partition. Those frontier areas were Baltistan (as part of Ladakh wazarat) known as Ghanche having its headquarters at Khalplu, area of Skardu having its headquarters at Skardu and the area of Gilgit consisting of Gilgit, Chilas, Diamir, Ghanzar, Astore and Hunza-Nagar. In addition to that, there was another area known as Aksai Chin which was almost uninhabited and situated on the eastern contiguous side of Ladakh district. By the mid-1950s, the Chinese army had entered the north-east portion of Ladakh. By 1956-57, they had completed a motorable road through Aksai Chin area to provide better communication between Xinjiang and western Tibet. India's belated discovery of this road led to border clashes between the two countries that culminated in the Sino-Indian war of October 1962. China has occupied Aksai Chin since 1962. In addition to that, an adjoining region known as the Trans-Karakoram track was ceded by Pakistan to China in 1963.

Kashmir is a province in the State which was added to the State in 1846. Maharaja Culab Singh started his career firstly as a soldier and then because of his Military and Administrative capabilities at a short time became an important General in the Sikh Army of Maharaja Ranjit Singh who is known in the history as 'Lion of Punjab'. From the debris of Maharaja Ranjit Singh's kingdom (after his death) the State which was carved out by Gulab Singh is known as the State of Jammu and Kashmir. When it was being ruled by his (Gulab Singh's) fourth descendant Maharaja Hari Singh (before October 1947) it had the territory of

86,023 sq miles (corresponding to 2,22,236 sq kms). Jammu, Kashmir, Ladakh, Baltistan, Gilgit, Hunza-Nagar, Aksai Chin and other areas as already stated above were the territories which constituted the State. At that time, its population was 40,21,616 which was the lowest in density in India. The territory starts from the plains in the south and ends on the north comprising the low, high altitude valleys and some are the loftiest inhabited hamlets in the world. There are vide variations in its soil, climate, vegetation and inhabitants. The Border of the State touches Pakistan, Tajikistan (erstwhile ceded State of Russia), Afghanistan, Tibet and China. The residents of the State profess different faiths, speak different languages and dialects. The State has a blended culture as they profess Muslim, Hindu, Sikh, Bauddh and Christian faiths. Such a blended culture of the inhabitants has been generally tolerant and free from communal conflict.

Maharaja Hari Singh ascended the throne of J&K State in 1925 and was the reigning monarch at the conclusion of British rule in the sub-continent in 1947. One of the conditions of the partition of India imposed by Britain was that the rulers of Princely States would have the right to opt for either Pakistan or India dominions with some advice. In 1947, J&K population was 77 per cent Muslims and it shared a boundary with the dominion of Pakistan and dominion of India. On 22nd October 1947, tribesmen backed by Pakistani Army invaded Kashmir Valley. The aggression was spearheaded by tribals of the frontier district of Pakistan known as Waziristan. They were aided and guided by Pakistani Army personnel in civil clothes. They targeted the Hindu and Sikh inhabitants of the State who were mercilessly massacred. The survivors had to flee away from their hearths and homes to safer zones in the State and a good number of them crossed over the territory of the State and settled in different parts of India. The refugees belonging to district Muzaffarabad which was a part of the Kashmir Division were not allowed to settle in the same Division because of ulterior motives of Sheikh Mohammed Abdullah who at that time was the Administrator of the Emergency Government and was given free handle by the Union Government headed by Pandit Jawaharlal Nehru (the first Prime Minister) who had personal dislikes against the ruler (Maharaja Hari Singh) and intimate friendship with Sheikh Mohammed Abdullah. Though at that time, Maharaja Hari Singh was the ruler of the State yet his position at the whim of Pandit Nehru was reduced to that of only a nominal figure-head. The people of Jammu province suffered the main brunt of Pakistani aggression because the districts of Mirpur, Poonch and tehsil Rampur alias Rajouri of erstwhile district Reasi and now made a district and exclusively renamed as district Rajouri, were virtually run over and destroyed. The territory of the frontier district consisting of Baltistan, Gilgit, Hunza-Nagar and other small principalities stated above were occupied by Pakistani Army in 1948 when in fact in the first week of November 1947, British Gilgit scouts who were at that time working as agents of Pakistan. Their presence as a military force of Britishers was established in 1935 during Maharaja Hari Singh's time after getting that area on lease for 60 years. This had been done in execution of a well thought over political game plan to have a foothold in those strategical areas. The Americans were also a party to this game plan with a hidden agenda to supervise the adjoining territories of China and Russia in order to combat menace of communism. Diplomatic relations between India and Pakistan soured for many other reasons and eventually resulted in two further wars and a conflict on Jammu and Kashmir, i.e. the Indo-Pakistan wars of 1965, 1971 and Kargil conflict in 1999 followed by proxy war started in the garb of terrorism which is going on for the last 25 years. India has control of less than 50 per cent of the area of the former Princely State of Jammu and Kashmir (Jammu, Kashmir and Ladakh) while Pakistan and China control the rest.

Jammu

In the east of this region flows river Ravi and to its west the river Jhelum. Chenab river flows in the centre and Jhelum touched its western territories. Jammu city is the winter capital of the State and it stands on the spur of a hill over-looking the picturesque Tawi rivulet. The prominent features of the city are its temples and imposing palaces. The first magnificent palace known as Mubarak Mandi was constructed by second Dogra ruler Ranbir Singh and now it is in a dilapidated condition. It has now been declared as National Heritage and the Central Government is giving funds to restore it to its original position. The remaining three palaces were built by his descendants. (One of them by Amar Singh who was the father of the last Dogra ruler Hari Singh and remaining two built by Maharaja Hari Singh himself.) The population of Jammu city has tremendously increased by influx of displaced persons caused after three regular wars fought with Pakistan (of 1947, 1965 and 1971) and the last one which is still going on in the shape of a proxy war started by Pakistan from 1989. The uprooted and terrified people from the militancy affected areas have flocked to the city. The city is connected with the rest of the country with rail head and a modern airport. The world famous shrine of 'Shri Mata Vaishno Deviji' is situated at a distance of about 64 kms from Jammu city which annually attracts about more than one crore pilgrims from throughout the country and even from abroad. The important towns of the region are Kathua, Basohli, Billawar, Hiranagar, Samba, Ranbir Singh Pura, Akhnoor, Nowshera, Rajouri, Poonch, Katra (Vaishno Devi), Reasi, Udhampur, Ramnagar, Ramban, Banihal, Doda, Bhaderwah and Kishtwar. Mirpur, Bhimber, Kotli, Rawlakot, Palandri and Bagh were also important towns of the region but they are situated in that area which is known as Pakistan occupied J&K of the Jammu and Kashmir State. Out of the above stated important towns Jammu, Samba, Kathua, Rajouri Poonch, Udhampur, Reasi, Ramban, Kishtwar and Doda are the district headquarters.

People

In the Jammu region, the hilly track extends to the plains of Punjab (both Indian and Pakistani). Its snowy mountains bound Kashmir Valley. The inhabitants of the region are known as Dogras who are hardy people divided into several castes and sects both Hindus and Muslims. They are of Aryan-race and their language is Dogri. During NDA regime in the Centre headed by Shri Atal Bihari Vajpayee, Dogri was recognized as one of the national languages under the 8th Schedule of the Indian Constitution. The main occupation of the Dogras has been agricultural pursuits and employment in the Armed Forces. The Jammu province has produced soldiers of par-excellence and the prominent ones include late General Zorawar Singh who extended the boundaries of the State up to Ladakh and Baltistan regions. Two living Chiefs of the Indian Army—General VN Sharma and General NC Vij (both now retired)—are natives of this region. Even third living retired Army Chief JJ Singh claims his migrated ancestry from Marwah area of the tehsil of Kishtwar. Besides the above stated named Retired three Army Chiefs, there are many retired and serving Lt Generals who owe their origin to Dogra soil of Jammu. The first recipient of Mahavir Chakra (given posthumously of Indian Army) was Brigadier Rajinder Singh (of J&K forces) and first recipient of Param Vir Chakra (given posthumously of Indian Army) was Major Som Nath Sharma of Garhwal Regiment of the Indian Army. Both of them were the sons of Jammu soil. Major Som Nath's father, elder brother of General VN Sharma, had migrated to Himachal Pradesh. In other words, the Jammu region is called the nursery of the Indian soldiers. The inhabitants of the region of middle mountains are called Paharis. Their spoken dialects are mixture of Dogri, Pathwari, Khasi, Bhadarwahi, Pogli, Suraji, Gojri and in some areas Pahari Kashmiri is also spoken by the descendants of old migrants from Kashmir province. Muslims converted from Hindu Brahmin and Rajput clans in large numbers are living in the districts of Poonch and Rajouri on both sides of the divided districts. In Pakistan occupied areas of J&K's erstwhile tehsils

Palandri and Bag (now made district headquarters), they are mostly convert Muslims of Brahmins known as Sudan tribe and Sattis tribes etc. Gujjars and Bakarwals are mostly migratory tribes and all are the descendants of Hindu converts into Islam. Amongst Gujjar community most of them live in every district of Jammu region. The predominant population is that of Hindus.

Kashmir

The people of Kashmir Valley are physically taller and of fair complexion in comparison to the inhabitants of the other two regions (Jammu and Ladakh). They are more shrewd and politically awakened. One theory is that Kashmiris are the descendants of the lost tribes of Israel, because in some cases there is similarity of Jewish-cut features. But the credible view which finds support in the 'Rajatarangini' and 'Nilamata Purana' (old scriptures written in Sanskrit) is that the valley was a big lake and was drained by Kashyapa Rishi who imported Brahmins and sages to live there. The third view held by some persons is that when river Saraswati dried, Brahmins and Kshatriyas who had settled on its banks migrated to the Himalayas and found abode in Kashmir.

Before the advent of Islam in the 14th century, the population in Kashmir was not entirely of Brahmins and Chandravanshi Rajputs. There are also found the names of several sects—Nishads, Khakhas, Darads, Bhauttas, Bhikshas, Damaras and Tantrins etc—who constantly gave trouble not only to the rulers but to the Brahmins also. Buddhism came into ascendancy in the 2nd century BC and during its heyday Buddhist kings and Ministers used to build 'Viharas' and temples simultaneously. There was no religious bigotry. Islam entered Kashmir without any conflict. Ranchan, a Buddhist fugitive from royal family of Ladakh was the first convert to Islam when he was not admitted to Hindu fold by Brahmins of Kashmir. He had adopted Islam religion after succeeding in usurping the throne of Kashmir. His rule was short-lived and after him first Muslim ruler was Shah Mir. Muslim saints like Sheikh Nur-ud-Din and Hindu saint like Lalleshwari were venerated alike by Muslims and Hindus. Even during the darkest days of religious persecutions by fanatical rulers such like Sikandar Khan (alias Butshikan) and Afghan Governors, the people of Kashmir lived amicably. Brahmins are known as 'Kashmiri Pandits' and are considered the purest specimen of Aryan settlers in the Valley. They have undergone various political vicissitudes and suffered at the hands of religious persecutors. The community has known en masse exodus during some periods of Sultan rule, Mughal rule and Afghan rule. Now because of the spurt of terrorism in Kashmir they have again seen en masse displacement. The literacy rate between them is above 90 per cent and their chief occupation is government services. The community has produced great saints, authors, administrators and politicians. The first Prime Minister of the Independent India was Pandit Jawaharlal Nehru (a Kashmiri Pandit by origin) followed by non-Kashmiri Shri Lal Bahadur Shastri for a short period and then his daughter Mrs Indira Gandhi stepped into his shoes.

Sikhs are another small community in the Valley having some pockets of the population in Baramulla district and Tral area of Anantnag. Most of them were originally Brahmins followed by Khatris from Punjab imported by Raja Sukh Jivan (1754)—who was an appointee Governor of Afghans. He declared independence and became Raja with the help of powerful Kashmiri nobles. This position he could maintain for a short period because Afghan ruler Ahmad Shah Abdali again invaded Kashmir and subjugated him. He was taken as a prisoner to Lahore where he was blinded and then mercilessly killed under the feet of an elephant. During the Reign of Maharaja Ranjit Singh (1819-1839), those Brahmins and Khatris embraced Sikhism. Some addition was made by migration from Punjab especially by Khatri trading community who too had become Sikhs. They are hardy people and mostly agriculturists. Recently they have taken to police and military services.

Overwhelming majority of the people of Kashmir Valley profess Muslim religion. The old surnames of Pandit community are still retained such as Pandit, Bhatt, Handoo, Taing, Koul/Kaul, Raina etc because they are all converts. The Sheikhs, Sayeeds and Pirzadas are considered more respectable amongst Muslims. The Muslim population is divided into Sunni and Shia sects, the former being in a prepondering majority. There are some settlements of Pathans and Mughals in certain parts of the Valley.

The valley is approximately 84 miles in length and 20 to 25 miles in breadth. The average height from sea level is about 5,000 ft to 6,000 ft. Lofty mountains guard the valley from all sides from the outer world. The river Jehlum arises from the spring of Verinag and transverses the whole length of the Valley. It is also known as Vitasta and it provides cheap mode of transport through boats and cargo boats. Kashmir is a land of lakes, rivulets, rivers, flowers and fruits. The Wular lake is the largest fresh water lake of India. It is 12.5 miles long and 5 miles wide. The Dal lake lies at the foot hills to the east of Srinagar city and is 4 miles long and nearly 2 miles wide. Presently its area has been squeezed by large number of encroachments.

Srinagar is the summer capital of the State and is situated in the centre of the Valley divided by river Jehlum. It is one of the oldest cities of

India founded by Emperor Ashoka. The city is connected by motorable road from the time of Dogra rulers and a modern airport. The Central Government is linking the Valley with rail service and the work is going on though not at a high speed. Railway link has been provided in the valley connecting the town of Anantnag with the town of Baramulla. Now it has been extended up to Banihal falling in Jammu region. Prime Minister Narendra Modi had on July 4, 2014 flagged off Shri Shakti Express train from Katra Vaishno Devi while commissioning the 25-km-long Udhampur-Katra line. Baramulla towards the north-west of the Valley is a town of importance because it is from here that the river Jehlum adopts rushing, roaring and foaming torrents by entering the hilly areas. Another town situated nearby is Sopore which was originally founded in 9th century and it is known as home of apples and a hub of terrorism. In the south of the Valley, Anantnag is an important town which has numerous springs. Martand (Muttan) is a spiritual place for Hindus because there is an ancient Sun Temple which stands on a spring. Besides the native Kashmiri Pandits, the other Hindus from other parts of the country also perform 'Shradh' ceremonies there. Shopian is an old town in the lap of Pir Panchal and is a starting point of an old Mughal Shahi Caravan Road which now has been made motorable from Poonch district of Jammu. It is a famous centre of fruit trade. Budgam is a new town of importance and is situated nearby the city of Srinagar. Anantnag, Kulgam, Pulwama, Shopian, Budgam, Srinagar, Ganderbal, Bandipora, Baramulla and Kupwara are the district headquarters. There are three universities in the Valley, i.e. University of Kashmir, Islamic University of Science and Technology (recently established during Mufti Mohammad Sayeed's coalition government) and Sher-e-Kashmir University of Agricultural Sciences and Technology. Engineering institute (NIT, Srinagar), Medical institute which is known as Sher-e-Kashmir Institute of Medical Sciences (SKIMS) are other important centres of professional learning and teaching. Gulmarg, Pahalgam, Sonamarg and Yus Maidan are the most famous picnic spots. The Muslim shrine of Hazratbal which houses one hair of Prophet Mohammad is venerated throughout the country. 'Charar-e-Sharief' is a famous Sufi shrine which was earlier destroyed by fire ignited by militants and now stands reconstructed by the government. The famous shrine of 'Kheer Bhawani' and cave of 'Shri Baba Amarnathji', Shankaracharya Temple are situated in the Valley.

Ladakh, Gilgit and Their People

Beyond the Valley is Ladakh and it lies to the east of the Valley. It is the land of 'Lamas'. The Baltistan and Dardistan (Gilgit) are on the north of the Valley. The whole region is mountainous. Formally, Leh was the district headquarters of the Ladakh region but after 1975 when Sheikh Mohammed Abdullah came into power for the second time on the basis of an accord with Mrs Indira Gandhi, he made the tehsil headquarters of Kargil as district headquarters which is predominantly inhabited by Shia Muslims. The Buddhists are in majority in the district of Leh and in minority in the district of Kargil. Ladakhis are known for their hearty laughter and hospitality. They rarely quarrel even when they are under the influence of common beverage known as 'Chang'. They are truthful people and crime rate amongst them is very low. Before opening of vehicular traffic and consequent travel by air service, the locking of houses amongst Ladakhis was an unknown feature. Now Leh is a very modern town having a modern Airport and a large number of hotels. It attracts large number of foreigners as visitors. Similarly, the people of Kargil who are Balti by race are also honest and truthful people and like Buddhists, they too are true patriots. The people of this region (Ladakh) like the people of Jammu region also feel being discriminated in the matter of governance and development. The people of Leh spearheaded an agitation and succeeded in getting the status of local self-governance in the allocation of funds and development activities. Similarly, the people of Kargil also got this benefit. After the Kargil conflict, the district of Kargil attracted world attention and despite large scale devastation by Pakistani shelling, the town of Kargil again has regained its repute as a modern town. Despite being co-religionist with Pakistanis they have never sided with their ideology and always have retained the good faith of Indian nationalism. During the wars of 1947, 1965, 1971. the Kargil conflict of 1999 and the present ongoing proxy war, they have remained true patriots. The inhabitants of the Leh region also possess these qualities and they too have opposed with all their might the Pakistani aggressions and in addition one Chinese aggression of 1962. A Ladakhi village has invariably a small or a big Gompa or Monastery according to its size. In a Gompa, the parents present their children in their childhood to do service as monks and nuns. The Muslim inhabitants of Kargil are also very much religious minded and they are under the influence of Aggas who get guidance from Iran.

The headquarters of erstwhile tehsil Kargil and now district headquarters which is re-occupied part of old Indus Valley from the occupation of Pakistan in 1947 covers an area of 6,222 sq miles. It is bounded on the north by Karakoram Mountains, on the east by Ladakh, on the south by Himalayas and on west by Dardistan (Gilgit). Skardu town of Baltistan was its tehsil headquarters during Dogra rule. The town of Kargil was a part of Skardu tehsil being a 'Niabet headquarters' and the people of Skardu and Kargil are of the same clan and all profess Shia Muslim faith.

Dardistan or Gilgit

Dardistan or Gilgit extends in the north to the Karakoram Range of high mountains and besides Gilgit, comprises Hunza-Nagar and small principalities of Chilas, Yasin, Punial, Ishkoman and Koh. Chitral was a tributary of the erstwhile Princely State of Jammu and Kashmir. Gilgit is 233 miles from Srinagar if linked by road.

Dardistan or Gilgit is inhabited by broad-shouldered, moderately stout built and active high-landers. The seat of Dards extends from Chitral and Yasin across the Indus regions of Gilgit, Chilas and Bunji to the Kishanganga Valley. Dards had been maintaining their independent status till the middle of 19th century when part of it was brought under his sway by Maharaja Ranjit Singh of Punjab. After his death when Maharaja Gulab Singh became the ruler of the State of Jammu and Kashmir, a Hindu Governor appointed by Maharaja Ranjit Singh showed his loyalty to Maharaja Gulab Singh but the natives revolted against him and he was murdered. Maharaja Gulab Singh succeeded in restoring his rule over that area by crushing the mutiny. After the death of Maharaja Gulab Singh in 1857, there was another revolt but his able successor Maharaja Ranbir Singh subjugated them by extending his suzerainty on the extended areas such as Chilas. Chilasis are a Dard tribe inhabiting a long Valley on the west of Nanga Parbat. Now, the whole area of Baltistan and Dardistan are under the illegal occupation of Pakistan and a big chunk of it has been illegally ceded by Pakistan in favour of China and, in lieu thereof, have got constructed a road linking this area with the Tibetan area occupied by China. Pakistan uses this road for getting arms supplies from China to their country. Majority of them are followers of Shia faith of Islam and remaining few are Ismailis and Sunnis. They were followers of Buddhism before conversion to Islam. There are some villages on the side valleys which still follow Buddhism.

The seat of power of this region is Gilgit. On October 26, 1947, Maharaja Hari Singh acceded to India and the Indian Army landed in Srinagar on 27 October 1947. By early November, the raiders were pushed back in significant numbers and vast areas were got cleared from their occupation. It was on November 4, 1947 when a British Major by the name of Major Brown of Gilgit scouts pulled off his audacious coup apparently on the plea that being Muslim majority area it must accede to Pakistan. The Gilgit scouts followed him and he raised Pakistani flag after arresting Brigadier Ghansar Singh, the then Governor of Gilgit appointed by Maharaja Hari Singh. Right from 1846, when the Britishers handed over the Valley of Kashmir to Maharaja Gulab Singh under the treaties of Lahore and Amritsar (to be discussed fully later on), they had an eye to capture this strategic area and to achieve the object they had been pressurizing Maharaja Ranbir Singh and Partap Singh to give the military control of this area to them but due to intervening obstacles, i.e. the outbreak of first war of independence of 1857, and then break of the first world war of 1914, they could not succeed in their designs. In 1930s the Britishers were worried that their friend, the Maharaja of Kashmir was too weak to safeguard the security of this region. They provoked the disturbances in order to harass the administration of the State and that forced the Maharaja to lease out the key territories of Gilgit for a period of sixty years in their favour. A special military unit called 'Gilgit Scouts' was formed to reinforce the hold in the areas which could have allowed the Britishers to keep this area in their hands till 1995 when the lease period would have expired. Anglo-American powers were worried about Stalin's communist thrust from Russia and in coming into power the Communists in China where the civil war was going on and the wind was in their favour. In order to keep their footholds they had done so. Under the terms of lease agreement, the civil administration which included the means of communication, roads, hospitals, education etc were allowed to remain under the control of Maharaja but security of the area was taken over by the Britishers. In other words, the financial requirements were to be met from the State exchequer but the hold of military was with the Britishers. They improved the communication system only for military purposes and had established an aerodrome. The Hindu civil servants of the Maharaja were massacred in large numbers including the personal security guards of the last Governor—Brigadier Ghansar Singh. Some of them were lucky to be taken as prisoners. Those prisoners along with their surviving family members and that of the slain officials were later on repatriated by Indian Government including imprisoned Governor Brigadier Ghansar Singh.

This was a sensational coup carried out by Major Brown who at that time was aged 32 years. About 12,000 sq miles of this key strategic real estate roughly 1/7th of the total area of Jammu and Kashmir State fell into Pakistani hands at one stroke. Major Brown could not carry out this coup at his sweet will until directed by his master's, i.e. the British authorities. For the Britishers Kashmir's real geopolitical importance lay in its northern frontiers. It formed a vital listening post at the pivot of Asia—the meeting point of Russia, China, India and

Afghanistan in the high Himalayas. The corroborative circumstantial evidence to hold such a view has been found recorded by eminent Lt Gen SK Sinha in his book, *A Governor's Musings: Soldier Statesman Speaks*. Lt Gen Sinha after his supersession as Army Chief of India had gone on retirement and afterwards when the Congress Government was not formed in the Centre, Inder Kumar Gujral, the then Prime Minister of India, appointed him as Ambassador to Nepal. The successor government appointed him Governor of Assam State and finally he had a full term of Governorship in the State of Jammu and Kashmir. He in his above said book has recorded: "The British had their strategic perception of national interests. Besides Churchill, the Chiefs of the Army staff of the eminence of Montgomery, Cunningham and Tedder lent their support of having a friendly Islamic land mass containing the new, 'Wells of Power' which means oil wells and also blocking Soviet approach to the warm waters in the south. Churchill as Prime Minister of England and Linlithgow had cultivated Muhammad Ali Jinnah to have a friendly territory in north-west Asia. This territory ipso facto included Jammu and Kashmir whose north areas, borders so close to Soviet Russia, China and Afghanistan. No wonder, the Labour Party including Attlee had fell in line with this thinking. The then Foreign Secretary Bevin, when partition had been announced on 3rd June 1947, stated that the division of India would help to consolidate Britain in the Middle East. Thus, the secession of 1947 was in essence a product of both communal sentiments exploited by Muhammad Ali Jinnah and the strategic perception of our erstwhile British rulers." At present, the boundaries of the State run for 750 miles with Tibet (now substituted by Peoples Republic of China), 300 miles with Union of India, 600 miles with Pakistan and 50 miles with Afghanistan. The Central Asian State of Tajikistan is separated from Jammu and Kashmir by a narrow strip of Wakhan. The maximum width of this strip is 40 miles, whereas, at some places it is only 10 miles wide. It was created by imperialist powers of Russia and Britain both. In an agreement with the British, the Emperor Czar of Russia had agreed not to advance beyond Pamir range of mountains in the south, Wakhan was annexed with Afghanistan and it remains as such until this day (*Geographical Realities of J&K* by GM Mir, Publication United Kingdom).

On August 15, 1947, the area of the State was more than the then State of Hyderabad, three times more than the State of Mysore, two times more than the States of Gwalior and Bikaner, five times more than the State of Jaipur, ten times more than Baroda and five times more than United Punjab. It was larger than 111 free countries of the world.

Population

In 1947, at the time of partition, total area of the State was about 2,22,236 sq kms, of which Jammu Division comprised of an area of 32,315 sq kms, Kashmir province 22,133 sq kms and frontier districts of Ladakh and Gilgit 1,64,139 sq kms. From this total area roughly speaking 79,000 sq kms from the erstwhile State is under the illegal occupation of Pakistan and the remaining area measuring about 42,000 sq kms is with China mostly occupied after the Indo-China war of 1962 and remaining area was ceded by Pakistan herself who built a National Highway connecting its territory with Pakistan in order to facilitate the supply of arms and ammunition to the latter and have an access to the ports of Arabian Sea of Pakistan. From the above stated authentic information, it transpires that out of the erstwhile State of Jammu and Kashmir, the Indian administered State is comprised of 1,01,387 sq kms. When we deduct this area from the total area of the State the remaining area which is left out comes to the extent of 1,21,064 sq kms which is more than half of the total area of the original state. The population of the State as per the Census of 1941, 1981 and 2011 is tabulated hereunder:

Population	*Kashmir*	*Jammu*	*Ladakh*	*Total*
Census 1941	17,28,686	20,00,157	—	40,21,616
Census 1981	31,34,904	27,18,113	1,34,372	59,87,389
Census 2011	69,07,623	53,50,811	2,90,492	1,25,48,926

As per the census of 1941 (done during Maharaja's time) the total population of the State was 40,21,616 and Jammu province accounted for 20,00,157 while Kashmir province excluding Gilgit, Skardu and Ladakh had population of 17,28,686. In the census of 1981, the total population of the State was 59,87,389. The Hindu population (including Sikhs, Buddhists and microscopic Christian community) was about 36 per cent. Muslims accounted about 64 per cent. The population of the Jammu region was 27,18,113 while Kashmir Valley counted for 31,34,904. The population of Ladakh region was 1,34,372. According to this census (1981) report the difference between the population of Kashmir Valley with Jammu region plus Ladakh region was 2,82,419 whereas, difference between Kashmir region and Jammu region was 4,16,791. According to the Census of 2011, the total population is 1,25,48,926 comprising the population of Jammu region 53,50,811 and that of Kashmir Valley 69,07,623. The difference between the two regions comes out to 15,56,812. The population of Ladakh region is 2,90,492. Even if Jammu region and

Ladakh region population is clubbed together, the difference of population with Kashmir Valley comes to 12,66,320.

During this gap of thirty years the population of Jammu region has not doubled whereas Kashmir Valley population has not only doubled but has added 6,37,815 souls to its double number of population. It is alarming and not trustworthy because during 1990-91 the Hindu Sikh population residing in Kashmir Valley had migrated numbering more than 3.50 lakhs. Not only that, a big chunk of population belonging to majority community who had threat from militants had also migrated to Jammu region. How it is possible that the population of Kashmir region has crossed more than double number even losing a big chunk of its population by way of migration? These migrants have not returned to Kashmir Valley till date. Not only that, some members of the majority community from Kashmir Valley for reasons known to them had migrated to Pakistan occupied area of the State after the eruption of militancy and have not still returned.

Subversion of Electorate's Fundamental Right on Regional Basis

Area of Jammu, Kashmir and Ladakh regions along with number of Assembly seats before the submission of J&K Delimitation Commission's Report as well as thereafter are tabulated below:

	Kashmir	*Jammu*	*Ladakh*
Area of regions (in sq kms)	15,948	26,293	59,146
Before submission of report, i.e. Assembly seats of 1987	42	32	2
After submission of report, i.e. Assembly seats of 1996	46	37	4
After submission of report, i.e. Assembly seats of 2002	46	37	4
After submission of report, i.e. Assembly seats of 2008	46	37	4

Under the J&K Representation of People's Act, five aspects are to be kept in mind while delimiting the constituencies: (i) Geographical compactness, (ii) nature of terrain, (iii) communication facilities, (iv) population and (v) welfare motive. While making the report, the Delimitation Commission should have considered all these above stated facts in favour of Jammu region which is 10,345 sq kms more than the area of Kashmir region. The Jammu region is heterogenous being mostly mountainous, sparsely populated, lacking motorable road connectivity and inhabited by people having different dialects and culture. Against this, Kashmir region is plane area, having a good network of roads, compact and densely populated, having comparatively more homogenous culture, common language barring some hilly areas inhabited by Gujjars and Pahari speaking people. These areas are tehsils of Uri, Tangdhar and Gurez. Pahari and Chhinna dialects are spoken there. Gujjar population who speak Gojri dialect is scattered in the hilly areas of valley such as of tehsil Pahalgam, Kangan and Pir Panchal range of mountains bordering with Jammu region.

Total number of electorates and average number of electorates per Assembly seat before the submission of J&K Delimitation Commission's Report (submitted by Justice KK Gupta (Retd)) as well as thereafter are tabulated below:

Total electorates, total number of Assembly seats and average number of electorates per Assembly seat	*Kashmir*	*Jammu*
Before submission of Delimitation report (Elections of 1987)		
Total number of electorates	19,21,179	15,39,269
Total number of Assembly seats	42	32
Average number of electorates per Assembly seat	45,742	48,102
After submission of Delimitation report (Elections of 1996)		
Total number of electorates	23,81,859	22,40,769
Total number of Assembly seats	46	37
Average number of electorates per Assembly seat	51,780	60,561
After submission of Delimitation report (Elections of 2002)		
Total number of electorates	28,84,852	31,06,280
Total number of Assembly seats	46	37
Average number of electorates per Assembly seat	62,714	83,954
After submission of Delimitation report (Elections of 2008)		
Total number of electorates	32,81,113	30,47,264
Total number of Assembly seats	46	37
Average number of electorates per Assembly seat	71,329	82,358

(During Assembly Elections of 1996—Jammu region had 1,41,090 less eligible electorates than Kashmir region. In 2002 Assembly Elections—Jammu region had 2,21,428 more electorates than Kashmir region. In 2008 Assembly Elections—Jammu region had 2,33,849 less eligible electorates than Kashmir region's eligible electorates. The phenomenal increase of 3,96,261 electorates (3,28,113 – 28,84,852 = 3,96,261) during a span of 6 years is alarming for tilting the balance of power in favour of Kashmir region).

If viewed from another angle, it is found that difference of average electorates per seat in the Assembly elections of 1987 between the two regions was 2,360. In 1996, Assembly elections despite migration of population as stated above the difference arose to 8,781 electorates. In the Assembly elections of 2002, the difference further swelled to 21,240 electorates. Lastly in the Assembly elections of 2008, there was an abnormal downward trend when the difference of electorates in Jammu region came to the extent of 11,029. It is a mystery to find out the reason why the Assembly electorates' strength decreased abnormally in the Jammu region in 2008 elections from the elections held in 2002 to the extent of 59,016 electorates (31,06,280 – 3,04,764 = 59,016) whereas, the electorates strength in Kashmir Valley during the above said period has increased to a number of 3,96,261 (32,81,113 – 28,84,852 = 3,96,261).

BREAK-UP OF THREE DISTRICT ASSEMBLY CONSTITUENCIES OF STATE IN ASSEMBLY ELECTIONS OF 2008

Name of district	*Number of assembly constituencies*	*Number of electorates*
Baramulla	10	7,09,906
Srinagar	8	5,60,679
Jammu	11	9,06,941

Note: Information has been received vide RTI/CEO/Pub/2012/4043 dated 4 October 2012 from PIO (Joint Chief Electoral Officer J&K).

The readers would themselves understand the discrimination of glaring nature when district Jammu having many fold areas of inaccessible nature comprising of 'Khuds' and hilly paths in 'Kandi belt' comprising of scanty scattered villages situated on lower hills having very less road connectivity stands allotted only eleven seats in the legislative Assembly against district of Srinagar having a small area and well connected system of motorable roads. In other words, amongst eight constituencies, six constituencies exclusively fall within the area of Municipal Corporation of Srinagar city. The remaining two Hazartbal (number 18) and Sonawar (number 24) have some small rural adjacent segments but all of them are well connected. The majority of the electorates even in these two constituencies reside in the city of Srinagar. The total number of electorates in the district as a whole is 5,60,679 and they have been allotted eight Assembly constituencies. For further clarification the names of those constituencies are: Hazartbal (number 18), Zadibal (number 19), Eidgah (number 20), Khanyar (number 21), Habakadal (number

22), Amirakadal (number 23), Sonawar (number 24) and Batmaloo (number 25). Out of eleven constituencies of Jammu district, Assembly constituency of Gandhi Nagar (number 71) has 1,43,629 electorates, Jammu West (number 73) has 1,39,965 electorates while Jammu East (number 72) has 51,660 electorates. Barring the above said two constituencies which exclusively fall under the jurisdiction of Municipal Corporation Jammu whileas the third one Gandhi Nagar (number 71) has substantial number of electorates residing outside the limits of Jammu Municipal Corporation area. The remaining eight are rural constituencies. Khanyar constituency of Srinagar district has 48,900 electorates and Habakadal constituency has 49,667 electorates. If we club the electorates of both these constituencies the total number of electorates comes to 98,567 which combined figure is less than 45,062 electorates from single constituency of Gandhi Nagar. One fails to understand how the Election Commission of India and the Hon'ble Prime Minister of India who are under oath of the Indian Constitution to ensure the governance throughout the country on the basis of equality before law which is one of the fundamental right of every citizen, this right has been allowed to be trampled by perpetrating injustice on the basis of domicile in one of the States of the Union of India. Similar is the case of Baramulla district. As an example, Gurez constituency (number 9) has only 15,390 electorates. Sangram constituency (number 12) has 59,659 electorates which number is less than half of the electorates of Gandhi Nagar and Jammu West constituencies of Jammu city. Baramulla town constituency which is a district headquarters has 73,112 electorates which number is slightly above half of the electorates of Gandhi Nagar constituency of Jammu city.

On 20 April 1951, Dr Karan Singh being the Regent of the State proclaimed for constituting the Constituent Assembly and for the 75 seats elections were held during the months of August-September 1951. On 31 October 1951, the first session of Constituent Assembly was held. The elections were held under the tenure of Sheikh Abdullah as Prime Minister. Out of these 75 seats Sheikh reserved 43 seats for Kashmir region, 30 for Jammu region and 2 for Ladakh region. Besides that, additional 25 seats were earmarked for Pakistan occupied area (POJK) of the State. There was only one political party which was challenging the autocratic behaviour of Sheikh Abdullah and that was Praja Parishad—a patriot party of Jammu region. The Congress Party had not opened its account in the State and was wholly supporting Sheikh Abdullah's National Conference. The Sheikh's mindset was to establish his personal rule over the remaining two regions of the State, i.e. of Jammu and Ladakh.

Out of 43 seats of Kashmir region, Sheikh Abdullah won 41 seats uncontested because the nomination papers of all those contestants were got rejected at the time of scrutiny. Out of the remaining 2 Assembly seats, two contestants remained in the field and they themselves withdrew from the contest. Thus, Sheikh had won all the 43 seats uncontested from the Kashmir region.

In Jammu region, 'Praja Parishad' had filed 28 nomination papers to contest the elections out of 30 seats but from 13 seats their nomination papers were rejected. As a protest Praja Parishad had boycotted the elections. There remained only 2 independent candidates for the contest from Kahna Chak seat and Akhnoor seat from Jammu district but they too withdrew from the contest. In this manner Sheikh Abdullah captured all the 75 seats in the Constituent Assembly. Yousef Korbel in his book *Danger in Kashmir* at page 222 has recorded that "such a success even a dictator cannot achieve." This was a very calculated move of Sheikh Abdullah to place Kashmir region at a dominant position over other two regions and then dictate terms to the Central Government for getting removed Maharaja Hari Singh as a ruler of the State and take all the Reigns of Governance in his hands as an Absolute Monarch. He had an eye to blackmail India over the trump card which he had in his hands for winning over the Plebiscite in favour of India in the United Nations. The case had been taken in the United Nations by India under a well thought conspiracy hatched by the Britishers through Lord Mountbatten who was Governor-General by giving a wrong advice to Pandit Jawaharlal Nehru on the pretext that Kashmir problem would be solved very soon. Lord Mountbatten and his wife Lady Mountbatten had influenced Pandit Nehru. Lady Mountbatten's influence over Pandit Jawaharlal Nehru was all pervading. In the United Nations, Anglo-American block got a ready made handle in their hands to blackmail India and help their Protege State of Pakistan which was created by them under a deep rooted conspiracy to have a check on Russia and China as well as protect their economic rights and interests in the oil wells of Muslim block of Arabian countries.

In Democratic Rule in the State, Sheikh Abdullah's elections of 1951 were boycotted by Jammu-based political party known as 'Praja Parishad'. This was done on the basis of revengeful attitude and discrimination of Sheikh Abdullah towards the inhabitants of Jammu region. There were allegations also that elections were a farce being based upon the census figures of 1941 which had lost their credibility after the disturbances of 1947 when Hindu population stood uprooted from about half of the area from Jammu region and from the whole

Muzaffarabad district and part of the Baramulla district from Kashmir region. Some of them were massacred in communal frenzy by the locals and Pakistani raiders. Similarly, some Muslims of Jammu district, part of Kathua, Reasi and Udhampur districts were massacred on the basis of majority of Hindu population. Some had migrated to Pakistan. There was no authentic record prepared by an independent agency of making all of them as electorates. There was no political opposition in the Kashmir Valley. But at the present scenario, the average electorate's strength for one Assembly seat in Jammu region is 82,358 (as per elections of 2008) against Kashmir regions electorate's strength of 71,329 per seat. It is for reader's information that the Constituent Assembly of the State while enacting the J&K State Constitution under Section 50 had provided that there shall be 11 elected MLCs from Jammu region as against 11 elected MLCs from Kashmir region in the Legislative Council by the elected members of Legislative Assembly. The Kashmir region's 11 seats included two seats for Ladakh region. In other words, only 9 MLC seats for elected members from Kashmir region stands allotted so far. This was done keeping in view the heterogenous nature of Jammu province, its area and other relevant factors as already stated above which are ingrained in the relevant provisions of the J&K Peoples Representation Act.

Pandit Prem Nath Dogra (a celebrated leader of Jammu region) called the elections of Constituent Assembly as a 'Drama' and demanded judicial probe. Four allegations were made against Sheikh Abdullah and they were:

1. Different dates for holding elections in Jammu region and Kashmir region. They were fixed in this manner in order to benefit the candidates of Kashmir region.
2. The constituencies were carved out in such a way so that Hindu-dominated areas are reduced to minority against Muslim population.
3. The nomination papers of Praja Parishad candidates were rejected without any basis.
4. In order to make the success of National Conference candidates, government machinery was used. (Reference book of MK Taing)

Kamal Ahmed Siddiqui in his book *Kashmir Ek Manjarnama* (page 536) has recorded the words of Sheikh Abdullah: "Bakshi Ghulam Mohammad was incharge of elections of Jammu region as that was his field. It is possible some irregularities might have been committed there as seeing the nature of Bakshi Ghulam Mohammad. This could not be impossible."

Graig Baxter, in his book *The Jan Sangh: A Biography of an Indian Political Party* (page 117) has written that "this was not unimaginable that Praja Parishad under those circumstances might have chosen other ways to achieve its objects."

Sheikh Abdullah was in a great hurry to take revenge with the royal family and with the aid of his selected and elected 75 members got a tainted and illegal report prepared on 10 June 1952 to achieve his life-long objectives. First of all, he abolished the autocratic rule of Maharaja Hari Singh under whose sovereign authority that Constituent Assembly was constituted under Constitution Act of 1939 which recognized the sovereign authority of the Maharaja even over the Legislature. He had totally forgotten the written pledge given to Maharaja in his Letter of Apology dated 29 September 1947 whereafter his conviction and sentence for an offence of sedition was pardoned by the Maharaja. Maharaja was the sole authority who on 5 March 1948 had appointed him as Prime Minister of the State by terminating the tenure of his duly appointed Prime Minister Mehr Chand Mahajan.

The elections of 1957 for Legislative Assembly were held under local Election Commission during Bakshi Ghulam Mohammad's time as Prime Minister and Praja Parishad could win 5 seats despite 17 nomination papers filed of the candidates to contest the elections. Election ballot boxes were tampered by opening them and keeping the seals intact. The election boxes were defective. They were kept for days together after the elections in the Government treasuries and ballot boxes were tampered by removing the votes. In one case of Assembly segment 12 boxes were found broken. In case of counting the votes of one of the Assembly seats of Jammu city where advocate Lala Dwarka Nath of the Jammu Bar Association had contested the election as a candidate of Praja Parishad on June 29, 1957, his polling agent in presence of Polling Officer had demonstrated the defects in the polling boxes by opening them along with the intact seals which were put upon them. This demonstration was made in respect of ballot box number 58 and 59. In order to quell the noise which was created all over the country about the dictatorial attitude of Sheikh Abdullah by way of an eyewash, a matriculate retired official by the name of Krishan Lal Kitchloo who was of 80 years old was appointed as one-man Commission. His relations were in Government Service. He himself was drawing pension from the government. During those days even pension could be stopped and relations could be dismissed from service. This shows the judicial nature of this Commission and Kitchloo gave a clean chit in his verdict regarding these elections. (Refer page 232 of *Jammu-Kashmir ki Anakahee Kahani* by Dr Kuldeep Chand Agnihotri.)

In 1962, the elections were held under the control of Election Commission of India. National Conference had contested 75 seats and out of them 14 nominees returned unopposed members in the Assembly. Praja Parishad nomination papers were 25 but only 3 could return to the Assembly. The old practice of tampering the election results continued. The writer of this book has his personal experience while appearing as an advocate on behalf of Praja Parishad candidate Moulvi Lateef from Mehandar constituency of Poonch district. The opposing candidate of National Conference was Peer Jamait Ali Shah. Tehsildar Mehandar was the Returning Officer. He rejected the nomination paper of Praja Parishad candidate without any reason. When Supreme Court ruling was cited before the Tehsildar, he openly declared that Election Law of India was not applicable in the State and consequently Election Commission of India had no jurisdiction. National Conference won 70 seats as it had lost 2 seats in the Valley in favour of Independent Candidates as those 2 candidates were not of the liking of Bakshi Ghulam Mohammad. One of them was a notorious land grabber and otherwise badly reputed. The other candidate was GM Sadiq's nominee. (Refer page 233 of Dr Kuldeep Chand Agnihotri's book.) The Handwara constituency was lost by National Conference candidate in favour of Independent candidate. About unfair means adopted by Bakshi Ghulam Mohammad, Pandit Nehru had written to him in case, he would have allowed few more seats for the opposition, the democratic position would have been strengthened. (Refer Fault Line Kashmir 223). On 30 December 1963, Praja Parishad merged with Jan Sangh.

Two seats have been allotted to Jammu region for the Indian Parliament, three for Kashmir division and one for Ladakh division. The total electors of these Parliamentary constituencies from 1999 to 2009 are tabulated hereunder:

Name of Constituency	*Total Electorates in 1999*	*Total Electorates in 2004*	*Total Electorates in 2009*
Jammu	14,46,792	18,51,838	17,19,868
Udhampur	10,16,952	13,48,721	13,63,060
Ladakh	1,43,719	1,75,768	1,52,491
Baramulla	7,63,639	9,40,998	10,54,496
Srinagar	8,54,081	10,57,733	11,06,729
Anantnag	8,04,911	9,98,905	11,76,474

From the above tabulated figures it is established that for Jammu Parliamentary constituency, there is a direct downward slash from 18,51,838 electorates in 2004 elections to 17,19,868 electorates in

2009 elections. Same is the position in respect of Udhampur constituency where the electorate's strength in 2004 was 13,48,721 while a very slight increase of electorates was up to the number of 13,63,060 in 2009 Parliamentary elections. In the same manner, the electorates strength has decreased in Ladakh region because in 2004 the electorates strength was 1,75,768 in 2004 and it decreased to the strength of 1,52,491 in Parliamentary elections of 2009. On the contrary, there is a constant upward rise in electorate's strength in three Parliamentary constituencies of Kashmir region. It is noteworthy that Parliamentary electorates had swelled in numbers in Jammu region on account of partition of the country in 1947. The Hindus and Sikhs numbering in thousands residing in the border areas of west Punjab (Pakistan) escaped for safety of their lives and honour after crossing over the nearby State border. They cannot hold any landed property in the State and are debarred from getting any government job as well as have no Voting Right in the State legislature. They are constantly raising their voice by holding demonstrations and even had taken their case in the Hon'ble Supreme Court which was decided in 1987 by urging the State Government to treat their case sympathetically. The Supreme Court could not give them their full rights as Citizens of free India because of insertion of special Article 35(A) in the constitution of India by the President of India to protect the State Subject's rights of J&K inhabitants. The continuous rise in the electorates list in Kashmir Valley raises a reasonable doubt that non-State Subject electorates have also been allowed to settle in the Kashmir Valley because it is a proven fact that thousands of halwai shop owners (as shopkeepers) and religious clerics hailing from Uttar Pradesh and Bihar States are residing there after the onset of militancy. The writer of this book has come across many militants while in custody as a member of the J&K Public Safety Act and as Judge High Court on hearing Habeas Corpus writ petitions that some militants were born from inter-State marriages of such parentages.

It is unfortunate that malady of discrimination has been made of permanent feature by amending Section 47 of the Constitution of Jammu and Kashmir. Sub-Clause (3) mandates that upon the completion of each Census, the number, extent and boundaries of the territorial constituencies shall be readjusted by such authority and in such manner as the legislature may by law determine. A provision has been added affecting amendment by Twenty-ninth Amendment Act, 2002 which provides that such adjustments shall not effect representation in the Legislative Assembly until the dissolution of the then existing Assembly provided that until the relevant figures for the first census taken after 2026 have been published. The readjustment of the total number of seats in the Legislative Assembly of the State and the division of the State into territorial constituencies have also been prohibited. This amendment would be a handle in the hands of concerned unscrupulous elements to manipulate the figures of the census in the same manner during 2021 till 2026 by increasing the population and electorate's strength of Kashmir region at the cost of Jammu region. By that time, much water would have flown down the river Jhelum in order to politically deprive the inhabitants of Jammu region from their basic fundamental right of having just and equitable share in the Governance of the State. This malpractice did not exist during the autocratic reign of Dogra rulers because the last ruler Maharaja Hari Singh had given equal right of voting to the inhabitants of both the regions.

Before parting with this topic, it would be advantageous for the information of the readers of this book that in Pakistan occupied area of J&K State, Old Mirpur district has been divided into three districts—Bhimber, Kotli and Mirpur. Old Muzaffarabad district of Kashmir region has been bifurcated into three districts comprising of Muzaffarabad, Hattian and Neelam. Poonch old wazarat area has been divided into four districts—Poonch having an area of 855 sq kms with a district headquarters at Rawlakot, Haweli district, Bagh district and Sudhnati having its headquarters at Pallandari. The population figure of these small districts in 1998 was 29,72,501. Seven small districts have been created from Baltistan and Gilgit areas which is also known as Dardistan. It has a population of 9,70,347. Pakistan occupied area has its own High Court and Supreme Court as well as Legislature but all these institutions are fully controlled from Rawalpindi where a separate department for Kashmir Affairs exists and is always controlled by a Military General. Pakistan has been changing the demographic composition of Baltistan and Gilgit areas by settling Sunni population from Punjab and other parts of the country. There is widespread unrest and upheaval. The people do not want Pakistani hegemony. Against these atrocities in the recent past, a hartal was also observed in the district headquarters of Kargil falling under the dominion of India because of ethnic sympathy. After a gap of 27 years, from the date of its forcible occupation by Pakistan, the people of this part of the J&K State could get enacted Constitution for themselves. It is known as, "The Azad J&K Interim Constitution Act, 1974." Some of the salient features of this Constitution are reproduced in Appendix 6.

Discrimination with Jammu

In 26,000 sq kms area of Jammu, there were 31,06,280 voters according to 2002 census. Two-third area of Jammu is hilly, inaccessible and does not have proper road-communication, connectivity. It has 37 Assembly seats and two Lok Sabha seats. In comparison to this the area of Kashmir Valley is 15,953 sq kms and there were 28,84,852 voters. Most of this area is plane and well connected with each other and they have 46 representatives in Assembly and three in Lok Sabha.

COMPARATIVE STUDY OF JAMMU AND KASHMIR

	Jammu	*Kashmir*
Voters per Assembly seat	83,954	62,714
Area per seat	710.6 sq kms	346 sq kms
Voters per Lok Sabha seat	15.29 lakh	9.61 lakh
District (10 + 10 + 2 = 22)	10	10
Area of each district	2,629 sq kms	1,594 sq kms
Length of road (in 2006)	4,571 sq kms	7,129 sq kms
Government employees	1.25 lakh	4.0 lakh
Employees in the Secretariat	462	1,329
Central Institution (10 including NIT and Central University)	1	9
Total Budget on Tourism	10% (of total budget)	85%
Number of Tourist in 2009 (including 5 lakh Amarnath pilgrims)	85 lakhs	8 lakh

In 2008, per capita central assistance was Rs 9,754 in the State whereas it was Rs 876 per person in backward states like Bihar. It includes 90 per cent as grants and 10 per cent as required to be given back, whereas the remaining states have to pay back 70 per cent.

Mess in Population

In 2001 census, population of Kashmir Valley was shown as 54,76,970 and the number of voters was 29 lakh. Whereas the population of Jammu was shown as 44,30,191 and the number of voters 30.59 lakh.

Mess in Higher Education

Due to terrorism, educational system of Kashmir Valley almost collapsed but the percentage of success from this area is competitive exams has gone up.

Admission in Medical Courses

Jammu had 60 per cent share in MBBS admissions in 1990 which has decreased every year to 17-21 per cent during the period from 1995 to 2010. This percentage is less than 10 in general category.

J&K Public Service Commission

When Omar Abdullah became the Chief Minister after the assembly elections in 2008, there was full strength of Public Service Commission consisting of Seven Members and One Chairman. From the Jammu region there were three Members and five from Kashmir region including Chairman. The number started decreasing when Dr Goswami retired in 2009. After that Roop Lal Bharti, the second member from Jammu region retired on May 29, 2011 and thereafter only one Member from Jammu region KB Jandial has remained to represent the Jammu region, whileas there are three Members including the Chairman from Kashmir region. Because of brute majority of the Members some times unfair selections are also made. Many such selections have been quashed in the High Court, but all of the aggrieved candidates cannot knock the doors of the High Court and discrimination in the recruitment of Gazetted Services in the government goes on unabated. Similar is the case in case of non-gazetted recruitments.

Discrimination with Ladakh

Sheer discrimination with Ladakh region has been going on in Jammu and Kashmir right from the Constitution of a democratic government in the State. In order to resolve this problem, Autonomous Hill Development Council, on the patter of Gorkhaland in West Bengal, was constituted for both districts of Ladakh. But even after that the discrimination with the region continued.

The Jammu and Kashmir Public Service Commission conducted an examination for the recruitment of KAS and KPS officers in 1997-98. One Christian, three Muslims and 23 Buddhist candidates cleared this examination. Interestingly, one Christian and three Muslims who cleared the exams were given appointment but from the 23 successful Buddhists only one person was given appointment. This one example is sufficient to gauge the discrimination being meted out to the Buddhists of Ladakh.

There is a separate cadre for the employees of State Secretariat who are called Secretariat Cadre Employees. They are about 3,500 today. A very nominal representation is from Ladakh region.

The number of State Government employees in 1996 was 2.54 lakh which increased to 3.58 lakh in 2000. About 1.04 lakh of them were recruited only during the regime of Farooq Abdullah as Chief Minister. Only 319 of them, which is just 0.31 per cent of the total recruitment, were from Ladakh.

The number of the employees working in public sector is 21,286. Out of it, only three Buddhists have been given job in the State Transport Corporation, No Buddhist was granted a job in the eight other PSUs.

Similarly, 24 Patwaris were recruited in the State in 1997. There was only one Buddhist among them and rest were Muslims. Similarly, 40 employees were recruited in the State education department under fourth class category and all of them, barring only one, were Muslims.

The height of injustice is seen when the Buddhist do not get permission to perform last rites of their dead one in Muslim-dominated areas. They have to take the dead body to Buddhist-dominated areas to perform last rites.

The State Government has been repeatedly making attempts to popularize this region as a hot tourist spot, but it does not take any step to preserve and promote the local Buddhist culture, Buddhist temples and heritage sites which are endangered due to infiltration and are also losing their importance and privacy.

Since all controls of the region are done from the Kashmir Valley, the Ladakhi language and culture are in danger. The Bhoti language of Ladakh has been very rich since time immemorial. Many highly significant Sanskrit texts which are not available in other parts of the country are still safe in Bhoti language. Since the State Government has made Urdu as compulsory language, majority of the Buddhist students from Ladakh are forced to study out of the region. The Bhoti language can be preserved only by including it in the 14th Schedule of the Constitution.

About 1,600 kms long border of India lies with Ladakh. Keeping in view the strategic importance of the region the only way to protect the borders and the protection and preservation of the Ladakhi culture is to declare it a Union Territory.

Note: The above stated facts of discrimination are taken from a book *Jammu-Kashmir: Facts, Problems and Solution* by Ashutosh. Recently some improvement has taken place after the establishment of Ladakh Development Council. The writer of this book subscribes to the later view and doubt about the authenticity of some of the facts and figures but not as a whole.

Wazir Commission Report

In order to remove the irritations in respect of administrative matters between two regions, Sheikh Abdullah who initially was the head of Emergency Administration and then Prime Minister under Maharaja from 5th March 1948 till August 1953 ruled the State as absolute ruler. His second term was as Chief Minister from 1975 to 1982. He was compelled to appoint Chief Justice JN Wazir (Retd) of the J&K

High Court to head the Commission which is known as Wazir Commission for the creation of new districts in order to remove the grievances of the people residing in far flung areas. This Commission remained on job for three years, i.e. from 12 November 1981 to 3 January 1984 and had taken into cognizance the historical aspects as well as other relevant facts while making the recommendations. It is appropriate to state here that during Maharaja Hari Singh's time due to the vastness of the Jammu region area it had five districts and two jagirs (Chenani and Poonch) and Kashmir region had three districts. Even up to 1975, when Sheikh Abdullah came to power after an Accord with Mrs Indira Gandhi, Jammu region had six districts (Udhampur, Jammu, Kathua, Doda, Rajouri and Poonch) and Kashmir region had three districts (Srinagar, Anantnag and Baramulla). Without waiting for the receipt of the commission's report, Sheikh Abdullah in a great hurry on 1 July 1979 as Chief Minister suo moto carved out three more districts in Kashmir region and one more district for Ladakh region, i.e. Kargil district. Wazir Commission had in 1984, recommended creation of nine districts for Jammu region and creation of seven districts for Kashmir region. After the death of Sheikh Abdullah his successor government headed by his son Dr Farooq Abdullah maintained this status during his tenure as chief minister but Congress coalition government supported by PDP (People's Democratic Party) and led by Congress nominee Chief Minister Ghulam Nabi Azad in order to gain political sympathy of Kashmir region added four districts in the kitty of Kashmir region making a total of ten districts. The Jammu region at that time had six districts and there was recommendation of Wazir Commission for increasing the number up to nine districts but without caring for the recommendations he (Ghulam Nabi Azad) added one more district and made the equal number of ten districts each in order to place the two regions at par. In other words, against the recommendation of nine districts in Jammu region, addition of only one district was made and for the recommendation of seven districts for Kashmir region three more districts were added. The Wazir Commission had taken into consideration the geographical compactness, ethnical similarity and other relevant factors into considerations. Location of Kashmir region is very compact as it has 75 per cent terrain as plane. Jammu region has not more than 25 per cent area as plane. Facilities of communications, percentage of area covered by roads in Kashmir region is almost double in number than that of Jammu region. The Commission appears to have taken cognizance of the area, backwardness, topography, geographical continuity and distribution of population and area of the regions. At the time, when Wazir Commission was on the job, road network was merely 5,000 kilometre in Kashmir region as less than 3,500 kilometre in Jammu region. The total combined area of present Baramulla and Kupwara districts is 6,977 sq kms whereas Doda district comprises of 11,691 sq kms. The recommendations of Wazir Commission if accepted would have made Jammu Division entitled for more funds allocations in comparison to Kashmir Division. This is a grave injustice by way of discrimination with the inhabitants of Jammu region and violative of constitutional guarantees granted under the Indian Constitution and J&K Constitution.

Report of Delimitation Commission, 1995 is Void Ab Initio and Setting up a New Delimitation Commission is a Constitutional Requirement

Section 3 of The Jammu And Kashmir Representation of the People Act, 1957 deals with the Constitution of Delimitation Commission and it reads:

> As soon as may be after the completion of each census, the Governor shall constitute a Commission to be called the Delimitation Commission which shall consist of 3 members:
>
> Two members, each of whom shall be a person who is or has been a judge of the Supreme Court or of a High Court in India; and
>
> A Deputy Election Commissioner nominated by the Chief Election Commissioner.
>
> Provided that until the relevant figures for the first census taken after 2026 have been published, it shall not be necessary to constitute a Commission to determine the delimitation of Assembly constituencies in the State under this sub-section.

The Governor shall nominate one of the members appointed under Clause (a) of Sub-Subject (1) to be the Chairman of the Delimitation Commission.

The Delimitation Commission shall determine the Delimitation of Assembly constituencies in the State within such period as may be specified by the Governor.

Section 3-A deals with associate members and it requires that five members of the Legislative Assembly to be nominated by the Speaker should be associated with the Commission but none of the associate members shall have a right to vote or to sign any decision of the Commission.

It is worthwhile to mention here that after the census of 1981, the State Government headed by Sheikh Abdullah constituted

Delimitation Commission and Chief Justice Wazir Janki Nath (Retd) was nominated its Chairman. After sometime Chief Justice Mian Jalal-ul-Din (Retd) succeeded him as a Chairman who already was a member of the said Commission. He remained Chairman for long time but did not give his report. Meanwhile, militancy erupted in the State and under militant's threat he resigned from the post of Chairman. He had a sitting judge from Jammu region Justice KK Gupta as a member and after his resignation Justice KK Gupta (Retd) was made the Chairman. In this Commission, TN Sheshan (Chief Election Commissioner of India) was the third member but for the reasons best known to him he neither attended any meeting nor signed the report which was prepared by the Chairman under his own signatures and of the second member Justice AM Mir who was a sitting judge of J&K High Court. The State was at that time under Governor's Rule (from 1990 to 1996). Prior to the nomination of TN Seshan as third member his predecessor Peeri Shastri was the third member who had been attending all the meetings. The President by way of an Ordinance amended Sub-Clause (b) and instead of the Chief Election Commissioner, substituted Deputy Election Commissioner as a third member to be nominated by the Chief Election Commissioner of India. The Ordinance was made a law in 1997 by the State Legislature when it came into existence after the general elections of 1996. After the induction of Deputy Election Commissioner nominated by the Chief Election Commissioner as a third member, a new delimitation commission was constituted by substituting Justice GA Kuchhay (Retd) as a member in place of Justice AM Mir. Justice GA Kuchhay (Retd) after few days tendered his resignation as a member because he had been receiving threats to his life from militants. The resignation was accepted and Justice Bilal Nazki who was then a sitting judge of the J&K High Court was nominated as a member under Sub-Section 1(a) of Section 3. Long back in 1988, Sub-Clause (2) of Section 4 had been amended and the number of seats in the Legislative Assembly was increased from 76 to 87.

Under Section 4 of the J&K Representation of People Act, the Delimitation Commission had to readjust the extent and boundaries of the Assembly constituencies and determine the number of seats to be reserved for Scheduled Castes. While doing so, Commission had to take due regard to the population of the last census which was held in 1981. In the census of 1981, Kashmir region had a population of 31,34,409 whileas Jammu region had 27,18,113 inhabitants. The difference of the population was 4,16,791. Ladakh region had a population of 1,34,372. There were 42 Assembly constituencies for Kashmir region and 32 for Jammu region. The Ladakh region had 2 Assembly seats. In other words, there was a difference of 10 seats between two regions Jammu and Kashmir. At this material time, the Delimitation Commission had 11 more seats at its disposal to be distributed amongst the three regions. The commission allotted 4 seats to Kashmir region, 5 seats to Jammu region and 2 seats to Ladakh region. In this way, presently the Kashmir region has 46 Assembly seats whereas, Jammu region has 37 seats and Ladakh region has 4 seats. Besides taking into account the population of the last preceding census four other factors had to be given due consideration by the Delimitation Commission which are geographical compactness, nature of terrain, facilities of communication, and the like consideration. The Commission had failed to take into consideration all the above stated ingredients of Section 4 and in a casual and perfunctory manner allotted five seats out of eleven seats in favour of Jammu region. It is noteworthy that this Commission was the first local functional Delimitation Commission headed by a majority of two judges of the J&K High Court whileas the third member was Deputy Election Commissioner of India. They had the ground reality knowledge to adjust the seats by carving out the Assembly constituencies after taking into consideration the injustice done in the past. It is worthwhile to mention here that the first two elections of 1952 and 1957 in J&K were conducted under the control of State Election and Franchise Commissioner. Later, the elections of 1962, 1967, 1972, 1977, 1983 and 1987 were supervised and controlled by Election Commission of India. Before 1967, nominated members were sent to the Lok Sabha from the State of J&K. During 1960, a Delimitation Commission was constituted under the Chairmanship of Justice GI Kapur with RC Soni, retired judges of the Punjab High Court and KVK Sundaram, Chief Election Commissioner as its members and PS Subramanian as Secretary of the Commission. The Delimitation Commission carved out the territory of constituencies. The Constitution of J&K was enacted in 1957 by the Constituent Assembly which had its source from the Constitution of J&K of 1939 enacted by the Maharaja and that time, the Constitution of 1939 was still in force. Under the Constitution of 1939, Democratic Rights for holding elections of the 'Praja Sabha' for electing the representatives were conferred by the Maharaja on the basis of equality of number of voters. After the accession of the State with dominion of India, Constituent Assembly was constituted under the Maharaja's Constitution of 1939 but Sheikh Abdullah's administration without any basis carved out 30 seats for Jammu region and 43 seats for Kashmir region and 2 seats for Ladakh region. This basic Human Right of Equality disappeared when reigns of powers were transferred in a democratic setup headed by Sheikh Mohammed Abdullah. The people of the State had no Fundamental Rights till 1954. They were extended when Bakshi Ghulam Mohammad had replaced Sheikh Mohammed Abdullah as Prime Minister of the State of J&K. The Constitution of J&K came into force on 26 January 1957. Prior to the Constitution of above stated Delimitation Commission, it is reiterated that elections were being held at the discretion of political executive headed by two successive Prime Ministers Sheikh Abdullah and Bakshi Ghulam Mohammad. Already it stands discussed in this book how they were arbitrary and discriminatory in giving equal representation to other two regions. When the first Delimitation Commission under the supervision of Election Commission of India was set up, the electorates of Jammu and Kashmir enjoyed the Fundamental Rights with some modifications as guaranteed in the Constitution of India along with other citizens of India. The first Delimitation Commission should have addressed itself to safeguard the Fundamental Rights such as Articles 13, 19 and 21 but the ground reality reveals that they stand trampled down. Unfortunately, the second Delimitation Commission without showing any compliance to all the ingredients of Section 4 of the Representation of People's Act perpetuated the injustice which already had been done. The result is that the report of the Commission of 1995, would have prospective adverse effect on the electorates of Jammu region beyond 2031 till new census would be held and the setting up of a Delimitation Commission thereafter takes place. In this way, the report of Delimitation Commission suffers from the vires of inherent patent illegality and as such is void ab initio.

Before the submission of the current Delimitation Commission's report, elections were held in 1987. At that time, the electorate's strength for Kashmir region was 19,21,179 while that of Jammu region was 15,39,269. Average number of electorate's per Assembly seat for Kashmir region was 45,742 and for Jammu region was 48,102. After the submission of the Delimitation Commission's report the electoral strength of 1996 Assembly elections for Kashmir region was 23,81,859 and for Jammu region was 22,40,769. Average number of electorates per Assembly seat for Kashmir region was 51,780 and for Jammu region 60,561. In the elections held in 2002 for the State Legislative Assembly, the total number of electorates for Kashmir region was 28,84,852 whereas for Jammu region was 31,06,280. The average number of electorates per Assembly seat for Kashmir region was 62,714 and for Jammu region was 83,964.

In the elections held for Legislative Assembly of 2008, the total number of electorate's in Kashmir region was 32,81,113 and in Jammu region was 30,47,264. The average number of electorate's for Kashmir region was 71,329 and for Jammu region 82,358.

From the above quoted figures, it becomes crystal clear that after the submission of the Delimitation Commission's Report in 1995, the average number of electorates per Assembly seat for the Jammu region is constantly on the increase. It is a matter of great concern that during the elections of 2002 Jammu region had 2,21,428 more electorates than Kashmir region but thereafter an adverse trend started and since then the strength of electorates of Kashmir region is constantly on the increase. Viewed from another angle on the basis of the available figures it is found that difference of average electorates per Assembly constituency seat in the census of 1981 was much less as the difference of population between the two regions was 4,16,791 and according to the census of 2011 the population of Kashmir region has shown an abnormal increase and it has swelled up to 69,07,623 whileas Jammu region's population has increased at a lower scale up to 53,50,811. In other words, Jammu region has not even doubled its numbers of population. On the contrary, the population of Kashmir region has reached more than double number of population from the census of 1981 to the census of 2011. To make it more clear the difference of population between the two regions has gone up to 15,56,812 in 2011 from a difference of 4,16,791 in 1981. The adverse effect for the denial of fair treatment in respect of electorate's rights is illustrated by a survey sample of the Assembly elections of 2008 while dealing with the elections of two capital cities of the regions of Jammu and Kashmir. Assembly constituency number 71 (Gandhi Nagar) had 1,43,629 electorates whileas Jammu West constituency number 73 had 1,39,965 electorates. Khanyar constituency of Srinagar district had 48,900 electorates and Habakadal constituency had 49,667 electorates. If the electorates of both these constituencies are clubbed together the total comes to 98,567 electorates which figure is less than 45,062 electorates of single constituency of Gandhi Nagar. The scale of injustice has tilted in favour of Jammu region because the Delimitation Commission had not given due regard to the five parameters enshrined in Section 4 of the Act while re-adjusting the extent and boundaries of the Assembly constituencies. The ruling party in the State took benefit of this lopsided report by perpetuating their political domination over the electorates of the Jammu region. At that time, National Conference (regional political party) had a majority in the Legislature. They amended Section 47(3) of the Constitution of Jammu and Kashmir in 2002 and incorporated a proviso therein which States, "that until the relevant figures for the first census taken after 2026 have been published, it shall not be necessary to readjust the total number of seats in the Legislative Assembly of the State and the division of the State into territorial constituencies under this sub-section." The Legislature in

2002 resorted to a dubious device for depriving the due share of the electorates of Jammu region that would have gone to them in accordance with the mandates of unamended Section 3 of the J&K Representation of People Act after the exercise of census of 2001. A Delimitation Commission would have been mandatorily constituted and its verdict had to be carried out. Section 3 (Representation of People's Act) was amended along with Section 47(3) of the Constitution of J&K and the bar for readjustment of the total seats available was imposed till the figures of the first census taken after 2026 have been published. In other words, the establishment of Delimitation Commission was totally banned at least up to 2031. Undoubtedly, it is established law that there cannot be equality of the numbers of electorates in each and every constituency of the State because Section 4 of the Representation of The People Act prescribes the method to readjust the extent and the boundaries. This Section envisages that besides taking into account the population figure of the last census, the geographical compactness, nature of the terrain, facilities of communication and the like consideration have to be kept in mind by the Delimitation Commission. After the census of 1981, next two censuses were held in the State, i.e. in 2001 and 2011. After the census of 2001, the electorate's strength had gone up in Jammu region because of large scale migration of population from Kashmir region due to disturbed law and order conditions from 1990 onwards. Major chunk of the migrated population is still residing outside the limits of Kashmir region. In this way, the population of Jammu region has unimaginably increased but the census of 2011 has turned the table in favour of the electorates of Kashmir region and the figure as published lacks credibility. The remaining four factors enumerated in Section 4 continuously weigh in favour of Jammu region ever since the J&K People's Representation Act was enacted. The gap of strength of electorates is constantly on the increase qua the electorates of Jammu region per Assembly seat. The fundamental right of equality guaranteed to every citizen of the country under Article 14 of the Constitution without just classification cannot be taken away. Article 13 of the Constitution States those laws inconsistent with or in derogation of the Fundamental Rights shall be void to the extent of inconsistency. Article 15 prohibits discrimination on grounds of religion, race, caste, sex or place of birth. The State Legislature has amended Section 47(3) and Section 3 of the J&K Representation of People Act by exercising its powers as conferred by Article 370 of the Indian Constitution.

The above stated amendments were challenged by a political party of the State by the name of J&K National Panthers Party by filing a

Public Interest Litigation in the High Court of J&K which was decided by the Division Bench in the case of J&K National Panthers Party *vs* Union of India and Others 2010 (1) SLJ 1. The plea of the petitioner that stoppage of readjustment of the extent and boundaries of the territorial constituencies affects democracy as enshrined in the Constitution was not accepted. By dismissing the writ petition, the court was swayed by the principle that "Delimitation for the purpose of dividing the State into single member territorial constituencies to the extent of number of members of the Legislative Assembly is the mandate of the Constitution and is basic feature of democracy contemplated in the Constitution, but readjustment of the extent and boundaries of such territorial constituencies upon completion of each census is not such a mandate, nor it is contemplated to be the basic structure of democracy contemplated in the Constitution." It was further held that right of equality as guaranteed to the Citizens of India does not entail exact equality in the matter of weight of the voter by reasons of the other provisions contained in the Constitution of India.

The petitioner felt aggrieved from the judgment of the Division Bench and filed Civil Appeal Number of 2010 (arising out of SLP (C) Number 22224/09) in the Hon'ble Supreme Court which was dismissed on 9 November 2010. The appellant petitioner had challenged the vires of the amendment of Section 3 of the J&K Representation of the People Act and amendment of Section 47(3) of the Constitution of J&K on the ground that in view of the postponing of the delimitation of the constituencies, the growing imbalance in the matter of composition of various constituencies would continue despite the census operation being carried out.

It is an admitted fact that Delimitation Report was given in 1995. In the electoral history of the State it was the first judicial verdict when the Commission had two judicial members as Judges of the J&K High Court. One of them who was the chairman was a retired judge and the other was still a serving judge. Both of them were in a better position to know about the regional aspirations of two regions but none of them addressed himself to redress the existing imbalances. Under the J&K Representation of People Act, the aims and objects for setting up a new Delimitation Commission after the prescribed time limit was to distribute the constituencies in the State by readjustment and extent to remove the imbalances caused due to demographical and other changes which subsequently had to occur in the normal course of events. Afterwards, because of amendments incorporated in the State Constitution and J&K Representation of People Act respectively, discriminatory and arbitrary distribution of Assembly seats already favouring the electorates of Kashmir region would last at least till 2031 when blanket ban imposed up to 2026 by the amendments for carrying the census operation would expire. The Delimitation Report of 1995 should have been based on the mandates of Section 4 of the J&K Representation of People Act read with the relevant provisions of the Indian Constitution and Constitution of J&K which protect the Constitutional Rights and Statutory Rights of all the inhabitants of three regions of the State but the factum of imbalances and injustice done to the electorates on regional basis was allowed to continue unaltered. The first elections of Constituent Assembly were held in 1951. Thereafter the State Assembly constituency elections were held in 1957 and at that time also the political executive power as well as Legislative power was overwhelmingly controlled by the leadership of Kashmir region. During the elections of 1951 even Fundamental Rights were denied by Sheikh Abdullah to the residents of the State and in an arbitrary and despotic manner he had fixed 43 seats for Kashmir region and 30 seats for Jammu region. He had allotted 2 seats for Ladakh region. Unfortunately, both the above mentioned Delimitation Commissions had failed to set aside the wrongs committed perpetually. To add insult to the injury the past adverse affects for the deprivation of Constitutional and Statutory Rights of the electorates of Jammu region for 35 years more from the date of second Delimitation Commission's verdict would continue. During 1991, the census operation was due but the same could not be held because of widespread disturbed law and order conditions on account of onset of militancy. During that period, large scale migration of the population from Kashmir region took place particularly of Hindu minority community as a whole and selectively amongst the members of the majority community who overtly or covertly had sided with national and secular forces of the country.

The grievances which the appellant had projected before the Hon'ble Supreme Court have been highlighted in the judgment and they are: postponing of the Delimitation of constituencies as a result of the aforesaid amendments, the growing imbalance in the matter of composition of various constituencies would continue despite the census operations being carried out. That as a result of census operation, the composition of the population is reflected and that gives rise to an exercise in Delimitation for a proper representation of the rights of the people in a democratic polity. Without these demographical changes being properly reflected in the composition of the constituencies by way of Delimitation exercise, the essence of democracy will be defeated in the elections. That last census was held in 2001 and without setting up a Delimitation Commission and accepting its report, the true voice and popular view of the democracy would not find proper representation.

During the course of arguments, the counsel of the appellant had urged that out of 37 constituencies in Jammu region, some are reserved for Scheduled Caste and Scheduled Tribes whereas, of 46 constituencies in Kashmir region, not even a single seat is reserved for Scheduled Caste and Scheduled Tribes when in fact on the basis of electorates strength some constituencies should have been reserved for Scheduled Castes and Scheduled Tribes. This means that reserved seats would not be rotated or changed for 35 years.

In para number 11 of the judgment, the Hon'ble Supreme Court has observed that no substantial challenge has been made to the amendment of the Constitution of J&K in the writ petition by the appellant. In para number 12 it is further mentioned, "We do not find adequate pleading challenging the amendment to Section 47 of the Constitution of J&K." During the course of arguments it was pleaded that not holding of a Delimitation exercise immediately after the completion of the census as a result of the aforesaid amendment is unconstitutional. That amendment was itself violative of the basic structure of the Constitution of India as applicable to the State as well as to State Constitution.

The appeal was dismissed after holding that Delimitation Laws made under Article 327 of the Constitution of India are immune from the judicial test of their validity and the process of allotment of seats and constituencies is not liable to be called in question in any court by virtue of Article 329(A) of the Constitution of India read with Section 142(A) of the Constitution of J&K. In holding so, the Apex Court was guided by the law laid down by the Constitution Bench of the Supreme Court in the case of RC Poudyal and others *vs* Union of India and others (1994), Supp 1 SCC 324 wherein it is held that perfectly arithmetical equality of value of votes is not a constitutionally mandated imperative of democracy and that even if the impugned provisions make a departure from tolerance limits and the constitutionally permissible latitudes, the discriminations arising are justifiable on the basis of the historical considerations peculiar to and characteristic of the evolution of Sikkim's political institutions and the same is true in case of J&K State.

Article 327 of the Constitution of India empowers the Parliament to make a law relating to Delimitation of constituencies. The mandate of Article 329(A) is that any law relating to the Delimitation of constituencies or allotment of seats to such constituencies shall not be called in question in any court. Identical provision has been made in Section 142(a) of the Constitution of J&K. While dismissing the appeal, it was held that challenge regarding basic structure of the Constitution is also not based on a sound principle.

With due respect to the Division Bench judgment of the High Court as well as that of the Apex Court, it can reasonably be said that the petitioner of this case had failed to project its case in its true perspective on factual and legal matrix. The historical and political background as well as constitutional aspects should have been set out in the pleadings in detail and amendments incorporated in Section 3 of the J&K Representation of People Act as well as in Section 47(3) of the Constitution of J&K should have been dilated at the touch stone of their constitutional propriety. At the outset, lopsided, arbitrary and discriminatory nature of the Delimitation Commission report which has shaken the constitutional structure of the Constitution of India as well as Constitution of J&K should have been discussed in detail within the parameters of law. The injustice done in the report of Delimitation Commission for the fair exercise of voting by the electorates of Jammu region had shown their adverse effects in the State Assembly elections of 1996, 2002 and 2008 whereby their Fundamental Rights were trampled. The injustice was done because of aforesaid amendments and the adverse effects whereof would last up to 2031 when census would be held and by way of fulfilling the statutory requirement a Delimitation Commission would be setup to readjust the constituencies and the extent of their boundaries. The ratio decidendi of the case of Kesavananda Bharati *vs* State of Kerala 1973 SC 1463 should have been reflected in the pleadings and reiterated in the arguments. The decision was rendered by the Constitution Bench of the Hon'ble Supreme Court consisting of 13 judges, wherein the basic structure of the Constitution was held to be of unalterable nature. The basis structure in its essential broader sense has been stated consisting of the following features:

Supremacy of the Constitution.

Republican and democratic form of government.

Secular character of the Constitution.

Separation of powers between the Legislature, the Executive and the Judiciary.

Federal character of the Constitution.

The Hon'ble Supreme Court in the said appeal (SLP 22224/09) in para number 29 has elaborated the concept of basic structure in a more explicit, transparent and exhaustive manner by stating, "it is hazardous to define what is Basic Structure of the Constitution as what is basic does not remain static for all time to come." They have referred 14th edition of Shorter Constitution of India by DD Basu and have noted down the basic features which have been culled out from various pronouncements of the Supreme Court. Although the above noted five ingredients of Basic Structures remain the genesis but their species have been enumerated in the judgment under heads (a) to (v). Shorn of unessentials which are not germane to the present controversy the remaining are stated hereunder:

(b) The principles behind Fundamental Rights.

(c) The objectives specified in the Preamble to the Constitution.

(i) Freedom and dignity of the individual.

(m) The 'essence' of other Fundamental Rights in Part III.

(n) The concept of social and economic justice—to build a welfare State.

(q) The principle of free and fair elections.

(r) Limitations upon the amending power conferred by Art. 368.

Adverting to the facts of the present case in hand, the amendments in question have violated the secular character of the Constitution of J&K as well as that of Constitution of India because the principles behind the Fundamental Rights, their essence and dignity of the electorates of Jammu region are denied in violations of the guarantees of Fundamental Rights enshrined in Articles 13, 14, 15 and 21 of the Indian Constitution. The secular character is one of the hallmarks of the basic structure but there is discrimination with the electorates of Jammu region in respect of the weight of their votes on the basis of religion and domicile. Hindus are of minority status in the State but in Jammu region they are in majority. Instead of protecting their minority status the value of their votes have been devalued. To add fuel to the fire, approximate equality in the voice of every voter irrespective of his/her religious faith in the Jammu region is a cry in the wilderness. The fundamental right of equality without any justification or classification runs contrary to the Preamble of the Constitution and basic fundamental structure. In other words, the electorates of Jammu region can claim equal or more weight of their votes because their case falls securely within the bounds of criteria laid down in Section 4 of the J&K Representation of People Act as they have more population in many defined areas of their respective Assembly constituencies. This can be said so because they do not have comparable geographical compactness, existence of hilly areas inclusive of barren and inaccessible terrain and less facilities of communication as compared to Kashmir region which has less number of electorates in their many constituencies and they have an advantage of geographical compactness, plane nature of terrain and more facilities of communication. The population of Jammu region is heterogeneous in contrast to the population of Kashmir region which is homogenous. Statistical figures regarding the vastness of the area of Jammu region along with other requisite criteria have been stated above and need not be repeated. It is worthwhile to mention here that State Legislature and Indian Parliament in the Centre have the powers to amend their Constitutions as well as Statutes falling respectively within their specified domains. This power is restricted to the extent of not rendering any fundamental right as redundant, extinct or abrogated but in the present case, the State Legislature has exercised this power without any justification or classification and thus, basic features of the Indian Constitution under above said heads (c), (m) and (n) stand denied. The Constitution does not allow any such amendments under Article 368 of the Indian Constitution which goes against any of the basic feature. On the same basis the principle of free and fair elections as envisaged under above stated head (q) can also be not altered. The above stated heads (q) and (r) are to be given harmonious construction in contrast to contradictory construction. The conclusion arrived at by the Hon'ble Supreme Court in para 31 of the judgment in appeal is the result of not presenting the case on true facts. This discussion would remain incomplete without referring to the Constitution scheme on the basis of historical facts when Constitution of J&K State was enacted because in the judgment in appeal, historical facts of Sikkim State were taken into consideration by allowing the reservation on less number of voters as a whole.

Before 26 October 1947, Maharaja Hari Singh who being the sovereign head of the State of J&K was the fountain head of administration and repository of all the powers of the governance, i.e. administrative, legislative and judicial. His word was final in all spheres. Being the sole sovereign head he could even transfer or lease any part of his dominion to a foreign power of course with the concurrence of Governor-General of the British dominion as he had done in case of Gilgit agency by leasing out the same to British Government for 60 years. In the exercise of his internal absolute sovereign power, he had pardoned the sentence imposed by a Court of Law upon Sheikh Abdullah and released him from jail in the month of September 1947 when unconditional apology was tendered to the former by the latter. He had appointed Sheikh Abdullah as Emergency Administrator at the biding of Pandit Jawaharlal Nehru, the then Prime

Minister of India. Under compelling circumstances while keeping in view the national interest Maharaja within a short period of five months had appointed Sheikh Abdullah as his Prime Minister in the month of March 1948 when the term of the already duly appointed Prime Minister Mehr Chand Mahajan had to expire in 1952. Maharaja had appointed his son Dr Karan Singh as his Regent who on 1st May 1951 issued a proclamation for convening Constituent Assembly for enacting the State Constitution. On 15th October 1951, National Conference of Sheikh Abdullah had won all the 75 seats which were not contested due to unfair electoral process. On October 31, 1951, first session of Constituent Assembly started in Srinagar. The Regent had exercised his delegated powers under J&K Constitution which was enacted by the Maharaja in 1939. The Constitution of J&K Constituent Assembly was an event of great importance in the political history of the State. It started its work on November 5, 1951 when Sheikh Abdullah was the Prime Minister under the sovereignty of Maharaja Hari Singh. In the Constitution of J&K of 1939, Maharaja had ensured the voting right on the basis of equality for all the regions of the State. The State of that time was also comprised of the territory which illegally is still in the occupation of Pakistan Sheikh Abdullah had arbitrary allotted the seats to each of the remaining three regions despite the fact that Maharaja Hari Singh still was de facto and de jure ruler of the State. Instead of getting his prior concurrence he was not even consulted or informed. The task of Constitution making in true sense of the term started in 1954 when in 1953 Sheikh Abdullah had lost the vote of confidence in the Constituent Assembly and his Deputy Prime Minister Bakshi Ghulam Mohammad was unanimously elected as leader of the Constituent Assembly. It entered a decisive phase when in the 12th session of the Constituent Assembly, held from September 29, 1956 to November 19, 1956, the Drafting Committee on October 10, 1956 presented a Draft Constitution which after detailed discussions was approved and adopted on 17 November 1956 and the Constitution came into force on 26 January 1957. The Preamble is clearly an adaptation of the Preamble to the Constitution of India which reads as under:

> WE, THE PEOPLE OF THE STATE OF JAMMU AND KASHMIR, having solemnly resolved, in pursuance of the accession of this State to India which took place on the 26th day of October 1947, to further define the existing relationship of the State with the Union of India as an Integral part whereof, and to secure to ourselves:
>
> JUSTICE, social, economic and political;

LIBERTY of thought, expression, belief, faith and worship;

EQUALITY of status and of opportunity; and to promote among us all;

FRATERNITY assuring the dignity of the individual and the unity of the NATION;

IN OUR CONSTITUENT ASSEMBLY this seventeenth day of November 1956, do HEREBY ADOPT, ENACT AND GIVE TO OURSELVES THIS CONSTITUTION.

Preamble of an Act is a key to unfold and understand the intent and objects of its enactment contained in its provisions. The Preamble of Constitution of J&K at the outset ensures justice, social, economic and political. It also saves the equality of status and of opportunity and assures the dignity of the individual. By making amendments in Section 47(3) of the Constitution of Jammu and Kashmir and Section 3 of the J&K Representation of People Act, justice has been denied in respect of social, economic and political matters as well as equality of status and dignity of the electorates of Jammu region as a whole. The Hon'ble Supreme Court while deciding the appeal in question was swayed by the principles laid down in the decision of Constitution Bench in the case of RC Poudyal's (Supra). Undoubtedly, the Apex Court has held that a perfect arithmetical equality of value of votes is not a constitutionally mandated imperative of democracy and, even if the impugned provisions which deny the equality make a departure from tolerance limits and the constitutionally permissible latitudes, the discriminations arising are justifiable on the basis of the historical considerations peculiar to and characteristic of the evolution of Sikkim's (State) political institutions. The provision in the Constitution indicating proportionality of representation is necessarily a broad, general and logical principle but not intended to be expressed with arithmetical precision. The principle of mathematical proportionality of representation is not a declared basic requirement in each and every part of the territory of India. Disregarding the statutory and constitutional dispensation based on historical reasons is not a justifiable right. While applying this principle to the facts of the present case in hand the appeal was dismissed.

It has already been said above that the appellant (Petitioner herein) had failed to bring into the kind notice of the Hon'ble High Court as well that of the Hon'ble Supreme Court that the basic structure of the constitutional scheme as applicable to the State has been eroded so far as the political right of voting is concerned along with other criteria as set out in the Preamble of the Constitution of J&K and the Constitution of India. The concept of social and economic justice to build a Welfare State is one of the requirements of the Preamble of Constitution of J&K and that has been eroded along with other basic structures as enumerated above so far as the electorates of Jammu region are concerned. The region has a little less than the double area of Kashmir region. It comprises of hills, mountains, having less connectivity and diverse culture and languages. On the basis of statutory criteria prescribed in Section 4 of the J&K Representation of People Act, the Jammu region electorates can claim more constituencies than the allotment made in favour of Kashmir region. The present allotment is a departure not from tolerance limits and the constitutionally permissible latitudes. This is not only a case of pure arithmetical exactness or precision of equality but departure from approximate equality in the voice of every voter residing in the Jammu region. The historical background also tilts in favour of the Jammu region because before the invasion of Pakistan in 1947, the Constitution of J&K of 1939 which was enacted by the ruler treated equally the residents of both regions in respect of the number of voters despite the fact the ruler belonged to Jammu region. The Jammu region was the worst sufferer on account of that invasion as it had lost its more area and population as compared to Kashmir region. Thousands of inhabitants belonging to both the communities were uprooted, massacred by invaders or mutually due to communal frenzy but Kashmir region which had minority status at that time, both in population and area-wise, gained an upper hand in taking the reins of government in their hands. The uprooted Hindus and Sikhs from Muzaffarabad district and part of Baramulla district of Kashmir region in 1947 were not allowed to settle in Kashmir region by Sheikh Abdullah. In 1949, the State Constituent Assembly was constituted by the ruler through the delegated power on his son (Dr Karan Singh) and he remained elected head of the State as Sadar-i-Riyasat for two consecutive terms. The Constitution of J&K was drafted, enacted and came into force during his tenure. Because of the existence of Delimitation Commission's Report and unconstitutional amendments in question even the status of Dr Karan Singh along with his descendants have been diminished because of lesser weightage of voting pattern when they are registered voters in their ancestral city of Jammu but the value would increase in case they become registered voters in the concerned Assembly constituency of ancestral Srinagar city where they too have ancestral property. In the back ground of the above stated history, the ratio decidendi of the Constitution Bench ruling (Supra) also favours the case of electorates of Jammu region on the historical background. Not only that, Pandit Nehru and Sheikh Abdullah at a joint conference on July 24, 1952 had declared that, "the State Government was considering Regional Autonomies within the Larger State." (Reference write-up by Balraj Puri, journalist, in the issue of *The Times of India*, July 23, 2002.)

The amending power conferred by Article 368 of the Constitution of India as per the mandates of the law of the land as well as of the Constitution of J&K illustrated in this judgment of the appeal cannot dilute the basic features of sub heads (r) and (q). In a nutshell, principles of free and fair elections have also been recognized as one of the basic feature. Both the basic features (r) and (q) have to be read not in contradiction to each other but in contradistinction to each other. In case the malady of amendments in question are properly re-agitated on the factual and legal matrix, it is quite possible in the humble view of the writer of this book, that the amendments incorporated in Section 47(3) of the Constitution of J&K and Section 3 of the J&K Representation of People Act may be declared as null and void.

In the case of Satwant Singh *vs* APO, New Delhi, AIR, 1967, SC, 1836, it has been held that such a law would be void, if it discriminates or enables an authority to discriminate between persons without just classification. The absence of arbitrary power is the first essential of the rule of law upon which the whole of Indian constitutional system is based. Equality is for equals, that is to say, those who are similarly circumstanced or entitled to an equal treatment. Article 14 applies where equal is treated differently without any basis. Article 15 mandates that State shall not discriminate against any citizen on grounds only of religion, race, caste, sex and place of birth or any of them in respect of the matters specified therein. Article 21 protects the dignity and honour of the life of a Citizen. The discriminations of unpalatable nature stare at the face of the Delimitation Report and subsequent amendments incorporated in Section 47(3) of the Constitution of J&K and Section 3 of the J&K Representation of People Act when one compares the electorates strength of two constituencies of winter capital of Jammu city with any of the eight Assembly constituencies falling in the limits of summer capital of Srinagar city. An example has been already given above how the electorate's strength of Gandhi Nagar constituency or that of Jammu West constituency excels in the total strength of two constituencies of Srinagar city. Before closing this chapter it would be appropriate to mention here that the electorates of Jammu region have been denied the benefits of Articles 6 and 7 of the Universal Declaration of Human Rights 1948. In this view of the matter, the amendments engrafted in Section 47(3) of the State Constitution and Section 3 of the Representation of the People Act require to be declared as ultra vires of the Constitution by a competent court by re-agitating the matter in its true perspective. It follows from above made discussion that for the sake of good governance based on upholding Rule of Law setting up of a fresh Delimitation Commission in the State is overdue after the completion of census of 2011. The full Bench of the Patna High Court in the case of Janardhan Paswan *vs* State AIR 1988 Pat 75 at para 42 has held that prohibition of discrimination on the grounds of race or caste enshrined in Article 15(1) permeates the electoral rights of franchise.

At the end of this discussion, it would be beneficial to state here that the report of Delimitation Commission runs contrary to the constitutional provision of Section 50 of the State Constitution wherein the Constituent Assembly of the State has provided more representation to the electorates of Jammu region than that of Kashmir region. The Section deals with the composition of Legislative Council. It is provided therein that Legislative Council shall consist of 36 members, chosen in the manner provided in this Section. Sub-Clause 2 states that 11 members shall be elected by the members of the Legislative Assembly from amongst persons who are residents of province of Kashmir and are not members of the Legislative Assembly inclusive of two Ladakh seats. Sub-Clause 3 states that 11 members shall be elected by the members of the Legislative Assembly from amongst persons who are residents of province of Jammu and are not members of the Legislative Assembly. From the above it transpires that Kashmir region returns only nine members in the Legislative Council.... The same constitutional criteria at least should have been adopted by the Delimitation Commission while fixing the number extent and readjustment of the State Assembly constituencies because at that time there existed no amendments in Section 47(3) of the State Constitution and Section 3 of the J&K Representation of People Act. In the same way, the State Legislative Assembly in 2002 while incorporating the above stated amendments should not have over reached the wisdom of their predecessors who were the members of State Constituent Assembly. They should have, in order to make the democracy more representative, democratic, equitable enduring, visible and transparent, given at least equal representation to the electorates of Jammu region although five parameters laid down in Section 4 of the J&K Representation of People Act increases their share.

In a democratic polity which is governed by written Constitution and where rule of law is paramount, judiciary is regarded as sentinel on the qui vive not only to protect the Fundamental Rights of the citizens but also to see that the democratic values as enshrined in the

Constitution are respected and the hope and faith of the people in the constitutional system are not atrophied. Sacrosanctity of Rule of Law neither recognizes a master and a slave nor does it conceive of a ruler and a subject but, in quintessentially, encapsules and sings in glory of the values of liberty, equality and justice in accordance with law requiring the present generation to have the responsibility to sustain them with all fairness for the posterity ostracizing all affectations.

CHAPTER 2

Appraisal of the History

History is a dialogue between the past and the present, addressed to the future. Walter Benjamin has said, "There is a secret agreement between the past generations and the present ones." India had never known the study of History but Kashmir is an exception where a great historian by the name of Kalhana (12th century) wrote his immortal work 'Rajatarangini' in Sanskrit poetry which gives some glimpses of the contemporary times as well as of the past.

Antiquity

It is narrated in 'Nilmatapurana' that the name of the Valley at one time was 'Satisar'—the lake. There is a myth that a devil by the name of Jalodbhava came to live here at the instance of Nila but when this devil started the destruction of the inhabitants living in the surrounding areas, Nila sought the help of his mentor Kashyap Rishi who sought the help of Brahma, Vishnu and Shiva. The Kashyap Rishi with their blessings cut the mountains from Baramulla side and thus, dried the lake. By this the devil could not get any hiding place for shelter and ultimately he was beheaded by Lord Vishnu with his 'Sudarshana Chakra'. The Nagas were the earliest known inhabitants. Aryans also moved to this area and they acquired dominance throughout the Valley.

Period of Hindu and Buddhist Kings

Gonanda is the first known king of Kashmir and he was a relation and friend of Jarasandha (king of Magdha). He had gone to help Jarasandha in a war against Lord Krishna and was killed by the latter. His son wanted to take revenge and he too was killed by Lord Krishna. His widow was made the ruler by Lord Krishna himself who was succeeded by her son known as Gonanda-II. After him, Kashmir was ruled by at least 43 kings.

Ashoka (273-232 BC)

He extended his control over Kashmir and encouraged Buddhism in the Valley and built Viharas and Stupas. He was not intolerant of Hinduism. He repaired old Shiva temples and constructed two new ones. He founded the ancient capital city known as Srinagari about five kilometres away from the present city of Srinagar. His son Jalauka after him became Monarch of Kashmir and he came under the influence of Hinduism. Three centuries later Kashmir passed under the control of Kushans. The most powerful monarch of this dynasty was Kanishka whose rule extended to north-western India and Central Asia. Buddhism was adopted as State religion. Kashmiri missionaries carried the messages of Buddhism to China and far of places in South Central Asia. The fourth Buddhist Council was held by Kanishka in Kashmir at a place called Kundalvara.

The Kushans were succeeded by a number of rulers and noteworthy amongst them were: Abhimanyu, Vhisana-I, Indrajit, Ravana and Vhisana-II. During the reign of these kings's Saivism progressed and Buddhism suffered. Hiuen-tsang the celebrated Chinese traveller came to Kashmir in AD 631. At that time, the Karkota dynasty was ruling over Kashmir and its founder, Durlabhavandhana, was the king. He held his sway over Taxila, Hazara, Poonch and Rajouri. He was under the suzerainty of emperor Harshavardhana whose capital was Kanouj. Hiuen-tsang thought poorly of the Kashmiris of the time. He recorded, "they are volatile and timid, they are good looking but deceitful. They are fond of learning and follow both Buddhism and Hinduism."

The most outstanding king of Karkota dynasty was Lalitaditya who ruled for 37 years from AD 724-761. Like Alexander the great, he was fervently motivated to be a conqueror. His kingdom extended up to the banks of river Cauvery in south India and to Kokan and Kathiawar in the west. In the east, he had his authority up to Bengal. In the east of the Kashmir Valley—Ladakh and part of Tibet were under his control. Some historians have expressed their doubt about his southern expeditions. The noble and memorable act of his life is the construction of Sun temple of Martanda near the present site known as Mattan (in South Kashmir). He was a staunch believer of Hinduism but equally liberal towards Buddhism. His successors proved incompetent and the dynasty collapsed by the middle of the 9th century. For the next one and half century the Kashmir history was influenced by women rulers. The first lady was Jayadevi who ruled the Valley as a mistress and succeeded in getting crown passed on to one of her brother's grandsons known as Avantivarman who founded the new dynasty of Uptala. Avantivarman ruled for 28 years (AD 855-883) and his period is known for developmental activities in irrigation and agricultural pursuits. He founded the town of Avantipur (situated on the National Highway) and the ruins of his two magnificent temples still attract the tourists. The rule of his dynasty ended in AD 939 when Yasaskaradeva—a Brahman was crowned as king and his rule lasted for 10 years as his Chief Minister enacted a coup and killed him. His name was Parava Gupta. His son Ksema Gupta (AD 950-958) ascended the throne and he married the daughter of Lorren King which is presently located in Poonch district. This lady dominated the Kashmir scene for fifty years, first as queen, then as Regent of her son and grandsons and finally as direct ruler. Her name was Didda. She was extremely beautiful, highly intelligent and uncommonly wayward. She favoured the politics of intrigues, murders and debauchery. At last, she succeeded in passing on the throne to the son of her brother Samgram Raja and this new dynasty of Kshatriyas came to be known as Lohara dynasty and they ruled the Kashmir from AD 1003-1101. The notable king of this dynasty is Jaya Singha (AD 1128-55). He ruled for 28 years and this period is considered as the age of 'Aryan Renaissance in Kashmir'. The next two hundred years saw only weak and selfish kings. During this period of moral decay, economic declines and political disruptions, foreign adventures started arriving in the Valley. The historical figures are Shahmir (alias Bulbul Shah) and Rinchin. Shahmir settled in a village near Baramulla and Rinchin in Lar. Both of them were helped by the Damra King by the name of Sahadeva, by grant of Jagirs.

Shahmir (Bulbul Shah) hailed from Turkistan and had stayed for a long period at Baghdad as a disciple of Shah Niamat Ullah Farzi of the Suhrawardi School of Sufis. Rinchin hailed from Ladakh and had taken a refuge in Kashmir after the murder of his father—a local chief in power struggle by the Baltis. Rinchin took undue advantage of the chaotic conditions created by weak king Suhadeva (forgetting the benevolent act done to him) and he plundered the area around the Lar Valley when king Suhadeva fled away at the time of foreign invasion in AD 1320, committed by one Mongol warrior hailing from Turkistan known as Dalacha. Dalacha had beheaded the men whosoever could be caught by him and taken away women and children as slaves. This invasion was the result because in Central Asia the Mohammedanized Turks had become more aggressive and the conversion as Muslims by coercion of Dards in the Indus Valley was taking place at a rapid speed. Islamic influence had been pouring in the populace of the Kashmir

Valley. After the flight of King Sahadeva, his Chief Minister (Ramchandra) had proclaimed him as king but Rinchin got Ramchandra murdered by deceitful means and thus, usurped the throne. In this manner, Kashmir Valley for the first time came to be ruled by a Ladakhi Buddhist.

Rinchin wanted to strengthen his position as a king by adopting the Hindu religion of his subjects and requested their revered head Shri Devaswami to admit him in the Hindu fold. The Pandits held a conclave and with one voice refused to grant him the privilege on the plea that the caste of his birth was doubtful. Rinchin was disappointed and he could not sleep during the night but early in the morning he heard a sharp and loud voice of the mauzin, "there is no God but God and the Mohammad is his prophet." He looked out from the window and observed Bulbul Shah at prayer. He went to him and embraced Islam. Due to the influence of Bulbul Shah alias Shah Mir, Kashmir came under the rule of first Muslim king—Rinchin and at that time, a small section of the local population had already embraced Islam. Rinchin got himself married with Kota Rani who was the daughter of slain Prime Minister Ramchandra. The rule of Rinchin lasted for three years (AD 1320-23). After his death the courtiers invited Udynadeva, real brother of the late King Sahadeva to accept the throne and he did so. To strengthen his position he married Kota Rani. The king was weak and lazy ruler and the real control of the kingdom was exercised by Kota Rani. At this time, second invader from Central Asia known as Achala appeared in the Valley and the king fled to Ladakh but Kota Rani and Shah Mir together defended the valley and compelled Achala to retreat. Shah Mir (Bulbul Shah) became the hero of the people and a de facto ruler. The King Udynadeva returned and died in AD 1338. Kota Rani kept his death a secret for four days. She moved to a safe place, i.e. in the fort of Indera Kot and proclaimed herself as the next ruler. Shah Mir challenged her position and came out in the struggle as victorious. After this, he asked Kota Rani to marry him. Kota Rani outwardly accepted the offer but before marriage could take place she committed suicide in the bridal chamber.

CHAPTER 3

Muslim, Sikh and Dogra Rulers

Muslim Rule

Shah Mir (Bulbul Shah) assumed the kingship under the title of Sultan Shamsh-ul-Din but he could also rule the Valley for three years (AD 1339-1342). His rule was humane and just. His dynasty is known in the history as 'Sultan Dynasty' and ruled the Valley for 222 years. During the rule of his one descendant Qutub-ud-Din (AD 1373-1389) Sayyid Ali Hamdani came to Kashmir and Islamic practices began to be adopted strictly. At this time, the king along with his converts to Islam had been following the Hindu customs, dresses and even performing the Yagyas. The king had no heir but in the old age was blessed by a Yogi named Brahmanath and obtained a son thereafter who was named Shingara. After ascending the throne he assumed the name as Sultan Sikandar (AD 1389-1413). He proved to be very cruel and bigoted king.

Sultan Sikandar

During his regime, a large number of Sufi saints and Islamic scholars came to Kashmir from Persia and Central Asia. About 700 Sayeeds accompanied Mohammad Hamdani son of Ali Hamdani. Through them the influence of Islam spread further in Kashmir. He also came in contact with Orthodox Sunnis and resolved to run the State on purely Islamic laws. He was actively assisted by a convert sadistic Kashmiri Pandit—Suha Bhat who adopted the name as Malik Saif-ud-Din. The Sultan banned all the un-Islamic practices such as drinking, gambling, dancing and playing of musical instruments. The Hindus were forbidden to apply 'Tilak' and they were subjected to pay the State Tax (Zizia). His Chief Minister (Suha Bhat) and Sultan himself threw into Dal Lake all the sacred books of the Hindus that they could lay their hands on and seven mands of sacred threads (Yagyo Paveets) of murdered Brahmins were burnt. From this period the population of Muslims came into prominence into the Valley. The Sultan is called 'Butt Shikan' (destroyer of idols). Many Hindus fled away from the Valley in order to save their lives and honour. He had even tried to pull down the famous Sun Temple of Martand. He was succeeded by his elder son who ruled the Valley for seven years and continued the policies of his father. After his death his younger brother succeeded him who ascended the throne under the title of Zain-ul-Abidin.

Zain-ul-Abidin (AD 1420-1470)

He completely reversed the policy of his father. All the restrictions against the Hindus were removed and cow slaughter was banned. Even the killing of fishes in sacred springs of Hindus was prohibited. He allowed the reconstruction of demolished temples and even he reconstructed some. He recalled Pandits who had fled the Valley due to religious persecution and assigned them responsible positions on the basis of merits. He laid down large number of canals and the annual rice production during his time arose up to 77 lakh Kharwars while in 1822-23 it could be 20 lakh Kharwars. He punished the corrupt officials and encouraged the honest ones. He revived old art and craft. His palace was the finest building in the east as it had twelve storeys with each storey having fifty rooms, halls and corridors decorated with carvings and frescoes. He introduced the use of gunpower and fabricated few cannons. He established control over Ladakh, Baltistan and subjugated the hill principalities of Nowshera, Rajouri and Lohara in Jammu province. He reigned for half a century and earned the reputation of being the greatest Sultan of Kashmir. Kashmiris still remember him as 'Bad Shah' (great king). The famous present square in Srinagar city has been named as Bad Shah Chowk.

His sons proved unworthy of his illustrious career as a king and kept themselves busy in intrigues and internecine quarrels. One weak sultan was followed by another and the courtiers comprising of Sayeeds, Magreys, Chaks and Dars indulged in their power games. Chaks were followers of Shia faith while Sayeeds and Magreys were attached to Sunni faith. The miseries of the people increased during the epidemic that swept the Valley in AD 1515-16. A large number of populations died because of this natural calamity.

In 1540, Mughal King Humayun was defeated by Sher Shah Suri and his one general Mirza Haidar Dughlat while in retreat entered the Valley with 4,000 soldiers. He got the aid of Magreys and Sayeeds and thus, without much resistance established his control in the Valley for eleven years in the name of Humayun (from 1541-51). There was a successful revolt against him led by Hussain Magrey who had established his headquarters at Khan Pur near Rajouri in Jammu province. Delhi throne had gone in the hands of Sher Shah Suri and after his death his son Saleem Shah Suri invaded the Kashmir but was defeated by the Kashmiris under the powerful noble known as Daulat Chak. Thus, the Kashmir throne went into the hands of Chaks but they kept themselves engaged in throwing away each other from the throne. One Ali Chak in the open court snatched the crown from the king and put it on the head of his brother Ghazi Chak. The last two Chak rulers were Yusaf Shah and Yaqub Shah. Yusaf Shah had married Haba Khatun, who is also known as Zooni (the moon). She was a gifted poetess and even today her mournful songs are sung in most of the Kashmiri households. The last Chak King was Yaqub Shah who after some resistance lost the throne to the Mughals on October 14, 1586.

Mughals

Mirza Haidar Dughlat had already ruled in Kashmir Valley in proxy on behalf of Mughal King Humayun from AD 1541 to 1551 when Humayun captured the Delhi throne from Sher Shah Suri's dynasty. He had appointed his brother Kamran as Governor of Punjab province. Kamran sent a force of 3,000 soldiers from Noushera (Jammu province) to subjugate the Valley and as there was no resistance his General occupied the throne. But this rule was temporary which lasted for one and half months only because the Kashmiri nobles who at the time of invasion were quarrelling patched up their differences and had started Guerilla warfare and that compelled the Mughals to leave the Valley. After Humayun, his son Akbar ascended the Mughal throne and on December 20, 1585 he sent a strong force of 5,000 soldiers under the command of Raja Bhagwan Dass to conquer the Kashmir Valley. At that time, Mohammad Yusuf Shah was the king and his son Prince Yaqub resisted the invasion. Finally a negotiation was entered between Raja Bhagwan Dass and the king to the effect that Yusuf Shah shall retain the throne but on the coins which were to be in circulation the name (Khubta) of the emperor Akbar should be recited. Raja Bhagwan Dass persuaded the king to pay obeisance to the emperor Akbar who at that time was camping at Attock (in west Punjab). Emperor Akbar refused to rectify the agreement and ordered the imprisonment of the king. His son (Yaqub Shah) issued the coins in his name. He started a rule of terror in the Valley. As the king belonged to Chak dynasty who were Shias, he started suppressing the Sunnis Muslims. Emperor Akbar was approached by the local people to invade Kashmir. Mughal forces under the command of Qasim Khan invaded Kashmir via Peer Panjal pass and as the people were annoyed with the cruel king so there was little resistance. The forces entered Srinagar city on October 14, 1586. Emperor Akbar spread his influence easily in the Valley because of prevalent conflict between Sunnis and Shias. At the intervention of Mughal General Maan Singh the imprisoned king—Mohammad Yusuf Shah was released after two years and he was ordered to live in the province of Bihar where an estate (Mansav of 500 horses) was granted in his favour. He died there. The Mughal rule remained in the Valley for a span of 160 years. The Valley was now linked with mainland by two roads, i.e. one through Jehlum Valley and the second through Peer Panjal (Naushera-Rajouri route). After Akbar Jahangir ascended the throne and he also loved the Valley, its streams and meadows. His son Shah Jahan (AD 1627-1658) was equally fascinated by Kashmir. During the rule of these two kings famous Mughal gardens including Shalimar, Nishat, Achabal, Chasma-e-Shai and Pari Mahal were laid.

Aurangzeb (AD 1658-1707)

He ruled India including Kashmir for 49 years and during his tenure Kashmir Valley saw 14 Governors. One Governor whose name was Iftikar Khan (AD 1671-75) persecuted the Brahmins. Wise men from their community under the leadership of Kirpa Ram Datt of Mattan intensely prayed at the holy cave of Shri Baba Amarnath and got directions in a dream to approach the 9th Sikh Guru Teg Bahadur. They went to him and complained, "We suffer great atrocities. Cows are killed. Janues (holy threads), a Maund and a quarter in weights are snapped in a single day." The Guru consoled them and said, "go and tell the Mughal rulers that if they converted Teg Bahadur they would all voluntarily accept Islam." On the receipt of this message Aurangzeb got enraged and he ordered the execution of the Guru. The martyrdom of the Guru changed the Sikh faith who thereafter became warriors and they waged a relentless war against Mughal Empire which ultimately got a corresponding support from Marathas in the west. The result was that the Mughal Empire started crumbling giving birth to Hindu independent States in the Punjab and surrounding areas and Maratha Empire in the western India. Ultimately, the crown was lost to the Britishers. After Aurangzeb's death the war of succession started in Delhi and the Governors appointed for Kashmir seldom came there as there was no accountability. In 1746-47, there was a devastating flood followed by a famine and it is said that three-fourth of the Kashmir population perished in hunger. During these chaotic conditions some influential leaders invited Ahmad Shah Abdali to invade Kashmir and establish his rule. On this invitation, he invaded Kashmir and defeated the last Mughal Governor who at that time was a local upstart known by the name of Abdul Qasim Khan.

Afghans

The decision of the wise people of Kashmir proved basically wrong because of their (Afghan's) rule which ended for 67 years but in the history it is remembered as the rule of barbarians and savages. They killed the people like flies and mosquitoes in order to satisfy their lust and greed for money. Ahmad Shah Abdali appointed first Governor of the Kashmir by the name of Abdullah Khan and being tortured by him, some people committed suicide by jumping into the Dal Lake. He left for Kabul after five months leaving Kashmir in the charge of Abdullah Khan Kabuli along with Sukhjiwan Mal—a Hindu Khatri from Punjab as Chief Advisor to Kabuli. A noble local Chief by the name of Abdul Hassan Banday thought of ending the cruel rule of the Afghans and incited Sukhjiwan Mal to declare independence. In the revolt, Kabuli was assassinated and Sukhjiwan Mal after assuming all the powers appointed Hassan Banday as his Chief Minister. Both of them worked well and twice defeated the Afghans in the battles. Even some of the Afghans were taken prisoners and paraded in the streets of Srinagar where the people jeered them and spitted at their faces. Sukhjiwan Mal declared his allegiance to the Mughal emperor of the time in Delhi who granted him the title of Raja. A devastating famine of 1755 ended the happiness of the people. Meanwhile, Ahmed Shah Abdali through his agents succeeded in spoiling the cordial relations between the Raja and the Prime Minister. He sent third expeditionary force in 1762 and major portion of the Army men of Sukhjiwan Mal deserted him. He was captured, taken to Lahore before Abdali where he was blinded and then mercilessly killed under the feet of an elephant. In this manner, Afghan rule was again established.

Second Governor whose name was Faqir Ullah got hundreds of Kashmiri Pandits killed under the suspicion that his father was killed by a noble man from their community by the name of Kailash Dhar. One of the Governors was Amir Khan who married a beautiful Kashmiri girl ha'ling from a low caste and indulged in merry making. He built a beautiful house in the middle of the Dal Lake after acquiring the building material by destroying so many Mughal gardens. The famous Amira Kadal bridge of Srinagar as well as the famous Sher Garhi building (where Dogra rulers had also lived for some generations and presently old secretariat is located) were built by him. He had declared himself as an independent ruler but was defeated by a punishing expeditionary force sent from Kabul because people had not supported him on account of his hostile attitude towards Sunnis. In 1783, George Foster who was an officer in East India Company visited the Kashmir and described in writing how the people for minor offences were tied in pairs and thrown in the river. The women were sexually abused. Another Governor by the name of Ata Mohammad Khan earned notoriety for his insatiable lust for women. The Hindu parents used to sully the good looks of their girls in order to evade his attention. Last Governor was Jabbar Khan who persecuted the Hindus relentlessly. A Pandit noble man by the name Birbal Dhar after dogging his security travelled from Srinagar on horse back along with his son to Lahore and approached Maharaja Ranjit Singh for help. Maharaja on earlier two attempts of 1812 and 1814 had been unsuccessful to capture Kashmir. This time Sikh forces under the command of Misr Diwan Chand and Raja Gulab Singh defeated Jabbar Khan at Shopian on July 15, 1819 and captured Srinagar on the next day, i.e. on July 16, 1819. The Afghans had ruthlessly broken the will of the Kashmiri people to such an extent that initially they required twenty thousand soldiers to hold the Valley but subsequently only three thousand soldiers were required for the purpose.

Sikhs

Muslim rule in the Valley lasted for 500 years and ended in 1819 when it was conquered by Maharaja Ranjit Singh. At that time, 9/10th of the population had accepted Islam. Sikh rule lasted only for 27 years (1819-1846). After annexing the Kashmir Maharaja Ranjit Singh lived up to 1839 but could not visit the Valley even once. During Sikh rule Kashmir saw ten Governors. Misr Diwan Chand who was the first Governor but he remained for a short time followed by Moti Ram who banned cow killing and the offence was punishable with death sentence. Prince Sher Singh also remained Governor who neglected the State duties and rendered no help to the people during the severe famine of 1832. He was followed by Col Mian Singh who arrived in 1833 and gave much relief to the people by immediately importing food grains from Punjab. After the death of Maharaja Ranjit Singh indiscipline and anarchy spread and on April 17, 1841, the Sikh troops mutinied in Kashmir and murdered their Governor (Mian Singh). At that time, Maharaja Sher Singh had succeeded his father and he dispatched Raja Gulab Singh to quell the mutiny and the latter effectively did so. The last Governor was Imam-ud-Din who after some resistance finally handed over the Kashmir Valley to Gulab Singh as a consequence of the treaty of Amritsar between Gulab Singh and Britishers in 1846. After the death of Maharaja Ranjit Singh, the Lahore Darbar had weakened and the last five years were full of intrigues and quarrels between the Governors and the Army commanders. The Sikh soldiers who were not getting their pays used to plunder the peasantry. A common man had to work free of wages for the government or for a petty official.

Dogra Rule

In the history, Jammu city has remained the seat of power being ruled by Rajput dynasties. It is recorded in the history that the foreign invader Timur, in AD 1398-99 had sacked the Jammu city. The rule of the Dogra kings used to be extended up to few kilometres or more according to the administrative capacities. During Mughal rule the Rajas of Jammu were their feudatories but enjoyed internal freedom for the rule. Raja Ranjit Dev ascended the throne in 1742 and had extended his territory between Chenab river and Ravi river and in the south bordering Sialkot. During his time, Haji Karim Dad was the Afghan Governor of the Kashmir Valley and he had been committing atrocities on Kashmiri people. At the request of some Kashmiri nobles, he had sent his forces to Kashmir via Banihal pass in order to tame the Governor but this information leaked before hand and the attempt met with stiff resistance at the mountain passes with the result that expedition had to be withdrawn. His descendents proved indolents and incompetents with the result that the kingdom was lost to Sikh Chief's and finally to Maharaja Ranjit Singh. Maharaja Gulab Singh comes of from the family of Ranjit Dev (as his father Mian Kishor was the grand son of Surat Dev who was younger brother of Ranjit Dev). Gulab Singh was born in 1792 and had got his early upbringing from his grandfather in a jagir near Samba town who gave him training in all military arts. At the age of 16, he went to Lahore in 1809 and was taken into service as a commander of a small force of Ranjit Singh. He proved himself as a fearless warrior and military leader. In the unsuccessful expedition of 1814 against Fateh Khan (Afghan ruler of Kashmir), he showed his soldier's worth which was recognized by Maharaja Ranjit Singh. Again he showed exemplary bravery and ability in the seize of Jalandhar and Multan. In 1819, he enabled Maharaja Ranjit Singh to capture Peshawar by subjugating warring tribes of Yusafzai. At that time, a brave Dogra freedom fighter by the name Mian Dido had been resisting the occupancy forces of Ranjit Singh around the area of Jammu city by waging a guerilla war with the help of local population and the authorities of the time had failed to quell his voice. Maharaja Ranjit

Singh entrusted the job of quieting the rebellious voice of this freedom fighter and Gulab Singh finally succeeded in getting him killed near the cave of Shri Mata Vaishno Devi. All these acts of military strategy convinced Ranjit Singh about the capacity of Gulab Singh to provide effective rule in the unruly difficult Jammu area. Ranjit Singh had an overall strategy to create a subordinate military power between the Sikh and Afghan domains. In 1820 Jammu was given as an estate (Jagir) to him and on his representation to collect the revenues he was permitted to keep an army of his own and he was given the hereditary title of Raja. With a military force at his command Raja Gulab Singh subjugated the small hilly principalities of Jammu region such as Reasi, Kishtwar, Rajouri, Bhimber, Chenani, Poonch, Bhaderwah etc. The installation ceremony of being Raja at the bank of river Chenab at Akhnoor (18 miles west of Jammu) was presided over by Maharaja Ranjit Singh who in 1820 personally put the Raj Tilak on Gulab Singh's forehead. Finally, Gulab Singh succeeded in extending his authority over the entire 22 hilly Rajas of Jammu region. He had the full authority to do so as his other two competent and influential brothers Dhyan Singh and Suchet Singh had attained the positions of eminence in Lahore Darbar of Maharaja Ranjit Singh (Dhyan Singh had become the Chief Minister at Lahore Darbar).

Conquest of Ladakh

In 1834, with the implied consent of Maharaja Ranjit Singh and the East India Company, Maharaja Gulab Singh thought of conquering the most strategic area of Ladakh having borders with China and Tibet. It was also a Central route of the wool trade with Central Asia. Buddhism had travelled to Ladakh via Kashmir Valley even before Tibet had not come under its influence. When Buddhism was dominated by Hindu revivalism in India, Ladakh came under spiritual and cultural influence of Tibet. Even for some time after the control of this area by a Kashmiri Hindu ruler Lalitaditya (AD 724-761) it came under the ruling control of Tibet but this paramount domination was of temporary nature. Famous Sultan of Kashmir, Zain-ul-Abidin (AD 1420-70) and after some time Mirza Haider who ruled Kashmir in proxy on behalf of the Mughal King Humayun (AD 1541-51) and then de jure Mughal rule over Kashmir, Ladakhi Rajas had accepted loose form of suzerainty over them by foreigners. Except these brief periods, Ladakh was being ruled by independent indigenous kings. One Sengge Namgyal (AD 1616-42) was its most outstanding ruler who had brought Zanskar area under his control and built a number of monasteries including the world famous Hemis Monastery.

To achieve his laudable object Maharaja Gulab Singh deputed his most brilliant General Zorawar Singh accompanied by most able military expert in mountain warfares and strategist General by the name of Mehta Basti Ram resident of Kishtwar, through Kishtwar route of Jammu province and invaded Ladakh in 1834 and the first battle was fought in Pushkyum Valley where the Ladakhis were defeated. Second battle was fought between Kargil and Suru where also Ladakhis were defeated. At that time, Gyalpo was the king of Ladakh and he made frantic requests to the Britishers for help which was denied. The king surrendered. After this conquest General Zorawar Singh subjugated Baltistan in 1841 and a disgruntled Prince was installed on the throne who had sought the help of the General. The credit for the Ladakh and Baltistan campaigns undoubtedly would go to Zorawar Singh, such great success could not have been achieved without outstanding and loyal officers such as Mehta Basti Ram.

In 1841, General Zorawar Singh set up to conquer Lahasa (capital of Tibet) and ran over two provinces Rudok and Gar. He established his army base in the company of 5,000 troops near the sacred lake of Mansarovar and from there sent detachments to all over Tibet for pillage. This was the month of December and because of severe cold which was more than minus 30 degrees he could not get fuel stocks in order to keep the troops warm. Because of severe cold, Dogra soldiers were losing their hands and feet from frost-bite. The army base was located at a height of 15,000 feet from the sea level. Tibetans under their able General by the name of Shastra delivered a sudden and fierce attack. His troops were better acclimatized. Zorawar Singh fought valiantly at the head of the troops and was wounded by a bullet but after falling on the ground from the horse back he continued his fight with the sword till he was killed by a spear thrust. This historic battle was fought on 12 December 1841. A small number of over 250 surviving soldiers could manage their return to Jammu via Almorah route (now falling in Uttaranchal State) with the capability of Mehta Basti Ram to tell the sad story to Maharaja Gulab Singh. Historians have also recorded that about 700 soldiers were taken prisoners by the Tibetans. This defeat of General Zorawar Singh was caused by bad weather conditions rather than by better valiant fighting spirit of Tibetans. In other words, the General had chosen a wrong timing of making an attack ignoring the factor of freezing cold. Had the weather conditions not disfavoured him, the history of Tibet and India would have been different.

Maharaja Gulab Singh did not yield to this defeat and next year he personally brought his troops to Srinagar and established his camp there. A punitive force of 6,000 soldiers under the command of Dewan Hari Chand and Wazir Ratnu was sent to reoccupy Ladakh because the Tibetan forces had taken the control of the administration of the areas which General Zorawar Singh had conquered. It is recalled that till this time, Kashmir Valley had not come under the rule of Maharaja Gulab Singh but a friendly Governor of Gulab Singh was incharge of the area on behalf of the Sikh rule of Lahore Darbar and these operations were being conducted in the name of Lahore Government.

After a brief skirmish at Skardu, the Dogra forces advanced to Leh and defeated the Tibetan commanders Achhanjit and Karam Shah. Achhanjit was taken prisoner and brought to Srinagar before Raja Gulab Singh. Negotiations were opened with the Tibetans and finally a treaty was signed whereby old frontiers were agreed to be the boundary line between Tibet and Gulab Singh's dependency of Ladakh. Traders of both countries were granted reciprocal concessions. Achhanjit was set free. (Copy of the Agreement Appendix 1 is attached.)

Note: For further details readers of this book are requested to read the contents of Appendix 8 of this book.

Founding of the State of Jammu and Kashmir (1846-56)

Gulab Singh had become the Raja of Jammu in 1820-21. The economy of Kashmir depended upon mostly in the trade of hand woven shawls and the raw material was available in Ladakh, Tibet and Central Asia. Baltistan and Ladakh regions were under his control and on the southward Jammu region were also with him. Maharaja Gulab Singh's one brother Dhyan Singh was the Dewan at Lahore and the second brother Suchet Singh was the commander of a large Sikh Force. In 1841 Gulab Singh was deputed by Lahore Darbar to Kashmir to punish the mutinous regiments who had murdered their own Governor Mian Singh and Gulab Singh had successfully restored the law and order by installing his own protege Ghulam Mohi-ud-Din as Governor of Kashmir. After Maharaja Ranjit Singh's death (1839) his son Kharak Singh had succeeded him and he had appointed Dhyan Singh as his Chief Minister. In 1841, British Garrison was besieged in Afghanistan and they made a demand of help for Sikh Forces. Lahore Darbar deputed Gulab Singh who at that time was at Hazara and he took full advantage of this opportunity to show his military ability to the distressed Britishers and saved their honour and lives. In this manner, he cultivated deep friendship with Major Lawrence (who later on became Sir Henry and helped a lot in passing on the administration of Kashmir Valley in favour of Gulab Singh). In 1842, Lahore Government fell into disorder after the death of Chand Kaur and a spree of murders started of the heirs of Maharaja Ranjit Singh and Chand Kaur who were ascending the throne. Prince Sher Singh who had ascended the Gaddi was murdered along with his Chief Minister Dhyan Singh and in revenge Suchet Singh and Hira Singh caught hold of the murderers and punished them. Another son Dalip Singh of Maharaja Ranjit Singh was put on the throne. Suchet Singh and Dhyan Singh's son Hira Singh after some time were murdered and Rani Jindan and her paramour Lal Singh now controlled the Lahore Government. They pushed the Sikh Army into war with the Britishers and at this stage Rani Jindan sought Gulab Singh's help to lead the Army but the latter declined on the plea that Lahore Darbar had been harsh to him as his brothers and sons had been murdered in 'Darbari intrigues'.

Transfer of Kashmir to Maharaja Gulab Singh

The battle between the Sikh forces and British forces is known as battle of Sobraon (fought on 10 February 1846). Though the victory was in favour of British yet they suffered heavy casualties. They wanted a negotiated peace. Had Maharaja Gulab Singh joined the war with disciplined force of Dogras against the Britishers, the consequences would have been disastrous. Being foresighted visionary Maharaja Gulab Singh had realized the futility of joining hands with Lahore Darbar which was replete with intrigues, treacheries and in total disarray and uncontrollable. The Britishers also wanted Maharaja Gulab Singh on their side. Sir Henry Lawrence (friend of Maharaja Gulab Singh) sent a note to Gulab Singh to meet him and when they met he told, "The Governor-General had promised to grant him the hilly district, together with the country of Kashmir, after having separated them from the Government of Punjab, and that Gulab Singh would be recognized as an independent ruler." Gulab Singh continued the negotiations on behalf of Lahore Government and succeeded for Dalip Singh (the then ruler)—the Treaty of Lahore which was signed on 9 March 1846. It contained a clause to the following effect:

> "In consideration of the services rendered by Raja Gulab Singh of Jammu to the Lahore State towards procuring the restoration of the relations of amity between the Lahore and British Governments, the Maharaja hereby agrees to recognize the independent sovereignty of Raja Gulab Singh in such territories and districts in

the hills as may be made over to the said Raja Gulab Singh by separate agreement between himself and the British Government with the dependencies thereof which may have been in the Raja's possession since the time of Maharaja Kharak Singh, and the British Government in consideration of the good conduct of Raja Gulab Singh, also agrees to recognize his independence in such territories and to admit him to the privilege of a separate treaty with the British government."

After seven days a separate Treaty was signed at Amritsar (on 16 March 1846) between Maharaja Gulab Singh and the British Government. According to Clause I of the Treaty, "the British Government transferred and made over forever in independent possession to Maharaja Gulab Singh and the heirs male of his body all the hilly or mountainous country with its dependencies situated to the eastward of the river Indus and westward of the river Ravi including Chamba and excluding Lahaul, being part of the territories ceded to the British Government by the Lahore State according to the provisions of Article-IV of the Treaty of Lahore dated 9 March 1846."

It was further provided in the Treaty that the eastern boundary of the area transferred to Maharaja Gulab Singh shall be laid down by Commissioners appointed by the British Government and the Maharaja respectively for that purpose and shall be defined in a separate engagement after survey. It was further agreed that the limits of the territories of Maharaja Gulab Singh should not be at any time changed without the concurrence of the British Government. Article-III of the Treaty provided, "in consideration of the transfer made to him and his heirs by the provisions of the foregoing Articles, Maharaja Gulab Singh will pay to the British Government the sum of Rupees seventy-five lakhs of Rupees (Nanakshahi), fifty lakhs on or before the 1st October of the current year, AD 1846." The Treaty also contained an Arbitration clause that in case of any disputes or questions that may arise between Maharaja Gulab Singh and the Government of Lahore or any other neighbouring State, the dispute shall be referred to the Arbitration of the British Government, whose decision shall be final and binding. Maharaja Gulab Singh agreed for himself and his heirs along with his military forces to join the British troops when deployed in the hills or in the territories adjoining his possessions. He undertook not to employ or retain in his service any British subject or the subject of any European or American State without the consent of the British Government. Maharaja Gulab Singh declared to respect, in regard to the territory transferred to him, the provisions of Articles V, VI, and VII of the separate engagement between the British Government and the

Lahore Darbar, dated 11 March 1846. The British Government agreed to give its aid to Maharaja Gulab Singh in protecting his territories from external enemies. Article-X of the Treaty provided, "Maharaja Gulab Singh acknowledges the supremacy of the British Government and will in token of such supremacy present annually to the British Government one horse, twelve perfect shawl goats of approved breed (six male and six female) and three pairs of Kashmiri Shawls.

Note: A copy of the Treaties of Lahore and Amritsar are attached as Appendix 2 and Appendix 3 respectively.

Despite signing the Treaty of Amritsar Maharaja Gulab Singh became the de jure ruler of the areas but had no de facto control over them. According to Huttenback (*The Journal of Asian Studies*, Michigan, Vol. XX, Number 4, August 1961, "Gulab Singh and the Creation of the Dogra State of Jammu, Kashmir and Ladakh"), "the final act of the drama was to be played in Kashmir itself, Gulab Singh still had to defeat the Sikh Governor who was unwilling to surrender the province." Maharaja Gulab Singh sent his two Generals, Lakhpat Rai and Rattnu along with some force to persuade his one time confide Governor of Kashmir Sheikh Imam-ud-Din but he became a turncoat and refused to give possession. A battle took place and Maharaja's General Lakhpat Rai was killed and his followers took shelter behind the ramparts of Hari Parbat fort. Maharaja Gulab Singh appealed to the British for the help and force was sent under Sir Henry Lawrence to help him to establish his rule. On hearing this, the Governor Imam-ud-Din left the Valley along with his troops and reaching Lahore produced written instructions on behalf of Lal Singh (confident of Rani Jindan) to oppose the forces of Gulab Singh. Lal Singh was dismissed as Chief Minister of Lahore Darbar and sent to dhiana under heavy guard.

The question arises as to why British parted away a beautiful land like Kashmir for a paltry sum of Rupees seventy-five lakhs? (Nanakshahi)

The answer to this question is found in a letter from Sir Henry Hardinge to Queen Victoria written about three weeks before signing of the Treaty. He had written, "to weaken the Sikh State which has proved too strong, by making arrangements by which, Kashmir may be added to the possession of Gulab Singh. Declaring the Rajput Hill States with Kashmir independent of the Sikhs of the planes."

The State of Jammu and Kashmir as it is officially designated differed from other Indian States as it was totally independent in its internal affairs. Maharaja Gulab Singh suppressed the crimes with iron hand. The rebellious leaders were publicly hanged by summary trials. In Kashmir Valley, hilly tribals from Muzaffarabad areas known as Khakhas and Bombas who were habitual trouble makers by resorting to loot, arson, robberies, murders etc were effectively driven away from the areas of their operations and strong garrisons were installed in the forts guarding the passes. Order was restored in every part of the State and every effort was made to make the trade and commerce free from any danger.

It is said that Maharaja on his first visit to Valley remarked in disgust that he had actually got nothing in return for seventy-five lakh rupees as two-third area was under hills and mountains and remaining one-third belonged to Jagirdars. The famous historian in his book (*Founding of the Jammu and Kashmir State* by KM Panikkar) has observed, "the great difficulty that the Maharaja experienced was with regard to Jagir grants. There were no less than 3115 Jagirs granted in Dharmarth besides numerous alienations of other kinds. A large number of them were unregistered. The last two Governors Sheikh Ghulam Mohi-ud-Din and Sheikh Imam-ud-Din were extremely lavish in their grants especially the latter, who for the sake of popularity signed away large tracks of land at the end of Sikh regime. As soon as the Maharaja took charge of his country he instituted an enquiry of quo warranto. The Jagirdars and other grantees greatly and loudly complained that the Maharaja was resuming their ancient possessions. Tyler, the head of the inquiry commission, conducted an independent enquiry records, "that the Maharaja was inclined to be just and reasonable. His point was that people being as revenue farmers should not claim the land they held in farms to be Jagirs, that grantees who were given one acre should not be allowed to possess two on the same 'sanad', and that in case of treason, rebellion and gross misbehaviour the Jagirs should be liable to resumption."

Maharaja Gulab Singh rationalized the civil administration and entrusted to it to the courtiers who were called Dewans or Ministers. Maharaja retained the power of government in him on foreign relations of the State, fines, revenue collection and taxation. For administrative convenience the State was divided into three Provincial Divisions Jammu, Kashmir and the frontier regions of Ladakh and Gilgit. Those Divisions were further divided into districts. Jammu Division was comprised of four districts, i.e. Jammu, Jhupal, Kishtwar and Jasrota. The Kashmir province was divided into the Divisions of Kamraj and Maraj. The frontier regions were divided into two, i.e. districts of Ladakh and Gilgit. (See Kashmir Constitutional History and Documents by MK Teng, RK Bhat and Santosh Koul.)

Maharaja Gulab Singh had three sons—Udam Singh, Randhir Singh alias Sohan Singh and Ranbir Singh. Udam Singh had died at Lahore by the fall of a wall apparently in execution of a conspiracy. Randhir Singh had been murdered in Lahore in the succession war of throne by the heirs of Maharaja Ranjit Singh. The only surviving son was Ranbir Singh. Gulab Singh was eager to ensure to put him on the throne during his life time as he was not keeping good health. Britishers consented to his request and Maharaja Gulab Singh made himself and his son during his life time Ranbir Singh as the Maharaja of the State of Jammu and Kashmir and himself served him as Governor of Kashmir. The Raj Tilak ceremony was performed in 1856. Maharaja Gulab Singh died thereafter on 12 August 1857 at the age of 65 years. During his life time, he did away with old tyrannical system of Beigar (free manual service from the subjects).

British Interference

A large number of British populations were treating the Treaty of Amritsar as a big blunder. Even when the ink of the Amritsar Treaty had not dried out, during the spring season of 1846 itself, Lord Hardinge visited the Kashmir Valley and sent a note to the Maharaja that he had some misgivings about the nature of his administration and claimed the right of the East India Company to interfere in his affairs. The hidden idea behind this move was to get a British Resident appointed in the State to act as their informer and dictate their terms to the king. To achieve this object, an attempt was made by sending a British Official to ascertain the wishes of the Kashmiri people. Maharaja's advisor Rajakak Dhar tutored the people beforehand and they with one voice praised the government before him and they liked continuance of Gulab Singh's rule. The mischievous game plan got thwarted, however, in order to save their face, they sent certain suggestions which were accepted by the ruler. The Maharaja got relief from these pressure tactics when in 1848 second Sikh war took place with the Britishers.

Rebellion in Gilgit

The Sikhs had annexed Gilgit in 1841 under the Army command of Nathu Shah of Gujranwala and Mathra Dass. When in 1846 Gulab Singh acquired Kashmir Nathu Shah transferred his services to him but this was disliked by the local Chiefs of the area and they rose in revolt by killing Nathu Shah. Similar trouble grew up in Chilas. Gulab Singh had to send his forces and these areas were reclaimed.

Maharaja Gulab Singh is the only Indian ruler to have carved out a State for himself during nineteen century out of the wreckage of Sikh empire. He is one of the few Indian rulers to have extended the frontiers of India. His conquest of Ladakh is a landmark for the safety of the modern India to keep the foreign inimical forces at bay.

Maharaja Ranbir Singh (1856-1885)

With the object of making the administration effective and result oriented he divided the State into a number of Divisions called 'Wazarats'. The Jammu province was divided into seven Wazarats: (1) Jammu Khas; (2) Jasrota; (3) Ram Nagar; (4) Reasi; (5) Udhampur; (6) Nowshera Khas and (7) Minawar. The pattern was borrowed from the adjoining Punjab. Similarly, the Kashmir province was divided into six 'Wazarats': (1) Shehar-i-Khas; (2) Anantnag; (3) Shopian; (4) Pattan; (5) Kamraj and (6) Muzaffarabad. The frontier areas of Gilgit including the areas of Dardistan were administered by creating a wazarat at Gilgit and Ladakh areas were administered by creating a wazarat at Leh. In 1860, he abolished the system of collection of revenue in kind and substituted it with cash collections in the province of Jammu. He setup three departments—the Revenue, the Civil and the Military—with clearly defined work. The judicial system was re-organised and a penal code was drawn up on the lines of Indian Penal Code which is known as Ranbir Penal Code. Appeal Courts were established at Jammu and Srinagar and nearly thirty Subordinate Courts functioned in the State. Justice was made inexpensive. He used to hear a case himself on a stamp of only half a rupee. He had started the construction of Cart road between Rawalpindi and Srinagar. A path between Jammu and Srinagar was built. Telegraph and postal services were instituted. Silk worm seeds were imported from China and distributed between villagers. He is thus the founder of famous silk industry in Jammu and Kashmir. He had even laid down experimental tea gardens in Katra Vaishno Devi area which existed even after 1947 and the local people used to consume that tea. Iron and coal mines were located in Jammu region. Money was spent on planting wine creepers which were imported from abroad and multiplied in the State to set up the system for making wine. He encouraged shawl industry. He established many schools, Maktabs and Pathshalas. Shortly after ascending the throne he constructed a splendid monument of Raghunath Temple in Jammu city which became a centre of learning and research for Sanskrit scholars who were being afforded free boarding and lodging. The magnificent building of

Raghunath Mandir is known throughout the world. He also built a famous temple of Ranbeshwar in Jammu city and many big and small mandirs in a religiously sacred place known as Parmandal in Jammu area which place was even personally visited by Maharaja Ranjit Singh during his life time. He also built up a magnificent building at a very short time to receive the Viceroy of India which was known as 'Ajaibghar'. This building even at present with some alterations and modification and repairs is serving as State legislature house nearby the Government Secretariat building Jammu. He even rendered help for the establishment of Punjab University by donating rupees one lakh and became its first fellow. He saved the lives of large number of population in Kashmir during the notorious famine of 1878-79 by procuring food grains from Punjab but the corrupt State officials had not fully cooperated in the movements of the grains which resulted estimated three-fifth of the total population of the Valley to have perished. The hostile elements levelled gravest charges of neglect and cruelty against him in order to lower his position before the Britishers but in the independent inquiry held by the British Darbar he was exonerated. Besides an able administrator, he was also a very shrewd military leader as he had sent his spies to Central Asia in order to study the political conditions. On the receipt of feedback, he asked permission from the Britishers to dispatch a military expedition to Yarkand and Kashgar with an attempt to incorporate these two important cities of the Central Asia into his kingdom but the British had their own long range policy of commercial penetration and they strongly disapproved of it. In AD 1870 the Britishers compelled Maharaja to appoint Englishmen as Commissioners of Ladakh district (in 1870 Mr Drew and then in 1871 Mr Johnson). They were appointed so for the upkeep of road and safe travel of the traders but Maharaja was deprived by the Britishers to levy any tax or any levy on the goods supplied from British India or abroad to Central Asia vice-versa. This eroded the authority of the Maharaja in Central Asia. After the death of Maharaja Gulab Singh which occurred in 1857, in 1859 again there was a revolt in Gilgit against the Dogra rule but Maharaja Ranbir Singh immediately sent a punitive force under the command of General Hoshiar Singh who ably punished the insurgents. Consequently, Gilgit was permanently annexed. The British were at war with Afghanistan and did not like Russian influence in the Chitral area. They persuaded Maharaja to take Chitral area under his influence and he tactfully did so as the Chief of that area (Mehtar) accepted the suzerainty of the Maharaja. After some time, he resiled but Maharaja applied force and finally brought him under sway. The Britishers deputed their officer as 'officer on special duty' who remained there for four years in order to inform the Britishers about the moves of Russia across the range of Pamir Mountains. When a ruler of the choice of Britishers was installed in Afghanistan they withdrew their officer.

Maharaja Ranbir Singh, at the young age of 28 years ascended on the throne of a State which was largest in area of all the States in the sub-continent having most strategic location for the whole of the country, but he so ably entrenched the roots of his dynasty, which yielded fruits up to two next generations in his posterity after his death. He is considered as the ablest administrator in the dynasty of Dogra rulers.

Maharaja Partap Singh (1885-1925)

Being the eldest son of his father (Maharaja Ranbir Singh) he became the ruler after his death and ruled the State for forty years. He further strengthened the Administrative, Judicial and Defence Reforms which were initiated by his father. He was responsible for introducing important British Indian Laws (Acts) to the State with the authority of Judicial Circular Number 201 passed under the Resolution Number 39 dated 11th January 1896. The number of courts was increased up to ninety. A first rate Cart road down the Jehlum Valley connecting Srinagar with Rawalpindi and another over Banihal pass connecting Srinagar with Jammu was constructed.

British Control Over the State

The Britishers had planned the appointment of a Resident in the State even during the life time of Maharaja Ranbir Singh and after his death they got the golden chance to execute this plan. Czarist Russia was extending its territories up to Afghanistan and the Britishers had apprehended danger to their colonial rule in the sub-continent. Their greed to rule prevailed over the moral and ethical values to respect the obligations of the Treaty of Amritsar. They also considered that the State was their own creation. The Britishers had the misgivings about the administrative abilities of Maharaja Partap Singh to rule the State because his personality was unimpressive. On the basis of these considerations they appointed Sir Olivier St John as the first Resident who was succeeded by a highly intriguing Resident by the name of C Plowen who at once planned the deposition of the Maharaja and annexation of the State of Jammu and Kashmir with English Union.

Deposition of Maharaja

The Resident joined the younger brother of Maharaja Amar Singh (father of Maharaja Hari Singh) with him in this mischievous game and prepared some forged letters allegedly written by the Maharaja to his trusted servants to poison the Resident and these letters also contained treasonable material addressed to Czar of Russia. The English Press readily gave wide publicity of this conspiracy but Indian owned press from Calcutta known as, *Amrit Bazar Patrika* got a wind of the secret note prepared by the then Foreign Secretary to the Government of India showing anxiety of the British to take control of the internal administration of the State particularly the frontier districts. On the exposure of this intrigue there arose a hue and cry throughout the country and because of public fear this morbid and nefarious game plan was given a final go by.

The Britishers adopted another mode to diminish the authority of the Maharaja and they issued an 'Irshad' whereby Maharaja was deprived of the effective rulership because the governance of the State was placed subject to the control of the Resident by constituting the council of Regency consisting of Raja Amar Singh, Raja Ram Singh (both real younger brothers of the Maharaja) an experienced European Officer, Rai Bahadur Pandit Suraj Koul and Rai Bahadur Pandit Bhag Ram. These members were appointed by the Government of India and held independent charge of their respective departments subject to the control of Resident who could pass the final decree in all the matters. He could veto any resolution.

British Political Agency in Gilgit

In their first attempt in 1877 during Maharaja Ranbir Singh's time, the Britishers had deputed an officer on special duty in Gilgit yet the State had retained complete control both in civil and political spheres. In 1889, the Britishers created Political Agency which was put solely in charge of the civil, political and military administration. They started training the troops which were already there and named them 'Imperial Service Troops'. The major part of the expenditure for administering the area which included making of roads, establishing dispensaries, running schools etc was to be borne by the State. After achieving the object of taking the full control of the strategic areas of Gilgit, the Britishers started slowly restoring the authority of the Maharaja. In 1891, Maharaja was appointed as President of the above stated council with Raja Amar Singh as its Vice President. In 1896, the Maharaja was given the power to, "send for proceedings of the council" and in case he did not agree with any of the decisions or orders he could refer it back to the council. Every member had to prepare synopsis of the work done by him outside the council and send it to the Maharaja. With the shifting of the Administrative headquarters of the Britishers from Calcutta to Delhi and consequent consolidation of their authority on the north-western frontiers of India in 1905, the State Council was abolished and Lord Curzon himself conferred the administrative powers upon the Maharaja. The Maharaja was assisted by a Chief Minister, three other ministers (Revenue, Home and Judicial). All the Ministers had to send the cases and their abstracts to the Maharaja through the Chief Minister. An abstract of the orders and their disposal was required to be sent to the Resident. In 1909, Raja Amar Singh who had played an important part in intrigues with the Resident passed away, while Raja Ram Singh had already died in 1899. During the First World War the Maharaja rendered all the possible help to the Britishers in fighting the war and in lieu thereof had gained their sympathy. On the close of the World War and on the repeated requests being made by the Maharaja, the Britishers restored the full administrative powers upon him on the confidential understanding that Maharaja would consult the Resident on all matters pertaining to the frontier districts and some other important administrative changes.

Important Achievements of Maharaja

In 1880, the work of laying down a Cart Road through Jehlum Valley was taken into hand by Maharaja Ranbir Singh and after his death in 1885, the work was completed in 1890 by the Maharaja. His able Minister Dr A Mitra worked out a plan to construct a Cart Road from Jammu to Srinagar and the work on it began in 1913 and a first vehicle (a horse driven carriage) crossed over it in 1915. It remained a private road of the Maharaja and a special permit was required to travel over it. In July 1922, however, the Maharaja vide an order threw open this road to public. He extended the railway line from Sialkot to Jammu in 1890. The credit for linking the city of Srinagar with railway heads at a distance of 200 miles via Jammu and at an equal distance of 200 miles with Rawalpindi goes to him. He had also prepared a comprehensive plan to take the railways from Jammu to Srinagar, a dream that the NDA Government under the leadership of Shri Atal Bihari Vajpayee materialized though the alignment area is not the same as was envisaged. He had also decided the Constitution of the Legislative Assembly and the establishment of a High Court of

Judicature. For effective organization of the Army he appointed his nephew, Raja Hari Singh, as Commander-in-Chief of the State Forces and Foreign Member of the Council. The Maharaja was a pious man having a religious bent of mind and generously made donations for religious and charitable purposes. He donated about one hundred and twenty-five kanals of land nearby the precincts of the then Jammu city which abutted on the Banihal Cart Road. This was meant for the study of Vedic culture and he constructed thereon a Mandir known as Ved Mandir which now lies in the heart of the city and is a centre of Hindu cultural organizations which provide free shelter and education to orphans, blinds and old people irrespective of their caste, creed, colour and domicile. A Cow shelter where hundreds of unattended cows are fed is also inside the premises including a modern Charitable Hospital. He had also donated money and lands for the benefit of Muslim community. He passed away in 1925. He had also donated some land to be used by the pilgrims of Shri Baba Amarnath near Pahalgam (health resort) which was known as 'Sadhu Pardaw' and big chunk of forest land simultaneously was donated in favour of famous shrine of Muslims known as Nand Rishi near the famous resort of Gulmarg. Unfortunately, during the democratic rule in the State, the above stated land of 'Sadhu Padaw' could not be preserved by the State after the onset of second tenure of Sheikh Abdullah's regime. The writer of this book who happens to be a founder member of Shri Amarnathji Shrine Board (SASB) from 2002 till 2014 have been regularly raising this issue in the Annual Board meeting of the Shri Amarnathji Shrine Board. With great efforts recently it could be ascertained that Tourism Department ofJ&K State has set-up a bus stand on that big chunk of land. Present Governor NN Vohra being the Chairman of the Board is very much inclined to relinquish the customary right of use of this land in favour of the government but the writer of this book is constantly creating hurdles for such illegal abandonment. The shrine of Nand Rishi is holding the donated forest land till now. The State Forest Department maintains the forest area and the income goes to the shrine.

Maharaja Hari Singh (1925-1947)

He was born in 1895 to Raja Amar Singh and ascended the throne in 1925 on the death of Maharaja Partap Singh who was the real elder brother of his father and had died issueless. His uncle (Maharaja Partap Singh) had given him sufficient grooming in the administration of the State. He was well educated and had modern ideas. He had even received training in Imperial Cadet Corps, Dehradun. During First

World War, he was sent to the front along with Dogra forces and they had won laurels in several battles in France, Palestine and East Africa.

After becoming the ruler, he realized the grievance of his subjects in general and that of Dogras of Jammu in particular that they had been deprived from getting the services in the administration of the State affairs during Maharaja Partap Singh's rule as a large number of educated bureaucrats from outside the State (particularly from neighbouring Punjab) had usurped the important posts and they were not treating the State Subjects with dignity and honour. There used to be some physical clashes between the wards of those outsider officials and businessmen settled in Jammu with the local educated youths. The locals had cherished the expectations from the ruler who was being depicted as the pride of the Dogras. The slogan, 'A State for the State People, was being heard in all parts of the State'. After ascending the Gaddi he favoured the appointment of State Subjects to all posts in the administration and placed equal faith in Muslim Officials. At the time of assuming the reigns of powers in the State he had declared that "though he was a Dogra Hindu yet as a ruler, his religion was justice." He quickly passed some revolutionary legislations such as Agriculturist Relief Regulations which released the cultivators from the clutches of the money lenders. He passed compulsory Education Act which made compulsory education up to 5th class for boys in the cities of Jammu and Srinagar. The prevention of Infant's Marriage Act and the Removal of Untouchability Act. He threw open the gates of all the temples for Harijans. When the family priest who was the head of famous Raghunath Temple objected to this move, he at once removed him as a head Pujari and with the consent of his younger brother opened the gates of the temple for the Harijans and appointed him as the head priest. High Court was established with powers of supervision over the Subordinate Courts. He used to appoint eminent jurists from outside the State as judges. He had established a Board of Advisors consisting of eminent judges from outside the State to hear the appeals to give him advice in respect of appeals filed against the judgements of the High Court as he himself was a figure head to approve those judgements as a final authority. He was very much opposed to corruption and was taking very strict actions against corrupt officials. Having appointed his Ministers, the Muslim contingent usually from Uttar Pradesh, he would not interfere with their working. His illustrious son Dr Karan Singh (first head of the State after independence of India, i.e. as Regent up to 1952, elected as Sadar-i-Riyasat from 1952 to 1965, and as Governor of the State from 1965 to

1967, a Member of Parliament continuously for next eighteen years from Jammu region and the youngest Cabinet Minister in the Centre during Indira Gandhi's regime—a world known great scholar particularly in Indian philosophy (a recipient of Padma Vibushan award) has noted in his *Autobiography* at page 40, "in fact when at the age of 30 he (his father) ascended the throne on 23rd September 1925. He had proclaimed, Justice is my religion and merit alone will be considered the deciding factor for all types of employment. Caste, creed, religion or sex will receive no consideration.... Indeed, there was a case when a citizen of Jammu living just outside our palace challenged in court my father's decision to acquire his property, and successfully prevented the move."

In 1927, he issued Notification Defining and Regulating the Rights, Powers and Privileges available to the Citizens of the State who were termed as State Subjects. In Notification 1-L/84 dated 20 April 1927 the term State Subject was defined to mean and include:

Class I: All persons born and residing within the State before the commencement of the reign of His Highness the late Maharaja Gulab Singh Sahib Bahadur, and also persons who settled therein before the commencement of Samwat year 1942 (AD 1885), and have since been permanently residing therein.

Class II: All persons, other than those belonging to Class 1 who settled within the State before the close of Samwat year 1968 (AD 1911), and have since permanently resided and acquired immovable property therein.

Class III: All persons, other than those belonging to Class 1 and II permanently residing within the State, who have acquired under a 'Rayatnama' any immovable property therein or who may hereafter acquire such property under an 'Ijazatnama' and may execute a Rayatnama after ten years continuous residence therein.

Class IV: Companies which have been registered as such within the State and which, being companies in which the government is financially interested or as to the economic benefit to the State or to the financial stability of which the government is satisfied, have by a special order of His Highness been declared to be State Subjects.

Note I: In matters of grants of the State scholarships, State lands for agricultural and house building purposes and recruitment to State Service, State Subjects of Class I should receive preference over other classes and those of Class II, over Class III, subject, however, to the order dated 31 January 1927 of his Highness the Maharaja Bahadur regarding employment of hereditary State Subjects in government service.

Note II: The descendants of the persons who have secured the status of any class of the State Subjects will be entitled to become the State Subject of the same class. For example, if A is declared a State Subject of Class II his sons and grand sons will ipso facto acquire the status of the same Class (II) and not of Class I.

Note III: The wife or a widow of a State Subject of any class shall acquire the status of her husband as State Subject of the same Class as her husband, so long as she resides in the State and does not leave the State for permanent residence outside the State.

Note IV: For the purpose of the interpretation of the term 'State Subject' either with reference to any law for the time being in force or otherwise, the definition given in this Notification as amended up to date shall be read as if such amended definition existed in this Notification as originally issued.

This Notification providing State Subjects preference to outsiders in cases of employment in government services was welcomed as it intended to give the employment to a large number of unemployed people in the State.

The Notification had categorized four classes in the term 'State Subject'. This Notification was followed by Notification Number 13-L dated 27 June 1932 under the command of the Maharaja for the purposes of determining the status of the State Subjects in foreign countries and to inform the concerned governments as to the position of their nationals in the State of Jammu and Kashmir.

(b) Notification dated 27th June 1932

The Notification reads as under:

Whereas it is necessary to determine the status of Jammu and Kashmir State Subjects in foreign territories and to inform the governments of foreign States as to the position of their nationals in this State, it is hereby commanded and notified for public information, as follows:

That all emigrants from the Jammu and Kashmir State to foreign territories shall be considered State Subjects and also the descendants of these emigrants born abroad for two generations:

Provided that, these nationals of the Jammu and Kashmir State shall not be entitled to claim the internal rights granted to subjects of this State by the laws, unless they fulfil the conditions laid down by those laws and rules for the specific purposes mentioned therein.

The foreign national residing in the State of Jammu and Kashmir shall not acquire the nationality of the Jammu and Kashmir State until after the age of 18 on purchasing immovable property under permission of an 'Ijazatnama' and on obtaining a 'Rayatnama' after ten years continuous residence in the Jammu and Kashmir State as laid down in Notification Number I-L/84, dated 20th April 1927.

Certificates of nationality of the Jammu and Kashmir State may, on application, be granted by Minister-in-Charge of the Political Department in accordance with the provisions of Section I of this notification.

Note: After the accession of the State with India, the Constituent Assembly framed the Constitution of Jammu and Kashmir which came into force with effect from 26 January 1957 and it has also recognized this prevailing legal position of the term permanent residence in the State and in Part III of the Constitution it incorporates Sections 6, 7, 8, 9 and 10 with wider scope. It is advantageous to reproduce these sections herein under:

Sec 6: Permanent Residents

(1) Every person who is, or is deemed to be, a citizen of India under the provisions of the Constitution of India shall be a permanent resident of the State, if on the fourteenth day of May 1954:

(a) he was a State Subject of Class 1 or of Class II; or

(b) having lawfully acquired immovable property in the State, he has been ordinarily resident in the State for not less than ten years prior to that date.

(2) Any person who, before the fourteenth day of May 1954, was a State Subject of Class I or of Class II and who having migrated after the first day of March 1947, to the territory now included in Pakistan, returns to the State under a permit for resettlement in the State or for permanent return issued by or

under the authority of any law made by the State Legislature shall on such return be a permanent resident of the State.

In this section, the expression 'State Subject of Class I or of Class II' shall have the same meaning as in State Notification Number 1-L/84 dated the twentieth April 1927, read with State Notification Number 13/L dated the 27th June 1932.

Sec 7: Construction of references to State Subjects in existing laws

Unless the context otherwise requires, all references in any existing law to hereditary State Subjects or to State Subject of Class I or of Class II or of Class III shall be construed as references to permanent residents of the State.

Sec 8: Legislature to define permanent residents

Nothing in the foregoing provisions of this part shall derogate from the power of the State Legislature to make any law defining the classes of persons who are, or shall be, permanent residents of the State.

Sec 9: Special provision for Bills relating to permanent residents

A Bill making provision for any of the following matters—

(a) defining or altering the definition of the classes of persons who are, or shall be, permanent residents of the State;

(b) conferring on permanent residents any special rights or privileges;

(c) regulating or modifying any special rights or privileges enjoyed by permanent residents;

shall be deemed to be passed by either House of the Legislature only if it is passed by a majority of not less than two-thirds of the total membership of that House.

Sec 10: Rights of the permanent residents

The permanent residents of the State shall have all the rights guaranteed to them under the Constitution of India.

Note: Fundamental Rights as guaranteed in the Indian Constitution along with other Constitutional Rights found in other Articles of the Indian Constitution were applied to the State in exercise of the powers conferred by Article 370 of the Constitution by the President of India under SRO 1610 and by CO 48 of 1954 with some additions and amendments. The Constitution (application to Jammu and Kashmir) order, 1950 was superseded. By this order only Article 1 and Article

370 were made applicable in the State and they remained unaltered by this subsequent order.

After Article 35 in the Indian Constitution, the following new Article was added for the sake of Jammu and Kashmir State:

> "35-A, Saving of law with respect to permanent residents and their rights. Notwithstanding any thing contained in this Constitution, no existing law in force in the State of Jammu and Kashmir, and no law hereafter enacted by the Legislature of the State:
>
> (a) defining the classes or persons who are, or shall be, permanent residents of the State of Jammu and Kashmir, or
>
> (b) conferring on such permanent residents any special rights and privileges or imposing upon other persons any restrictions as respects:
>
> (i) employment under the State Government;
>
> (ii) acquisition of immovable property in the State;
>
> (iii) settlement in the State; or
>
> (iv) right to scholarships and such other forms of aid as the 'State Government' may provide, shall be void on the ground that is inconsistent with or takes away or abridges any rights conferred on the other citizens of India by any provision of this Part."

Note: Before the full bench decision of the Jammu and Kashmir High Court given in the case of 'The State of Jammu and Kashmir and others *vs* Dr Susheela Sawhney and others', (203 KLJ 282) the prevalent legal position was that upon marriage to a non-State Subject, a woman who was a State Subject by birth, lost her special status of a State Subject to acquire or inherit immovable property and ineligible for a government job. By a majority judgement (two judges concurring and third one dissenting) it has been laid down that on marriage with a non-permanent resident, the daughter of the permanent resident of the State shall not lose her status as a Permanent Resident of the State for any purpose. In the minority judgement, however, one judge differed from this view and the result is that the majority view of the full Bench prevails. In respect of adoption of a non-State Subject by a State Subject, the Division Bench of the State High Court in the case of 'The State of Jammu and Kashmir *vs* Vijay Manchanda', LPA Number 70 of 1987 decided on 21st of November 1988, has held that a person by adoption cannot acquire the status of the Permanent Resident of the State of Jammu and Kashmir.

Against the backdrop of the constitutional safeguards spelled out above, the legal position which emerges is that, a resident of the State of J&K can become President of India, Prime Minister of India, Chief Justice of India, Chief of the Armed Forces, Speaker of the Indian Parliament but a non-State Subject cannot become even a peon in the State. A State Subject can acquire immovable property throughout the country but even the First Citizen of India (President of India) cannot acquire even an inch of immovable property in the State except for affairs of the Indian Union. The State laws having a bearing on this topic have preferential value over the relevant provisions of the Indian Constitution. According to the personal opinion of the writer of this book Article 35(A) in the Constitution has been incorporated by the Presidential Order and not inserted by the Indian Parliament which required 2/3rd majority. This is a grey area for discussion.

The Maharaja had progressive ideas about freedom and self-rule. He expressed these ideas/sentiments at the Round Table Conference held in London in 1930. Speaking on behalf of Indian Princes, he observed: "As Indian and loyal to the land whence we derive our birth and infant nature, we stand as solidly as the rest of our countrymen for our land's enjoyment of a position of honour and equality in the British Common Wealth of Nations." He withdrew some of the privileges which had been guaranteed to British resident and started putting pressure for the abolition of the political agency in Gilgit, but the British did not like it and he had to withdraw his moves. On the contrary, the British understood that he was an enlightened ruler and difficult to tame. On account of the constant and rigorous pressure of the British, the Maharaja withdrew his administration from Gilgit and in 1935 handed over Gilgit Wazarat on a lease to the British for a period of sixty years. The British improved the security of the area by building some air fields and setting up wireless stations in that area and as stated earlier they were imparting military training to Gilgit scouts which were under their command. They used their services and started sending military missions to Central Asia. This was being done to contain the advancement of Russian Communism. They had started giving aid help to maintain and restore the authority of the overthrown local chiefs known as Amirs.

Upsurge in the State

The British had been annoyed by the Maharaja on account of his political statement issued in the round table conference at London and wanted to teach him a lesson. In the Indian Union, they had introduced the policy to divide the Indians on communal lines by adopting to hold elections on the basis of communal representations and this policy had started the creation of hatred between the two communities. With the birth of Muslim League as a political organization, the young Muslim students from Jammu and Kashmir State were receiving education in Lahore and Aligarh Muslim University and they got influenced by the propaganda and as a consequence thereof, 'All Kashmir Muslim Conference' was founded and its first annual session was held in December 1930 in Lahore. The youths who attended this session on their return to the State started propaganda on communal lines and they were supported by several other youngmen returned from Universities. Those who were still receiving the education and particularly in Muslim Aligarh University also came in contact with Muslim leaders and propagators of Pan-Islamism. They organized themselves for holding meetings in a room set up as, 'Muslim Reading Room, Srinagar'. These youths had the tacit support of British Government and a British Minister serving in the State Administration of the Maharaja. Old religious Muslim leader known as Moulvi Mirwaiz had died in 1931 and was succeeded by new Mirwaiz by the name of Yousaf Shah, who had received his theological education at 'Deoband' in Uttar Pradesh and he too was influenced by the aims and objects of the Reading Room Party. The younger members of this party started organizing mammoth meetings in villages and particularly in various mosques. Sheikh Mohammed Abdullah had obtained his MSc degree from Aligarh University in 1930 and after returning to Kashmir he had succeeded in getting only a teachers' job in Government High School Srinagar and not as a Lecturer (Gazetted) in a college. Meanwhile, Maharaja had constituted Civil Service Recruitment Board for the selection of candidates to higher posts on the basis of merit. The Hindus and particularly Kashmiri Pandits were advanced in studies and they were getting selected in higher percentage on the basis of merit than the Muslim candidates. It is noteworthy that even during the cruelest Afghan rule the Kashmiri Pandits because of their learning habits, adaptability to the circumstances and shrewdness had succeeded in grabbing many posts in the Administration and this trait even now exists in this community in the changed circumstances. This policy of recruitment on the basis of merit was also opposed by Sheikh Mohammed Abdullah who himself felt a victim of non-selection for a gazetted post. He resigned the post of a science teacher and became active member of the Reading Room Party and added fuel to the burning fire of organizing mammoth meetings and delivering fierce speeches in the mosques. Communal tension had reached to the zenith which required explosion at the ripe time.

Incident of July 13, 1931

This incident requires a deep study in order to know about the mindset of Sheikh Mohammed Abdullah who has been proclaimed by some followers as 'Baba-e-Kaum' which means Father of the Nation. A European visitor had come to Srinagar on a holiday trip along with a non-State Subject Abdul Qadir and both of them were staying in Srinagar. On June 21, 1931, Abdul Qadir made a highly seditious speech in the premises of a Muslim holy shrine 'Khanqah of Shah Hamdan'. He was arrested and criminal trial against him started in the Sessions Court, Srinagar. During the trial a large number of people started visiting the court and taking part in hearing the proceedings. In order to avert the law and order problems the venue of the trial was shifted to Srinagar Central Jail. On July 13, 1931 an estimated crowd of 4,000 to 5,000 people had collected outside the premises of the Central Jail Srinagar and they started raising slogans impressing upon the government that case should be withdrawn. On instigation of some communal elements, the gathering became unruly and they started pelting stones towards the enclosure of the jail and made an attempt to break open the doors of the jail forcibly. Meanwhile, the inmates of the jail including the prisoners became restive and showed their sympathy towards the rioters. The then District Magistrate ordered the police to open fire on the crowd as a result thereof twenty-one persons died and many more were wounded. Dead bodies of the killed people in firing were taken in procession to the Jamia Masjid, Srinagar. The communal Propaganda was already hot in the Valley which produced immediate result of reaction on the minority Hindu community. In the sparsely Hindu inhabited localities, their shops were looted and three people were also killed. There were many cases where Hindu women were disgraced. The Maharaja immediately appointed an enquiry committee to be headed by the Chief Justice of the J&K High Court but the agitators boycotted the enquiry by making allegations that it would be of partisan nature. The Maharaja understood the nefarious designs and promptly promulgated ordinances and in consequence thereof wholesale pre-emptive arrests were made. There were police firing on the crowds in the important towns of the Valley such as Anantnag, Shopian, Baramulla and Sopore. Under these ordinances public floggings in the squares of the Srinagar city were introduced. Because of adoption of such an effective policy, certain innocents may have also suffered.

The British Government immediately reacted and their Resident in the Kashmir delivered a pre-emptive note to the Maharaja demanding its acceptance within twenty-four hours. The concessions which were demanded in this note were:

Definite and immediate steps should be taken to remedy the more obvious grievances of Muslim subjects such as cow killing ordinance, the prohibition of khutba, the stoppage of Azan etc.

A competent and unprejudiced British Officer deputed by the Government of India should hold a full inquiry into Mohammandan grievances and demands. They advised the Maharaja to ask for the loan of the services of such officer without delay.

A European Indian civil service officer, be appointed as Chief Minister and

The sooner Sir Daya Krishan Kaul (the brother of Raja Hari Krishan Kaul) left the State, the better as his presence was definitely against His Highness interests."

The Maharaja had to yield to the pressure from the people below and the Government of India from the above.

This communal virus spread in Jammu province too and in Mirpur district Hindus in the villages and particularly those who were doing the money lending business became the victims of the loot and arson. In the Punjab 'Ahrar Party' of the Muslims which had sympathy with Indian National Congress started sending Jathas (bands of volunteers) into the State territory and they even penetrated in the capital of Jammu. To cope up with the situation request was made to the British to send the troops and accordingly the British sent one company of British soldiers to the district of Mirpur and two companies to Jammu district. The British Government accepted the request of the Maharaja to send an officer to head the inquiry commission and spared the services of Sir BJ Galancy of the Foreign and Political Department of Government of India who was appointed the Chairman of the Commission consisting of four members. These four members had to be one Muslim and one Hindu from Kashmir province and same ratio applied to Jammu province. After few months of the setting up of this Commission, the Hindu representative of Jammu resigned but the Commission continued its work and submitted its report recommending that minimum qualifications for appointment to a government post should not be high and effective measures should be taken, "to present the due interests of any community from being neglected."

The Commission also recommended the grant of proprietary rights in respect of all land, "of which the ownership is retained by the State and the right of occupancy is enjoyed by private persons."

After the submission of the report by the Commission, Galancy was requested to head the Kashmir Constitutional Reforms Conference for giving effect to the wishes of the ruler to associate his people with the Administration of the State. The Conference submitted its report on April 1932 recommending that a Legislative Assembly be established as early as possible. The Maharaja issued a Notification on 22 April 1934 (Constitution Number 1 of Samwat 1991 corresponding to 1934) providing for the establishment of the Legislative Assembly. The Jammu and Kashmir Constitution Act Number 1 of 1934 consisted of 46 sections and it envisaged the establishment of the Legislative Assembly for the State called the 'Praja Sabha'. The Regulation provided that all powers, legislative, executive and judicial were retained by the Maharaja. The council of ministers was comprised of the Prime Minister and such other Ministers of the State as the Maharaja may appoint. The Prime Minister and the other Ministers were to hold office during His Highness' pleasure. The Assembly was to consist of members nominated or elected under the Regulation. The total number of non-elected members was to be forty-two which were to include the ministers. The number of elected members was to be thirty-three and thus, the total was seventy-five. (Note: this figure of seventy-five was also adopted by the ruler for the representatives of the Constituent Assembly constituted in 1950 and it remained so till the last report of the delimitation commission whose recommendations were accepted in conducting the elections of 1996 at a fixed number of 87 and thereafter.) The elections were to be held for the constituencies and for the communities as specified in the J&K Assembly Electoral Regulations. The President of the Assembly was to be appointed by the Maharaja and the term of the Assembly was fixed for three years. The first elections of the Prajasabha were held in 1934 and vide Order Number 132 dated 13 October 1934 the Maharaja appointed the following Ministers to be the members of the State Assembly:

Colonel EJD Colvin, CIE, Prime Minister.

Major General Nawab Khusru Jung Bahadur, Minister-in-Waiting.

Wajahat Hussain, ICS, Home Minister.

VN Mehta, ICS, Revenue Minister.

Rao Bahadur Thakur Kartar Singh, Finance Minister.

All these Ministers except Rao Bahadur Thakur Kartar Singh (who was basically from State Judicial Service) were the officers of the Indian Civil Service and thus the control of Administration quietly passed into British hands. After these developments, the British withdrew the support to the communal agitations.

(Jammu and Kashmir Government Gazette, Vol. 46 dated 7th Baisakh 1991 (19th April 1934).

The main political party at that time was 'Muslim Conference' headed by Sheikh Abdullah and the leadership of this party had been demanding a responsible government with conferment of more financial powers to the State Legislature which should be constituted on the basis of only elected members. Second elections to the Praja Sabha were conducted on 31 May 1937 in which Muslim Conference captured nineteen out of 21 seats for which it had setup its candidates. The remaining two could not be elected as their nomination papers had been rejected. Maharaja and his Prime Minister Gopalaswami Ayyangar were frightened with this result.

Jammu and Kashmir Constitution Act, 1939

To save his power, prestige and authority, but keeping in view the pressure of the public opinion, the Maharaja promulgated the Jammu and Kashmir Constitution Act, 1939 on 7 September 1939.

The Constitution provided for a council consisting of Prime Minister and such other members of the State as the Maharaja may appoint by Royal Warrant of appointment. The Prime Minister and other Ministers were responsible to the Maharaja and were to hold office during his pleasure. The Legislature of the State was again named 'Praja Sabha' comprising of the President, (Prime Minister) and 75 other members. Out of 40 elected members, 33 were to represent the communities and the constituencies as specified in Schedule II and seven to represent the special constituencies shown in Schedule III. These thirty-three members who were to be elected by different communities on a franchise did not cover more than 3 per cent of the population. Those who had passed middle school examination or its equivalent could vote. Women were not given right to vote. The life of the Prajasabha was fixed for three years from its first meeting. The High Court was made court of record and vested with jurisdiction to hear and determine any original civil suit or other proceeding of which the value was not less than rupees ten thousand and every such suit or proceeding was to be instituted in the High Court. The High Court had jurisdiction to entertain and dispose of such appeals, revisions and other cases-civil, criminal or revenue-as it might be empowered to do under any enactment in force in the State. The Constitution consisted of 72 sections. Note: After the accession of the State with India by the Maharaja, Sheikh Abdullah was appointed by the Maharaja as Emergency Administrator of the State under the Provisions of this

Constitution and on 5 March 1948 as Prime Minister. Not only that, Constituent Assembly of the State to frame new Constitution was also enacted under the above said Constitution by Maharaja's son. (Dr Karan Singh being his Regent with powers and authority as well as consent derived from the Maharaja.)

The Praja Sabha could make laws for the whole State or any part thereof but it was not an absolute power. The Act provided that it was not lawful for Praja Sabha to consider or deal with any matter or enact any law relating to or affecting:

(a) His Highness or any member of the royal family or the management of the royal household, etc. The other such matters from head (b) to (j) were fully elaborated. Head (b) related to treaties, foreign policy etc and the remaining from (c) to (j) need not to be reproduced herein. The most note worthy ungrateful act which Sheikh Abdullah did after getting Maharaja exiled from the State to his person as well as to his progeny which he could not hide in the inner layers of his subdued mind was that after holding tainted elections for constituting Constituent Assembly and thereby capturing all the seventy-five seats, Sheikh Abdullah on August 9, 1953, with one stroke got abolished the hereditary rulership of the Maharaja when State Constitution was in the process of enactment. This was an arbitrary act which no conscientious man would have done. The Constitution of Jammu and Kashmir was approved and adopted on 17 November 1956 and it came into force on 26 January 1957. By virtue of the Deed of Accession executed by Maharaja in favour of dominion of India which was accepted by the Governor-General of India, the State had fully acceded to Union of India and as a temporary measure to enable the State Government to establish democratic rule, Article 370 as a temporary measure was engrafted in the Indian Constitution. On 26 January 1950, when Constitution of India came into force by virtue of Deed of Accession, Article 1 and Article 370 of the Indian Constitution applied in the State along with some other Articles and this aspect has been fully discussed in this book. It is for the future generations to judge how in an unconstitutional manner a patriot king like Maharaja Hari Singh was removed from the scene of the State administration and in his place a Prime Minister having no respect for democracy and who could be judged in history as despot stepped into his shoes in order to establish his personal rule and the rule of his family. This happened because of historical facts as Kashmir problem had been created initially to some extent by Maharaja who could not understand the British game plan at proper time that they wanted his state as a part of newly created Muslim dominion. He blindly believed his Prime Minister RC Kak who was a Muslim League agent and giving him wrong advise of remaining independent. His army chief and police chief too were British agents. This initial stage of indecision subsequently was made most complicated by the then Prime Minister of India who because of his personal liking for Sheikh Abdullah had taken Kashmir problem in his own hands from the Department of duly established Ministry of States headed by Sardar Patel who smoothly settled the problems of all other Princely States which numbered about 365 and got them smoothly Acceded to India. The dismissal, detention and subsequent trial of Sheikh Abdullah under the law of land have been hereinafter fully discussed in this book. When Sheikh Abdullah for second time assumed the powers as Chief Minister, after the Accord of 1975, he made attempts to establish his personal rule but in a subtle manner. As an instance, his advisors in a very clever manner had bodily lifted Section 50(2) of Maharaja's enacted Constitution Act of 1939 and got it incorporated in 1975 in the J&K High Court rules. At that time, Sheikh could not get the J&K Constitution amended because he was wholly and solely holding the chair as a Chief Minister with the support of Congress MLAs on account of Indira-Sheikh Accord. Section 50(2) of Constitution of 1939 provided that all other judges of the State High Court (at that time there were only 3) shall have rank and precedence according to the seniority of their appointment. When during the elections of 1977 which were held in the State under Janata regime in the Centre and they were the only one which were fair elections held so far, as far as rigging was concerned Sheikh Abdullah's lieutenants could achieve absolute majority for him by fanning communalism by showing Pakistani salt in their one hand and administering oath of Holy Quran in the other to bring Sheikh into power in order to save the State. The above said provision of Maharaja's Constitution 50(2) was got utilized by the ruling National Conference in their favour by winning the case of Mian Bashir Ahmed *vs* State of Jammu and Kashmir (AIR 1982 J&K 26). The then Chief Justice Mufti Bahauddin Farooqi who was Sheikh's protege and later joined National Conference party constituted Full Bench of only 4 judges when 5 judges were available at the full strength of the State High Court. Anti-Defection Act enacted by Sheikh Abdullah for his political game was challenged. Full Bench was constituted which was evenly divided—Chief Justice and Justice Mir taking one view and Anand J and Kotwal J taking a different view. By evoking the High Court rule, the opinion of the Chief Justice prevailed. The judgement was challenged in Supreme Court but the controversy remained unresolved.

Formation of Political Parties

In 1932, a political organization was founded under the name of 'All J&K Muslim Conference' and Sheikh Abdullah was elected as its first President. The aims and objects of this organization were to work for social, economic and cultural betterment of Muslims and to secure a large share in civil and army services. In 1934, differences arose in the Working Committee of the Conference as a result thereof it was dissolved and Chaudhary Ghulam Abbas was appointed sole dictator of the Muslim Conference. Abbas' talks with the Prime Minister failed. He gave a call for civil disobedience movement which evoked very little response. Abbas was arrested and after trial was sentenced to six months' imprisonment.

In other Princely States, the freedom movement launched by Indian National Congress was having its impact. Indian National Congress was the motivating force behind it and the Congress took deep interest in what was happening in J&K. In 1938, the working committee of All J&K Muslim Conference met at Srinagar and after a heated discussion lasting 52 hours passed a resolution recommending to the general council to allow all people to become its members, "irrespective of their caste, creed or religion." Next year, i.e. in 1939, the recommendations of the working committee were accepted and the J&K National Conference came into existence.

Great affinity grew between the ideology of National Conference and Indian National Congress. Jawaharlal Nehru's visit to Kashmir in 1940 was liked by the Kashmiris.

In 1944, National Conference adopted a programme of socialistic pattern of society as its goal with the elective principle of responsible government and the elective principle applied from the local Panchayat right up to the legislative Assembly. This was known as programme of 'Naya Kashmir', i.e. of new Kashmir.

Jinnah did not like the ideology of National Conference and he preferred Chaudhary Ghulam Abbas who was a lawyer by profession and a member of Bar Association Jammu. He had become President of the All J&K Muslim Conference. When after accession of the State with

India, Sheikh Abdullah came into power Chaudhary Ghulam Abbas migrated to Pakistan and died there as a refugee as nobody gave him a recognition as being a leader.

In the summer of 1944, Jinnah came to Kashmir in order to create some footing for his party though publicly he had proclaimed the visit on health grounds. A reception was given in his honour by National Conference and dais was shared by Sheikh Abdullah. The speech which he delivered there was "The Muslims have one platform, one 'Kalma' and one God. I would request the Muslims to come under the banner of the Muslim Conference and fight for their rights."

Jinnah also presided over the annual session of the 'Muslim Conference'. In his address, he described the National Conference as a 'band of gangsters'. Later on, when National Conference had launched the 'Quit Kashmír' movement, Jinnah levelled it as "an agitation carried on by a few malcontents who were out to create disorderly conditions in the State."

Sheikh Abdullah had realized that his political future with Jinnah was bleak and thus, did not join with the dominion of Pakistan. Jinnah was a man of great ego and possessed hauty temperament. Sheikh had come in close contact with Indian leaders like Mahatma Gandhi, Jawaharlal Nehru, Abdul Ghaffar Khan, Maulana Abul Kalam Azad and he had read their mind-set which was of tolerant and benevolent nature.

His hatred for Jinnah has found expression in his biography *Atish-e-Chinar*. He writes, "At that time, Jinnah was intoxicated with power. He thought it beneath his dignity to talk to a poor and resourceless nation. When this equation of power went against him, he woke up in panic from his dream. But by this time, the snake had passed, only its line remained."

In the summer of 1945, a unique session of National Conference was held at Sopore (a town in the Valley) and the important feature of this session was the meeting of the Standing Committee of the All India States People Conference under the President ship of Pandit Jawaharlal Nehru. It is noteworthy to unfold the mindset of Sheikh Abdullah because even at this crucial juncture he had a hidden agenda in his mind to make Kashmir Valley as his fiefdom by nourishing an idea that Kashmir Valley was inhabited in majority by his co-religionist and ultimately they would be supporting him to retain the seat of power as he had no other political adversary of significance. OP Saraf, veteran journalist and a close confide of Sheikh Abdullah hailing from Jammu province was appointed by Sheikh as Emergency Publicity Officer in

1948 after resuming the charge by the latter (Sheikh Abdullah) as Emergency Administrator of the J&K State, has published an article in the local daily newspaper of Jammu *Daily Excelsior* in its issue of May 3, 2012 which reads: "I was an activist of National Conference in 1940 and continued to be so. The Sheikh was enamoured by the Communist Party of India (CPI) line especially of its concept of the right of self-determination. However, in Sopore convention of National Conference (NC) in 1945, Nehru had said that unnecessary importance was given to the idea. The Communist had supported, 'Two Nation Theory' through Adhikari thesis, which described the creation of Pakistan as an expression of the right of self-determination. The CPI had sent BPL Bedi and Freda Bedi to play up the 'Independent Kashmir Card'. Freda, of Irish extraction with British connections tried to influence the Sheikh for independent Kashmir. She wrote the first ever Biography of the Sheikh titled *Sheikh Abdullah and His Ideas*. Communists described Kashmir accession to India as 'Treachery' (Refer The Cross Road, 6th January 1950). They supported a Telangana type of movement." This theory Sheikh Abdullah practised during his first tenure as Prime Minister of J&K State till 1953. He met with his nemesis, firstly losing the confidence of the Representatives of the Constituent Assembly and then getting dismissed as Prime Minister by the Head of the State Sadar-i-Riyasat and subsequently getting detained under the Preventive Law for his anti-national activities and secondly after sometime by facing a criminal charge of conspiracy to get the State ceded from Union of India and an attempt to wage war against the duly established government in the State and Union of India. He was put on trial for more than five years. The committal court presided over by NK Hak, had committed him along with co-accused to stand their trial before the specially created court of District and Sessions Judge which was presided over by MK Tikko who as a lawyer had remained as an activist of National Conference and Sheikh Abdullah after coming to power had inducted him in judicial service. The trial of the case was scuttled en route because of political reasons even after some evidence was recorded. The case was withdrawn. (This aspect has been discussed with more details in this book). After a gap of 21 years, while remaining in wilderness, he realized his mistake and joined the mainstream politics after entering into an Accord in 1974 which came into force on February 1975. The Political Accord is known as Indira Gandhi and Sheikh Abdullah Accord of 1975 and in this way Sheikh Abdullah secured the seat of power for the second time not as Prime Minister but as Chief Minister. After sometime, he committed a volte-face in breach of the said agreement by declaring elections and becoming the Chief Minister without the support of the Congress(I). His basic idea of independent Kashmir was carried on by his son Dr Farooq Abdullah in the garb of Regional Autonomy when he had succeeded as Chief Minister though it was somewhat soft and diluted than the original idea of Independent Kashmir. When Dr Farooq Abdullah became Chief Minister he got the Bill passed in the Legislature for Regional Autonomy. He was an ally of NDA Government in the Centre and his son Omar Abdullah was a State Minister in the NDA Government. The NDA Government out rightly rejected this agenda of Regional Autonomy though it is still followed by Sheikh's grandson Omar Abdullah who is presently the Chief Minister of coalition government with Congress(I) support. This aspect of the matter has been discussed in some detail in latter part of the book. Representatives of many Indian States took part in that session of Conference. Speeches were also made regarding the political and social ideologies of the people of Kashmir on the basis of similarities with the people living in the rest of India. As the Second World War was going on and the Maharaja had rendered all sorts of help to the British including his personal visit as an Army General in the war front, the British were very happy with him and in the result he enjoyed full powers as a ruler without any hindrance or check. During this period N Gopalaswami Ayyangar relinquished the post of Prime Minister and an era of orderly and stiff government came to an end. Many Prime Ministers in quick succession were appointed and they were: Raja Sir Maharaj Krishan, Col Sir KN Haksar and Sir BN Rai. None of them could contribute anything substantial for good governance. In the summer of 1945, BN Rai handed over the charge and the Maharaja appointed RC Kak who was a local Kashmiri Pandit as his Prime Minister. He had entered into the government service as a Librarian in a local government college, and had second marriage with a foreign lady of British nationality because his first wife who was from his own community had died. His meteoric rise to the post of Prime Minister though speaks of his intelligence yet the part played by him in contributing to the delay for the accession of the State with Union of India by ill advising the Maharaja on the basis of secret links with Jinnah has been proved on the basis of authentic record mentioned in this book and he was acting as an agent of the British-American block through Lord Mountbatten who was also advancing the idea of a bigger Muslim block comprising J&K State in the dominion of Pakistan to safeguard the British interests to keep a watch on the activities of Communist Russia and China which was also likely to become a Communist State. RC Kak also had a close liaison with Muslim League which would be discussed later on and had become a supporter of Independent Kashmir or accession with Pakistan. Maharaja Hari Singh at a later stage had come to know about the designs of his Prime Minister RC Kak, who was therefore, unceremoniously divested of the coveted post of Prime Minister. Maharaja put him under house arrest. Mehr Chand Mahajan (third Chief Justice of the Supreme Court) had agreed to take over the charge as a Prime Minister of the J&K State on 13th September 1947 from Major General Janak Singh Katoch who had succeeded RC Kak by way of interim arrangement. However, formal charge as Prime Minister was taken by Mehr Chand Mahajan on 15 October 1947 and on the same day he had a Press Conference in his official room.

Quit Kashmir Movement and Detaining of Pandit Nehru

In March 1946, came the Cabinet Mission to India for negotiating with Indian Leaders the manner in which the transfer of power was to be made. After a careful examination of Muslim League's demand for Pakistan, the Commission came to the conclusion that it was not practical to setup a sovereign Muslim State and instead suggested a federal Union of India with a weak Centre. With regard to the Princely States, the Cabinet Mission made it clear that while it would not be possible for the British Government to carry out its obligations of Paramountcy over such States after a new self-governing government, or governments, came into being in British India, the British Government could not and would not in any circumstances transfer such paramountcy to the Indian Government. The Paramountcy was, therefore, to lapse on India attaining Independence and the Princes were to be free to decide their future.

This policy statement of the Cabinet Mission provoked Sheikh Mohammed Abdullah to challenge the validity of the Treaty of Amritsar, because under that scheme the paramountcy was to revert to the Maharaja of Kashmir after the departure of Britishers from the sub-continent. On May 15, 1946, he launched quit Kashmir movement. In his speech on May 17, 1946 Sheikh Abdullah said, "The tyranny of Dogras has lacerated our souls. It is time for action. You must fight slavery and enter the field of 'Jihad' as soldiers. Every man, woman and child will shout, 'Quit Kashmir'. The Kashmiri Nation has expressed its will. I ask for plebiscite on this question."

This was a total reversal of the earlier policy of the National Conference seeking a responsible government under the aegis of the Maharaja as the constitutional monarch as envisaged in the new Kashmir concept of 1944 (Naya Kashmir). Evidently, Sheikh Abdullah had found an opportunity to end the dynastic Dogra rule by invoking the communal slogan consisting of the virus of (a) Jihad, (b) Kashmiri Nation and (c) Idea of Plebiscite. In fact Sheikh Abdullah had shown his true colours even after taking the powers as emergency administrative head of the State after independence by ignoring the superior constitutional authority of the duly appointed Prime Minister Mehr Chand Mahajan and even the Maharaja who was the sovereign head vested with all the powers. Before, getting his appointment as Emergency Administrative head from the Maharaja, Sheikh Abdullah had pledged his loyalty and obedience in writing to the person as well as family of the Maharaja. He had adopted his autocratic behaviour by exploiting his closeness with Pandit Nehru and subsequently his special position to win plebiscite for India. When he was deprived of his autocratic and despotic rule in 1953, with the support of responsible colleagues of his National Conference like Bakshi Ghulam Mohammad, GM Sadiq and others he again raised the issue of plebiscite by floating new political party known as Plebiscite Front which was confirmed as secessionist organization by judicial verdict given by the then Chief Justice of the State Hon'ble Justice Murtaza Fazal Ali under the provisions of the Prevention of Unlawful Activities Act. This issue has been fully discussed in this book with relevant extracts of government order and subsequent confirmation of that order by the Competent Tribunal constituted under the Act. Not only that, after the demise of Pandit Nehru when Sheikh Abdullah had signed the accord with the late Prime Minister Mrs Indira Gandhi in 1974 (which came into force in February 1975) he had not hesitated to fight elections to the State Assembly on the Question of 'Kashmiriat'. Unfortunately, Pandit Nehru could not understand the hidden traits of his character. All these dictatorial acts Sheikh Abdullah could do by getting liquidated the position and status of Maharaja Hari Singh who was the absolute ruler of the State with the help of Pandit Nehru. The Instrument of Accession which Maharaja had scribed as a sovereign ruler of his State was breached and finally given a go by along with promises subsequently made with him including those with the Minister of States Sardar Patel who was Deputy Prime Minister. The last Prime Minister of Maharaja Hari Singh, Mehr Chand Mahajan who had facilitated the accession of the State as Prime Minister of Maharaja at a very crucial time in his book *Looking Back* has fully described the scene how unusual and unwanted great importance was given to Sheikh Abdullah by Pandit Nehru at the time of accepting the Instrument of Accession executed by Maharaja, sovereign head of the State, with sovereign dominion of India. At that time Sheikh Abdullah was only a head of a political organization which had its following in Kashmir region and negligible influence in Jammu region which was the biggest region population-wise and area-wise in the State. Even area-wise Ladakh region, inclusive of Gilgit agency and Baltistan had the biggest area of the State. In other words, Sheikh Abdullah was only a persona non grata except a fast friend of Pandit Nehru and representing a regional political party. At his bidding the accession was accepted with a unilateral clause without the knowledge of Maharaja that wishes of the people shall be ascertained after law and order is restored. This clause gave a special status to Sheikh Abdullah to blackmail the accession which was factually and legally perfect. The Instrument of Accession was of the same nature containing all the clauses which all other rulers of the country had offered to the Indian dominion for accepting their accessions. Lord Mountbatten as Governor-General of India had no statutory authority neither under the Indian Independence Act of 1947 nor the Act of 1935 to insert this Clause unilaterally. Under the Indian Independence Act, the Union of India could either accept or reject the accession made by the ruler and there was no provision for acceptance of Provisional Accession. This point on its legal aspect has been discussed by Mehr Chand Mahajan in his above stated book as well as by the writer of this book in detail in this book at proper place.

> "On May 20, 1946 Sheikh Abdullah was taken into custody along with other prominent leaders under the relevant law. Pandit Nehru set afoot his journey to meet his detained friend and raised protest for his detention. He was refused permission to enter State. God knows what designs he had, the consequences of which he himself was not aware. He forced his entry by pushing the guard of State Administration who under the wise leadership of Bhagwan Singh (an official of Maharaja) tactfully allowed him to enter and then escorting him to the Dak Bungalow provided all facilities including a car of the State to return to India. It was only his three days stay." (Refer page 42 of *Maharaja Hari Singh: The Troubled Years* by Harbans Singh.)

This incident permanently spoiled the relations between Nehru and Maharaja and Sheikh Abdullah always exploited the hatred in his favour. Nehru had come for the help of his friend on his own and was not deputed by the Congress Working Committee. On June 21, 1946, Maulana Abul Kalam Azad who was the Congress President appealed to Nehru to return to New Delhi for discussions in connection with the approaching independence. This fact is corroborated from a letter written in reply by Sardar Vallabhbhai Patel to the All Ceylon Neta Ji Valibar Sangam, Colombo in reply to their expression of regret over the official silence of the Congress over the issue. The letter dated 25th June 1946 of Sadar Patel is reproduced herein as under:

> "About your advice to the Congress to take immediate steps to crush the arrogant and autocratic spirit of the Kashmir Government I can only say that the whole Working Committee is in session all the while and the Committee has thought fit to express no opinion on it nor has Pandit Nehru thought fit to consult the Working Committee about the affairs. He has taken action individually as President of the All India States People's Conference on his own responsibility."

Pandit Nehru went in a sullen mood by promising that he would come again soon. He did return as one of the Defence Counsel's member comprising of Messrs Asif Ali and Dewan Chaman Lal advocates. He stayed in a House Boat in Srinagar and made discrete inquiries about the happenings following Sheikh's detention. The Trial Court had found Sheikh Abdullah guilty of the charge and awarded three years imprisonment. (Refer Supra Harbans Singh page 42.)

Nehru's ego was certainly hurt and this injury was expressed by him during a visit to Jammu after becoming the Prime Minister of India. By this time, Maharaja had been exiled from the State at the insistence of Sheikh Abdullah who firstly had entered the portraits of power in the duly established Government of Maharaja with his consent and authority as Emergency Administrator and later on with the constant pressure exercised by Pandit Nehru on Maharaja he was made the Prime Minister of the State by the former in place of Mehr Chand Mahajan whose term would have expired in 1952 as per his Order of Appointment referred in this book. Sheikh Abdullah immediately had forgotten the written Oath of Allegiance to the person of Maharaja and his family members in his Letter of Unqualified Apology dated September 26, 1947 written from the prison reproduced in verbatim herein after. The writer of this book fails to understand how the Indian Government of the time representing veteran freedom fighters and men of integrity and morality without giving any opportunity to the Maharaja of being heard could become a privy to such tyrannical act against a patriot who was the main architect and sole legal authority for making the edifice of accession of his State with the dominion of India. Even the world colonial power like Britain during their rule in India had not caused such a horrendous injustice to any of their subjects except the one who was their enemy during the war of independence of 1857 (last Mughal Emperor Bahadur Shah Zafar). Pandit Nehru is the main villain of the piece. A bare reading of the Instrument of Accession would make it crystal clear that the Government of India committed blatant breaches of the Articles of the Instrument of Accession. The attention of the readers of this book is drawn to Article 7 and 8 of the Instrument of Accession and those Articles would amplify the fact that Maharaja Hari Singh was the de facto and de jure sovereign head of the State when he was treated like a traitor later on at the bidding of Sheikh Abdullah and unceremoniously was compelled to resile outside from his own State for good in the same manner in which the East India Company in 1857 had externed the last Mughal ruler Bahadur Shah Zafar who had waged war against the British. The Nizam of Hyderabad who had entered into an armed conflict with the dominion of India was not treated with any sort of disrespect or dishonour but with all dignity and honour. Jammu people greeted Pandit Nehru with banners and placards demanding the return of the Maharaja because of love and affection of the latter. In return, Pandit Nehru was beyond himself with rage and said in Hindi in these words, "mein usko ane dun jisne mujhe qaid kiya—mein Jo wazir-e-Azam Hind banane wala tha." (I will not allow him to come back who had arrested me. I was at that time future Prime Minister of India.)

Some prominent leaders of the National Conference, including Chaudhry Ghulam Abbas, joined the Muslim Conference. In October 1946, the Muslim Conference launched direct action campaign under the leadership of Mirwaiz Moulvi Yusaf Shah. Mirwaiz Moulvi displayed extreme hostility to the Indian National Congress and the National Conference.

In his statement on September 25, 1946 Moulvi Yusaf Shah had deplored the interference of the Congress and stated, "The Hindu capitalists want to get the State into their grip, but I warn that if the Government of J&K gets terrified at the might of the Congress and strikes an unholy alliance with the National Conference fascists, it will have to face the terrific opposition of the Muslims. And this, sinister alliance will be smashed to pieces. The Muslims of Kashmir have warded off Pandit Nehru's invasion in 1940, 1945 and 1946. Now he is again out to make a fresh attempt and it is the duty of the Kashmiri Muslims particularly and all the well-wishers of the country to smash up his onslaught."

Under the direct action programme some prominent leaders including Chaudhry Ghulam Abbas were arrested and this shows increasing influence on the Muslims of Jammu and Kashmir. Politically very interesting statement was issued on May 10, 1947 by Chowdhary Hamidullah Khan (President of Muslim Conference) who urged the

Maharaja to declare himself independent. He said, "if Kashmir has to keep itself aloof from carnage and bloodshed, it should lose no time in adopting a strong and bold policy. His Highness the Maharaja Bahadur should declare Kashmir independent immediately. A separate Constituent Assembly to frame the Constitution for the State, according to the wishes of the people should be established at once. His Highness the Maharaja Bahadur will receive the cooperation of the Muslims in carrying out this policy. The Muslim form 80 per cent of the population. They are represented by the Muslim Conference. The Muslims will welcome the Maharaja Bahadur as the first constitutional ruler of independent and democratic Kashmir."

Gandhiji's Visit to Kashmir and Lord Radcliffe's Report for Partition

The British Government had announced the transfer of complete power to the Indians. The partition of India was in the offing. Gandhi came to Kashmir in the month of July 1947 and returned back in August 1947. He was impressed by the communal harmony which prevailed in the State. Mahatma Gandhi had a meeting with the Maharaja. This meeting was followed by a visit by the head of the RSS (Rashtriya Swayamsevak Sangh) Guru Golwalkar. The Maharaja had been made aware by the latter about the game plan of Muslim league for the sub-continent of India. Dr Karan Singh in his autobiography has written at page 51, "All I was able to gather from Gandhiji's words was that he was urging my father to ascertain the wishes of his people, to take his people into confidence, and to align himself with rather than against them in the political turmoil that was engulfing the country." Besides that in June 1947, Lord Mountbatten as Viceroy of India had also paid four days visit to Kashmir and according to his own version (though denied by Maharaja) advised Maharaja to join any of the two dominions before August 14, 1947 and assured him that Indian leaders would have no objection in case he would join Pakistan. In one of his speech contained in the book *Time Only to Look Forward* (pages 268-269), Lord Mountbatten has told a different story and recorded that Maharaja dodged him every time during this period of visit and when matter was finally to be discussed the Maharaja pretended an attack of colic and the meeting was cancelled. This visit was a link of British game plan which would be unfolded with details in this book. Maharaja Hari Singh himself has revealed the purpose of his visit and the advice which he had received in totality from Lord Mountbatten. This revelation has been made by Maharaja Hari Singh himself in his letter sent to Dr Rajendra Prasad from Pune in 1952 (summary thereof reproduced in this book) after his exit from the State. In a nutshell he has revealed that Lord Mountbatten was compelling him to join the dominion of Pakistan. Be that as it may, the tangible result of Mahatma Gandhi's visit to Kashmir was replacement of RC Kak as Prime Minister by Major General Janak Singh Katoch on August 10, 1947. Katoch was replaced as Prime Minister on 10 October 1947 by the appointment of a great lawyer and jurist Justice Mehr Chand Mahajan who at that time was a judge of the Lahore High Court (undivided Punjab) and later on in 1954 became the Chief Justice of India. He is at number three in the seriatim list of the Chief Justices of India. Before assuming the charge as Prime Minister of the J&K State, he had acted as a nominated judge along with Justice Teja Singh a colleague judge of Lahore High Court from the side of Indian National Congress in the Boundary Commission which was appointed by the British under the Chairmanship of a great jurist of Britain Lord Cyril Radcliffe to chair two Boundary Commissions one for Bengal and one for Punjab. The Boundary Commission under discussion here relates to the division of undivided Punjab province which had Muslim majority. The Muslim League had nominated Justice Din Mohammad who was the then Chief Justice of Bhagalpur High Court as well as Justice Muneer of Lahore High Court who later on became the Chief Justice of Pakistan Lahore High Court. The Commission in principle was appointed by the British in June 1947 in order to determine exactly which territories to assign each country after coming into force the Indian Independence Act. Each Commission also had four representatives—two from the Indian National Congress and two from Muslim League. Given the deadlock between the interests of the two sides and their rancorous relationship, the final decision was essentially that of Lord Cyril Radcliffe. After Commission's sittings in Lahore were over, the members were taken to Shimla under police escort and lodged in Cecil Hotel for writing the report. Every member had written a separate report. Justice Mahajan has recorded at page 115 in his book "Jusitce Din Mohammad frankly told me at the outset that so far as he was concerned he would write the report coinciding the demands of Muslim League and I could do what I liked." He was the senior most judge among the four Indian Judges of Punjab Boundary Commission. Lord Cyril Radcliffe was given five week's time to decide on a border. On July 15, 1947, the Indian Independence Act 1947 of the Parliament of United Kingdom stipulated that British rule in India would come to an end on August 15, 1947. Before partition, some 40 per cent of the area of India was covered by Princely States. These States except the State of J&K were covered by a part of Sir Radcliffe Agreement. They were not in British possession and did not form part of British India though were in subsidiary alliances with the British who were responsible for their external affairs. They were left free to accede to one of the new dominions. Muslim majority provinces such as North-West Frontier, Sindh and Balochistan were to become the foundation of Pakistan. However, two provinces did not have overwhelming majority—Bengal in the north-east (54.4 per cent Muslim) and the Punjab in the north-west (55.7 per cent Muslim). Pakistan was intended as a Muslim home land, while the new India was secular with a Hindu majority. After the completion of the assigned work of this Commission on the sub-continent as a whole, Mahajan in his book at page 117 has recorded, "it is said that about 4 million people went from one side to the other and about a million killed on each side. The people had left their homes and set out by every means of communication to seek refuge with their own kind. Reliable opinion which was gathered thereafter was that one million on each side had died by massacre, diseases, starvation, fatigue etc." So sensitive work was completed by the British Jurist in a great hurry within three week's time in a haphazard and casual manner because he himself was eager to leave India in great hurry as the climate was not suitable to him. There are instances when some houses in villages were falling divided between the boundaries of two dominions. Also, the relationships were so tendentious that the "judges could hardly bear to speak each other." The atmosphere was so tense and anarchic that the wife and two children of a Sikh judge of Lahore High Court had been murdered by Muslims in Rawalpindi a few weeks earlier. Justice Mehr Chand Mahajan had played an active and important role in getting one Hindu-dominated tehsil Pathankot and two Muslim-dominated tehsils of present Gurdaspur district, tehsils of Batala and Gurdaspur on the side of India leaving the fourth Muslim-dominated tehsil Shakargarh of old Gurdaspur district to form part of Pakistani Sialkot district in order to provide a corridor to Maharaja for establishing means of communication to join with the dominion of India. Of course, this could not be done without the final opinion of Lord Cliff who too had accorded his final seal in a judicious manner. There was hostile propaganda which was let loose by Pakistan and some British writers that Lord Mountbatten had helped Maharaja Hari Singh because he was his old acquaintance and a batchmate in getting training in the British Army School in London. This allegation is divorced from the truth. The fact of the matter is that terms of reference of the Boundary Commission had enshrined in it that Commission would, "Demarcate the boundaries of two parts of the Punjab province on ascertaining the continuous majority areas of Muslims and non-Muslims. In doing so, it will also take it into account other factors."

When Lord Radcliffe found this clause in the reference, he sent a query to the Secretary of State for India, asking, "What other factors might mean." The Secretary replied that Punjab Boundary Commission must include the location of Sikh shrines. He considered this clause in a judicial sense without caring who would be beneficiary. The reason why three tehsils of old Gurdaspur district were never intended for Pakistan was that had they been made part of west Punjab, Amritsar, the Sikh holy city, would have been completely surrounded by Pakistan. (Refer Karpal Singh on Punjab.) Lord Radcliffe was giving Nankana Saheb in Sheikhupura district—the birth place of Guru Nanak Dev to Pakistan as well as Lahore Gurudwara of Sheeshganj and four other important shrines related to Guru Arjun Dev and Guru Ram Das. This decision was judicious and not political as he had kept open a corridor for the State of J&K to join dominion of India having a link in the plane territory suitable for establishing means of transportations and communications. Only because of this wise decision, Indian help could be provided to the J&K State during foreign aggression committed by Pakistan. The road link and railway link from its territory with the State contributes for its all around development since 1947. It can easily be inferred that other two members of the Boundary Commission Justice Mehr Chand Mahajan and Justice Teja Singh might have also lent support to this decision in their separate awards. Justice Mahajan had his property in Pathankot as well as in nearby tehsil of Nurpur of Kangra district which was his birth place. Justice Teja Singh must be attached in his heart to safe guard the most sacred religious place of the Sikhs. Guided by judicial conduct by keeping aside personal and religious interests and feelings, it was expected in all fairness to give weightage to the clause, "Take into account other factors" as term of the reference. Rather, there is evidence to the contrary of authentic nature that Lord Mountbatten was favourably inclined for Pakistan as directly has been disclosed by Maharaja Hari Singh to the President of India in his letter written from Pune (Maharashtra) in the month of August 1952. Prime Minister Mahajan was also of the same view that after having a meeting with Lord Mountbatten as Prime Minister of the J&K State at the time of having negotiations for accession, Lord Mountbatten had expressed his views that State should join the dominion of Pakistan. Lord Radcliffe had arrived in India on July 8, 1947 and much before August 17, 1947 he had prepared his report which was officially published on 17 August 1947. The division of united province of Punjab was to be made on the basis of population which comprised of 1,62,17,242 (Muslims) and 1,22,01,577 (non-Muslims). The North-West Frontier Province had a population of 27,88,797 (Muslims) and 2,49,270 (non-Muslims). Maharaja Hari

Singh showed the quality of a great Statesman when he immediately after signing of the Radcliffe's report hired the services of Justice Mehr Chand Mahajan to use him as his Prime Minister of the State in order to facilitate the accession with India where the future Prime Minister (Pandit Nehru) was permanently hostile to him. Maharaja released Sheikh Abdullah from the prison after pardoning his remaining conviction and imprisonment for a term of about one and a half years (total three years) on September 29, 1947 after receiving a letter of 'unqualified apology' written by Sheikh Abdullah on September 26, 1947, which reads as under:

> "May it please Your Highness,
>
> It is after about one and half years incarceration that—as long wished—I had an opportunity of having detailed talks with Thakur Nachint Chand. What unfortunate things happened during this period in the State I need not mention. But this is now realised by every well-wisher of the State that many of the regrettable happenings of the past have mainly been due to the misunderstandings which appear now to have deliberately been created by interested people in order to achieve their own ends. Rai Bahadur Ram Chandra Kak, the ex-Prime Minister through his mischievous methods and masterly man-oeuvrings brought these misunderstandings to a climax and succeeded in his attempt, though temporarily, to a certain extent. He painted me and my organization in the darkest colours and in everything that we did or attempted to do to bring Your Highness and your people closer, baseless and selfish motives were attributed to me. But God be thanked that all these enemies of Your Highness and the State stand exposed today.
>
> In spite of what has happened in the past, I assure your Highness that myself and my party have never harboured any sentiment of disloyalty towards your Highness' person, throne or dynasty. The development of this beautiful country and the betterment of its people is our common aim and interest and I assure your Highness the fullest and loyal support of myself and my organization. Not only this, but I assure your Highness that any party within or without the State, which may attempt to create any impediments in our efforts to gain our goal, will be treated as our enemy and will be treated as such.
>
> In order to achieve the common aim set forth above, mutual trust and confidence must be the mainstay. Without this, it would not be possible to face successfully the great difficulties that beset our State on all sides at present.

Before I close this letter I beg to assure your Highness once again of my steadfast loyalty and pray that God under your Highness' aegis bring such an era of peace, prosperity and good government that it may be second to none and be an ideal for others to copy.

Your Highness's Most Obedient Subject
SM Abdullah"

Note: The name mentioned in the above stated letter at the outset of Thakur Nachint Chand has figured because he was elder brother-in-law of Maharaja Hari Singh and had great influence on his sister (Maharaja's wife). He had been working as advisor to Maharaja. Dr Karan Singh in his autobiography at page 82 has recorded, "This hopeful letter led to Shiekh Abdullah's release from jail and was followed up by a meeting between him and my father (Maharaja Hari Singh) at Gulab Bhawan at which, I was told he even offered my father a gold sovereign in the traditional court manner."

Thereafter, the whole situation under went a sea change as a result of Pakistani invasion and subsequent accession of the State with the Union of India. Shiekh Abdullah rode the crest of a popular wave with the full support of Jawaharlal Nehru on account of two qualifications. The first one was his close friendship with Jawaharlal Nehru and the second was that Pandit Nehru was genuinely convinced that on account of Muslim Majority of the population in the State, Sheikh Abdullah should be fully involved in the governance of the State for national and international reasons. The corroborative evidence in this behalf is a letter written by Pandit Nehru on 13th November 1947 (after the accession of the State with India) to Maharaja Hari Singh, He wrote:

"As I pointed out to you, the only person who can deliver the goods in Kashmir is Sheikh Abdullah. He is obviously the leading popular personality in Kashmir. The way he has risen to grapple with the crisis has shown the nature of the man. I have a high opinion of his integrity and his general balance of mind. He has striven hard and succeeded very largely in keeping communal peace. He may make any number of mistakes in minor matters, but I think he is likely to be right in regard to major decisions.

But the real point is that no satisfactory way out can be found in Kashmir except through Sheikh Abdullah. If that is so, full confidence must be placed in him. There is no half-way house between full confidence and a half and half affair which has little advantage and many disadvantages. Even if a risk has to be taken in giving this full confidence, that risk has to be taken. There is no other way as far as I can see it both from the short-term point of view and the long-term one. Sheikh Abdullah is earnestly desirous of co-operating and is amenable to any reasonable argument. I would suggest to you to keep in close personal touch with him and deal with him directly and not through intermediaries."

CHAPTER 4

Era of Independence and Lapse of British Rule

On June 17, 1947, the Indian Independence Act was passed stating that on August 15, 1947, the British would relinquish their authority in India which was to become an independent country. A part of its territories with a prepondering Muslim majority was to be constituted into Pakistan and recognized as an independent and sovereign State. Three major political forces were operating in the State of J&K at that time. In Kashmir Valley, the majority of the Muslims were with Sheikh Abdullah who was the head of the National Conference but this party had very little influence in the regions of Jammu and Ladakh. Mirwaiz Moulvi Yusaf Shah had religious and fanatical followers in the down town of Srinagar city and they had a recognizable nuisance value. There used to be frequent street fights between the followers of National Conference and Moulvi Yusaf Shah (the first one was called as Sher Party (Lion's Party) and the second one was called as Bakara Party (Goat's Party) by the public. Muslim Conference had little following in the Valley after the split in 1939 and the formation of National Conference but it was becoming more popular day by day amongst the people of small part of Jammu region because of ideological affinity with Muslim League which was a dominating force amongst the Punjabi Muslims in the neighbouring Punjab province. These Muslim League elements had started polluting the peaceful atmosphere firstly in two border districts of Mirpur and Poonch areas which were predominantly inhabited by Pathwari speaking people which too some extent resembles Punjabi. The other dialect is Poonchi. Sixty thousand ex-military men of Second World War consisting of 'Sathis and Sudans' clans convertees from Brahmins were available for fanning the virus of communalism in these two districts and particularly in tehsil Plandari of old Poonch district. They are of rebellious nature because after occupation of Pakistani forces an establishment in papers as Headquarters of Pakistan Occupied Kashmir at Plandari they had even revolted against Pakistan. The Pakistan Government much before the accession of the State had clandestinenly started arming them with arms and ammunition and had also infiltrated some army men from their regular force.

On the urgent pleas of Muslim League leaders of the State, Jinnah had sent his Private Secretary Khurshid Hussain to assess the Kashmiri's potential field for his activities who had reported that it will require considerable effort, spread over considerable long period of time, to reform Kashmiris and to convert them into true Muslims (refer Copland, page 233, Taken Over from a Secret Report of Jinnah dated August 20, 1943 Jinnah's book page 17). By contrast the Muslims of Jammu and Poonch were Sunnis and racially akin to Punjabi Muslims. In Ladakh and Baltistan there were Shias and Buddhists. In Gilgit there were Shia's and in hunza Ismailis. This bewildering complexity was also in mind of Maharaja not to accede to any dominion. In a nutshell, majority of the Muslims had a good deal in common with the 'Bhakti' tradition in Hinduism. The Dogra Muslims, Gujjars and Bakarwals were not very much akin to Punjabi Muslims and have their distinct Dogra culture. More importantly Maharaja was not sure about the Partition Report of the Commission regarding the areas of his States boundaries touching the boundaries of both the newly created dominions. The Report of the Boundary Commission was made public on 17 August 1947. Already a mention has been made by reproducing the letters of the leaders of Muslim Conference who had been constantly advising the Maharaja to declare independence in free India and become an independent ruler. The Dogras of Jammu in general considered the Maharaja as their leader and wanted him in power.

Maharaja Hari Singh's son Dr Karan Singh in his autobiography has recorded at page 41, "to this party (National Conference) my father was hostile mainly because of Jawaharlal Nehru's close association with his arch enemy Sheikh Abdullah. Then there was the Muslim League led by Muhammad Ali Jinnah. Although this party supported the rights of the rulers to decide the fate of their respective States and in Kashmir opposed Sheikh Abdullah and his National Conference tooth and nail, my father was enough of a Hindu not to be able to stomach the aggressive Muslim communalism of the League and this led him to spurn tempting offers from Pakistan. Mountbatten (the then Governor-General) had visited Kashmir during the month of June as has already been recorded and his purpose was to persuade the Maharaja to make up his mind well before 15th August 1947 and had brought an assurance from the Indian leaders that they would not take objection to his deciding in whatever way he thought fit, even if it was accession to Pakistan. The Maharaja evaded the discussion and he first sent the Viceroy out on a prolonged fishing trip to Thricker (a famous fishing spot in Kashmir Valley) and then—having fixed a meeting just before his departure got out of it on the plea that he had suddenly developed a severe attack of Colic."

On this attitude being depicted by Maharaja to Lord Mountbatten, he in an ex-parte manner is generally being defamed as a villain of whole drama regarding delayed accession. This is being done as there is nobody to plead his cause of Patriotism at the cost of his Personal honour and position as Head of the State. He had purposely evaded any commitment with Lord Mountbatten who in the gist of his advice was compelling him to join the dominion of Pakistan on the basis of facts and figures which Maharaja had later on spelled out in his letter addressed to President of India.

Prem Shankar Jha at page 107 of his book, *The Origins of a Dispute: Kashmir 1947*, has recorded from the British official records that bureaucrats of the Labour Government at the India office in London wanted Kashmir to accede to Pakistan. It was they who drafted the letter to Nehru in which Attlee sought to persuade to him not to accept Maharaja's accession even when the raiders were a bare seventeen miles from Srinagar. When Kashmir acceded to India, they kept their doors open for the reversal of the decision. The Principles had been explained by Lord Mountbatten to the rulers of India in his speech given in the chamber of Princes on July 17, 1947 that they should bear in mind geographical continuity, economic interdependence and the composition of their population, while deciding which dominion to accede. In Kashmir, the British officials working for the Maharaja within their small circle had gathered authentic information that RC Kak was advising Maharaja to remain Independent and in case this was not acceptable to British, then accede to Pakistan. At page 108, Jha has recorded that "Maharaja's Army Chief Mr Scott in his last written report at Karachi had disclosed that in the month of September 1947 when it became certain that Maharaja was joining India, he refused to accept extension in his term of office offered by Maharaja on the idea in his heart that he would not serve under Congress and would leave for London." The writer of this book is disclosing the mindset of British Government which is recorded in para 151 at page 60 of the White paper on Indian States wherein mentioned that, "engagements of the crown had been with rulers and not with the people." At para 152 of the same page, it is recorded that, "Since 1929, the Congress had openly declared that States should be brought in line with British India by the introduction of responsible government. Furthermore, White Paper on Indian States records that Pandit Nehru in 1952 had made it clear in Indian Parliament that to ascertain the wishes of the People was not a special policy for the State of J&K but a general policy adopted for other Indian States. This statement was repeated by Pandit Nehru in a Public meeting in Hyderabad after Nizam of Hyderabad had acceded to dominion of India." From this it transpires that the wishes were to be ascertained in every State by not holding a Plebiscite or Referendum amongst the People but through their elected members of the Legislature such a ratification was required. The elected members of the J&K State in the Legislature which was constituted as Constituent Assembly under Maharaja's Constitution Act of 1939 had ratified the accession firstly before 1950 when it had sent its four appointed members of Parliament to the Indian Constitution Assembly where the Constitution was being enacted and thereafter when it was enacted the President of India passed an order in 1950 to make applicable certain articles of the Indian Constitution from 26 January 1950 when the Indian Constitution came into force. This order has been discussed in this book. The stability of Pakistan dominion was essential for British in order to have a watch on Russia and China. It was a well-thought policy to have the accession of J&K State with Pakistan. The important cities of Pakistan—Sialkot, Rawalpindi and Peshawar—were located nearby the boundary of the State of J&K. The important Mangla Hydroelectric Dam was also a few miles away from the border of Mirpur district of J&K State. Supreme Headquarters of the Joint Military Committees working has been revealed by Prem Shankar Jha at page number 110. It is recorded that before Pakistani attack on 22 October 1947 in the Kashmir territory the Delhi Government eight weeks earlier had promised the State Government on the request made on behalf of Maharaja to supply the arms and ammunition. On that request Sardar Patel had discussion with Pandit Nehru and thereafter instructed defence minister to supply the same at top priority. The Defence Minister had ordered the supreme headquarters to supply the arms and ammunition accordingly but General Lockhart had intentionally withheld the supply on the plea that they were not available in Delhi but were throughout the depots all the country. This decision was on their own and even Lord Mountbatten was kept in dark. However when final decision was taken on 26 October 1947 they were collected in one day and army was dispatched on 27 October 1947. At page 111 of that book Jha has written from the secret record of British office in London that, "if Pakistan was to remain politically viable and serve as a sheet anchor for

Britain's strategic interest in middle east, the South-East Asia, Kashmir had to serve as a buffer between the NWFP and India. If Kashmir became a part of India, the 'Khudai Khidmatgars' would gain a safe heaven from which to foment rebellion in NWFP and raise the demand for an Independent Patkhtoonistan."

At page 115 of his book, Prem Shankar Jha has referred Pandit Nehru's telegram sent to Prime Minister Attlee informing him about accession of J&K states to India explaining all the attending circumstances for sending Military help. The reply of telegram was, "I do not think it would be helpful if I were to comment on the action which your government has taken." He had suggested that it may not become a cause for the breakdown of the two dominions. That you and Prime Minister of Pakistan should try to concert plans to ascertain the wishes of the people. All this correspondence Jha has quoted from UK High Commissions records of India from British library.

Larry Collins in his book *Mountbatten and Independent India* at page 56 has recorded that the task of Lord Mountbatten for getting referred the Kashmir dispute to UNO had finished and on 21st June 1948, he left India along with his wife to London but he had remained at pains at his heart that he could not merge J&K State with the dominion of Pakistan. According to him, for this incomplete task the Pakistan's policy was defective. He has quoted Lord Mountbatten in his words, "Could anybody ever think that Pakistan would do such a foolish act that she would not recall the raiders from the territory of J&K State. I had told Liaquat Ali Khan, Prime Minister of Pakistan, that he had simply to recall the raiders and after that Plebiscite would be held. You would win and get Kashmir back. By not doing so you are getting yourself entrapped in the net of Pandit Nehru and on my telling for holding Plebiscite now are retracting from the promise and getting criticised amongst your well-wishers."

The other hidden force working behind the scene was the Prime Minister of the State of J&K—RC Kak who from the position of a petty librarian in a local government college had managed to occupy the highest administrative post in one of the largest State in the country. His links with the Anglo-American block stand established. He had married a British national after the death of his first local wife. He had his hidden connections with Muslim League which have been exposed in this book. Not only that, Maharaja Hari Singh had admitted with his last Prime Minister Mehr Chand Mahajan that he had been misguided by RC Kak for remaining an independent State. Mahatma Gandhi's visit to the Valley during the months of July-August 1947 and his meeting with the Maharaja brought the result of RC Kak's unceremonial dismissal and subsequent replacement by way of a stop gap arrangement by handing over the charge of Prime Minister to General Janak Singh Katoch which ended within two months time because formal appointment for five years term as Prime minister was made of Mehr Chand Mahajan who arrived in the State on 10 October 1947. This aspect has been fully discussed in details under a separate chapter. Sheikh Abdullah's release from the prison after his unqualified apology vide letter dated September 26, 1947 was also a first step in the right direction to facilitate the accession. It may be noted that revered Hindu leader Guru Golwalkar (head of Rashtriya Swayamsevak Sangh) had also visited the Valley during those days of turmoil and impending political changes in the sub-continent and he had a meeting with the Maharaja. Despite an olive branch shown by Pakistan and its political organization Muslim League to the Maharaja for a secure future exalted position in Pakistan, he did not fall into the trap but showed his sense of patriotism of not losing the sight of the stark reality that accession with the dominion of Pakistan would result into large scale massacres of the Hindus and Sikhs. During this period of uncertainty Maharaja strengthened the road link between Jammu and Pathankot and he had envisaged a scheme to construct a boat bridge over the river Ravi. The State was not linked with any communication system with the narrow strip of the area which was to fall in the Indian dominion on partition of the country except tehsil of Pathankot which as a single unit of four tehsils of old Gurdaspur district had majority Hindu population. The only hope was that in case tehsil Pathankot falls in the share of India then a plane road link and railway link is possible. Two existing road links of the State along with one railway link connecting Sialkot was definitely to end in the future territory of Pakistan. One of such existing road was running parallel with railway line from Jammu to Sialkot. The other motorable road link starting from Srinagar had to meet at the ending points falling in the areas going to the share of Pakistan in the Rawalpindi area. This shows that there was a scheme to accede to India. The allegation of Pakistan that accession was obtained under coercion is not based upon any evidence as this allegation stands refuted not only by the assertion of Lord Mountbatten but also by the unambiguous statement of three service Chiefs of Armed Forces of India who were all British nationals—General RM Lockhart, Chief of the Indian Army; Air Marshal TW Elmhirst, Commander of the Royal Indian Air Force; and Rear Admiral JTS Hall, Chief of the Royal Indian Navy. (Reference: *Time Only to Look Forward*, Mountbatten's Speeches). In a joint statement, they said, "On 24 October the Commander-in-Chief, Indian Army, received information that tribesmen had seized Muzaffarabad.

This was the first indication of the raid. Prior to this date, no plans of any sort for sending Indian forces into Kashmir had been formulated or even considered."

Jawaharlal Nehru has written in *India's Tryst with Destiny*, that on August 14-15, India woke to light and freedom but in Kashmir, the Maharaja was having dreams of independence—dreams that had been planted in his mind by ambitious advisors and flatterers. A mention has to be made in this book about his two prominent advisors, the powerful dubious characters—Swami Santdev and unfaithful Prime Minister RC Kak. The latter had also links with Muslim League and toying with the idea of Independent Kashmir or accession with Pakistan. The Swami being a sycophant and flatterer of Maharaja in order to always show a rosy picture of his future may be uttering about the rise of his kingdom up to Lahore as Dr Karan Singh has made a mention in his autobiography but it cannot be digested that Maharaja was so credulous to believe him totally as he was an educated and enlightened ruler. Jagmohan in his book *My Frozen Turbulence in Kashmir*, has recorded, "when the Maharaja left for Jammu at 2 AM on October 27 (actually 26) 1947, in a great hurry he found that the Swami who had been advising him to stay at Srinagar, was going ahead of the Caravan." Dr Karan Singh (Maharaja Hari Singh's son) in his autobiography has corroborated this fact by stating that when he along with his father had reached at Kud after leaving Srinagar at the instance of KPS Menon (a senior officer in PMO and later on Indian Ambassador in Russia), Swami Santdev joined them in his white fiat car at Kud on the National Highway.

In response to the telegram of August 12, 1947 from the Prime Minister of Jammu and Kashmir, Pakistan agreed to enter into a 'Stand Still Agreement' with the Maharaja w.e.f. August 15, 1947. On the same day, an identical telegram was also sent to Government of India that, "the J&K Government would welcome standstill agreement with the Union of India on all matters on which these exist at the present moment with outgoing British Indian government. It is suggested that the existing arrangements should continue pending settlement of details and formal execution of fresh agreements." These arrangements according to the Treaty of Amritsar of 1846, comprised the use of Indian forces if there was internal rebellion or invasion by a foreign government. The Government of India however, did not accept the offer immediately and telegraphed back:

> "Government of India would be glad if you or some other Minister duly authorised in this behalf could fly Delhi for negotiating Stand Still Agreement between Kashmir Government and Indian

> dominion. Early action desirable to maintain existing agreements and administrative arrangements."

By this time, the temporary charge of Prime Minister which was with General Janak Singh Katoch which had been taken over formally by Justice Mehr Chand Mahajan on 10 October 1947. Before the Prime Minister of the State could go to Delhi to discuss these matters, the State was invaded by Pakistan with the help of tribals from its frontier areas by way of skirmishes. Not only that the border areas from Kathua to district Mirpur of the length of 250 miles had also become volatile.

After Pakistan had accepted the 'Stand Still Agreement' (see Appendix 4), side by side it imposed the economic blockade in respect of essential commodities, i.e. petrol, food, cloth, salt and other items. Communications were tampered and transit of people was hindered. After receiving the information from Major General Scott who was incharge of J&K forces that there were incursions of the armed raiders from Pak territory, the Maharaja on October 15, 1947 sent cable to British Prime Minister that proved an exercise in futility. The Maharaja realized the helplessness of the British though in the inner layers of his mind, he was hoping a helping hand from the British in case of need on becoming an independent ruler.

Maharaja had released all the National Conference leaders including its head Sheikh Abdullah from September 1947 and they had started the deliberations as to the fact whether State should accede to Union of India or to Pakistan or remain independent. GM Sadiq—a senior National Conference leader who later on became Chief Minister of the State also went twice to Pakistan with a request to give them the time to think and not precipitate a hurried decision. Pakistan replied in imposing an economic blockade and sending invaders of the tribal areas under her occupation guided and assisted from the personnel of armed forces into the State territory. Before the tribal invasion, Major General Scott (who was only a Brigadier in the Indian British Army but was later conferred the honorary rank of Major General by Maharaja Hari Singh) and Mr Powell (a British police officer), who was the head of the J&K Police in the rank of Inspector General had left the State. He too was promoting Anglo-American block's policy which has been discussed in this book.

When the Government of Britain had decided to end her rule in India, then for discussion Cabinet Mission had visited India and informed the members of the 'Chamber of Princes' that after the lapse of British rule, the Princes would not be under their suzerainty. As already has been discussed in this book that on 25 July 1947, Lord

Mountbatten had addressed the Princes that in practice the States would not be Free or Independent because they previously were also not independent as many of their administrative departments were under the control of British Raj. They had only one option of either joining any of the two dominions. Lord Mountbatten had made it clear that while taking decision, the Princes had to take into consideration their geographical continuity and wishes of the people. There is no record available that it was necessary for a ruler that before taking any opinion, the wishes of his subject had to be necessarily ascertained. The British had established a department for this purpose which was known department of States. (See White Paper on Indian States, pages 160-164). This Department had sent a communication to every State which envisaged that after accession the States had to surrender three subjects to the dominion of India—Foreign Affairs, Communications and Defence. This decision had been taken by the State Department which was under the control of Sardar Patel. With these efforts many States had acceded to the dominion of India before 15 August 1947. Out of the remaining States, the State of J&K was one which acceded to India on 26 October 1947 and that accession was accepted by Governor-General. In this way, it was a complete accession. (Refer HS Gururaj Rao, *Legal Aspects of Kashmir Problem*, page 19.)

The writer of this book would draw attention of the readers of this book to Section 6 of the Indian Independence Act, 1947 which deals with Legislation for the new dominions. Sub-Section (1) of Section 6 had given the Legislative authority to the Legislature of each of the two new dominions to have full power to make laws for that dominion, including laws having extra territorial operation. Under Sub-Section 2 no law and no provision of any law made by the Legislature of either of the new dominions shall be void or inoperative on the ground that it is repugnant to the law of England. Sub-Section 3 had fully authorized Governor-General of the new dominions to assent to any of the law of the Legislature of that dominion. Sub-Section 6 reads that the power referred to in Sub-Section (1) of this section extends to the making of laws limiting for the future the powers of the legislature of the dominion.

Section 8 was the temporary provision as to government of each of the new dominions. Sub-Section (1) gave the powers to each of the two dominions to make their constitutions. Sub-Section (2) had enabled the legislatures of both the dominions to add other provisions in accordance with the law mad by the constituent assembly of the dominion under Sub-Section (1) of this section which should be in accordance with the Government of India Act 1935. There were restrictions imposed in the proviso from (a) to (e). The aims and objects of the above said Act was to make provision for setting up in India of two independent dominions, to substitute other provisions for certain provisions of the Government of India Act, 1935, which apply outside those dominions and to provide for other matters consequential on or connected with the setting up of those dominions. This Act was enacted in the British Parliament on 18 July 1947.

Neither in the Government of India Act of 1935 nor in the Indian Independence Act of 1947 there was any provision which enabled either the Governor-General of India or a ruler of an acceding State to make any provisional accession. Also there was no power to withdraw or allowed to be withdrawn the accession once made. Once on 26 October 1947 the Governor-General had accepted the Offer of accession made by Maharaja Hari Singh it was final and complete. The letter which Governor-General of India had written to the Maharaja that after the restoration of the peace in the State, the opinion of the people shall be ascertained that was a part and parcel of the political policy which had been adopted by the Government of India as adopted by Congress in 1929 and discussed above.

During the freedom movement Congress Party had framed a policy towards helping the movements launched by various political parties in different States of Indian dominion that democracy should be established in Autocratic States. The will or wish of the people is the foundation of the democratic institution.

From the above discussion made regarding Section 8(2) of the Indian Independence Act of 1947 read with Section 6 when the Governor-General of India had accepted the accession of the State, the accession was complete. The authority was with the ruler and Governor-General had to accept it or reject it and inform the ruler. In the State of Jammu and Kashmir, Maharaja Hari Singh had exercised his authority of making the accession and Governor-General of India had accepted it so it is final and complete and nobody under law has any authority like our present Chief Minister Omar Abdullah to declare publicly that State had not merged with the Union of India.

Appointment of Mehr Chand Mahajan as Prime Minister of Kashmir

At the end of the month of April or on 1st May 1947, Maharaja allowed Maharani and Dr Karan Singh to visit Lahore. Maharani arranged a meeting with Justice Mehr Chand Mahajan of Lahore High Court at Faletti's Hotel in Lahore and offered to the latter the post of

Prime Minister of J&K State. Mahajan remained non-committal and renewed the offer at the end of August 1947 (see page 123 and 124 of the book *Looking Back*—Mahajan). On 7th September 1947 Mahajan showed his willingness from Dharamshala (now district of HP State) where he was staying with his family on account of disturbed conditions in Lahore where he was working as judge of the Lahore High Court. He left Dharamshala on 10th September 1947 in heavy rain for Kashmir and after two days of journey with great difficulty was able to reach Jammu at night-time. The shape of the motorable road from Kathua to Jammu was so bad that he had to disembark from the vehicle at two places and cross the flooded rivulet 'Ujh' on Cavalry horse's back assisted by Cavalrymen flanked by both sides. He had to halt for the night in a military camp situated at a distance of one mile from rivulet Ujh. From Jammu it took him two days to reach Srinagar. After meeting the Maharaja and Maharani, he stayed in Srinagar for three days. He has made a mention of this fact in his above stated book at Page 125 how sensational news was in circulation that dismissed Prime Minister RC Kak with the help of the then Chief of the Staff of Army an Englishman (General Scott) had made an attempt to make his escape successful from the State but his attempt was thwarted by the administration. At that time, General Janak Singh was acting as officiating Prime Minister and Ramlal Batra a retired member of Punjab's provincial Civil Service was the Deputy Prime Minister of the State.

The terms of Mahajan's appointment as Prime Minister were discussed with General Janak Singh and were embodied in the order of His Highness' dated 18th September 1947.

It said:

"I herewith offer you the post of Prime Minister of my State on the following terms:

You will be given as salary of Rs 5,000 per month. This will be free of income tax, which you may have to pay on this amount.

You will be given a free and furnished house.

You will have a free car with a driver but without petrol.

The tenure of your service will be a period of five years.

In case of earlier termination of service you will be paid the salary for the rest of the period."

Mahajan accepted the offer saying that as soon as he would be released by the Government of India and given leave and permission to serve the State, he would come and take up the office of Prime Minister. He then left for Delhi. There on 19 September 1947, he met the Defence

Minister (Sardar Baldev Singh) and Home Minister (Sardar Patel). The latter ordered him to immediately accept the offer of Maharaja. Mahajan then met the Prime Minister Pandit Nehru and apprised that Maharaja was willing to accede to India and also to introduce necessary reforms in the Administration which would be taken later on. Pandit Nehru wanted an immediate change in the internal Administration and felt somewhat annoyed. Pandit Nehru also asked Mahajan to see that Sheikh Abdullah was set free. Mahajan was advised to see Mahatma Gandhi and he remained with him for an hour. It is recorded at page 126 by Mahajan in his book that, "he (Mahatma) had no desire to liquidate the Maharaja or to do any harm to him and that if possible this State should accede to India and that administration should have democratic setup," Mahajan had informed the Maharaja the gist of the talks he had held with the leaders.

On the midnight of 10 October 1947, Mehr Chand Mahajan received two telephone calls from Sardar Patel calling him immediately to Delhi. Simultaneously, in the early morning, he also received a telephone message from the Governor granting him eight months leave and direction to take up the employment with affect from 10th October 1947. On 11 October 1947, Mahajan reached Delhi and called on Sardar Patel, Pandit Nehru, Mahatma Gandhi and Lord Mountbatten. At page 128 of his book Mahajan has specifically recorded that Lord Mountbatten had, "clearly told me that my position was unenviable and that he did not know what advice I should give to His Highness. He resented His Highness's attitude to him when he had visited the State earlier as the Maharaja had refused to meet him for discussing the question of accession. I guessed that his view (Lord Mountbatten's) was that Kashmir had no alternative but to accede to Pakistan though he said that as Governor-General of India he would be very happy if I advised Maharaja to accede to India...."

Mehr Chand Mahajan arrived at Srinagar on 12 October 1947 and duly conveyed the message of Pandit Nehru to Maharaja. Maharaja gave the requisite permission to Sheikh Abdullah to go to Delhi and meet Pandit Nehru but suspected that the visit would give trouble to him (Maharaja) as well as to Mahajan. At page 129 of the book Mahajan has recorded:

> "Panditji had a soft corner for the Sheikh and was very friendly with him and as the Sheikh's ambition was to become the Prime Minister of Kashmir, he would take the earliest opportunity to prevail upon Pandit Nehru to put him in power. Once in power he would revive his 'Quit Kashmir Movement' and become all powerful himself. The Maharaja wanted to keep Sheikh Abdullah

> within the State after his release and not permit him to go to Delhi to see the Prime Minister"

Before leaving for Delhi on 13th or 14th October 1947, Sheikh Abdullah and Begum Abdullah sought an interview with His Highness. The Sheikh had desired an interview with His Highness alone but Maharaja insisted the interview in presence of Mehr Chand Mahajan, Prime Minister and Deputy Prime Minister RL Batra. Sheikh showed his resentment not only in his talk but also in his rude behaviour towards Mahajan and Batra. The burden of his talk was that His Highness should trust him and handover the administration to him. "He would then behave like a dutiful son and a loyal subject. Though he was swearing allegiance and loyalty to His Highness, he desired that Maharaja should remain only a constitutional ruler and real power should be delegated to him." (Page 130, Mahajan)

Mehr Chand Mahajan has recorded his impression regarding Sheikh Abdullah in the following words:

> "This was my first good look at Sheikh Abdullah and my impression was that he was out to gain power at any cost. To acquire it he would try to influence his friend, the Prime Minister of India, but would not disdain the use of any other means such as creating some kind of an uprising in the State."

Before the appointment of Mehr Chand Mahajan as Prime Minister, Jinnah had made at three occasions attempts to come to Srinagar and stay there ostensibly for reasons of health. He had sent his personal secretary a Britisher twice with a personal letter to Maharaja. He was willing to come as a private citizen and to make his own arrangements. Maharaja suspected that he would coerce him to secure Kashmir's accession with Pakistan and celebrate coming Eid there as Governor-General of Pakistan. Jinnah's private secretary was also already in Kashmir for the last three months and creating communal tension. Maharaja politely refused the visit that he was not at that time in a position to make due arrangements according to the status of a head of the neighbouring State. But Jinnah had openly proclaimed that legally speaking the question of accession depended entirely on the choice of the ruler and the people of the State had no right to question his choice. That Maharaja was an independent sovereign and should not care a fig for National Conference and Sheikh Abdullah. That Pakistan would not touch a hair of his head, nor would require him to delegate any powers to the peoples of the State. That after accession, he would continue to be an absolute ruler of the State. Mahajan at page 131 of his book has recorded: "Ram Chandra Kak the Prime Minister of

Kashmir at that time, had, it was believed, never made any secret of his pro-Pakistan leanings. He had been, it is said, hobnobbing with Pak politicians promising them Kashmir on a platter." Mahajan has frankly admitted at page 132 that, "if the Maharaja had decided the question of accession before 15th August 1947, much of the trouble and bitterness may well have been avoided. But British declarations about the status of the States after independence seemed to the Maharaja—and to some extent to his advisors—to open the way to an independent Kashmir. He fondly believed that with the help of his Dogra forces he might achieve this end."

Though Mehr Chand Mahajan had arrived in Srinagar on 12th October 1947 and along with Deputy Prime Minister of the State RL Batra had on the insistence of Maharaja participated in the meeting held with Sheikh Abdullah as discussed already but on 15th October 1947, Mahajan had formally taken the oath of office and entered the office of Prime Minister. On the same day, he held a press conference which was well attended and dealt with the prevailing circumstances in the State. On the same day, Major Shah, a responsible officer of the Pakistan Government who had arrived in Srinagar a week or ten days before sought an interview with him. Before the arrival of Major Shah, Pakistan had started an effective blockade of the State. Food, clothing, petrol, ammunition and other articles of necessity which had been bought by the State had been seized by Pakistan authorities either at Sialkot or at Kohala. The object of blockade was to bring pressure on Maharaja and coerce him to accede to Pakistan. Major Shah armed with this weapon and with the threat of a tribal raid was there to negotiate the accession with Pakistan. From the talks with Major Shah, it had come out that he was suggesting immediate accession with Pakistan and if that was not agreed there was bound to be trouble. Mahajan had told him that he was serious to consider this question keeping an open mind whether accession to Pakistan would be more purposeful than its accession with India. As a condition precedent to this consideration, that blockade must end and lorries waiting entry to the State should be allowed to proceed. Major Shah thought that proposal was reasonable and he would find out from Jinnah who was in Lahore. He accordingly sent him a telegram. Jinnah was not agreeable and Shah again met Mahajan in the afternoon. He conveyed to Mahajan the suggestion of Jinnah to visit Lahore for discussion which invitation was outrightly turned down by Mahajan. Towards, the close of interview, the attitude of Shah became aggressive and he told Mahajan that refusal to decide accession immediately might result in serious consequences. Mahajan blurted out that a threat of that kind would throw the State into the lap of India.

Mehr Chand Mahajan conveyed the purport of the interview to Maharaja who was now of the view that Kashmir should not accede to Pakistan even if he have to built a road through Bhaderwah, Kishtwar via Chamba and Dalhousie to connect the State with India. At this time Mahajan asked a question to Maharaja, "if this was his idea why he did not take that decision before 15 August 1947 which might well have avoided all this trouble? His answer was that he had been differently advised by his former Prime Minister and that he was all the time hoping that Kashmir State could retain an independent status without acceding to any dominion." (See page 142, Mahajan.)

Alongside this blockade to starve the people of the State and frighten the Maharaja an all out effort was made by Pakistani agents to create communal trouble inside the State just as it has been created in India before and after partition. The State of J&K was absolutely free from outburst of communal frenzy even when the Punjab on both sides of the border was having a full dose of it. Lakhs of refugees from Pakistan were in Jammu and Kashmir territory and were passing from Gujarat (name of the area included in Pakistan of west Punjab province), Sialkot and Rawalpindi to Pathankot in India on foot unmolested by the Muslim residents of the State. This had been the state of affairs when Mahajan had travelled from Dharamshala (Kangra) to Srinagar in early September that is from 10 October 1947 to 13 October 1947, but the situation completely deteriorated soon after Jinnah got news about the rejection of his several requests by the Maharaja for accession. Muslims of the Jammu province were incited to create communal trouble inside the State and Jammu became a seat of communal killings. Communal raids were organized from Pakistan on Jammu border villages on a border of 250 miles running with Pakistan. When this information had reached to the Maharaja and Prime Minister Mahajan in Srinagar from the Governor of Jammu, they decided to come down with the hope to restore communal harmony. They were in Jammu province between the 18th and 23rd of October 1947. They received deputations of Hindus and Muslims. Their presence in Jammu created some order in the city. They had decided to visit border villages from Mirpur, Kotli to Kathua in jeeps with full risks and dangers. They had seen on the border a scene of inhuman butchery and cruelty. Platoons of Dogra army patrolling the border were helping in repulsing these raids but their strength was too insignificant for the long stretch of the border.

There was a plan to kidnap and abduct the Maharaja and Mehr Chand Mahajan to take forcible accession from them at the point of bayonet. All their movements were reported to Pak authority because the superintendent of police of Jammu had become a Pak agent so was the Muslim chief of the staff. The plan was to capture them during lunch at the Bhimber Dak Bungalow. Bhimber town was situated nearby the Pakistan border on the Gujarat side and motorable road runs alongside the border. The original plan of visit was to go on 21st of October to Bhimber side. Pak people had organized an armoured car raid on Bhimber for the 21st but a providential help came in the mind of the Maharaja who suddenly changed his programme form the way and instead of going to Kathua first proceeded towards Bhimber. On 20 October 1947 they witnessed a scene of total destruction and Hindu population was migrating to places of safety. Maharaja assured them of safety and had a lunch at Bhimber Dak Bungalow and after giving instructions to the administration returned by 10 O'clock at night to Jammu. As was scheduled by Pakistan and her agents the Dak Bungalow of Bhimber was attacked by armed car raids organized from Gujarat on 21st October where an important minister of Pakistan Government himself was present. The presentiment or foreboding of the Maharaja had saved them from falling into the Pak hands. The next day they went to Kathua and noticed similar scenes. The whole border was in a State of tumult and excitement engineered by Pak authorities from inside and outside the border to force the Maharaja to sign a letter of accession in favour of Pakistan. India was a silent spectator of this game, meanwhile giving whatever meagre help it could give, by air, on humanitarian grounds and still negotiating a Stand Still Agreement. The Maharaja along with the Prime Minister returned to Srinagar on 23rd of October 1947 by air when Pakistan had already launched a full-fledged attack from Kohala side during the night of 22 October 1947 and after getting full support of Muslim armed forces of Dogra Army Battalion who at Kohala had butchered their Col Narayan Singh and Hindu Comrades, the raiders captured the district headquarters of Muzaffarabad on 23 October 1947. In the way Maharaja and Prime Minister saw the towns of Bhimber, Kotli and Mirpur burning with fire as Pakistani raiders had completely overrun the administration. They could not see the town of Muzaffarabad due to bad weather. When they landed at the airport of Srinagar, they learnt about a regular raid being conducted by Pakistan Army with the help of tribal men of North-West Frontier which was also a part of Pakistan. Efforts were made to blow up the bridges but no dynamite was available in the State and could not be procured because of blockade imposed by Pakistan. The Maharaja and the Prime Minister sent the military aid that was possible. On 24th and 25th of October British Prime Minister was approached but no help came from his side. Bakshi Ghulam Mohammad was organizing the bands of his partymen to stop the people from leaving the city of Srinagar due to panic without knowing the consequences that if the raiders would have captured the city all of them would have been mercilessly butchered. During this crisis Sheikh Abdullah quietly left for Delhi in the evening of 25 October 1947 after he got accommodation in the airflight. He only returned to Srinagar on 27 October 1947 when military aid from India had arrived in Srinagar. The Maharaja's administration had only a cavalry of battalion, the personal guards of Maharaja and a disbanded company of Muslim Soldiers at their disposal to save the city in case of emergency (pages 272-275, Mahajan).

Further Mahajan has recorded at page 150 of his book that on 24th October 1947, the Deputy Prime Minister (RL Batra) had left Srinagar for Delhi carrying a letter of accession to India from the Maharaja and a personal letter of accession to India from the Maharaja and a personal letter to Pandit Nehru and another to Sardar Patel asking for military help in men, arms and ammunition. Mahajan had also wrote to both requesting them to save the State from Pakistan's unprovoked aggression.

In the afternoon of 25 October 1947, the Prime Minister Mehr Chand Mahajan held a meeting with officer commanding Srinagar, the Inspector General of Police and the Governor of Kashmir that raiders should be given a receding battle to secure that State's depleted forces should suffer few casualties as possible. The Maharaja had instructed Mahajan to fly to Delhi if he could secure a plane. As they were groping for a way out, VP Menon, Secretary of the Ministry of States, Government of India arrived in Srinagar by plane. He came straight to the residence of Mahajan and told him that he had come to take him to Delhi. Nothing about military aid, he said, could be decided till his arrival there. He was told that Deputy Prime Minister of the State had been sent to Delhi with letter of accession. Mahajan reminded him that Pandit Nehru had promised about military aid whenever he would demand but Menon told him that the aid could not be provided without his availability at Delhi. Both of them went to the Maharaja and apprised him about the situation. Maharaja asked Mahajan to accompany Menon in the early morning of 26 October 1947. Maharaja had also told them to send Maharani and Yuvraj to Jammu but himself would stay in Srinagar to protect the city from invaders. Mahajan and Menon suggested that Maharaja's presence in Jammu is necessary as the situation may require his personal negotiations with India and it would be convenient in Jammu rather than in Srinagar. Eventually, he was persuaded to leave Srinagar at about 2 AM on the morning of 26 October 1947. After His Highness had left at 2 AM, an officer of the

State forces came from the front and informed Mahajan that Chief of the Armed forces Brigadier Rajinder Singh had been wounded and was lying on the road with six or seven bullet injuries in his body. Next morning, i.e. on 26 October 1947 Mahajan and Menon arrived at Safdarjung Airport at 8 AM where a car was waiting and Mahajan was taken to Prime Minister's house where Sardar Patel was also waiting. They were apprised of the situation with a request of military help. Nehru observed that it was not possible at the spur to send troops as such an operation required considerable preparation. Mahajan was adamant in his submission but the Prime Minister was sticking to his view. At last Mahajan said, "Give us the military force we need. Take the accession and give whatever power you desire to the popular party. The army must fly this evening to save Srinagar or else he would go to Lahore and negotiate terms with Jinnah." Nehru when heard that Mahajan had orders to go to Pakistan in case military aid was not given immediately, he became upset and in angry tone said, "Mahajan go away." He got up and was about to leave the room when Sardar Patel detained him by saying in his ear, "Of course Mahajan you are not going to Pakistan." Just then a piece of paper was passed over to the Prime Minister. He read it in loud voice said, "Sheikh Sahab also says the same thing." It appeared that Sheikh Abdullah was listening to all this talk while sitting in one of the adjoining bedroom. Prime Minister's tone changed at once after reading that slip. Mahajan was told to go to the house of Defence Minister and take rest and he would be informed the result after holding a meeting before lunch. At 12.45 PM, the Defence Minister came and informed Mahajan that decision has been taken to send two companies of Indian troops to Srinagar. He also told Mahajan to provide necessary information to the commander of the troops and luckily Mahajan had taken the plan where clash of the raiders and State forces had taken place (page 152, Mahajan).

CHAPTER 5

Invasion of Kashmir by Pakistan

In the book titled *Operations in J&K 1947-1948*, Ministry of Defence, Government of India, it is recorded that invasion of the Kashmir Valley from Pakistan was planned with meticulous care and showed considerable strategic and tactical insight. The plan was first to split up the State Army into tiny groups by means of hit and run attacks all along the long frontier with Pakistan. The defending force was compelled to distribute itself into garrisons of Platoon strength spread indeed along the entire southern frontier. Pakistan also allured the tribal Pathans for the beauty of Kashmir and its wealth to loot it and enjoy the women folk. The British had been paying the unruly Pathans crores of rupees from Indian revenues for their appeasement which Pakistan could not pay. The invasion would have kept them busy and Pakistan would get a big beautiful and fertile chunk of State territory within her dominion.

The main invasion was planned and launched by the Army Headquarters of Pakistan and was called, 'Operation Gulmarg'. Orders were issued through DO letters marked Personal/Top Secret and signed personally by the British Commander-in-Chief (C-in-C) of Pakistan Army, within few days of Pakistan coming into existence. Conclusive proof of Pakistan Army's direct role in the invasion of J&K came into light through two different sources. The first was Major Onkar Singh Kalkat, then serving as Brigade Major at HQ Bannu frontier Brigade group, under Brigadier CP Murray (a British). The Brigadier being away at Mirali outpost, Major Kalkat on 20th August 1947 received an envelope marked Personal/Top Secret and he opened it. The contents thereof inside that letter from C-in-C Pakistan Army revealed a detailed plan of Operation Gulmarg. He hastily called up the Brigadier and was advised not to breathe a word about it to anybody else he would not be allowed to leave Pakistan alive. Pakistan Army had got scent of Major's

Kalkat's knowledge of the Operation Gulmarg Plan. Consequently, he was put under house arrest in his residence. But the officer made a daring escape and reached Ambala on 18th October 1947. At night he boarded a goods train to reach Delhi in haste. The following day he met Brigadier Kalwant Singh, the acting CGS, Col Thapar the acting DMO and Sardar Baldev Singh, the Defence Minister and told them about the Pakistani Plan for Operation Gulmarg. But this did not cut any ice with them. While Major Kalkat was making efforts to find out his missing family members who were left by him in Mianwali (Pakistan). The family had been shifted to east Punjab with the help of local Deputy Commissioner. Operation Gulmarg had already started on 22nd October 1947. The Indian Authorities now realized their folly in showing indifference to Kalkat's invaluable information and could trace him in Amritsar on 24th October 1947. He was taken to Prime Minister Pandit Nehru who shouted at the Defence Minister and the acting DMO for not taking necessary action in the light of Major Kalkat's revelation.

The second source was GK Reddy, a journalist. On 21st October 1947, he took a trunk call and found it was from Lt Col Alavi (the PRO of GHQ, Pakistan Army to API, Lahore). Alavi not suspecting that he was speaking to anyone but a Muslim clearly stated that the attack on Ramkot (J&K Border post) would begin that night. The subsequent progress of the invasion would be given to API Lahore by GHQ Rawalpindi every evening on phone, but must be published as communique from 'Azad Kashmir Government' under Palandri date line, Palandri being given out as HQ of Azad Kashmir Government. After escaping from Pak, Reddy gave out his story which was published in *Blitz*, weekly of Bombay dated 9th June 1948.

These two independent testimonies based on first-hand knowledge conclusively prove Pakistan's complicity with active guidance of British to her Army Officer's in the invasion of J&K, apart from the fact that the strictly controlled supply of ration and petrol could not have reached the invaders without official help or connivance.

According to 'Operation Gulmarg' plan as described by Major Kalkat every Pathan tribe was required to enlist one Lashkar of 1,000 tribesmen. After enlistment these Lashkars were to concentrate at Bannu, Wana, Peshawar, Kohat, Thal and Nowshera by the first week of September 1947. The Brigade Commanders at these places were to issue them arms, ammunition and some essential items of clothings but on papers they were to be shown to have been issued Pak Army units. Every tribal Lashkar was also to be provided with a Major, a Captain and ten JCOs of the regular Pak Army. The Major was to be the actual

Commander of the Lashkar and act as the 'adviser' of the Tribal Malik nominally in command of the unit. These Pak regulars were to be Pathans and to dress and live like other Pathans. The entire force was to be commanded by Major General Akbar Khan who was given the code name Tariq. He was to be assisted by Brigadier Sher Khan. Their headquarter was located in the same building as the C-in-C of the Pakistan Army and General Sir Frank Messervy was, of course, privy to the whole plan. (Pages 17 and 18.)

All Lashkars had to be concentrated at Abbottabad by 18th October 1947. They were to be moved in civil buses at night. A detail plan was chalked out to capture the whole State fully given at pages 18 and 19 of the above said book titled *Operations in J&K 1947-1948* and need not to be reproduced here. All this shows that there was no internal revolt as was being claimed by Pakistan but it was a well calculated invasion by the Government of Pakistan after getting assistance from Tribals and seeking a little help from the elements of Muslim League party who were locals.

The State Forces comprising a total of nine Infantry Battalions, two Mountain Batteries and a Cavalry Regiment were thinly spread out along the entire boundary with Pakistan stretching from Mirpur, Poonch, Nowshera and Rajouri in Jammu and Kohala/Domel in Kashmir. Some of the raiders were also hired from the tribal territory of Afghanistan. All the raiders were armed with modern weapons including Bren-guns, Stenguns, grenades, heavy mortars, anti-tank rifles and land mines.

Brigadier Rajinder Singh had replaced General Scott as Chief of the Army Staff on ad-hoc basis. Domel/Kohala the gateway of Kashmir Valley from Rawalpindi route was defended by fourth J&K Infantry commanded by Lieutenant Col Narayan Singh. The Battalion comprised two companies of Dogras and two of Muslims mostly hailing from Mirpur area. It was said that Maharaja Hari Singh who had himself supervised troop deployment had doubts about the loyalty of his Muslim troops after the formation of Pakistan on the religious base, but Lt Col Narayan Singh assured him that their loyalty was undoubted as he had commanded and seen them during Second World War when the Battalion was deployed in North Africa. This blind faith of Lt Col Narayan Singh was betrayed by the Muslim troops when they got the signal from across the Kohala Bridge about the impending raid by the Muslim raiders as they mutinied and with the first shot of a bullet killed their own Commander Lt Col Narayan Singh and simultaneously other Hindu colleagues who were unarmed were also massacred. This full-fledged invasion had taken place on October 22,

1947 and prior to that there were stray infiltrations and raids. Such infiltrations were witnessed even in Kathua, Jammu sectors of the border because some armed men in civil clothes had infiltrated near the town of Samba within depth of about 10 kilometres and resorted to loot and arson. They were pushed back by a party of the State force, and civilian population had also shown resistance. Similar type of infiltration had started in RS Pura sector and there were frequent skirmishes between the deployed State forces and the infiltrators across the border. The British Chief of the Army Staff Mr Scott and Inspector General of J&K Police Mr Powell had the knowledge of these infiltrations and they had informed the Maharaja. The fact that they left the State in great hurry raises a doubt that they may be having some prior secret information from their original Masters (British) about the Pakistan plan with implied support of the British to grab the State by force. It is noteworthy that on 27 October 1947, when Jinnah came to know about dispatch of Indian troops to Srinagar, he became furious. That night he sent instructions to General Sir Douglas Gracey, the acting Commander-in-Chief of Pakistan Army (General Messervy, the C-in-C was away on leave) to move the Pakistan Army into Kashmir to seize Baramulla, Srinagar and Banihal pass as well as to move into Mirpur district of Jammu region. However, General Gracey replied that he could not take such action without consulting the Supreme Commander Field Marshal Auchinleck. Next morning, the Field Marshal came to Lahore to explain Jinnah that in view of the accession of J&K to India, the despatch of Indian troops to Srinagar was perfectly legal, and if the Governor-General of Pakistan (Jinnah) insists on sending his Army to J&K, all British men serving in Pakistan Army would have to be pulled out at once. Consequently, Jinnah had to climb down and cancel his orders. There was, thus, a free run for the raiders towards the Valley without the least resistance. Jinnah was desperate that Srinagar city should be taken without any loss of time but the raiders took their own time enjoying themselves in unprecedented orgies of loot, rapes and killings and were not willing to listen to their Pakistani masters. This may be thought only as a divine intervention which saved the Srinagar city because when the Indian Army landed in Srinagar by air, the raiders had advanced even up to the outskirts of Shaltang and only few kilometres away from the Srinagar Airport.

While the raiders were still near Uri, Maharaja Hari Singh issued a command, "Brigadier Rajinder Singh will proceed to Uri forthwith whatever troops he can muster and fight the raiders, to the last man and the last round of ammunition." There were few troops at Badami

Bagh Cantonment to organize except for about one hundred and fifty who were on guard duties including the palace guards. Thereafter, a mechanized convoy of some ten to twelve vehicles commanded by Brigadier Rajinder Singh proceeded to Uri. Brigadier's strategy was now only to somehow delay their advance by positioning his party on the highway and preventing them from moving the vehicles. With military tactics of the highest order, the Brigadier kept the raiders engaged for about two days but they were in thousands and had encircled his forces. After giving bloody battles to the raiders and sacrificing their lives only half a dozen soldiers had survived with the Brigadier whose both legs were fractured and was rendered unfit to drive a vehicle. He asked his men to seat him reclining against a tree, removed his rank badges and held a pistol in his outstretched hands. He then asked his men to save their lives. On their refusal to forsake him, he commanded them in a firm voice repeating the words of his Maharaja, "the last man and the last round of ammunition." When the Indian Army re-occupied that area the only human remnant which was available on the spot was a necktie which was hanging with a bush and nothing else. One version is that this valiant Dogra soldier was killed on the spot when he was killing the raiders with his pistol but the other version which has appeared in the local newspaper (*Daily Excelsior*, Jammu of October 23, 2005 penned by RK Koul who according to him has remained with the Brigadier as a civilian staff member of Kashmir Brigade headquarters of which he was the commander) that "in the Civil and Military Gazette of the time, after the Brigadier had shot dead a couple of raiders he was captured and carried away to Peshawar where he was brutally tortured before being killed." (Note: The writer of this book has his personal doubts about this version as severely injured Brigadier could not survive for long to undertake such an arduous journey). On October 23rd 1947, a large force of raiders had entered Muzaffarabad in three hundred lorries (motor vehicles) and started looting murdering and raping women. The raiders killed Hindus and Sikhs in thousands. Some of them who could not flee to save their lives to the mountains committed suicides. Duni Chand Mehta who was the Wazir-e-Wazarat (SDM of Muzaffarabad) was done to death but his family members consisting of wife and three minor kids were spared. His widow Mrs Krishna Mehta along with other survivors of the massacre were taken as prisoners and later on were repatriated through Red Cross Organisation. The town of Baramulla was completely ransacked by October 26th 1947 after killing about three thousands inhabitants which included mostly Hindus, Sikhs and few Christians and Muslims. Jagmohan, author of *My Frozen Turbulence in Kashmir*, has at page 87 recorded, "as noted by Father Shanks, the tribesmen—great, wild, black beasts they were—came shooting their way down from the hills on both sides of the town. A 20 year old Indian nurse Philomena, tried to protect a Muslim patient whose baby had just been born. She was shot dead first. The patient was next." Even the St Joseph Convent was destroyed, and the Assistant Mother Superior and three nuns were brutally murdered. After visiting Baramulla, the correspondent of the New York Times wrote, "Surviving residents estimate that 3,000 of their fellow townsmen, including four Europeans and a retired British officer and his pregnant wife, were slain." VP Menon in his book *Integration of the Indian States*, has recorded at page 406, "On 8 November 1947 Indian forces under the command of Major General Kulwant Singh occupied Baramulla. When the Indian troops entered the city they found that it had been stripped by the tribsmen of its wealth and women. Out of a population of 14,000 only 1,000 were left. The devastation by the raiders was indeed ghastly, reminiscent of Nadir Shah's sacking of Delhi." The raiders hardly realized that the time spent by them in committing their abominable crimes would turn out to be their punishment, as it enabled the Indian forces to land at Srinagar airport on October 27th 1947 and ultimately push back the raiders inflicting heavy casualties on them. Without the gallant resistance shown by 150 men of Dogra Army under the able command of Brigadier Rajinder Singh and their sacrifices, the city of Srinagar would have fallen into the hands of the raiders and then it would have been impossible for the Indian army to land in Srinagar by air. The consequences would have been that the whole Valley would have been devastated and its re-occupation would have been a thing of the past. Brigadier Rajinder Singh was the first recipient of Maha Vir Chakra (posthumously) of Indian Forces. He belonged to the State Forces which at that time were not a part of the Indian Army. Equally important was the role played by a young activist Master Maqbool Sherwani (who was a tailor by profession) of National Conference. He helped the Indian Army indirectly by misleading the raiders as well as organized the villagers to show resistance to them. This was done to delay the capture of the city of Srinagar by the raiders. The raiders ultimately caught hold of him and tortured him by nailing his body and brutally murdered him. India cannot forget his supreme sacrifice and every patriot still owes him a debt for saving the lives and honour of lakhs of inhabitants of the State. Every Indian should adore him as a National Hero. On October 24, 1947, the Mohara Power Generating Station was captured by the raiders and the Srinagar city plunged into darkness. On October 24th 1947, Maharaja Hari Singh approached the Government of India for military assistance. On October 25, 1947, Secretary of the Ministry of States (VP Menon) flew to Srinagar and after few discussions with him Maharaja offered for accession. In his letter dated 26 October 1947, Maharaja Hari Singh wrote to Lord Mountbatten (the then Governor-General of India):

"My Dear Lord Mountbatten,

I have to inform your Excellency that a great emergency has arisen in my State and request immediate assistance of your government. As your Excellency is aware the State of J&K has not acceded to the dominion of India or to Pakistan. Geographically my State is contiguous to both of dominions. It has vital and cultural links with both of them. Besides my State has a common boundary with the Soviet Republic and China. In their external relations, the dominions of India and Pakistan cannot ignore this fact. I wanted to take time to decide to which dominion I should accede, or whether it is not in the best interest of both the dominions and my State to stand independent, of course with friendly and cordial relations with both. I accordingly approached the dominions of India and Pakistan to enter into stand still agreement with my State. The Pakistan Government accepted this Agreement. The dominion of India desired further discussions with representatives of my government. I could not arrange this in view of the developments indicated below. In fact, Pakistan Government are operating post and telegraph system in the State. Though we have got a Stand Still Agreement with the Pakistan Government that government permitted steady and increasing strangulation of supplies food, salt and petrol to my State. Afridis, soldiers in plain clothes, and desperadoes with modern weapons have been allowed to infiltrator into the State at first in Poonch and then in Sialkot and finally in mass area adjoining Hazara district on the Ramkot side. The result has been that the limited number of troops at the disposal of the State had to be dispersed and thus had to face the enemy at the several points. Simultaneously, that it has become difficult to stop the wanton destruction of life and property and looting. The Mohara power house which supplies the electric current to the whole of Srinagar has been burnt. The number of women who have been kidnapped and raped, makes my heart bleed. The wild forces thus let loose on the State are marching on with the aim of capturing Srinagar, the summer capital of my government, as first step to over running the whole State.

The mass infiltration of tribesmen drawn from the distant areas of the North-West Frontier coming regularly in motor trucks using Mansehra-Muzaffarabad Road and fully armed with up to date weapons cannot possibly be done without the knowing of the

Provincial government of the North-West Frontier Province and the Government of Pakistan. In spite of repeated requests made by my government no attempt has been made to check these raiders or stop them from coming to my State. The Pakistan Radio even put out a story that Provisional Government has been set up in Kashmir. The people of my State both Hindus and the Muslims generally have taken no part at all. With the conditions obtaining at present in my State and the great emergency of the situation as exists, I have no option but to ask for help from the Indian dominion. Naturally they cannot send the help asked for by me without my State acceding to the dominion of India. I have accordingly decided to do so and I attach the Instrument of Accession for acceptance by your government. The other alternative is to leave my State and my people to free booters. On this basis no civilized government can exist or be maintained. This alternative I will never allow to happen as long as I am ruler of the State and I live to defend my country.

I am also to inform your Excellency's Government that it is my intention at once to set up an interim government and ask Sheikh Abdullah to carry these responsibilities in this emergency with my Prime Minister. If my State has to be saved immediate assistance must be available at Srinagar. Menon is fully aware of the situation and he will explain to you, if further explanation is needed.

In haste and with kind regards.

The Palace Jammu — Yours Sincerely
26th October 1947 — Hari Singh"

Maharaja Hari Singh dispatched the Instrument of Accession for acceptance by the Government of India along with this letter. In the Instrument of Accession the Maharaja had declared,

1) "I, hereby declare that I accede to the dominion of India with the intent that the Governor-General of India, the dominion Legislature, the Federal Court and any other dominion authority established for the purposes of the dominion shall, by virtue of this my Instrument of Accession but subject always to the terms thereof, and for the purposes only of the dominion exercise in relation to the State of Jammu and Kashmir (hereinafter referred to as 'this State') such functions as may be vested in them by or under the Government of India Act, 1935, as in force in the dominion of India, on the 15th day of August 1947 (which Act as so in force is hereafter referred to as 'the Act').

2) I hereby assume the obligation of ensuring that due effect is given to the provisions of the Act within this State so far as they are applicable therein by virtue of this my Instrument of Accession.
3) I accept the matters specified in the Schedule hereto as the matters with respect to which the dominion Legislature may make laws for this State.
4) I hereby declare that I accede to the dominion of India on the assurance that if an agreement is made between the Governor-General and the ruler of this State whereby any function in relation to the administration in this State of any law of the dominion Legislature shall be exercised by the ruler of this State, then any such agreement shall be deemed to form part of this Instrument and shall be construed and have effect accordingly.
5) The terms of this my Instrument of Accession shall not be varied by any amendment of the Act or of the Indian Independence Act, 1947, unless such amendment is accepted by me by an Instrument supplementary to this Instrument.
6) Nothing in this Instrument shall empower the dominion Legislature to make any law for this State authorizing the compulsory acquisition of land for any purpose, but I hereby undertake that should the dominion for the purpose of a dominion law which applies in this State deem it necessary to acquire any land, I will at their request acquire the land at their expense or if the land belongs to me transfer it to them on such terms as may be agreed, or, in default of agreement, determined by an arbitrator to be appointed by the Chief Justice of India.
7) Nothing in this Instrument shall be deemed to commit me in any way to acceptance of any future Constitution of India or to fetter my discretion to enter into arrangements with the Government of India under any such future Constitution.
8) Nothing in this Instrument affects the continuance of my sovereignty in and over this State, or, save as provided by or under this Instrument, the exercise of any powers, authority and rights now enjoyed by me as ruler of this State or the validity of any law at present in force in this State.
9) I hereby declare that I execute this Instrument on behalf of this State and that any reference in this Instrument to me or the ruler of the State is to be construed as including a reference to my heirs and successors. The Instrument of Accession had a Schedule wherein the matters with respect to which the

> dominion Legislature could make laws for the State, were specified. The matters regarding which the dominion Legislature was given the power to legislate were relating to defence, external affairs, communications and ancillary matters."

Accepting the accession, Lord Mountbatten wrote to the Maharaja on October 27, 1947:

> "In the special circumstances mentioned by your Highness, my government has decided to accept the accession of Kashmir State to the dominion of India. It is my government's wish that, as soon as law and order has been restored in Kashmir and her soil cleared of the invaders, the question of the State's accession should be settled by a reference to the people. Meanwhile, in response to your Highness's appeal for military aid, action has been taken today to send troops of the Indian Army to Kashmir to help your own forces to defend your territory and to protect the lives, property and honour of your people."

Note: The 'Instrument of Accession' in original form is attached as Appendix 4A at the end of this book.

CHAPTER 6

Responsibility for Delayed Accession of J&K with India

Preponderant established view on one sided available evidence is that Maharaja Hari Singh was solely responsible for not acceding to the dominion of India before 15th August 1947 and is the piece of villain for the creation of subsisting Kashmir problem. The first Prime Minister of India, Pandit Nehru, has also said that when the dawn of freedom was imminent in the sub-continent the Maharaja of Kashmir was dreaming of his independent autocratic existence. The writer of this book does not fully concur with this view because of the availability of the surrounding circumstances and the evidence to the contrary. The first circumstance against Maharaja was on account of his inherited disadvantage being a Dogra Hindu of the State while his subjects constituted about 65 per cent Muslim population. His State was surrounded by communicable border which as a whole was to fall into the share of newly created dominion of Pakistan. The State had only one rail link from Jammu to Sialkot (now in Pakistan). Besides that there was one motorable road leading from Jammu up to Sialkot and then to Lahore. The capital cities of the State, i.e. Jammu and Srinagar had also been linked with motorable road during the reign of Maharaja Pratap Singh. A fair weather road existed near the international border with Pakistan from Jammu to Kathua and that only link with some minor realignment was improved with Lakhanpur in order to connect the motorable link up to river Ravi which Indian forces connected after making a bridge of make shift arrangement with Pathankot. The summer capital of Srinagar city had a motorable road with Rawalpindi (surely falling in the share of dominion of Pakistan). The apparent area surely going to the share of dominion of India had no plane boundary touching with the boundary of the J&K State nor there existed any motorable link which could be used to get military aid or help from

India in case of need. The State had major revenue generating source from the timber extracted from its majestic jungles, and sale markets (Jangalat Mandis) were located in most likely areas to go to Pakistan. The timber was transported through its three rivers Jhelum, Chenab and Ravi which have their natural plane flow through Pakistan territory where the transported timber was catched and stored for sale. By luck one Hindu majority tehsil of Pathankot and two Muslim-dominated tehsils of Batala and Gurdaspur from Muslim-dominated district of Gurdaspur had come to the share of Indian dominion and they could provide a corridor for linking the State with a motorable road but the great hurdle was that river Ravi which formed a boundary line had no bridge over it. The second circumstance was that Maharaja had an insincere and unfaithful Prime Minister Pandit RC Kak who had established rapport with Muslim League, of course, with the prior approval of Muhammad Ali Jinnah. All of them showed him (Maharaja) an olive branch of remaining an independent state. RC Kak constantly advised Maharaja to remain independent. This fact has been admitted by MY Saraf, Chief Justice of Pakistan Occupied Kashmir High Court who originally belonged to the town of Baramulla in his book *Kashmiris Fight for Freedom*. He in his first incarnation had remained a staunch activist of National Conference up to 1946 and subsequently switched his loyalty to Muslim League and had high connections with the Muslim League party dignitaries including access with Muhammad Ali Jinnah. The other factor was that at that time Prime Minister Kak had a British wife and she had established her contacts with Lord Mountbatten who before the formation of two independent dominions was then common Governor-General of the whole sub-continent. When Maharaja came to know about these facts, he immediately unceremoniously dismissed Kak as his Prime Minister and put him under house arrest. The third circumstance was that in the month of June 1947, when Lord Mountbatten as Governor-General of undivided India had visited Kashmir, he had given categorical assurance to Maharaja to accede to Pakistan on the pretext that he had an assurance from Indian leaders that they would not object for it. No such assurance was given by him to Maharaja that he could join Indian dominion without any danger from Pakistan. He could give such assurance for free exercise of discretion because Muhammad Ali Jinnah had always been a protege of Britishers. Lord Mountbatten's frame of mind was disclosed when Mahajan as Prime Minister of the State had met him in official dealings relating to the accession of the State and after discussion Mahajan had formed an opinion that from the inner layers of his heart Mr Mountbatten wanted that State should have acceded to Pakistan. (Refer *Looking Back*, Mahajan.) Not only that, in his book *Jammu-Kashmir ki Anakahee Kahani*, Dr Kuldeep Agnihotri at page 11 has referred a book *Jammu and Kashmir 1949-64* (page 112) written on Kashmir affairs by Javed Aslam. It is recorded in this book in the words of Maharaja Hari Singh himself, "Lord Mountbatten on the basis of ideas and figures had discussed the current affairs from that it appeared that he was compelling him to accede to Pakistan.... Lord Mountbatten had also given the assurance that the State of J&K is Muslim-dominated and with the accession of dominion of Pakistan the latter would become more stable." This aspect has also been already discussed and shall be discussed more in Maharaja Hari Singh's letter. The fourth circumstance was that Maharaja was having a permanent enemy in his sleeves in the incarnation of Sheikh Abdullah who despite showing his regrets for past deeds in his above letter of apology dated September 26, 1947 reproduced herein above had promised to remain loyal throughout his life personally as well as through his political organization, National Conference, to the Maharaja but in the inner layers of his heart had always been polluting the mind of Pandit Nehru against Maharaja who always nourished hatred against Maharaja for his arrest/detention in 1946 for entering the State territory to render help to Sheikh Abdullah for his detention. Last but not the least, the leadership of Muslim League in the State with prior approval of Jinnah was trying their best to win over Maharaja for joining the dominion of Pakistan with guaranteed safety and honour and status of his position as Head of the State. In his letter dated 26th October 1947 reproduced above which accompanied the Instrument of Accession, Maharaja has made an admission, "I wanted to take time to accede to which dominion I should accede or whether it is in the best interest of both the dominions to remain independent of course with friendly and cordial relations with both." It is noteworthy that at that time India and Pakistan had a joint Supreme Commander of the Forces by the name of Field Marshal Auchinleck. The Commander-in-Chief of Pakistan Forces was General Messervy while Commander-in-Chief of Indian Forces was Sir Robert Lockhart. Pakistan Army had a large number of British officers. It has been fully discussed in this book that immediately after August 14, 1947, Pakistan Army under British General was hatching a conspiracy to grab J&K State through rendering external help by engaging tribesmen of North-West Frontier led by Pakistani Army personnel and instigating some Jamaat-e-Islami elements found in numbers in the frontier districts of Poonch and Mirpur. Lord Mountbatten was surely in the knowledge of all these developments but he did nothing to check the aggression and failed to give any breathing time to Maharaja for making a final decision at the appropriate time.

Over the years, two completely different versions of Kashmir have come into being. Prem Shankar Jha in his book *The Origins of a Dispute: Kashmir 1947* has critically examined both versions using the recently classified transfer of Power Documents as well as Personal Accounts of the main Participants in the events of that period. In Chapter 3 under the caption, 'Accession Under Duress', he has admitted the stark reality that Kashmir was not a communally polarized State and there had been no spontaneous uprising of Muslims against the Maharaja. It can safely be said that Maharaja had never used his State forces to cleanse the State of the Muslim Population. Prior to the month of September 1947 there had been no breakdown of the State administration. Rather, it was engineered by Pakistan after breaking the Stand Still Agreement (Appendix 4). Pakistan had started breaking down the Law and order machinery by sending military and civil marauders in the State and especially the tribal people of North-West Frontier Province. Jha from the perusal of the Transfer of Power Documents, the India Office Records, and contemporary accounts has come to the view:

> That the Indian Government did not have any special designs on Kashmir prior to the invasion by raiders on 22nd October 1947. On the contrary, it did nothing to persuade or coerce the Maharaja, but went out of its way to assure him that it would not object if the State acceded to Pakistan.

That few Congress leaders and amongst them Sardar Patel was the most important, like Muslim League and Jinnah had made some attempts to persuade Maharaja to accede to India when the latter were putting pressure and holding out tempting inducements to make him accede to Pakistan.

Pandit Jawaharlal Nehru was emotionally much more involved with Kashmir than Sardar Patel. He, therefore, put all the pressure he could muster on the Maharaja to release Sheikh Abdullah and other political detenus and hold an election or at the very least brought the Sheikh into his government as a prelude to holding it because Sheikh would prefer to join India rather than Pakistan as he professed secularism. Patel by contrast was more legalistic in his approach and was far less bothered with ascertaining the wishes of the people first, once the Maharaja had made up his mind.

There was conclusive evidence that before any body could have plotted to seize Kashmir, Maharaja was the first who decided on his own in September that he had no option but to accede to India, and Nehru had rebuffed him. He had released all the convicts including Sheikh Abdullah and other detenus by that time. Not only that, in

September 1947 after the visit of Mahatma Gandhi to Kashmir, he had immediately sacked his Prime Minister Pandit RC Kak and had been taking all the steps to strengthen the road from Jammu to Kathua (Lakhanpur) and made arrangements for a pontoon bridge over river Ravi. Much earlier to that, in the month of May 1947 he had sent Maharani Tara Devi and Yuvraj Karan Singh to Lahore for having parleys with Justice Mehr Chand Mahajan of Lahore High Court. The primary reason for his long delay was his aversion to both Pandit Nehru and Sheikh Abdullah because of their close and intimate relations with each other. This would mean the end of his rule over Kashmir with the blessings of Pandit Nehru. This was a prophetic understanding. In his book *Gandhi's Emissary*, page 260—Mahatma Gandhi has said about Pandit Nehru:

"He was very magnanimous man, who on occasions would act like an elephant which did not forget." This is proved from the fact that having being prevented at Kohala State Guest House on the border of the State, in June 1946 by Hari Singh's Government he was more than enough injured in his personal vanity and it is confirmed had become an inveterate enemy of Maharaja Hari Singh and the latter was vanished from the administrative scene within two years after the accession. Later on, Pandit Nehru in the company of two lawyers was allowed to defend Sheikh Abdullah during his trial for sedition when ultimately he was convicted and sentenced for three years imprisonment.

Pandit Nehru in order to counter the rival propaganda and hostile world opinion that Kashmir had about 2/3rd Muslim population in normal course should have gone to the share of Pakistan on the basis of two nation theory having foundations on religion though India had opted to be a secular State. Pandit Nehru had cherished the idea before and after accession that people of the State should be involved through Sheikh Abdullah but Sardar Patel was of the view of taking the aid of Indian Independence Act which envisaged that only Maharaja had the right to accede to the dominion of his choice. This remained Patel's consistent position, both before and after the accession.

Pakistan's consistent propaganda is that Lord Mountbatten had colluded with Indian Government in hatching a conspiracy to deny the Kashmiri's their right to accede to Pakistan. There is no evidence in support of this view except the visit of Lord Mountbatten as Viceroy of undivided India for a short holiday trip from June 18 to June 23 (1947), two weeks after announcing the Partition plan. Lord Mountbatten had urged Maharaja and his

Prime Minister Pandit RC Kak not to make any declaration of Independence, but to ascertain one way or another, the will of the people of Kashmir as soon as possible and to announce their decision by 14 August 1947. He told them that the newly created States Department headed by Sardar Patel as Minister of States and VP Menon as his Secretary was prepared to give an assurance that if Kashmir went to Pakistan this would not be regarded as an unfriendly act by Government of India. Mountbatten wanted to repeat all this at a formal meeting with the Maharaja's Staff, with official note keeping but after fixing the meeting for the last day of the Viceroy's visit, Maharaja Hari Singh called it off pleading colic. Lord Mountbatten's notes are the evidence that the Indian Government had no designs on Kashmir other than Nehru's obsession with getting the Sheikh released and somehow pressuring the Maharaja into holding an election. In his final report on Kashmir, General Scott (CNC) of the State forces wrote that there was no evidence of any specific activity by the Government of India to persuade Kashmir to join India. He however, noted that Maharaja's household, consisting of Maharani and her brother Thakur Nachint Chand, and his astrologer (Swami Sant Dev) were persuading him to join dominion of India. On the contrary as has already been mentioned in this book that there is conclusive evidence that Britain wanted Kashmir to be a part of Pakistan all along, the reason lies embedded in Britan's strategic goals after the Second World War."

If one reads in between the lines, alleged offer was made by Lord Mountbatten that Maharaja should have declared his intention before 14th October 1947 when neither the dominion of Pakistan nor that of dominion of India had come into existence. The dominion of India came into existence on 15 August 1947. On 14 August 1947, the dominion of Pakistan would have been a reality on the basis of a Muslim theocratic State and Maharaja's about 65 per cent Muslim population mostly Punjabi speaking of some parts of Jammu region and border region of Kashmir would have opted in favour of Punjabi Muslims being ethnically and culturally and religiously inclined to them. There were Muslim League elements in Kashmir Valley also in his administration. They were in large numbers in the province of Jammu including some in the capital city of Jammu. The Amirs of small States of Gilgit Frontier Area of the State, namely, Hunza, Haveli and Nagar etc were sending threats to Maharaja to invade Kashmir Valley with 20,000 rebels. Note: This fact has been fully disclosed by Maharaja in his letter addressed to President of India in the month of August 1952.

He has disclosed that those Amirs were doing so at the instigation of the Britishers who had their vested interest in that area to have their permanent presence in order to keep a watch on the activities of Communist Russia and China which was going to be a Communist country as well as volatile Afghanistan. The report of the partition was disclosed on 17 August 1947. In Punjab province of British India communal riots and bloody uprising was at the full swing, how Maharaja with a meagre Army of 13 thousand consisting of more than 2/5th mostly Punjabi Muslim soldiers of Jammu region could contain spontaneous revolution. No external help for security reasons as was mandated under Treaty of Lahore and Treaty of Amritsar entered between founder of the State Maharaja Gulab Singh with the Britishers could be available to quell the uprising as the Britishers were leaving the sub-continent. Muslim forces of Maharaja after the Tribal invasion abetted by Pakistani army had undoubtedly sided with enemy forces and at many places had butchered their Hindu comrades in uniform with whom they had fought shoulder to shoulder during Second World War. Two glaring examples are of the cold blooded murder of Col Narayan Singh and his Hindu subordinate soldiers by 4th Battalion Muslim soldiers posted at Kohala Bridge at the end of the State Border. They had also murdered another commander and his subordinate Hindu soldiers at some other place by the name of Ram Singh. The capture of Muzaffarabad and Baramulla and massacre of Hindu and Sikh population speaks for itself about the genuine apprehensions of Maharaja regarding total chaos of administrative machinery, and under those circumstances according to the writer of this book he should not be condemned ex parte as a scapegoat for delayed accession. Besides the Muslim rival soldiers of Maharaja there were other potent actors who contributed more in the delayed accession and the creation of present day Kashmir problem. History cannot forgive them because ultimately truth and justice has to prevail which is the law of the nature to sustain this world. Truth adheres while falsehood falls apart. Had Pandit Nehru been pragmatic in dealing with Maharaja with kind heart without any egocentric hatred and shown magnanimity as administrative head of a vast country like India by assuring him to preserve his honour, dignity and status and not insisting to make Sheikh Abdullah as repository of sole authority of the State, the history of the country would have been different. Subsequent events have shown how Sheikh Abdullah acted in a more autocratic manner than the Maharaja who despite being sovereign ruler had great respect for rule of law but Sheikh Abdullah as a Prime Minister of democratic government became law unto himself. In order to take revenge with the landlords who had been supporters of Maharaja he enacted a draconian law known as Big Landed Estates Abolition Act in 1950 when there was no legislature in the State. Principles of natural justice were violated by forcibly snatching the landed property mostly belonging to the Hindu population of Jammu and Kashmir. Undoubtedly, a large section of landless tillers were benefited but some of the constituents of big landlords such as widows, old people, illiterates, having large size of family members were thrown on the road sides with one stroke of the pen by depriving them any amount of compensation—an action of the government that could not be justified by any constituent Unit of State comprised in the dominion of India, where Right to Property had been recognized as one of the Fundamental Rights guaranteed under the Indian Constitution. Even at that point of time in 1950 State of J&K Constitution Act of 1939 enacted by the Maharaja on September 7, 1939 was in force and at that time Maharaja was the de jure head of the State being the Monarch. The law of the State envisaged that without the consultation and consent of the Maharaja no Act or law could be passed or any administrative order could be issued. In other words, Maharaja was the fountain head of every authority of the State including the judiciary. At that time, Maharaja's son Dr Karan Singh was only a Regent appointed by Maharaja himself. Dr Karan Singh in his autobiography at page 120 and 121 has fully described his tug of war as Regent with Sheikh Abdullah reminding him not to pass this Legislation in the absence of a Legislature but he (Sheikh) did not budge even an inch. Sheikh had even wrote a threatening letter to Dr Karan Singh and in reply thereto Dr Singh had informed him that he had sought the advice of the Central Government vide his letter of 12th July 1950. Despite this, on the next day, Sheikh Abdullah made a long speech at Lal Chowk in Srinagar in which he went ahead and announced the measures, despite the fact that he had been called to Delhi to discuss the matter. The measures were not legal without Regent's signatures. This was first of the series of differences of approach of opinion between him and the Government of India which grew over the next few years and culminated in the dramatic events of August 1953. The aggrieved deserving landlords mostly belonging to the hilly areas and Kandi belts of Jammu region were badly hit because the lands in Jammu region are not as much fertile and productive as that of Kashmir Valley. The people of Ladakh region were also badly hit in the same manner. Sheikh Abdullah filled high posts in the government and in the subordinate judiciary without the existence of a recruitment authority which during the autocratic regime of the Maharaja's time did exist. Every gazetted post was referred for selection to the duly constituted Public Service Officers Selection Board and Maharaja never interfered with its functions. The very same Board had found Sheikh Abdullah lacking in merit for the selection against a gazetted post in a college as Sheikh Abdullah was holding a postgraduate degree in science stream. Sheikh Abdullah was allowed to enjoy more autocratic powers and Maharaja had ever exercised. Sheikh was able to appoint one of his political colleagues, Pandit Jia Lal Kilam as judge of the J&K High Court and in the same manner made Gulam Nabi who was a practising lawyer in sub-judge's court Anantnag as Governor of Kashmir province. Mian Jalal-ud-Din and Pandit MK Tikku who were junior lawyers of Srinagar Bar Association were directly recruited as Munsifs by over-jumping the seniority at the lowest ladder in the hierarchy of J&K Judicial Service. They, thus, became seniors to many other judicial officers who were already in service and ultimately Mian Jalal-ud-Din retired as Chief Justice of the J&K High Court and Pandit MK Tikku after some time became District and Sessions Judge. Both these lawyers were activists of Sheikh Abdullah's political party National Conference. MK Tikku was picked up to try the conspiracy case against Sheikh Abdullah when he had become Sessions Judge. The Committal Court was manned by Special Magistrate Pandit NK Hak. MK Tikku who at that time was posted as Additional Sessions Judge Jammu was transferred and made incharge of Special Trial Court for the trial of Sheikh Abdullah. The conspiracy case of treason and other serious offences had almost reached its final stage but due to some political developments that had taken place after the creation of Independent Bangladesh, the case was withdrawn as Sheikh Abdullah realized that his Independent Kashmir was a Day Dream. Immediately thereafter, when Political Accord between Mrs Indira Gandhi and Sheikh Abdullah came into existence as a consequence thereof Sheikh Abdullah was completely given the reins of the Governance of the State. After some time, MK Tikku was made a Minister by Sheikh Abdullah in his cabinet. He had remained as an activist of National Conference as a lawyer and his induction in judiciary was also made by Sheikh Abdullah himself. There are many examples when Sheikh Abdullah had during his first rule outrightly appointed the activists of his political party as Deputy Commissioners and Superintendents of Police such as Amin who was posted Deputy Commissioner Doda and later on was arrested with Sheikh Abdullah in 1953. Many prominent activists of his political party were given gazetted posts in the Civil Secretariat and various other wings of the administrative services including education department both at lower and at the higher levels. In the State forces, the Maharaja had given two fifth representation to the Muslims mostly hailing from Jammu province but in the newly created J&K Militia by the Sheikh a negligible representation was given to the inhabitants of

Jammu and Ladakh regions. Sheikh had used J&K Militia personnel to suppress with brute force the agitation of Jammu people started in 1952 which is known as Praja Parishad Agitation. This blatant misuse of power was done by Sheikh Abdullah during his first incarnation as Prime Minister of J&K State from 1948-1953.

Dr Karan Singh in his *Autobiography* at page 154 has mentioned about the aggressive anti-Dogra attitudes of Sheikh Abdullah and MA Baig. Both of them were promoting Kashmiri Chauvinism. Apart from Jammu Agitation, there was the broader question of implementing the 'Delhi Agreement' on the constitutional relationship between the State and the Centre. Delhi Agreement had been earlier worked out after prolonged negotiations between Sheikh Abdullah's team and representatives of Government of India. While the decision regarding abolishing the Monarchy had been rapidly implemented because it suited Sheikh, he had started dragging his feet as far as other items were concerned. From this it transpired that he was strengthening his position. Dr Karan Singh had been meeting Pandit Nehru in order to apprise him about the genuine demands of Jammu people who were being victimized by Sheikh but the latter was deeply opposed to Praja Parishad Agitation launched by Jammu people saying that it was of communal nature and going against the national interest. When Sheikh Abdullah started avoiding the implementation of Delhi Agreement of 1952 and purposely avoided going to Delhi for discussions at the first point of time Pandit Nehru finding himself helpless had remarked in the presence of Dr Karan Singh the fact which he has recorded on page 154 of his *Autobiography* that:

> "He (Pandit Nehru) was particularly hurt, even bewildered at the hostile manner in which his old protege and friend Sheikh Abdullah was acting and agreed with me when I remarked that unlimited power seemed to have brought out Sheikh's worst fascist and totalitarian tendencies."

After the sudden death of Dr Syama Prasad Mookerjee in detention, a great resentment and suspicion was caused amongst the people of Jammu in particular and in the country in general. Thereafter, Sheikh was on war path. Despite repeated suggestions to visit Delhi and an invitation from Pandit Nehru to do so on 3rd July 1953, he refused to go down to capital (Delhi) and discuss the whole situation. Maulana Abul Kalam Azad had purposely come down to Srinagar but Sheikh ignored him and he was virtually insulted by National Conference workers. Sheikh's speeches became more stringent and it became clear that he was working for Independent Status for Kashmir which would imply a virtual negation of the accession to India. At about that time Adlai Stevenson (a British important national) visited Srinagar and had long talks with Sheikh. It appeared he was encouraged for Independence Theory. (See page 156 of Karan Singh's *Autobiography*). Dr Singh has given a graphic account of conflict in Sheikh's Cabinet about his attitude and a mention of the fact that the Sheikh was still a popular figure in the Valley despite the fact that corruption and maladministration had to some extent eroded his stature (page 161, ibid). At this page, Dr Karan Singh has elaborately stated the reasons for his dismissal as Prime Minister in his letter addressed to Sheikh. The order of dismissal was passed on August 8, 1953. It is also mentioned at page 164 of the autobiography that Sheikh was given two hours time to say his Namaz of the early morning as he was served with the order in early morning at Hill Resort of Gulmarg where Sheikh had gone. He was also given time within this period to pack his necessary luggage but during that period he succeeded in burning a number of documents which he had taken with him. He was taken into custody and at early hours of 9 August 1953, was escorted in a car and driven out of Kashmir Valley.

In his second incarnation when he got the seat of power after the Accord of 1974 with Mrs Indira Gandhi the same tactics were followed but in a more clandestine and subtle manner. This period started from 1975 and ended in 1982 when Sheikh Abdullah expired. During this period, he too recruited many of his party activists of Plebiscite Front which legally had been declared as Unlawful Organization and subsequently was confirmed in a judicial verdict (fully discussed in the judicial order in this book at proper place). They found their entries in a surreptitious manner in government services particularly in the Civil Secretariat where the representation of the Dogras of Jammu and Kashmiri Pandits started diminishing in a systematic drastic manner. Prior to this period of his second regime when Bakshi Ghulam Mohammad was at the helm of the affairs from 1953-1964, he had maintained a ratio of 40 per cent and 60 per cent representations in government services for Jammu and Kashmir region respectively. Ladakh region formed a part of Kashmir region and the inhabitants were the most sufferers. This arrangement continued even during the time of his successor GM Sadiq who merged the National Conference (regional party) with the mainstream Congress Party. Sadiq was succeeded by Syed Mir Qasim as Chief Minister in 1971 who proved to be a weak administrator and facilitated the accord of Sheikh Abdullah with Mrs Indira Gandhi in 1974 which came into force in February 1975. Thereafter, the tables were turned and the Jammu region as well as

Ladakh region were at the receiving ends during Sheikh's tenure as well as the tenures of his descendants Dr Farooq Abdullah, GM Shah (his son-in-law) and grandson Omar Abdullah. These assertions of the writer of this book stand corroborated from a simple instance regarding the appointments of retired judges of the State High Court where almost all the post-retiral constitutional assignments had gone in favour of the judges belonging to Kashmir region and this practice at present is followed by his grandson with a brazen manner of blatant favouritism. There is authentic official record which shows that recently two retired High Court judges hailing from Kashmir region who despite being disqualified have been bestowed favours to occupy respective two new constitutional posts of different Commissions.

In a letter written by Sardar Patel to Sardar Baldev Singh Defence Minister on 13 September 1947, the release of Col Kashmir Singh Katoch (son of Major General Janak Singh Katoch last but one Prime Minister of the State in the Maharaja's regime) from the Indian Army for secondment to the Kashmir State forces was ordered. Sardar Patel had suggested, "it would be best therefore, to lend his services for a period of three years on the condition that if the State decides to join the other dominion, Col Katoch will revert to the Indian dominion." (*Sardar Patel's Correspondence, 1945-50*, Durga Das, Navjivan Publishing House, Ahmedabad, Doc. 3, page 87.)

The Indian Government was not trying to persuade the Maharaja to accede to India but this did not mean that the Congress Party was indifferent to the issue. However, it was not till July that the Congress Party established formal contact with the Maharaja. After meeting Rai Bahadur Gopal Das (a prominent Hindu leader of Lahore) Sardar Patel wrote to the maharaja that there is considerable misapprehension in your mind about the Congress. He further wrote that allow me to assure your highness that the Congress is not your enemy as you happen to believe.... It is unfortunate that none of the Congress leader has got any contact with your Highness. Patel went on to assure him that the Congress has no intention of interfering in Kashmir's domestic affairs. I wish to assure you that the interest of Kashmir lies in joining Indian Union and its constituent Assembly without any delay. Patel's letter apparently broke the ice between Congress and Maharaja Hari Singh. It was followed by detailed discussions between Maharaja Hari Singh and Rai Bahadur Gopal Das. Maharaja had promised to declare general amnesty and dismiss his Prime Minister Pandit RC Kak who had a leaning for independence or accession to Pakistan. (*Patel's Correspondence*, Vol. 1, page 36.) Maharaja was under the pressure from his family to accede to India. This pressure had started from the month of March or April as on 1st May 1947, when Maharaja allowed Maharani and Dr Karan Singh to visit Lahore. Maharani met Justice Mehr Chand Mahajan of Punjab High Court at Faletti's Hotel in Lahore and offered the latter the post of Prime Minister. Mahajan remained non-committal and renewed the offer at the end of August 1947. (Mahajan, page 123.) Mahajan's takeover as the Prime Minister of the State has been discussed in detail in the book at a proper place.

The very first task that the Maharaja entrusted to Mahajan was to secure Delhi's acceptance of Kashmir's accession, without insisting on a referendum or any other step of internal administrative reform designed to bring Sheikh Abdullah into the government what happened thereafter is a matter of history and fairly disclosed by Justice Mahajan and which requires no further discussion. From all the above mentioned historical facts and the attending circumstances it can safely be said that it was Maharaja who had firstly made up his mind to accede to India but Pandit Nehru remained the main stumbling block for accession, on his instance that the Maharaja must first get the backing of the Majority of the people through Sheikh Abdullah. Had Nehru been more accommodating, as Sardar Patel clearly wanted to be, Jammu and Kashmir would have acceded to India well before the raiders invaded the State. The accession would have been incontestable not only on legal grounds, which were never in doubt, but what is more important because it would demonstrably not have been under Duress (this is precisely what Jinnah was insisting upon in the case of Junagadh State in Gujarat at that very movement). British were also of the same opinion because they continued to regard Junagadh as part of Pakistan after it had been liberated by India. Mahajan had reached Srinagar braving floods by road on 13 September 1947 in response to the letter of Maharani dated 25 August 1947 and Mahajan had started meeting Pandit Nehru and Sardar Patel between 19 and 21 September 1947. Mr Scott who was State forces head and Mr Powell who was police chief (both British nationals) had decided to leave the State services as they had come to know that Maharaja was going to join Indian dominion. On 26 September 1947, the *Pakistan Times* newspaper whose owner was a prominent member of Muslim League had reported in the first page that Kashmir was going to join India. KH Churched who was Jinnah's secretary and knew the Kashmir Valley very well had been in Srinagar monitoring political developments since the beginning of the month of July 1947.

A reference has been made to the State of Junagadh. Its accession with India has been fully discussed by VP Menon in his above referred book from page 124-150. Sir Mahabat Khan Rasul Khan was the ruler but he was an eccentric of rare vintage. He had reared hundred's of dogs and was even at times arranging their marriages. One instance is the marriage of two pups and after celebrating the marriage, he declared a holiday in his State. He had his constitutional advisor Navi Baksh who on July 25, 1947 had agreed with Lord Mountbatten while in a meeting of Princes in Delhi that his State would accede to India. Same impression he had given to Sardar Patel and Jam Saheb of Bhavnagar. He had fallen ill and during his absence the charge was taken over by Sir Shah Nawaz Bhutto (father of Prime Minister of Pakistan late Zulfikar Ali Bhutto) who was a Muslim League politician and in the month of early May he had joined the State Council of Ministers under some scheme. He had succeeded in winning over the ruler to join Pakistan by making an announcement on August 15, 1947 that State had joined Pakistan. After this there was internal revolt because 82 per cent of the population was Hindu and they were being tortured by this foolish ruler. The Indian Government also started exerting pressure and when the situation was becoming worse the ruler stealthily fled away to Pakistan along with major part of wealth from the government treasury. He had left one of his wives along with her minor son in hurry in his palace to provide them a place to board his plane to Pakistan whereas he had boarded a pet dog with him. When the situation was getting out of control Bhutto also followed the foot steps of his master and went away to Pakistan. There was no blood shed of serious type and with the timely handling and intervention of the Government of India with neighbouring Hindu rulers in the first week of November 1947 the law and order was restored. On 13 November 1947, Sardar Patel as Home Minister of India addressed a mammoth public meeting at the invitation of the public in the grounds of Bahauddin College. By that time democratic government had come into existence. When normal conditions were fully restored by the public representatives, the Government of India fulfilled her promise to hold a referendum which was held and supervised by CB Nagarkar who was neither a Hindu nor a Muslim. He was a senior judicial officer of ICS cadre serving in the State. There were 2,01,457 registered voters and out of them 1,90,870 exercised their franchise. From them, only 91 cast their votes in favour of accession with Pakistan.

Operation on the Kathua-Jammu Road

At page 981 of his book MY Saraf (Chief Justice POJK) has recorded this fact in the following words, "this sector was opened in September 1947 with Headquarters at Sialkot. To start with, there were 8 ex-INA officers headed by Col IK Kiani (ex-ADC with Netaji Subhas Chandra

Bose) and a few hundred men, also of former INA with volunteers particularly from tehsil Khushab, the number soon increased to 3,500 men armed with 3,000 Dara-type rifles. The sector's primary task was to disrupt enemy movement and help Muslim population. Such sector headquarters were established at Chaprar, Bijragarhi, Rupo Chak and Shamal in Shakargarh tehsil and mujahids had started harassing and attacking the enemy convoys on Jammu Kathua Road from 2nd October 1947 onward. As fighting in this sector had started tribal lashkars were also introduced and in the beginning of 1948 their number had swelled up to 25,000. At page 988, MY Saraf had stated his opinion based upon the report of Lord Birdwood who made a special study of Kashmir dispute "that sending of tribesmen to Kashmir by provincial Governor administrating NWF Province was not possible without the approval of Central Government, i.e. Quaid-e-Azam and Prime Minister Liaquat Ali Khan. The Chief Minister of Punjab could not allow the territory to be used for their passage, arrange for their arms, transport and supplies."

CHAPTER 7

Governance of J&K After Accession with India

On 27 October 1947, military assistance had been dispatched to Srinagar. Earlier to that, Mahajan along with VP Menon had left Srinagar in the first flight of the morning of 26th October 1947 and immediately on their arrival at Delhi, Menon went straight to a meeting of the Defence Committee and reported his impressions about the situation. Soon after the meeting of the Defence Committee, he flew from Delhi to Jammu accompanied by Mahajan. The Maharaja was asleep, as he had left Srinagar in the early morning of October 26th, 1947 and had been driving all along the journey. Menon woke him up and told him what had taken place at the Defence Committee meeting. Maharaja was ready to accede at once. He then composed a letter to the Governor-General describing the pitiable plight of the State and reiterating his request for military help. Maharaja had informed the Governor-General that it was his intention to set up an interim government at once and to ask Sheikh Abdullah to carry the responsibilities in this emergency with Mehr Chand Mahajan, his Prime Minister. He signed the Instrument of Accession. At page 400 of his book *Integration of the Indian States*, VP Menon has recorded, "Just as I was leaving, he (Maharaja) told me that before he went to sleep, he had left instructions with his ADC that, if I came back from Delhi, he was not to be disturbed as it would mean that the Government of India had decided to come to his rescue and he should therefore be allowed to sleep in peace, but that if I failed to return, it meant that everything was lost and, in that case, his ADC was to shoot him in his sleep." With the Instrument of Accession and the Maharaja's letter, Menon flew back at once to Delhi. Sardar Patel was waiting at the aerodrome. Thereafter, meeting of the Defence Committee was held and after a long discussion at the end of which it was decided that the accession of J&K

should be accepted subject to the proviso that a referendum by the people would be held in the State when the law and order situation allowed.

After the failure of Pak attempt to capture both Maharaja and Mahajan at Bhimber when they were on tour there on 20 October 1947, Jinnah become impatient. He ordered his British Commander-in-Chief to move two Brigades of the Pak army into Kashmir on 27 October, one from Rawalpindi and another from Sialkot. The Sialkot army was to march to Jammu, to take the city and the Maharaja as a prisoner. The Rawalpindi column was to advance to Srinagar and capture the city. All this was thought that State should be saved the anarchy that tribesmen's raid had produced. This aspect has been discussed in detail in this book at a proper place how British Commander refused to carry out the orders. The only additional disclosure made by Mahajan in his book *Looking Back*, is regarding sending of one brigade of Army from Sialkot also to march to Jammu and take the Maharaja as prisoner.

Mehr Chand Mahajan in his book at page 155 has reproduced the conditions which Pandit Nehru had given to him in his own handwriting on which Maharaja had been given military help at that critical time. They are reproduced as under:

> "The first one was that His Highness should accede to India with regard to three subjects: defence, external affairs and transport. This he had already done. The second was that the internal administration of the State should be democratized and new constitution be framed on the lines of the model already set out for the State of Mysore. The third condition was that Sheikh Abdullah be taken in Administration and made responsible for it along with the Prime Minister."

Mahajan had enquired from Pandit Nehru that he would be misfit in a democratic setup as in a democratic government a popular Prime Minister had to take his place. Nehru said, "No, you will have to stay as Prime Minister." Mahajan had shown these conditions to Maharaja who accepted them. Prime Minister Pandit Nehru confirmed these terms in typed letter the next day.

When military situation improved Prime Minister Mahajan invited Sheikh Abdullah to Jammu to share Administration with him and had sent his Deputy Prime Minister RL Batra to carry on his duties in Srinagar with the help of other Ministers. This arrangement did not work. Sheikh came after few days and bluntly told Mahajan that he would act as Prime Minister as advised by Sir Gopalaswami Ayyangar.

For elucidation Mahajan and Sheikh Abdullah went to Delhi and a conference was held at the residence of Pandit Nehru in which Sardar Patel and VP Menon joined. Sheikh demanded that he should be made Prime Minister and Mahajan be made a glorified dummy as 'Dewan' with no powers. After 3 hours of discussion it was decided that Sheikh should be designated as 'Head of Emergency Administration' and Mahajan should carry on as Prime Minister.

The Sheikh was duly sworn in as head of Emergency Administration and he took all the leading members of National Conference in administration.

Sheikh Abdullah could attain this position after securing his release from the jail by virtue of letter written from jail dated September 26, 1947 to the Maharaja and that letter in its original form has been reproduced earlier. Justice Mehr Chand Mahajan, who at the time of execution of the accession agreement had been appointed by Maharaja as his Prime Minister has termed the above said letter as 'qualified apology'. In this letter he had expressed that neither he nor his party had ever harboured any sentiment of disloyalty to Maharaja's person, throne or dynasty. At the end of the letter he, had written, "Before I close this letter I beg to assure Your Highness once again of my steadfast loyalty and pray that God under Your Highness' aegis bring such an era of peace, prosperity and good government that it may be second to none and be an idol for others to copy."

After the invasion of the State by Pakistan and accession with India, Sheikh Abdullah, rode the crest of a popular wave with the support of Jawaharlal Nehru. Apart from his close personal friendship with the Sheikh, Jawaharlal was genuinely convinced that in the peculiar circumstances of Kashmir with its Muslim majority it was absolutely essential both for national and international reasons for Sheikh Abdullah to be fully involved in the government of the State. This fact finds supporting evidence from the letter dated 13th November 1947 written by Pandit Jawaharlal Nehru to Maharaja Hari Singh and the said letter already has been produced in its original form earlier in this book. Pandit Jawaharlal Nehru had showered praises on the integrity and loyalty of the Sheikh Abdullah and made a suggestion to the Maharaja, "to keep in close personal touch with him and deal with him directly and not through intermediaries." This shows Pandit Jawaharlal Nehru as a gentleman of impeccable nature genuinely trusted Sheikh Abdullah but the latter proved to be not loyal to both, i.e. Maharaja Hari Singh as well as to Pandit Jawaharlal Nehru. The fact of the matter is that Pandit Jawaharlal Nehru understood him after few years when already he (Sheikh) had damaged the national cause but Maharaja Hari Singh who had been dealing with him since 1931 had already traced out the hidden traits of his personality. From the very beginning Sheikh Abdullah had become leader of Kashmiri masses by exploiting their religious sentiments knowing fully well for political reasons that they were a majority community in the valley and ensured his position by tilting balance of majority population in his favour keeping in view the regionalism and religion of Kashmir Valley over political adverse position of truncated Jammu region which had been reduced to minority status on the yardstick of population criterion. This was purposely done by halting the advancement of Indian forces who with the passage of time would have liberated the whole of the area of district Mirpur and the remaining areas of Poonch Estate (district) as well as remaining parts of the then tehsil Rajouri which formed part of erstwhile district Reasi. These areas along with their Muslim population still remain under the illegal occupation of Pakistan and they have named it as Azad Kashmir. After securing the chair as Emergency Chief Administrator of the State, Sheikh Abdullah immediately changed his obedient and docile attitude and came out openly in his true colours by adopting a belligerent despotic attitude towards Maharaja as well as towards Indian dominion.

Dr Agnihotri in his book *Jammu-Kashmir ki Anakahee Kahani* at page 39 (after referring reliable evidence from the quoted books written by (1) Prof Balraj Madhok, ex-President of Akhil Bharatiya Jan Sangh, (2) Alex von Tunzelmann, *Indian Summer*, page 298) has recorded that Hindu and Sikh refugees from west Punjab in large numbers along with local Hindus and Sikhs had been trapped in the western part of Jammu region of the State adjoining the territory of Pakistan on account of aggression made by Pakistan and particularly district Mirpur of J&K was in great danger and being immediately run over by invaders. That Indian Army was present in the State and where to depute it, it was in the hands of Chief Emergency Administrator, i.e. Sheikh Abdullah. In order to save the lives and honour of those unfortunate human beings on 15 November 1947, Prof Balraj Madhok along with Pandit Prem Nath Dogra (a proclaimed Dogra leader who later on also became President of Jan Sangh for one term) met Pandit Nehru at the Jammu Airport in order to make him aware of the grave situation. Pandit Nehru asked them to meet Sheikh Abdullah. Sheikh Abdullah was approached but he did not send any Army there. It was widely believed in Jammu that Pandit Nehru and Sheikh Abdullah were interested in vacating the aggression in Kashmir Valley and had no interest in falling the areas of district Mirpur along with other above said areas in the hands of Pakistan. Mehr Chand Mahajan on 2 November 1947 had made a fervent request to Pandit Nehru to get retrieved the encircled State forces personnel from the towns of Mirpur, Kotli, Poonch and Nowshera. Sheikh Abdullah in the real sense was not interested to retain those areas in the State as the inhabitants were not followers of his National Conference. On 21 November 1947, the town of Mirpur fell into the hands of the enemy. The Hindus and Sikhs were mercilessly butchered. Most women folk committed suicides. Five thousand women were captured alive by the raiders and they were taken to Pakistan. Very less number of survivors reached Jammu to tell their stories of mayhem and butchery.

Lord Mountbatten was not interested to get those areas liberated including the top hierarchy of the military British Generals who were holding the control of Army. All of a sudden Lord Mountbatten had to leave for London in connection with attending a marriage ceremony of his relation and remained out of India from 9 November 1947 to 29 November 1947. During his absence (of twenty days), the Indian Army had vacated some areas of the above said region from the occupation of enemy. Immediately Lord Mountbatten wrote a letter to Pandit Nehru, "Indian Government forcibly wants to thrust its will and authority over the inhabitants of Mirpur and Poonch through the help of Army. Majority of the population is Muslim therefore they should not be forced to join India otherwise it will result into causing irreparable injustice to them." The raiders had abducted Sydney Smith, a reporter of *Daily Express* newspaper. He after release had disclosed the three common motives of the raiders and they were:

(i) To finish the rule of Hindu Maharaja Hari Singh (by beheading him and hanging his head on Kohala Bridge).
(ii) To raise to the ground the biggest Sikh State which was of Patiala in Indian Punjab and capture the holy shrine of Amritsar.
(iii) In case possible, to capture Delhi. (Translated by the writer of this book from Hindi version.)

Sheikh Abdullah started issuing ordinances on his own without the consent of His Highness. Mahajan had objected that law making power was with the Maharaja and not in him. As Chief Emergency Administrator of the State, Sheikh came in open clash with Prime Minister Mehr Chand Mahajan when in early December 1947, he ordered the transfer of Governor of Jammu province (equivalent to present Divisional Commissioner) Lala Chet Ram Chopra. The then Prime Minister Mahajan had to yield after initial opposition because of opponents' political position. For some time, they were not on speaking terms. Later on, Sheikh Abdullah dismissed Lala Chet Ram chopra from service and stopped his pension which was restored by the successor government. He along with ex-Prime Minister Pandit Ram Chandra Kak were taken for sometime for interrogation and kept in the servant quarters of Naidu's Hotel owned by Sheikh Abdullah's in-laws where they were physically and mentally tortured. Maharaja's ex-ADC Capt Dewan Singh who is presently alive at the age of 93 years and continuously had served the Maharaja in that capacity form 1942 till 1961 when Maharaja expired in Bombay has told the writer of this book that even human excreta was thrown upon both of them in order to forcibly extort evidence against Maharaja that Maharaja had ordered the massacre of Muslims in the districts of Jammu, Kathua, Reasi and Udhampur. Both of them had tolerated the inhuman treatment but did not become a part of the concocted falsehood of defaming Maharaja (orally told by late Chet Ram Chopra to Captain Dewan Singh). When Gopalaswami Ayyangar as a Central Minister learnt about the pitiable plight of late Lala Chet Ram Chopra, he called him from Jammu to Delhi and gave a temporary appointment for rehabilitating the Hindu and Sikh refugees from Pakistan who had taken shelter in Madhya Pradesh. After the expiry of this temporary arrangement, he was called by Maharaja in Bombay and given employment in his personal staff till the time his pension was released by the State Government under Bakshi Ghulam Mohammad's regime. Pandit Ram Chandra Kak was tried as an accused by Sheikh Abdullah but no charge was proved against him. His real elder brother Pandit Amar Nath Kak who was one of the leading lawyers of Kashmir Bar Association was so much harassed that he left his legal practice for good and started his career afresh as an advocate in the State of Madhya Pradesh where he remained till the end of his life. His fault was not confessed to the fact that he was advising Pandit RC Kak against Sheikh Abdullah but the real fact was that he was totally in favour of joining the Union of India while his brother RC Kak preferred independence of the State or in the alternative merger with Pakistan. He was a staunch nationalist and during the communal rights of 1931 generated by Sheikh Abdullah's Muslim Conference after the incident of Jail break, his house was attacked by the goons of Muslim Conference and some damage was done to his house and library. Sheikh Abdullah's vengeance was so high against the Maharaja that forgetting all the written pledges given by him to remain loyal and obedient throughout his life along with his political organisation National Conference, he during the month of February 1948 started demanding the abdication of Maharaja Hari Singh from the State. On his persistent demands Pandit Nehru sent his personal emissary, Brijlal Nehru and advised the Maharaja to abdicate the State in the national interest. In the first week of March 1948 Prime Minister Mahajan was summoned to Delhi and told in a meeting attended by Ayyangar and Sardar Patel that Proclamation appointing Sheikh Abdullah as premier had to be issued. Consequently, on 5 March 1948, the Sheikh took over a Prime Minister in the national interest as the case of Kashmir was pending in the Security Council. Patel and Ayyangar prevailed on Maharaja Hari Singh in May 1949 to abdicate in favour of his son (Dr Karan Singh). Maharaja left for Bombay on 20 June 1949 and never returned even once to his State of which he was the absolute ruler. Once he had made an attempt to come to his State temporarily along with Maharani to inquire about the well being of his subjects but Pandit Nehru dissuaded him to do so (*Autobiography* of Dr Karan Singh). He died in 1961 and as per wishes expressed in his will, his ashes were scattered over the city of Jammu. As a true son of the Dogra Soil, he loved the Dogra land so much being the place of his birth and ancestral soil which is evident from the last wish of his life expressed in the will to perform this last remaining ceremony of mortal coils of body (ashes) to mix with Dogra soil. In the holy Bible, it is said: "From dust you have been raised and to dust you will meet." He maintained intact his personal dignity and honour till his death and never allowed Sheikh Abdullah to dominate his status as a ruler. A political analyst has put it, "where the Maharaja was required to be consulted, he was bullied and where he was needed to be informed, he was ignored." When he died no respect was shown to his departed soul by the State who had sacrificed his Monarchy to save the lives, honour, dignity and culture of his State Subjects which was at the stake of annihilation at the hands of foreign marauders. He had spurned unconditional Offer which had been made by Jinnah to preserve his rule at any cost after the dominion of Pakistan was established. No such offer had been made by the newly created dominion of India. On the contrary, the Prime Minister Pandit Nehru was coercing him to make Sheikh Abdullah as Prime Minister and bestow all the powers on him of governing the State. His personal status and position as a ruler was always at stake which he had understood and that was the main reason for delaying the accession in time. At the time of his (Maharaja's) death, Bakshi Ghulam Mohammad was the Prime Minister of the State and he was occupying the chair because of the benevolent act of accession made by Maharaja in favour of the dominion of India. In case, Maharaja had acted to preserve his status as a ruler and joined dominion of Pakistan, Bakshi Ghulam Mohammad would have found himself in jail as he was considered enemy number two in the National Conference organization by the political party of Jinnah—Muslim League. Two student leaders of

Jammu Bhim Singh and late Raj Kumar showed courage and guts as they climbed over the Civil Secretariat building of Jammu and reached the top floor. There they lowered the National and State flags which were hurling in order to show respect to the departed soul. Both of them were arrested on spot and beaten mercilessly. Bakshi Ghulam Mohammad detained them under the Preventive Laws and foisted other offences also but a patriot and a great social cum political figure of Jammu Lala Ram Nath Bhalgotra advocate came to their rescue without charging any professional fee. He fought their case tooth and nail in the High Court and ultimately they came out from the jail.

The second noteworthy conflict with Mehr Chand Mahajan was when he had got the house of a Superintendent of Police of Jammu city searched. That Superintendent of Police at his heart was a Pakistani. Beside other objectionable articles, a transmitter was found in his house. Everything that happened at Jammu was being transmitted by him to Pakistan. Mahajan put him under arrest. The Sheikh came to Mahajan several times and asked him to release him. Similarly, the Chief of the General staff who had run away from a place raided by Pakistanis at midnight had been put under military guard. The Sheikh was very anxious for his release as well. (Mahajan, page 163.)

There were other two factors which were polluting the mind of Sheikh Abdullah and they were ideological and regional. The ideological conflict encompassed the desire of the Sheikh Abdullah to become unchallenged Sultan of Kashmir and to achieve this object his autocratic behaviour is manifested from the facts that immediately he wanted to do away with the Jammu and Kashmir forces but Maharaja Hari Singh legally had been their Commander-in-Chief. After becoming the Prime Minister, he wanted the administrative control of the forces under his thumb but this was strenuously objected by the Maharaja and in reply to a memorandum of Sheikh Abdullah, Maharaja raised two important points which are reproduced hereunder:

"(1) Firstly in case the administrative control of the State Army is transferred to the Union of Government as suggested by you (Sheikh), the Pakistan propagandists will make capital out of it and make a plausible case that the State has been completely annexed to Indian Union by taking over complete Military control. Such an impression should not be permitted to be created.

(2) Secondly, Pakistan's suggestion that at the time of Plebiscite the Forces of Indian Union should be sent away may to some extent be forced on us. In case, the administrative control of

> the State Forces is handed over it will be difficult for us to make out a case for the retention of the State Forces because administratively there will be no distinction between the two."

Sheikh was adamant and he informed the Maharaja that he had decided to stop the salaries and allowances to these troops w.e.f. 16th August 1948. This conflict continued for a long time and later on, the merger of the State Forces with the Indian Army took place. Another source of conflict was the 'Reserved Subjects' which were supposed to have been left under Maharaja's authority, including pensions of various types to the members of the ruling family, the hospitality (Tawaza) department, and so on. Then there was the question of land reforms and the Sheikh Abdullah was pressing for radical changes even without following the proper due course of law. Sheikh was also eager to take over the Dharmarth Trust—a religious endowment created by the founder of the State Maharaja Gulab Singh, which administered over a hundred Hindu temples and shrines in different parts of the State. The trust was spending several lakhs of rupees for the feeding of refugees in Jammu from Pak-occupied area but Sheikh Abdullah was making the allegation that this money was used for political purposes. This allegation was false and frivolous but was being made only to grab the properties of the Hindus by the Sheikh's administration. Ultimately, Sardar Patel had to personally intervene and these properties could be saved. The second area of conflict was that Sheikh Abdullah really represented Kashmiri opinion which although numerically was in majority at that time because of Pakistani invasion and grabbing of the areas of Mirpur and major parts of Poonch districts as well as Rajouri tehsil of erstwhile Reasi district but this majority was confined to one region of the State, i.e. Kashmir Valley. Maharaja Hari Singh in turn commanded the traditional loyalty of the Dogras who constituted a majority in the Jammu region.

After Muhammad Ali Jinnah's death in September 1948, Sheikh Abdullah became more haughty and aggressive. The annoyance of Maharaja with Sheikh and frustration with the proceeding in the Security Council stand expressed in his letter dated January 31, 1948 to Home Minister Sardar Patel in these words: "There is an alternative possible for me and that is to withdraw the accession that I have made to the Indian Union. The union only provisionally accepted the accession and if the Union cannot recover back our territory and is going eventually to agree to the decision of the Security Council which may result in handing us over to Pakistan, then there is no point in sticking to the accession of the State to the Indian Union and that may kill the reference to the UNO because Indian Union will have no right to continue the proceedings before the council if the accession is withdrawn. The result may be a return to the position the State held before the accession."

The insulting attitude of the Sheikh Abdullah has found expression in his letter dated April 20th 1948 where Maharaja said:

(1) "As I have mentioned to you and to Menon and Shankar also once or twice, there is one aspect of propaganda against me which has distressed me beyond words, particularly as it affects not only my position as a ruler but my personal honour. I refer to the wild and baseless allegations that are being made against me that I left the capital at the dead of night and removed truckloads of furniture and other belongings. I would ordinarily have dismissed these allegations but to my great regret and profound shock, they have found expression in some of the utterances of my present Prime Minister (Sheikh Abdullah). I would invite your attention to the speech which Sheikh Abdullah made before the Security Council in which he said the following words:

The Maharaja in the dead of night left the capital along with his courtiers and the result was absolute panic. There was no one to take over the control. This is the manner in which administration changed hands and we were de facto in charge of the administration. The Maharaja later on gave it a legal form.

(2) How entirely divorced from facts this allegation is would, I am sure, be borne out by your Secretary Menon at whose instance I reluctantly left Srinagar for Jammu. The other allegation that truck loads of belongings were removed is absolutely false and fantastic. The fact is that some lorries carrying the families of those officers who had already moved to Jammu on government work and families of servants followed me. I felt morally responsible to afford transport facilities to these families. All my household effects which usually remain permanently at Srinagar have been and are still there. I am sure you will appreciate that such speeches and allegations when made by responsible and highly placed persons in the administration and by members of the National Conference are bound to create disaffection and promote feelings of estrangement between the ruler and his people.

(3) You might ask why I am resuscitating this matter after so much lapse of time since the speech was made, but apart from the

> fact that those allegations are still being persisted in and are being given credence under continuous propaganda, the speech of my Prime Minister is being distributed in a pamphlet form headed 'Kashmir: Appeal to World Conscience'. I hope your Ministry will succeed in giving a lie to this propaganda by means of an authoritative pronouncement or communique explaining the correct facts and by persuading Sheikh Abdullah to make amends for the lapse which he has made."

To straighten the record the writer of this book reiterates as already noted in this book that Sheikh Abdullah himself had flown to Delhi on 25th October 1947 before Maharaja Hari Singh had left Srinagar with his family and did not return until after the Indian Army arrived in the Valley, i.e. on 27th October 1947. This fact has been mentioned at page 86 by Dr Karan Singh in his autobiography also. Maharaja Hari Singh had left by road from Srinagar to Jammu at 2 AM of the morning of 26th October 1947, whileas Maharani and Yuvraj had set out for Jammu two hours earlier.

In another letter of May 6, 1949 to Sardar Patel, the Maharaja said: "Nor would it be fair on my part to conceal from you my own feeling that while Sheikh Abdullah has been allowed to depart from time to time as suited his inclinations from the pledged and written word, to act consistently in breach of the loyalty which he professed to me prior to his release from jail and oath of allegiance which he took when he assumed office, and to indulge openly along with his colleagues in a campaign of vilification and foul-calumny against me, both inside the State and outside, I should have had to be driven from position to position—each of which I thought I held on the advice of the State's Ministry."

The facts and the circumstances show that even Sardar Patel who till now is being considered as the iron man of India and the most competent then Minister of States-cum-Home Minister could not rein Sheikh Abdullah because of his close proximity with Pandit Jawaharlal Nehru who was the Prime Minister and a trump-card in his hands to blackmail India on the issue of plebiscite. Sheikh Abdullah had attained this position by committing breach of trust of loyalty committed in writing by him with Maharaja and to his family members and in response Maharaja had reposed faith in him. This he had partly done because of qualified apology shown in his letter dated 26th September 1947 already reproduced in original form supra and partly on the assurance given by Pandit Nehru to Maharaja in the letter (already reproduced above) whereby Nehru had advised the Maharaja to place implicit faith in him as he was a trusted friend of India and of nationalist views. Mehr Chand Mahajan who had been already appointed as Prime Minister by the Maharaja on 18 September 1947 with the approval of Government of India and by 15 October 1947 he had taken the formal oath was an eye sore for the Sheikh. Mahajan was a bridge between Maharaja and Government of India and was a seasoned lawyer and a very competent judge. He had fully understood the Machiavellian game plans of the Sheikh. He had a five years term as Prime Minister. According to the agreed terms between the Maharaja, the Government of India and Sheikh Abdullah (already reproduced at page 115 of this book), the Sheikh Abdullah had to work as, 'Head of Emergency Administration', till the democratic government could be established. In 1951, elections for Constituent Assembly were held to frame the State Constitution and thereafter the members had elected Sheikh Abdullah as their leader. In other words, he could become Prime Minister and replace Mahajan in 1951. By taking up unnecessary and baseless cudgels with Mahajan and side by side spreading false propaganda against the person of the Maharaja, Sheikh Abdullah chalked out a well thought plan to ease them out systematically. The first soft target was Mahajan. All the false accusations made by Sheikh against Mahajan had been rebutted by him effectively and discussed in this book but the strongest weapon of blackmailing them with Central Government was his unshakeable stature projected by Pandit Nehru to win the Plebiscite. Ultimately he succeeded in getting ousted Mahajan during the month of February 1948, i.e. within a span of four months from the date of his appointment made by Maharaja as Prime Minister of the State. Under the compelling circumstances, Maharaja had to appoint Sheikh Abdullah as his Prime Minister on 5 March 1948 with a Council of Ministers and a Dewan to be nominated by the Maharaja. This was done by Maharaja by a Royal Proclamation which was the first step for the integration of the State with Union of India. After becoming the Prime Minister of the State he acquired a higher position and status to defame Maharaja and blackmail India. The result was that the Maharaja was constantly humbled and was, thus, forced to abdicate his authority in favour of his son. On June 20, 1949, the Maharaja issued a proclamation vesting all his powers in Yuvraj Karan Singh as his Regent. Thereafter, Sheikh took everything for granted in his favour and went on taking all decisions despite the fact there was still no legislature to which he could be held responsible. The readers of this book would themselves judge the morality of Sheikh Abdullah and traits of his personality who still is called by some gullible people as 'Baba-e-Quam'. In order to falsely defame Maharaja, he had no hesitation in weakening the case of India in Security Council where falsely he had stated that Maharaja had abdicated administration in lurch while fleeing from Srinagar to Jammu and he along with his organization de facto were incharge of the administration. This statement is factually false and legally wrong. The fact of the matter is that Sheikh Abdullah was appointed Chief Emergency Administrator in the beginning by the Maharaja while Mehr Chand Mahajan was his Prime Minister. Sheikh Abdullah in the beginning turned his guns against Prime Minister Mahajan by falsely painting him a communalist. At page 829 of his book *Kashmiris Fight for Freedom*, MY Saraf, Chief Justice of POJK High Court has recorded their correspondence and relevant extracts from his book are:

> "Prime Minister Mahajan has stated the Sheikh accused me of being a party to the shooting of some Muslim personnel of the State Forces who were being evacuated by the Indian Army from Kotli tehsil (now in POJK). They were rebels and had been disarmed. Some of them misbehaved while coming to Jammu under Military Escort and naturally there was some shooting. I had no knowledge of the incident till the Sheikh told me.
>
> Though Sheikh boasted that he was a nationalist, really he had a communal outlook on things. Any harm done to the Hindu population or their property did not affect him at all, but the slightest injury to a Muslim touched the very core of his heart. He complained against me to the Prime Minister (Pandit Nehru) on this score. The matter however concerned the Army and as the commander had already appointed a court of inquiry, nothing more could be said about it."

At page 836 of the above said book Saraf has quoted Mehr Chand Mahajan from Mahajan's book (page 176) by stating that, "Sheikh Abdullah had made a complaint with Pandit Nehru that Mehr Chand Mahajan instead of giving .303 rifles sent by India for the training of National Conference workers had handed over to the workers of RSS. Pandit Nehru did not hold any inquiry and took the words of Sheikh Abdullah as gospel truth and wrote a very nasty letter to the Maharaja against me.

His Highness gave the letter to Mehr Chand Mahajan for reply. I wrote a letter to Pandit Nehru that I did not receive a single rifle from him, the rifles sent were in the possession of Commanding Officer of the Indian forces in the State who had not given any rifle to the RSS workers. Pandit Nehru promptly withdrew the allegations. He expressed regrets and said he was sorry to learn that he was misinformed."

Furthermore, Mahajan in his book at page 158-159 has stated:

> "The Sheikh also made an attempt to poison the Mahatma Gandhi against me. He wrote to the Mahatma that Muslims were being killed in Jammu at the instigation of Maharaja and myself. Mahatma without asking me, charged us with these killings, in one of his post-prayer speeches."

Writing to Gandhi in protest to his speech Mehr Chand Mahajan wrote as under:

> "It is undoubtedly true that a very large number of Hindus and Sikhs were killed and their women abducted. It is also true that a considerable number of Muslims were killed and their women abducted.... After 30 October 1947, killings continued. Since then the Muslims suffered the most in parts of Udhampur and parts of Reasi districts. They also suffered in Jammu district and part of Kathua district. The Muslim population in a part of Reasi district across the Chenab river including whole part of Rajouri tehsil, in Bhaderwah and Kishtwar areas became very aggressive after 30th of October. In these parts the Hindu and Sikh population has been practically wiped out in a very large number. Their women have been abducted and are in possession of the local Muslim population. In the Mirpur district, the Hindu and Sikh population has been exterminated. Similar was the case in district Poonch. If a proper estimate is ever made of these happenings and of the killings on either side, it seems to me that the loss of life of the Hindus and Sikhs and the number of their women abducted will come out to be considerably more than the loss in these two matters suffered by the Muslims. Even at the present moment, though aggression on the part of Hindus has completely stopped, the Muslim population is still out of control and cases of abduction of Hindu women and killings of Hindus and Sikhs by the Muslim population are still going on. The loss of property of Hindus and Sikhs is several times more than that of Muslims. In the circumstances stated above, all that can be said is that on the reasoning employed by you, whatever communal trouble took place between the 15th to 30th October, the responsibility for it, in the absence of extenuating circumstances, is on the then government of His Highness. One of the extenuating circumstance is on the then government of his Highness is that after 30 October 1947 up to the date whatever has happened including loss of lives, property or abduction of women the responsibility was on the Emergency Chief Administrator (Sheikh Abdullah) as he was in control of Administration. However, so far as I can see neither the government of His Highness before the 30th nor that of the Administrator/Dictator subsequent to that

date be made responsible for any happenings as in the circumstance in which the government was placed whether before or after 30 October, it was humanly impossible to stop all that took place when men had become insane and started behaving like jungle animals. In view of the extent of the territory no effective steps could be taken to completely stop the mutual killings." (See Mahajan, pages 159-60.)

Nowhere Sheikh Abdullah during that period mentioned in his speech that about 30,000 Hindus were massacred in the town of Rajouri and surrounding areas. He never made a mention of the fact that more than twenty-five thousand Hindus who had collected in the town of Mirpur were put to sword except about two thousand who were lucky to save their lives. About 5,000 women were abducted. (Note: This incident of massacre has been discussed already in this book). In addition to this, thousands of Hindus were massacred with the help of some Muslim League elements in collaboration with Raiders or some where even independently. Women folk were abducted and raped. Some of them were subsequently recovered with the help of Red Cross Organisation. All this had happened when Sheikh Abdullah was Prime Minister of the State and after the above stated holocaust he was able to visit that area. As head of the Administration he should have equally criticized the insane and brute behaviour of communal-minded elements found in both the sections of society—Hindus and Muslims—and thus, had failed to discharge his moral and legal duty impartially.

Though Maharaja Hari Singh appointed his only son Yuvraj Karan Singh as Regent, constitutionally speaking he remained the ruler because of the Treaty of Lahore entered with Lahore Darbar and Treaty of Amritsar entered with Britishers. The dominion of India was the Successor State of the British Raj and was bound under international law by those treaties. Under the treaty of Amritsar, the Britishers were under obligation to secure the borders of the State by rendering all sorts of help on demand being made by the ruler. They had even being sending their own forces as mentioned earlier to help the Maharaja in restoring the law and order which Sheikh Abdullah had disturbed by fanning communalism after 1931. Under the Jammu and Kashmir Constitution Act of 1939, all the executive, legislative and judicial powers were vested with the ruler. The Indian Independence Act of 1947 recognized the ruler of a State and nobody else could make an accession of the State either with the dominion of India or dominion of Pakistan. Maharaja Hari Singh's fault was that he did not exercise this discretion within the deadline of August 15th 1947 because he grievously misjudged the political situation in the country. To the

Indian National Congress, Maharaja was hostile mainly because of Jawaharlal's close association with his arch enemy Sheikh Abdullah. This hostility had increased because of a grave folly committed by Maharaja at the advice of his Prime Minister RC Kak when in 1946 Nehru's entry was banned in the State and in defiance thereof he was symbolically prevented to proceed ahead. Then there was the Muslim League led by Muhammad Ali Jinnah. Although this party supported the right of rulers to decide the fate of their respective States and in Kashmir opposed Sheikh Abdullah and his National Conference tooth and nail, but Maharaja was enough of a patriot not to be able to stomach the aggressive Muslim Communalism of the League, and this led him to spurn tempting offers from Pakistan. Finally, there was the main political party in the State itself, the National Conference led by Sheikh Abdullah, with whom Maharaja was at loggerheads for decades because he looked upon it as a major threat to his throne and Dogra rule. The net result was that when the crucial movement came, all the forces that counted were arrayed on the opposite side of the fence. It is suspected that Maharaja did not believe that British would actually leave or at least come to his rescue because of the presence of their high ranking military officers at the helm of affairs in both of the newly created dominions. The only positive reaction to the rapidly approaching partition was to offer to sign a standstill agreement with both the dominions. The Kashmir Valley was inhabited predominantly by Sunni Muslims with a sizable community of Shias, Sikhs and the redoubtable Kashmiri Pandits, Paharis and Punjabi speaking Muslims of whole of the district of Muzaffarabad and hilly areas of the district of Baramulla. Jammu province predominantly by Dogra Hindus with a significant Muslim component, the western strip from Muzaffarabad to Mirpur by Punjabi Muslims; Gilgit, Skardu and Kargil by Shia Muslims, and Ladakh by Lamaistic Buddhists. By and large the people of the State were united in their loyalty to the ruling family, although Sheikh Abdullah's bitter anti-Dogra movement in the thirties and forties had succeeded in making an impression upon politically aware sections in the Kashmir Valley. But when the British intention of withdrawal from the sub-continent became established, and the establishment of Pakistan a certainty, the whole situation underwent a fundamental change. Political movement led by Sheikh Abdullah was pro-Jawaharlal Nehru but against Maharaja Hari Singh, while the Muslim Conference was pro-Maharaja but also pro-Pakistan. Hidden forces also influenced the mind of Maharaja for remaining indecisive and they were represented initially to marginal extent by spiritual Guru Swami Sant Dev and greatly unfaithful RC Kak who was the Prime Minister and internally sided with Jinnah.

MY Saraf (Chief Justice of Pakistan Occupied Kashmir) in his already referred book at page 715 has written that, "in a written note, RC Kak had advised the Maharaja to remain independent at least for one year and then take an appropriate decision in the light of developments and requirements. Kak had a meeting with Quaid-i-Azam in Delhi on 19th July 1947 and Jinnah had not shown any displeasure about Kak Plan." The author of that book is a Kashmiri by birth belonging to the town of Baramulla and has remained a close associate of General Zia-ul-Haq chief of the Army staff. He was previously an active member of National Conference because he was picked up by Sheikh Abdullah and made General Secretary of the reception committee of National Conference's Sopore annual session of 1945 which was attended by Pandit Nehru. He joined J&K Muslim Conference in August 1945. When it (committee) was dissolved, he became a founder member of J&K Liberation League. It is recorded in his book by way of inferences that he had been carrying on open and clandestine activities to promote the cause of Pakistan in Kashmir by creating liaison with government servants having leaning for Pakistan and responsible British nationals who were watching the Anglo-American interests. He had access with British agent posted in J&K State which fact he has recorded in his book. He had come to know through him before 14 August 1947 that Maharaja was joining the dominion of India. Same thing had been told to him by the British Principal who was running St Joseph's College in Baramulla and his name was G Shanks. He was an admirer of Pakistan. Saraf was able to hurl Pakistan's flag on the post-office building in Baramulla district headquarters with the active connivance of then Wazir-e-Wazarat Faiz Ullah who was the elder brother of Chaudhary Hamidullah Khan the then Muslim League President of J&K State by ignoring the strict order passed by Prime Minister Janak Singh. This treacherous act was done on 14 October 1947. The writer of that book could occupy the high offices in POJK and last one was that of Chief Justice of POJK High Court. He recorded his opinion at page 715 of above referred book that, "RC Kak had been in touch with Muslim League high command and may have suggested the course of remaining independent to distract the attention of Indian National Congress." He has also admitted that when Maharaja had become aware of these facts, he had at once dismissed him. It is noteworthy that RC Kak's second wife was a British national and Lord Mountbatten through her was polluting the mind of her husband to join the dominion of Pakistan. She was also under the influence of Lord Mountbatten. Within week's time after the visit of Mahatma Gandhi in Kashmir, RC Kak was replaced as Prime Minister by Major General Janak Singh Katoch who at that time was a minister in Maharaja's Cabinet.

Even after the deadline of 15 August 1947, Maharaja Hari Singh had remained the sole authority to accede to any of the dominions and after he made an unqualified accession with the dominion of India but its Clause VIII (accession document) was an exception which saved the continuance of his sovereignty in and over the State. The dominion of India was given the powers to legislate only in respect of defence, external affairs, communications and ancillary matters. The Union of India by a unilateral act incorporated the clause of referendum while accepting the Instrument of Accession and it was not binding upon the Maharaja because he had not consented for ascertaining the wishes of people. This legal position, the writer of this book has discussed in length while judicially confirming the bans imposed by the State Administration on all the eight Militant Organizations operating in the State under Governor's rule during the years 1990-1992 as well as at relevant places of this book. The summary of these judicial findings is in the relevant chapter of this book under the head 'Banning of Militant Organisations'. In a nutshell, it has been held that militant organizations had no legal locus standi to challenge the accession of the State made with India by a sovereign power (the ruler) accepted by a sovereign country (the dominion of the Republic of India). This view holds the field in national and international fora. The unilateral clause inserted in the Instrument of Accession by the then Viceroy of India (Lord Mountbatten) gave a handle in the hands of hostile foreign blocks for their vested interests to raise the boggy of holding a plebiscite and this has also proved a breeding ground for the anti-national elements including political blackmailers to whip up communal hatred. Reference of the dispute made by Pandit Jawaharlal Nehru in the UNO is the main cause for keeping this Kashmir problem alive and this is a self-created trouble at the instance of Lord Mountbatten. It is noteworthy that all the other States in the territory of British rule who joined the Indian dominion under the provisions of India Independence Act were successfully dealt with by Sardar Patel who was the Minister of States of Independent India except the State of J&K which the Prime Minister Pandit Nehru had made a special case to be dealt with exclusively by him for his love and affection for Sheikh Abdullah. This act of benevolence for a personal friend till date has become a messy and ticklish national problem which is constantly keeping the two dominions at hostile positions. Both the countries are suffering human and financial losses in this conflict over which three open wars were fought and one armed conflict which is known as the war of Kargil took place. Thousands of human lives have been lost and the number is increasing day by day in the proxy war which has been launched by the Pakistani rulers and now they are finding themselves incapable of containing it. Pakistani rulers also now reaping the fruits of their misdeeds as uncontrolled militants are attacking their civil population and the establishment but the strongest wing of the State ISI (Inter-Services Intelligence) is still running and helping training camps to create militants mainly on the plea of liberating J&K State. The people of the State are the worst victims and sufferers. The Hindu minority of Kashmir province who belong to the clan of late Prime Minister Pandit Nehru have become migrants from the place of their birth and are living as refugees. Kashmir Valley has been purged of Hindu population and it is very dangerous for secular India. Even a section of majority community of Kashmir too has become migrants and many of them lost their lives along with Hindu brothers. Plebiscite being a watchword at that time, this became the trump card in the hands of Sheikh Abdullah also. As the man who was supposed to win the plebiscite for India, he could virtually demand India's pound of flesh and this he did repeatedly, not only by assuming powers but also by defaming and harassing the Maharaja. He made accusations against the Maharaja for having organized the massacres of Muslims in Jammu. He was so revengeful that even after the exit of Maharaja from the scene of Kashmir Administrative set up from 20th June 1948, he went on concocting false stories against him. The writer of this book at the age of 12 years had himself heard a vituperate speech given by Sheikh Abdullah in his village Panthal which is situated in the lap of sacred Trikuta Hills where Shri Mata Vaishno Devi University (SMVDU) has now been set up by the Shri Mata Vaishno Devi Shrine Board. In the month of April 1951, Sheikh Abdullah had come there in connection with the inauguration of a small hilly canal (Kohul) and had said without any provocation from anyone: "I want to tell those people who are anxious to bring back the Maharaja that Hari Singh will never return to the State. He has massacred the Muslims of this place. His wife was an accomplice in these nefarious actions. There is no room for any murderer in this State." This statement has been reproduced by MY Saraf in his above referred book as a piece of corroborative evidence when Saraf has levelled a false accusation against Maharaja to defame him internationally that "near Mishriwala village on Jammu Akhnoor road, Maharaja Hari Singh had seen two Muslim women hiding for safety by the side of the road and that he came down from his car and with his own weapon shot them dead." Such type of false propaganda against the honour and dignity of Maharaja who was above religious considerations as a ruler was the dirtiest malicious propaganda not expected from persons holding constitutional posts both inside the country and outside the country, i.e. either from Sheikh Abdullah or from MY Saraf. Saraf had remained a State Subject and his changed domicile in a hostile country while holding a responsible post of the higher judiciary, i.e. Chief Justice should not have killed his conscience which is not expected from the fraternity of judges because of the oath of the office administered to them. Same principle applies to Sheikh Abdullah who was appointed by the Maharaja as his Prime Minister and was under oath either in the name of God or his religion to uphold the truth. The people in large numbers who had gathered there (in Panthal) to hear the sane voice of their Prime Minister were emotionally hurt as some residents of that village had also been murdered by some unruly Muslim League elements who temporarily had shifted their residences for earning their livelihood across the areas of Chenab river in the same district (Reasi). He went on to the extent of telling Jawaharlal Nehru that Maharaja distributed sweets when Gandhi was assassinated. This fact has been recorded by Dr Karan Singh in his book *Heir Apparent*. He was able to convince Pandit Nehru that as long as Maharaja remains in the State he could not possibly win the Plebiscite. Though Sardar Patel, Rafi Ahmed Kidwai, Maulana Abul Kalam Azad, Dr Rajendra Prasad and other senior leaders had understood the mind-set of Sheikh Abdullah yet Pandit Jawaharlal Nehru was not amenable to heed any advice as he was obsessed by the fear of plebiscite. The patriotism in the Maharaja prevented him in the national interest and people of the country in general and of the State in particular not to act in violent reaction against the legal and moral infringements committed by the Union of India and Sheikh Abdullah against his person. He sacrificed his authority and freedom in the national interest by abdicating the State forever and did not pay even a single visit to the State till his death which occurred in 1961 in Bombay. The unfair and unjust treatment meted out to him by Government of India can be judged from the fact that Maharaja Hari Singh got punishment by leaving the State on account of delayed accession and not toeing the line of action of Sheikh Abdullah who wanted to become an independent monarch by acts of treachery and sedition for which he was later on arrested and tried by a Court of Law, and alternatively giving an honourable and dignified treatment to the Nizam of Hyderabad who got murdered thousands of his Hindu subjects and entered into an armed conflict with Union of India. The future generations of this country and of the world will judge the sense of justice, equity and good conscience of the regime of Pandit Jawaharlal Nehru.

In August 1952, Maharaja Hari Singh wrote a letter to Dr Rajendra Prasad, President of India in order to straighten the record as his honour and dignity had been lowered to a great extent on the basis of false and concocted propaganda done in breach of oath of loyalty shown to Maharaja by Sheikh Abdullah for the sake of getting himself appointed as Emergency Administrator and subsequently Prime Minister of the State. The Prime Minister of India, Pandit Nehru had also given assurances to the Maharaja that Sheikh Abdullah would act as Emergency Officer under Maharaja's Prime Minister. He had also been assured that his status would be protected and the pattern of future Constitution as was envisaged for the Maharaja of Mysore. Even in his own hand written note given to Prime Minister Mehr Chand Mahajan when on 26 October 1947, the signatures of Maharaja Hari Singh were obtained on accession this was assured. Sardar Patel had also given assurances to Maharaja. All these assurances given by the Central leaders had paled into insignificance because of commitment made by Pandit Nehru at the bidding of Lord Mountbatten to hold Plebiscite in order to ascertain the wishes of the people of J&K because according to them only Sheikh Abdullah could win the Plebiscite in favour of the dominion of India. Sheikh Abdullah after capturing all the 75 seats in the Constituent Assembly by holding tainted elections and sidelining the constitutional head Maharaja Hari Singh had started blackmailing India with a dominant intention of becoming Independent Sultan of J&K State. He had been encouraged by Anglo-American block which facts have surfaced and led to the unceremonial dismissal of Sheikh Abdullah. Regular speeches were given to humiliate and malign Maharaja in order to paint him black and unpatriotic. If Sheikh Abdullah said Maharaja could not return to his State, Prime Minister of India with all authority and prestige was endorsing it. With this weapon in his hand Sheikh Abdullah had got the termination of the engagement of Mehr Chand Mahajan as Prime Minister of the State with a span of four months and exile of Maharaja from the State within a period of two years. Through the medium of this letter Maharaja Hari Singh had enumerated 30 points in detail supported by documents how in an ex-parte manner he had been maligned without his fault and has given his version how the Kashmir problem has been unnecessarily created and blown out of proportions. The writer of this book does not want to make this book lengthy and as such only a summarized form of that letter has been reproduced. The readers in case are interested, can read the full text of his letter which is reproduced in verbatim in the book titled *Maharaja Hari Singh: The Troubled Years* by Harbans Singh, page 292. Maharaja himself in paragraph 31 of that letter has summarized his position and that is reproduced hereunder in verbatim:

(1) "The Government of State of Jammu and Kashmir was more advanced and enlightened than that of any other Indian State in the pre-Partition days;

(2) I employed men of undoubted ability and standing to be my Ministers from time to time;

(3) In August 1947 Lord Mountbatten gave me the impression that I should accede to Pakistan, Government of India was undecided about the matter, wanted every step by me endorsed by Sheikh Abdullah, the people of Jammu and Kashmir were divided in their opinion and I decided to enter into Stand Still Agreement with both India and Pakistan in order to have time for things to settle down;

(4) Pakistan did not act up to the Stand Still Agreement, blocked supplies to the State and aided and abetted the raiders;

(5) I released Sheikh Abdullah as advised by Sardar Patel and relied on the assurance given by Sheikh Abdullah backed by the assurances given by the Government of India;

(6) I took Sheikh Abdullah in my government;

(7) I issued the Proclamation on 5 March 1948;

(8) Sheikh Abdullah with the connivance of the Government of India started tinkering with the Constitution after 5 March 1948;

(9) Sheikh Abdullah persuaded the Government of India to drive me out of the State;

(10) I left the State and appointed the Yuvraj, my Regent;

(11) My rights of personal property and the affairs of Dharmarth Trust were interfered with by Sheikh Abdullah;

(12) Sheikh Abdullah by maligning me created an impression that the people of Kashmir were against me;

(13) The Constituent Assembly was set up;

(14) The will of the people of Jammu and Kashmir is now judged by the whims and caprices of Sheikh Abdullah;

(15) Sheikh Abdullah having made up his mind to get rid of the ruler and his dynasty, persuaded the Government of India to see eye to eye with him and to lay down that this could be done even before the new Constitution was framed much less approved by you on behalf of India;

(16) I get no redress and am told that I am in the wrong, the will of the people is all that counts and I must abide by such will;

(17) The Press carries reports from day to day creating feelings against me. False reports are not contradicted;

(18) The Prima Minister got angry as evidenced by his letter dated 5th July 1952 because I stated facts;

(19) The States Minister avoids giving a proper reply to me and yet the Press says I have been asked and have not replied;

(20) The Yuvraj is being coerced by the Prime Minister and Sheikh Abdullah to accede to their suggestions.

In Para 32 of the letter which is fully reproduced hereunder, he has stated:

> Finally, I have to say that I had my range of controversy with Sheikh Abdullah and Prime Minister and I am bitter about the fact that the Government of India have been unable to afford me protection and safeguard my rights in spite of the fact that throughout these four and a half years, I have given full cooperation and the fact that my pre-1947 conduct did not compare unfavourably with that of the other rulers who at present enjoy Government of India's protection and favour. During the last three years of my enforced absence from the State I have given them no cause for grievance and at the most, I have been charged with delay in permitting the Yuvraj to take action which having regard to the consideration involved and my better experience, was natural and understandable. Even in this matter ultimately, I did fall in line with the Government of India. If the result of all this is the final stage has again to be a betrayal by the Government of India of their assurances and promises etc and is to result not only in my final removal from the State but also on the sacrifice of the Yuvraj whom I had entrusted to the Government of India's protection. I can only say that it would be an ill return for the faith which I and the Yuvraj placed in the government and the help and cooperation to the extent of self-effacement that we rendered to it. Only history and posterity will be able to do justice to our respective points of view.

(33) In these circumstances, I appeal to you to consider the matter impartially in all its aspects with all your sagacity and wisdom and guide me as to what would be in the best interests of the State.

I remain,
Yours faithfully,
Hari Singh

Without reproducing some of the observations made by Mahajan in his book *Looking Back* contained at pages 173 and 174, full account of the cause of J&K Problem would remain deficient. Those crucial statements are:

"An account of my career in Kashmir would be incomplete without mention of the kindness, love and affection with which His Highness the Maharaja treated me. He reposed implicit faith in my judgement and not once did he decline to accept my advice. I gave him unquestioned loyalty and did what I could to maintain his prestige and position in the State. After the raid and the collapse of State forces, he was absolutely dependent on India for saving the State. India could dictate to him whatever terms she liked and he offered no resistance. At the initial stage, I was able to secure from the Prime Minister of India and Sardar Patel a position for him similar to the one that the Maharaja of Mysore was to hold in his State. Before the raid, I had been assured by Sardar Patel that the Maharaja of Kashmir would, in his constitutional status, occupy the same place as the Nizam of Hyderabad. At that time the Nizam was offered very attractive terms but he was riding the high horse and wanted to carve for himself an independent State. If the Government of India and Pandit Jawaharlal Nehru had struck to the terms of the letter they had given to me at the time of accession and had given to the State a Constitution on the then proposed Mysore State model, the Maharaja's position would have been quite secure and Sheikh Abdullah would not have been able to displace him and become practically the autocratic ruler of the State.... In the correspondence that followed, the Prime Minister gradually tried to dilute the Mysore State model, leaving the Maharaja merely as a constitutional head, I strongly resisted this attempt. We wanted to hold the Prime Minister of India strictly to his promise. He was trying to back out of it on the ground that the circumstances had completely changed since that promise was made. We felt that nothing had changed so far as Kashmir was concerned except that Sheikh Abdullah was demanding more powers. For the Maharaja, the Sheikh had neither affection nor goodwill. Pandit Nehru rightly thought that so long as I was in the State fighting the Maharaja's battle he could not easily hand over the State's administration entirely to Abdullah. That was the reason why he was for a democratic set up in the State. It became necessary that I should be eased out of my office. After I left, Sheikh Abdullah also thought that it would be much easier for him to drive out the Maharaja. Events proved that he was right.

I have had the highest respect for the Maharaja and the friendly relations thus started between us continued till his death. My only regret is that the Government of India did not treat the Maharaja in the manner that he deserved."

It is noteworthy that the position of Raja of Mysore was in due course of time diluted and the State was completely merged with Union of India, of course, with the consent of Raja.

At page 163, Mahajan has made his remarks about Bakshi Ghulam Mohammad who was then Deputy Prime Minister and they are:

> "As in the rest of India, we had to evacuate a large number of refugees from Jammu to Pathankot. Bakshi Ghulam Mohammad, as Deputy Prime Minister, did splendid work in this matter. Working day and night, he was able to evacuate a very large number of persons from Jammu to Pathankot. He gave me full co-operation in all administrative matters and was very courteous and friendly both towards His Highness and myself. If Bakshi Sahab had then been chosen as Prime Minister in place of Sheikh Abdullah, most likely the history of these days might have been differently written. People would have been much happier than they were under the regime of Sheikh Abdullah. Power went to his head and he started behaving like Hitler and Mussolini."

The above stated observation of Mahajan is prophetic as it was during the premiership of Bakshi Ghulam Mohammad that the Constituent Assembly which had been constituted by Sheikh Abdullah, had enacted the State Constitution wherein many constitutional provisions of the Indian Constitution were made applicable which were in the benefit of the general public and in bringing the State nearer to the mainstream of the country. On the contrary, Sheikh Abdullah was very possessive for his personal authority in order to become the unchallengeable Sultan of Jammu and Kashmir because of the reference of the dispute being pending in the United Nations. Not only that, Bakshi diverted many developmental funds towards the development of State which has been to some extent discussed in this book later on. It is unfortunate that a nationalist and a public oriented leader Bakshi Ghulam Mohammad was axed under the 'Kamraj Plan' like Sardar Partap Singh Kairon Chief Minister of Punjab who too was very popular in the masses for development works. The matter did not end here because Bakshi Ghulam Mohammad was indicted by setting up an inquiry commission against him which was headed by a retired Supreme Court judge. The commission is known as Justice Ayyangar Commission. The fact of the matter is that charges of corruption against Bakshi were not of as much alarming nature as would surface in case a Commission of Inquiry is set up against successive governments which came into power after the Indira-Sheikh Accord of 1975. The glaring examples are setting illegal colonies around the city of Jammu by illegally encroaching upon the government and forest lands. The colony of Bhatindi stares at the face when so many ministers, judges, Members of Parliament, Chief Ministers etc have encroached upon the said lands. In the State on a whole hundreds of thousands of Forest and State lands have been encroached in this manner.

CHAPTER 8

Indications of Unconstitutional Statements of Chief Minister Omar Abdullah

The statements are:

1. On November 2, 2013, while addressing a Public meeting in Bandipura (a town in Kashmir Valley), he had said: "The problem of J&K is not going to be solved by financial and employment package. It is a political problem and needs political solution." (Reported in a local daily of Kashmir Valley newspaper *Greater Kashmir* in its issue of November 3, 2013).
2. He has also said that, "There has not been a complete merger of J&K State with India like Other States. There were certain conditions for the merger which have not been fulfilled by India." (Refer *The Times of India*, September 26, 2013.)
3. *Deccan Chronicle* in its issue of August 16, 2013 has reported that Chief Minister Omar Abdullah while speaking about violence in Kishtwar had said, "People of his State are being treated in a different way forcing them to feel separate." "I am often asked why do people of J&K feel different from the people of the rest of the country. He said whenever he pondered over the question, he was not able to reach a conclusion, but the way the Kishtwar communal clashes were presented before the rest of the country, provided the answer." He had quoted figures from the Union Home Ministry on the deaths in communal riots that counted 34 deaths in Utter Pradesh and 13 deaths in Maharashtra during 2012. He had further stated, "were these incidents discussed in Parliament?" He had made the above statement in his Independence Day Speech at Bakshi Stadium, Srinagar.

4. About holding discussion about Article 370 the *Indian Express* newspaper in its issue of December 4, 2013 has reported, "Any move to abrogate Article 370 will re-open Jammu and Kashmir's accession to India."

The writer of this book has tried to understand the purpose lying behind the inner layers of the above stated statements. Viewed from a common man's understanding they have a tendentious affect to feed fat to the ongoing anti-national movement launched in the State by the anti-nationals after the final and irrevocable accession of the State which was made by Maharaja Hari Singh.

The reply to statements number 2 and 4 regarding accession and complete merger is as follows:

> As per the Government of India Act, 1935, which was included in the Indian Independence Act, 1947, the right of taking a decision regarding accession and then merger was given to the ruler of the State and any Indian State would be treated as acceded and merged into either of the two dominions only when the Governor-General accorded the approval to the Instrument of Accession prepared by the Administration of the respective State. There was no provision for conditional accession and then merger in the Indian Independence Act, 1947.

On October 26, 1947 Maharaja Hari Singh acceded/merged Jammu and Kashmir State into Indian dominion on the basis of the same legal Instrument of Accession under which the other States had Acceded/merged into Indian dominion and the then Governor-General of India Lord Mountbatten had signed the same. In case of J&K State he had done so by stating: "I do hereby accept this Instrument of Accession, dated October 26, 1947." The acceptance was made on 27 October 1947.

The relevant clauses of the Instrument of Accession signed by Maharaja Hari Singh, which show the 'full and final merger' of Jammu and Kashmir into Indian dominion, are as follows:

> **Clause 1:** "**I hereby** declare that I accede to the dominion of India with the **intent that** the Governor-General of India, the dominion Legislature, the Federal Court and any other dominion authority established for the purposes of the dominion shall by virtue of this my Instrument of Accession, but subject always to the terms thereof and for the purposes only of the dominion."
>
> **Clause 9:** "I hereby declare that I execute this Instrument on behalf of this State and that any reference in this Instrument to me or to

the ruler of the State is to be construed as including a reference to my heirs and successors."

According to the above stated Clause-I of the Instrument of Accession, the State of Jammu and Kashmir is a permanent part of India. Not only that, it is an integral part of India. The Jammu and Kashmir State stands as State in the list of States of Indian Union at number 15.

Maharaja Hari Singh had further stated in this Instrument of Accession that:

"The terms of this my Instrument of Accession shall not be varied by any amendment of the Act or of the Indian Independence Act, 1947, unless such amendment is accepted by me by Instrument Supplementary through this Instrument."

Note: Under the Indian Independence Act, 1947, even Pandit Nehru, Lord Mountbatten, Mohammad Ali Jinnah, Queen of England, British Parliament and residents of States concerned did not have any right to raise any objection with regard to the accession and subsequent merger made by the ruler himself.

In 1951, the Jammu and Kashmir Constituent Assembly was constituted. All the 75 elected members were from National Conference and Maulana Masoodi became its Speaker. This very Constituent Assembly made applicable Article 1 and Article 370 and certain other Articles. This was done on January 26, 1950, when the Indian Constitution was made applicable to the whole country. Four nominated members from the State had participated in the process of making Indian Constitution. (See Constitution Application Order of 1950 Appendix VII.) Subsequently, the Constituent Assembly of the State which was constituted in 1951 under the sovereignty of Maharaja Hari Singh, it had ratified the accession/merger of the State with India on February 6, 1954. On May 14, 1954, the President of India issued Constitutional Order 'applicable to Jammu and Kashmir' under Article 370 of the Indian Constitution, through which some remaining part of the Indian Constitution to the limited extent were made applicable to Jammu and Kashmir State with certain exceptions and amendments.

The State's own Constitution 'Constitution of Jammu and Kashmir' came into force from January 26, 1957.

Section 3 of the Constitution of Jammu and Kashmir says:

The State of Jammu and Kashmir is and shall be an Integral Part of India and Section 5 prescribes the extent of Executive and Legislative power of the State. It is provided therein that such

> Executive and Legislative powers extend to all matters except those with respect to which Parliament has power to make laws for the State under the provisions of the Constitution of India. The State of Jammu and Kashmir acceded to India under Indian Independence Act, in the manner as prescribed by the Government of India Act, 1935 as in force on that day.

Section 4 of the Constitution of Jammu and Kashmir says:

> That the Territory of the State comprises all the Territories which on 15th day of August 1947 were under the sovereignty or suzerainty of the ruler of the State. Section 147 of the Constitution of Jammu and Kashmir deals with Amendment of the Constitution and last proviso states that no Bill or Amendment seeking to make any change in this Section or provisions of Section 3 and 5 or the provisions of the Constitution of India as applicable in relation to the State shall be introduced or moved in either House of the Legislature.

The State Constitution was adopted on 17th day of November 1956 and Sections 1 to 8 and 158 which deal with the Territory, Permanent Residents, the Relationship of India and the State and the application of the General Clauses Act, 1920 for the interpretation of the Constitution came into force at once, i.e. on 17 November 1956. The remaining Sections came into force on January 26, 1957. The People of Jammu and Kashmir had chosen January 26, the Republic Day of India, as the date for 'full and final' enforcement of their Constitution is the evidence of the emotional integration of the State with the rest of India. The use of the word 'merger' as is being often quoted by various leaders for their political agenda is not of any importance because in legal terminology this term is generally used when two companies merge with each other. The State of Jammu and Kashmir being a sovereign State under the relevant Laws had acceded to sovereign dominion of India and the word of 'accession' as was used under the relevant Laws covers the commutation of the word 'merger'. It is an admitted fact that after accession of a State nobody had any legal right of secession.

Be that as it may, it has been reiterated in Indira-Sheikh Agreement/Accord of 1974 that:

> The State of Jammu and Kashmir, which is a Constituent Unit of the Union of India shall, in its relation with the Union, continue to be governed by Article 370 of the Constitution of India. In the Resolution adopted in Parliament on November 14, 1962 after China's aggression and in the Resolution adopted unanimously in

> Parliament on February 22, 1994, We have stated time and again that We will definitively take back the area occupied by China (1962) and by Pakistan (1947).

Unwanted and illegal comments:

> On October 27, 1947 Lord Mountbatten, while accepting the Instrument of Accession of Maharaja Hari Singh, had sent a letter in which he had made an unwanted and illegal remark "My government has taken a decision to accept the proposal of merger of Kashmir with India. Keeping in view the policy of my government that where there is dispute and in that case the final solution of this issue of merger should be found out according to the wishes of the people of the State. My government wants that when law and order situation is restored in the State and its area is freed from the invaders, then the issue of State's merger should be resolved according to the wishes of the People of the State."

On November 1, 1947, Lord Mountbatten held discussion with Muhammad Ali Jinnah in Lahore and had accepted the plea of holding plebiscite in Jammu and Kashmir State. On November 2, 1948 in his Radio Broadcast the then Prime Minister of interim Indian Government Pandit Jawaharlal Nehru had also given assurance to hold plebiscite in Jammu and Kashmir. The Government of India placed a proposal before the United Nation Organization in January 1, 1948 appealing to declare Pakistan an invader, that the land be liberated and also to know the peoples' opinion in a peaceful atmosphere. In fact this suggestion and proposal were illegal because Maharaja Hari Singh had Acceded/merged Jammu and Kashmir State with India under the same Indian Independence Act of 1947 under which the partition of India took place, Pakistan was formed, and all the 569 princely States were merged either with India or with Pakistan.

The Instrument of Accession did not contain any requirement for taking into account the wishes of the people and its legality was independent of this condition. The popular leader Sheikh Abdullah went to United Nations and in his speech before Security Council on 5 February 1948 stated that accession of India is complete and unquestionable. Maharaja Hari Singh wrote a letter to Sardar Patel on July 15, 1948 in which he had clearly stated, "that we are interested in the progress of whole of India...." This also means that he had fully and finally Acceded and merged his State with the dominion of India.

Prime Minister Dr Manmohan Singh has also tried to create an atmosphere by giving indication regarding need of political solution, relaxation of Armed Forces Special Powers Act, withdrawal of forces from certain areas, and implementation of the proposal of Autonomy with consensus.

In this way, it is found that there are efforts to generate an atmosphere in the country that the solution of Kashmir problem is not possible without giving anything. On the other hand, an atmosphere is being created amongst the people of Kashmir that the time to take final decision is approaching. The Security Forces have been directed to use minimum force. Over 3500 Security Personnel have been injured so far, besides hundreds have lost their lives. There is an agitation like atmosphere created in the Kashmir Valley by observing frequent *Bandhs* and pelting of stones as well as hurling of grenades and firing on the security forces with sophisticated arms. This type of whole agitation is confined only to Kashmir Valley which consists of 14 per cent of the area of the State and that too mainly in five of the 10 districts, i.e. of Baramulla, Srinagar, Pulwama, Anantnag and Shopian. Majority of the Gujjars, Shias, Pahari people, Sunni Kashmiri Muslims, Kashmiri Sikhs, Kashmiri Pandits, Ladakhis, refugee groups, Dogras, Buddhists and Baltis etc are not involved in such type of agitations.

The above type of unwanted statements coming from the mouth of Chief Minister who is under oath administered to him under the Constitution to uphold the Rule of Law as well as unity and integrity of the country are least expected. These statements are made purely for the sake of creating 'Vote Bank' policy. They create unnecessary suspicion in the minds of gullible people in general and provide a handle in the hands of anti-national elements about the question of accession of the State with India, which is 'Full and Final'. The only exception is that 135 Articles of the Indian Constitution are not yet made applicable in the State and there exists temporary Article 370. They can be made applicable whenever well meaning Public oriented Legislators having an agenda of all round development of the whole State without any regional prejudices want to do so. Instead of playing vote bank politics there should be politics of eradication of all around corruption and making the State a viable industrial State. We can copy the developmental activities of our neighbouring hilly State Himachal Pradesh where industrial units have been established at a rapid speed in 'Baddi area'. Some of the industrial units which initially had been established in the State of Jammu and Kashmir were compelled to shift their units to Himachal Pradesh because of non-co-operation of the State Government. That State has made a rapid progress in horticulture and production of electricity which is supplied there without interruptions. This is the result of good governance. It is noteworthy that nature is more bountiful to J&K State as compared to the State of Himachal; but in our State all around corruption is eating the vitals of the society and there is no accountability. The alienated youth can be brought back in the mainstream of the nation by providing it job opportunities including professional engagements in industries, agriculture, horticulture etc on modern lines. The industry of tourism can be augmented which has great potential in our State as compared to other States. The statements which are being made regarding non-merger of the State in the Indian Union encourage the anti-national elements existing in the State as well as in the rest of the country. Whenever there is government of the people and for the people such statements ought not to be made by constitutional functionaries who are bound by the oath under the Constitution to uphold the security and sovereignty of the State and country. We have the shining examples in the State when there were well meaning administrators with maturity and commitment to the Nation at the helm of affairs such like Bakshi Ghulam Mohammad and GM Sadiq. The anti-national elements were at the receiving end and there were no frequent hartals and stone peltings. When a strong government is in the Centre such type of statements are never allowed to be made and the example is of the rule of Mrs Indira Gandhi, who had liberated Bangladesh from the clutches of Pakistan in 1971 and because of that success the Doctrine of Separatism at that time had been given a decent burial. The Indira-Sheikh Accord of 1974 was the result of that success. There are more such examples when the Centre had remained strong.

Be that as it may, Maharaja Hari Singh himself would have completely merged the State with Union of India for all intents and purposes by entering into supplementary agreement as was provided under the Indian Independence Act. In the real sense of the term of then prevalent law, the sole authority to do so, was vested with Maharaja but unfortunately injustice was done to his sovereign authority at the behest of Sheikh Abdullah by Pandit Nehru and he was removed from the scene of the State in an illegal and unceremonial manner. On the contrary against the provisions of the Indian Independence Act and Act of 1935 this power was given to the Constituent Assembly and later on has automatically devolved in the State Legislature. But our elected representatives are not sincere and eager to attract the application of remaining above stated Articles of the Indian Constitution.

Dr Karan Singh in his autobiography has recorded that on January 31st, 1948, Maharaja had written a lengthy letter to Sardar Patel with whom he had friendly relations describing the unsatisfactory military situation and volunteering to lead his own forces and if permitted the

Indian Forces. He had expressed this desire in the eventuality the Union Government cannot recover the territory of the State then to save it at last from the adverse decision of the Security Council for handing over the State to Pakistan in a plate.

In a nutshell he was not prepared to go beyond the Mysore Model after becoming constitutional ruler and giving governance to leaders of National Conference as the latter were not able to command confidence of Hindus and Sikhs and even a large section of Muslims. He wanted to have a Dewan of his choice as a member of the Cabinet and in case possible as President and wanted to preserve certain reserve powers. Then he wrote another letter on 6 May 1949, in continuation of earlier two letters dated 29 April 1949 and 1 May 1949 to Sardar Patel. The Maharaja had stated, "Nor it would be fair on my part to conceal from you my own feelings that while Sheikh Abdullah has been allowed to depart from time to time as suited his inclinations from the pledge and written words to act consistently in breach of the loyalty which he professed to me prior to his release from jail and the oath of allegiance which he took when he assumed office, and to openly indulge along with his colleagues in a campaign of vilification and foul calumny against me, both inside the State and outside...."

From the above stated facts it has been established cogently that Maharaja Hari Singh would have been satisfied on the position which Maharaja of Mysore had obtained from the dominion of India but unfortunately because of close friendship of Pandit Nehru with Sheikh Abdullah he was not accorded this position. Dr Karan Singh at page 100 of his autobiography has recorded that, "although Sardar Patel never criticized Jawaharlal in his presence, but it was clear from his conversation that he did not approve of his special relationship with Sheikh Abdullah, whom he evidently distrusted and disliked."

During Prime Ministership of J&K State up to 1953, Sheikh Abdullah was not even prepared to make applicable Chapter III of the Indian Constitution which guarantees the Fundamental Rights. He had not even allowed the Government of India to make applicable Agreement of 1952 which he had fully discussed but retracted later on under the dream of becoming Independent ruler of the State with the help of Anglo-American block. Maharaja of Mysore had executed the Instrument of Accession on 9th day of August 1947, which was accepted by Governor-General of India on 16 August 1947. On 23 June 1949 he entered into supplementary Instrument of Accession and made some variations in the terms and conditions of the earlier Instrument of Accession. On 25 November 1949 he had made a declaration stating therein that by virtue of his earlier proclamation dated 29 October 1947 he had ordained that his Ministry should set up a Constituent Assembly composed of elected representatives of the people and entrusted it the task of framing the Constitutional Bill for the State of Mysore. Then on 25 November 1949 he made further declaration that Constitution of India should be adopted as the Constitution of his State. In this way after a period of little over two years from the date of accession he completely merged his State with dominion of India. (Refer Page 339 and 370 of the White Paper on Indian States.) In a similar manner some other States like Patiala and United States of Rajasthan by its Raj Pramukh Maharaja Sawai Man Singh had also merged his States. (Refer Page 368 of The White Paper on Indian States.) Even the Nawab of Hyderabad who had entered into an armed conflict with Union of India in 1950 had completely merged his State with dominion of India. The fault for not getting supplementary agreement under relevant laws lies with the then Central Government at the behest of Sheikh Abdullah and after that on the elected representatives in the State legislature who are not allowing the application of the Indian Constitution as a whole. In this way legally speaking the State had completely merged as there is irrevocable accession made by Maharaja Hari Singh and the term accession encompasses in it the term 'merger'. Under Article 370(3) the then Constituent Assembly and now State Legislature can at any time make recommendation to the President of India for the abolition of Article 370 and thereby resulting into the complete merger of the State with Union of India. Even without it there is complete merger and the above stated statements are of hollow nature.

The other two issues, i.e. Number 3 and 4 raked up by Omar Abdullah also have no relevance. The communal riots of Kishtwar cannot be compared with riots of the States of Utter Pradesh and Maharashtra. We have to bear in mind that the boundary of Kishtwar district on the whole north side meets with the boundary of district Anantnag of Kashmir Valley where already there is complete purging of the people of minority community. The riots of Kishtwar seems to be a part of that extended game-plan. Secondly, the State Home Minister who is local MLA of Kishtwar was very much present in the town for the last few days when the rioting in question took place. Every patriot citizen of the country has a right to ask Omar Abdullah what his State Minister was doing there despite the fact sufficient availability of para-military forces and the police personnel. How could he not get any prior information about rioting from intelligence Agencies? The other issue is regarding re-opening of the question of accession which statement prima facie falls within the definition of sedition. At the cost of repetition it is stated that accession of the State was full and final on

27 October 1947 when Government of India had accepted the offer of Maharaja to Accede to the dominion of India.

The writer of this book is of confirmed opinion that the people of J&K State can still preserve their special status for getting employment in State Government jobs to the exclusion of outsiders. They can retain their agricultural holdings because of the existing laws enacted by Maharaja Hari Singh such as State Subject definitions which doctrine was adopted by Maharaja in 1927 and 1932 and subsequently amended from time to time, coupled with the enforcement of various Revenue Laws. The present J&K Agrarian Reforms Act which was enacted in 1976 can also be of utmost use for preventing the alienation of the lands to non-residents of the State. The inhabitants of the State can preserve their separate identities of all the three regions from unwanted exploitations.

CHAPTER 9

Ejection of Raiders

As soon as raiders invaded the State on October 22, 1947, some fifth columnists belonging to Muslim community in the State Forces started desertions and majority of them were hailing from Mirpur and Poonch districts. There were some incidents when they were massacring their own fellow soldiers. The glaring example is that of Colonel Hari Singh who was murdered during his sleep as he had not taken precautionary measures to disarm these elements but professionally trusted them on the past good record of Second World War. Similarly, these elements had eliminated Lt Col Narayan Singh at Kohala. Even against these odds, the remaining majority of the troops fought valiantly and the shining example is that of Brigadier Rajinder Singh. The delay of two days in the advance of hordes of raiders by the troops under his command and then one day's more delay of such advance caused by destruction of Uri bridge by the retreating troops of his command were the most crucial three days. The time, thus, saved enabled the Maharaja to complete the accession of the State with Union of India. VP Menon at page 397 has paid tributes in his book to Brigadier Rajinder Singh and his martyred men in these words, "But he and his colleagues will live in the history like the gallant Leonidas and his three hundred men who held the Persian invaders at Thermopylae. It was but appropriate that when the Mahavir Chakra decoration was instituted the first award was given posthumously to this Heroic soldier," i.e. Brigadier Rajinder Singh.

On October 27, 1947 Lt Colonel D Ranjit Rai commanding the first batch of Indian troops landed at the airport of Srinagar. It was not certain at that time whether the airport was still held by the State forces. This small contingent of troops carried in few planes was from first Sikh battalion which was then deployed on internal defence duties at Gurgaon. Lt Col Rai had the orders to defend the air field and in case it was under the occupation of the enemy then fly back. At that time, invaders estimated three thousand to five thousand were in Baramulla which was only at a distance of 35 miles by a fine Tarmac road. With inadequate force at his command, he dug his defences at Pattan and engaged the raiders near Baramulla. He lost his life in this bold venture which unnerved the invaders as they thought that Indian army in large numbers had arrived. He sacrificed his life on 28 October 1947 and was the first Military Officer of the Indian Army to have suffered casualty at the hands of the raiders. He was posthumously given the award of Mahavir Chakra.

In another bold incident Major Som Nath Sharma of Kumaon Regiment engaged the raiders in Budgam on November 3rd 1947 when they reached near the Srinagar airport. He was out-numbered seven to one. He very valiantly engaged them in action and inflicted heavy casualties. This brave soldier of Indian army belonged to the Dogra soil of Jammu being elder brother of Gen VN Sharma, who some years back retired as Chief of the Indian Army. Their grandfather was a State Subject and father who was in medical core of Indian Army had shifted his domicile in Himachal Pradesh. He was awarded Param Vir Chakra posthumously and was the first soldier of the Indian Army to have received a highest gallantry award of the land. In the intervening time reinforcements arrived and the Srinagar airport was saved. The supreme sacrifices of three soldiers—Brigadier Rajinder Singh, Lt Col Ranjit Rai and Major Som Nath Sharma have made unforgettable contribution in saving the Kashmir Valley. Major Som Nath Sharma had sent the following memorable message to his Brigade Headquarters—"The enemy is only 50 yards from us. We are heavily outnumbered. We are under devastating fire. I shall not withdraw an inch but will fight to the last man and the last round."

Brigadier Sen in a highly professional army operation brought the raiders in his net at Shalteng near the outskirts of Srinagar city and attacked them from three sides, with the Indian Air force landing air support. Three hundred raiders were killed on the spot and they were completely routed. They retreated in panic and this battle proved decisive in causing their perpetual retreat. This victory was achieved on November 7, 1947 and three days thereafter the Indian troops captured the town of Baramulla. Had shortage of petrol not occurred the forces would have captured Muzaffarabad. In the Jammu theatre of military action Brigadier Usman is considered as saviour of Nowshera in Jammu region. He laid down his life while defending Jhangar area. He was posthumously awarded Param Vir Chakra.

CHAPTER 10

Take-Over of Gilgit by Pakistan

The British-Indian Government in 1935 had virtually forced Maharaja to give strategic area of Gilgit on lease to them for sixty years. With the lapse of paramountcy, the Britishers declared to give back the possession of Gilgit to Maharaja. On this development Maharaja sent his senior most and trusted army officer Brigadier Ghansara Singh as Governor to Gilgit in the month of July 1947. The handing back of the area took place in a function held in Gilgit on 1st August 1947 with Major General HL Scott Chief of the Army staff and Brig Ghansara Singh Governor Designate, representing the State Government. Raja Noor Ali Khan hailing from Bhimber tehsil of Jammu Division who at that time had been posted at Skardu tehsil headquarters was appointed as Wazir-e-Wazarat (SDM) of the Agency and was allowed a free hand in the setting up of the Civil Administration. The 6th J&K Infantry Battalion reinforced by two Sikh companies raised after the month of April was ordered to Boonji which was the principal cantonment in the region before 1935. The total strength of the Dogra Army in the region did not exceed 1200, of whom 500 were Muslims and they could be expected to rally the support of local population which was 100 per cent Muslims. The Gilgit Scout officers Major Brown and Captain Mathieson were there at the time of Partition and continued there because of their experience and knowledge of the area. But unfortunately, their presence proved to be of disastrous nature as they conspired, abetted and executed the cession of the State. Both took part in demolition of Dogra Administrative Structure.

No sooner Brigadier Ghansara Singh did arrive in Gilgit than he was faced with catalogue of demands from the officers and JCOs of Gilgit scouts who were Muslims and few Britishers. He tried to win over their sympathies but of no avail. The local population excluding some British agents amongst Mirs and Rajas of those small principalities were not against the Maharaja and had no hand in the revolt. It was

Pakistan who was instigating some of them through the medium of British officers. The Muslim army officers mutinied on October 31st 1947 and took the Governor prisoner. Hindu civil servants and some guards of the Governor were either massacred or taken prisoners along with their family members. Before leaving his official residence, Brig Ghansara Singh asked his captors what they intended to do with their prisoners and requested if the policy was to repatriate them to Jammu, the first batch should consist of men with families while he would prefer to be sent last of all. He also requested that they should be given some cash to enable them to reach their destinations and undertook, personally, to refund the amount, after reaching Jammu. He was transferred to Attock Fort located in Pakistan territory along with two thousand or so Indian prisoners. They were later exchanged through International Red Cross. The Garrison Commander, Major Brown—a British officer, hoisted the Pakistani flag formally on November 4, 1947. As has been narrated earlier one-seventh of the total area of the State thus, was given illegally in plate to Pakistan by the intriguing English officer.

Gilgit-Baltistan region has had chequered history ever since the partition of the sub continent. Pakistan's control over the area began after tribal invasion, sponsored and aided by Pakistan Army in 1947. The area is under Pakistan's control. Now it is neither independent nor integrated or federated. However, in 1953, Pakistan separated the region from the rest of the J&K Occupied Area and gave it a new name of 'Northern Areas'. This was done by Pakistan in breach of the Karachi Agreement arrived at between Pandit Nehru Prime Minister and Prime Minister of Pakistan. This illegally detached area was administered by Pakistani bureaucracy in collaboration with Pakistan Army under the loose framework. Twice did New Delhi shoot heated missives to Pakistan. One was about Pakistan's ceding 5,000 sq kms area in Shaksgam Valley to China and the other was when Pakistan completed the Karakoram Highway that changed the entire strategy of the region in military and political terms. But the entire spectrum of our northern border strategy changed when with the tacit agreement of Pakistan, China sent in thousands of her People's Liberation Army (PLA) personnel disguised as technicians, skilled workers and labourers. For more than few years in the past, they were engaged in working on numerous developmental and infrastructural projects in the strategic region with Beijing making major investments. Building of link roads, bridges, tunnels etc has been taken up on large scale. China has sounded Pakistan that she is interested in having a regular military base in Waziristan. Among other prospective enterprises are a link with Afghanistan through the Wakhan Corridor.

However, Baltistan and Gilgit remained in focus when India pre-empted Pakistan's impending adventure of capturing Siachen Glacier in 1984. The Kargil war of 1999 could also be linked to segregate this region from the hold of India. China in collaboration with Pakistan has a blue print of extending Railway line there and supply the electricity to Pakistan from Rougan Mega Hydroelectric Power Generation Plant in Tajikistan. China wants its influence to continue in Central Asia and approach to Arabian Sea and monitor the affairs of Iran. Pakistan is systematically changing the demographic composition of Shia population by inhabiting Sunni Punjabi and Pakhtoon Muslims of North-West Frontier Province. There are conflicts and fundamentalism can grow unless economic developments take place and youths are provided jobs and work. The Western world is thinking of its tourism potentialities and unexploited mineral wealth. Legally speaking, it is an integral part of erstwhile Princely State of Dogra ruler Maharaja Hari Singh and in illegal occupation of Pakistan. The recent incursions made by China up to the deep area of about 19 kms in the State territory during the month of April 2013 was an attempt to realize India her capability to secure safety of the Karakoram Highway linking China with the Gwadar Port located in Balochistan region of Pakistan in order to have access as stated above in the hot waters of Arabian Sea and strategically encircle India from the western side in the sea. China has taken this port on lease from Pakistan on an excuse of making it a modern Port. Recently, China has gone to the original position by vacating the occupied area when there was huge protests, hue and cry in the whole of India.

The Pakistani raiders also made a determined bid to occupy Ladakh. The most amazing feat of Air Commander Mehr Singh to fly his plane on May 24, 1948 at 23,000 feet above the sea level without oxygen and landing at the rough strip of Leh airport located at the height of 11,555 feet enabled the Indian forces to be airlifted to Leh and build up defences for Ladakh which was totally so far undefended. This is an unparallel act of bravery. The second unique feat was of Major General Thimayya who took his tanks to snow covered Zoji La pass at the height of 11,578 feet on November 1, 1948. This act of the General has been compared in the military history to Hannibal crossing the Alps with his elephants as no one so far in the history had taken tanks to such a height in such inaccessible high altitude snowy areas. Twenty-five enemy bunkers were destroyed and their occupants ran away in hurry. With these two daring acts Ladakh was made safe from any further incursion. It is noted that some raiders had reached near Khalsi town but one column of Indian Army from Himachal side after crossing Rohtang pass headed by Major Hari Chand (who was the real brother of the late Rani Parvati of erstwhile royal family of Leh) hailing from present Himachal Pradesh State greeted them with bullets and forced their retreat to reach the town of Leh. He got the full support from the locals who never liked those barbarous elements in their areas. He raised a local force of volunteers and cleared the interior area of Ladakh from the raiders. The heroic deeds of the Major were heard by the writer of this book verbally from the local people during his posting in 1982-83 as District and Sessions Judge Ladakh region which was a judicial district comprising of the areas of both administrative districts, i.e. of Kargil and Leh. His valiant deeds are also recorded in the military annals of Indian Army as to how he with the help of some chosen commandos and the consent and help of his commanding officer had cut the supply lines of the raiders in Ladakh area by conducting surprise attacks on them. Colonel HS Parab was then acting as Officer Commanding Leh and was responsible for all the operations to be carried in Leh. He was an officer of Second Battalion 8th Gorkha Rifles and was also appointed administrator for the district of Leh until further orders. He was given extraordinary powers under the signatures of Bakshi Ghulam Mohammad who was the Deputy Prime Minister of the State. He had been given complete control over the civil administration, both executive and judicial in the district. He had to execute all Civil, Revenue and Criminal powers which the Wazir-i-Wazarat of Ladakh has heretofore been exercising. He and Major Hari Chand who was made the head of Commando force were responsible for pushing back the infiltrators who had reached about fifty kilometres from the town of Leh. Major Hari Chand's brilliant exploits behind the enemy lines were acknowledged by the grant of Maha Vir Chakra to him after the campaign.

Rajender Puri writes in his book that Pandit Nehru was in a position to over-run Kashmir and clear the state of Pakistani aggression. But he was guided by British interest and on Lord Mountbatten's advice he halted the march of Indian Army. The British wanted to keep Kashmir divided as a permanent bone of contention between India and Pakistan. The order of ceasefire in 1948 was the first major disagreement between General Cariappa and Pandit Nehru. General Cariappa recalls, "If we had been given three weeks there would have been no Kashmir problem now. But Pandit Nehru was adamant. He did not tell the British Commander in Chief General Roy Bucher but told me directly to stop firing."

Mohd Yusuf Saraf, Chief Justice of Pakistan occupied area of J&K at page 1017 and at page 1018 of his book has admitted that Pakistan has the dominant intention not to allow India to occupy the international border of the State because 'Mangla Head Works' in the State area on Jhelum river, the only important cantonment then, besides Rawalpindi hardly ten to twelve miles from various points on the State border and strategically important town of Gujarat is hardly six to seven miles away. At page 1036, it is stated that, "a British Officer Lt Col Harvey Kelly who had served so well in area of Baramulla in Pandu ridge came back from the front because orders had been received that British officers were to be entirely withdrawn from Kashmir." By construction of Mangla Dam about 90,000 people were uprooted. Bala Gala town population of 50,000 submerged the town of Mirpur, and Dadyal is to irrigate about 30 lakh acres of land and generate 10 lakh kilowatts of electricity.

CHAPTER 11

Kashmir in the Security Council

While pushing back the raiders, the Indian Army had captured prisoners, arms and documents and it proved that Pakistan was directly involved. *London Times* newspaper of Britain in its issue of January 13, 1948 reported that, "Pakistan is sufficiently involved in aiding the raiders is certain. Our correspondent has first-hand evidence that arms, ammunition and supplies are being made available to the Azad Kashmir Forces. A few Pakistani officers are also helping to direct their operations. And however much, the Pakistan Government may disown intervention; moral and material support is certainly forthcoming."

India had two options, i.e. either to destroy the bases of support of the invaders or to lodge a complaint in the UNO. India adopted the second course with the active advice of Lord Mountbatten who had Anglo-American interest in his mind to black mail India in the UNO which was at that time in their full control. In the complaint it was stated, "In order that the objective of expelling the invader from Indian Territory and preventing him from launching fresh attacks should be quickly achieved, Indian troops would have to enter Pakistan territory; only thus could the invaders be denied the use of bases and cut off from their sources of supplies, and reinforcements in Pakistan. Since the aid which the invaders are receiving from Pakistan is an act of aggression against India, so the Government of India are entitled, in international law, to send their armed forces across Pakistan territory for dealing effectively with the invaders. However, as such action might involve armed conflict with Pakistan, the Government of India, ever anxious to proceed according to the spirit of the chapter of the United Nations, desire to report the situation to the security council in accordance with the provisions of Article 35 of the charter. They felt justified in requesting the council to ask the Government of Pakistan:

1. To prevent Pakistan Government personnel, military and civil, participating in or assisting the invasion of J&K State;
2. To call upon other Pakistan nationals to desist from taking any part in the fighting in J&K State;
3. To deny to the invaders:
   (a) Access to and use of its territory for operations against Kashmir;
   (b) Military and other supplies;
   (c) All other kinds of aid that might tend to prolong the present struggle."

When the Security Council took up the matter for consideration, Pakistan emphatically denied that it had any part in the invasion of J&K. In pursuance of the UN Security Council resolution of April 17, 1948, United Nations Commission on India and Pakistan was set up and the Commission arrived in Karachi. Pakistan admitted the presence of its troops 'since May' and 'in self-defence'.

Sir Owen Dixon headed this Commission as representative of the United Nations. His choice was of a single mediator. He was a judge of Australian High Court and a Jurist of repute. He was appointed on 14th March 1950. After having many meetings with Pandit Nehru and other leaders, he came to Karachi on 1st June 1950 and met Sir Muhammad Zafarullah Khan. He met Sheikh Abdullah also. The Prime Minister of India Pandit Nehru and Prime Minister of Pakistan met him jointly on 20th July 1950 at Delhi and meetings continued on day to day basis. His final opinion as observed in the report was,

> "when the frontier of the State of J&K was crossed by the hostile elements, it was contrary to international law and when, in May 1948, units of the regular Pakistan forces moved into the territory of the State, that too was inconsistent with international law."

The UN Security Council passed four resolutions on Kashmir. The first resolution of January 1948 urged the two Nations to take measures to improve the relations. The second resolution of April 17, 1948, recommended setting up a five member commission "to proceed to the sub-continent and there place their good offices and mediation at the disposal of the governments of India and Pakistan." The third resolution of August 13, 1948 was the most significant. It has been reproduced as Appendix 5. The resolution has three parts. Part I related to the 'cease fire'. Part II made it incumbent upon India and Pakistan to withdraw all its forces, regular and irregular, while India was required to reduce the strength of its forces. Part III said,

"The Government of India and Government of Pakistan reaffirm their wish that the future status of J&K shall be determined in accordance with the will of the people and to that end, upon acceptance of the Truce Agreement, both governments agree to enter into consultation with the Commission to determine fair and equitable conditions whereby such free expression of the will be assured."

The fourth resolution was merely a supplement to the third resolution. Before India could agree for 'cease fire' some assurances were given to it during the course of discussions and correspondence with the UN Commission for India and Pakistan. These have been listed as Appendix 6. One of the assurances was that the Plebiscite proposal shall not be binding upon India if Pakistan does not implement Part I and Part II of the resolution of August 13, 1948.

On March 21, 1949, Admiral Nimitz was designated Plebiscite Administrator. The UNO Military Observers were also deputed to assist in settling the cease fire line and supervising it. On July 27, 1949, the Karachi Agreement was drawn up on the basis of which the cease fire line was delineated and ancillary points settled.

President of the Security Council, General McNaughton separately proposed demilitarization of the entire area and this proposal equated India and Pakistan on the same footing and was contrary to the spirit of resolution of August 13, 1949 hence rejected by India.

On March 14, 1950, the Security Council appointed Sir Owen Dixon as its representative of the Commission after having various discussions as stated above with both the countries, he carried out his work. He with the discussions of India and Pakistan envisaged the partition of the State. He divided the State into three regions:

(i) the region about which there was no doubt about the wishes of the people to accede to India;
(ii) the region the inhabitants whereof undoubtedly wished union with Pakistan;
(iii) the region regarding which there was doubt about the wishes of the people and he recommended that plebiscite should be held there.

This 'Dixon Plan' was rejected by India and Pakistan. In April 1951, the Security Council appointed another representative Dr Graham. He laboured for two years and his recommendations were rejected by both the contesting countries. The stalemate continued thereafter. Pakistan started getting military and economic aid from USA and became a member of the western block. With the intensified cold war between USA and USSR the latter started giving strong support to India in the Security Council and openly accused USA and UK for causing interference in the internal affairs of Kashmir. The Russian leaders such as Bulganin and Khrushchev openly declared that, "the question of Kashmir as one of the States of India has already been decided by the people of Kashmir."

CHAPTER 12

Land Reforms in Kashmir

In April 1949, the State Government appointed a land reforms committee to prepare a plan for the abolition of big landed estates and transfer of the land to the tillers. Before the report of the standing committee could be submitted to the administration, Sheikh Abdullah suo motu announced drastic and sweeping reforms ignoring the Maharaja who was the head of the State. This was intentionally done to deprive the mostly Hindu Population of the State who held land in large numbers as landlords. The number of such landlords exceeded twelve thousand. Though some of them held the land in feudalistic conditions yet many were physically disabled widows, or not settled in lives. All these people were deprived to hold not more than 182 kanals of land and rest was taken by the State without paying any compensation. The jurisdiction of the Privy Council (the predecessor of the Supreme Court in Indian dominion) did not extend to the State even after accession and thus, the landlords were left to rub their heels in the cool. The Big Landed Estates Abolition Act was got passed in 1950 by Sheikh Abdullah by an administrative order issued in the name of Yuvraj Karan Singh in whose favour Maharaja Hari Singh had passed the crown at his forced abdication of the State in 1949. At that time, J&K Constitution Act of 1939 was in force which did not provide writ remedy in favour of a native of the State. The aggrieved landlords could not challenge this Act in a Constitutional Court because the writ jurisdiction of the Apex Court (Supreme Court) was extended to the State in 1954 and then Fundamental Rights guaranteed under Chapter III of the Indian Constitution were made applicable with certain amendments. The State High Court under Constitution Act of 1939 had no writ jurisdiction. The new Constitution of J&K State came into force on 26 January 1957 and Section 103 of that Constitution has given the power to the High Court of writ jurisdiction. At that time, Article 1 and 370 along with other some Articles as specified in the

Constitution Application Order dated 26 January 1950 were made applicable in the State. After that, there was Delhi Agreement of 1952 which is discussed fully herein after along with order dated 26 January 1950 and attached as Appendixes 7 and 8, respectively. (Note: Vide SRO 1610 dated 14 May 1954, the President of India made order CO 48 by virtue of which the provisions of Articles dealing with Fundamental Rights and other Articles were made applicable. This order along with other orders which were subsequently passed relating to the application of constitutional provisions have been discussed in detail in Appendix 9). This appeared to be the first act of brazen disloyalty, breach of trust committed by Sheikh Abdullah towards Maharaja Hari Singh as well as to the Union Government of India. The lands owned or held by or on behalf of the Maharaja were also taken away in excess of the prescribed limits without making any compensation. This is a unique and unprecedented example of a State act in the Indian Union when the Executive and Political State authority was used to deprive the citizens in one part of its territory depriving them the benefits of their Fundamental Rights regarding right to hold property and right to livelihood. This is also an example of usurping the sovereign power of the Legislature by an Executive Order against the provisions of the State Constitution of 1939 which then had application and Maharaja was then the constitutional head and no executive order could be passed without his signatures. It would be for the future enlightened generations to judge whether the rule in J&K State was democratic or despotic!!

Sheikh Abdullah wanted to make some dramatic announcements on 13th July 1950 as he stated this day to be celebrated as a National Day in order to gain maximum political mileage and a month before he sent to the Regent for signatures two proposals regarding abolition of Jagirdari (the feudal land-grant system) and of landlordism, without any compensation at all. The Regent seemed to have understood the game plan of Sheikh Abdullah as being against the interests of non-Muslim population and particularly Dogras who had not supported him during his movement and correspondingly given benefit to win the sympathy of co-religionists. Vishnu Kant Sahay, Secretary for Kashmir Affairs of Central Government, had come to Srinagar on a visit and the Regent referred the matter to him for obtaining the opinion of Government of India and the Regent had accordingly informed Sheikh Abdullah about this course of action being taken by him. This enraged Sheikh Abdullah and he wrote to the Regent, "It appears that the obvious limitations of the constitutional head of the State have escaped the attention of Yuvraj. The action taken by Yuvraj is entirely opposed to the spirit of the Proclamation dated 5th March 1948 under which the present government was set up. It has all along been understood that the ruler or his Regent will act strictly as the constitutional head of the State and it is on this distinct understanding that the present government hold their office. He went on, significantly, to add: It is also clear that the subjects in regard to which the submissions were made did not relate to a matter in which the State had acceded to the dominion of India and, therefore, in the existing constitutional set up the Government of India has no jurisdiction in this matter." The Regent received the drafted reply from the Central Government by hand and in this behalf the Central Government had also consulted Gopalaswami Ayyangar who had served as Prime Minister of the State under Maharaja Hari Singh and dealt with Sheikh Abdullah and knew Sheikh's mental make up. At this time, Ayyangar was a Central Minister in the cabinet of Pandit Nehru and therefore wanted that such an illegal piece of legislation as an Act which was being passed in the absence of Legislature in the State would be declared null and void by the Centre. Pandit Nehru did not permit it and Sheikh Abdullah succeeded in enacting this Draconian law. The Regent had written to Sheikh Abdullah with the draft which was appended to this communication and the communication is reproduced, "I appreciate the constitutional position under the Proclamation of March 5, 1948. Nonetheless it seems to me that these very far reaching proposals, which will drastically affect the economy of very large sections of the population and for the sanctioning of which there is no properly functioning legislature at present, should, in the existing delicate political situation, be first examined in concert with the Government of India, and that we should not rush this legislation without satisfying that government."

Note: Source of information reproduced above is from Dr Karan Singh's *Autobiography*.

Despite this, on the next day, Sheikh Abdullah made a long speech at Lal Chowk in Srinagar in which he went ahead and announced the measures, despite the fact that he had been called to Delhi to discuss the matter. The measures were not legal without the signature of the Regent. This was the first of the series of differences of approach between Sheikh Abdullah and the Government of India that grew over the next few years and culminated in his arrest in August 1953 and subsequent trial in the Court of Law. Ultimately, Sheikh Abdullah grudgingly made some amendments in the Act on the advice of New Delhi. It must be remembered that at that time, the Kashmir issue was still alive one at the United Nations, where Jawaharlal's overriding idealism and sense of fair play had made the whole matter embarrassingly complicated for India. The aggrieved inhabitants of the State had no remedy available at that time except for rising in revolt. Sheikh Abdullah by that time had also started showing discrimination in giving employment in government services to the inhabitants of the Kashmir region at the cost of the interests of the inhabitants of Jammu region and one glaring example was his lopsided recruitment from Kashmir Valley in J&K Militia. All these factors of victimization, neglect and discrimination led to agitation by a nationalist party formed in Jammu by the name of 'Praja Parishad'.

CHAPTER 13

Article 370 of the Indian Constitution

Jammu and Kashmir acceded to India on 26th October 1947 while Article 370 was adopted by the Constituent Assembly on 17th October 1949 as purely temporary provision. It always nourishes a feeling of exclusion among a certain section of the populace giving rise to fissiparous tendencies. It has led to the belief that Jammu and Kashmir can be put outside the constitutional organization of the Union of India.

Temporary Provisions with respect to the State of Jammu and Kashmir—

'(1) Notwithstanding anything in this Constitution,—

(a) the provisions of Article 238 shall not apply in relation to the State of Jammu and Kashmir;

(b) the power of Parliament to make laws for the said State shall be limited to:

(i) those matters in the Union List and the Concurrent List which in consultation with the Government of the State, are declared by the President to correspond to matters specified in the Instrument of Accession governing the accession of the State to the dominion of India as the matters with respect to which the dominion Legislature may make laws for that State; and

(ii) such other matters in the aid List as, with the concurrence of the Government of the State, the President may by order specify.

Explanation: For the purposes of this Article, the Government of the State means the person for the time being recognized by the President as the Maharaja of Jammu and Kashmir acting on the advice of the Council of Ministers for the time being in office under the Maharaja's Proclamation dated the fifth day of March 1948;

(c) the provisions of Article 1 and of this Article shall apply in relation to that State;

(d) such of the other provisions of this Constitution shall apply in relation to that State Subject to such exceptions and modifications as the President may by order specify:

Provided that no such order which relates to the matters specified in the Instrument of Accession of the State referred to in paragraph (i) of Sub-Clause (b) shall be issued except in consultation with the Government of the State.

Provided further that no such order which relates to matters other than those referred to in the last preceding proviso shall be issued except with the concurrence of the government.

(2) If the concurrence of the Government of the State referred to in paragraph (ii) of Sub-Clause (b) of Clause (1) or in the second proviso to Sub-Clause (d) of that clause be given before the Constituent Assembly for the purpose of framing the Constitution of the State is convened, it shall be placed before such Assembly for such decision as it may take thereon.

(3) Notwithstanding anything in the foregoing provisions of this Article, the President may, by public notification declare that this Article shall cease to be operative or shall be operative only with such exceptions and modifications and from such date as he may notify:

Provided that the recommendation of the Constituent Assembly referred to in Clause (2) shall be necessary before the President issues such a notification."

Note: In exercise of the powers conferred by Article 370 the President, on the recommendation of the Constituent Assembly of the State of Jammu and Kashmir, declared that as from the 17th day of November 1952, the said Article 370 shall be operative with the modification that for the Explanation in Clause (1) thereof, the following explanation is substituted:

"*Explanation:* For the purpose of this Article, the Government of the State means the person for the time being recognized by the President on the recommendation of the Legislative Assembly of the State as the Sadar-i-Riyasat of Jammu and Kashmir, acting on the advice of the Council of Ministers of the State for the time being in office."

Pakistan attacked the State of J&K with the aid of raiders on October 22nd 1947 and on October 26th 1947; Maharaja Hari Singh surrendered the jurisdiction of three subjects—Defence, Foreign Affairs and Communication to the Union Government. The format of this Instrument of Accession was the same as that of the other heads of the States. The Government of India had insisted that the wishes of the people of J&K State shall also be ascertained. In other words, it was unilaterally committed by the latter that the final decision with regard to accession would be taken by Constituent Assembly of the J&K State. For the intervening period, temporary provision had to be made in the Constitution of India. This was done by incorporating Article 370. In the Congress party other than Pandit Nehru and other few were strongly opposed to the engrafting of this provision. In the biography of Sardar Patel, it is recorded by V Shankar who was his Private Secretary that Pandit Nehru had finalized the draft of the provision in consultation with Sheikh Abdullah, before going to foreign visit. He left it to follow Congress leader Gopalaswami Ayyangar to defend it in parliamentary party. Though Sardar Patel was against this idea, he went ahead. However, due to stiff opposition from Congress members who shouted down even Maulana Abul Kalam Azad on the issue Patel said, "due to international complications, only a provisional approach could be made."

The sum and substance of this Article is that the Indian Parliament can undoubtedly legislate with regard to Defence, Foreign Affairs and Communication and with regard to the items in the Union and Concurrent lists it can legislate with the concurrence of State Government. The Constituent Assembly of J&K ratified the State's accession to India in February 1954. The first order issued by President of India under Article 370 in 1950 applied these provisions of the Indian Constitution which were related to the three subjects stipulated in the Instrument of Accession (Defence, Foreign Affairs, and Communication). Regarding the application of other provisions, discussions were held by the Central Government with Sheikh Abdullah who was then the Prime Minister of the State. An understanding was arrived between the Union India and the State Government and it is known as the Delhi Agreement of 1952. (Note: Constitution Application Orders of 1950 is annexed as Appendix 7.)

Historical Background of Article 370

By virtue of Clause 8 of the Instrument of Accession, Maharaja Hari Singh had given the jurisdiction to the Union of India in matters of external affairs, defence and communications. The Union Parliament had no jurisdiction in any other matter. The sovereignty, in so far as the internal administration of the State was concerned, remained with the ruler, i.e. Maharaja Hari Singh as provided for by virtue of Clause 8 of the Instrument of Accession. This clause has already been reproduced in this book in the 'Instrument of Accession'. In other words, the internal administration of the State even after the accession was governed by Jammu and Kashmir Constitution Act 1939 in which all the powers as a head of the State vested with Maharaja Hari Singh. Under the above said Act, Maharaja had appointed Sheikh Abdullah as Emergency Administrator for the State in 1947 and then as Prime Minister w.e.f. 5th day of March 1948. These matters have already been discussed in detail in this book.

In 1949, the Indian Constituent Assembly was coming to the end of its task. A large number of Indian States had been represented in the Indian Constituent Assembly from the beginning and had taken their share in the framing of the Constitution. When the States entered the Constituent Assembly, it was envisaged that the States would have separate Constitutions for their internal administration but soon it became clear that it was a legacy of the past and have no place in a democratic setup. The rulers and Rajpramukhs of the respective States made the Constitution applicable with some modifications operative in their States by issuing proclamations roundabout on 25th November 1949.

On October 17, 1949, the then Kashmir Affairs Minister Gopalaswami Ayyangar had introduced Article 306(A) (presently Article 370) in the Constituent Assembly of India. Article 306(A) was not included in the original draft of the Constitution presented by the committee set up under the chairmanship of Dr Ambedkar. Dr Ambedkar did not speak a single word in Constituent Assembly on this subject.

When Pandit Nehru asked Sheikh Abdullah to approach Dr Ambedkar on this matter, Dr Ambedkar clearly told Sheikh Abdullah,

> "You want that India should protect Kashmir, Kashmiris should enjoy equal rights in the whole of India, but you don't want to give any right to India and Indians in Kashmir. I am Law Minister of India and cannot betray and deceit my country in this regard."

Except Gopalaswami Ayyangar and Maulana Hasrat Mohani, nobody else took part in the discussion held in this regard in the Constituent Assembly. Even the four members from Jammu and Kashmir did not speak anything and remained mute spectators.

A few days before the discussions in the Constituent Assembly, a discussion was held on this issue in Congress Working Committee. Gopalaswami Ayyangar was isolated in the entire working committee. Only Maulana Abul Kalam Azad was his supporter but he was also asked to keep mum by all others. It is considered that Nehru was aware of this resentment. That is why he had gone on a foreign trip after giving his charge to Sardar Patel. In the end, in order to give respect to Nehru unwillingly Sardar Patel had to come in support of Ayyangar and the Congress Party had taken the decision to include this Article in the Constitution with a view to giving respect to Nehru's will.

In June 1949, the Yuvraj, Dr Karan Singh (as Regent of the State) on the advice of his Council of Ministers nominated four representatives to the Union Constituent Assembly to represent the participation of the J&K State. Under Clause 7 of the Instrument of Accession, Maharaja had not committed himself to the acceptance of any future Constitution of India or to fetter his discretion to enter into arrangements with the Government of India under any such future Constitution. Sheikh Abdullah during his tenure as Prime Minister of the State stressed these two Clauses in favour of the State (that is for himself) but had refused to accept the sovereignty of the ruler (Maharaja Hari Singh) who was the sole authority for making the accession to the Union of India. Sheikh Abdullah's position had been made over the head of the ruler by a unilateral act of the Government of India as in the Instrument of Accession; a clause was inserted without the consent of Maharaja that wishes of the people shall be ascertained. This clause later on proved a handle in the hands of Sheikh Abdullah to blackmail India. The Constitution of India was made applicable by the proclamation issued by Yuvraj Karan Singh which was issued on 25 November 1949. Till then, he had the delegated sovereign authority of the State vested in him as Regent by Maharaja Hari Singh who in the real sense was still a sovereign Head. The first act of retraction and disloyalty done by Sheikh Abdullah in the Constituent Assembly was that he abolished the sovereignty of Maharaja Hari Singh and his progeny despite one written and many oral assurances given from time to time which already stand enumerated and discussed at proper places in this book. The Sheikh could do so because Government of India herself had committed to ascertain the wishes of the people of the State and the trump card was in his hands to win the wishes of the people. The second compulsion was the reference made by the Government of India in UNO regarding the aggression and the threat of holding a Plebiscite which could only be won by Sheikh Abdullah at that time. The other Indian States merged in the sovereign republic of India after the Constitution was made applicable on 26 January 1950 while Sheikh Abdullah was even giving threats that the accession was not complete and the people of J&K had the power of ratification or abrogation. These were only hollow and illegal statements as the accession in the legal way had been made by Maharaja Hari Singh which was final and complete. Sheikh Abdullah at that time had no constitutional or legal status but only qualification which he possessed was that he was a close friend of Pandit Nehru who blindly reposed faith in him in all matters including loyalty to Indian dominion and having secular credentials. The real qualification of Sheikh Abdullah was that he was the head of that political organization National Conference which was opposed to the ideology of Muhammad Ali Jinnah's Muslim League and had affinity with Congress ideology. It had some leaders such as Bakshi Ghulam Mohammad and GM Sadiq who in their core of hearts were secular. During their respective rules as heads of the State administration they tried to treat other two regions of the State at par with Kashmir region. This trust and friendship was misused by Sheikh Abdullah at the first instance against Maharaja Hari Singh who was compelled to go in wilderness. This aspect shall be discussed hereinafter in the next chapter of this book in detail. The foisting of conspiracy case against Sheikh Abdullah by the Government of India is a tell told story. When Constitution of India came into force on 26th January 1950, Article 370 was to cover the case of Jammu and Kashmir State alone. Sardar Patel, the then Minister of States in India, in the Indian Constituent Assembly declared, "in view of the special problem with which the Jammu and Kashmir Government is faced, we have made special provisions for the continuance of the State with the Union on the existing basis." The existing basis were the basis of Instrument of Accession and the Special Provisions were embodied in Article 370 of the Constitution of India.

The Article has been described as Temporary Provision because the power to finalise the constitutional relationship between the State and the Union of India had been specifically vested in the Jammu and Kashmir Constituent Assembly. The Constitution of India clearly envisaged the convening of a Constituent Assembly for Jammu and Kashmir State and also provides that whatever modifications, amendments or exceptions that might become necessary either to Article 370 or to any other Articles in the Constitution of India in their application to Jammu and Kashmir State were subject to the decision of that Assembly. Taking advantage of the word 'Temporary' in the above said Article, Sheikh Abdullah started saying that Article is not capable of being abrogated, modified or replaced temporarily. In the

Constituent Assembly of the State, in the debate held on 11th August 1952, Sheikh Abdullah had said, "I would like to make it clear that any suggestions of altering arbitrarily the basis of our relationship with India not only constitute a breach of the spirit and letter of the Constitution, but it may invite serious consequences for a harmonious association of our State with India." Since the State of Jammu and Kashmir had become an integral part of India after the execution of the Instrument of Accession, therefore, Clause (1)(c) of Article 370 provides for the application of Article 1 of the Constitution of India which defines the territory of India. The State was shown in the Constitution as a Part B State, but the provisions of Article 238, which generally governed the relationship of Part B States with the Union of India, were not applicable to this State (Note: The distinction between Part A, B and C States has since been abolished by the States Reorganization Act, 1957).

Clause (b)(ii) provides for the addition to the matters in the Instrument of Accession with the concurrence of the Government of the State. After this sub-clause followed explanation in the original context of the Article 370 that Government of the State meant "Maharaja of Jammu and Kashmir acting on the advice of Council of Ministers." In 1952, the Constituent Assembly of Jammu and Kashmir, on the recommendations of the Basic Principle's Committee, abolished the hereditary rulership and substituted in its place an elected head designated Sadar-i-Riyasat. This necessitated the change of the explanation of what the Government of the State meant. Accordingly, the President of India on the recommendations of the Constituent Assembly of Jammu and Kashmir, modified the explanation to read:

> *Explanation*: For the purpose of this Article, the Government of the State means the person for the time being recognized by the President on the recommendation of the Legislative Assembly of the State as the Sadar-i-Riyasat of Jammu and Kashmir, acting on the advice of the Council of Ministers of the State for the time being in office.

The amendment accepted the act of the Constituent Assembly of Jammu and Kashmir for abolishing hereditary rulership and substituting the elected head of the State.

Note: This is the only amendment so far made from 1950 till date in Article 370. The amendment is a shining example for every patriotic Indian to think over the aspect that Government of India had totally forgotten the assurances given to the ruler of the State Maharaja Hari

Singh which are contained in Clauses (7) and (8) of the Instrument of Accession. These assurances were of bilateral nature and carried more weight and sanctity both legal and moral against unilateral assurance which was being exploited by Sheikh Abdullah regarding ascertaining the wishes of the people. The clauses clearly recite that without the consent of Maharaja nothing could be added or subtracted in the Indian Constitution. The unilateral clause was outside the scope of Indian Independence Act of 1947 read with Government of India Act, 1935 because only the rulers of the States in the undivided India had been given the absolute power to accede to any of the newly created two dominions. The policy adopted by Indian National Congress was a political policy to ascertain the wishes of the people through their representatives and not by holding a Referendum. The concerned dominion under law could either accept the offer of accession or reject the same but there was no scope for Conditional Accession. The elected representatives of the State in the J&K Constituent Assembly had expressed their wishes in respect of State of Jammu and Kashmir. This was a special concession illegally given to please Sheikh Abdullah which in due course of ltime was fulfilled in the prescribed manner. But Sheikh Abdullah on his part after abolishing the sovereignty of the Maharaja had started challenging the accession itself and for such an act of collusion with foreign powers in 1953 he had to be removed from the scene of power by the same Constituent Assembly by passing vote of No Confidence Motion.

Not only that, 1974 Indira-Sheikh Accord mentions that, "The State of Jammu and Kashmir which is a Constituent Unit of the Union of India, shall, in its relation with the Union, continue to be governed by Article 370 of the Constitution of India." Article 370 in 1974 in practice had not remained the same as it was during Sheikh Abdullah's first rule when he was Prime Minister from 1948 to 1953. 'The State Government' as defined in the amended Article 370 with explanation substituted at the end was done at the behest of Sheikh Abdullah. At that time, he did not even conceive that this very amendment would in future allow application of many beneficial provisions of the Indian Constitution in favour of the people of the State to strengthen the democracy and weaken the self-rule which Sheikh Abdullah had imposed in the State even in a more vigorous manner than the autocratic rule of Maharaja Hari Singh. This aspect of arbitrary functioning has been discussed in details already in this book. In his absence, the people became lucky to enjoy the Fundamental Rights with very few modifications as contained in Part III in the Indian Constitution. These rights are akin to natural rights which were not in existence during Sheikh's rule. The jurisdiction of Supreme Court of India was extended along with the jurisdiction of Auditor-General and Controller of Government of India and Election Commissioner of India etc. It is unfortunate that the successors of Sheikh Abdullah, i.e. his son and grandson after the Accord of 1974, many a times to pamper the separatist elements in the society in the State are raising the issue of taking the State back to the position of 1953 when Sheikh Abdullah was ruling the State. Recently Chief Minister Omar Abdullah is repeatedly issuing statements that State of J&K has not merged with Union of India. (The writer of this book has already discussed this topic in Chapter 8 (pages 186-87) of this book.) During Sheikh's rule because of constitutional order of 1950 and Agreement of 1952 only few Articles of Indian Constitution were allowed to be extended to the State of Jammu and Kashmir. These orders would be discussed hereinafter. This is a nefarious political game plan to keep intact the vote bank of anti-nationals and thereby allow the pot of separatist's elements boiling in the State as well as creating uncertainty and encouraging the alienation of the people from joining the political mainstream of the country. At times such like leaders who resort to this unholy and unethical political utterances when find themselves in adverse conditions they approach the State High Court and the Supreme Court of India for getting their grievances redressed including enforcement of statutory and Fundamental Rights.

Clause (b)(ii) provides for the addition to the matters in the Instrument of Accession with the concurrence of the Government of the State. This was provided for subsequent enlargement of the Union power if this were deemed necessary in the interests of the Union or the State.

According to Clause (1)(c), the only Articles of the Constitution of India which applied for their own force to the State are Articles 1 and 370; Clause (1)(d) provided that the other provisions of the Constitution of India applicable to the State could be determined by the President of India in consultation with the Government of the State. Exceptions and modifications could be made in the same manner and the provisions could be enlarged too. The High Court of Jammu and Kashmir in the case of Sant Singh *vs* State (AIR 1959 J&K 35) had held, "Power to modify includes a power to enlarge or add to an existing provision."

Clause (2) provides that, if the Government of Jammu and Kashmir recommended to the President of India an enlargement of the powers of the Union Parliament by including matters other than those referred to in the Instrument of Accession, such recommendations should be placed before the Constituent Assembly of the State. Thus, in effect the power to extend the scope of the Union power or otherwise change the basis of relationship of Jammu and Kashmir with India was vested in the Constituent Assembly of the State. The arrangement made under Article 370 was to continue until the Constituent Assembly of the State made a decision to the contrary.

Clause (3) provides that the Constituent Assembly could recommend the President of India to abrogate, modify or to make it applicable with exceptions. The President could not, however, take these steps without the previous recommendations of the Constituent Assembly of the State.

Under Article 370(1)(ii), the President of India in consultation with the Government of Jammu and Kashmir, issued *"The Constitution (Application to Jammu and Kashmir) Order, 1950* specifying the matters on which the Union Parliament would be competent to make laws for the State. This order was to govern the constitutional relationship of Jammu and Kashmir with India after the Indian Constitution came into force on 26th January 1950.

Some argue that the President may, by Public notification under Article 370(3), declare that Article 370 shall cease to be operative and no recommendation of the Constituent Assembly is needed as it does not exist any longer. Others say it can be amended by an Amendment Act under Article 368 of the Constitution and the amendment extended under Article 370(1). Section 147 of the Constitution of Jammu and Kashmir states no Bill or amendment seeking to make any change in the provisions of the Constitution of India as applicable in relation to the State, shall be introduced or moved in either house of the legislature. As per Section 5 of the Constitution of Jammu and Kashmir the executive and legislative power of the State extends to all matters except those with respect to which Parliament has power to make laws for the State under the provisions of the Constitution of India as applicable in relation to this State.

Section 3 of the Constitution of Jammu and Kashmir states that the State of Jammu and Kashmir is an and shall be an integral part of Union of India. The Constitution of the State was adopted and enacted on 17th November 1956. Around 260 Articles of the Constitution of India has been applied in the State of Jammu and Kashmir from time to time.

Jammu and Kashmir Constituent Assembly was constituted in 1951. The separate Constitution of the State of Jammu and Kashmir is the product of Article 370. Because of inclusion of Article 370 in the

Indian Constitution, the provisions of remaining Articles cannot be made applicable in the Jammu and Kashmir State by any Presidential Order until it is ratified by the J&K Constituent Assembly. This is why J&K Constituent Assembly was constituted in 1951. It was after the assent of the J&K Constituent Assembly under the powers rest in Article 370 that the President of India promulgated the implementation of Article 370 in the State on November 17, 1952. Under Article 35(A) of the Indian Constitution, only those Jammu and Kashmir residents residing there before 1954 could have Permanent Resident Certificate and can avail all the basic rights of citizenship in the State. The persons of rest of India cannot be Permanent Residents of the State. That is why the residents of rest of India can neither get employment, nor purchase property in the State of Jammu and Kashmir and they cannot have the right to vote in the State. Article 35(A) was inserted by Section 2(4)(j) of the order, 1954 and not enacted by Indian Parliament.

Consequential Effects of Article 370

1. Hindu refugees (presently about 2 lakh) migrated from West Pakistan into J&K State in 1947 are still deprived of the basic rights of citizenship; whereas the then Prime Minister Sheikh Abdullah had settled them in the areas for the security of unprotected borders. Most of them are Harijans and of other backward classes. Their children neither get any scholarship nor are entitled to get admissions in the Professional courses in J&K State. They are living like slaves in their own country even after 66 years of Independence.
2. Senior administrative and police officers who come here from rest of India through their official postings are also deprived of the basic rights of citizenship in the State. Some years back they had formed a housing cooperative society to get residential plots in the State but all the political leaders primarily from Kashmir Valley and backed by Jammu leaders of the coalition party in the Government (Congress) raised hue and cry and their action was severely condemned. The scheme ended in damp squib.
3. In 1956, Bakshi Ghulam Mohammad the then Prime Minister of J&K, duly invited 70 families of Valmiki community (sweepers) to get their services for cleansing the city of Jammu because of dearth of local sweepers. Now their families have increased up to 600 family units but they have not been

confirmed against those menial jobs. Even their residential colony has not been regularized.

4. Backward classes cannot enjoy the benefits of reservation of non-implementation of the recommendations of Mandal Commission.
5. Harijans in Kashmir Valley known as sweepers and Mochis etc, did not get any reservation benefit from 1947 to 2007. In 2007, the Supreme Court by its order had found them entitled for reservation benefits in Kashmir Valley but the State Assembly passed a law and thereby rendered the Supreme Court judgment not relevant for the State of Jammu and Kashmir.
6. Even the useful laws such as Wealth Tax, Gift Tax, Urban Land Ceiling Act are not made applicable in the State.
7. The 73rd and 74th Constitutional Amendment Acts regarding decentralization of administration have also not been implemented so far. Even though the Panchayat elections were held in the State after a long gap but still so many years have passed, the present government is creating every hurdle in the way to make them fully functional.
8. Even today 135 Articles of the Indian Constitution are not applicable in the State. The amendments made in the Indian Penal Code, Criminal Procedure Code, Civil Procedure Code in the centre are made applicable to corresponding State Acts to the extent which suits the rulers of the State and not as a whole for the benefit of residents of the State.
9. Tenure of State Assembly is 6 years, whereas in the rest of country it is 5 years. The minority community of Hindus has been deprived by not constituting a Commission for Minorities in the State whereas in all other States because of the mandates of Supreme Court judgments such Commissions have been set-up for the protection of minorities.
10. Even the emergency powers of the President of India are not applicable here.
11. The Central Public oriented benevolent Acts such as Right to Information Act and Consumer Protection Act are not applicable but the State has enacted its own Acts which are not at para materia with those Acts on all matters relating to Public Welfare. The State is very slow in affecting amendments which are made in these Central Acts to remove some defects and make them more beneficial for the Public. In order to curb

corruption amongst the public functionaries (both politicians and bureaucrats), in the rest of the country every State has appointed Lokayuktas giving them plenary powers to get the offences of corruption investigated by the investigating agency under its control and then accordingly recommend the convictions for the guilty but in Jammu and Kashmir, the Accountability Commission is only of a recommendatory nature which means a teethless institution. It is a defunct institution without the requisite strength of staff members. At present there are hardly 10 pending cases before it. The Accountability Commission has filed writ petitions in the High Court of Jammu and Kashmir seeking relief in the nature of mandatory nature to provide it the required staff members. There are instances that when in the beginning it was one-man Commission headed by a retired Supreme Court judge, some recommendations were made against some guilty persons but in response some of them were given promotions and plum postings. The authority of the Commission was diluted by increasing the number of members (retired High Court judges) making a total of three including Chairman but subsequently substituted by two members. The jurisdiction was curtailed by taking away the public servants from its purview. A retired Additional High Court Judge has also functioned as its Chairman. All this can happen in the State of Jammu and Kashmir.

12. There is gender discrimination in the State as the offsprings of the female residents married outside the State cannot inherit the properties of their respective mothers.

13. The salient features of the following Articles of the Indian Constitution made applicable in the State with certain modifications are highlighted which are detrimental from the security point of view of the nation as well as for the interests of the residents of the State as a whole:

    (i) In Article 3 of the Indian Constitution, further proviso is added in this manner:

    "Provided further that no Bill providing for increasing or diminishing the area of the State of J&K or altering the name or boundary of that State shall be introduced in Parliament without the consent of the Legislature of the State."

    (ii) In Article 7 of the Constitution the following further proviso was added:

"Provided further that nothing in this Article shall apply to a permanent residents of the State of J&K who having so migrated to the territory now included in Pakistan, returns to the territory of the State under a permit for settlement in the State or permanent return issued by or under the authority of any law made by the Legislature of that State, and every such person shall be deemed to be a Citizen of India."

The Supreme Court in the case of Rehman Shagoo *vs* State of J&K (AIR, 1960, SC, 1) said: "When certain subjects were made over to the Government of India by the Instrument of Accession, the State retained its power to legislate even on those subjects so long as the State law was not repugnant to any law made by the Central Legislature." Again the Supreme Court of India in the case of Puran Lal Lakhanpal *vs* Resident of India 1962 SCR 1 in a Constitution Bench case dealt with the scope of Article 370 and held that State Legislature has to be consulted for the application of the provisions of the Constitution of India which exclusively do not fall under list 1 and within the ambit of Instrument of Accession. In another case, which is also a decision rendered by the Constitution Bench of the Supreme Court in the case of Mohd Maqbool Damnoo *vs* State of J&K 1972 1 SCC 536. It has been held:

"The essential feature of Article 370, Sub-Clauses 1(b) and (d) is the necessity of concurrence of the State Government or the consultation of the State Government.

Article 370(1)(b) and Article 370(1)(d) place no limitation on the framing or amendment of the Constitution of J&K. If there is any limitation it is found in the Constitution of the State. Section 147 of the Constitution of J&K provides that under that Section, the Indian Constitution cannot be amended.

Now, the Governor instead of Sadar-i-Riyasat is competent to give the concurrence stipulated in Article 370 and perform other functions laid down by the J&K Constitution. He is successor of Sadar-i-Riyasat."

(iii) Article 21 and 14 are excluded by Article 35(A) of the Constitution of India to some extent in respect of Citizens of India. Article 21 gives a Fundamental Right for the protection of life and liberty. The Supreme Court in a number of its judgments has accepted that, "Life to its expanded horizon includes all that give meaning to a man's life including his tradition, culture and heritage and protection of that heritage in its full measure would certainly come within the compass of Article 21." In the case of Madhu Kishwar *vs* State of Bihar (1996) 5 SCC 125, the Supreme Court has held, 'Denial of Right' to succession to Scheduled Tribe women amounts to deprivation of their Right to livelihood under Article 21. The progenies of the daughters of Jammu and Kashmir State are denied the right of inheritance. Similarly, the citizens who are residents of the State stand discriminated on this basis of sex and this disqualification has been discussed above. In this way, the protection of Fundamental Rights guaranteed to every citizen of India under Article 14 and Article 15 also stand denied.

According to the view of the writer of this book the insertion of Article 35(A) in the Indian Constitution falls within the grey area to be debated in a Constitutional Court for its legality. The Article provides for saving of laws with respect to the permanent residents of their rights. This Article runs in the teeth of the Preambles of the Indian Constitution as well as that of the Jammu and Kashmir State Constitution.

When Sheikh Abdullah came into power after withdrawal of support given by Congress party to provide him seat of Chief Ministership, the elections were held and he secured the seat of Chief Ministership on his own by playing the communal card which fact has already been discussed herein fore. He had secured 2/3rd majority in the legislature. A significant event took place, when in 1980; the Resettlement Bill was introduced for the return of those persons who were Class I and Class II State Subjects before May 14, 1954 and had migrated to the territory of Pakistan after March 1947. Those migrants, their widows, wives or descendants could return and settle in the State. The Bill was sent to Governor for his signatures so that it becomes an Act. But the Governor did not sign it and referred to the Attorney General of India for his opinion. The Governor after receiving the opinion sent back the Bill pointing out the defects requiring the legislature for reconsideration under the provisions of Section 78 of the J&K Constitution.

On 30 September 1982, the President made a reference to the Supreme Court under Article 143 seeking its advisory opinion. The reference remained pending for about nine years but on 6 November

2001 when Dr AS Anand a State Subject himself was the Chief Justice of India, the matter was referred to a Constitution Bench of the Supreme Court which declined to answer the question in the affirmative as the State Assembly after heated debate had re-passed the Bill and the same in 1982 had become an Act. In less than one week after the Constitution Bench had returned the reference unanswered, the J&K National Panthers Party filed writ petition (Civil number 578/ 2001 in the Supreme Court) challenging the constitutionality of the Act. The operation of the Act was stayed. The final verdict is awaited but the present government headed by Sheikh Abdullah's grandson Omar Abdullah with the support of coalition government of Congress(I) has formulated a more dangerous rehabilitation policy for the militants who were residents of the State before exfiltration to Pakistan or Pakistan occupied area of J&K State even after 1954 for receiving militancy related training and now want to come back and join the mainstream of the political administration in the State. Those persons under this policy even can bring back their wives who are Pakistani residents and children born out of them. This is being done under the aid of Article 7 of the Constitution of India. Of course, there is a rider that their return would be outcome after proper scrutiny by a competent authority appointed by the State. This is a policy impregnated with great security risks but is being carried out to make the vote bank in favour of the ruling coalition partners.

Why Article 370 was Included in the Constitution?

Article 370 was included in the Constitution as stated above because at that time war was going on in the State with Pakistan and a dispute regarding accession was pending in UNO. Because of these special conditions the Article was inserted on temporary basis. Later on, the situation was normalized and the Instrument of Accession was ratified by the Constituent Assembly. Thereafter, many elections have been held even under the supervision of Election Commission of India after 1962 and in the Preamble of the J&K Constitution which came into force on 26 January 1957, it has been clearly stated:

> "We, the people of the State of J&K, having unanimously resolved in the presence of accession of this State of India which took place on the 26th day of October 1947 do further define the existing relationship of the State with the Union of India as an integral part thereof and to secure to ourselves: Justice, social, economic and political, liberty of thought, expression, belief, faith and worship;

> equality of status and of opportunity and to provide among us all; fraternity assuring the dignity of the individual and the unity of the Nation...."

The Special Status should have come to cease after 1954 as the situation had normalized and Constituent Assembly made the ratification of the accession in the Assembly which was the policy of the Central Government, expressed in the unilateral clause inserted by the then Governor-General of India after accepting the accession. This clause was not the requirement of the relevant law governing the accession contained in Indian Independence Act of 1947 read with Government of India Act of 1935. The continuations of Article 370, separate flag of the State are symbols of separatism under the protection of Article 370. Maharaja Hari Singh who had made the absolute accession with the dominion of India had wrote a letter to Sardar Patel on July 15, 1948 in which he had clearly stated that we are interested in the progress of whole of India. His words are reproduced hereunder:

> "Everybody is aware of my view on this issue and I have expressed it on several occasions. In brief, we want due place in the new constitutional structure of India. We hope that India will emerge as a great country in the world and will contribute in the solution of problems of mankind through its influence and global fraternity as well as great culture."

In the Security Council on 5 February 1948, Sheikh Abdullah had made a speech that accession to India is complete and unquestionable. Thereafter when Constitution of Jammu and Kashmir was enacted, Sections 5 and 147 had reiterated this position that Integration of the State is legally and politically complete.

The continuation of the Article suits the Kashmir Valley centric mainstream political organisations to rule over the peoples of other two regions, i.e. Jammu and Ladakh and this is happening because of weak government in the Centre except for few intervals but because of paucity of time they could not achieve this object. Now, with a strong government in the Centre a golden opportunity is available when by discussions and debates it should be churned out whether abrogation or amendments are required to be made in this Article to do away with the sense of segregation from the mainstream lurking in the minds of some segments of society. The report of Gajendragadkar Commission has taken cognizance of irritations and tensions. In Paragraph 7.16 of the report it is stated, "the government and the people of the J&K State may themselves decide when Article 370 should be abrogated." The

State has remained most backward for industrialisation and outside investment in the State. The educated youth want job opportunities which can be provided in large numbers in the private sector. The Valley very soon be connected with rail service. In case the youths are involved in developmental activities they shall not fall prey to separatist elements. All the inhabitants of three regions want to preserve their separate entities and the existing laws are sufficient to protect and preserve alienation of land wealth of the State. When peace and tranquillity would be pervading under an effective and honest government Article 370 which is of purely temporary nature would lose its significance.

Before this chapter is closed it is reiterated that Article 370 is only of temporary nature and was engrafted in the Constitution by way of a stop gap arrangement. It can be abrogated as it does not have any qualification to be called as one of the basic features of the Indian Constitution.

The Constitution (Application to J&K) Order 1950 dated 26 January 1950

In exercise of the powers conferred by Article 370(1)(ii), the President of India issued this order in consultation with the State Government and specified the matters with respect to which the Union Parliament would be competent to make laws for the said State.

Mainly it was elaboration of the subjects already specified in the 'Instrument of Accession', but certain additions were also made. Two Schedules were added.

The first Schedule related to the jurisdiction of the Union Parliament over the State and enumerated the appropriate items in the Union list of the Seventh Schedule to the Indian Constitution. The power of Parliament to make laws for the State was limited to the matters specified in this Schedule. The items were:

(1) Defence Entries 1 to 6.
(2) Preventive detention for the reasons connected with defence, foreign affairs and the security of India: Entry 9.
(3) Foreign Affairs: Entries 10 to 22.
(4) Communications: Entries 25 to 31.
(5) Trade and commerce with foreign countries: Entry 41.
(6) Matters relating to Parliament: Entries 72 to 74.
(7) Union Executive and Supreme Court: Entries 93 to 96.

Some other entries like those of 'Audit of Accounts' (Entry 76) and Railways (Entry 22) were applied with modifications.

The result of the application of this Schedule was that both the concurrent and the State list were not applicable to J&k State. Also, anything not contained in the First Schedule was within the exclusive powers of the State. The effect was that unlike other States, the residency power belonged to the State.

The Second Schedule tabulated to the provisions of the Constitution which in addition to Article 1 and Article 370, were to apply in relation to Kashmir. The parts of the Constitution of India made applicable to the State were:

Part V: This part deals with the Union Executive.

It was made applicable to the State with some exceptions and modifications. The main exceptions related to the powers of Supreme Court. The Supreme Court could have jurisdiction in respect of disputes under Article 131 only and Fundamental Rights were not applied, therefore no jurisdiction. The reason for such exclusion was that there was Board of Judicial Advisors in the State of which the appeals of High Court lay. The Draconian Law known as Big Landed Estates Abolition Act would have been struck down as it infringed Fundamental Rights guaranteed under Article 31 and Act would have been struck down.

This might suggest that there was no security for life and liberty in the State and that case infringing the recognized democratic liberties were not liable to avoidance for unconstitutionally. This was the game plan of Sheikh Abdullah.

Article 80 and 81, which deal with the composition of the House of the People and the Council of States was to apply with some modifications, the result was that representatives of the State in both the above said houses were to be appointed by the President of India in consultation with the Government of the State unlike other State where they were elected directly by the People in the House of People and in the Council of States by the Legislative Assemblies of the States.

Articles 54 and 55 deal with the election of President were also applicable with modification as appointed members had to give their votes.

Parts XI and XII deal with the relations between the Union and the States. Parts XI was made applicable with some exceptions and modifications with effect being that Legislative power over matters not enumerated in the Legislative list which vested in the centre, in case of

J&K vested to the State itself. Although item 14 on the Union list gives Parliament Legislative power with respect to agreements and treaties with other countries but this could not be done in respect of dispose of the territory of the State because of the commitment of Government of India that the power to finalise the future of the State vested in the State Constituent Assembly. (Nehru's Broadcast from the All India Radio on November 2, 1947. He had said, "We had declared that the fate of Kashmir is ultimately to be decided by the People.")

Part XII deals with finance. The appropriations from them was in its application to J&K restricted to the funds and Accounts of the Union. Article 282 and 283 had also thus, restricted application.

The Income Tax Department of the State was free from central controls. (Later on Income Tax Act was made applicable.) The State had its own Customs Department established during British period. Later on it was amalgamated with the Indian Excise Department on the initiative of the State.

Under Article 257, the Union Government has no power to give directions to J&K State to ensure compliance with Acts of Parliament or to ensure that Executive power of the Union Government is not prejudiced.

Part XV: It deals with elections. This was made applicable to the State Subject to some exceptions and modifications. Article 324 deals with the superintendence, direction and control of elections. It applied to the State only to the election of the President and Vice President of India. The Election Commission of India had no other jurisdiction in Kashmir. The jurisdiction has been extended from 1962. Article 334 which places a time limit on reservation of seats in the House of the People and the State Legislature applied only in so far as it related to House of the People. Article 335 which calls for special consideration of the claims of Scheduled Castes and Tribes to appointment in the Public Services applied only in so far as it related to the Union Services.

Part XVIII: Relates to the official language. The provisions were applicable so far they related to the proceedings in the Supreme Court. The official language had to be decided by Constituent Assembly of the State. Article 351 which relates to the promotion of Hindi language did not apply to the State.

Article 361 provides that the President, Governors are not liable to answer in any court for acts done or purported to be done in the exercise of their official duties. The application was done partial applicable to the President only. At the time of this order, there was in force in the J&K State, the Constitution Act 1939 and according to its provisions the acts of the ruler could not the questioned at all. Now this Article has been made applicable in 1954 when Sadar-i-Riyasat was elected. Article 364 which relates to the powers of the President to exclude or modify the legislation to ports and aerodromes was to apply to the State only so far as it applied to the laws made by the Parliament. The President had no power to modify or declare inoperative any law made by the State.

Article 365 which empowered the President to suspend the Government of a State on failure to comply with a direction given by the Union was not to apply to J&K.

Article 368 which sets out the procedure for amending the Constitution. In its application to J&K, it is subject to further proviso, viz provided further that no such amendment shall have effect in relation to the State of J&K unless applied by order of the President under Clause (1) of Article 370. This meant that the amendment of the Constitution of India can apply to J&K State only if the State Government (and later the Constituent Assembly of the State) agreed. This was a safeguard ensuring the continuance of relationship of State with India on the existing basis.

Of the nine Schedules in the Constitution of India only five were made applicable to the State.

Directive principles as contained in part IV of the Indian Constitution were not made applicable because the Constituent Assembly of the State had to determine them. Now, the Constitution of J&K contains Directive Principles according to the National Conference's manifesto of 1944. It is noteworthy that Constitution of J&K does not say anything about the concept of secularism as is contained in Indian Constitution.

In the application of Article 352 to this State, the President of India had no power to issue a proclamation in case of general emergency arising from internal disturbance. Article 356 enables the President to issue proclamations of emergency on the "failure of constitutional machinery in the State," empowering the Union to suspend the State Legislature and control the State Executive did not extend to the State.

From the discussion of this order, it is evident that the powers of the Union Parliament with regard to this State were extended beyond what was originally surrendered under the Instrument of Accession.

The constitutional relationship of the State in the Union immediately after the inauguration of the Constitution of India was to be governed by this order of 1950.

On 1st May 1951, Yuvraj Karan Singh issued proclamation to constitute Constituent Assembly consisting of representatives of the People, elected on the basis of adult franchise for framing the Constitution and for that purpose of the election, the State had to be divided in to territorial constituencies.

A Delimitation Committee shall be setup by the government to make recommendations as to the number of constituencies and the limit of each constituency.

The elections to the Assembly were completed by the month of August of the same year and on 31st October 1951, the first meeting of the Assembly was held in Kashmir. Sheikh Abdullah called this day as the 'day of destiny'. A day which comes only once in the life of a nation. (Refer Opening address of Sheikh Abdullah). He called the Assembly a 'Sovereign Authority' and told the members that whatever they decided had, "the irrevocable force of law."

He then listed the main objects and functions of the Constituent Assembly as follows:

(1) To frame a Constitution for the further governance of the country;
(2) To decide about the future of royal dynasty;
(3) To decide whether compensation should be paid to landowners for the expropriation of the Big Landed Estates, carried out in pursuance of the Land Abolition Act;
(4) To declare its reasoned conclusion regarding accession and future of the State.

He enumerated these alternatives: accession to India, accession to Pakistan or Complete Independence.

Committee was formed and the Assembly turned to its tasks. By August 9, 1953, it had made the following major decisions:

(i) On the recommendations of the Basic Principles committee, no compensation should be paid for the expropriation of the Big Landed Estates;
(ii) On the recommendations of the 'Basic Principles Committee':
  (a) That the basis of the political set up of the State should be fully democratic;
  (b) That the 'Hereditary Rulership' should be abolished and instead there should be an elected head of the State to be designated as 'Sadar-i-Riyasat';
  (c) That the State should have its own flag.

With these decisions, two functions of the Assembly were complete, the future of the royal dynasty and compensation to the landowners.

The Assembly, however, did not take any decision with regard to the accession, but set up a Drafting Committee, for drafting the Constitution for the State.

Note: It is noteworthy that on 8 August 1953, Yuvraj Karan Singh as Regent of the State had dismissed the government headed by Sheikh Abdullah and he had been arrested. He was succeeded by his number 2 in the Cabinet Bakshi Ghulam Mohammad who proved his majority in the Constituent Assembly. The rest of the development changes have been discussed in this book in full details.

Delhi Agreement 1952

After the Constituent Assembly of the State had taken important decision referred to immediately above, it was deemed necessary to receive the concurrence of the Union of India. Accordingly, representatives of the State Government conferred with representatives of Indian Government and arrived at an agreement. This agreement was later on known as the 'Delhi Agreement, 1952'.

The main features of this agreement are:

(i) in view of the uniform and consistent stand taken up by the Jammu and Kashmir Constituent Assembly that sovereignty in all matters other than those specified in the Instrument of Accession continues to reside in the State, Government of India agreed that, while the residuary powers of Legislature vested in the centre in respect of all States other than Jammu and Kashmir, in the case of the latter they vested in the State itself;

(ii) it was agreed between the two governments that in accordance with Article 5 of the Indian Constitution, person who have their domicile in Jammu and Kashmir shall be regarded as Citizens of India, but the State Legislature was given power to make laws for conferring special rights and privileges on the 'State Subjects' in view of the 'State Subject Notifications of 1927 and 1932: the State Legislature was also empowered to make laws for the 'State Subjects' who had gone to Pakistan on account of the communal disturbances of 1947, in the event of their return to Kashmir;

(iii) as the President of India commands the same respect in the State as he does in the other units of India, Articles 52 to 62 of the Constitution relating to him should be applicable to the State. It was further agreed that the power to grant reprieves, pardons and remission of sentences etc, would also vest in the President of India;

(iv) the Union Government agreed that the State should have its own flag in addition to the Union flag, but it was agreed by the State Government that the State flag would not be a rival of the Union flag; it was also recognised that the Union flag should have the same status and position in Jammu and Kashmir as in the Rest of India, but for historical reasons connected with the freedom struggle in the State, the need for continuance of the State flag was recognised;

(v) there was complete agreement with regard to the position of the Sadar-i-Riyasat; though the Sadar-i-Riyasat was to be elected by the State Legislature, he had to be recognised by the President of India before his installation as such; in other Indian States the head of the State was appointed by the President and was as such his nominee but the person to be appointed as the Head, had to be a person acceptable to the Government of that State; no person who is not acceptable to the State Government can be thrust on the State as the Head; The difference in the case of Kashmir lies only in the fact that Sadar-i-Riyasat will in the first place be elected by the State legislature itself instead of being a nominee of the government and the President of India. With regard to the powers and functions of the Sadar-i-Riyasat the following argument was mutually agreed upon;

(a) the head of the State shall be a person recognised by the President of the Union on the recommendations of the Legislature of the State;

(b) he shall hold office during the pleasure of the President;

(c) he may, by writing under his hands addressed to the President, resign his office;

(d) subject to the foregoing provisions, the head of the State shall hold office for a term of five years from the date he enters upon his office;

(e) provided that he shall, notwithstanding the expiration of his term, continue to hold the office until his successor enters upon his office;

(vi) with regard to the Fundamental Rights, some basic principles agreed between the parties were enunciated; it was accepted that the people of the State were to have Fundamental Rights. But in view of the peculiar position in which the State was placed, the whole chapter relating to 'Fundamental Rights' of the Indian Constitution could not be made applicable to the State, the question which remained to be determined was whether the chapter on Fundamental Rights should form a part of the State Constitution or of the Constitution of India as applicable to the State;

(vii) with regard to the jurisdiction of the Supreme Court of India, it was accepted that for the time being, owing to the existence of the Board of Judicial Advisors in the State, which was the highest judicial authority in the State, the Supreme Court should have only appellate jurisdiction;

(viii) there was a great deal of discussion with regard to the 'Emergency Powers', the Government of India insisted on the application of Article 352, empowering the President to proclaim a general emergency in the State; the State Government argued that in exercise of its powers over defence (Item 1 on the Union List), in the event of war or external aggression, the Government of India would have full authority to take steps and proclaim emergency but the State delegation was, however, averse to the President exercising the power to proclaim a general emergency on account of internal disturbance.

In order to meet the viewpoint of the State's delegation, the Government of India agreed to the modification of Article 352 in its application to Kashmir by the addition of the following words:

> but in regard to internal disturbance at the request or with the concurrence of the Government of the State.

At the end of Clause (1) both the parties agreed that the application of Article 356, dealing with suspension of the State Constitution and Article 360, dealing with financial emergency was not necessary.

The facts analysed above make it clear that the State of Jammu and Kashmir enjoys a special position in the Union of India, and this position of the State has been permitted by Article 2 of the Constitution itself. "In arriving at this agreement," declared Sheikh Abdullah, the then Prime Minister of Jammu and Kashmir, "the main consideration before our government was to secure a position for the State which would be consistent with the requirement of maximum autonomy for the local organs of the State power which are the ultimate source of authority in the State while discharging obligations as a unit of the federation."

The Jammu and Kashmir Constituent Assembly discussed this agreement and finally adopted a motion of approach on August 21st, 1952.

The Agreement was discussed in the Union Parliament on August 7, 1952 and accepted. (Refer Lok Sabha debates, August 1952.)

Despite this mutually accepted Agreement Sheikh Abdullah was causing intentional delay in its implementation. He started advocating secession, which would make Kashmir an Independent State. It has been discussed in this book that USA was instigating him to take this course. He was accused both by his colleagues in the Cabinet and Public outside of trying to create a State for himself. Three members of his cabinet submitted in a memorandum accusing him of various charges (Current Affairs Publication, Kashmir, August 7–September 17, New Delhi 1953). Sadar-i-Riyasat, Dr Karan Singh took cognizance and on August 9, 1953 dismissed Sheikh Abdullah from the post of Prime Minister and dissolved the Cabinet. In a nutshell the above said Agreement was not implemented during Sheikh's rule as Prime Minister.

The relevant portion of the order of dismissal read:

> "I, Karan Singh, Sadar-i-Riyasat, functioning in the interest of the people of the State who have reposed the responsibility and authority of the Headship of the State in me, do hereby dismiss Sheikh Mohammed Abdullah, from the Prime Ministership of the State of J&K, and consequently the Council of Ministers headed by you. (As reproduced in current Affairs Publication, Kashmir, August 17 New Delhi).

On the same day, the Sadar-i-Riyasat invited Bakshi Ghulam Mohammad, the erstwhile Deputy Prime Minister, to form the new Cabinet. On 9th August 1953, Sheikh Abdullah was arrested at Gulmarg, a health resort in the valley under the Preventive Detention Act. He was released about 4 years later in 1958 but was shortly re-arrested on a charge of 'Conspiracy to overthrow the Government'. His staunch follower Mirza Afzal Beg, Revenue Minister along with some others were also arrested. A case against him and few others was tried by a Special Magistrate in Jammu and committed to the Court of Sessions Judge. This case has been discussed in this book at appropriate place.

This was a special case where 'No Confidence Motion' was not required because Head of State was obliged to ensure the continuance of State Government in case he had reasonable grounds to believe that Chief Minister (then Prime Minister) had lost the confidence of the people or if he was engaged in treasonable activities. This was a time when Assembly was not in session. The Sadar-i-Riyasat wrote to Bakshi Ghulam Mohammad, "the continuance in office of new cabinet will depend upon its securing a vote of confidence from the Legislative Assembly during its coming session." The State Legislature met on October 5, 1953, and passed a unanimous vote of Confidence in new Cabinet.

The National Conference had earlier approved the change of government. A convention of about 400 delegates from the National Conference throughout the State met in Srinagar from September 13, 1953 and approved the change of government as inevitable in the interest of the country and the national movement and expressed complete confidence in the new government, promising their fullest co-operation.

Bakshi Ghulam Mohammad immediately upon taking in oath of office, went before the microphone to make a policy statement. In his statement he bitterly deplored the idea of an 'Independent Kashmir', under the patronage of the United States of America, which he said, "would be a threat to the freedom and Independence of Indian and Pakistani people." He praised India with which Kashmir had entered into 'indissoluble links'. (*The Times of India*, Bombay, August 11, 1953.)

The Assembly met on February 6, 1954, and adopted the reports of the Basic Principles Committee on Fundamental Rights and Citizenship, thereby fulfilling one of the major tasks with which it had been charged.

The 'Drafting Committee' presented its report on February 12, 1954 and it was adopted on February 15, 1954. The adoption of this report embodied the ratification of the State's accession to India. (According to the Statesman, Calcutta, February 17, 1954, of the 75 members, 64 present voted unanimously. Of the 11 absent members, six were under detention).

The Basic Principles Committee reported on the regulations concerning the relations between the State and Union and they were: In order to enable the centre to discharge the responsibilities, which devolve upon it under the Constitution, those provisions of the Constitution of India which may be necessary for this purpose should be made applicable to the State in an appropriate manner. While preserving the internal autonomy of the State, all obligations which flow from the fact of accession and also its elaboration, as contained in the Delhi Agreement, should find appropriate place in the Constitution. The Committee is of the opinion that it is high time that finality in this respect should be reached and the relationship of the State with the Union be expressed in clear and precise terms (Report of the Basic Principles Committee and the Advisory Committee on Fundamental Rights and Citizenship (1954) page 4.

The immediate outcome of this Report was that barrier between Kashmir and India was removed from April 13, 1954 at the initiative of J&K Government.

On May 14, 1954, the President of India, acting under Article 370, issued an order endorsing the relationship of the State with India as defined in Delhi Agreement of 1952. By this order the powers of the Union Parliament in relation to State were enlarged and most of the provisions of the Indian Constitution were made applicable, yet the internal Autonomy was not interfered. This order is known as Constitution (Application to J&K) order 1954, CO 48 (see Appendix 9 which also incorporates subsequent orders passed for the application of the Constitution to the State). More provisions of the Indian Constitutions were made applicable with certain modifications/ omissions including the Fundamental Rights.

Formation of Constituent Assembly

Ratification of the accession of the State of J&K in respect of remaining subjects like some other States of the sub-continent was still to be determined by Maharaja Hari Singh as per the remaining Clauses of the Instrument of Accession. Initially, Maharaja was vaguely attracted to the idea of Independence but only for some time in order to ascertain the wishes of all the inhabitants of all regions of the State—Jammu, Kashmir, Ladakh, Baltistan and Gilgit. He was waiting for this appropriate time of course after taking into confidence both the newly created dominions, i.e. India and Pakistan. For that purpose he had tried to enter into Agreement of Stand Still as was provided in the Indian Independence Act. As a step in aid he had requested both the dominions to enter into Agreement and as a consequence thereof the dominion of Pakistan had entered into Agreement of Stand Still as a sovereign State with sovereign Maharaja but the dominion of India had asked the Maharaja to enter into discussion either personally or through recognized authority. The dominion of Pakistan was having other plans, i.e. to grab the State somehow or the other such as inciting communal virus in the predominantly Muslim population or by committing an aggression in proxy. When Pakistan had started squeezing the supply lines of the State, Maharaja had understood that the intentions were bad and he was frantically requesting the dominion of India to send him help. The dominion of India had no plan to get acceded the State as the Prime Minister Jawaharlal Nehru himself had taken the case of the State of Jammu and Kashmir in his own hands and was committed to get the power before administration transferred in favour of his friend Sheikh Abdullah. This idea was subsequently overwhelmed by events such as invasion made by Pakistan in proxy with the help of tribal people under the command of her army and that resulted after due course of time in ceasefire because of United Nations intervention. Sheikh Abdullah in the inner layers of his mind was also not averse to the concept of independent Kashmir under his Sheikhdom. He started hobnobbing with Anglo-American block and the glaring example is his long discussions with US Ambassador Loy Henderson during the summer of 1950. Before he could move in that direction, he wanted to remove all the obstacles from his way and the greatest one was Dogra ruling dynasty. Dr Karan Singh in his autobiography has recorded regarding the then President of India, Dr Rajendra Prasad at page 122, "A kindly and cultured man, he always received me with affection and listened with interest to my reports on the situation in the State. It was clear that his approach was closer to the Sardar's than to Jawaharlal's, and he was particularly concerned about the difficult position in which the Hindus of the State were placed." Dr Karan Singh in the capacity as Regent of his State was more aware because of his personal experiences about the game plans of Sheikh Abdullah than any other leader and as a step in aid for the legal integration of the State, he on 25 November 1949 issued proclamation stating that Constituent Assembly of India can adopt the mode for the application of Constitution of India so far as it is applicable to the State to govern the relationship of the State between the State and contemplated Union of India. He repealed the relationship of the State and the dominion of India as was applicable under the provisions of Government of India Act 1935. The Proclamation is attached as Appendix 5A. As per the policy of the Congress party framed by it in respect of all States in India, its importance was necessitated to have a concept of forming a Constituent Assembly to frame Constitution for the State as that would make the question of Plebiscite redundant. Although on several occasions Pandit Jawaharlal had reassured the United Nations and Pakistan that India stood by her earlier commitment, it was clear that if a Constituent Assembly did meet and reaffirm the State's accession to

India it would have an impact on public opinion abroad. Sheikh Abdullah seemed to be working against the interests of the Dogra Dynasty in order to fulfil his life's most cherished ambition. During 1950, there were discussions about this Assembly between the State Government and the Union Ministry for Kashmir Affairs. Although Maharaja Hari Singh had designated Dr Karan Singh as the Regent, yet he had not abdicated and still remained legally the ruler. It was therefore, incumbent upon the Government of India to consult him about the Constituent Assembly, and on 30th November 1950 Vishnu Kant Sahay, Secretary for Kashmir Affairs wrote to the Maharaja enclosing a draft proclamation to be issued by the Regent and asked his comments. On December 10, 1950 Maharaja Hari Singh wrote a long letter to Sardar Patel in which he made several points and they included his assertion that proclamation can only be issued by him and not by his son who is Regent. He was also emphatic in asking the Government of India that powers and functions of the Constituent Assembly should be expressed, well defined and accurately worded and should exclude from the purview of their inquiry and consideration matters not expressly entrusted to them. That Constituent Assembly should report to the ruler who shall seek the advice of the Parliament of India in the matter.

Soon thereafter, Sardar Patel passed away leaving a vacuum in the national life that could never really be filled. Sheikh Abdullah strongly reacted to these assertions of the Maharaja and entered into correspondence with Vishnu Kant Sahay (Secretary of Kashmir Affairs Government of India) who wanted the comments of the Regent. The Regent in response wrote to Sheikh Abdullah that the ruler had directed him not to append any signature on any proclamation on the subject without his express approval. Then the matter was taken to the Government of India and Prime Minister's Secretary VP Menon met Maharaja Hari Singh at Bombay. On April 5, 1951. Gopalaswami Ayyangar wrote a letter to Maharaja not to delay the proclamation for the formation of Constituent Assembly because of the developments taking place in the State and at Lake Success (headquarters of UNO). Since the Government of India was committed to the convening of a Constituent Assembly so Maharaja Hari Singh being a true patriot did not press these points and yielded to the national interests. He had been assured in the above said letter that Constituent Assembly shall not take decisions against his apprehensions about the continuance of the accession of the Jammu and Kashmir State or part thereof to India and the connection of Headship of the State with his dynasty. A few days thereafter the Regent received a letter from VP Menon urging him to sign the proclamation and Dr Karan Singh on April 21, 1951 issued the proclamation for convening the Constituent Assembly.

Sheikh Abdullah seemed to have a pathological aversion to the ruling Dogra family and he launched a bitter personal attack on Maharaja Hari Singh and his son the Regent of the State Dr Karan Singh. The bittressed attack of vituperate nature was made on 9th April 1951. Dr Karan Singh has recorded in his autobiography at page 127 and 128, "he and DP Dhar (State Minister in the State and later on Cabinet Minister in Indira Gandhi's regime) had direct access to Jawaharlal and "they were able to counteract to some extent the belligerent Muslim Kashmiri chauvinism represented by the Sheikh and the hardliners in the National Conference led by Mirza Afzal Beg. Jawaharlal's psychology in this regard was interesting. If he rejected a person's bona fides, then any view or advice from those quarters would at once be suspect. Thus, he had a particular dislike for the Praja Parishad leaders in Jammu because he thought they were communalists and that their actions only jeopardized India's position vis-a-vis Kashmir."

On 5th November 1951, the Jammu and Kashmir Constituent Assembly met. The elections were held earlier but the only affective opposition group—Praja Parishad in Jammu—boycotted the elections because of rejection of nomination papers of 13 candidates. As a result of this, 72 out of 75 members were elected unopposed on National Conference ticket, and no Praja Parishad member was elected including the veteran and widely respected leader Pandit Prem Nath Dogra. Sheikh Abdullah in a somewhat pompous and flamboyant opening address pointed out framing a Constitution for the future governance of the country, it would declare its 'reasoned conclusion regarding accession' and also deal with the Land Reforms passed by the government. He also in a relished manner touched about the future of the royal dynasty. This shows how the assurances as given by the Central Government through the earlier quoted letter dated 5th April 1951 from Gopalaswami Ayyangar (a Cabinet Minister) to the ruler Maharaja Hari Singh were flouted in breach rather than in observance by Sheikh Abdullah. Every sensible Indian would view this development with dismay and contempt how the constitutional authority of the person who made the accession was eroded against all the norms of a democratic and civilized government which was bound to follow the rule of law. The legal and constitutional validity of Jammu and Kashmir's accession to the Indian Union rested upon the

Instrument of Accession signed by Maharaja Hari Singh and now that very person was being unceremoniously pushed out by an Assembly which had been convened through a proclamation signed by his son being the Regent. The legality of this decision was inquired by Dr Rajendra Prasad (President of India) from Pandit Nehru who had recognized Maharaja Hari Singh as Raj Pramukh like in respect of other States in India and how he could be by-passed. The fundamental question was the constitutional structure of the State and its compatibility with overall frame work—political, legal and financial—laid down by the Constitution of India.

The hidden agenda of Sheikh Abdullah it seemed was to carve out a Sheikhdom for himself and his coterie. He started exploiting India's difficulty with regard to holding a Plebiscite. Indian Citizenship Act was made applicable to the State. President of India was empowered to declare in the State emergency in case of external danger, but in case of internal disturbance, the power could be exercised only at the request, or with the concurrence of State government. President of India was empowered to grant reprieve and commute death sentences. Central Government agreed that confiscation of Jagirs without compensation shall permanently stand. The State was allowed its own flag which was the flag of National Conference. It was also agreed that Jammu and Ladakh should have cultural and regional autonomy. This may be added that new slogan that emanated from Sheikh Abdullah was found in his address in a public meeting in Srinagar on April 26, 1952 as he said: "the Constituent Assembly would decide whether to accede to India or remain independent or join Pakistan." At this time, *The Times of India* newspaper wrote, "Someday the atom bomb which Sheikh Abdullah plans to hurl, may explode in his hands and then there will be no independent Kashmir and there may also be no Abdullah." Differences had arisen between him and the Central leaders in regard to Fundamental Rights, Citizenship, jurisdiction of the Supreme Court, Election Commission, Comptroller and Auditor General, Emergency Provisions etc. After considerable irritation a broad agreement, known as Delhi Agreement was arrived at. Some of the salient features are reproduced herein under for ready reference.

The provisions of the Delhi Agreement included abolition of the hereditary rulership; vesting of the residuary powers in the State; continuance of Special Citizenship Rights for the 'State Subject'; flying of a separate flag for the State with national flag also finding a supremely distinct place; and subject to certain restrictions and limitations, extension of provisions of the Indian Constitution in respect of Fundamental Rights, emergency powers of the President and jurisdiction of the Supreme Court. After the completion of its report by the Basic Principles Committee a delegation consisting of Sheikh Abdullah, Bakshi Ghulam Mohammad, Afzal Beg and GL Dogra went to Delhi to thrash out the details of the relationship between the State and the Centre. After several days of parleys with Indian leaders headed by Pandit Nehru an agreement known as Delhi Agreement was signed and later on ratified by the Constituent Assembly. It was announced in the Parliament on July 24, 1952 by Pandit Nehru and on August 19, 1952, the Constituent Assembly of the State also approved it. The Constituent Assembly immediately thereafter on August 21, 1952 passed a formal resolution and abolished the hereditary institution of monarchy substituting the head of the State as Sadar-i-Riyasat. He was to be elected by the State Legislative Assembly for a period of five years amongst the persons who were 'State Subjects of Class-I'. He was to be recognized by the President of India and hold office at his pleasure. With regard to the other items of the Delhi Agreement, Sheikh Abdullah turned out to be insincere. He referred the remaining clauses of the Agreement to the sub-committees of the constituent Assembly, causing intentional delay.

Pandit Nehru wrote a letter to Sheikh Abdullah that his position in Parliament would become untenable in case Kashmiri leadership changes the clauses of Agreement. In another missive he stated "my honour is bound up with my word." Sheikh Abdullah was invited by Pandit Nehru himself for discussion but he avoided and remained unmoved. His frame of mind was understood by Mr Jan Stephens a foreign correspondence of eminence and a relevant extract from his observations which have a bearing on the point is reproduced, "Pre-eminently he appeared to me a Kashmiri patriot: full of zeal to improve his countrymen's plight, preoccupied with the value, the centre and motive of his whole political life, little concern with the rest of sub-continent affairs...." (See *Horned Moon*, pp. 210-213.)

Sheikh Abdullah had started committing a volte face when in January 1950, he gave interview to two foreign correspondents Davison and Ward Price. They reported that Sheikh Abdullah had said that Independent Kashmir was the best solution. He had given similar interview to Karanjia of *Blitz*. A senior intelligence officer posted in Kashmir by the Government of India also submitted such a report. When Sheikh Abdullah came to know about it, he demanded immediate withdrawal of the officer and threatened to jail him if demand was not accepted. His successor had also to be withdrawn on the ground that he had been sent without prior clearance. Sheikh

Abdullah had realized that Indian government and the people would become aware of his game plan so for the time being, he changed his idea of pursuing Independence. Pandit Nehru had sent Mullick, then Assistant Director Intelligence, for secret enquiry and he submitted a favourable report stating that Sheikh Abdullah wanted special status. (See MY Saraf's book *Kashmiris Fight for Freedom*, pages 1195-1196.)

CHAPTER 14

Dreams of Independent Kashmir

Jagmohan, in his book *My Frozen Turbulence in Kashmir*, has recorded at page 136 that, "Basically, Sheikh Abdullah was neither for India nor for Pakistan. It was his power game that got precedence over everything else. What suited him at a particular moment was all that mattered. From 1947 to 1952, he went on proclaiming that accession of Kashmir to India was based on fundamental principles and was irrevocable. In 1948, he told Jawaharlal Nehru, 'We have made our choice and linked our destiny with India, and nothing can separate us now.' On March 7, 1949 he announced, 'We have decided to work with and die for India.' He had recited a Persian couplet in public address at Lal Chowk Srinagar in the presence of Pandit Nehru the meaning whereof stands translated above in English."

While he was making such solemn declarations, he was sounding various quarters for support to the idea of having an independent Kashmir. As early as January 28, 1948, Sheikh Abdullah discussed the subject of independence with the American officials. This is evident from the note sent by Warren Austin to the State Department after an interview with Sheikh Abdullah on January 28, 1948. Again, on April 14, 1948, Sheikh Abdullah gave an interview to Michael Davidson of Scotsman in which he said, "Independent Kashmir, guaranteed by United Nations, may be the only solution." Sheikh Abdullah suggested to Sir Owen Dixon in 1950 that one possible solution of the Kashmir issue would be independent Kashmir. At that time, Sheikh Abdullah also wanted to enter into bilateral talks with the leaders of 'Azad Kashmir'.

This was the working of the mind of a person whom Nehru, in a letter to the Maharaja on November 13, 1947, described as "the only person who could deliver the goods in Kashmir." On April 10, 1952, Sheikh Abdullah made an aggressive speech at Ranbir Singh Pura, a nearby town of Jammu city bordering Pakistan and accused the Indian Government and Indian Press of Communalism. He had stated, "We want to join India without any kind of mental reservations but how can we do it as long as we are not convinced about the complete elimination of communalism in India? We are prepared to welcome application of India's Constitution to Kashmir in its entirety, once we are satisfied that the grave of communalism has been finally dug in India: of that we are not clear.... It is very well for people in India to think that communalism in the country has been finally eliminated but no one can deny that the communal spirit still exists in India. Many Kashmiris are apprehensive as to what will happen to them and their position if, for instance something happens to Pandit Nehru.... We have acceded to India in regard to defence, foreign affairs and communications and not in respect of other subjects because we wanted some kind of Autonomy for ourselves in internal matters. If there is a resurgence of communalism in India, how we are to convince the Muslims of Kashmir that India does not intent swallow up Kashmir" (See S Vashisht, page 88). On June 10, 1952, while speaking in the Constituent Assembly on the report of the Basic Principles Committee, Sheikh Abdullah said, "The people under the guidance of National Conference have sacrificed their lives, have gone to jails, and have lived in narrow cells inhabited by serpents and scorpions. Hundreds of women have been dishonoured, hundreds made to crawl on their bellies and thousands rendered martyrs by shedding their blood." Such an utterance was exaggerated to the greater extent. During 'Martyrs Day' speech delivered on July 13, 1952, he declared that the interference of the Central Government in the affairs of the State would not be tolerated. On July 13, 1953 while speaking on 'Martyrs Day' he again commented, "it is not necessary that our State should become an appendage of either India or Pakistan." On May 3, 1953 an American influential personality Adlai Stevenson had come to Kashmir and had a long meeting with the Sheikh. The New York Times in its issue of July 5, 1953 published a map hinting at the independent status of the Valley. On July 10, 1953, speaking at Mujahid Manzil, Sheikh Abdullah said, "A time will therefore, come when I will bid them goodbye." Sheikh had started giving this idea of Independent and neutral State at the encouragement of several foreign individuals. Clement Attlee made a statement on November 11, 1953 in London that "Kashmir should belong neither to India nor to Pakistan but be independent." A foreign writer Korbel in his book *Danger in Kashmir* (page 237) wrote that "came the highly inflammatory rumours that the United States was backing the idea of Kashmir independence and that Sheikh Abdullah had been encouraged in it when Adlai Stevenson had visited Srinagar in May." The ultimate cumulative result of the above stated acts of Sheikh Abdullah was the dismissal of his government on 9th August 1953 because of no-confidence motion and his detention as has been discussed already in this book.

Praja Parishad Agitation

The Jammu people were humiliated, marginalised and ignored in every field. Thousands of landlords who genuinely depended on the share of the land produce were thrown on the road side without making any compensation of the lands held in ownership by them. An agitation in Jammu was led by Praja Parishad. By 1952, the party had an excellent organization. On 27 November 1952, Dr Karan Singh arrived in Jammu after his taking oath as Sadar-i-Riyasat. His first visit was chosen by the Praja Parishad's high command as a suitable occasion to demonstrate their strength. Business was suspended all over the province. Students absented themselves from their classes and the local newspapers *Ranbir*, *Chand* and *Amar* published special editorials to awaken the people. By December 1952, the whole Jammu province was ablaze. Business remained suspended for about a week. Income from the custom house at Pathankot and earnings from government transport operating between Pathankot and Srinagar had been listed among the principal sources of revenue in the budget for 1952-1953 but the agitation led almost to a suspension of traffic. In addition to that, loss of revenue, heavy expenditure had to be incurred in meeting the disturbed situations. The main plank of the agitation was "in one country two Constitutions, two flags, two Prime Minister's, would not be tolerated." At national level, the agitation got support from Jan Sangh. Delhi Agreement was severely criticised with the allegations that it was not likely to gain Kashmir for India but would endanger the security of the country and hamper the development in the State. Dr Syama Prasad Mookerjee, President of Jan Sangh himself proceeded to Jammu. Sheikh Abdullah had unleashed a reign of terror and started crushing the agitation. Thousands of 'Satyagrahees' were arrested and many of them were jailed in Srinagar during winter season without providing proper facilities. Pandit Nehru used to issue statements condemning the agitation and Sheikh Abdullah used to get encouraged. Eighteen people had died in police firings. The killings at Jourian, Hiranagar, Sunderbani and Ramban showed how force was brutally applied. Dr Syama Prasad Mookerjee was arrested on May 11, 1953 and he died in custody on June 23, 1953. At that time, his age was 52 years. He had not been suffering from any serious ailment which could cause his instant death. His mother also addressed a letter to Pandit

Nehru to hold an inquiry but unfortunately nothing was done. The circumstances in which he died in the custody of the State Government were a cause of grave resentment and suspicion. The whole of India was shocked at this event, especially the people of Bengal, who held Dr Mookerjee in the highest regard. Dr Karan Singh in his autobiography at page 155 has recorded, "I was not informed of his illness or his removal to hospital, and only learnt of his death from unofficial sources several hours after his dead body had been flown out of Srinagar." There were protests, hartals in Jammu region. Nehru's own standing in public suffered. Mookerjee's body was taken to Calcutta where he was given the biggest funeral in the history of the city.

Central leadership started realizing the duplicity and conceit of the Sheikh. Sardar Patel from the very beginning had understood the true personality of the Sheikh but Pandit Nehru did not allow any harm to be caused to him. It was a great misfortune for the Indian Nation and particularly for the people of J&K that Pandit Nehru could not understand Sheikh Abdullah in his true colours after the dawn of Independence. He had placed full faith in him but in turn got being betrayed by the latter. This fact needs no other evidence in the presence of an admission made by Sheikh Abdullah himself in his book *Atish-e-Chinar* (pages 351-355) in Urdu recorded by Jagmohan in his book *My Frozen Turbulence in Kashmir* (page 138). The relevant translated portion is reproduced, "Nehru used to call himself an agnostic. But he was also a great admirer of the past heritage and the Hindu spirit of India. His interpretation of the Indian history, though not always based upon accurate knowledge, approximates to the interpretation of revivalists like KM Munshi and Dayanand Saraswati. He considered himself as an instrument of rebuilding India with its ancient spirit. In Nehru's outlook, therefore imprints of Machiavelli's political philosophy and jugglery are found. That is why the disciple of the principled philosopher and saint, Mahatma Gandhi, was at the same time very much fond of Chanakya. Jawaharlal Nehru employed Machiavellian approach towards us in Kashmir. He dealt with Pakistan in the same fashion. At international level also he exhibited that same Machiavellian outlook with regard to Hungary and other issues."

The attitude of Sheikh Abdullah caused concern to the Central leadership and a sharp rift in the State Cabinet. On August 7, 1953, majority of the Cabinet Ministers led by Bakshi Ghulam Mohammad started accusing him for creating uncertainties and expressed their inability to work with him. As already stated in brief at page 236 of this book Dr Karan Singh who was the Sadar-i-Riyasat immediately dismissed him and during the wee hours of August 9, 1953 he was arrested from Gulmarg and Bakshi Ghulam Mohammad sworn as Prime Minister. In a radio broadcast Bakshi justified the arrest in these words: "Betrayal of the country's interests was in the offing. The slogan of independence was highly misleading. An Independent Kashmir, under the influence of an imperial power, will be a grave threat to freedom and independence of the Indian and Pakistani people. Another Korea may be staged here."

There were disturbances after his arrest but Bakshi Ghulam Mohammad, who was an able administrator firmly established his rule though seventy lives were lost. Bakshi realized that without establishing constitutional strong links with the Centre there cannot be any development. The obstructive attitude of the Delhi Agreement was put to an end. On May 14, 1954, the first constitutional (application to J&K) order was issued by President of India and Provisions of Chapter III of the Indian Constitution dealing with Fundamental Rights with some modifications were made applicable to the State. This aspect to some extent has already been discussed at page 237 of this book. The operations of Customs, Central Excise, Civil Aviation, Posts and Telegraph extended. On April 1, 1959, the Permit System for entry into and exit from the State was done away with. This order (Presidential order) was amended from time to time and more provisions of the Indian Constitution were made applicable. (See page 237 of this book along with Appendix 9). The Constitution of J&K was amended in 1966 (during GM Sadiq's rule) to change the denomination of Sadar-i-Riyasat to that of Governor and of Prime Minister to Chief Minister.

In view of these amendments, the jurisdiction of the Supreme Court, the Election Commission, the Comptroller and Auditor General was extended. Article 356 also stands extended. Article 352 which enables the President to declare a proclamation of National Emergency, is applicable in a limited way. Article 360 which empowers President to proclaim financial emergency is not made applicable. The President cannot give any direction under Article 365 and he also cannot suspend the State Constitution. The Constitution of J&K has the jurisdiction in the State to the exclusion of Indian Constitution to the right to hold property, right to citizenship, and right to settlement. The Constitution of India recognises only one Citizenship but residents of the States enjoy double benefits. In the existence of such constitutional provisions the separatist elements are breeding in the State and in order to draw political mileage Sheikh Abdullah had not changed his attitude even after Indira-Sheikh Accord of 1974 but again started old Machiavellian game of Independence by creating uncertainties. As an instance to encourage separatists elements he enacted the J&K Grant of Permit for Resettlement in (or Permanent Return to) Act, 1982 (Act X of 1982) authorising the migrants of J&K of the years 1947 to 14th May 1954 gone to Pakistan to come back and settle in the J&K State and eject the Hindu/Sikh migrants of Pak-occupied areas from the evacuee properties duly allotted to them without any claim or right accrued to them. Apart from this, gross injustice is being done to displaced persons (Hindus/Sikhs) from the neighbouring area of West Pakistan who settled in the State in 1947. They have been living here for a period of more than six decades but they, their children and grandchildren have no Citizenship Rights in J&K State. Even Sheikh Abdullah had no interest or moral obligation in a democracy established in the State not only by Indian Constitution but also Constitution of J&K about the houses and landed properties left over in Pakistan occupied area of the State by fleeing Hindu and Sikh State Subjects in 1947.

To assert their rights, the refugees from Pakistan approached the Supreme Court and in its judgment dated February 20, 1987, the Apex Court recognized the injustice being done to them but could not provide any relief on account of Article 370 and the provisions of State Constitution. The pertinent observations made in this judgement are:

> "They are not entitled to be included in the electoral rolls of the State Assembly, they are not entitled to be elected to a Village Panchayats; they are not even entitled to purchase any land and they are also not entitled to be appointed to any service under the State Government. All these denials and deprivations are the consequences of the definition of a permanent resident under Section 6 of the J&K Constitution. It is to be noticed here that these provisions are not open to challenge as inconsistent with the rights guaranteed by Part III of the Constitution of India because of the Constitution order 1954 issued by the President of India under Article 370(1)(d) of the Constitution by which Article 35(A) was added to the Constitution in relation to the State of J&K. The petitioners have a justifiable grievance. Surely they are entitled to expect to be protected by the State of J&K."

The suggestions of the Supreme Court to amend the unfair laws by the Legislature have been ignored and the underlying motivation of the State rulers is to play petty politics and create imbalances in the three regions to create their hegemonies.

Birth of secessionist organization Plebiscite Front goes to the credit of Sheikh Abdullah who first of all gave such idea of a separate Nation of Kashmiri Muslims and right to have a Plebiscite in his speech on May 17, 1946 when under Maharaja Hari Singh's rule he had launched an agitation of 'Quit Kashmir'. Some of the extracts of his speech are reproduced, "the tyranny of the Dogras has lacerated our souls. It is time for action. You must fight slavery and enter the field of 'Jihad' as soldiers. Every man, woman and child will shout 'Quit Kashmir'. The Kashmiri nation has expressed its will. I ask for plebiscite on this question." Sheikh Abdullah remained in office as Prime Minister for five years and five months (from March 1948 to August 1953) and during this period, he had succeeded in increasing tremendously the percentage of Kashmiri Muslims in the government services by brushing aside the relevant recruitment service rules which were in vogue during Maharaja's time. He had not even cared to establish an independent recruitment body for providing government services for the sake of fair selection. This he had done even though people of Jammu region had launched a forceful agitation against his misdeeds and partisan rule under the regional political party Praja Parishad. As a possible precaution against the merger of Jammu province in east Punjab as a result of such an agitation, he created a new Muslim majority district in Jammu province by grouping the tehsils of Kishtwar, Ramban and Bhaderwah out of erstwhile Udhampur district having an area of 4,162 sq miles. The population of Muslims and Hindus, in the newly created district, was tilted to some extent in favour of Muslims. In this newly created district the migrated Kashmiri population from generations together had a substantial population though they were not in majority amongst the local Muslims. He abolished the district of Reasi and made it a tehsil of Udhampur district. His government established a National Militia and recruited thousands of Muslim youths hailing in majority from Kashmir Valley and few Kashmiri speaking Muslims from Jammu province and a very negligible number of Hindus and Sikhs almost excluding Buddhists and Christians. The cumulative effect of all these misdeeds was his dismissal from power as a Prime Minister and followed by launching a criminal prosecution against him for conspiracy and other offences.

After-Effects of Sheikh Abdullah's Removal as Prime Minister of J&K

Along with Sheikh Abdullah his many close diehard associates including Mirza Afzal Beg were arrested. Baig was released in November 1954 on health grounds. He started giving seditious speeches and BN Mullick has claimed that entire record of Indian intelligence network operating in certain parts of the Kashmir was removed by his agents and sent to POJK area. It is an established fact that an underground movement supporting the propounded cause of Sheikh Abdullah was operating in Kashmir Valley. There was a serious charge levelled in intelligence reports against Sheikh Abdullah while in power that he was going to meet a high ranking Pakistan spy during his stay in Gulmarg from where he was arrested in the wee hours. Soon after his release Mirza Afzal Beg founded the 'All J&K Plebiscite Front' with the blessings of Sheikh Abdullah who was still in detention. This organisation was declared as unlawful under the relevant Central Act and the order judicially confirmed by the Special Tribunal. Full discussion on this aspect has been made in separate chapter. Afzal Beg was re-arrested in 1955.

Bakshi Ghulam Mohammad as Prime Minister

In the new Cabinet of Bakshi Ghulam Mohammad, GM Sadiq, Sardar Harbans Singh Azad (a pleader from Baramulla), Pandit Sham Lal Saraf (a Kashmiri Pandit), Girdhari Lal Dogra and Ghulam Nabi Saugami were included. In a broadcast Bakshi announced the following concessions:

The State purchase of paddy, maize and wheat to feed urban areas, was completely abolished which gave relief to the peasantry.

Salaries of all government servants were substantially raised.

Education was made free from Class 1 to MA and compulsory up to primary classes.

A permanent ration system was introduced in the towns.

Wages of labourers and work charge employees were also raised. He came off from a poor family and was under matriculate but was a man of high vision, possessed practical intelligence and a philanthropist at heart.

He tried his best to assuage the hurt feelings of Jammu people during Sheikh Abdullah's rule of vengeance. Though he himself had committed most of the atrocities. He undertook equitable development works in all the three regions of the State. He had developed great personal regard and respect for the great leader of Jammu province Prem Nath Dogra who had valiantly fought against the misrule of Sheikh Abdullah and even had gone to jail. Bakshi on occasions used to consult him on important national issues. Bakshi as a shrewd administrator had successfully subdued the agitation which the followers of Sheikh Abdullah had tried to start in the valley only with the help of State Administration, i.e. Police and Magistracy. He established Engineering and Medical Colleges at Srinagar and an Agricultural Research Institute at Pampore. Primary Schools were opened at a distance of 2-3 miles from each other and a High School not more than a distance of 5 miles from each other. Large seats were secured at national level in the technical colleges and Universities in the rest of the country for the education of students from State. They used to be officially sponsored by the State Government. Refundable loans were advanced to those students free of interest for securing education even in medical and engineering disciplines. He made number of roads, bridges and public Rest Houses in all the three regions and till date none of his successors has proved to his worth. People still remember him as an embodiment of developmental works. Both the Secretariat buildings at Jammu and Srinagar are the gifts from his government to the State from the financial aid given by the Central Government.

Kashmir Conspiracy Case

In the Kashmir Conspiracy case, Sheikh Abdullah and 25 others, ten of whom were hiding or in Pakistan, were charged with conspiracy to overawe by force and show of force the duly constituted government of the State of Jammu and Kashmir, with the object of overthrowing it and facilitating annexation of the State's territory by Pakistan (quotations from Guardian London 19th September 1962). Sheikh Abdullah the former Prime Minister of Kashmir was dismissed and detained under the State Preventive Detention Act on August 9, 1953. He was released in January 1958, but re-arrested on April 1958, for allegedly making anti-India speeches.

The prosecution case was that no sooner was Sheikh Abdullah arrested in 1953 than he began to organize a conspiracy through letters smuggled by his wife and other visitors. The conspirators are alleged to have been in contact with Pakistani intelligence agents and secured from them money, typewriters, printing machines, arms, hand grenades, and other explosives. The prosection evidence rests on witnesses and on letters written to the accused which have been seized. They claim that the letters were written in a simple code. The final charges were brought against Sheikh Abdullah and others on August 31, 1962, in the court of NK Hak. The accused were committed for their trial in the Special Session Court, Jammu as has been already stated above. The offences alleged against the accused were under Sections 121-A and 120-B of the Ranbir Penal Code and Rule 32 of the Security Rules.

On January 8, 1958, when Sheikh Abdullah had been released before coming out from custody his trusted lieutenant Mirza Afzal Beg who already had been released in November 1954, on August 9, 1955 with his (Sheikh's) blessings had founded All J&K Plebiscite Front. After his release he started instigating the masses to create law and order problems insisting that the accession was provisional, and that it could only be settled after the Kashmiri Muslims had exercised their 'right of self-determination'. Hazratbal shrine in Kashmir was the venue of his political speeches after the Juma Namaz, i.e. the Friday prayers. It is really quite extraordinary how this blatant politicization of a holy shrine became accepted as part of life in Kashmir, whereas, if any Hindu were to make a speech within the premises of a temple he would at once be dubbed communal and probably arrested on the spot.

On February 1958, Sheikh Abdullah gave a provocative speech at Hazratbal shrine which resulted in causing the death of one person and injuring twenty-one. Plebiscite Front became his main political vehicle for capturing power. This was undoubtedly an anti-national organization and subsequently was banned under law. The ban was judicially confirmed by the Tribunal constituted under Central Act 'Prevention of Unlawful Activities Act'. The then Chief Justice of J&K High Court late Justice Murtaza Fazal Ali was appointed as Chairman of the one man Tribunal under the above said Act and he confirmed the ban. This judgment has been discussed in this book under appropriate heading. The whole valley was disturbed and there were frequent clashes between the Plebiscite Front and National Conference workers a party that was then under the control of the Prime Minister Bakshi Ghulam Mohammad. Almost all the mosques were used to whip up feelings against 'Hindu India' and Sheikh Abdullah began touring the Valley extensively. After three months it was decided that his activities were compromising the national interest, and he was again taken into custody under the Preventive Detention Act on 29th April 1958. Bakshi Ghulam Mohammad took a bold stand and got the criminal proceedings instituted against 80 accused of the Hazratbal incident. Out of these, 68 accused were committed to the Court of Sessions to withstand the trial and they included three ex-Parliament Members and two ex-Deputy Ministers. He had been fighting the Plebiscite Front politically. On his (Sheikh's) detention as stated earlier after prolonged considerations and legal consultations it was decided to prosecute him along with his trusted lieutenant Mirza Afzal Beg and twenty-two others. The whole case against him was built around his letter to the Security Council and the mystery surrounding its receipt at New York. By the end of March 1958, the material consisting of 1600 page dossier had been prepared. Bakshi Ghulam Mohammad who was Prime Minister, was summoned for consultations in Delhi and according to

BN Mullick he had said, "Bakshi at this stage declared that whatever might be the strength of evidence against Begum Abdullah, he could not agree to her prosecution. Muslim opinion in Kashmir Valley would not excuse him for dragging this lady, who was known as 'Madar-e-Mehrban' to the courts. Mullick had argued that without her in the trial we would miss one of the main connecting links with Pakistan and this would greatly weaken our case; but on this question Bakshi would not budge and Pandit Nehru also agreed with him." BN Mullick in his book which was banned for any entry in J&K State has strongly recorded the evidence gathered against Madar-e-Mehrban.

Nageshwar Prasad, an ex-Judge of the Patna High Court, one of the top criminal practitioners in India was appointed senior counsel. At Pandit Nehru's request, GS Pathak, a member of the Indian Upper House and Gopi Nath Dikshit, a leading advocate from Delhi, assisted Prasad. Mr Dingle Foot, British Lawyer of international fame appeared as Chief Defence Counsel but as the prosecution was still at the committal stage, he left his junior, JO Kellock at Jammu. Several local lawyers also appeared for the defence, but the main brunt was borne by Mirza Afzal Beg a co-accused and Abul Latif advocate of Kashmir Bar who had a good practice as a criminal lawyer. Khwaja Mubarak Shah advocate of Baramulla had also been appearing for Sheikh.

Before the start of the trial of Kashmir Conspiracy Case, differences arose between the panel of counsel and the Law Minister about the trial of the case on certain factual and legal aspects. During the discussions Pandit Nehru suddenly burst out and gave expression to his inner most and hitherto unknown opinion about Sheikh Abdullah which has been recorded by BN Mullick in his book *My Years with Nehru*. Says Mullick: "then suddenly to our utter surprise Pandit Nehru started talking bitterly against Sheikh Abdullah's communalism. He traced the Sheikh's history from 1930 onwards and mentioned how he had started his career with the Muslim Conference, which was an out and out communal organization. He said that as a result of pressures from outside and also seeing the development of the States Peoples Movement in the rest of India and for purely tactical reasons and probably under the advice of some of his more liberal followers, the Sheikh had converted the Muslim Conference into the National Conference of Jammu and Kashmir to give it a non-communal appearance. At this time, Pandit Nehru suddenly looked at me and enquired whether I had not come across some information of possible British connivance in that movement. I replied in the affirmative. He continued his talk against the Sheikh and mentioned all his communal activities throughout the period he had acted as the National

Conference leader. It was the Pakistani aggression which had mellowed him a little for a short time, because the tribals had committed gruesome atrocities on the Muslim population in the valley. But, as soon as he became the Prime Minister, he came out in his true colours once again and started his anti-Hindu activities. In contrast, he praised Bakshi and Sadiq for their completely non-communal outlook and said that these two were really secular minded persons who required all support from India. Pandit Nehru said that all trouble in Kashmir was due to the Sheikh's communal outlook and it was he who was not allowing the State to settle down to peace and stability. The Sheikh always talked about the rights of the Muslims forgetting that the Hindus also formed nearly 35 per cent of the population of the State and he never showed any consideration for them. Pandit Nehru mentioned that politically he and other Indian leaders had to go along with the Sheikh for a considerable period and they had also helped him and played him up hoping that coming in contact with secular India, where Muslims and Hindus and persons of all other denominations were living together and enjoying a peaceful life, Sheikh Abdullah would be able to get rid of his communalism; but communalism was a disease with him and he could never get rid of it and is based on the fact that Kashmir Valley had a Muslim majority."

They were charged for conspiracy to cause forcible annexation of the State to Pakistan. That he and his colleagues had received illegal aid from Pakistan for anti-national activities in the State, both through individuals as well as through All J&K Plebiscite Front. The case went on for some years before it was withdrawn on political reasons. There was incontrovertible evidence that the All J&K Plebiscite Front had received large sums of money from Pakistan and this was much later corroborated by none other than Zulfikar Ali Bhutto in his memoirs.

Unfortunately, this able administrator (Bakshi Ghulam Mohammad) allowed the existence of a coterie including relatives around him which developed a system of personal and political patronage resulting in rise of nepotism and corruption. Meanwhile, All J&K Plebiscite Front had started virulent propaganda against him and there were some detractors also in his cabinet who carried tales against him. An atmosphere of suspicion was developed against him. When Pandit Jawaharlal Nehru prepared a plan known as 'Kamraj Plan' to weed out undesirable administrators in the Congress Organization, Bakshi in a fit of bravado offered to resign and his resignation was accepted. The saga of developing the State at a high speed and curbing the anti-national elements effectively with iron hand and carrying the masses with the administration came to an end. Let it not be forgotten, however, that Bakshi rendered signal service to the nation at a very crucial juncture. Had he not stepped into the breach after the dismissal of Sheikh Abdullah and consolidated the nationalist forces in the State, India would have been faced with a much more difficult situation. The process of integration was continued by him right down to the end. While laying down the robes of the office, he in defiance to the wishes of the Centre got his protege Khwaja Shamsuddin elected as leader of the legislative party.

CHAPTER 15

Framing the Constitution of Jammu and Kashmir

As per the adoption of the policies for all Part B States in the Independent India, the State of Jammu and Kashmir being Part B State at number 15 was also required to have its own Constitution. During the initial rule of Sheikh Abdullah, Yuvraj Karan Singh on May 1, 1951 had issued a proclamation for instituting the Constituent Assembly to be elected from adult franchise on the basis of one electoral constituency of 40,000 electorates. Elections were held in the middle of October 1951. The Jammu Praja Parishad was forced to boycott the elections due to rejection of 13 nomination papers of important leaders out of 28. Out of the 75 seats, 73 were won by National Conference unopposed. Only two seats were contested and the elected members too were won over by National Conference. On October 31, 1951, the Constituent Assembly held its first meeting under the Chairmanship of Maulana Masoodi. As has been stated earlier Sheikh Abdullah had his hidden agenda of Independent Kashmir for himself and had been creating hurdles for the extension of the jurisdiction of Supreme Court, Election Commission, Comptroller and Auditor General, Emergency Provisions of the Indian Constitution. For the time being a broad agreement known as Delhi Agreement of 1952 was arrived at and that Agreement was approved by the Constituent Assembly. Immediately thereafter, the Constituent Assembly proceeded to abolish the institution of hereditary monarchy. By formal resolution the head of the State was named Sadar-i-Riyasat to be elected by the State Legislative Assembly for a period of five years. The leader of the Legislative House was designated as Wazir-i-Azam.

After the arrest of Sheikh Abdullah, the Constituent Assembly met in Jammu in the month of February 1954 and passed unanimous vote of confidence in Bakshi Ghulam Mohammad and his Cabinet. On

February 6, 1954 the Constituent Assembly confirmed the State's accession to India. The reports of the Basic Principles Committee inclusive of its report on fundamental rights were also adopted on the same day. The basic Principles Committee report stated that, "in order to enable the Centre to discharge its responsibilities, which devolve upon it under the Constitution, these provisions of the Constitution of India which may be necessary for this purpose should be made applicable to the State in an appropriate manner. While preserving the autonomy of the State, all obligations which flow from the act of accession and also its elaborations as contained in the Delhi Agreement should find appropriate place in the Constitution."

In consequence of this report, the customs barrier was removed on April 13, 1954 and thereby Kashmir became economically an integral part of India. The Centre compensated the loss of revenue to the State by a subsidy amounting to twenty million rupees a year.

On May 14, 1954, a Presidential order was issued incorporating the recommendations of the State Constituent Assembly in the Indian Constitution. The drafting committee presented the draft of the new constitution to the Assembly on October 10, 1956. It was unanimously adopted on November 17, 1956 and came formally into effect on January 26, 1957, the Seventh birthday of the Republic of India.

The State Constitution provides a Parliamentary form of government, a Legislature, adult suffrage, an independent judiciary, a Public Service Commission and other democratic institutions. In the matter of Fundamental Rights, the jurisdiction of the Supreme Court and the authority of the Comptroller and Auditor-General of India, the State is like any other in the Union. The official language is Urdu. The Directive Principles of the State Policy are also modelled after those of the Constitution of India. The State has to establish and preserve a socialistic order of society. The secularism is the basis of the Constitution though the specific word, 'secularism' is missing in the provisions of the Constitution. For this omission, elected members of the Legislative Assembly hailing from Jammu region and belonging to two opposition parties (Bharatiya Janata Party and Panthers Party) often raised this issue with the object of getting this word engrafted in the Constitution but the ruling political class from Kashmir Valley irrespective of political affiliations are not extending the support to incorporate this word for adopting the pattern of Indian Constitution. The elected members of coalition Congress party are remaining mute in order to share the power of governance.

In 1957, the State entered into financial arrangements with the Union Government which brought it on par with other States in respect of financial matters including proportionate allocation of funds from the centre. In order to make the administration of the State at par in efficiency with other States in the country, the allotment for fixed quota in posting IAS and IPS officers was legally allowed along with provision of a fixed quota to get inducted by promotion in the above stated two services from the cadre of State administrative and police officers. The accounts and Audit Department of the State is now under the Auditor General of India. Revenue and Expenditure are subjected to audit and scrutiny of the Auditor General. In 1959, the State Assembly unanimously decided to seek amendment of the State's Constitution to provide for the extension of the jurisdiction of the Election Commission of India and the Supreme Court over the State of Jammu and Kashmir. The system whereby even Indian citizens needed a permit from the prescribed State Authorities to enter the State was abolished from April 1, 1959 which was an important political and psychological step in the direction of closer integration. A bill was passed amending the State Constitution, bringing the status of J&K High Court Judges at par with those in the rest of the country with regard to salary, perks and retirement age etc. The recommendations of the State Legislature have been incorporated in the Indian Constitution through a Presidential order issued on January 26, 1960. The State Legislature passed an Act authorising the government to permit those non-State Subjects to purchase land and other immovable property in J&K who intend to set up industries in the State. The State Legislature passed the J&K Peoples Representation Act providing for the delimitation of constituencies for the purpose of elections to the Legislative Assembly and Legislative Council. Elections to the new Legislature were held in March 1957. Unfortunately, a trend was set in the Valley which remained formally established for decades and crossed all the limits during Dr Farooq Abdullah's time for unprecedented rigging of elections held in 1987 resulting alienation of the youths in large numbers from mainstream of politics of the State. They were prevented to enter the portraits of the Legislative Assembly on merits and ultimately they were exploited by the anti-national local and foreign elements to exfiltrate to Pakistan in order to receive the arms training and wage the on going proxy war of terrorism from within and outside the State including from foreign soils. Syed Salahudeen, who is now the head of the dreaded terrorist organization Hizb-ul-Mujahideen, is a shining example. It is alleged his success in the polls forcibly turned into a defeat by a heavy weight of National Conference candidate from Srinagar city constituency is an eye opener contribution towards the subversion of rule of law. That particular Legislator during his life time enjoyed maximum power in the hierarchy of Dr Farooq

Abdullah's administration. In the elections of 1957 held during Bakshi Ghulam Mohammad's time, of the 43 seats, 35 went uncontested to the National Conference, thus virtually pre-empting the results in the 75 member Assembly. This was because the nomination papers of opposition candidates were in several cases rejected on flimsy grounds. Bakshi Ghulam Mohammad, with all his administrative ability was an expert in getting and managing the elections rigged. In the final result, Praja Parishad (regional party) in Jammu led by Pandit Prem Nath Dogra was able to win only five seats and the rest went to National Conference, ensuring another five years term for the Bakshi Ministry. The pro-Abdullah forces could not even dare to contest the elections. All the integration of the State with India was done during Bakshi's regime. He ruled the State with popularity and benevolence. When he laid down the reins of the government in pursuance of Kamraj Plan of Pandit Nehru, the Pakistani elements were seeking an opportunity to disturb the conditions. Shamsuddin, the protege of Bakshi Ghulam Mohammad, who succeeded him with the support of Bakshi was a weak administrator and Bakshi had been doing the back seat driving. In order to create chaotic conditions in the State on December 27, 1963, the Holy Relic of Prophet Mohammad enshrined at the Hazratbal mosque was stolen. With the timely help of the Central Government it was recovered on January 4, 1964 and the inimical forces failed to fan communalism in the State. In order to establish the genuinity of the dramatically recovered holy relic, a committee of fourteen members known for their integrity and piety was made by the Action Committee but their names were not made known with the idea that government may not use its immense resources to win over them. Maulana Masoodi known for his incorruptibility was negotiating with Shri Lal Bahadur Shastri on behalf of the Action Committee. Shastri was specially sent by Pandit Nehru to resolve the crisis as the whole valley was religiously disturbed for this sacrilege act and people in thousands were day and night coming on the roads even during the months of December, January and February 1963-1964. The first to give the verdict was Faqir Mirak Shah, "the holiest of the holy men in Kashmir," who uttered the single word, 'Haq', meaning right. On 3 February 1964, at 2 PM, the identification parade was held at the Dargah. The fact as to who committed this theft still remains shrouded in the thick layers of mystery although the investigation of the case had been personally supervised by BN Mullick, who was the Director of the Intelligence Bureau. However, at that time, the Home Minister of India Shri Gulzarilal Nanda had announced that three persons were connected with the theft of Holy Relic and they were Abdur Rahim Bandey, Abdul Rashid and Kabir Butt, of which the first was a

Mutwalli or priest of the shrine. He also announced that a judge from outside the State would try the case. But this statement remained on the papers and was not put into practice at all.

The shortcomings of Shams-ud-Din were revealed and on the advice of the Central Government, National Conference Legislature elected GM Sadiq as their leader who assumed the office of Chief Minister in February 1964. With this change in the government, the State came more nearer to the Centre. The designation of the head of State was changed from Sadar-i-Riyasat to Governor. He was now to be appointed by the President and not elected by the State Legislature as previously. Sheikh Abdullah had faced trial for six years in the conspiracy case and there appeared no end to it. Sadiq initiated a policy of 'liberalization' which involved a change in the government's attitude vis-a-vis Abdullah. Quite soon after he assumed office, he had detailed consultations with the Prime Minister as a result of which there was a major policy shift and a decision taken to withdraw the conspiracy case against Abdullah, Afzal Beg and others and to release them unconditionally. An application for withdrawal of the case was made on 8th April 1964 before the court of the Additional Sessions Judge (Special Judge appointed for the case). The application was allowed and Sheikh Abdullah and his colleagues were released on the same day. Describing Sadiq as 'an old comrade' in his press conference the next morning, Sheikh Abdullah said that, while it was the people of Jammu and Kashmir who had to decide their future, he had no ready made solution for the Kashmir problem. He did, however, say that he was definitely against the division of the State. After release, Sheikh Abdullah received tumultuous welcome in the Valley.

Pakistan of course was jubilant at Abdullah's release, though the jubilation was not unqualified because they knew him well enough to realize that he was far too significant a political personality to act as anyone's pawn. Bhutto invited him to meet President Ayub, and when questioned about this at his press conference Sheikh Abdullah said, "Let us wait and watch. This is a matter between the two governments (India and Pakistan). This may arise when I meet Nehru." His speeches, however, were ambiguous. While on the positive side, he laid great stress on the maintenance of communal harmony and urged the Kashmiri Muslims to safeguard the life and property of non-Muslims. He refused to accept that the accession of the State to India was permanent and final, he came out openly in favour of the Plebiscite Front which had been founded by his main lieutenant Afzal Beg, and he seemed to equate India and Pakistan by reiterating that a solution of the Kashmir dispute should be found which is acceptable to all three parties. His tour and speeches created a tremendous impact in the valley.

Sheikh Abdullah came to Delhi at the end of April 1964 and had an emotional meeting with Jawaharlal with whom he stayed at Teen Murti House as his personal guest. He had prolonged meetings with the Prime Minister as well as number of Cabinet Ministers and other political leaders, including Jayaprakash Narayan who had always been friendly and favourably disposed to him. Sheikh Abdullah succeeded in persuading Pandit Jawaharlal to let him have one more try at building a bridge between India and Pakistan. Pandit Jawaharlal was no doubt disturbed at the growing rift between the two countries after the ill-fated border war with China. Also, USA and Britain had kept up their strong pressure on him to come to some sort of an agreement with Pakistan, and perhaps he saw in Sheikh Abdullah a person who might possibly achieve this. Sheikh Abdullah issued a statement on May 12, 1964 from Delhi in which he mentioned about his various meetings and discussions, reiterated the importance of India and Pakistan coming to an agreement over Kashmir, and announced that he was visiting Pakistan shortly to have discussions with President Ayub Khan and other leaders there. Pandit Jawaharlal Nehru also made statements in Parliament and at the AICC supporting these moves. Speaking at AICC Pandit Nehru had said that Sheikh is wedded to the principles of secularism. He does not believe in the two Nations theory which was the basis of formation of Pakistan. This was a dramatic change in Jawaharlal's policy vis-a-vis Kashmir. Only a few weeks earlier, Sheikh Abdullah was in the dock facing the charge of treason. After giving the statement from Delhi, Sheikh Abdullah returned to Srinagar on the next date, i.e. on 13th May 1964 and addressed a public meeting. His emphasis shifted from 'self determination' to Indo-Pakistan reconciliation, and he announced that he would leave for Delhi on 21st May 1964 en route to Pakistan. The future generations will laugh at this curious dichotomy well illustrated in the basic ambivalence that has characterized Indian approach ever since 1947. India on the one hand had claimed that the whole State of J&K ruled by Maharaja Hari Singh in 1947 was Indian territory and a major chunk of that was under the illegal occupation of Pakistan by an act of aggression and yet nothing could be done in practice to recover even an inch of the territory. A person who was being tried for treason and waging war with the country was being made as a judge for the purposes of reconciliations and final settlement with the hostile country. To add fuel to the fire, even some areas which were re-claimed after fighting two wars with Pakistan, i.e. of 1965 and 1971 were returned back on the negotiating table for buying the peace. Such things have never happened in the history of any other country in the world. On 27th May 1964 Sheikh Abdullah reached Muzaffarabad and what would have been the outcome of his visit that remains a matter of speculation because on 27th May 1964, a great historical event happened on account of the death of Pandit Jawaharlal Nehru who was a great patriot, politician, historian, litterateur, administrator and world statesman. It is said that Sheikh Abdullah in the company of Afzal Beg had met President Ayub Khan and broached the idea of making a confederation between India, Pakistan and Kashmir. After returning to Valley Sheikh Abdullah also changed his stand and started virulent propaganda against India. After Nehru's death Pakistan got opportunity to make war preparations with the idea to disintegrate India.

On February, 1965, Sheikh Abdullah and his wife went abroad ostensibly showing on Haj Pilgrimage but indulged in political propaganda. Indeed this blatant exploitation of religion for political purposes was one of his special techniques ever since he emerged into prominence in 1931. Despite his much-professed secularism, it was almost invariably on a religious platform that he enunciated his political policies. Before he left he had succeeded in creating a good deal of anti-Indian sentiments in the valley, and the social boycott was beginning to have a disturbing effect on pro-Indian elements among the Muslims. There were cases in which dead relations of Congress workers were refused burial space, and many other cases of harassment and discrimination began taking place. On March 28, 1965, he even met Chou En-lai (Prime Minister of China). His passport was immediately cancelled and on return was arrested at Delhi Airport on May 9, 1965 along with Mirza Afzal Beg. They were flown to Ootacamund in south India where they were ordered to remain within municipal limits. So, for the third time since 1947, Abdullah found himself under detention. His two main failings were his unwillingness to accept that Jammu and Kashmir would have to continue as part of India like other States even though it may enjoy special status in some matters, and also his inability to come to grips with the tri-regional character of the State in which the aspirations of the people of Jammu and Ladakh were often contradictory to those of the Valley. The aspirations of the people of these two regions till date remain suppressed and subdued. By this time, Pakistan had organized a force of 30,000 men consisting of Regulars and Mujahids and they made infiltration in large numbers under the command of General Malik. When they had reached the outskirts of Srinagar, the authorities came to know about it. After some skirmishes on the border on September 1st, 1965 the Pakistani Army launched a massive attack in Chamb Jourian sector. Lal Bahadur

Shastri was then the Prime Minister of India and under his leadership counter offensive on Lahore Sector and Sialkot Sector was launched and thus, the pressure on the Chamb Jourian sector ceased. Our army moved effectively into Pakistan Occupied Jammu and Kashmir (POJK), the most important operation being the capture of the bulge between Uri and Poonch which involved over-running about two dozen Pakistani posts. This gave India a much stronger strategic position and made it more difficult for the infiltrators to enter both the valley and the Jammu region. The major problem in Jammu region was the huge influx of refugees from the border tehsils of Akhnoor and Ranbir Singh Pura as well as the influx of Hindu population from remote areas to the towns in Poonch and Rajouri. These unfortunate refugees were for the second time in two decades uprooted from their hearths and homes. By and large, the Congress and the Jan Sangh (erstwhile incarnation of present Bharatiya Janata Party) overcame their political differences in the face of the grave threat to national security. In the Valley, however, it was different story. Maulvi Farooq openly espoused the cause of the raiders in his religious sermons, and wily Maulana Masoodi came out with a statement that a plebiscite was the only solution to the Kashmir problem, and demanded the release of Sheikh Abdullah and other political detenus. While Sheikh Abdullah himself was silent, one of his younger sons, who was living in England, made a statement strongly attacking India and supporting the 'freedom fighters' who were attempting to 'liberate Kashmir'. Security Council succeeded in making both the parties agree to a cease fire on September 22, 1965. Meanwhile, China was also adopting aggressive posture against India and put up his claim on territories of Sikkim State of India. In order to lessen its influence in the area, Russia tried hard to bring both the parties on negotiating table. On January 10, 1966, the Tashkent Declaration was signed in the presence of Russian leader Kosygin by Indian Prime Minister Lal Bahadur Shastri on behalf of India and President of Pakistan Ayub Khan, on behalf of Pakistan. Both the parties agreed to withdraw their troops to the position held by them on August 5, 1965. The text of the Tashkent Declaration is at Appendix 10.

After the Tashkent Declaration, the interest of the world community decreased and Pakistan also learnt a lesson of such a misadventure. Sheikh Abdullah was released from the custody. GM Sadiq faced him politically in the public. Because of the changed political scenario and liberal administrative approach adopted by GM Sadiq, the influence of Sheikh Abdullah in the public considerably decreased.

Sheikh Abdullah increased anti-national activities through his political organization All J&K Plebiscite Front. Consequently, on January 8, 1971, Sheikh Abdullah, Mirza Afzal Beg and GM Shah were expelled from the State. On January 12, 1971, the Plebiscite Front was banned under unlawful Activities (Prevention) Act of 1967 which is a Central Act having extended jurisdiction in the State of J&K. This administrative ban order was referred to the Tribunal constituted under the said Act which was headed by the then Chief Justice of J&K High Court Hon'ble Murtaza Fazal Ali who confirmed the ban and declared the Front as unlawful organization having secessionist aims and objects.

Note: The full discussion of this unlawful organization has been made in the chapter 'Unlawful Organizations'.

During the regime of GM Sadiq, in 1967 Delimitation Commission gave its report fixing the Assembly seats numbering 42 for Kashmir Valley and fixing 31 Assembly seats for Jammu Division. Two seats were given in the Assembly for Ladakh. Major groups in the Plebiscite Front claiming the blessings of detained leaders Sheikh Abdullah and Mohammad Afzal Beg declared its policy of non-participation in the elections on the plea that their motto is for right of self-determination through a Plebiscite. The second group supported by Maulana Masoodi and Mohiuddin Qurra decided to contest the elections on Independent tickets. Both of them had remained close associates of Sheikh Abdullah during his Kashmir Freedom Movement against the autocratic Dogra rule. Till date, GM Sadiq is considered as the best Chief Minister for providing comparatively clean governance in the State so far as components of corruption and nepotism are concerned but unfortunately he could not hold free and fair election. In the Assembly elections of 1967, the Kashmir region had three districts. Amongst them district Anantnag figures at the top for the misuse of election machinery and government authority which is unparalleled in the election history of the State because no predecessor had done it so patently and brazenly. In this district the candidates of the ruling party Congress(I) to which Sadiq belonged after he had merged the National Conference political party in it had returned most of their candidates unopposed because the nomination papers of opposition candidates had been rejected at a large scale on technical grounds. Opposition parties were furious; there were a series of angry protest meetings and processions. An opposition delegation consisting of Bakshi Ghulam Mohammad (National Conference), Pandit Prem Nath Dogra (Jan Sangh) and Dhanraj Badgotra (PSP) went to Delhi to protest against the rejection of nomination papers en mass. They demanded the dismissal of Sadiq's government and the imposition of President's rule to ensure fair elections. The Election Commissioner of India Mr Sundaram personally came to Srinagar and scrutinized the record but found no cogent official material in his hands to order any administrative interference because all the relevant record was either fabricated or destroyed in a very clever and expert manner. In most of the cases the prescribed oath forms were got removed from the accompanying nomination papers. The result was that Election Commissioner advised the concerned parties to challenge the election results by filing Election petitions before the Competent Election Tribunal. This unfair practice was started by Sheikh Abdullah in 1951 by getting his seventy-two candidates returned unopposed in the elections of Constituent Assembly, the practice that was followed by his successor Bakshi Ghulam Mohammad in the Assembly elections of 1957 and 1962. Their successor GM Sadiq in the elections of 1967 had surpassed their record of rigging elections. The major opposition party Praja Parishad (Jan Sangh and present Bharatiya Janata Party) from Jammu region could send only three members in the Legislative Assembly which included the veteran leader of Jammu region Pandit Prem Nath Dogra, Lala Shiv Charan (Udhampur), Rishi Kumar Koushal (Reasi). In the Kashmir region, the National Conference (headed by ex-Prime Minister Bakshi Ghulam Mohammad) was able to win seven seats, while two seats went to independent candidates including an ebullient young journalist Shamim Ahmed Shamim. Bakshi Ghulam Mohammad also surprised the Congress by winning the Parliamentary seat of Srinagar while defeating Congress candidate AM Tariq. Thus, over all, the Congress won fifty-nine of the seventy-three Assembly seats for which elections were held, twenty-two of them unopposed. For the Ladakh two Assembly seats elections were held in the month of June and they too were pocketed by Congress.

Differences among the members of the council of Ministers came to a head on collision with the resignation of Syed Mir Qasim, and other colleagues. In Kashmir, Indian National Congress was activated by Mohammad Shafi Qureshi (who later on became State Minister in Indira Gandhi's Central Cabinet). Syed Mir Qasim was President of the Indian National Congress and he took it to the grass root level. Later, Bakshi Ghulam Mohammad too advised the National Conference to officially merge with the Congress. While the transformation of the Congress was in progress, GM Sadiq breathed his last on December 12, 1971. At that time, the country was in the mid of war with Pakistan. By this time, Syed Mir Qasim had rejoined the Ministry and he was called to assume the office of Chief Minister which he occupied till 1975. In 1975 he was mainly responsible to persuade Mrs Indira Gandhi to hand over the reins of the government in favour of Sheikh Abdullah after entering into an Accord with him though the latter had not a single member in any of the Legislature. This is an unprecedented event in an elected democratic government in the world.

Earlier to that in 1971, the military dictator of Pakistan President Yahya Khan had started an unwarranted war with India when East Pakistan was getting out of control from his hold because people in general had arisen in revolt against the atrocities of the Pakistani ruler's who belonged to West Pakistan wing. The war with Pakistan ended with spectacular victory for India and the creation of an Independent State of Bangladesh which used to be known as East Pakistan. Pakistani troops numbering more than 90,000 were arrested. On the Western Front also India was on advantageous position. After losing the war, the Military Junta was discredited and it invited Zulfikar Ali Bhutto, leader of the majority party of the National Assembly of West Pakistan, to take over the Government of Pakistan. He immediately released Sheikh Mujibur Rehman from the detention in West Pakistan who was leading the revolt. Prime Minister Indira Gandhi and President of Pakistan Zulfikar Ali Bhutto held bilateral discussions which led to the execution of Shimla Agreement dated July 3, 1972. The full text of this Agreement is reproduced.

Shimla Agreement

Shimla Agreement on Bilateral Relations between India and Pakistan signed by Prime Minister of India, Mrs Indira Gandhi and President of Pakistan, Zulfikar Ali Bhutto in Shimla on July 3, 1972.

In order to achieve this objective, the Government of India and the Government of Pakistan have agreed as follows:

That the principles and purposes of the Charter of the United Nations shall govern the relations between the two countries.

That the two countries are resolved to settle their differences by peaceful means through bilateral negotiations or by any other peaceful means mutually agreed upon between them. Pending the final settlement of any of the problems between two countries, neither side shall unilaterally alter the situation and both shall prevent the organisation, assistance or encouragement of any acts detrimental to the maintenance of peaceful and harmonious relations.

That the pre-requisite for reconciliation, good neighbourliness and durable peace between them is a commitment by both the countries to peaceful co-existence, respect for each other's territorial integrity and sovereignty and non-interference in each other's internal affairs, on the basis of equality and mutual benefit.

That the basic issues and causes of conflict which have bedevilled the relations between the two countries for the last 25 years shall be resolved by peaceful means;

Indian and Pakistani forces shall be withdrawn to their side of the international border.

In Jammu and Kashmir, the Line of Control resulting from the cease fire of December 17, 1971, shall be respected by both sides without prejudice to the recognised position of either side. Neither side shall seek to alter it unilaterally, irrespective of mutual differences and legal interpretations. Both sides further undertake to refrain from the threat or the use of force in violation of this line.

The withdrawls shall commence upon entry into force of this agreement and shall be completed within a period of 30 days thereof.

This agreement will be subject to ratification by both countries in accordance with their respective constitutional procedures, and will come into force with effect from the date on which the instruments of ratification are exchanged.

Both governments agree that their respective heads will meet again at a mutually convenient time in future and that in the meanwhile the representatives of the two sides will meet to discuss further the modalities and arrangements for the establishment of durable peace and normalization of relations, including the questions of repatriation of prisoners of war and civilian internees, a final settlement of Jammu and Kashmir and the resumption of diplomatic relations.

Note: Due to contradictory interpretation of Shimla Agreement of 1972 about Siachen Glacier (74 km long), believed to the world's largest in the non-polar region has now turned into a battle ground at altitudes ranging from 15,000 to 20,000 feet from the sea level since June 1984. It remained un-demarcated as no troops had ever been deployed there. Later Indian troops moved in when Pakistan was discovered encouraging foreign expeditions to go there. Much blood of the troops from both the sides stands shed on this world's highest battle field for the control of 4,000 sq kms inhospitable area. After the peace talks started by ex-Prime Minister Shri Atal Bihari Vajpayee of the NDA Government which are being pursued by the present UPA Government a truce for the time being have been established in this area with Pakistan.

On 2 July 2012, forty years elapsed when this agreement was signed. It ended in the east with the excision of East Pakistan and emergence of Bangladesh. In the West, Pakistan gained some territory across the 'Cease Fire Line' beyond the Munawar Tawi rivulet in Chamb sector of J&K and some 'Pimples' of territory across the international border in India. A Status quo ante situation was agreed upon under the Shimla Agreement along the international border. Captured territories were exchanged. But the areas gained across the 'Cease Fire Line' in Jammu and Kashmir would be retained. India lost territory in Chamb, but acquired valuable strategic depth in the Kargil Drass Sector, which was the theatre of the Kargil Conflict in 1999. Incidently, the 'Cease Fire Line' was deliberately redesigned as the 'Line of Control', in the Shimla Agreement, a change in nomenclature that enabled India to end the tenure of the United Nations Military Observers Group in India and Pakistan. It was charged with maintaining peace along the Cease Fire Line established by the 'Karachi Agreement' (1949), what was found very irksome by New Delhi with its frequent calls for site inspections and constant nit-picking about border violations. The return of the captured territory and POWs numbering about 93,000 (mostly military but few civilians) to Pakistan undoubtedly paved a way for the return of besieged Bengalis in Pakistan and Biharis from Bangladesh to Pakistan yet Pakistan proved unfaithful in implementing the decisions taken though India (Indira Gandhi) moved ahead to seize the tension by entering into an Accord with Sheikh Abdullah and brought him to power in 1975. Had advisors of Mrs Indira Gandhi like PN Haksar, DP Dhar and PN Dhar acted with some foresight much advantageous result could have been elicited from Pakistan which is an unreliable State.

This Agreement remained cornerstone of Indo-Pakistan relations till the onslaught of militancy in 1989 which is a outgoing proxy war Subsequently it was supplemented by Pakistan when she started giving different interpretations to its provisions. Incursions of 1999 during NDA regime were the serious violations of this Accord which resulted in a war type skirmish in which ultimately Pakistan was a loser.

Kashmir Accord of February 1975 (known as Indira-Abdullah Accord)

The Kashmir Accord of 1974 enforced on February 1975, was another manifestation of blunders which have created Kashmir problem. After Bangladesh war of 1971, Pakistan suffered humiliating defeat as it lost its half of the eastern territory and more than ninety thousand army personnel were taken prisoners. This has never happened earlier in the military history of a country. Sheikh Abdullah and his coterie realised their futile attempts to create an Independent State for themselves with the help of Pakistan. After prolonged negotiations between Mirza Afzal Beg and G Parthasarathy, the Kashmir Accord was signed. Syed Mir Qasim was then the Chief Minister of the State. He was very helpful in making the award successful. After the Municipal elections some seats in the valley were won over by the supporters of Sheikh Abdullah. Negotiations began between Sheikh Abdullah and the Indian Government which resulted in the coming out of the above Accord. By now, Pakistan had lost the 1971 war as a result of which not only had East Pakistan been separated, a People's Represented State was established in Dhaka by New Delhi and West Pakistan had been saved from being run over, mainly by the intervention of President Nixon of America who had sent the Atomic Monster, Enterprise to the way of Bengal, to put teeth in his intervention. The armed separation of East Pakistan as well as the Indian inroads on the Western Fronts, operated as a most demoralizing factor in Occupied Kashmir. The leadership of the banned All J&K Plebiscite Front felt that Pakistan could no longer be expected to liberate Kashmir by force and this lead them to the idea of seeking a settlement with New Delhi. Sheikh Abdullah and his colleagues chose to ignore the idea of an Independent Kashmir State. As a result of the negotiations, an Agreement was signed between the two sides in New Delhi on 13 November 1974. It is reproduced below:

> "The State of J&K which is a constitutional unit of the Union of India, shall in its relation with the Union, Continue to be governed by Article 370 of the Constitution of India.
>
> The Residuary powers of Legislation shall remain with the State. However, Parliament will continue to have power to make laws relating to the Prevention of activities directed towards disclaiming, questioning or disrupting the sovereignty and territorial integrity of India or bringing about cession of a part of the territory of India from the Union or causing insult to the Indian National flag, the Indian National Anthem and the Constitution.

Where any provision of the Constitution of India had been applied to the State of J&K with adaptations and modifications, such adaptations and modifications can be altered or repealed by an order of the President under Article 370. Each individual proposal in this behalf to be considered on its merits but provisions of the Constitution of India already applied to the State of J&K without adaptations or modifications are unalterable.

With a view to assuring freedom to the State of J&K to have its own Legislation on matters like Welfare measures, Cultural matters, Social security, Personal law and Procedural laws, in a manner suited to the Special Conditions in the State, it is agreed that the State government can review the laws made by Parliament or extended to the State after 1953 on any matter relatable to the concurrent list and may decide which of them in its opinion needs amendment or repeal. Thereafter appropriate steps be taken under Article 254 of the Constitution of India."

This Accord was reached by the Centre to win over influential section of public opinion in J&K to join the mainstream of Indian nationalism. Pakistan's Prime Minister Zulfikar Ali Bhutto gave a call for hartal to protest against the Accord. Bhutto was of the view that the consequences of the December war caused frustration in Kashmir and resulted in bridging the gulf between Sheikh Abdullah and New Delhi (page 1277 of Saraf's book).

After the Agreement was signed, Mubarak Shah who was a practising lawyer of district Baramulla Bar and an old faithful associate of Sheikh Abdullah already had been inducted in Mir Qasim's Cabinet as a Cabinet Minister as a Preliminary step for transfer of State administration. Mubarak Shah had left his legal practice with the purpose of defending Sheikh Abdullah in the conspiracy case which was pending in Jammu as already stated. In other words, he was one of the members of the local panel of the defence lawyers. This team of lawyers was headed by Mirza Afzal Beg. Mubarak Shah was a secular minded pleasing and gracious personality possessing sagacity. He had developed his personal relations with some leading and influential segments of Jammu society. He had also developed very friendly relations with the writer of this book, when he was pursuing Sheikh Abdullah's conspiracy case in Jammu as at that time both of them were members of the legal fraternity as lawyers.

However, all differences between Sheikh Abdullah and the Indian Government could not be resolved. These differences came into open when Sheikh refused to dissolve the National Conference and instead demanded the dissolution of Indian National Congress. In 1965 during the Chief Ministership of GM Sadiq, National Conference had become J&K branch of Indian National Congress. Sheikh Abdullah's apparent argument was that people had no such faith in Indian National Congress as in National Conference which had a distinct history of its own and was known in every home. The writer of this book is of the view that Sheikh Abdullah disliked to become a common leader like others from the core of his heart, to act within the discipline of Indian National Congress organization being a national party but wanted to remain unchallenged independent head of his Kashmir-centric regional organization National Conference and wanted to rule the State according to his pre-planned schemes which already he had tried to materialize during his first tenure as Prime Minister of the State. The full text of the Kashmir Accord is annexed as Appendix 11.

CHAPTER 16

Rule of Sheikh Abdullah

(1948-1953 and 1975-1982)

World known spiritual saint late Swami Chinmayananda in his written discourse on Bhagwat Geeta while describing the scene of ongoing Mahabharata war has commented about the conversation of Dhritarashtra and Sanjay in the following words—"when our motives are impure and cause unjust, however, well equipped we may be, our minds should necessarily feel restless and agitated. This is the mental condition of all tyrants and lusty dictators. The war of Mahabharata which lasted for 18 days only could have been avoided had the all powerful grandsire king Dhritarashtra followed the Raj Dharma by giving the just due share of governance to his nephews (Pandavas) but he wanted the kingdom in perpetuity for himself and thereafter for his progeny." According to the writer of this book, in case Sheikh Abdullah, who was the tallest political leader of Kashmir region in 1947, followed his Raj Dharma by fulfilling the written and oral promises given to Maharaja Hari Singh, Pandit Nehru, Mrs Indira Gandhi and not shown disloyalty to all of them at the material times, the Kashmir problem would have been solved at the earliest. Maharaja Hari Singh, Pandit Jawaharlal Nehru and finally Mrs Indira Gandhi had reposed full faith in him before bestowing the crown of whole Jammu and Kashmir State on his head. As a result, the prolonged ongoing Mahabharata like conflict between the Government of India and Government of Pakistan would have ended although not within eighteen days but within eighteen months or at the most within eighteen years. But the motives of Sheikh Abdullah from the very beginning have remained impure and his cause unjust to keep the crown for himself throughout his life and thereafter for his progeny. He despite suffering incarceration for long years became one of the major causes for placing the two countries always at tenterhooks of war like situations by changing his political stands. Even after entering into Accord of 1974 with Mrs Indira Gandhi and accepting the question of accession as final and application of Indian Constitution to greater extent, the slogan of Autonomy is being raised till date. In other words, after 1947 two full-fledged wars were fought in 1965 and 1971 and third major conflict in 1999 in Kargil sector. The low intensity proxy war which was started in 1990 by the alienated segment of society with full support of hostile neighbouring country is still going on. The human lives loss on all sides goes up to lakhs leaving aside the material losses. Lakhs of inhabitants of the State have become homeless. There is no near hope of the end of present ongoing Mahabharata. Had Sheikh Abdullah acted in tandem with Maharaja Hari Singh according to the pledges incorporated in his letter of 26 September 1947 already discussed and reproduced, the self-created problem of Independence during Pandit Nehru's time and thereafter in a refined manner that of Autonomy would have died its natural death. Adverting to the period of his rule, Sheikh Abdullah remained Prime Minister from March 1948 to August 1953. During this period of rule, he acted as an unchallenged dictator or monarch and was law unto himself. He kept himself mostly engaged to take personal revenges with Maharaja Hari Singh. This aspect has already been discussed. Dogras, members of Maharaja's clan, were also not spared as their share in the State governance started diminishing. Some of them lost their landed properties by the enactment of a draconian law known as Big Landed Estates Abolition Act. After the Indo-Pak war of 1971, he realized that Independence or complete Autonomy for him through Plebiscite was a distant dream so he compromised. When Indira Gandhi and Sheikh Accord was enforced in February 1975, the Congress Party elected Sheikh Abdullah as its leader. He was sworn in as Chief Minister on February 25, 1975 (but not as Prime Minister). Three other non-Congress Ministers joined his Cabinet. They were Mirza Afzal Beg, DD Thakur (a leading lawyer of Jammu Bar) and Sonam Narboo (retired Chief Engineer of the J&K State and a native of Ladakh). Neither Sheikh Abdullah nor his three ministers were the elected members of the Legislative Assembly nor elected or nominated members of the Legislative Council. The transfer of Chief Minister's 'Gaddi' in favour of Sheikh Abdullah according to one opinion of a sizeable section of the society was the result of a wrong medical opinion based on false and fabricated record showing him suffering from serious ailments and resultant short span of life. This opinion lacks credibility in absence of authentic corroborative evidence. At least this is certain that Sheikh Abdullah fulfilled his last ambition of life to rule the State but the slot was not as glamorous as the previous one when he was the unchallenged Prime Minister of the State under the protective umbrella of Prime Minister Jawaharlal Nehru. He had compelled Pandit Nehru by way of a political card for securing a victory in the UNO when Plebiscite would be held in the State which was a self-created problem by the Government of India in a unilateral manner. This was without the consent of the ruler of the State Maharaja Hari Singh who was the sole authority to make the accession of the State under the Indian Independence Act of 1947. The accession could either be accepted or rejected totally by the Union of India and conditional acceptance was irrelevant. This time, Sheikh Abdullah became a common Chief Minister like any other Chief Minister of any other Indian State. Also, he was liable to be removed by the President of India by invoking the powers vested in him under Article 356 of the Indian Constitution read with Section 92 of the Constitution of the J&K. By this time much water had flown down from river Jehlum because almost many other Articles of the Indian Constitution had been made applicable in the State including the jurisdiction of the Supreme Court of India and the Comptroller and Auditor General of India. The Provisions of the Kashmir Accord make it clear that Sheikh Abdullah accepted the accession of the State as a settled issue and holding of Plebiscite had ceased to be a live issue. The subsequent events have proved that instead of giving a fair and equitable representation to the other two regions of the State for achieving socialistic all around development as agreed in one of the conditions, he had tried to advance his family rule in the State. The other two regions of the State, i.e. Jammu and Ladakh became the worst sufferers for discrimination of their inhabitants in all the spheres of governance which fact has been already discussed in detail. At the fag end of his life, Sheikh Abdullah should have fulfilled the obligation of giving Regional Autonomies within the framework of the constitutional law to those regions as he had made a joint statement to fulfil this obligation with Pandit Nehru in early fifties which facts already stand stated in this book. Not only that, during Poonch Agitation which started from district Poonch and was fully backed by the people of whole Jammu region as Jammu city had become its centre, Sheikh Abdullah out of fear had made public statement to remove the regional imbalances and set up a commission but when the agitation was withdrawn nothing tangible was done to fulfil this promise.

The Indira-Sheikh Accord turned out to be a love and hate affair. Immediately, Sheikh turned down the suggestion to join the Congress Party. On April 13, 1975, he revived the National Conference and became its President. On July 5, 1975, he dissolved unlawful organization All J&K Plebiscite Front and merged it with National

Conference. On August 15, 1975, he openly caused desertion of ten members from the Congress Legislative Party and joined them in the National Conference. Temporarily, the differences were resolved by appointing a co-ordinating committee from both the parties. On October 21, 1975, he announced the expansion of his Cabinet in which he included four Congressmen without consulting Mrs Indira Gandhi. Mrs Indira Gandhi retaliated by not allowing those four members to join the cabinet and this resulted into cancellation of the swearing in ceremony.

The National Conference leaders frequently described 23 years (from August 9, 1953 to February 25, 1975) as a "dark patch in the history of Kashmir." Sheikh Abdullah immediately started picking his Plebiscite Front workers in the State Administration including in the police department in a systematic and calculated manner, as he already had done of course more openly during his first tenure up to 1953.

In the Parliamentary elections of March 1977, the Congress Party was routed in northern India. The Congress Party sensed that Sheikh Abdullah would join hands with Janata Party. The Congress had strength of 45 members in the house of 75 and on March 25, 1977, it withdrew the support and put up a claim to form the Ministry. Sheikh Abdullah got the house dissolved from Governor LK Jha. The Congressmen decried the decision as "undemocratic, morally indefensible and constitutionally questionable."

At that time, there was Janata wave in the country. Party unit was set up in the State with Maulana Masoodi as its Convener. Maulvi Farooq of Awami Action Committee also joined it. This made Sheikh panicky and he started raising parochial feelings. He also raised false propaganda for the abrogation of Article 370 of the Indian Constitution. The propaganda included that the State would cede from India if Kashmiris were not given the place of honour and dignity. In the Muslim-dominated rural areas, the leaders of National Conference administered oaths to the electorates by holding Koran in one hand and Pakistani salt in the other to cast votes in their favour (See *My Frozen Turbulence in Kashmir* by Jagmohan). During the period of elections, he fell sick and his detractors say that this was a ploy to win the sympathy of the masses. This semi-fascist propaganda yielded results as in the elections of June 30, 1977; he won 39 seats in the Valley out of 42, seven seats from Muslim majority area of Jammu region out of total 32 seats and both seats from Ladakh. The Janata Party got two seats in the Valley and eleven in the Jammu. The Congress was routed in the Valley but it won 14 seats in Jammu region and that too because of infighting between the members of Janata Party.

In the history of elections so far held in the State this was the fairest election because Prime Minister Morarji Desai and other important leaders in his cabinet including Shri Atal Bihari Vajpayee of the Janata Party did not allow any rigging of the elections which could easily be done by them because the State was under the spell of Governor's Rule. However, from the above stated facts it is established that the tallest leader from Kashmir Valley, i.e. Sheikh Abdullah despite his last days of life did not desist from the old habit of playing a religious card in order to win a victory in the elections. These tactics adopted by him could be termed as unfair practice under the Election Law but because of the paucity of available evidence and in fighting and disunity in other political parties, the matter could not be taken up in the Election Tribunal by way of filing election petitions.

Sheikh Abdullah was sworn in as Chief Minister on July 9, 1977. Small caucuses in political and administrative arena ascended around him and this generated corruption and regional discrimination. He withdrew criminal cases against 30 hardcore activists of Al-Fatah (a militant organization). The Sessions Judge who was designated as Special Judge at that time to try this case was known for his honesty and possessed accommodating disposition of mind towards lawyers as well as litigants. He had been trying this case in the premises of Central Jail Srinagar where a small separate portion of the jail building had been converted as a court complex for the trial of anti-nationals. This had been done for security reasons as important and dreaded anti-nationals normally could not be taken on every date of hearing in the court complex of Srinagar which was situated in the heart of the city. In 1980, the writer of this book was promoted as District and Sessions Judge and posted as First Additional District and Sessions Judge Anti-Corruption for Kashmir Division (including Ladakh region) with additional powers to try the anti-nationals under the Enemy Agents Ordinance of the Samvat year 2007 (AD 1950) promulgated by the then Sadar-i-Riyasat (Dr Karan Singh). At least twice or thrice in a month, the court proceedings were held in Central Jail premises. The staff members had told the writer of this book that the accused of this notorious anti-national organization were being treated as State guests in the court on every date of hearing. They were being served sumptuous tea along with fried chicken and 'Kashmiri kebabs'. The accused were getting long adjournments according to their wishes and convenience. At this stage, it will amount to do injustice to the patriotic zeal and fervour of late Peer Ghulam Hassan Shah, ex-Director-General of Police (J&K) in case his professional ethics performed with sense of duty as a patriot police officer is not given a space in this book. This heroic deed of Police Officer of rare competence and moral courage with full dedication to safe guard the disintegration of the State from Union of India, unfortunately faded away after passage of time. The successor political bosses at the helm of the affairs inclusive of administrators and concerned members of the judiciary had succumbed to some hidden pressure to prolong the legal process set afoot by him. He had done so without caring for the future risk to his life and family member's safety. With utmost professional competence he had unearthed the underground network of the above said anti-national organization. The result was that all the accused got an opportunity to avail the pre-planned escape route and were away from the clutches of law. Had the case been tried in a fair manner with all promptitude it could be possible the result would have been otherwise. MY Saraf of POJK in his book has tremendously praised the network of the above stated organization from his own Pro-Pakistan point of views. After the end of this one of the sensitive anti-national case, Sheikh Abdullah accommodated some of the accused at vantage political and administrative positions including in the judiciary. In order to ensure the successful accession of Chief Ministership in favour of his son Dr Farooq Abdullah, he asked the potent contender Mirza Afzal Beg to resign. He did so on September 25, 1978 and four days later was expelled from the party. Throughout his life, Baig had stood like a rock with Sheikh Abdullah and advanced his mission of life. He was recognized as number two leader in the hierarchy of leadership. After his unceremonious expulsion, he fell sick and remained on death bed for a pretty long time. Late DD Thakur on Baig's exit occupied his senior position in the government as a minister and in his autobiography he has recorded that when he (Thakur) suggested Sheikh Abdullah to pay a courtesy call jointly at the house of Afzal Beg, Sheikh Abdullah opposed this idea but with great persuasion he made him to agree to see the ailing ex-minister along with his other colleagues. It is not sure whether Sheikh Abdullah himself had accompanied them or not.

Anti-defection law was enacted to strengthen his coterie. In order to keep the emotional fervour of the Kashmiri masses boiling he passed the controversial Resettlement Bill which discriminates the inhabitants of the State on the ground of religion. At the time of partition of India in 1947, many Muslims having Muslim League's leanings had migrated from the State to the territory of Pakistan. The Bill envisaged their safe return including their successors in the State of J&K but Hindus and Sikhs who became refugees from the Pakistan occupied areas had not been given any compensatory relief. Rather, they had to surrender their properties occupied as allottees of the evacuee properties on the claims of proprietary rights of those anticipated returnees from Pakistan. In other words, again for the second time they had to become refugees on the basis of being Hindus/Sikhs. Even hardcore descendant militants of those migrated families could return to the State under the protection of that proposed Bill as Real Migrants. Sheikh Abdullah passed away on September 8, 1982. He got a mammoth funeral. Dr Farooq Abdullah as expected succeeded him as Chief Minister. This was a smooth affair as there was nobody in the National Conference to challenge Sheikh Abdullah's last wish. Mrs Indira Gandhi (Prime Minister of India) and Governor of the State BK Nehru had also participated in the funeral procession. The writer of this book who at that time was in Kargil Headquarters as District Judge Ladakh also came to witness the funeral procession which was a sea of human beings. Undoubtedly, people of Kashmir gave him great love and affection in the last journey of his life.

The Resettlement Bill had raised fierce controversy as the Central Government and the Governor received hundreds of representations. The Governor sent the Bill back to the Legislative Assembly pointing out the constitutional infirmities. At this time, Dr Farooq Abdullah had become the Chief Minister. He persisted and got the Bill passed second time on October 4, 1982. The Governor was left with no option but to give his assent. From here, the Central Government held discussions with new Chief Minister Dr Farooq Abdullah and made a Presidential reference to the Supreme Court for its advice. In 2002, the Supreme Court dismissed the reference by holding that it had already become an Act so the reference was not maintainable. Two Public Interest Writ Petitions were filed in the Supreme Court. (Writ Petition of 2001 titled 'Shiv Sagar Tiwari and another *vs* State of J&K' and others; writ petition of 2001 titled 'J&K National Panthers Party *vs* Union of India and others'). The Apex Court has granted the interim relief by staying the operation of the Act and the writs stand admitted for hearing. The thinking of the protagonists of the Resettlement Act and the thinking of the J&K Liberation Front spring from the same root, i.e. separatist psyche. The passing of the Autonomy resolution in the J&K Assembly in 2001 by Dr Farooq Abdullah gives credence to this view. The resolution also speaks of discrimination and communalism. It divides the State into eight Divisions out of which only one Division would be Hindu-dominated and one Division Buddhist while six would be Muslim-dominated. It dissects the Jammu region on communal lines. The Central Government headed by Shri Atal Bihari Vajpayee outrightly rejected this resolution though Dr Farooq Abdullah and his partymen were most unhappy being the partners in the coalition NDA Government.

Sheikh Abdullah as Ruler of the State

During his second incarnation as head of the State Administration, Sheikh Abdullah took up the robes to switch his remaining unfinished political goals of the first regime. Side by side during this period he had allegedly started collecting wealth in order to enrich himself and his near relatives at the fag end of his life. Soon after his relations with Congress(I) organization had become very sour and there was a rat race for winning political upper hand in the State. Allegations and counter-allegations were made for corrupt deeds against each other. A printed booklet in Urdu language was circulated amongst the major Heads of the Departments of the State and amongst the public figures in the name of one Abid Hussain Khan under the title *Open Book of Sheikh Abdullah's Life* (Part Fourth). The full particulars of the printer and publisher of this booklet were not given. The writer of this book when was posted as District and Sessions Judge Rajouri also received a copy of this booklet which was commonly known as *Lal Kitaab* or *Red Book of Sheikh Abdullah*. The allegations made in this book are mostly supported by official record and at no point of time they were politically controverted either through Press or taking legal action in a Court of Law. So in a bona fide manner it is presumed in the public interest that they contain iota of truth. Furthermore, the writer of this book stands to be corrected if what has been stated in this booklet is either factually or legally incorrect; even though he has reproduced only that which he has found to be genuine and factually correct. Remembering the famous saying of Winston Churchill (one of the illustrious Prime Ministers of England) that, "History will be kind to me for I intend to write it"; I have ventured in good faith for the interest of general public to translate the original version from Urdu language into English and to reproduce some of the extracts for historical records from that booklet copy whereof is still in my possession.

At page 3 of the above said booklet, it is recorded that after assuming the power in 1975, Sheikh Abdullah made a declaration: "My first duty would be to clean the public life from all sorts of evils and misdeeds. For strengthening the moral values in the State such a policy would be adopted where every public servant and public figure (man) would be held accountable for his acts. This would be my first object." It is alleged that all this was a hollow statement but the following categorised acts would speak for themselves. The first heading of the alleged misdeeds of Sheikh Abdullah is titled, 'How showers of wealth had started percolating in the house of the Chief Minister?'

1. The first allegation is that when in 1975, Sheikh Abdullah came to power, he was not a wealthy man. He had neither paid any Income Tax nor any Wealth Tax. Within a span of six years he became 'Crorepati' by usurping the government lands. On those usurped lands buildings were raised in a systematic manner by utilizing the services of government contractors at the cost of public funds meant for development purposes.
2. The second allegation is regarding illegal allotment of 'Dhanjiboy Properties' on Nazool land situated in the Estate of Kothibagh Srinagar in favour of Chief Minister Sheikh Abdullah. This property is situated in the heart of Srinagar city's commercial centre nearby the bank of river Jhelum in Polo Ground area. This land is State land owned by Nazool Department and during the regime of Dogra ruler Maharaja Pratap Singh was given on lease for forty years with effect from 13 October 1921 in favour of Dhanjiboy. The lease was both for residential and commercial purposes. The full history of this property from the very start till its allotment in 1981 in favour of Sheikh Abdullah is attached by way of authentic government record with that book (*Red Book*). It remained in safe hands till the end of Congress rule in 1975 when the last Congress Chief Minister Syed Mir Qasim by Cabinet order had approved it for the construction of a government hotel with commercial complexes. The tables were turned when Sheikh Abdullah came into power, the main portion of the building along with commercial complexes built thereon extending on more than two acres was resumed by making a payment of meagre amount of Rs 3,60,000 to the last surviving heir of Dhanjiboy who was a widow. The payment was made to her through a person in proxy whose name was Ghulam Mohi-ud-Din but he was immediately ousted and by a Cabinet order. The Chief Minister Sheikh Abdullah himself became an allottee. It is stated that the value of the land, building and commercial complex standing thereon at that time was about a crore. This is a clear case of misuse of official power.
3. The third allegation relates to the house which is situated behind Nedous Hotel on Maulana Azad Road and was valued at that time Rs 10,00,000 in that booklet. The ancestral house of Sheikh Abdullah which is situated near Sher-e-Kashmir Institute of Medical Sciences Srinagar was given on a monthly rent of Rupees Two thousand to the Institute. The residential house of then Chief Minister Sheikh Abdullah which is situated

as stated above behind Nedous Hotel started fetching rent from government along with the furniture which was converted as Chief Minister's house. A mention is also made of a Farm House situated in Tangmarg near famous resort of Gulmarg and allegation is made about the constant encroachments being made on the nearby State and Forest Lands.

4. The next allegation is with regard to 16 kanals 8 marlas of land situated in 'Gupkar Road' which is the most posh locality in the city of Srinagar. The price of the land has been estimated at Rs 40,00,000. This is also Nazool Land and the original allottee was a forest contractor who was made to surrender the possession along with one bungalow constructed thereon because of official influence. The whole plot along with the existing bungalow thereon was allotted on lease in favour of 'Begum Abdullah' at a very nominal fee. Immediately thereafter, another building was raised by Begum Sahiba on that piece of land at State expenses. Copy of the government allotment order is attached with that *Red Book*. The cost of the buildings was assessed at Rs 10,00,000. At present its value may be approximately Rs 30-40 crores.
5. The next allegations pertains to Dr Farooq Abdullah who lived for fourteen years in England on the pretext of acquiring higher knowledge in medical profession but returned with his old MBBS degree obtained by him from Rajasthan University where his nomination had been made by Pandit Nehru himself for admission from government reserved quota. While coming back along with his Begum, he brought two foreign cars on which the alleged custom duty payable was in the sum of Rupees Two lakhs. Dr Abdullah got the exemption on the plea that those vehicles would be plied for public benefit in the Sher-e-Kashmir Medical Institute but they were exclusively used by him. On the basis of possessing simple MBBS degree, he was appointed in 1980 as Director of the Sher-e-Kashmir Medical Institute at the monthly pay of Rupees Two thousand. His Begum was appointed as Chief Matron on the equivalent pay. Such a high pay was not payable at that time in the State to a Head of the Department.
6. The allegations pertains to Ghulam Mohammad Shah, son-in-law of Sheikh Abdullah, who was a Cabinet Minister in Sheikh Abdullah's Cabinet and holding a very lucrative department—Public Works and Roads Department. Allegations are that he openly was charging money for affecting transfers of the officials

of the department according to their ranks. Similar types of allegations are made against the deceased son of Sheikh Abdullah (Tariq) who was made incharge of tourism department. There is also allegation about illegal allotment of half acre of land near Zero bridge in favour of the official newspaper of National Conference *Nawai Subah* at a yearly rent of Rupee One.

7. This allegation relates to the allotment of State land made in favour of in-laws family of Sheikh Abdullah. The land in question measures fifteen acres and its allotment period had yet to expire in 1985 but in hot haste on 1 June 1980, allotment was extended for ninety years. In corroboration of this allegation copy of Cabinet decision numbers 117-A dated 24 March 1976 and copy of cabinet decision 264 dated 9 June 1980 are attached with that *Red Book*. According to the prevalent rule practice, the allotment order could be for forty years but vide government order number REV (NDK) 387 of 1980 dated 21 October 1980 it was made for ninety years according to the very convenient conditions favouring the allottee. The market price of the land has been assessed more than Rupees One Crore. At that time, arrears of rent in the sum of Rupees Eight lakh were due from the allottee but no consideration for this serious breach of agreement condition was taken for cancelling the allotment but on concessional rates the allotment was extended for ninety years more. Similarly, Government Order number 673 UD dated 31 October 1980 has been mentioned whereby land measuring more than sixty-five kanals was again allotted for forty years for that family when the allottee was in illegal possession from 1961. In case some body else would have been in this situation his allotments would have been cancelled. At present the market value of those properties runs approximately into hundred of crores.

8. The illegal allotment of property worth hundreds of crores of rupees relates to leasing out eight kanals of land situated at Malabar Hill in Mumbai for Rs 5,00,000 per annum in 1981 by the J&K Government when Sheikh Abdullah was the Chief Minister. The allottee of this land is Singhvi Construction Company which had also been favoured by supplying timber at cheap rates in the name of Pencil making factory in J&K State. After the death of the Maharaja Hari Singh in 1961, this property was taken by the J&K Government and converted into a State guest house. The property was intact till 1981, but

Sheikh Abdullah on June 17, 1981 leased out to M/s Singhvi Construction Company Private Ltd (a non-State Subject) for 90 years. A premium was charged at the initial stage of a meagre amount of Rs 2,05,00,000 with a future yearly premium payable at the rate of Rs 5,00,000. Against the terms and conditions of lease agreement, the allottee (construction company) demolished the Haveli and constructed a multi-story building consisting of 12 duplex flats in 24 floors with a swimming pool adjacent to it. The allottee started litigation with the government. In order to prolong the litigation, the allottee (construction company) had taken the matter in SLP to the Hon'ble Supreme Court which was not being properly prosecuted on behalf of the State government despite the allottee had obtained stay order after getting appointed Arbitrator—a retired judge of the Supreme Court Justice Tulzapurkar. At the end of 1996, the matter was listed in the State High Court roster before the writer of this book. An opportunity was thus available in routine to peruse the record. It was found that the government advocates were not serious to pursue the matter. The writer of this book passed effective interim orders and forced the then Chief Secretary Ashok Jaitley to get the matter pursued seriously both in the High Court as well as in the Supreme Court. This coercive course bore the required fruit and the concerned government advocate started appearing in the Supreme Court as well as before the arbitrator. The result was that a supplementary agreement was entered between the State Government and the allottee Singhvi Construction Company on April 8, 2002 in respect of the said property. One duplex flat on the second floor measuring 700 square feet was acquired by the State. For the general enlightened people of the society it was not a fair deal as the fishy matter is still being agitated in the public fora. In the last session of the Legislative Assembly in 2013 which was held in Jammu some MLAs raised the issue and compelled the government to appoint Public Accounts Committee which was headed by PDP MLA Rafi Ahmed Mir as Chairman. The Committee has made the observations: "the situation of the State in 1981 was not so bad which would have compelled thev government to reach such a poor Agreement at throw away prices and putting the state for great recurring loss for decades together." It is reported in the local newspaper *Daily Excelsior* of Jammu in its issue of 16 April 2013 that Public Accounts Committee appointed by the Assembly had asked the

> government to conduct on spot inspection of the property. A future responsible government with honest intentions will look into the matter when it comes into power and this misdeed of glaring misuse of official position and authority is hoped to be settled within the framework of law by redressing the grievances of the people of the State in general who are its owners and not any particular Chief Minister. There are more allegations supported by concerned government record delineated in this booklet which also speak of pecuniary benefits conferred on Sheikh's family and his near relations but they need not to be mentioned here as the above stated examples are sufficient to bring home the point at issue for the information of the readers. Moreover, there is generally no accountability in the whole of the country and particularly in this part of the country for such misdeeds committed by politicians of even lower strata and not to talk of high and mighty.

Dr Farooq Abdullah inherited the crown from his father after his death in September 1982. He surrounded himself with the Ministers in his cabinet of his own choice and made many prominent colleagues of the cabinet of his father to leave the berths of ministership. The most notable casualty was DD Thakur who was the sole choice from Jammu region of Sheikh Abdullah while occupying the chair of Chief Minister for the first time. He was the first Deputy Chief Minister to have been appointed from 1947 till that date hailing from Jammu region. Sheikh Abdullah had been using his persuasive advocacy skills in dealing with Government of India and bringing the finances to the State but Farooq Abdullah's cabinet did not comprise many talented or educated people. In fact, there were very few graduates in his ministry.

The relations between Indira Gandhi and Dr Farooq Abdullah strained and became bitter during the course of Assembly Elections of June 1983. In these elections National Conference won 46 seats and Congress 26. There was spurt in anti-national activities. The Punjab events also started casting their long shadows. Farooq Abdullah as usual took little interest in the administration of the State and allowed corruption to increase. He was seen playing Golf sometimes in Srinagar and sometimes in Chandigarh. As Chief Minister he was even found enjoying at the marriage parties of wealthy businessmen. The glamourous city of Mumbai was also a favourite place for him to be in the company of film stars. He was generally known as Disco Chief Minister. The fundamentalist elements which were in the State even during Maharaja's time got a God sent opportunity to strengthen their bases after the demise of Sheikh Abdullah with full strength. Up to 1974, such elements had been subdued. Bakshi Ghulam Mohammad as Prime Minister of National Conference up to the end of his rule had suppressed them with heavy iron hand and thereafter GM Sadiq as Chief Minister of Congress Party had politically marginalized them.

Religious and regional feelings were unscrupulously exploited. To strengthen his position in the Valley Farooq Abdullah joined hands with Mirwaiz Maulvi Farooq though the latter had not shed his pro-plebiscite stand even temporarily. He (Dr Abdullah) had been speaking different languages at different places and at different occasions. He had been propagating that elections were a Plebiscite. Because of such behaviour, there was a sharp polarization of the electorates on communal and parochial lines. The Kashmiri and Muslim-inhabited areas of Jammu and Ladakh regions voted for the National Conference and Hindu-dominated areas of Jammu for the Congress. In Leh district of Ladakh, Congress won while as in Kargil district assembly constituency, National Conference candidate won. Mrs Indira Gandhi's meeting on June 3, 1983 was violently disturbed and obscene gestures were made at her in Iqbal Park, Srinagar which was the venue of the meeting. This incident was headed by Mohd Shafi Bhat, advocate, who earlier had instigated the Members of the Kashmir Bar Association to agitate against the installation of the statue of Mahatma Gandhi in the complex of new High Court building, Srinagar. Mohd Shafi Bhat was rewarded to become MLA and then Member of Parliament on National Conference tickets. (Note: these facts have mentioned in details in the book *My Frozen Turbulence in Kashmir* by Jagmohan). Besides that the writer of this book also has some personal knowledge. During the elections of 2002, when National Conference ticket was denied to Shafi Bhat, he was admitted by the Congress Party in its fold and was given party ticket as a Congress candidate to contest from the city of Srinagar Assembly constituency and he returned successful member of Congress(I) Party in the State Legislature. Such is the moral character of the political parties as well as of some of the legislators. During the elections of 1983, the Centre had sent large number of paramilitary forces for election duty, but State Authorities allotted them inconsequential work and managed the polling booths exclusively by their own staff. The allegations of rigging in the elections were not without any substance because 40 election petitions were filed in the State High Court. At some polling stations more than 90 per cent polling had taken place. Mufti Mohammad Sayeed (ex-Chief Minister and now PDP patron) at that time was the Chief of the Congress Party in the State and he bemoaned, "This is like Bhutto's 1978 election in Pakistan. It has no legitimacy. It is based upon fraud."

Terrorism Surfaces in the Valley

Though during Sheikh Abdullah's regime, the separatist elements were being encouraged in getting government jobs and distribution of all sorts of government largesse yet he had not abdicated his sovereign authority in their favour as it happened after his death. His full control over the affairs of the State finds support from an incident narrated to the writer of this book during his posting in the years 1978-79 as Chief Judicial Magistrate Udhampur by the area commander of the Northern Command (General Buch) at latter's residence. The General had expressed his ignorance for not getting any prior information from the military intelligence agencies regarding the large scale destruction of the properties of the activists of Jamaat-e-Islami in Kashmir Valley by the workers of National Conference during one night's silent operation.

In 1980, the writer of this book after his promotion as District and Sessions Judge and subsequent posting in Srinagar, as already has been stated in this book, got an opportunity to try the case of Maqbool Bhat, founder of JKLF militant organization, along with his four associates (one local and three Pakistanis). They were charged for committing dacoity with murder of the Bank Manager (of J&K Bank Branch, Langate) read with violating the Provisions of J&K Enemy Agents Ordinance. The said Maqbool Bhat at an earlier occasion also had infiltrated into Kashmir Valley in 1966. In execution of the terrorist related activities, he had killed Chaman Lal, CID Sub-Inspector of the J&K Police Force. He was apprehended by the law enforcing agencies. The trial of the case was held by Neelkanth Ganjoo, the then concerned Sessions Judge and he had awarded death sentence to Bhat. The judgment had been confirmed by all the concerned superior courts. In 1968, Maqbool Bhat escaped from Srinagar Jail after getting full support from some concerned authorities. This incident throws floodlight over the pitiable control of the State administration and that of the then Central government headed by Congress party. After his escape from the Srinagar Central Jail to Pakistan, he was detained from suspicion angle by Pakistani intelligence agencies of being an Indian intelligence agent but was released by the Competent Tribunal where he was tried. After Indira-Sheikh Accord of 1975, the anti-national elements found a golden opportunity to step-up their subdued activities. Maqbool Bhat availed this opportunity at the first instance and for the second time infiltrated into the State along with his associates and committed a dacoity in the J&K Bank Branch Langate in the Kashmir Valley. The Bank Manager (a Kashmiri Muslim) showed resistance and met a heroic end by sacrificing his life at their cruel hands. Local people apprehended some of the accused on the spot including Maqbool Bhat. Before the writer of this book had taken over the charge of the office (as First Additional District and Sessions Judge Srinagar as stated above), Bhat had already been shifted to Tihar Jail, Delhi on getting before hand information from intelligence agencies about the existence of a secret plan to facilitate his second time escape to Pakistan by jail breaking. The team of his defence lawyers headed by Abdul Gani Lone, advocate (who subsequently had floated a terrorist organization and lastly in 2000 was killed by the militants of some other organisation) moved an application to bring back Maqbool Bhat from Tihar Jail to Srinagar to face the joint trial of the case. Additional prayer was also made to initiate contempt proceedings against the authorities who had shifted him and that trial of the case should be stayed. None of the above stated reliefs as prayed for was granted. The order was not liked by Maqbool Bhat's cohorts and supporters. GM Shah who was the son-in-law of Sheikh Abdullah and remained a leading light of Banned Unlawful Association 'Plebiscite Front' was holding the charge of Housing and Urban Development Department. He was one of the most aggrieved and annoyed persons along with his Deputy Minister late BA Kitchloo. Both of them conspired and cancelled the allotment of a government quarter of the writer of this book without following the prescribed law and procedure. The writer of the book at that time was in Jammu on leave and when went back to join the duty found the quarter locked and sealed by the Estate Department. All the household articles were lying inside. This shocking incident is one of the unforgetful sad event of his life. A noble and spiritual minded honest IPS Officer (Ram Parkash) who at that time was holding the charge as Commandant of IVth J&K Police Battalion was writer's neighbour. He accommodated the writer of the book along with his family members for 3-4 days till the writer of the book could hire a private accommodation. Bahauddin Farooqi was at that time holding the charge of Acting Chief Justice of the J&K High Court (who later on was transferred on complaint basis to Sikkim High Court as Chief Justice but he did not join and resigned and then for some time remained a guiding figure of the separatist organizations. He had even filed a writ petition in their favour on his name regarding accession of the State and other allied matters in the High Court of Jammu and Kashmir). On the next day, the writer of the book informed the then Acting Chief Justice (Farooqi) telegraphically whose headquarters at that time was in Jammu. Telegram was given on

19 April 1981 containing the following contents: "my allotted flat sealed by Estate Department during my absence without recourse to law." A detailed letter highlighting the conduct of the above stated two ministers was sent to the Chief Minister at Jammu (Sheikh Abdullah). Neither the Acting Chief Justice nor the Chief Minister took any cognizance because GM Shah was the son-in-law of Sheikh Abdullah. The Jammu Bar Association and Udhampur Bar Association condemned this diabolical, brutish and fiendish act of the government by passing resolutions. The writer of the book had no other option but to take out the household articles in a private rented accommodation. Without any support from the High Court, it was impossible to enter into a legal battle with the high dignitaries of the government.

In 1981, the Income Tax Authorities simultaneously carried out raids throughout the Kashmir Valley in the business premises of some top carpet dealers. Mattoo and Sons is a business concern and deals in carpet business having head office establishment in the posh locality of Hari Singh High Street, Srinagar. This family is very affluent and politically well connected as Sheikh Abdullah's younger daughter is married in the family. The business of the family also came under the scrutiny of the Income Tax Department. Sheikh Abdullah at that time was the Chief Minister and his son Dr Farooq Abdullah was a Member of the Indian Parliament of National Conference ruling party. When the raiding party of the income tax department had started the operations at different localities of the targeted business houses, Dr Farooq Abdullah as a Member of the Parliament came out openly to the help of business fraternity. He started inciting the mobs to rise in revolt against the Income Tax Authorities and the Union of India. The people started manhandling the Income Tax Officers when they were discharging their official duties. Forty-seven out of a total of sixty-nine Income Tax Officials which included female officers were injured in the violent clashes. At few places, the seized documents were forcibly snatched. After this incident the Income Tax collective raids in the valley have become a thing of the past.

During Dr Farooq Abdullah's regime, militancy seemed to gain impetus much more than it did during the regime of his father (Sheikh Abdullah). Because of such a wanton administrative laxity ultimately the whole administration collapsed and the common people are still paying the price by becoming refugees and getting themselves killed like flies and mosquitoes. Given below are some of the glaring examples where the government failed to provide effective administration. Rather, pro-Pakistani elements and a sizeable section of the National Conference workers including ministers and bureaucrats were working at the same emotional wavelength. During the month of October 1983 one day international cricket match between India and West Indies took place in Srinagar. Indian players were hooted, heckled, abused and assaulted with sticks. Rotten eggs and vegetables were thrown upon them.

A nexus had developed between some ultra Sikh youths (who were hostile to the Union Government) and Kashmiri anti-nationalists. On June 7, 1984, a combined procession was organized in Srinagar city where naked swords were brandished. The crowd went on rampage and a number of shops including Arya Samaj school building and the Nirankari Bhavan were set on fire. The Pujari of Hanuman Temple at Amira Kadal was beaten and the idol thrown into the Jhelum river. Prior to this, a number of bomb explosions had taken place in the city of Srinagar. The common man stood terrorized and the administration was gradually losing its hold on the affairs of the State.

Split of Sheikh Family

Khalida Shah, eldest daughter of Sheikh Abdullah was equally politically ambitious as her brother Dr Farooq Abdullah. Her husband GM Shah who had stood through thick and thin with his father-in-law and also felt betrayed like Mirza Afzal Beg—a life long associate and partner in all his trials and tribulations. The husband and wife could not reconcile with Sheikh Abdullah's decision to pass on the crown to his son Dr Farooq Abdullah. GM Shah had managed to get at least eight tickets of the Assembly through his mother-in-law during the elections of 1983 and they had become legislators. Farooq Abdullah for the first time became Chief Minister in September 1982 after Sheikh's death and he had unceremoniously dropped about half a dozen Cabinet Ministers of his Father's Cabinet. They too clandestinely joined hands with GM Shah.

Congress(I) started public agitation against rigging in elections and misrule of Dr Farooq Abdullah. A booklet known as *Lal Kitaab* (*Red Book*) as previously discussed in this book, was published which contained documentary evidence against Sheikh Abdullah and his family members for acquiring immovable property worth crores of rupees by illegal and corrupt means. Many demonstrations were held throughout the State. In one such demonstration which was held on January 15, 1984:, four Congress supporters were killed in police firing. Mohd Shafi Qureshi leader of Congress(I) gave a statement, "if you raise a slogan 'Azad Hindustan Zindabad' you get killed and in case you shout 'Pakistan Zindabad', 'Indian dogs go back', you prosper and make money." Janak Raj Gupta a Congress(I) leader who later on became Member of Parliament had openly declared that Farooq was in league with terrorists. KC Pant, Central Minister had said that Farooq was a "willing prisoner in the hands of anti-national forces." In rejoinder Dr Farooq said that in case Central Government did not give financial assistance he would turn to Saudi Arabia for help and termed the Congress(I) a party of 'goondas and chors'. There was also the allegation that Farooq Abdullah had allowed the territory of the State to be used for running clandestine training camps for Sikh terrorists. He had openly sided with Akalis in the elections of 1983. PC Sethi was at that time Home Minister of Central Government and he too expressed deep apprehensions over such training camps. Congress(I) MPs of Lok Sabha had been describing him as security risk and a traitor. Rajkumari Bajpai for instance said, "Dr Farooq Abdullah had always contacts with people who thought in terms of separating Kashmir from India. He has personal relations with leaders of J&K Liberation Front. After coming into power also, he continued his contacts with these people and that was why he had started giving encouragement to Jamaat-e-Islami and Jamaat-e-Tulba which were their militant wings. These people started raising slogans which had never been heard earlier." BR Bhagat had said, "facts had borne out clearly that Dr Abdullah was indulging in anti-national activities. He had aligned himself with Maulvi Farooq who did not believe in accession."

Janak Raj Gupta, then a leader of Congress(I) and subsequently Member of Parliament of Congress(I) (who later on joined ruling National Conference during the last spell of Dr Farooq Abdullah's rule) and now again a Congress leader quoted extensively from Urdu weekly *Insaf* published simultaneously from Muzaffarabad and Rawalpindi that, "On his visit in 1974 at the invitation of Ansari Group of Plebiscite Front Dr Farooq Abdullah had pleaded for independent Kashmir. He had gone to the extent of saying that if Sheikh Abdullah did not accept his view he would revolt against his father." The above said allegations and counter-allegations also find a place in the book written by Jagmohan in *My Frozen Turbulence in Kashmir*.

Twelve MLAs of the ruling party National Conference chose GM Shah as their leader and an independent MLA, Ali Mohd Naik also joined them. He also got the support of twenty-six members of the Congress(I) Legislature Party. They through documentary evidence presented their claim before the Governor and prayed for the dismissal of the minority government of Dr Farooq Abdullah.

The then Governor Jagmohan wanted to issue proclamation under Section 92 of the J&K Constitution assuming to himself all the powers of the government and under Sub-Section 5 of Section 92 of the State

Constitution he sought the requisite concurrence of the President of India. The concurrence was refused and GM Shah was asked to form the government after dismissing Farooq Abdullah with an assurance from him that he would convene the Assembly within one month and prove his majority. He did not prove his majority because of the obstacles created by the then Speaker Ali Mohammad Yatoo who was also removed from that post.

CHAPTER 17

GM Shah's Rule

(July 2, 1984 to March 6, 1986)

By causing the defections in the manner stated above and collecting all the disgruntled elements from the party of his father-in-law (National Conference) and with the blessings of the Central Government ultimately GM Shah established his rule by proving majority in the Legislative Assembly. Janak Raj Gupta then Congress(I) leader played an important part in destabilizing Dr Farooq Abdullah's government and the allegations levelled against him by the supporters of Dr Farooq Abdullah were that he brought crores of rupees from Centre in causing the defections of the MLAs. This government of defectors as alleged had immediately started minting money by all foul and unfair means. (Reference: *My Frozen Turbulence in Kashmir* by Jagmohan).

In the period following the Lok Sabha elections in 1984, GM Shah's cabinet went on a looting spree. Senior officers were recklessly transferred and swapped with undeserving officials. In 1985, the cabinet decided to confer proprietary rights to the lessee's of the State lands at half of the market value and also to regularise all unauthorized occupations of 'nazool lands'. The Governor tried to stall these transactions but it had partial effect. As an instance prime land of immense commercial value on the BC Road in Jammu city was transferred in favour of a very influential business family of Jammu city where a commercial complex was established against Municipal and other relevant by-laws. Later on, Dr Farooq Abdullah when after assuming the powers of government, set up a Commission headed by Justice IK Kotwal to go into all the irregularities and find out the acts of corruption in the political set up. This case was also referred to him for enquiry. Late Justice IK Kotwal had confided privately with the writer of this book being a senior member of the Advisory Board constituted under Public Safety Act of which the former was Chairman that some of the cases referred to his Commission had the evidence of clinching nature and many hi-fi politicians and bureaucrats could be implicated but when the rule of Dr Farooq Abdullah ended this Commission was bound up and consequently the record also became untraceable. Some Sales Tax cases were also settled through settlements benefiting the influential defaulters worth crores of rupees. Shah was known for his short temper and at times he used to abuse the public servants in the full public view. As Chief Minister once he slapped a Traffic Police Officer in Srinagar who was in official uniform. The reason for such a criminal action was that Chief Minister had formed the opinion that the officer was not performing his official duties with due diligence. There are many instances of such an erratic and undignified behaviour which no other Chief Minister ever did or exhibited. At times, there were collective protests from the public servants but then he used to bow down. This whimsical misrule of GM Shah lasted from July 2, 1984 to March 6, 1986 and was replaced by Governor's rule for six months. After his ouster from power, GM Shah floated his political party known as Awami National Conference. His communal credentials are established from his single utterance when out of power, he once gave a statement on family planning programme by undermining it that, "the official birth control programme is aimed at reducing the State Muslim majority to a minority. The Muslim constituted 80 per cent population of the State in 1947, they have now been reduced to only 54 per cent. In another ten years time they would be reduced to minority of 48 per cent of the total population." This is statistically wrong and false and reflects GM Shah's communal mind set. During his life time, he at many occasions made utterances that seemed to be in favour of the terrorists and the terrorist organizations despite the fact that he had remained as an important Cabinet Minister in Sheikh Abdullah's regime and then as a Chief Minister after securing the vote of no confidence against Dr Farooq Abdullah.

GM Shah's rule was replaced by Governor's Rule and Shri Jagmohan administered the State for six months, i.e. from March 7, 1986 to September 6, 1986.

CHAPTER 18

Dr Farooq Abdullah's Rule
(November 1986 to January 18, 1990)

The second stint of Dr Farooq Abdullah's rule may be known in the State history as deficient governance. All pervading casualness had the tendentious effect of causing inefficiency, ineffectiveness and in due course of time it proved as main factor for eroding administrative authority resulting in the rise of open militancy in this peaceful State. Prior to this, the culture of violence was uncommon. An intentional murder caused with violent means was unknown feature in the Kashmir Valley. A glaring instance of casual and cavalier approach in running the government can be well illustrated by an instance of allowing a procession on January 13, 1989 in the Jammu city on the eve of birth day of Guru Gobind Singh. 'Akal Takht' which is the highest spiritual seat of the Sikhs had given a call for the observance of protest week from January 6 to January 13, 1989 after the hanging of the killers of Mrs Indira Gandhi slain Prime Minister of India. The death by hanging of the killers was caused in pursuance of the verdict of the Supreme Court of India. As a retaliatory act of revenge the Khalistani militants had a few days earlier hanged four innocent civilians (Hindus) in the neighbouring district of Gurdaspur (Punjab). In the background of this tension, surcharged atmosphere, the administration had taken no precautionary measures to avoid any law and order problem.

Some mischievous elements in the procession had exhibited the portraits of the assassins—Satwant Singh and Kehar Singh as martyrs. Anti-national slogans were raised by those elements when the procession reached the heart of the city. In Purani Mandi area of the city these hooligans set on fire about fifty kiosks (khokhas) and damaged dozens of parked vehicles. A portion of Hanuman Temple was also damaged. There was instant reaction of this hooliganism in which twelve processionists lost their lives and many were injured. There was no response from the police side as not even a single tear gas shell was exploded. Special Branch of Police had not made any report about preparations of the subversive's activities. Why the administration had become so indolent and incompetent is a question to be answered by Dr Farooq Abdullah. At that time, the Congress(I) was also sharing the power with Dr Farooq Abdullah in consequence of unwritten Rajiv Gandhi and Dr Farooq Abdullah Accord which was aimed at to work together and form a coalition government of National Conference and Congress(I) to share power in the ratio of 60:40 respectively. The Accord proved discord for good governance because of absence of healthy opposition and consequent spurt in militancy.

The second instance is the holding of Assembly Elections which were held on March 23, 1987 and they created unparalleled misgivings about their fairness. The margins of victories in some constituencies were very small than the votes rejected. It is alleged that some victorious contestants were declared unsuccessful and some were beaten with the help of police. Many people cite the example of dreaded militant Sayeed Salahudeen (chief of the militant organization Hizb-ul-Mujahideen now operating from Pakistan). He was a cleric in a small mosque in the city of Srinagar and fought elections against an influential candidate of National Conference on one of the Assembly segment of Srinagar city. People in general allege that actually he had won the election but after getting him beaten by the police he was declared as unsuccessful candidate. He became a disgruntled politician and crossed the border and received training in arms and ammunition in Pakistan. Many such humiliated and disgruntled politically ambitious youths crossed the border and went to Pakistan for receiving training in handling arms and ammunitions in order to avenge them. Yasin Malik (chief of JKLF), Showkat Bakshi, late Abdul Gani Lone and Syed Ali Shah Geelani (a hardcore separatist leader of Jamaat-e-Islami) and many other militant leaders have narrated their personal experiences of maltreatment meted out to them at the hustings to the writer of this book when they had appeared personally before him during the trial of Banned Association Cases as Chairman of the Tribunal constituted to adjudge regarding those bans as well as subsequently as a Senior member of the Advisory Board constituted under the J&K Public Safety Act and finally as Judge of the J&K High Court.

The third example is a tell tale story regarding the total collapse of the administration both judicial and executive. The incident relates to a personal incident which happened with the writer of this book while discharging the judicial functions as Principal District and Sessions Judge, Jammu. The factual matrix of the case is that some members belonging to the 'Balmiki Christian Community' had filed a civil suit in a representative capacity under the title of "John Peter and Ors *vs* Mohan Lal Motial and Others" for declaration that the decree obtained by the defendants in the earlier suit was a nullity. During the pendency of the suit an application for grant of interim injunction was made by the plaintiffs. The trial court (City Judge, Jammu) had issued an interim injunction restraining the defendants from executing the decree obtained by them. Against that interim order, appeal was filed which was heard by the writer of this book as an Appellate Court. After hearing the counsel for the parties, the order of the trial court was set-aside holding that plaintiffs had failed to make out a prima facie case and that the balance of convenience was also against them. The order was announced on May 29, 1989 in the open court at about 10.30 AM. Ladies and men numbering about twenty along with their advocates from the plaintiff's respondents side were present in the court when the order was announced. The counsel of the defendants (respondents) and one defendant respondent in person were also present. After hearing the verdict, the plaintiff appellant's party did not leave the court and started making noise. Within few minutes, the court room was packed with more supporters. The writer of this book tried his best to pacify them by stating that they have the right of challenging this order in the High Court and this was not the permitted course under law to challenge it. After hearing the commotion, the senior prosecuting officer (of the police department) along with two or three police constables in uniform came in the court room from the adjoining court room of Chief Judicial Magistrate, Jammu. He also tried to pacify them but the mob became furious and started raising slogans in the court room that injustice had been done with them because the judge being a Hindu had decided the case in favour of the opposing party who were also Hindus. The subject matter of the dispute was a religious place where the Christian community had set up a claim that it was a Church and the Hindu Balmiki community had a counter claim that it was a Hindu Sun Temple. Meanwhile, a large number of Christians started pouring in the court room by ascending the stair cases of the court building. The writer of this book apprehended physical injury and immediately got up from the chair along with the staff members. Dinesh Maini, Private Secretary of the writer of this book, with all alacrity was able to shift the record of the listed cases in the retiring room and bolted the doors from inside. The writer of the book immediately rang up the Director-General of Police (Geelani Pandit) who responded spontaneously and dispatched a police force under the command of the then Deputy Superintendent of Police. By that time, Members of the Bar Association also started pouring in the court room and their presence deterred the rioters from breaking open the doors of the retiring room. Ex-member Legislative Assembly Wazir Massi of the Christian community had set up a stage below the stairs by standing on an elevated place and started giving an inflammatory speech scandalizing the court verdict. When the police party reached he was in the process of delivering the speech. The Deputy Superintendent of Police made a lathi-charge and dispersed them. He also got the court room cleared where some members were sitting in dharna. The court room had remained in their control for about one hour. Later on, it was revealed from some sources that this unruly mob which consisted of more female members than males was the result of a pre-planned and organized conspiracy apprehending an unfavourable verdict in appeal as the case had no merit. In this behalf later on the fact surfaced that some meetings were held at private places and one in the main Church of the city. The CID wing of the police had totally failed to gather any prior information about all these nefarious preparations. On the same day (i.e. May 29, 1989) a detailed report of the incident in writing was submitted by the writer of this book to the Hon'ble Chief Justice Dr AS Anand even reciting the names of the material witnesses of the incident which included the names of some prominent members of the Bar Association. A specific request was made to take legal action against the rioters but it goes as a black day in the history of the State judiciary when Hon'ble Chief Justice Dr AS Anand (who later on retired as Chief justice of India) instead of upholding the rule of law and to maintain the honour and dignity of the court (institution) sided with the rioters in protecting them as no action was taken.

The members of the Bar Association Jammu immediately rose to the occasion to save the honour and dignity of the court (institution) and went on strike. This strike was historical one as it lasted for fifty-eight days. Some of the members of the Bar had sat on hunger strike for days together and they had to be hospitalized. Even the courts at district level remained locked for some days by the agitating lawyers. This strike got the support from the Bar Associations of the whole State of J&K including other States such as Himachal Pradesh, Punjab and Haryana and Delhi as they also went on token strikes and passed the resolutions by condemning the failure of the administration to protect the dignity and honour of the institution of the courts. Even country-wide reaction about the attack on the judicial working system failed to awaken the judicial conscience of the Hon'ble Chief Justice. However, the government had to yield to the pressure of the legal fraternity and public at large with the result Divisional Commissioner (NR Gupta), Deputy Inspector General of Police Jammu Range (Mr Ali) and Senior Superintendent of Police (Jaswant Singh) were simultaneously transferred.

It is worthwhile to disclose here that Chief Justice Dr AS Anand did not decide the revision petition filed by the plaintiffs petitioners (John Peter and Others) challenging the order passed in the above said appeal but the same was decided by his successor Chief Justice SS Kang. The revision petition was dismissed as devoid of any merit. The unsuccessful plaintiff party went to the Supreme Court by filing Civil Appeal which was registered under Civil Appeal Number 3024 of 1990 titled 'John Peter and Others vs Mohan Lal Motial and others'. The Hon'ble Supreme Court dismissed the appeal on November 28, 1991 by appreciating the order of the writer of this book in these words, "The learned District Judge has recorded elaborate findings in holding that the appellants had failed to establish a prima facie case and the balance of convenience was also against them. The findings recorded by District Judge are findings of fact which could not be interfered with by the High Court. In this view, we uphold the order of the High Court although on facts and not on the question of law."

Note: The full text of the judgement of the Hon'ble Supreme Court is attached as Appendix 12.

Furthermore, it turned out that the Chief Minister and the Chief Justice were working at tandem to promote the service careers of those who were undeserving and ineligible. A District Judge from Kashmir region who was at serial number 15 in the seniority list of District and Sessions Judges had been selected as Law Secretary to the J&K Government. His immediate junior District Judge hailing from Jammu region who was at serial number 16 in the seniority list had been made Registrar of the J&K High Court against the established practice that a senior-most suitable District and Sessions Judge should occupy that post. One was the blue-eyed boy of the Chief Minister and the other of Chief Justice. Both the high dignitories chose this incident as convenient time to strike the deal in order to that both of the above mentioned District Judges to be elevated as Judges of the J&K High Court at the cost of less privileged fourteen senior District and Sessions Judges. Accordingly, Career Demolition Operation was launched for spoiling the service records of all the fourteen senior District and Sessions Judges. In a clandestine manner, false and damaging entries in the service records of all the fourteen senior District and Sessions Judges were made. Those adverse entries were not communicated to any of the concerned victims. Top of it even all the colleague judges of the High

Court were kept in dark about this morbid exercise. This was all an illegal unprecedented operation loaded with ulterior motives. The favoured duo overnight became officers of high integrity and outstanding merit and most suitable to be elevated as High Court Judges. All the senior judges were dubbed as indolents and of doubtful integrity. On the basis of fabricated record recommendations for the elevation as Judges of the J&K High Court were forwarded on the same day through the office of the Governor. Meanwhile, Dr AS Anand, Chief Justice was transferred from J&K High Court to Madras High Court. The judicial officers of the district of Srinagar wanted to give him a farewell party and when they approached the Chief Minister Dr Farooq Abdullah with an invitation to participate in the dinner he casually disclosed to them that two vacant posts of the High Court Judges are being filled and the recommendations stand forwarded. There was sudden commotion and the immediate reaction thereof was that the farewell party was cancelled. After unearthing unprecedented and unethical conspiracy in the whole system of judicial history in the country between a Chief Justice and a Chief Minister of a State, judicial officers raised their voice against the illegal recommendations which got stalled in the Centre as well as in the Supreme Court. The result was that the recommendations were turned down. The new Chief Justice of the High Court Hon'ble Justice SS Kang held full court meeting and all the brother judges were unanimous in cancelling adverse entries made in a unilateral manner as already stated above. Amongst the aggrieved District and Sessions Judges, the writer of this book was one of them in a seriatim manner. The writer of the book along with other two left out senior colleagues got opportunities for their elevation as High Court Judges in the due course of time. There is no precedent of such an unethical and illegal administrative conduct of a Chief Justice of this High Court which was established by Maharaja Hari Singh in 1927.

In 1988, against fourteen cadre posts of Deputy Commissioners in the State only six IAS officers had been selected to be suitable for the appointments as Deputy Commissioners by Dr Farooq's government and the remaining posts were filled by the local officers mostly hailing from Kashmir Division. Likewise, against fourteen cadre posts of Superintendents of Police, only five IPS officers were working and the remaining were occupied by locals. All the locals in the above stated streams were chosen from the trusted and faithful cadre. This had been purposely done in order to create unhealthy nexus between the politicians and the local public servants who knew the art of sycophancy in a better manner. The administration expenses in the State of Jammu and Kashmir are at the top in whole of the country and at that time there were ten Additional Chief Secretaries, three Director-General of Police and more than a dozen Inspector Generals of Police. In the J&K Road Transport Corporation over staffing is an exemplary instance where at that time there were six drivers and eight conductors for a Bus. This number has undoubtedly increased many folds till now, i.e. in 2014.

Corruption in the Administration

The percentage of securing the government jobs by unfair means increased during National Conference regime. Such appointees usually possessed low merit and easy virtues. Their main objects and aims are to secure the government jobs or to make up the loss incurred in getting entries in the jobs from the public. During Governor Jagmohan's rule, private professional practice by doctors who were in government service was banned and that order was judicially upheld by the High Court but as soon as Shri Jagmohan descended from the 'Gaddi' the ban was lifted by Dr Farooq Abdullah. A doctor who has good private practice does not remain fully fit to discharge his official duties during the duty hours. Similarly, in the education profession a teacher can resort to tuition work privately after office hours. He is left high and dry to pay due attention in discharging his duties in the school. There is no check on private tuition work.

The Union Government from Pandit Jawaharlal Nehru's time till date has turned a blind eye on the widespread corruption in Jammu and Kashmir. Bakshi Ghulam Mohammad ranks first as Prime Minister of the State to use the Central aid substantially on developmental works but he faced inquiry commission to inquire into allegations of corruption against him and this commission is known as 'Ayyangar Commission' headed by a Supreme Court Judge. The findings confirmed most of the allegations and he was thus, politically finished though he was most popular secular Kashmiri leader and was liked equally by the people of all the three regions of the State. There was least discrimination on regional basis during his time. The experience has shown that he was more sinned against than he was a sinner. Now, the recent survey conducted by some famous NGO organisations of the country has established that during Dr Farooq Abdullah's regime from 1996 to 2002, merit-wise position in corruption prevalent in the State was at 18th serial number but during the coalition government (from 2002 to 2005) headed by Mufti Mohammad Sayeed with Congress it increased and our State has occupied the 2nd most corrupt State in the whole country. During the present coalition government of National Conference and Congress, it is generally said that our State has acquired first position in the country for corruption and inefficiency as there is no accountability.

Dr Farooq Abdullah during his rule permitted the erection of a hotel at the most commanding hill site of the famous Dal Lake on one of the ridges of 'Chashma Shahi Complex' which could have caused maximum pollution to the Dal Lake and uglification of the beautiful landscape. Thank God, Governor's Rule was imposed and Governor Jagmohan understood the impending danger from this unwanted construction. He at once stopped it and it remained incomplete as a structure till President's Rule which ended in 1996 when again Dr Farooq Abdullah came to power. Much damage had been stopped to the ecology. Unfortunately, during Dr Farooq Abdullah's regime from 1996 onward followed by subsequent coalition governments, the owners of that hotel somehow or the other have succeeded in completing the construction of the hotel. Motorable road connectivity was provided to the hotel complex by making available State and forest land from the Boulevard Road of Dal Lake. Presently, this hotel is functioning and opening ceremony was done during Omar Abdullah's regime which was attended by some top most politicians in power and some high ranking bureaucrats.

Land Colonising Private Company was floated in 1987 known as 'Asra Builders' by Raman Mattoo (son-in-law of late PL Handoo, the then Revenue and Urban Development Minister in Dr Farooq Abdullah's regime) and his associate partner Asgar Ali (then an Assistant Commissioner in the Revenue Deptt). Residential plots were carved out by this private company after getting the land in possession against Revenue Laws, Municipal Laws and Town Planning Regulations. The State Anti-Corruption Department after investigations had proved corruption cases against them. Mattoo had become Minister in the coalition government led by Mufti Mohammad Sayeed. Asgar Ali had been getting promotions and plump postings during all the subsequent regimes till he became Director in the Rural Development Department for Kashmir and was caught in a scam by the J&K Accountability Commission. Governor Jagmohan during his tenure had been receiving many complaints against this duo for malpractices and he had sent some complaints along with his notes to the then Chief Minister Dr Farooq Abdullah. Dr Farooq Abdullah had sent the whole record along with the note of Governor to the House Committee of the Legislature specially set up for this purpose and till date nothing has been heard about the outcome. The only inference which can reasonably be drawn is that Legislative Assembly too was infested by the virus of shielding the corrupt deeds. It is hoped that in the future some responsible public welfare oriented government may lift out the protective curtains of such mysteries. Governor Jagmohan in his book *My Frozen Turbulence in Kashmir* has recorded some more facts about these corrupt deeds of the above said duo and thrown sufficient light how they were getting shelter from the corridors of power.

In 1947, when Maharaja Hari Singh was ruling the State more than 30 per cent area was under the cover of forests. During Bakshi Ghulam Mohammad's rule followed by GM Sadiq and that of Sayeed Mir Qasim some influential persons got the leases to extract timber on concessional rates but during Sheikh Abdullah's family rule virtually licensed massacre of the green gold wealth started till the ban was imposed by the Supreme Court in 1996 by its historic judgements including Awareness Forum *vs* State of J&K (1999) 1 SCC 210. The felling of the trees were declared prohibited by the Supreme Court in 1998 (AIR 1998 SC 2553). There are other judgements also to this effect. During the period of independence the forest area has diminished approximately from 30 per cent to 12 per cent or 10 per cent from the protected area of the time of Maharaja's rule. About four crore cubic feet of timber stood extracted. Even Dr Farooq Abdullah had criticised the working of J&K Forest Corporation. The study has shown that during 1952 to 1976 about 91 thousand hectares of forest land was lost to various development projects. Majority of the private forest lessees with the connivance of unscrupulous politicians and corrupt forest officials have denuded the forests against the J&K Forest Act which was enacted during Dogra family rule. Under law, allotment of only 3 marlas of land in the forests for the construction of seasonal huts can be made out for nomads but this law now has been observed in breach rather than in observance because some people belonging to 'Bakarwals' and 'Gujjar' communities have been permanently allotted big chunks of lands where some pacca structures have come up in large numbers. This policy has contributed to the denudation of forests. Even vacant State lands and banks of nallahs mostly nearing the border areas with Pakistan have not been spared for making allotments of lands to the members of the above said community. This practice was in vogue at a high speed during the National Conference regime and it continued even during coalition government of PDP.

During Governor Jagmohan's rule, Dr Farooq Abdullah made a statement which was published in the national newspaper *The Times of India* in its issue of February 7, 1991. Prima facie, the statement constituted the commission of the offence of 'Sedition' as defined under the Indian Penal Code (in the State Ranbir Penal Code) as well as it violated the provisions of POTA (which at that time was made applicable in the State). A portion of the statement is reproduced, "I directed my partymen to lie low, go across the border, get training in arms handling; do anything but do not get caught by Jagmohan." He had also alleged, "That Governor Jagmohan was out to wipe out the National Conference and the Congress from the State so that he could prop up other political parties and hand over the power." A Public Interest Writ Petition had been filed by one public-spirited young man by the name of Sukesh Khajuria (OWP Number 101/1991) wherein relief was claimed in the nature of direction to the police to register a case against Dr Farooq Abdullah for the violations of the relevant provisions of law. The court had issued process to secure the service of the respondents arrayed in the petition including that of respondent Dr Farooq Abdullah who at that time was living in United Kingdom. On the basis of the report made at the back of notice without ensuring its receipt, the then dealing judge of the case presumed that notice stood duly served. In 1996, the registry of the High Court listed the above stated writ petition before the writer of this book and at that time Dr Farooq Abdullah had become the Chief Minister of the State. The record revealed that service was defective in law and the writer of this book ordered the Registry of the court to issue fresh summons for affecting service on the respondents. Dr Farooq Abdullah was personally served the summons and he filed reply on affidavit in which he denied all the contents of his published statement. The Union of India was also a party respondent and her counsel sought time to file the reply while the publisher (*The Times of India*) was yet to be served through its administrative head office. In the interim order the writer of this book had directed the Registry to post the writ petition before him on the date which was specified in that order. Meanwhile, the headquarter of the writer of this book was changed to Srinagar wing of the High Court. The writer suspects this was done so that the writ petition did not come up before him for adjudication. The order for shifting the headquarters of the writer of this book is attached as Appendix 13.

The concerned judge heard the matter on the next hearing without waiting for proper serving of the notices on the remaining respondents, *The Times of India* etc, and held, "no case was mader out against Dr Farooq Abdullah even on its prima facie value on the allegations made against him because until and unless a person so sent across the border does not come back in the State and commits the offence, he cannot be held guilty for the commission of any offence." The interim order passed by the writer of this book regarding affecting the service on the newspaper *The Times of India* is attached as Appendix 14 and the full text of the judgement given by the concerned judge is attached as Appendix 15.

Note: The judgement of the learned Justice was not challenged by the petitioner by filing LPA in the Division Bench for the reasons best known to him. According to the view of the writer of this book, the judgement runs contrary to the established principles of law. Dr Farooq Abdullah could only be declared not guilty of the charges in case on the factual matrix it could be indubitably proved on the sole plea that he was not the author of the alleged statement. The Supreme Court in the case of Nazir Khan and Others *vs* State of Delhi 2003 (6) Supreme 234 has held, "that Section 124-A IPC deals with Sedition which is a crime against the society nearly allied to that of treason, and it frequently proceeds treason by a short interval. Sedition embraces all those practices, whether by word, deed, or writing, which are calculated to disturb the tranquillity of the State and lead ignorant persons to endeavour to subvert the government and laws of the country. It is disloyalty in action, and the law considers as Sedition all those practices which have for their object to excite discontent or dissatisfaction, to create public disturbance, or to lead to civil war, to bring into hatred or contempt the sovereign or the government, the laws or the Constitution of the realm, and generally all endeavours to promote public disorder." Besides the offence of Sedition, the statement in question also falls within the infractions of the provisions of POTA. This judicial verdict leads some people to think how high and mighty managed to remain outside the reach of law. Legally admitted dictum says: "when a judge quails, only then justice wails." Findings of the learned judge that the allegations contained in the statement were, "at the most slanderous for Jagmohan and he could take action," are according to the view of the writer of this book not in consonance with law because the allegations as attributed were against Governor Jagmohan while he was discharging sovereign functions of the State and not in his personal capacity. Besides the constitutional head of the State all the legislative and administrative powers were also vested in him at that time. Being Governor of the State, he enjoyed constitutional immunity of being sued or proceeded against in any legal action.

Steps taken to Change Demographic Composition of Jammu Division

The glaring examples of encroachments made on State lands and Forest lands by the members of majority community even hailing from

Kashmir region have been discussed to some extent in the previous chapters but here a discussion is being made on how these criminal acts are being justified with the aid of legislature by enacting the law by the name of, 'The Jammu and Kashmir State Lands (vesting of ownership) to the Occupants Act, 2001'. The hidden agenda in this Act is to legalise the unauthorized allotments or trespasses committed on the State and Forests lands in the border belts as well as in the hilly areas. Some of these allotments and encroachments suggest that the borders with Pakistan stand connected by these new settlements through 'khuds and nullahs' up to the hilly areas so that infiltrators can easily reach from the areas of district Kathua, district Jammu and district Rajouri to the hilly areas of more heights where there are safe hideouts for militants and the members of the minority community have migrated in large numbers. The mushrooming growth of the mosques seen on the National Highway at odd places also raises a doubt about the nefarious designs. To bring home this assertion, the cogent and convincing piece of evidence is the coming up of unauthorised and illegal colonies on the Forest and State lands nearby the city of Jammu known by the name of 'Bhatindi', 'Sunjawan' and the forests of 'Sidhra'. They are of strategic importance as situated on imposing hillocks surrounding the city of Jammu. Once, they were the living lungs for the inhabitants of the Jammu city to provide fresh air and preserve the natural ecology. Let it be known to every body who is concerned with the Rule of Law that under the prevailing law an act of trespass committed by a person on the State land constitutes an offence under Section 447-A of the Ranbir Penal Code punishable for an imprisonment of one year and fine. Similarly, trespass on forest land and felling of trees in the demarcated areas are also cognizable offences under the Forest Act punishable with imprisonment and fine. Felling of trees in a forest area is also an offence. The Supreme Court in the case of Environment Awareness Forum *vs* State of Jammu and Kashmir and others (1999) 1 SCC 210 has made applicable the provisions of Central Act of 1980 for the conservation of Forests. The State also has its own protection and conservation of Forest Act. The colonies having unauthorized houses built thereon numbering thousands are the shinning examples of anarchy and lawlessness. Some of the settlements provide safe hideouts to the anti-nationalists from where the subversive activities are carried out. By felling the trees in thousands from this lush green areas the environment and ecology of the Jammu city is threatened. In the Bhatindi Colony, Dr Farooq Abdullah has built his palatial house when he was Chief Minister even by making encroachments on the State land. He was followed by some of his cabinet colleagues, ex-legislators of the State and Members of the

Parliament, judges, bureaucrats, scribes, businessmen, influential party workers and above all some anti-social and anti-national subversive elements. The writer of this book has the personal experience of dealing with some cases of militants where they had found safe hideouts to protect themselves after committing acts of militancy in these illegally built-up colonies. The notorious massacre carried out against Hindus by killing 29 of them and injuring more than 30 in Rajeev Nagar/Qasim Nagar in the vicinity of Jammu city which is nearby the unauthorized dwellings of the Bhatindi Sidhra Colonies is a shining example. This incident had taken place on July 13, 2002. In the month of June 2003, a fidayeen attack was carried out by two militants on the Army establishment located in Sunjawan area where twelve army personnel were killed. The militants had fled from the spot and took shelter in the nearby colony abutting on State/Forest Land. The militants had got the logistic support from this area to launch the attack. Similarly, one militant who caused carnage on August 7, 2001 at Railway Station, Jammu was seen by the people running towards Bhatindi Colony and found a safe shelter there. Despite best efforts by the security forces he could not be traced out. In this incident five security personnel and seven civilians were killed while thirty-four civilians were injured. Only a symbolic opposition was shown some times by the public representatives of the Jammu region but that was not seriously taken by the ruling Junta.

The aims and objects of the above stated Act, in the preamble are, "for purposes of generating funds to finance power projects in the State." The salient features of this Act are that an encroacher/trespasser of the State Land from 1990 onwards would be conferred the proprietary rights on the land even held in possession by him as a trespasser. To achieve the sales of the Lands to these persons a committee was set up under Section 12 of the Act, headed by District Collector (Chairman) and Assistant Commissioner (Revenue) as its Member. The territorial Tehsildar and Director Land Management of the Development Authority were the member secretaries. This Committee had to determine the market value and then sell the land to the encroachers/trespassers. The coalition government of PDP headed by Mufti Mohammad Sayeed went many steps ahead in liberalizing the Act in favour of the trespassers by enacting the Jammu and Kashmir State Lands (Vesting of Ownership to the Occupants) (Amendment) Act, 2004. The previous Act was amended to facilitate the sale of State Lands even to those trespassers/encroachers who are found in actual possession at any time. Thus, the rider that a trespasser/encroacher should be in possession from 1990 was lifted. However, under the amended Act the Status of the committee which had to sell the State

Land to the unauthorised occupants (in the real sense criminals) was upgraded and instead of the 'District Collector' the name of Divisional Commissioner concerned was substituted. The District Collector was kept as member but above him Special/Additional Secretary to Government Revenue Department is added as a member. This Act is also known as 'Roshni Act' (Act of Light). The encroachers/trespassers had started making applications before the authority constituted under the Act for the sale of the land in their favour. The trespassers/encroachers are taking steps to reap the benefits of this Act. In a letter recently written by a nationalist citizen of Kashmir region and published in the local newspaper *Daily Excelsior* (May 28, 2013), it is revealed that under the above said Act 6,75,230 kanals of land have been approved for granting of ownership to the applicants across the length and breadth of the State. This much land has been approved by the price fixation committee for vesting of ownership to the occupants under the above stated Act. That according to the applications available in the Revenue Department, 1,47,752 applications seeking ownership of land have been disposed off by the Department. It is also stated that so far the proprietary rights have been transferred at the cost of Rs 303.99 crore but out of this Rs 72.90 crore have been deposited by the beneficiaries. The scibe of this letter has fully disclosed the names of influential politicians, retired judges, bureaucrats (both serving and retired) and doctors, since they have paid peanuts while acquiring huge chunks of lands and other properties located in the prime localities of the Srinagar city. Some influential business men have also been named. The details of areas of lands and price paid thereon which proves that above said Act has turned out to be a gold mine for the above stated beneficiaries. During the last Assembly Session held in Jammu in 2013 it was revealed by the Revenue Minister that maximum encroachments stand made on forest lands in Jammu region and Rajouri district figures at the top. The above stated Act, according to the view of the writer of this book, is an illegal piece of legislation because it advances the mischief of the commission of crimes instead of suppressing/punishing them. During the Chief Ministership of Mufti Mohammad Sayeed, the Revenue Minister Qayoom affected the transfers of 25 Patwaris and Girdawars belonging to the districts of Doda, Poonch, Rajouri and Udhampur. The Revenue Minister was not competent to issue those transfer orders under the government business rules and this is a breach of the Oath and actionable under Law. Under the relevant rules only the Divisional Commissioner of Jammu Division was the competent authority to affect those inter-district transfers on the existence and availability of valid legal grounds which have to be specified for judicial scrutiny in case of any challenge. The reasonable inference from this transfer order which can be drawn is that it was also a step in aid to rehabilitate the category of the above stated trespassers/ encroachers over the State and Forest lands. In this manner the demographic, ethnical, cultural, political and economical balance is intentionally titled. What is the explanation of importing Revenue Officials at the ground level from other districts to the district of Jammu? Why are the inhabitants of the Jammu region irrespective of their religious beliefs also not afforded such a golden opportunity to occupy State and forest lands in Kashmir region and particularly in Srinagar district? A copy of this transfer order is attached as Appendix 16.

However, some awakened people on individual basis had been applying breaks to these nefarious games by filing Public Interest Writ Petitions in the High Court. In 2002 such a petition in the nature of PIL was filed by Iqbal Hussain Bhat and others and the Division Bench on May 16, 2002 restrained the State not to allow the Forest Area of the Bhatindi Colony which was destroyed by fire to be used for residential purposes. A fire was intentionally broken in the forest area to clear it from the trees for setting up illegal colony but the stay order of the court stood in the way as an impediment. It may be noted that thousands of kanals of forest land has been encroached in this area in addition to State Land but here is no accountability.

In its Sunday issue of March 9, 2014 *The Tribune* newspaper has repeated about the 'Roshni Act of J&K State': Mr Subash Chander Pandey, Principal Accountant General (CAG) detects irregularities worth over Rs 25,000 crore. Against the target of over Rs 25,000 crore government realised only Rs 76 crore. Twenty lakh kanals of State land still under encroachment. Ten lakh kanals encroached upon in past decade. The Act was enacted during the regime of the then Chief Minister Dr Farooq Abdullah in 2001. The next government of PDP and Congress amended it in 2004 and framed rules also to finance various hydel power projects in the State from money generated via conferring ownership rights upon persons who had been occupying State land. However, against a target of Rs 25,448 crore that was to be realised by November 2006, the State Government could only realise a paltry Rs 76 crore, thereby failing to meet the purposes of legislation.... The rules which were framed in 2005 and 2007 during the tenure of Ghulam Nabi Azad were not in harmony with the Act. Before amendment in 2004, a total of 10 lakh kanals was under encroachment but after amendment another 10 lakh kanals were encroached."

Infiltration of Subversive Elements in Government Services

The mentors of militancy first of all made the police force as its target because it provided ready made nursery for the spread of the virus in the recruits which belonged to the cadre of plebiscite front Association. Sheikh Abdullah after coming into power in 1975, in a systematic planned manner started raising additional police force from the rank and file of his party workers of the said unlawful association. Some activists of the said Association had even found berths in other departments including Civil Secretariat and Legislature. The proportional representation of the minority—Hindu Community—started diminishing at a faster rate. His son Dr Farooq Abdullah and son-in-law GM Shah continued to follow his footsteps. The object had been fully achieved by 1989 when the bureaucracy stood almost politicised. The representation of Jammu province in the Civil Secretariat had been lowered up to about 10 per cent.

After the death of Sheikh Abdullah which occurred in 1982, his son Dr Farooq Abdullah became the Chief Minister for the first time. His casual personal traits of character started seriously influencing the State administration in eroding the authority of rule of Law. A coterie of like-minded and inexperienced bureaucrats surrounded him and overnight became powerful. Against these growing chaotic conditions Sheikh Jabar, National Conference MLA from Kangan, was the first to raise the banner of revolt. He submitted a memorandum to the President of India listing the misdeeds of Farooq Abdullah. He was intimidated and hounded by the supporters of Farooq Abdullah. Khalida Shah (daughter of Sheikh Abdullah) went to Kangan in support of his claims. She was assaulted in the way and injured.

GM Shah and Dr Farooq Abdullah held separate conventions. There were thus, tensions all around i.e., between the State and the Centre, between the National Conference and Congress as well as amongst Sheikh Abdullah's family. Pro-Pakistan and pro-Khalistan elements were nursing their own designs.

During the Parliamentary elections of 1989, the militants gave a call for the boycott of elections which was carried. Prof Saifuddin Soz (ex-Cabinet Minister in the UPA Central Government from Congress(I) and now State President of Congress(I)) had fought the elections on 2nd term as a candidate of National Conference from Baramulla Parliamentary constituency. He could get only five votes from Sopore town and not a single vote was cast in the main city of Baramulla town although he was a native of that place. Some other polling stations also showed the same type of results. Late Mohammad Shafi Bhat (an advocate by profession and lastly MLA of Congress Party from one of the Srinagar city Assembly constituencies) was the National Conference candidate from one of the Srinagar city constituency and he returned in the Assembly as unopposed candidate. Before the elections, the coalition partners National Conference and Congress were issuing damaging statements against each other. Mohammad Shafi Qureshi was the State President of Congress and he had even gone to the extent of saying that unless separatist tendencies and forces of terrorism are not curbed the security of the State and the country will be threatened. He complained of step motherly treatment for Congress. Mustafa Kamal, younger brother of Dr Farooq Abdullah retarded that Rajiv-Farooq Accord had outlived its utility. Time had come when both the parties should take a re-appraisal of the situation." Dr Farooq Abdullah had said that, "Kashmiri Muslims were not trusted by New Delhi."

Mohammad Shafi Bhat after Parliamentary elections became Member of Parliament and in the house he had given the statement, "Centre is treating Kashmir as its colony and Kashmiri as second class citizens. The centre has not fulfilled the promise given in 1947."

Immediately after the elections the militants brutally murdered Saidullah, SHO Maisuma Bazar Police Station Srinagar and his dead body remained unattended for hours in the market. He was a very dedicated and patriotic police officer. On October 27, 1988, a bomb exploded in parked Maruti van at Lal Chowk, Srinagar. A passer-by was injured and a lady judicial Munsiff Magistrate (Miss Warkoo) and a woman advocate accompanying her were injured along with other passers-by. On July 13, 1989, a bus of CRPF was fired at in which two jawans were killed and 10 were injured. In retaliatory firing four innocent civilians were injured. Pak Independence Day of August 14 was celebrated with gusto and gaiety. On 15 August 1989, bomb blasts injured about 60 persons. No street light was allowed to burn even on the Civil Secretariat building at Srinagar. Mohammad Yusuf Halwai on the Independence Day had burnt a candle in his place of business in Mohallah Safakadal of down town Srinagar but he had to pay the price for his life by getting bullets from the militants. He was an activist of National Conference and first political worker to become the victim of militants. Although militants have killed hundreds of National Conference workers to gain upper hand over this organisation yet Mohd Yusuf Halwai ranks first in this list and he is a national hero in the real sense of the term like National Conference's martyr master Maqbool Sherwani of 1947 who was killed with nails by Pakistani raiders. This national martyr deserves all praise and a suitable place in the history for combating terrorism in Kashmir. Mohammad Shafi Qureshi President of the State Congress Committee experienced bomb blast in his garage and his Maruti car was completely destroyed. On September 8, 1982 when Sheikh Abdullah died, the whole Kashmir Valley was crying 'Sayno-Shero' (our lion) is gone but on September 8, 1989 his death anniversary was celebrated as deliverance day.

On September 14, 1989 Pandit Tikka Lal Tiploo advocate who was Vice-President of BJP (Bharatiya Janata Party) and a bold out-spoken patriot of the first order was shot dead near his house in broad day light. He was the solitary local voice in the Kashmir Bar Association who in 1981 had openly condemned the undignified and totally illegal exercise of executive order passed by GM Shah, Housing Minister in Sheikh Abdullah's Ministry regarding the cancellation of the allotment of the government residential quarter against the writer of this book. GM Shah had got annoyed because the writer of this book had passed an adverse order for the lodgement of Maqbool Bhat (founder of JKLF) in Tihar Jail, Delhi, who along with other accused were facing trial of murder charge and illegal infiltration into the State. Maqbool Bhat had hatched a conspiracy with his political supporters in power and bureaucracy of jail breaking and at the request of the government he was lodged in Tihar jail Delhi. No other member in Kashmir Bar Association because of fear could come out openly against this uncivilized and despotic act of GM Shah except late Tikka Lal Tiploo advocate who had to sacrifice his life for national cause at the hands of militants. He lived as a lion in the Kashmir Bar Association. Of course, some other well meaning members of the Bar Association of Srinagar were clandestinely siding with him but they could not open their mouths out of fear. The first death anniversary of Ajaz Dar who was the first militant killed while attacking the house of Wattali, then DIG Kashmir was celebrated with a halo of martyrdom. On this day, DIG CRPF Tiwari was attacked with grenades and J&K Bank's branch at Safakadal was attacked.

On September 27, 1989, Shabir Shah President of Peoples League (a Secessionist Association) was arrested near Ramban and brought to Srinagar but then DC Srinagar refused to sign his arrest warrant. That officer later on was given constant promotions and retired as a senior officer in the government. Advocate-General and Additional Advocate-General had refused to appear in such cases and passed the liability on junior government advocates. On October 27, 1947, the first Batch of Indian Army under the command of Col Dewan Ranjit Rai had landed in Srinagar Airport and this day is being observed as 'Black Day' by the militants. On this day, complete hartal was observed in the Valley and the house of Sub-Inspector Shabir Ahmed was attacked in his village killing his wife and 10 year old daughter. This Sub-Inspector had done commendable job in containing the militancy.

On November 4, 1989, NK Ganjoo retired District and Sessions Judge who had passed death sentence against Maqbool Bhat (founder of JKLF Subversive Association) in his trial for murdering Sub-Inspector Chaman Lal of CID wing of J&K Police was killed in broad day light near High Court building in Srinagar. His dead body remained unattended for more than an hour at Jhangir Chowk. Revenge was taken on his life after about eighteen years gap (from the date of announcement of the judgement). This dastardly and fiendish act instilled a sense of fear among fellow members of the judiciary. On the arrest of Shabir Shah, processions were taken in the towns of Doda, Bhaderwah and Kishtwar in Jammu province. In the district headquarters of Doda town Islamic Flag was hoisted. The National Conference and Congress coalition regime was allowing these incidents without showing least resistance. Paid advertisements were published in the local newspapers showing many people's dissociation with the above stated two political parties.

On December 8, 1989, terrorists of JKLF kidnapped Dr Rubaiya Sayeed, daughter of then Home Minister of India Mufti Mohammad Sayeed (later Chief Minister of the State in coalition government of PDP and Congress from 2002 to 2005). Dr Farooq Abdullah at that time was abroad. About 20 Muslim organizations condemned this savage act in the country. Amanullah Khan who at that time was the head of JKLF militant organization issued a threat from Pakistan to kill Dr Rubaiya and in reaction the State government gave in and freed five top terrorists—Hamid Sheikh, Sher Khan, Javed Ahmed Zargar, Mohammad Kalwal and Mohammad Altaf Bhat—to secure the release of Dr Rubaiya. This was a turning point in the history of Kashmir Terrorism as terrorists established their upper hand because public gave a rousing welcome to the freed terrorists.

The terrorists' related incidents increased and security forces were being fired upon during curfew hours. On December 20, 1989, two police officers were shot at. On December 27, 1989 a police constable was shot dead in Khanyar and on December 27, 1989 Pandit Prem Nath Bhat advocate (advocate-cum-journalist) of Anantnag was killed when he was returning home after attending a case in the District and Sessions Judge Court, Anantnag. He was a very brilliant erudite scholar not only in the field of law but also in Hindu and Muslim theologies. Because he commanded considerable respect in both the communities so 'Jehadi' elements chose him as a target from Hindu minority community in Anantnag district to terrify them with the ultimate object of cleansing the Hindu population. At page 108 of the book *The Truth Foretold*, the author PN Bhat, whose work is based upon the collected material from the articles of martyer PN Bhat, advocate has recorded:

"Prem Nath Bhat who was one of the leading lawyers of Anantnag District Court and a respected social activist commanding respect in both the communities—majority and minority that secularism was the hallmark in Kashmiri society because of common blood coursing through the veins from conversion which took place five centuries back was dried because of dirty prevailing politics in Kashmir. Prem Nath had been raising his voice by writing many articles, write-ups in different newspapers and journals. He was chosen as an important target for killing by the anti-nationalists in order to frighten the members of minority community on the principle, "kill one and frighten one thousand." Bhat was killed in broad day light in December 1989. This day is annually celebrated as Martyr's Day in Jammu and all Kashmiri Pandit martyrs are remembered. According to the author of the above mentioned book, the Kashmir Congress is the worst sinner in this game and their paid workers and the so called freedom fighters receiving five hundred rupees from the Government of India each month and with special privilege to their sons and daughters in the matter of admission to educational and technical institutions and appointment in government services were in the vanguard of the arsonists and looters of February 1986 under the command of Mufti Mohammad Sayeed (who was then Minister in the Central Government). They raised to ground thirty temples and three villages of the Hindus. In spite of this loss, Congress could only rule the State indirectly through GM Shah. Not a single real culprit of February 1986 riots was touched with the result that this lawless element was encouraged and it continued its pass time of teasing and troubling the minority community. All the fanatic fundamentalists got entrance in administrative services and the police forces were infested by anti-Indian elements from top to bottom. The line thinned with the result that no action is taken against acts of vandalism and hooliganism by the miscreants against the docile and mild community.... Suffice to say that acts of arson, stoning and loot have followed an unbroken succession. From Swami Nand Lal's Ashram in Tikkar to Somyar complex in Srinagar there were many sporadic acts of violence against this community. The latest is the 'Vicharnag murder of Keshav Nath

> Mahant' who refused to get converted and was killed by the policemen on duty for his refusal. It was followed by a call for march to Goutamnag, a Hindu shrine of Goutam Rishi of Naya School of Philosophy. It is here that communal politics again surfaced and minority organ 'Martand', carried the head line in 24th March issue, 'Will Qazi Nissar Farooq Abdullah collusion set Kashmir Ablaze'. On the same day, a Deputy Superintendent of Police was injured near Kashmir University and five bomb blasts were caused in the city of Srinagar at different places. Earth satellite station at Hari Parbat was damaged by hand grenades.

On January 1, 1990, a powerful blast injured seven persons. On 2 January 1990, two persons were killed and on January 3, 1990, Inspector of Intelligence Bureau (IB) RNP Singh was shot dead. On January 6, 1990, six explosions occurred in which 30 persons were injured. On January 8, 1990, thirteen persons were killed and one hundred injured. To spread more terror—a police official was blind-folded, gagged, brutally tortured and then hanged from a tree in Hyderpura locality of Srinagar city. One Imam of village Saller was also tortured in the same fashion. All the leading national newspapers reported their opinions that State had abdicated its law and order authority in favour of the Militants because in 1989, sixteen hundred violent incidents including 351 bomb blasts had occurred. The identity of IB officers was being disclosed in order to dry up all sources of information. A Head Constable of J&K Police working as a Wireless Operator at joint Interrogation Centre was passing all important information. A driver of Governor's pilot car was also found involved in this racket. Militants, as well as arms and ammunition was sometimes transported in police vehicles.

Be that as it may, Dr Farooq Abdullah is answerable to every patriotic citizen of the country as to why between July and December 1989, he released seventy hardcore terrorists. Some of them were highly motivated who had gone to Pakistan and received extensive training in handling arms and ammunition. As instances Mohd Afzal Sheikh, Rafiq Ahmed Ahangar, Farooq Ahmed Ganai, Gulam Mohd Gojjri had held important positions in different militant organizations and had caused number of blasts and number of firing incidents on the security forces causing death and destruction to human life and property. The Advisory Board (constituted under the J&K Public Safety Act of which subsequently the writer of this book had also remained as a member for more than three years) at the material times had confirmed their detentions but Dr Farooq Abdullah had released them with one stroke of his pen for reasons best known to him.

One Inspector of electricity posted in Pulwama functioned as Commander of Hizb-ul-Mujahideen and while remaining absent from duty was being marked present in the office and drawing his pay. From the house of one IVth class employee, 13 bombs were recovered. Twelve dangerous detenus escaped from Central Jail, Srinagar. Sher-i-Kashmir Institute of Medical Sciences was a hub of militant activities where Dr Guru who later on was killed by rival militants was the beacon light of subversive elements. At the same pattern militants were getting shelter and preferential treatment in SMGS Hospital, Srinagar and Lal Deed Hospital, Srinagar. This was happening mainly because of fear psychosis from the militants and partially out of sympathy owned by some fifth columnists amongst the medicos.

In every Department the writ of the militants was running. Many government employees who had crossed the border for receiving training in handling arms and ammunition were being shown present in the office and their month-wise pays were drawn and distributed at homes. Police Department stands in the first row. Education, Hospital Services, Revenue, Electricity and Rural Development Departments are the other shining examples which deserve special mention.

Some judges of the Srinagar Wing of the J&K High Court actively rendered the help for the spread and sustenance of militant activities. Division Benches were being constituted by these judges themselves without the consultation of the Chief Justice. Some lawyers of the Srinagar Bar Association under the Presidentship of Mian Qayoom advocate had set the time of their watches half an hour behind the standard Indian time which synchronized with Pakistan's time. Those judges were frequently staying the executive orders whenever action was taken against Militancy related activities including media persons who were openly propagating for 'Jihad'. Before issuing the stay orders, the State side generally was not heard. Legal powers to impose the curfew at times were restricted by passing prohibitory orders. Even anticipatory bails were frequently granted to the detenus to be arrested under the provisions of the J&K Public Safety Act. Some times, even arrests were restrained. The State and the Union Government as the case may be usually had to come to Jammu for filing LPA or SLPs were filed in the Supreme Court. The judicial functioning of the Subordinate Courts in the Valley had come to a grinding halt. In militancy prone areas Shariat courts had been set up and the writ of the militants swayed in criminal and civil matters. Even cognizance of heinous crimes such as murders and rapes were taken by those Shariat courts (Islamic courts). Matrimonial disputes were being settled including land disputes involving the operation of Revenue laws. The processes issued by courts for summoning the parties or witnesses could not be executed by its own agency or through the agency of the police. Against the backdrop of all these chaotic conditions finally on January 19, 1990, Governor's rule was imposed in the State and Jagmohan took over the reins of government.

Imposition of Governor's Rule

Jagmohan who had earlier remained Governor of J&K from 26 April 1984 to July 1989 and was replaced by General KV Krishna Rao from July 1989 to 19 January 1990. During the intervening period from 1989 to 1990, the militancy had raised its ugly head and hijacked the administration during Dr Farooq Abdullah's regime. The Government of India on 19 January 1990 brought Governor Jagmohan for second time as Governor because on earlier occasion he had remained very popular in the State. He had taken the administration of Shri Mata Vaishno Devi shrine by setting up a Statutory Board and this is his most notable achievement for the development of the 'Yatra'. When Farooq Abdullah's government had totally failed, Governor's Rule was imposed and keeping in view, the administrative skills of Jagmohan, he was specially brought to restore the authority of the State. Unfortunately, his tenure was short-lived, i.e. w.e.f. 19 January 1990 to 26 May 1990. During that period services of hundreds of anti-national government employees were terminated under Section 126(3) of the J&K Constitution read with Article 311(2)(C) of the Indian Constitution for their involvement in anti-national activities. He was succeeded by Girish Chandra Saxena (26 May 1990 to 12 March 1993) followed by General KV Krishna Rao (second term from 12 March 1993 to 2 May 1998). During General Rao's time Assembly elections were held in 1996. Dr Farooq Abdullah came to power in 1996 with two-third majority and he absorbed hundreds of above stated dismissed employees and notable instance is from police department when with one order more than two hundred dismissed police personnel were taken in J&K Fire Services Organization. Initially, he had tried to take them back in the police department but there was a resistance from the side of then Governor Girish Chandra Saxena who had also consulted the writer of this book on the subject because of implicit faith. Ultimately, some good sense prevailed and they were absorbed in J&K Fire Services Department. Some of those employees had even crossed the border for receiving training in militant relating activities. Governor Jagmohan had imposed ban on eight prominent subversive militant Associations under the local law known as J&K Criminal Amendment Act of 1983. A high powered Judicial

Tribunal under that Act was constituted and the writer of this book was made the Chairman along with two members of the ranks of District and Sessions Judges. This aspect has been fully discussed under the Chapter 'Banning of Militant Organisations'. He retrieved the lost State authority to some extent from the militants hands and made them to suffer for the crimes which they were perpetuating against the innocent civilians including the personnel of the para-military forces. The militants virtually were on the run and their agony was echoed by the late Prime Minister of Pakistan Mrs Benazir Bhutto who dubbed Jagmohan as a most cruel despot and murderer of humanity. Some pseudo-secularist political leaders for the game of vote banks and immature thinking also joined the chores. Lastly, late Prime Minister Rajiv Gandhi also turned his inveterate adversary. The result was that Jagmohan was withdrawn by the Central Government from the scene of power and replaced by General KV Krishna Rao as the Governor who after completion of tenure was replaced by Girish Chandra Saxena as Governor for second time during popular rule of National Conference. The above stated three Governors got the opportunity of serving as Governors in the State for two terms each and all of them in their own way have combated the menace of militancy in the ongoing proxy war during Governor's Rule. Their role in the history would remain worthy of appreciation.

CHAPTER 19

Regional Imbalances

Maharaja Gulab Singh founded the State of Jammu and Kashmir with his uncanny foresight. He was an able military General, versatile administrator and a shrewd politician. The present State comprises three distinct regions Jammu, Kashmir and Ladakh besides areas of Baltistan and Gilgit. Before Pakistan's aggression of 1947 two culturally distinct regions known as frontier districts comprising Baltistan and Gilgit had remained in the territory of the State and those parts had also acceded to the Union of India by virtue of composite instrument of accession executed by the sole ruler Maharaja Hari Singh with his sovereign authority. The factors of geography, language, race, religion and culture had separated all the regions. The only common bond was the rule of the Maharaja.

The Central leadership right from Pandit Jawaharlal Nehru till date has lacked vision to safeguard the economic, political and cultural fabric of the inhabitants of the present three regions which could not be completely occupied by Pakistan. Many people make allegations that Sheikh Abdullah influenced Pandit Jawaharlal Nehru during the conflict of 1947 with Pakistan not to reclaim the POJK areas of Jammu region as well as Pahari- and Punjabi-speaking areas of district Muzaffarabad and Baramulla in Kashmir Valley by halting the advancing Indian Army. It is a stark reality that Sheikh Abdullah had only a nominal influence in the inhabitants of the above stated areas including the frontier districts of Baltistan and Gilgit and they always had been opposing his political supremacy. It is an admitted fact based on history as discussed in earlier chapters that Sheikh Abdullah had started his political career on the basis of Kashmiri Muslim card but when he realised that Muhammad Ali Jinnah who was too egoistic would not tolerate him, he sided with Pandit Nehru and other Congress leaders. The Galancy Commission was set up by Maharaja Hari Singh against the alleged discrimination of Kashmiri Muslims only and

Sheikh Abdullah was the most vocal Kashmiri leader for the achievement of this Commission.

After 1947, the State Government has always remained dominated by Kashmiri Muslim leadership and neither the Indian National Congress nor the regional dominating political party National Conference ever gave a chance to a Jammuite to become the Chief Minister. In the election of 2002, PDP (Kashmir-based political party) won sixteen Assembly seats from the valley and Congress had won twenty seats which include five seats from the valley also. The Congress was thus, the largest political party in the State but even then Chief Minister's slot went to the share of PDP and Mufti Mohammad Sayeed succeeded to become the Chief Minister for the first three years. He had retained all the important portfolios for the ministers belonging to his political party. With the intervention of Congress central leadership a Kashmiri speaking Muslim from Jammu region (Ghulam Nabi Azad) whose ancestors had migrated from Kashmir region became the Chief Minister for the first time in the history but in his government the majority of the Cabinet Ministers were still from Kashmir region holding all the important portfolios. He had started putting efforts to give due representation to Jammu region but the coalition party (PDP) did not give him a chance to complete his full term of three years as was agreed in the minimum programme of governance before forming the government. The support was withdrawn on a very sensitive religious issue raised for acquiring political gains at the cost of national integration regarding the alleged Land Row which related to the use of the State land in Baltal area of Kashmir region for setting up temporary settlements to provide facilities to the pilgrims of Shri Amarnathji shrine. Ghulam Nabi Azad had to resign and Governor's Rule was imposed. This had happened after the exit of General SK Sinha as Governor (from 4 June 2003 to 25 June 2008). The present Governor NN Vohra had recently taken over the charge as Governor of the State and he had given the charge of the above said land in an illegal and arbitrary manner in order to win favour from the government for his secure tenure to government. An agitation of great intensity was started by the inhabitants of Jammu region in 2008 which lasted for two months. This aspect has been dealt in detail separately in this book.

Against such type of patent regional discrimination which started after the dawn of Independence in 1947, the people of Jammu region had started an agitation by forming a regional party known as Praja Parishad. During 1953, this agitation bore the fruit of removing Sheikh Abdullah from the seat of power. Again tension had started brewing up from 1960 onward. To satiate these feelings a Commission known as Gajendragadkar Commission of enquiry was appointed by then Government of Jammu and Kashmir, headed by Congress party in consultation with the Union Government, vide government order number 878-D of 1967, dated 6th November 1967.

Gajendragadkar Commission

The terms of reference of this commission were as follows—

"(i) To make an assessment of the development programmes apportioned to the various regions of the State and to recommend measures necessary to give assurance that the resources available to the State Government are being shared equitably and also to convey a feeling of equal participation in the integrated development of the State.

(ii) To examine the recruitment policies of government and to recommend measures for giving an equitable share in government employment to the various regions and communities, having special regard to the claim of the Scheduled Castes and other economically, educationally and socially backward communities, classes and groups among the citizens of the State consistently with the maintenance of efficiency of administration.

(iii) To examine the policies of the State Government regarding admissions to institutions of higher education and the schemes of assistance by way of scholarships and loans, with a view of ensuring an equitable distribution of the available facilities to the various regions and communities, and having special regard to the claims of the Scheduled Castes and other economically, educationally and socially backward communities, classes and groups among the citizens of the State.

(iv) To consider generally the causes that lead to irritations and tensions and to recommend remedial measures."

In considering the above matters, the Commission was required to take note of the provisions contained in Part III 'Fundamental Rights' as well as other provisions of the Constitution of India as made applicable to the State of Jammu and Kashmir and of the Directive Principles of State Policy laid down in Part IV of the Constitution of Jammu and Kashmir and particularly of Section 23 thereof.

Of the 93 memoranda received by the Commission, a little over one third were from the Kashmir region, 51 from the Jammu region, four from Ladakh and six from outside the State. An analysis of the memoranda and the oral evidence recorded by the Commission could be broadly classified under four major Heads pertaining to (i) Development, (ii) Employment, (iii) Education and (iv) Conditions giving rise to irritation and tensions. The Commission at page 25 of the report remarked, "that during the second five year Plan period, the levels of expenditure in the Jammu and Kashmir regions were not markedly different and it was only in the third Plan period that a substantially higher expenditure was incurred in the Kashmir region. A scrutiny of the expenditure tables showed to the Commission that major regional disparities had occurred in agriculture, irrigation, power, transport and communication, education and health and family planning. Agricultural programmes in the Kashmir region was approximately 50 per cent more than in the Jammu region. Further, while the gross area under cultivation in Jammu region is much larger than the Kashmir region, the investment in agriculture in the former had been substantially less than in the latter. At page 31 of the report it was recorded, "the table showed that though the livestock population in the Kashmir region is considerably smaller than in the Jammu region, the veterinary hospital facilities were better in the former and very much larger sums of money had been spent there than in the Jammu region or Ladakh. Similarly, at page 32 of the report it is recorded that in the field of forestry, the Kashmir region has received more attention than the Jammu region. In Jammu the emphasis has been on soil conservation. One wishes that more attention was paid to afforestation in Ladakh. At page 33 of the report it is stated that much higher investment was made in the Kashmir region than in either of the other two regions in the Fisheries Department. Under the head of irrigation the finding is, "in irrigation, therefore, the Kashmir region is much better served than Jammu or Ladakh." In the power sector the Commission gave the finding at page 34 in the following words, "At the end of the Third Plan period, therefore, the availability of power in the Kashmir region was considerably more than in the Jammu region. In Ladakh it was almost negligible. The number of towns and villages electrified in the Kashmir region was almost double the number of those electrified in the Jammu region." In the industries sector the Commission came to the finding, "Jammu region has received less attention than the Kashmir region in industrial development." In the field of transport and communication the finding was that in both the Jammu and Kashmir regions a number of places have been opened up and connected by new routes and the State and the Union Governments have applied themselves with vigour to this developmental activity. In the education sector the finding at page 40 was, "in education, the Kashmir region has done better than the other regions. The student teacher ratio for high and higher secondary schools is smaller in the Kashmir region than in the Jammu region, though for colleges it is higher in the former. Enrolment in colleges is much higher in the Kashmir region—almost twice the enrolment in the Jammu region, though the former has only two more colleges. Professional institutions also are located mostly in the Kashmir region." In the health and family planning sector the Commission gave the finding, "The number of Doctors was, however, almost 60 per cent more in the Kashmir region than in the Jammu region at the end of the Third Five-Year Plan period. It is also to be noted that even though the Kashmir region had only nine hospitals at the end of the Third Plan period as against ten in the Jammu region, the bed strength in the former was about 50 per cent more than in the latter. In Ladakh the facilities available appear to be extremely poor."

After considering these aspects the Commission came to the view that the people of each region should have a feeling of equal participation in the integrated development of the State. The Commission expressed its feelings of disgust and dismay in these words, "Irrespective of the criteria that are adopted for the purpose, it is important that the people of each region should have a feeling of equal participation in the integrated development of the State. From the various memoranda and the oral evidence, we came to realize how strongly Jammu nurses a feeling of being discriminated against in development matters."

Recruitment Policy

The Commission received several memorialists and representatives who complained before it that in the matter of recruitment to government services there was discrimination on communal or religious grounds, or a lack of reservation for the Scheduled Castes and for those who claim to be economically, educationally and socially backward. This grouse has a long history because in the late twenties and early thirties there were complaints that the Muslims, who formed the great majority of the population, were not adequately represented in the State services. Maharaja Hari Singh on these complaints, in November 1931, appointed a Commission which is known by the name of 'Galancy Commission'. The recommendations of this Commission were mostly accepted by the Maharaja but after the dawn of independence the people of Jammu and people of Ladakh irrespective of their religions became the victims of the discriminatory policy, though by an order dated 31st December 1954 the government appointed a Recruitment Board as well as framed the Jammu and Kashmir Civil Services (Classification, Control and Appeal) Rules, 1956. The irritations and tensions continued to swell and during the regime of National Conference more injustice started to be perpetuated against the Jammu and Ladakh regions. On the facts which were available at that time before the Commission it gave its finding that though the Kashmir region's population was 53.3 per cent of the total population of the State, its share in the services as on 1st April 1967 was 60.9 per cent. The Jammu region's population at that time was 44.2 per cent of the total population of the State but its share in the services on 1st April 1967 was only 36.1 per cent. The rate of recruitment of Ladakhis had been shown a decline from 2.5 per cent in 1961-62 to 1.4 per cent in 1965-66. The recruitment of Sikhs in the services had been fluctuating from year to year but their share on 1st April 1967 was considerably in excess of but was due to them on a population basis. According to the 1961 census, the Scheduled Castes of the Jammu and Kashmir State formed 7.98 per cent of the total population of the State but their share in the services of the government was very much lower than is justified on the basis of their population.

The Commission scrutinized the statistical data pertaining to admissions of students to institutions of higher education furnished by the State Government and noted that as between the Jammu region and the Kashmir region, the number of students belonging to Jammu selected for study in higher institutions was much smaller than the number of those belonging to Kashmir, but the share of the Hindus had been much larger than that of Muslims in all the important courses of the study. (Note: This position would had been the result of overwhelming rate of literacy amongst the Hindus of the Kashmir.) The Commission recommended special concession, quotas or reservations for admission to educational and professional institutions as well as grant of scholarships and study loans in favour of the socially and economically backward classes of the State. The Commission considered the causes of irritations and tensions existing at that time among certain sections of the population in spite of the authoritarian nature of Dogra rule, certain section of the population flourished and prospered during that period. The State army was composed almost entirely of Dogra Rajputs for whom it provided the main source of employment. The educated and advanced Kashmiri Pandit community gradually came to monopolize the ministerial posts in the government and occupy positions of influence in the Civil Administration. In 1925, Maharaja Hari Singh after becoming the ruler came under the pressure from the inhabitants of the State and accepted the principle of recruiting only

State Subjects in government posts. These two communities were the main beneficiaries of Dogra rule along with a large number of Jagirdars, Chakdars and Shahukars (moneylenders). With the introduction of democracy and power going in the hands of Sheikh Abdullah, he in his first populous political action deprived the 'Jagirdars' and 'Chakdars' from holding big chunks of lands. He promulgated the Big Landed Estates Abolition Act and deprived thousands of people to hold excess of 182 Kanals of land without making any provision for compensation. A large number amongst them were poor because of indolence, being crippled or widows etc. This act has been elaborately dealt in a previous chapter. Bakshi Ghulam Mohammad had unequivocally stated before the Commission that merit could not be the only criterion for the recruitment in services because if merit was made the sole criterion there would be no place for Muslims, Jammu Dogras and other backward people in the State. He, therefore, introduced communal and regional representation for filling government posts and making admissions to educational institutions. When the Public Service Commission was established in 1957, it was also advised to keep these considerations in view. Because of this policy Kashmiri Pandits could not easily adjust themselves to the changed situation. Jammu Dogras who had traditionally sought their career in the armed forces of the State lost this source of employment when the State army ceased to exist as a separate entity.

The ambivalence in regard to political policy also has contributed for generating irritations. The people living in Kashmir Valley mostly feel that there is a certain degree of ambivalence about the political policy of the Union Government towards the State. Constant hostile propaganda from the other side of the sub-continent, and secessionist doctrines propagated by certain political leaders and parties of the State and the attempts of some political leaders of India to mediate in Jammu and Kashmir affairs have created doubts in the minds of the people of the State about their political future. All the political parties which appeared before the Commission were however, unequivocal in their stand that the accession of the State to the Indian Union was final and irrevocable. The existence of Article 370 in the Indian Constitution which was primarily of temporary nature is also according to a large section of the population one of the reasons for creating regional tension. Representations were also made before the Commission about unfairness of the elections being held in the State. They had pointed out that in the last general elections of 1962, 141 nomination papers were rejected and 26 members were returned unopposed to the State Legislative Assembly and that the whole of Anantnag district failed to get an opportunity to go to the polls for electing its representatives to Parliament or the State Legislature. The Commission was of the firm view that, "even if all the matter were equitably settled, we feel that there would still be a measure of discontent unless the political aspirations of the different regions of the State are satisfied." In fact we considered that the main cause of irritation and tension is the feeling of political neglect and discrimination, real or imagined from which certain region of the State suffer. Although the Jammu and Kashmir State has been a single political entity for over a hundred years, it cannot be denied that geographically, ethnically, culturally and historically, it is composed of three separate homogenous regions Jammu, Kashmir and Ladakh. In fact, the Pir Panjal range forms a natural dividing line between the Jammu and Kashmir regions. A convention should be established that if the Chief Minister belongs to one region, there should be a Deputy Chief Minister belonging to the other region, by another convention, the number of Cabinet Ministers belonging to the regions should be equal. There should also, in addition, be a full-fledged Cabinet Minister belonging to Ladakh. Recommendation was also made that the functions of each head of the department should be divided on a regional basis; in other words, each department should have a head and an additional head, one of them functioning in one region and the other in the other region. The members of Kashmir Administrative Service, the Kashmir Civil Service (judicial) and the Kashmir Police Service should work for a minimum specified period in each of the three regions. The Commission expressed its opinion for the rehabilitation of Refugees from non-liberated areas.

The Commission had made forty-two recommendations at the end of their findings which are reproduced hereunder:

Development Programmes

1. There should be a statutory State Development Board and Statutory Regional Development Boards for the three regions—Jammu, Kashmir and Ladakh. The Regional Boards should be headed by the Chief Minister or the Planning Minister and should consist of legislators from the regions, economists, experts and concerned officials. The regions should be adequately represented on the State Development Board which should be headed by the Chief Minister.

   The functions of the Regional Development Boards will be—

   (a) to draw up the regional plans;

(b) to assign priority to schemes and projects included in the regional plans; and

(c) to supervise the implementation of the regional plans.

In discharging these functions it should be the special responsibility of the Regional Development Boards to pay due regard to the special needs of the backward areas of their respective regions.

The State Development Board will scrutinize the regional plans, prepare a residuary Plan of schemes and projects which transcend regional boundaries or happen to be of an all-State interest and allocate plan funds equitably (after taking into account the population, area and the specific needs of each region) to the regional plans and the residuary plan of all State interest (Paragraphs 4.26 to 4.28).

2. The State Development Board and each of the Regional Development Boards will prepare at the end of each year a report of their respective activities giving details of the progress of the Plan programmes and Plan expenditure. At the end of each Plan, similar detailed reports should be prepared by the Boards indicating the physical and financial targets and the physical and financial achievements. All these reports should be laid before the Legislature as soon as may be after they are prepared (Paragraph 4.29).
3. Recruitment rules for all the State services for which they do not exist at present should be framed and promulgated as early as possibly. Recruitment Rules for other services also should be speedily framed (Paragraph 5.17).
4. Complete, tabulated results of all competitive examinations held by the Public Service Commission and other Recruitment Board that may be set up, should be published. These results should be sent to all candidates who have taken the examinations or, if this is not always feasible, the results should be at least made available for scrutiny on request (Paragraph 5.18).
5. Seniority lists for all services should be drawn up correctly and maintained up to date (Paragraph 5.19).
6. The annual confidential reports on all government servants should be written up regularly and objectively and maintained properly. There should be provision for the review of the confidential rolls by an authority superior to the reporting officer. A proper procedure should be prescribed for dealing

with representations of government servants against adverse entries in their confidential rolls (Paragraph 5.20).

7. The following multiple criteria should be adopted for determining which classes should be treated as backward;-
   (a) the economic backwardness of the class.
   (b) the occupation or occupations pursued by that class of citizens.
   (c) their place of habitation.
   (d) the average of student population per thousand in that class,
   (e) Caste, in relation to Hindus. (Paragraph 5.33 and 5.34)
8. The existing list of backward classes should be revised and a fresh list drawn up by a high-powered committee after applying the multiple criteria, mentioned above, relating to social, educational and economic backwardness (Paragraph 5.35).
9. Article 335 of the Constitution of India should be made applicable to the Jammu and Kashmir State and reservation for the Scheduled Castes made in the services in proportion to their population (Paragraph 5.38 and 5.39).
10. Reservation in the services should also be made for the backward classes, as freshly determined, in proportion to their population, subject, however, to the condition that the total reservation for the backward classes and the Scheduled Castes should not ordinarily exceed fifty per cent. The balance of the posts should be filled strictly and solely on the basis of merit. In filling the posts reserved for the backward classes and the Scheduled Castes, persons belonging to each of these categories should be selected on the basis of merit (Paragraph 5.35).
11. Reservation of places in educational and professional institutions should be made for the backward classes and the Scheduled Castes in proportion to their respective population, subject to the condition that the total reservation does not ordinarily exceed fifty per cent. The balance of the places in such institutions should be filled strictly and solely on the basis merit. In filling the places reserved for the backward classes and those reserved for the Scheduled Castes, merit should be the criterion for selecting the persons in each of these categories (Paragraph 6.18).
12. A certain proportion of the provision available for the grant of scholarships and study loans should be set apart for the

backward classes and the Scheduled Castes. The provision should be separate for each of them and should not be less than the proportion that either of them bears to the population of the State (Paragraph 6.20).

13. The balance of the provision for the grant of scholarships and study loans should be made available to the rest of the student population. In giving scholarships or loans, the means of the parent or guardian should be an important factor for determining the eligibility of the applicant and, other things being equal, merit should be the sole criterion for granting them (Paragraph 6.20).
14. The government and the people of the State of Jammu and Kashmir may themselves decide when Article 370 of the Constitution of India should be abrogated (Paragraph 7.16).
15. The State Government should immediately take all steps to arrange for the holding of elections to the local bodies as early as possible. These elections should be held regularly in future (Paragraph 7.18).
16. A convention should be established that if the Chief Minister belongs to one region, there should be a Deputy Chief Minister belonging to the other region. By another convention, the number of Cabinet Ministers belonging to the two regions should be equal. There should also be a full-fledged Cabinet Minister belonging to Ladakh (Paragraph 7.30).
17. The functions of each Head of Department should be divided on a regional basis; in other words, each Department should have a Head and an Additional Head, one of them functioning in one region and the other in the other region. The Department will be under the overall control of the main Head who will also be responsible for the coordination of work between him and the Additional Head (Paragraph 7.31).
18. When the High Court of Jammu and Kashmir functions at Srinagar, there should be at least one High Court Judge stationed at Jammu to dispose of the cases there. Similarly, when the High Court is functioning at Jammu, there should be at least one High Court judge stationed at Srinagar to deal with the cases arising in Kashmir (Paragraph 7.32).
19. Some of the cadres should be district-based, certain others region-based and the balance State-based. In district-based cadres transfers should be permissible only within the district and in region-based cadres transfers should be permissible only within the region. Members of State-based cadres alone should

be transferable anywhere within the State. Generally speaking, the incumbents of inferior and non-gazetted (other than supervisory) posts should be district-based. Supervisory non-gazetted posts, both clerical and non-clerical, should belong to the regional cadres. Class III and Class IV gazetted posts should also generally be in the regional cadres. The residents of the entire State shall be eligible for appointment to the posts included in any of these cadres (Paragraph 7.33).

20. The incumbent of a district-based post on promotion to a post in the regional cadre will become transferable anywhere within the region. Similarly, a person on promotion from a post in a regional cadre to a post in all State cadre will become liable to transfer to a place anywhere in the State (Paragraph 7.34).

21. Members of the Kashmir Administrative Service, the Kashmir Civil Service (Judicial) the Kashmir Police Service and such other State services as the State Government may consider necessary, shall be liable to serve for a minimum specified period (say, 5 years in each of the three regions of Jammu, Kashmir and Ladakh (Paragraph 7.35).

22. A Regional Recruitment Board should be set up for each of the Jammu and Kashmir regions and a District Recruitment Board for each district in the State including Ladakh. The function of the Regional Recruitment Board will be to make recruitment to the regional cadres, and that of the District Recruitment Boards to make recruitment to the district cadres. These Boards will concern themselves with filling those posts which are outside the purview of the Public Service Commission. These Boards could function part-time and be manned by suitable officer's drawn from the regions or districts, as the case may be (Paragraph 7.36).

23. There should be a separate full-fledged university in both the Jammu and Kashmir regions. One of them, preferably the one in Jammu, should immediately start a faculty of law. Subsequently, law classes will also have to be started in the other university (Paragraph 7.37).

24. As all the professional colleges are located in Kashmir (the Agricultural College at Ranbir Singh Pura also having been closed down recently) it will be proper to open a new medical college at Jammu. The question of starting an engineering college in the Jammu region may also be considered when the need for turning out a larger number of engineering graduates is felt (Paragraph 7.38).

25. The State Government should review the entire policy of food grains prices, both for procurement and for issue, and introduce uniform prices for food-grains throughout the Jammu and Kashmir regions (Paragraph 7.40).
26. The quantum of rations issued at Srinagar and Jammu should be the same (Paragraph 7.41).
27. In the matter of rations issued to government servants in the Ladakh district, no distinction should be made between 'local' and 'non-locals'. If, however, non-locals want to take the whole part of the rice ration in the form of wheat Atta, this should be permitted (Paragraph 7.42).
28. Some supplementary rationing of foodgrains should be introduced at Leh and Kargil on a basis similar to that adopted for the towns of the Jammu and Kashmir regions other than the cities of Srinagar and Jammu (Paragraph 7.43).
29. The system of collection of tolls and the location of the toll barriers in the State should be re-examined and rationalised so that neither the Jammu region nor the Kashmir region is placed at a disadvantage compared to the other (Paragraph 7.44).
30. A degree college should be established immediately at Leh. Subsequently, a second college should be established at Kargil (Paragraph 7.46).
31. The transport facilities available to Ladakh should be improved. In particular the number of buses and trucks plying between Srinagar and Leh should be substantially increased and transport facilities made available for access to the interior places in Ladakh (Paragraph 7.46).
32. Suitable arrangements should be made for the stay at Kargil of persons travelling between Leh and Srinagar (Paragraph 7.46).
33. Stable and satisfactory arrangements for providing electricity to Leh and Kargil and other places of importance in Ladakh should be made (Paragraph 7.46).
34. The single-line administration which was introduced in Ladakh some time ago should be revived in its entirety. The post of Development Commissioner should be merged with that of the Deputy Commissioner and the incumbent of the post should function as the Head of all Departments in Ladakh Affairs Secretary should be the Secretary for all subjects so far as Ladakh is concerned. He should work under the Ladakhi Minister who could hold charge of the portfolio of Ladakh Affairs (Paragraph 7.46).

35. The status of Leh should be accorded due recognition as the headquarters of a vast region by the construction of suitable buildings and roads, improving sanitary arrangements and other such measures (Paragraph 7.46).
36. The sanctioning of roads, irrigation and hydel schemes for Ladakh entails much delay as they have to pass through several stages both in the State Government and in the Central Government. As the passage through these different stages is unavoidable, all the authorities concerned in the State and Central Government should be instructed to deal as expeditiously as possible with the schemes relating to Ladakh (Paragraph 7.47).
37. The State Government should consider the request of the people of Ladakh for giving its due place in the formal name of the State (Paragraph 7.48).
38. There are some obvious anomalies in the Big Landed Estates Abolition Act and the Tenancy Act. The Wazir Committee had in 1953 made certain recommendations for dealing with some of them. The Land Commission appointed in 1963 has recently submitted its report. The State Government should consider the recommendations of the Wazir Committee and the Land Commission and take action to remove the anomalies, wherever possible (Paragraph 7.52).
39. The notification staying the disposal of applications made by the land-holders on grounds of resumption for personal cultivation should be rescinded, the Act under which the notification has been issued should be repealed and all pending applications for ejectment should be disposed of as expeditiously as possible (Paragraph 7.53).
40. The outstanding problems of refugees from non-liberated areas of the Jammu and Kashmir State should be examined sympathetically so that their apprehensions may be allayed (Paragraph 7.55).
41. Fresh appointments to posts should, as a rule, be made only on the recommendation of the Public Service Commission or the Regional/District Recruitment Boards and the tendency to make ad hoc appointments against newly created posts should be discouraged (Paragraph 7.58).
42. Regular meetings of the Departmental Promotion Committees, presided over by a member of the Public Service Commission, should be held so that panels of officers eligible for promotion to posts within the purview of the Commission are always

available. Ad hoc promotions pending the approval of the Public Service Commission should be avoided. The Departmental Promotion Committees should invariably have a representative of the Service Department as a member (Paragraph 7.59).

The report was signed on November 29, 1968 and the State of Jammu and Kashmir remained under the rule of Congress up to 1975. At the time when this report was given GM Sadiq was the Chief Minister and after his death in 1971 Syed Mir Qasim was the Chief Minister till 1975 when under Indira-Sheikh Accord the power was handed over to Sheikh Abdullah despite the fact that neither he nor anyone from his political party was a member of the State Legislature. It is very disgusting and dismaying that even during Indian National Congress rule the most of the recommendations of this Commission were not accepted and whatever was accepted was not implemented.

On October 12, 1977, Sheikh Abdullah made a statement and assailed the report of the Gajendragadkar Commission. In December 1978, the reaction of the Jammuites gave vent to the start of a serious agitation started by the students in which the public of the districts of Poonch, Rajouri, Udhampur, Kathua and Jammu got deeply involved. The agitation continued for 94 days in which at times curfew had to be imposed and there was police firing as well. This agitation was speared by 'All Parties Jammu Action Committee'. To cool the feelings of the public, Sheikh Abdullah with all his political cleverness appointed another Commission under the Chairmanship of retired Chief Justice of India Hon'ble Justice SM Sikri. The other two members of this Commission were Dr Malcolm and S Adisesniah. Dr M Zaheer was the Member Secretary. To summarise, the task of the Commission under the terms of reference was as follows:

1. To recommend measures for equitable share in securing government employment.
2. These measures may involve changes in the Constitution also.
3. The share in employment is to be determined by regions and also by distinct administrative units.

In a nutshell, the thrust of regional imbalances was sidetracked by the appointment of this Commission which had to mostly concentrate on distinct administrative units. The Commission submitted its report on August 25, 1980 but the recommendations have been shelved. The Commission had found regional imbalances apart from imbalances in individual items recorded in para 5.4.1. at page 117. The Commission had found imbalances in financial expenditure and in development programmes at the regional level in the IV Plan period and had proposed State Development Board composed of the Chief Minister as Chairman. However, the Commission was of the view that it would be drastic remedy to recommend a change in the Constitution by creation of regional committees and according to its view the imbalances could be remedied by executive or legislative actions. The enlightened public men from Jammu had projected their case before the Commission by urging, "The cardinal point that has to be grasped is that it is not simply a question of a job here or a road there, it is a much deeper problem of giving the people of Jammu and Ladakh a feeling of equal participation and involvement in the affairs of the State."

During Sheikh Abdullah's time on July 1, 1979, the State Government suddenly decided on its own for the creation of three districts in Kashmir Valley, i.e. Budgam, Pulwama and Kupwara and one in Ladakh region Kargil. There was a reaction on this which resulted into agitation which is known as 'Kishtwar Agitation'. This agitation was tried to be crushed by violence but the inhabitants of Kishtwar tehsil fought against injustice with courage and determination.

On November 12, 1981, the State Government appointed Commission under the chairmanship of Justice JN Wazir (Retired Chief Justice of J&K High Court) to go into this question. The Commission in its report of January 3, 1984 recommended the creation of three districts in the Jammu division—Kishtwar, Samba and Reasi and one district Bandipur in the valley but these recommendations were ignored and in 2006 when there was coalition government led by Congress(I) with PDP, without caring for this recommendation equal number of 10 districts were created in each of the two regions. This topic to some extent has already been discussed.

In the month of October 1987, Dr Farooq Abdullah in hot haste and without any cabinet agenda made an order modifying the normal pattern of shifting the State government secretariat and other offices from Srinagar to Jammu. This practice is known as, 'Darbar move', and is in vogue since 1870. Though this is expensive and causes some inconvenience for the disposal of official work yet it has its advantages of cementing the relations between Kashmiris and Jammuites. Climatically also it suits the both. The Jammuites apprehended that it was a move to make Srinagar city as permanent capital of the State and it would damage the economy of the Jammu region. Total bandh was observed in Jammu, Udhampur and number of other towns. Student community had also plunged into this agitation which resulted in the closure of educational institutions. The agitation prolonged for five weeks. It was being headed by Bar Association Jammu and its elected president was DK Khajuria, advocate. The agitation was so forceful that Union Government had to send her Home Minister Sardar Buta Singh to Srinagar who landed there on November 12, 1987 and after discussing the matter with Dr Farooq Abdullah the latter yielded to cancel his order. The restoration of the status quo-ante was to the disliking of the Kashmir Bar Association and they gave a call to public to avenge the lowering of the status of the government before the agitators. The public responded and the agitation lasted for five weeks leaving behind bitterness and tension between the two regions. Regional parochialism increased and some people since then are raising the voice for separate Statehood for Jammu region. A movement had been launched to achieve the object under the name of Jammu State Morcha which fought the Assembly elections of 2002 and won one seat within one month's time from the date of its formation. The writer of the book had also strongly felt about discrimination with Jammu region and remained for sometime patron of Jammu State Morcha. In the Assembly elections of 2008, again the seat won in 2002 by Jammu State Morch fell into the kitty of the same legislator. The national parties Indian National Congress and BJP also fought this election of 2002 on the basis of discrimination with Jammu and both parties in their election manifestoes had promised with the people to get the reports of Gajendragadkar Commission and Wazir Commission implemented after the formation of the government. These elections ended the family rule of National Conference after 1975 and a coalition government with the support of People's Democratic Party (PDP), a regional party, was formed in the State. To rule the State on the basis of a coalition government Minimum Common Programme was agreed between these two major political parties and other small supporting parties with an object of implementing the reports of these above stated two Commissions. The Chief Minister for the first three years term under the agreement was from PDP (Mufti Mohammed Sayeed) but he did not implement even a single recommendation of the Gajendragadkar Commission but on the contrary had been issuing parochial political statements against the recommendations of Wazir Commission. It is noteworthy that a few recommendations of the Gajendragadkar Commission such as setting up a separate Jammu University, a Medical College and an Engineering College were set up during National Conference regime. The only major achievement is that a Chief Minister belonging to Jammu region Ghulam Nabi Azad for the first time after Independence could sit on the chair for the contemplated remaining three years period but unfortunately that was not allowed to be completed. During this period the aggrieved people of Jammu and Ladakh region were hoping to get some justice from him.

His ouster on the row of Baba Amarnath Land Row stands discussed in this book.

On the basis of the recommendations of the Wazir Commission demand was made for the creation of Reasi district and when it was not met, in September 1988, an agitation was started by the people who were led by veteran political leader Rishi Kumar Koushal. Initially, the government took no notice of it. The agitators declared the creation of the district and appointed their own Deputy Commissioner and other officers. The Government then (headed by Dr Farooq Abdullah) applied force and tried to suppress it. Despite this brutal repression the agitation continued for two months. On some assurance given by the State Government, the agitation was suspended. Afterwards, sub-district status was given to Reasi and Kishtwar. The Court of Additional and Sessions Judge was created at Reasi. Later on, as has been discussed earlier during the coalition government of Congress(I) and PDP, Ghulam Nabi Azad as Chief Minister created 10 districts each for two regions against the recommendations of Wazir Commission Report. In order to specify the boundaries of the newly-created districts, Ghulam Nabi Azad appointed a committee headed by Chief Secretary (Retd) of the State SS Bloeria comprising of retired officers of the Revenue Department as members. This committee was appointed in the month of August 2006 with a stipulation that committee should submit its report within a period of 6 months which accordingly was submitted.

The Jammu people have been meeting out discriminatory treatment ever since 1947. Large number of institutions such as Institute of Medical Sciences, Institute of Engineering, Cable Car Project etc have been located in valley. Some time back a Dental College and an Agricultural University were established in Jammu region. The head offices of more than twelve Corporations are situated in the Kashmir region.

Besides these imbalances, a significant inroad has been made in the Constitutional Judicial Commissions which are set up under the various State Acts. The glaring examples are that Dr Farooq Abdullah during his rule had ensured that every Judicial Commission should be headed by a retired judge of the J&K High Court hailing from Kashmir region but the only exception was that Justice IK Kotwal (Retd) was allowed to hold the post till his death which after wards has been continuously occupied by retired judges for the last more than 13 years hailing from Kashmir region. A year ago when the term of that judge had expired Omar Abdullah as Chief Minister again got it filled by a Retired Additional Judge hailing from Kashmir Valley. The other examples of these Commissions are: (1) Chairman of the Advisory Board constituted under the J&K Public Safety Act. (2) President of the State Consumer Redressal Commission under the J&K Consumers Protection Act. Note: The only exception is that when this commission was set up in 1987, it was in 2005 the writer of this book on the recommendation of Governor SK Sinha to the then Chief Minister Ghulam Nabi Azad was appointed for the first time as President of the State Consumer Redressal Commission initially for two years which was later on extended for remaining three years. His successor is an Additional Retired judge of the High Court hailing from Kashmir region. He was appointed at the initial stage for five years term. All the President's of this Commission hailing from Kashmir region have been given at the initial stage for a term of five years but this was an exception for the reasons best known to the authorities when the writer of this book was given initially two years term and then extended for three years. (3) Chairman of the Jammu and Kashmir Human Rights Act. (4) Chairman of the J&K State Subjects Inquiry Act. (5) Chairman appointed under the J&K Backward Classes Act. (6) Chairman of Fee Regulatory Authority for Educational Institutions. (7) Of course for about last two years, coalition partner the Congress Party, by putting pressure on National Conference got appointed a retired Justice hailing from Jammu region as Chairman State Accountability Commission whileas the other member hails from Kashmir Valley as a retired Justice. This was the result of statutory provision which envisages that out of two members one should hail from either of the two regions. To add fuel to the fire, some retired judges hailing from Kashmir region who having once served for full terms against a particular post under the relevant Act are getting re-appointments against the Statutory bars imposed under those very different relevant Acts. Nobody who is concerned with the Rule of Law is giving any attention against such legal abuses. During Mufti Mohammed Sayeed's coalition rule any post which fell vacant from the above stated Commissions was swapped by a Kashmiri.

Chapter 20

Terrorism

Political violence in society when viewed from the victim's point of view is called terrorism. This is resorted to by anti-national groups to obtain political goals. Terrorism comprises violence aimed at brutal and random intimidation, coercion, destruction of human lives and properties. Striking terror and fear in the heart of every member of the society including soldiers is the basic aim of all terrorist acts. Twenty first century is facing the dreadful destabilising capabilities of its satanic capabilities after the scientific advancements.

Types of Terrorists

(i) State-supported, (ii) non-State supported, (iii) State-directed groups.

State-supported terrorist groups receive direct and indirect support from one State or group of States for perpetration of acts of terrorism in target State. This support is political, diplomatic, moral and economic. Our neighbouring country Pakistan has sponsored this type of terrorism against the Union of India using the territory and the people of J&K State. Non-State supported groups of terrorists do not have any national level, political aspirations including any demand for secession. These groups have in their ranks radical intellectuals and furious youths who lack training and infrastructure. State-directed groups of terrorists are used to crush dissident and rebellious elements in the State. Pakistan has achieved the invidious distinction of using both State supported and State directed terrorists groups against India in J&K State.

Terrorist Organisations

Every terrorists group is led and inspired by a charismatic leader. The leader does not expose himself to dangers. The group has under ground fighters and over ground supporters.

Classification of Terrorists—Hardcore/Non-Hardcore

The hardcore terrorists are highly motivated youths who indulge in killings and destruction with an easy conscience to carry forward the cause of movement. They disassociate themselves from friends, parents, relatives and society in general showing total faith in their leader. Non-hardcore terrorists live in underground lives waiting for their blooding experience and hardcore status.

Terrorism Support Structure

There has to be a sizeable strength of people outside the organisation to provide moral and material support. These people do not carry out any terrorist action and keep their usual lifestyle but are supporters of the cause. They are the life line of the movement. These supporters act as harbours and guides, publish inspiring accounts of terrorists and spread disinformation about combative actions of the government. They provide money and medical treatment.

Victims

Terrorists want to kill the leaders in society. Intellectuals who denounce the ideological basion of terrorist's campaigns are prominent targets. Soldiers of all hues are the prime targets. Soldiers in the terrorist's environment are the most visible components of a national power. Political leaders rush to the places of carnage perpetuated by the terrorists but nobody sends a word of condolence to soldiers killed in ambush or by mine explosion. Terrorists groups in J&K State are espousing the cause of Pakistan and they are indulging in wanton killings sending chills down the spine of a once integrated peaceful society. The spread of militancy will be discussed in a next chapter at the appropriate place and it would be relevant to deal with the militant organisations after this chapter.

Formation of Militant Organisations and Imposition of Bans on their Functioning

In the earlier chapters, the mindset of Sheikh Mohammed Abdullah to create a Sheikhdom for himself has been discussed in details. This idea has its genesis on the communal card of Kashmiriat. In 1932, Sheikh Abdullah had become the first President of the political organisation floated under the name, 'J&K Muslim Conference' and its aims and objects were set out for social, economic and cultural betterment of Muslims. It already stands discussed in this book how Sheikh Abdullah parted his ways with J&K Muslim Conference and formed his own political organisation under the name of National Conference having great affinity with the ideology of Indian National Congress. Till his death (which took place in 1982) he did not allow anybody to challenge his authority in this political organisation. It is still a family concern up to the third generation of Sheikh Abdullah. Furthermore, it also stands discussed that after the visit of Cabinet Mission to India in March 1946, it was made clear by the mission that it would not be possible for the British Government to carry out its obligations of paramountcy over Indian States after a new self-governing government or governments come into being in British India. It had been thus, made clear that British Government would not be in a position in any circumstances to transfer paramountcy to Indian Government. This policy statement of the Cabinet Mission provoked Sheikh Abdullah on May 15, 1946, and he launched Quit Kashmir Movement. His clear slogan was that Kashmiri nation had expressed its will and he asked for plebiscite on this question. In the rest of the country Quit India Movement had been started in 1942, but at that time Sheikh Abdullah did not join his hands with his friendly national organisation Indian National Congress. When the Britishers changed their policy of handing over the power to Indian National Congress and Muslim League on the basis of two nations theory, the circumstances had forced him to join hands with Indian National Congress in strengthening the accession of the State made by Maharaja. After the aggression of Pakistan on Kashmir, the circumstances were in favour of Sheikh Abdullah to take over the administration but he did not remain fair to the faith reposed upon him by the Central Government as well as the written promises made by him to Maharaja Hari Singh to remain loyal to him and his family. It also stands discussed that after his arrest and the commencement of his trial he again came out in true colours and floated an anti-national and subversive political organisation known by the name of All J&K Plebiscite Front. The Indian Government headed by Mrs Indira Gandhi was compelled to declare this political organisation under Section 3 of the Unlawful Activities (Prevention) Act, 1967 as Unlawful Organisation. The Front was declared to be an Unlawful Association by Notification Number SO 227 dated 12 January 1971 which was published in the Gazette of India Extraordinary, Part II. The Notification referred to above runs thus:

"SO 227—Whereas, the All Jammu and Kashmir Plebiscite Front is an Association—

(a) Which encourages or aids persons and its sympathisers to undertake unlawful activities within the meaning of the Unlawful Activities (Prevention) Act, 1967 (37) of 1967;

(b) The members of which undertake such activities:

(c) Such persons and sympathisers or members aforesaid, for example Sheikh Mohammed Abdullah, Mirza Mohd Afzal Beg and GM Shah have on diverse occasions, for example, Sheikh Mohammed Abdullah at Kishtwar on 1st May 1970, and at Naqshband Sahab, Srinagar, on 13 September 1970, Mirza Mohd Afzal Beg at Nowbug, October 1970, and at Hazratbal, Srinagar on 2nd October 1970, and GM Shah at Damhal, Anantnag district on 26th October 1970, by words either spoken or written or by signs or visible representation supported a claim to bring about the secession of a part of the territory of India, Jammu and Kashmir (hereinafter referred to as the State), from the Union and asserted claim to determine whether or not such part will remain a part of the territory of India;

(d) Such persons and sympathisers or members have on such or other occasions, either disclaimed or questioned the sovereignty and territorial integrity of India, by making speeches or in writing to the effect that the State is not a part of India and that the question of accession of the State to India remains to be decided;

(e) Which has for its object a so-called settlement of the question of the accession of the State to India through Plebiscite and the said object which amounts to an assertion of a claim to determine whether the State is or will remain a part of India, is an unlawful activity within the meaning of the said Act. And whereas, for all or any of the grounds set out in the preceding para as also on the basis of other facts and materials in its possession which the government considers to be against the public interest to disclose, the Central Government is of opinion that the said Front is an unlawful Association:

Now, therefore, in exercise of the powers conferred by Sub-Section (1) of Section 3 of the Unlawful Activities (Prevention) Act, 1967 (37 of 1967), the Central Government hereby declares the All Jammu and Kashmir Plebiscite Front to be an unlawful association. (Number F. 11/1/71-K. Part 1)

(Sd.) Ashoka Sen,
Joint Secretary to the Government of India."

On 8 February 1971 the Central Government in pursuance of Sub-Section (1) of Section 4 of the Act, made a reference to the Tribunal for the purpose of adjudicating whether or not there is sufficient cause for declaring the Front as an Unlawful Association. The Tribunal was constituted by virtue of a notification Number SO 572 dated 28th January 1971, by the Central Government by virtue of the powers conferred on it by Sub-Section (2) of Section 5 of the Act. Late hon'ble Syed Murtaza Fazal Ali (the then Chief Justice of J&K High Court) was appointed as Chairman of the Tribunal. The Central Government also filed a large number of documents in support of the imposed ban before the Tribunal as documentary evidence in support of the detailed statement of facts. The Tribunal issued notices against the leaders of this organisation and in consequence thereof Messrs MA Baig and GM Shah advocates appeared on their behalf to contest that it was not an unlawful association. BB Lal, senior advocate appeared for the Central Government.

After hearing the arguments of the parties and considering the nature of the pleadings, the Tribunal framed the following issues:

"1. Whether All Jammu and Kashmir Plebiscite Front is an Unlawful Association within the meaning of Section 2 of the Unlawful Activities (Prevention) Act?
(OP Central Government)
2. Whether on the facts and circumstances of the cases there is sufficient cause for declaring the aforesaid Front to be an Unlawful Association? (OP Central Government)
3. Whether the Unlawful Activities (Prevention) Act is not constitutionally valid and has not been properly applied to the State? (OP Defendants Plebiscite Front)
4. Relief."

Issue number 3 was not pressed by the counsel of the Front.

The Tribunal held many sittings in Delhi and recorded the evidence led by the parties before it both documentary as well as oral. After the appreciation of the evidence and hearing the legal arguments in depth the finding of the Tribunal was that the Front was an Unlawful Association. The conclusions of the Tribunal are reproduced hereunder in verbatim:

"16. Conclusions: It has been found by the Tribunal that some allegations of a serious nature against the Front have not been proved (vide Paragraph 14 Supra). The Front has also been found to have employed peaceful and constitutional methods to promote its object and it is essentially an organisation of a secular character. It has also been found that the Front has on many occasions helped and contributed a lot in the maintenance of law and order and communal harmony. Baig argued the plea of bona fide claim of right to get out of the consequences of the Act, but the Tribunal has over-ruled this plea for the reasons given hereinbefore. The Act has already been applied to the State in 1969 and the Tribunal on a full and complete interpretation of Ss. 2 and 4 of the Act has held that the Front falls within the mischief of Sections 2 and 4 and is therefore an unlawful Association indulging in unlawful activity. Baig in his evidence on re-examination categorically stated that his stand was not rigid, and observed:

> "Publicly we had said that our attitude on plebiscite is not rigid and that through Sheikh Mohammed Abdullah the Central Government could explore other alternatives for finalising the dispute."

In view of these special circumstances, the Tribunal is constrained to observe that if the Front and its leaders accept the accession of Kashmir to India as a fait accompli; change their stand and alter their ideology in face of the changed situation and are prepared to throw themselves into the mainstream of the political life of the country and its body politics and the government is convinced of the genuineness of the Front's intentions the government may seriously consider the desirability of withdrawing the ban forthwith or in the near future so as to allow the defendants to participate in the democratic process of our great country.

Before concluding this judgment, the Tribunal would take to express its great appreciation of the valuable assistance received from Baig for the defendants and Lal counsel for the government. The Tribunal feels highly indebted to Baig for his ingenious, pointed and persuasive argument and for giving full cooperation to the Tribunal in completing the proceedings within the shortest possible time. The Tribunal is also thankful to the State for having given every possible assistance in terminating the proceedings in the shortest possible time.

Result: For the reasons given above, issues 1 and 2 are decided in favour of the Government and the declaration that the Front is an unlawful Association made in the impugned Notification Number SO 227 dated 12th January 1971 (22nd Pusa, 1891 SF) is hereby confirmed and the references is accepted. Let the judgement be sent to the

Union Home Ministry for publication in the Government Gazette. Let the records of the case be also sent to the Union Home Ministry for safe custody.

New Delhi (Sd) S Murtaza Fazal Ali
15th June 1971 Chairman Unlawful Activities (Prevention) Tribunal
(Number F. 11/1/71-K Part I), Ashok Sen, Joint Secretary

At the time of termination of Dr Farooq Abdullah's rule in the State (on 19 January 1990), by the imposition of Governor's rule, the anti-national elements had virtually seized the livers of the State machinery and the State authority had collapsed. Central Government had sent Jagmohan, one of the most able administrators of the country, as Governor of the State. In order to restore the State authority, the Governor had to impose bans on eight prominent militant associations/organisations although at that time 44 Unlawful Associations were operating in the State (Appendix 17). In the first instalment, only six Organisations/Associations were declared unlawful and subsequently two more such Organisations were declared unlawful. Vide SRO 146, dated 16 April 1990, Jamaat-e-Islami J&K was declared as Unlawful Association. Vide SRO 147 dated 16 April 1990; Islamic Students League was declared as unlawful Association. Vide SRO 148 dated 16 April 1990; Islamic Jamiat Tulba was declared Unlawful Association. Vide SRO 149 dated 16 April 1990; Mahaz-e-Azadi was declared as Unlawful Association. Vide SRO 150 dated 16 April 1990; Peoples League was declared as Unlawful Association. Vide SRO 151 dated 16 April 1990; Jammu Kashmir Liberation Front was declared as Unlawful Association. These SROs were published in the J&K Gazette (Special edition) on 16 April 1990. The Organisations were declared Unlawful Associations by the Government of J&K by virtue of the powers conferred in the State Government under the Jammu and Kashmir Criminal Law Amendment Act of 1983. Sub-Section (1) of Section 3 of the Act empowers the State to impose ban on any Association if it is of the opinion that such Association is or has become unlawful. Sub-Section (2) of Section 3 requires that every such notification issued under Sub-Section (1) shall specify the grounds on which it is issued and such other particulars as the government may consider necessary and fix a reasonable period for any office bearer or member of the Association or any other person interested to make a representation to the government in respect of the issue of the Notification.

After fulfilling all legal formalities, the State Government vide Order Number 427-GR-LD(A) of 1990 dated 30 May 1990, created the Tribunal after sanctioning the staff and vide SRO 200 dated 11

June 1990 appointed the writer of this book as Chairman of the Tribunal (whole time) by virtue of the powers vested in her under Section 5 of the above said Act. At that time, the writer of this book was posted as Principal District and Sessions Judge Jammu. Two junior District and Sessions Judges were appointed as part time members of the Tribunal. Vide the same SRO, i.e. 200, Qazi Muzaffer-ud-Din was appointed as a member and the third member was subsequently appointed and he was Sardar Harcharan Singh Bahri. This event has happened for the first time in the history of the Indian judiciary when a Chairman of such an important Tribunal which only had not national ramifications but international also was selected from the cadre of District and Sessions Judges. The criteria for the appointment was that the incumbent should not succumb to the physical threats issued or harms caused by the militants or succumb to the huge monetary allurements offered by them. Qazi Muzaffer-ud-Din member of the Tribunal resigned after he received threats of physical harms from the militants after attending only one preliminary meeting of the Tribunal and he was replaced by Harbans Lal, District and Session Judge as a member.

The Jamaat-e-Islami J&K was declared to be an unlawful Association by Notification Number SRO 146 dated 16 April 1990. It was published in the Government Gazette on 16 April 1990. The Notification runs thus: SRO 146 whereas, the Jamaat-e-Islami J&K is an Association:

Which encourages or aids persons and its sympathisers to undertake unlawful activities within the meaning of the Jammu and Kashmir Criminal Law Amendment Act of 1983;

Such persons and sympathisers and members aforesaid have for its objects, activities and actions which interfere and aim at interference with the public administration, the administration and the maintenance of law and order and which constitute a danger to the public peace;

Such persons and sympathisers and members aforesaid have for its objects, activities and actions which are intended to encourage and which encourage, aid and incite the people to undertake activities which are offences punishable under Section 153-A and 153-B of the State Ranbir Penal Code;

Such persons and sympathisers and members aforesaid have for its objects, activities and actions which are intended or which may form a part of the scheme intend to threat or likely to threat or disrupt or likely to disrupt harmony between different religious groups of the State;

Such persons and sympathisers and members aforesaid have for its objects, activities and actions which are intended or which form part of the scheme intend to cause or likely to cause, fear, alarm and feeling of insecurity amongst members of different religious groups and communities in the State;

Such persons, sympathisers and members aforesaid by words, either spoken or written, or by signs or visible representation have indulged in activities e.g., on 3rd January 1989, Ashraf Sahrai General Secretary in a statement criticised Shimla Agreement as a conspiracy and claimed that Kashmir issue could be settled only through self-determination. Similarly, on 1st February 1989, Syed Ali Shah Geelani asserted that elections were no substitute for self-determination; and

Whereas, for all or any of the grounds set out in the preceding paragraphs as also on the basis of other facts and materials in the possession which the State Government considers to be against the public interest to disclose, the State Government is of opinion that the said Jamaat-e-Islami is an Unlawful Association.

Now, therefore, in exercise of the powers conferred by Sub-Section (1) of Section 3 of the Jammu and Kashmir Criminal Law Amendment Act 1983, the Government of J&K hereby declares the aforesaid party to be an unlawful association.

Any person, whether an office bearer or a member of the aforesaid Association or otherwise interested, can make a representation in respect of this Notification to the Government of Jammu and Kashmir within a period of thirty days from the date of issuance of this notification, if he so desires.

By order of the Governor

Sd/-

Addl Chief Secretary to Government Home Department"

The plaintiff/State had filed documents comprising of (1) Annexure-A to SRO 146, (2) Dossier, (3) Details of some anti-national and prejudicial activities, (4) constitution, (5) Lists of schools, (6) Battle Order, (7) Extracts of relevant DSIS, (8) Besides this, the plaintiff/State had also filed a plaint stated to be statement of facts.

In the plaint the government had arrayed Jamaat-e-Islami J&K as defendant Number 1. Hakim Ghulam Nabi, S/o Mubarak Shah, R/o Muloo Chitragan-Shopian C/o Addl DG, Prisons, J&K, Jammu (Amir of Jamait) was arrayed as defendant Number 2. Mohammad

Ashraf Sahrai C/o, Addl DG, Prisons, J&K, Jammu, General Secretary of Association, was arrayed as defendant number 3. Syed Ali Shah Geelani, C/o Addl. DG Prisons, J&K Jammu. (Known as Leader of the Association in question) was arrayed as defendant Number 4.

Service on defendant Number 2 could not be affected by the Tribunal because it was pleaded by the State that he had gone underground. Notice was published in the local newspaper and in the media to secure his presence but he did not attend the proceedings. He was proceeded ex-parte. Service of defendant number 3 was affected through Superintendent District Jail Kathua and the copy of the notification, plaint and the statement of facts along with all other record produced in the court were handed over to him personally and he stated not to take part in the proceedings. The service was affected on defendant number 4 through the superintendent Central Jail Naini (Allahabad) as he was lodged there. The Tribunal held its proceedings on 19 February 1991 in the premises of Central Jail Naini Allahabad where all the relevant record of the case was handed over to him for filing the written statement. His written statement was received in the Head Office of the Tribunal at Jammu on 27 March 1991. Defendant number 3 had also filed the written statement.

On 4 September 1991, the proceedings were held in the premises of Tihar Jail Delhi and defendant Syed Ali Shah Geelani was personally present along with his advocate MH Baig (Deputy Chief Minister of the ex-coalition government of Congress(I) and PDP). At the request of MH Baig advocate the proceedings were adjourned on the plea that he wanted to go through the record and again on 7 September 1991, the proceedings were taken up in the premises of Tihar Jail Delhi. On this date, that is on 7 September 1991, MH Baig advocate made a statement that defendant number 4 (Ali Shah Geelani) had withdrawn his presence from the proceedings and that he did not like to associate himself with the proceedings. A written request in this behalf was also made and that formed a part of the record. Permod Kohli Advocate-General assisted by BS Slathia, Presenting counsel and LN Chadha, Presenting Counsel appeared for the plaintiff/State.

The case of the plaintiff/State consisted of the dossiers of the defendants, annexures, the Constitution of the Association and other documentary evidence. The factual matrix on the averments of the plaint and the accompanying factual statement with it is produced in verbatim.

1. The Association encourages or aids persons and its sympathisers to undertake unlawful activities within the meaning of the

Jammu and Kashmir Criminal Law Amendment Act of 1983;

2. Such persons and sympathisers and members aforesaid have for its objects, activities and actions which interfere and aim at interference with the public administration, the administration and the maintenance of law and order and which constitute a danger to the public;
3. Such persons and sympathisers and members aforesaid have for its objects, activities and actions which are intended to encourage and which encourage, aid and incite the people to undertake activities which are offences punishable under Section 153-A and 153-B of the State Ranbir Penal Code;
4. Such persons and sympathisers and members aforesaid have for its objects, activities and actions which are intended or which may form a part of the scheme intend to threat or likely to threat or disrupt or likely to disrupt harmony between different religious groups of the States;
5. Such persons and sympathisers and members aforesaid have for its objects, activities and actions which are intended or which form part of the scheme intend to cause or likely to cause, fear alarm and feeling of insecurity amongst members of different religious groups and communities in the State;
6. That on 3rd January 1989, Ashraf Sahrai General Secretary (defendant number 3) in a statement criticised Shimla Agreement as a conspiracy and claimed that Kashmir issue could be settled only through self-determination. Similarly on February 1st, 1989 Syed Ali Shah Geelani asserted that elections were no substitute for self-determination;
7. The Association aims to carve out, Islamic State out of the present government established by law.
8. The Association disputes the accession of J&K State with India and preaches time and again secession of the State from Union fold. It induces the youth that it would be Kashmiris who have to decide about the fate of Kashmir and none else;
9. The Association criticised the centre and the State Government for measures taken to reduce the Muslim majority complexion of the State into minority. It further criticised the special status conferred on the State vide Art. 370 of the Indian Constitution which stands eroded from time to time;
10. The Association does not accept the constitution of the State and describe it as fraud committed by undemocratic governments.

11. The Association alleges that Kashmir issue is still unsolved and needs to be decided in accordance with the resolutions of UNO.
12. Ghulam Mohd Bhat (Amir-e-Jamat) on June 13, issued a press release in Srinagar, wherein he stated that Kashmir was disputed territory. Earlier to it; Ghulam Qadir Wani (Amir-tehsil-Bandipore) while addressing the congregation had enjoined upon the Kashmiris to liberate their land. He had questioned the accession and stated that late Jawaharlal Nehru, Sheikh Abdullah and Mrs Indira Gandhi had cheated the people of the State. Similar views were expressed on August 19, 1986 by GM Saifi (Amir Zilla Baramulla), M/s Abdul Majid (an activist of the Association) and Ghulam Nabi Nowsheri on August 29, 1986 vehemently resented the taking of Dargahs by the government. On April 1987, they had assailed the conception of socialism and secularism as they were anti-Islam and had emphasised that Islam was the complete code of life. Syed Ali Shah Geelani, on May 13, 1987; had criticised bunglings in elections and remarked that government would crumble under its own weight.
13. Abdul Majid Bhat on May 20, in Sopore addressed Friday congregation and stated that the policies of State and Central Government were anti-Islamic. He had remarked that beaf was 'Halal' for Muslims yet slaughter of bovine was banned in the State. On the other hand, consumption of liquor was banned in Islam but it was permitted. It was also alleged that there was no freedom of religion by allowing simply prayer five times a day.
14. On June 3, 1988 in Srinagar, the Association issued a press-release and made public its resolution which enjoined that India and Pakistan should concede the demand of Kashmiris for the exercise of their right of self-determination.
15. In the premises of Tahama Eidgah, Sopore on June 25/26, M/s Abdul; Majid Bhat, Syed Ali Shah Geelani and Prof AG Bhat exhorted the congregation not to yield to the pressure of 'Batil Nizam' (non-Muslim rule). Geelani had stated accession of State to India was a wrong decision.
16. Syed Ali Shah Geelani on July 1, 1988 while addressing the Friday congregation at Baramulla had stated that they were prepared to make all sacrifices relieving Kashmiris from the shackles of slavery. He also criticised the Presidential Ordinance which separated religion from politics by remarking

that the said Ordinance has caused interference in the affairs of the Muslims and it should not be made applicable to Muslims.

17. GM Bhat had stated that Kashmir issue could not be resolved unless Muslims in general and Muslim youth in particular assemble under one banner and struggle for its settlement.
18. On June 25, 1988 at Sopore Syed Ali Shah Geelani while addressing Eid-ul-Zuha congregation had remarked that Islam was not free in Indian Union and that they have to strive hard for getting it emancipated from slavery chains.
19. Mohd Ashraf Sahrai on July 25 had stated extension of Presidential Ordinance to J&K State which bans the misuse of places of worship would be resisted by the Association.
20. Nazir Ahmed Kashni in a press statement dated August 13, 1989 had urged the government not to introduce the Presidential Ordinance as behind the Ordinance there was a conspiracy against religion.
21. GM Saifi while addressing congregation in Sopore on September 2, condemned the leaders who mislead the Muslims by assuring that Islam was quite safe. Regarding the adoption of religious institution prevention of misuse Bill by the parliament he had stated that how Laws made by man could be imposed at the house of God (Mosque). He induced the audience by saying that such a thing could be possible in the case of a temple or a Gurdwara but not in the case of a Mosque.
22. On September 9th, 1988 AS Geelani, while addressing public meeting at Vilgan (Handwara) had stated that Muslims in India did not enjoy freedom of religion and they were being distanced from religion through conspiracies. The aim and object of the Association in question was to replace the present political system through the establishment of Nizam-e-Mustafa.
23. On September 16, while addressing Friday congregation AS Geelani assailed the ideas of Socialism and secularism by alleging that minorities are maltreated in India. That Muslims are dubbed as second class citizens and whereas Sikhs are treated as third class citizens.
24. Daily mouth piece 'Azan' of Association in question in its issue dated 3 January 1989; published a threat given by Syed Ali Shah Geelani and GM Sumji to start a public row in case

government established by law ventured to have created three new districts in Jammu Division against the one in Kashmir.

25. On January 3rd, 1989 Mohd Ashraf Sahrai (defendant) criticised the Shimla agreement and stated that it as conspiracy. He had claimed that Kashmir issue could be settled only by the exercise of right of self-determination.
26. Daily official organ *Azan* of the Association in question in its column January 1989 condemned the arrest of Kashmiri youths by the government. In its editorial of January 11, issue it was remarked that while the whole country would celebrate its Republic Day with gaiety the people of Kashmir would be lamenting over their plight.
27. On January 13, 1989 GM Sofi and Saifi while addressing a Friday congregation criticised the action of local police against local butchers for slaughtering of bovine animals. He had suggested clandestinely to them not to carry on this part of trade openly. While referring to the remarks of late Rajiv Gandhi made at the end of SAARC conference, they criticised and said that Kashmir issue could not be solved under the Shimla Agreement but could be solved giving the opportunity to the Kashmiri people to exercise the right of self-determination.
28. M/s Hakim Ghulam Nabi, Ghulam Qadir Wani and Abdul Hamid Fayaz, activists of the Association on January 16, in Shopian criticised the constructive programme of family planning and said that it was well-planned conspiracy to reduce the Muslim majority to the microscopic minority.
29. On January 20, Moulvi Ghulam Mohd Kakashi while addressing Friday congregation appreciated the crusade of Afghan rebels and called upon the Kashmiris to emulate the spirit of struggle in order to shake off slavery shackles.
30. M/s Ghulam Mohd Sofi and Saifi on February 3, 1989 at Sopore exhorted the gathering to foil the attempts of forces inimical to Islam and prayed for the success of Afghan Mujahideen, Palestinian and Kashmiri people
31. On February 17, 1989 Mohd Ashraf Sahrai while addressing a public meeting and condemned the part of Indian Government in supporting the Soviets in Afghanistan and remarked that conspiracies to hurt the sentiments of the Muslims in India are going on. He criticised the alliance between the National Conference and Congress(I) and said by arresting the Muslim youths, their future is being ruined.

32. M/s Mohd Ashraf Sahrai, GM Saifi during the Zuhr prayers in Eidgah Qadeem Bala, on April 6, had stated that they would bring out an Islamic revolution in the State on the pattern of Afghan Mujahideen.
33. Ghulam Mohd Saifi alleged that Kashmir was a disputed territory and JKLF was in favour of an independent Kashmir. He had held Dr Farooq Abdullah responsible in the execution of Maqbool Bhat.
34. Syed Ali Shah Geelani on April 7, in Sopore called upon youths to be prepared to lay down their lives in order to achieve their freedom. On April 14, 1989 at Sopore again he asked the people to continue their struggle for liberating Kashmir. He had also said that Kashmir was under illegal occupation of India. He also threatened that any attempt to close down their Dargahs, would be met with dire consequences. He exhorted the youths for launching struggle to free themselves from shackles of slavery.
35. On April 7, 1989 Syed Ali Shah Geelani at Jamia Masjid Sopore in an Iftar party stated that recent activities of separatist/subversive elements in Srinagar was an expression of growing misrule of the State Government. He had stated that accession of State to India was not final. He had condemned the people of Pakistan to the extent, they voted in favour of secular and socialistic elements at the general elections in the country.
36. On April 21, In Baqa Sahib mosque Batmaloo, Srinagar, GM Bakshi criticised the Central Government and remarked that India was only place where the worship places of minority communities were usurped by the majority community.
37. While addressing Friday congregation at Jamia masjid Sopore, GM Saifi disclosed that if Kashmiri Muslims would act like Afghan Mujahideen Indian rulers would have to inevitably retreat from Kashmir. Imam of the mosque Ishaq Naziki also said like that.
38. Syed Ali Shah Geelani at Sopore on May 12, declared that present hartal/strike was a beginning of so called 'Quit Kashmir Movement' and asked the people to lend support for observing hartals.
39. Syed Ali Shah Geelani in the company of Abdul Ahad Bhat visited the families of those persons who had been involved in terrorist and disruptive activities and paid Rs 3,000/- as assistance to each family.

40. On May 27/28, 1989; Syed Ali Shah Geelani had stated while addressing a gathering at Eidgah Langate that the Association would not rest at peace unless socialism and secularism were eradicated from the State.
41. Syed Ali Shah Geelani while addressing a public meeting at Beerwah on July 19, 1989 said that Kashmiris were living as slaves since last four decades. He had asserted that the Association in question was in agreement with the aims and objects of terrorists and they had sympathies with them.
42. On July 29/30, 1989 in a congregation at Eidgah Zaloora Sopore, Syed Ali Shah Geelani and others had said that Muslims continued to get raw deal and were victimised in communal violence. Later on; GM Saifi had stated that the Association would launch an armed struggle to seek settlement of so-called Kashmir issue.
43. On August 19/20, 1989, Syed Ali Shah Geelani while addressing a congregation at Shalimar, had claimed that Kashmir issue was unresolved and demanded its settlements in accordance with UNO resolution. He had also said that besides setting up of Islamia Nizam, the Association wants freedom of J&K.
44. On August 26/27,1989, while addressing a gathering at Eidgah in Anantnag, Syed Ali Shah Geelani said that militants were on true path as per their own ideology and thinking.
45. On December 8, 1989 Syed Ali Shah Geelani while addressing a Friday congregation at Sopore had asked the participants to support the freedom loving youths and join their ranks.
46. On February 15, 1990 Syed Ali Shah Geelani while addressing a gathering at Malabagh Srinagar disputed the State's accession with India and demanded its settlement in accordance with UNO resolutions. He also stated that Kashmiri youths were left with no option but to pick up arms and fight for restoration of their rights. He refuted the charge that Pakistan was in any way involved in the present situation in Kashmir.
47. In the plaint/which was filed subsequently on 11 February 1991, it is alleged in Para 5 that the Association in question has been preaching, promoting, organising and committing acts which are prejudicial to the maintenance of communal harmony between different religions. In doing so, the Association indulges in disturbing the public peace and tranquillity from time to time. The Association has also been

publishing and circulating the published material appealing thereby to cause disharmony and feelings of enmity, hatred and ill-will between Muslims and other non-Muslims residents of the State of Jammu and Kashmir.

48. In Para II, it is alleged that the Association has been indulging directly or indirectly in killing of innocent people causing thereby a feeling of insecurity amongst members belonging to different communities and this exercise was undertaken by its members with a view to achieve its unlawful objects.

Defendant number 3 Mohd Ashraf Sahrai before absenting himself in the proceedings had filed the written statement wherein he had taken the preliminary objections to the effect that notification in question had not been published by the government in the manner prescribed by law as well as not have been communicated to the Association. According to him, the provisions of Section 3 and Section 4 of the Act had not been fully complied with. On facts of the case, he took the pleas which are summarised hereinunder:

In the sovereignty of God. In the total surrender of the man before God. Man has to account for his act. Prophet Mohammad is a prophet of God through whom God has ordained to follow the teachings of Holy Quran, which is a complete code of life revealed by almighty God to his last messenger.

That the aims and objects of the Association in question are to strive for the establishment of God's sovereignty in all spheres of life and to spread the teachings of Prophet Mohammad for the welfare and betterment of mankind.

The message of God for which the Association has to strive, is meant for every human being irrespective of his colour, creed, caste, race, religion or group. For the purpose of spreading the message of God, the Association in question has decided to act and has acted and shall act within the ethical, moral and truthful and honest limits. It has never adopted any method or means which would endanger peace and tranquillity of mankind. It has never discriminated amongst the man and woman on the basis of groupism, language, colour, creed or nationality. The Association is of the view that divine message is for all the mankind. The Association has not in any manner encouraged the undertaking of unlawful activities or any person connected with it never interfered with the public administration or the maintenance of law and order or has endangered public peace. On the other hand, the Association in question strives for the establishment of eternal peace by preaching the message of God as revealed by holy prophet. It is denied that any person connected with the Association has ever intended to threat or disrupt harmony between different religious groups or has caused fear, alarm or the feeling of insecurity amongst members of different religious groups and communities of the State. He has also pleaded that before issuance of notification in question; the Association was a recognised political party and had taken part in the elections held in the State Assembly and Parliament. The Association in question is registered and recognised political party with the Election Commissioner of India and it has been issuing policy statements on national and international issues. Regarding the accession of the State with Indian union he had stated that no representative of the people of J&K State was present at the time of signing the said agreement so it is not binding upon the people. He has further stated that neither the criticism of Shimla Agreement entered between the Government of India and the Government of Pakistan nor claiming self-determination as a solution for Kashmir issue per se constitute an act which falls within the purview of unlawful activities. That the criticism against the Indian Government for having forged a political alliance between the national ruling party Indian National Congress with regional party National Conference with an avowed object to harass the Muslim youths by frequently arresting and interrogating them is not an offence and the Association cannot be held responsible for doing unlawful and illegal activities.

Case of Defendant Number 4 (Syed Ali Shah Geelani) before the Tribunal which could be made out from his sketchy and lengthy objections prepared in Urdu language, replete with parables quoted from holy Arabic literature and Urdu poetry was summarised as follows:

"He had not specifically given any reply to the allegations which were contained in SRO 146 and enumerated from (a) to (g), however, he specifically dealt with the allegations contained in annexure 'A' to said SRO as well as to some allegations contained in the plaint. With regard to the allegations that Association in question has the aims and objects to carve out an Islamic State from the present government established by law he pleaded that the object of the Association was to strengthen the faith of Islam and this was devotion towards Almighty God for achieving the salvation by the activists of the Association. That in this regard, the directions of the holy prophet are considered of paramount consideration. That Association had taken part in the Assembly elections of the State and in 1969, it also took part in Panchayat elections against two rival political parties—All J&K Plebiscite Front and Congress Party. Thereafter, the Association had taken part in the J&K State Assembly elections held during the years 1971/1972, 1977, 1983 and 1987. As all these elections were rigged by corrupt electoral practices so the faith of the majority of the people in the democratic system of the government was eroded and as such the Association never took part in any subsequent election. He disputed the accession of the State with the Union of India and stated that it was only provisional. That according to the UNO Resolution passed on 13 August 1948, the fate of J&K State had to be determined by holding Plebiscite and the dominions of India and Pakistan had to withdraw their armed forces from the territory of J&K State. That the Constituent Assembly of the State which framed the State constitution in 1952 and ratified the accession was not properly constituted. The Kashmir problem is not a border dispute between two dominions of India and Pakistan but concerns the people of Jammu and Kashmir who number 1,20,00,000 and they have the sole right of self-determination with regard to the accession of the State. That non-residents of the State of Jammu and Kashmir are being granted fake J&K Permanent Resident Certificates with an intention to change the balance of population. The Central Government has also been pressurising the State Government to accord the status of permanent residents to the Hindu refugees from West Pakistan who settled in the State in 1947. That in Kashmir Valley, family planning programme is being propagated vigorously by offering money and sex in order to reduce the percentage of Muslim population. In the National Census reports, the Muslim population is not correctly reflected. The laws enacted by the Indian Parliament are extended to the State of Jammu and Kashmir without the ratification of State Legislature. The jurisdiction of the Election Commissioner of India and Supreme Court of India has wrongly being extended to the State. The nomenclature of the head of the State from 'Wazir-i-Azam' has been wrongly changed as Chief Minister. The entry and exit from State without a permit as was in vogue has wrongly been abolished. He also denied the allegations contained in para 25, 26 and 27. With regard to the allegations contained in para number 28, he stated that in 1947, when the State was divided in two parts, the Muslim constituted 80 per cent of the total population which now has been reduced to 60 per cent only. On the allegations contained in Para 29 he stated that Moulvi Ghulam Mohd Bakshi was only a well-wisher and supporter of the Association. He on behalf of the

Association appreciated the cause of Afghans and sacrifices made by them and criticised the Russian dominion. While replying to the allegations contained in para number 30 he stated that Kashmiris have humanly and Islamic relations with the Afghans and Palestinians. In reply to the allegations contained in para number 31, he has endorsed the spirit of the criticism and also stated that atrocities were being committed on the innocent youths after the said alliance. With regard to the allegations contained in para number 32, his reply is that nobody should worry about Islamic revolution on the pattern of Afghan Mujahideen in the State. That the Association has also been struggling in the State for the last 42 Years for the establishment of democratic constitutional Islamic revolution.

He endorsed the allegations contained in para number 33, as well as admitted the allegations contained in para number 34. He also admitted the allegations contained in para number 35, 36, 37, 38, 39, 40 and 41. With regard to the allegations contained in para number 42 he admitted the fact that Muslims are victimised. With regard to the allegations contained in Para 43, he denied for holding a public meeting at Shalimar on August 19 and August 20, 1989. However, he admitted the other allegations. He admitted the allegations of para number 44 and para 45. With regard to the allegations contained in para number 46, he admitted categorically that he tells the Kashmiri youths not to become desperate with their struggle which has been yielding results. That the population of J&K State is equal to the population of one district of UP State and India has captured the State being a big power but it can't crush the Kashmiris. Allegations contained in para number 47 have been denied by him and further stated that the Association in question was formed in November 1953, and it never took part in any communal riot or ever showed any disgrace to any temple, Gurdwara or Church. According to him, migration of Hindus/Sikhs from valley took place for achieving political ends and the Association had no hand in it. He denied the allegations of para number 49.

From the pleadings of the parties, on 20 August 1991 the following two issues were raised:

1. Whether on the facts and in the circumstances stated in the impugned notification (SRO 146 dated 16 April 1991) and the pleadings of the parties, there is sufficient cause for declaring Jamaat-e-Islami to be an unlawful Association within the meaning of the provisions of J&K Criminal Law Amendment Act, 1983? OPP.

2. Whether there has been no compliance of the provisions of Section 3 of the J&K Criminal Law Amendment Act 1983? If so, what is its effect on the proceedings there under? OPD.

The burden of proof of Issue number 1 was on the Plaintiff and burden of proof of Issue number 2 was on the defendants. At the first instance, the Plaintiff/State was directed to produce the evidence. Defendants withdrew their presence from the proceedings and they were proceeded ex-parte. The Plaintiff/State produced ex-parte evidence.

After carefully appreciating the voluminous evidence both documentary and oral led by the Plaintiff/State the Tribunal came to the view that it was proved beyond doubt that the Association in question 'Jamaat-e-Islami' J&K is preaching, propagating and advocating the following feelings, theories, ideologies, cults and claims:

> "The Association aims to carve out Islamic State out of the present government established by law. The Association disputes the accession of J&K State with India and preaches time and again Secession of the State from the Union fold and induces youth by exhorting them that it would be Kashmiris who have to decide about the fate of Kashmir and none-else. The Association levels unfounded allegations that the Central and the State Governments are taking measures to reduce the Muslim majority character of the State. The Association had also been criticising the authorities that the special status conferred on State vide Article 370 of the Indian Constitution stands eroded from time to time. The Association does not accept the validity of the J&K Constitution. The Association had been alleging that Kashmir issue is still unsolved and needs to be decided in accordance with the resolutions of UNO. The Association had been carrying on propaganda, which was spreading communal hatred in the State. Its activities and actions had an objective which was likely to threat or disrupt harmony between different religious groups of the State. The activities of the Association had been causing fear, alarm and feelings of insecurity amongst different religious groups and communities in the State by exhorting the general public to observe frequent hartals. The Association had been interfering with the maintenance of supplies and services essential to the life of the people at large. Furthermore, the aims and objects of the Association are also to earn the odium of the people in general against the established government by levelling unsubstantiated charges of atrocities. These activities resulted in the interference with the public administration, administration of law and the maintenance of public order.

Conclusion

The aiding, undertaking and the propagating of the above stated feelings, cults, objective, claims etc as stated above by the Association in question or by its office bearer or activists fall squarely within the ambit of Section 2(b) and (c) of the Act as being the Commission of 'Unlawful' activities by the Association in question.

Result

For the reasons given above, the reference is accepted and the declaration that the Jamaat-e-Islami J&K is an 'Unlawful Association' made in the impugned notification number 146 dated 16 April 1990 is hereby confirmed. Let the copy of the judgment be sent to the Home Secretary, Government of J&K Jammu, for publication in the Government Gazette. Let the records of the case be also sent to the Home Ministry for safe custody.

Before parting with the judgement, we are constrained to observe it with a sincere hope that militancy in the Kashmir Valley a heaven on this earth would end sooner than expected. Violence is no solution to any problem. It only breeds hatred and adds to the miseries of innocent common people. The unity and integrity of the country must be preserved at all costs. It is above politics, above individual gain and above the interests of one group or another. It is fundamental to the prosperity of the nation as a whole. Communalism is an extremely dangerous virus, India is a multi-religious nation and communalism adds to the miseries of all. Much of our nation's energy and resources have to be diverted to the containment of communal violence. The nation can ill afford this. And lastly, let there be no doubt that India belongs to all of us, we are citizens of this great country. All of us to whatever religion we may belong are equally the children of India with equal rights; privileges and obligations. Let us all play our role to fulfil the basic objectives of our Constitution which include strengthening communal harmony and national integration.

sd/-	sd/-	sd/-
(Harbans Lal, Member)	(HS Bahri, Member)	(GD Sharma, Chairman)

SRO 147

Vide this SRO the Association by the name ISLAMIC STUDENT'S LEAGUE was declared as Unlawful Association. In the plaint presented by the State before the Tribunal the Association Islamic Student's League was arrayed as defendant number 1 and Shakeel Ahmad Bakshi (head of the Association) as defendant number 2 and Mohammad Nayeem alias Firdous (second head of the Association) as defendant number 3.

Permod Kohli, Advocate-General assisted by BS Slathia, presenting counsel and LN Chadha, presenting officer had appeared for the Plaintiff/State while no counsel appeared for the defendants. Defendant number 2 (Shakeel Ahmad Bakshi) after filing the objections absented and was proceeded ex-parte along with defendants 1 and 3.

The case of the plaintiff in a nutshell made out from the SRO and the plaint as well as the annexures attached therewith was summarised thus:

"That the league is an Association which encourages or aided persons and its sympathisers to undertake unlawful activities. That members of this Association undertake such activities.

That such persons and sympathisers and members aforesaid have for its objects, activities and actions which interfere and aim at interference with the public administration and the administration of maintenance of law and order and which constitute a danger to the public peace.

That members of the Association and its sympathisers have for their objects, activities and actions which are intended to encourage and which encourage aid and incite the people to undertake activities which are offences punishable under Section 153-A and 153-B of the State Ranbir Penal Code.

That the members of the Association and its sympathisers have for their objects, activities and actions which are intended to form part of the scheme intended to cause or likely to cause, alarm and feeling of insecurity amongst members of different religious groups and communities in the State.

That on January 15, 1987, the Association called a meeting at Baramulla and exhorted the people not to participate in the Republic Day's celebrations. Mohammad Abdullah Sherani on 23-1-1987 said that the Central Government was responsible for launching aggression on the Muslim society. On 10th April 1989, the League demanded the release of Shakeel Ahmad Bakshi and Niyam Khan and also said that festival of Eid should not be celebrated by the Kashmiri Muslims as their brothers were in Jails.

That the Association does not accept the factum of accession of the State of Jammu and Kashmir with the Union of India and its members preach and propagate and practise secession and demand right of self-determination. That they are thus having recourse to unconstitutional methods. That the Association wants to establish Islamic Society in the valley.

That the Association has been actively organising supporting and giving calls for strikes and 'bands', observing civil curfew, civil disobediences and unleashing a reign of terror by resorting to gun culture.

That the Association propagates the commemoration of the Independence Day of the Union of Pakistan.

The case of defendant number 2 Shakeel Ahmad Bakshi before the Tribunal.

In his written statement, he at the outset pleaded that the league is a "purely non-militant reformist organisation which has its aim to bring into lime light and acquaint the authorities of genuine and legitimate problems of the society." That the 'league' has always opposed undemocratic and unlawful actions and never participated or abetted any commission of militancy related offences. That the ban imposed by the government on the Association "has not affected its few office bearers but has affected the entire society also by curbing their voice and that too is one of the factors which forced the oppressed to resort to militancy." That the basic values of Indian democracy such as fraternity and social equality have been denied to the ten million people of the J&K State. That by setting up bunkers at every twenty or fifty yards, the Armed Forces have beleaguered the valley. This has been done to crush the just voice of the people. Incidents of indiscriminate shooting by firearms at the citizens such as at Gowkadal in Srinagar, by pass at Bemina, at Handwara, at Zakura in the city of Srinagar have been mentioned. It is also alleged that the houses of people have indiscriminately been set ablaze by the personnel of security forces without any rhyme and reason. That the members of the security forces have become debauchers as they commit gang rapes. That the perpetuation of such crimes inspire the youth to join the cult of militancy. Lastly, it is alleged that Kashmir has forcibly been annexed by India and Pakistan. That this unnatural division of the territory has separated some people from their kiths and kins. In other words, this has caused ethnic, emotional segregation and demographic homogeneity has been broken. That on Kashmir, the United Nations has passed many resolutions from 1947 to 1951 empowering the Kashmiris to determine the accession of the J&K State by expressing their will but Government of India has failed to implement these resolutions. It is also pleaded that security forces should be withdrawn from Kashmir Valley and human rights and civil liberties be restored. Since ban on the Association was imposed without giving any opportunity of being heard and that now any such like offer will be an exercise in futility.

The Tribunal on a careful consideration of the evidence both documentary as well as oral led by the plaintiff/State and the admission made by defendant number 2 in his objections held that, "it was proved beyond doubt that the Association 'League' is preaching, propagating and advocating the following feelings, theories, ideologies, cults and claims:

> The League stands for the right of self-determination for the rights of Kashmiris.
>
> That the future of the Kashmir can only be decided by the people and none else.
>
> That the past assurances given by the political leaders of India from time to time regarding a fair and impartial Plebiscite have not been fulfilled and must be carried out.
>
> That the accession of Kashmir with India is only provisional and therefore, Kashmir cannot be said to be an integral part of India.
>
> That the League is carrying on propaganda which is spreading communal hatred and creating insecurity among the different religious, racial and regional groups. Its aim is also to earn the odium of the people in general against the established government by levelling unsubstantiated charges of oppression and excesses which adversely result in the interference with the public administration, administration of law and the maintenance of public order."

Conclusion

The aiding, undertaking and the propagating of the above stated feelings, cults, objects, claims etc as stated above by the Association in question or by its office bearer or activists fall squarely within the ambit of Section 2(b) and (c) of the Act as being the commission of 'unlawful activities' by the Association in question.

Result

For the reasons given above, the declaration that the League is an 'Unlawful Association' made in the impugned notification number 147 dated 16 April 1990, is hereby confirmed and reference is accepted.

Let the Judgment be sent to the Home Ministry, Government of J&K, Jammu/Srinagar, for publication in the Government Gazette. Let the records of the case be also sent to the Home Ministry for safe custody.

sd/-	sd/-	sd/-
(Harbans Lal, Member)	(HS Bahri, Member)	(GD Sharma, Chairman)

SRO 148

Vide this SRO Islamic Jamiat Tulba was declared as unlawful Association. In the reference made by the government to the Tribunal accompanied by a copy of the plaint, documents, and annexures, the Tribunal arrayed the State of Jammu and Kashmir through Additional Chief Secretary Home as plaintiff and Islamic Jamiat Tulba (Association) as defendant number 1. Sheikh Tajmul Islam S/o Sheikh Abdul Ahad resident of Shaheed-Gung, Srinagar (head of the Association) as defendant number 2.

Permod Kohli Advocate-General assisted by BS Slathia presenting counsel and LN Chadha presenting officer appeared for the plaintiff/ State. Nemo appeared for the defendants.

The case of the Plaintiff/State as was summarised in the judgement is reproduced hereunder:

> "That the Jamait is an Association which encourages or aids persons and its sympathisers to undertake unlawful activities within the meaning of the Jammu and Kashmir Criminal Law Amendment Act, 1983.
>
> Such persons and sympathisers and members aforesaid have for its objects, activities and actions which interfere and aim at interference with the public administration, the administration and the maintenance of law and order and which constitute a danger to the public peace;
>
> Such persons and sympathisers and members aforesaid have for its objects, activities and actions which are intended to encourage and which encourage, aid and incite the people to undertake activities which are offences punishable under Section 153-A and 153-B of the State Ranbir Penal Code;
>
> Such persons and sympathisers and members aforesaid have for its objects, activities and actions which are intended or which may form a part of the scheme intend to threat or likely to threat or disrupt or likely to disrupt harmony between different religious groups of the State;

Such persons and sympathisers and members aforesaid have for its objects, activities and actions which are intended or which form part of the scheme intend to cause or likely to cause fear, alarm and feeling of insecurity amongst members of different religious groups and communities in the State;

The sympathisers and members of the Association have indulged in such like activities that is on 22 July 1982 at Eidgah Srinagar, the defendant Sheikh Tajamul Islam said that his party would continue to struggle for the establishment of the Muslim State and on 5 November 1982 the workers of the Association demanded that Kashmir question was still unresolved;

The aims and objects of the Association is to install Islamic rule in the J&K State, in utter disregard to the Constitution of India/ J&K.

In March 1980, Dr Yousaf-ul-Umar and Tajamul Islam criticised the Government of India by stating that India has captured Kashmir after inducting its army, usurped the right of self-determination of Kashmiris.

On 5 August 1980, Sheikh Tajamul Islam addressed a press conference at Jehangir Hotel, Srinagar and stated that Indian Constitution was not accepted and his party wanted to bring an Islamic revolution.

On 17 June 1981, Tajamul Islam commanded the Muslims to stand under the banner of Islam so that Islamic type of government could be established after removing the present lawfully established government.

On 2 August 1981, at Eidgah Srinagar, Tajamul Islam challenged the accession of Kashmir to India.

On 27 July 1982, on the eve of the Eid-ul-Millad, the workers of the Association exhorted not to accept the Constitution of India.

On 1 June 1988, Sheikh Tajamul Islam, while addressing the press conference in Srinagar stated that his party was interested in establishing Islamic government.

On 18 September 1983, at the occasion of Eid prayers, Sheikh Tajamul Islam said that India had forcibly occupied Kashmir and the solution was by having Plebiscite.

On 20 December 1984, the followers of Jamait addressed a press conference at Hotel Bizone, Srinagar and stated that they wanted to bring Islamic revolution in the State and that the accession to India was illegal.

The activists of the Association managed to paste Urdu posters entitled Muslims in India to take revenge against Hindus.

On June 13, 1989 at Srinagar in a press statement Inayatullah Indrabi, Chief Organiser stated that revolution minded youths had taught a lesson to the pro-Indian and irreligious forces on the event of Jama Masjid episode on June 9, 1989.

On June 16, 1989 Inayatullah Indrabi asked the people to indulge in revolutionary activities.

In the first week of August 1989, a book published by the Chief of the Association was circulated in which it was held that the position of India over Kashmir was the same as was of Britain over India prior to 1947."

The case was not contested by the defendants and the Plaintiff/State in support of its case adduced ex-parte evidence.

On a careful consideration of the evidence both documentary as well as oral led by the Plaintiff/State, the Tribunal held that it was proved that the Association in question (Islamic Jamiat Tulba) is preaching, propagating and advocating the following feelings, theories, ideologies, cults, and claims:

"The aims and objects of the Association are to install Islamic rule in the Jammu and Kashmir State in utter disregard to the Constitution of India/J&K.

The Association holds the view that J&K State has not legally acceded to the Union of India and that the people of Kashmir has a right to get them emancipated from the clutches of India.

The people of Kashmir have a right to determine their future by holding the Plebiscite.

The Association (Islamic Jamiat Tulba) had been carrying on propaganda which had been spreading communal hatred in the State. Its activities and actions had an objective which was likely to threaten or disrupt the harmony between different religious groups of the State. Also fear, alarm and feelings of insecurity amongst different religious groups and communities in the State was caused by the activities of the Association and that there was likelihood of causing further such effects. By exhorting the people to observe frequent hartals, the Association had been interfering with the maintenance of supplies and services essential to the life of the people at large.

The actions and activities of the Association its office bearers and activists were directed to destabilise the lawfully established government and the object was to interfere with the public administration as well as maintenance of law and order.

Conclusion

The aiding, undertaking and propagating the above stated feelings, cults, objects, claims etc as stated above by the Association in question or by its office bearers or activists fall squarely within the ambit of Section (2)/(b) and (c) of the Act as being the commission of 'Unlawful Activities' by the Association in question.

Result

For the reasons given above, the reference in question is accepted and the declaration that the Jamait is an 'unlawful Association' made in the impugned notification number 148 dated 16 April 1990, is hereby confirmed.

Let the copy of the judgement be sent to the Home Secretary, Government of J&K, Jammu for publication in the Government Gazette. Let the records of the case be also sent to the Home Ministry for safe custody."

sd/-	sd/-	sd/-
(Harbans Lal, Member)	(HS Bahri, Member)	(GD Sharma, Chairman)

SRO 149

Vide this SRO Mahaz-e-Azadi (Association) was declared as Unlawful Association on 16 April 1990, and the reference was made to the Tribunal constituted under Section 5 of the Jammu and Kashmir Criminal Law Amendment Act of 1983, for the purposes of adjudicating whether or not there is sufficient cause for declaring the Association unlawful.

On the presentation of the Plaint accompanied by relevant record the Tribunal arrayed the State of Jammu and Kashmir through Additional Secretary Home as Plaintiff and Mahaz-e-Azadi (Association) as defendant number 1. Altaf Khan Azam Inqulabi, S/o Abdul Rashid Khan, R/o Hawal-Khanyar, Hazratbal Colony-Nagin, Srinagar (Presently underground) (Head of the Association) was arrayed as defendant number 2.

Permod Kohli Advocate-General assisted by BS Salathia, presenting counsel and LN Chadha, presenting officer appeared for the plaintiff/ State.

Nobody appeared for the defendants despite the substituted service affected upon them. At page 10 of the judgement the tribunal summarised the case of the Plaintiff/State from the contents of the Notification as well as from the Plaint and the annexures attached therewith in the following manner:

> "The Mahaz-e-Azadi is an Association which encourages or aids persons and its sympathisers to undertake unlawful activities within the meaning of the Jammu and Kashmir Criminal Law Amendment Act 1983;
>
> Such persons and sympathisers and members aforesaid have for its objects, activities and actions which interfere and aim at interference with the public administration, the administration and the maintenance of law and order and which constitute a danger to the public peace;
>
> Such persons and sympathisers and members aforesaid have for its objects, activities and actions which are intended to encourage and which encourage, aid and incite the people to undertake activities which are offences punishable under Section 153-A and 153-B of the State Ranbir Penal Code;
>
> Such persons and sympathisers and members aforesaid have for its objects, activities and actions which are intended or which may form a part of the scheme intend to threat or likely to threat or disrupt or likely to disrupt harmony between different religious groups of the State.
>
> Such persons and sympathisers and members aforesaid have for its objects, activities and actions which are intended or which form part of the scheme intend to cause or likely to cause, fear, alarm, and feeling of insecurity amongst members of different religious groups and communities in the State.
>
> That defendant Mohd Azam Inqulabi on July 20, 1986 declared at Shamaswari (Srinagar) that his party would struggle for freedom of Kashmir. On 7 August 1986, he addressed a meeting in Lal Chowk and demanded Independence of Kashmir. He had also given a call for hartal on February 2, 1989 to mark the death anniversary of Mohd Maqbool Bhat.
>
> That the aims and objects of the Association is that Kashmir issue is yet to be solved and needs to be resolved according to the UNO resolution to exercise the right of self-determination.
>
> That on the night of May 15/16, 1984, the Association pasted posters 'Azadi-Ke-Parwane-Garibon-kay qaidian'. The spokesman of

the Association alleged that they could continue their struggle for freedom of Kashmir.

That on December 11, 1984, defendant Mohd Azam Inqulabi had stated that Kashmir issue was unsolved and he had a comprehensive plan about its peaceful settlement in case people extended their support.

That on 18 May 1985, the workers of the Association and its activists Hamel Indrabi and Mohd Iqbal instigated shopkeepers to observe hartal and processions were organised for which pro-Pakistan and anti-national slogans were raised.

That on 14 July 1986, defendant Mohd Azam Inqulabi alleged that Indian National Congress and RSS were responsible for the partition of the country in 1947. He had also called upon the leadership to stop the changing Muslim majority character of the State. On August 7, 1986 he had stated that the Association intended to establish an autonomous Kashmir.

On January 17, 1988; handbills/posters were issued on behalf of the Association in question urging the people not to celebrate Republic Day and boycotted it. Instead it was stated that black-flags should be hoisted.

On February 10, 1988; defendant Azam Inqulabi was found persuading shopkeepers in and around Jamait market Srinagar to observe Maqbool's Day on February 11, 1988 by hoisting black flags.

On July 21, 1989; defendant Azam Inqulabi appealed to the Kashmiri to adopt the path of arms and struggle against India.

On November 8, 1989, defendant Azam Inqulabi in a press statement at Srinagar alleged that Kashmiri youths have been forced to take arms when they were denied the right of self-determination.

On January 3, 1990; the Association through press in Srinagar had asked the people to observe January 5, 1990 as a right of self-determination Day.

The Plaintiff/State in support of its case produced ex-parte evidence. The Tribunal discussed the legal aspects of the case under the provisions of the relevant Law and after analysing the documentary and oral evidence within the parameters of the Evidence Act held at page 34 of the judgement, it is proved that Association in question (Mahaz-e-Azadi) is preaching, propagating and advocating the following feelings, theories, ideologies, cults and claims:

"The Association stands for the right of self-determination of Kashmiris regarding the accession of the J&K State made with India. This act of the Association per se falls within the purview of unlawful activities as envisaged under Section 2 of the Act.

The Association is carrying on propaganda which is part of the scheme to threaten or likely to threaten or disrupt or likely to disrupt harmony between different religious, racial, language or regional groups or caste or communities. Its activities are intended to cause fear or alarm or feelings of insecurity amongst members of different religious, racial, language, regional groups, castes and communities. Its activities interfere and also have the object of interference with the public administration and the maintenance of supplies and services essential to the life of the communities and activities constituted a danger to public peace as well as maintenance of law and order.

Conclusion

The aiding, undertaking and the propagating of the above stated feelings, cults, objects, claims etc as stated above by the Association in question or by its office bearer or activists fall squarely within the ambit of Section 2(b) and (c) of the Act as being the commission of 'Unlawful Activities' by the Association in question.

Result

For the reasons given above, the reference in question is accepted and the declaration that 'Mahaz-e-Azadi' is an 'Unlawful Association' made in the impugned notification Number 150 dated 16 April 1990, is hereby confirmed.

Let the copy of the judgement be sent to the Home Secretary, Government of J&K Jammu, for publication in the Government Gazette. Let the records of the case be also sent to the home Ministry for safe custody."

sd/-	sd/-	sd/-
(Harbans Lal, Member)	(HS Bahri, Member)	(GD Sharma, Chairman)

SRO 150

Vide SRO 150; the government banned the militant Association by the name of People's League. Before the Tribunal, the State of Jammu and Kashmir through Additional Chief Secretary Home became the plaintiff and the Association People's League was defendant number 1. Farooq

Ahmad Shah Rehmani, S/o Abdul Ahad Shah, R/o Una Gam, Bandipora who was acting as head of the Association and had gone underground was arrayed as defendant number 2. Shabir Ahmad Shah, S/o Ghulam Ahmad Shah, R/o Keri-Pura, Anantnag who was at that time under detention and also was head of the Association was arrayed as defendant number 3.

Permod Kohli Advocate-General assisted by BS Salathia presenting counsel and LN Chadha presenting officer appeared for the State. Defendant number 3 Shabir Ahmad Shah was served with a notice by the Tribunal through concerned Superintendent jail to appear in the Tribunal on 5 February 1991 but the State made a request that proceedings may be conducted in the premises of Tihar Jail, New-Delhi where he was lodged as a detenue. The request was accepted and on 18 February 1991, the Tribunal held its sitting in the premises of Tihar Jail New Delhi. Copy of the statements of facts (stated to be plaint filed by the plaintiff/State) along with copy of the Constitution of the Association in question, copy of the notification in question (number 150) and copy of Annexure A were supplied to him. He had undertaken the liability to submit his reply in the Tribunal in its principal place of sitting that is Jammu on or before 11 March 1991, but no such reply was received. Thereafter, the proceedings were held again on 16 March 1991, in the premises of Tihar Jail, New Delhi where he filed the reply to the show cause notice.

The case of the Plaintiff/State in the Notification as also in the plaint was summarised as follows:

> "That the League is an Association which encourages or aids persons and its sympathisers to undertake unlawful activities within the meaning of the Jammu and Kashmir Criminal Law Amendment Act, 1983.
>
> Such persons and sympathisers and members aforesaid have for its objects, activities and actions which interfere and aim at interference with the public administration and the administration of maintenance of law and order and which constitute a danger to the public peace.
>
> Such persons and sympathisers and members aforesaid have for its objects, activities and actions which are intended to encourage and which encourage aid and incite the people to undertake activities which are offences punishable under Section 153-A, 153-B, of the State Ranbir Penal Code;
>
> Such persons and sympathisers and members aforesaid have for its objects, activities and actions which are intended or which may

form a part of scheme intended to threat or likely to threat or disrupt or likely to disrupt harmony between different religious groups of the State;

Such persons and sympathisers and members aforesaid have for its objects, activities and actions which are intended or which form part of the Scheme intended to cause or likely to cause, fear, alarm and feeling of insecurity amongst members of different religious groups and communities in the State;

That the leaders of the Association desire to have arms training imparted to their workers secretly on the pattern of Chinese Guerrillas. In 1984 such an incitement was made. In May 1985, Farooq Rehmani provoked the Religious sentiments of the Muslims and tried to provoke people on the Writ Petition filed in the Calcutta High Court on the issue of Holy Quran. The group also had given a call for boycotting 'Republic Day' celebrations.

That the aims and objects of the Association in question are also to achieve the right of self-determination and the settlement of Kashmir issue on the light of UNO Resolution of 1948. By taking recourse to unconstitutional methods, the leaders exhorted the party members to oppose State's accession to India.

In 1987, the activists of the Association gave a call for boycotting celebrations of Republic Day. In January 1988, such activities were repeated.

On February 17, 1988, a call for observing Hartal on the death anniversary of Maqbool Bhat was given and thus interference with the maintenance of supplies and services essential to the life of the people at large was made.

On July 10/11 at Kadipura (Anantnag) some activists of the party decided to incite fear and alarm and feelings of insecurity amongst members of different religious groups in Kashmir.

On August 28, 1988; Shabir Shah (Defendant) urged the youths to continue their struggle for the establishment of Nizam-e-Mustafa in the State. Thus, ousting the secular character of Indian policy.

On October 27/28, 1989, the party gave a call for observing two day's hartal as a mark of protest against landing of Indian Troops in the J&K State in 1947, thereby arousing anti-national feelings among the people.

That on December 22, 1989, hand bills depicting the Association's message of freedom and Islamisation was found in circulation in the city. This caused insecurity in the minds of the minority community.

Posters were circulated by the activists of the Association to observe January 26, 1990 as a 'Black Day'. Defendant Shabir Shah had desired that Indian Constitution was unacceptable and only the Holy Quran was the code of human beings. This caused panic in the mind of non-Muslims.

Furthermore, it is reiterated in the plaint that members of the said Association have been preaching, propagating and practising Secession and demanding right of self-determination and settlement of alleged Kashmir Issue in the light of UNO Resolution of 1948.

The case of defendant Shabir Shah is as under:

India by referring the Kashmir dispute to UN Security Council converted it as an international issue and the Security Council by adopting resolution granted to the people of J&K the right to determine their future through a plebiscite under the auspices of United Nations.

That India and Pakistan are legally and morally committed to implement the Resolution in letter and spirit.

That the then Governor-General of India Lord Mountbatten in his letter dated October 27, 1947, had written to the Maharaja of Kashmir (Hari Singh) that as soon as the law and order has been restored in Kashmir, the question of State's accession should be settled by a reference to the people.

That the United Nations Security Council in another resolution had in unequivocal terms declared that constituent Legislative Assembly of Kashmir could not decide on the future of the State and such action should be considered null and void.

That Jawaharlal Nehru, Prime Minister of India had even stated in the Parliament that Kashmir Assembly's action was one sided and it could not subvert the UNO Resolutions.

That the atrocities are being perpetrated by the security forces on the people of Kashmir which will breed hatred and contempt and (from this attitude), dangerous consequences shall follow. In Kashmir human rights are ruthlessly suppressed, voices outrageously muffled and movements are revengefully restricted. In Kashmir, human blood flows like the holy waters of Ganga river and rapes and arsons are frequently committed.

In respect of other allegations of the Plaintiff/State contained in the SRO annexure and plaint, the defendant has taken no notice and in a perfunctory manner replied that those details are 'tendencious and carry no substance and weight'. The levelling of such like accusations, according to him, is an exercise in futility.

Shabir Shah (defendant number 3) did not enter appearance, so he was proceeded ex-parte.

Defendant Number 3 (Shabir Shah) after filing the objections to the show cause notice absented himself and took no step to prove any allegation made by him. Also, he had not specifically denied the allegations of the plaintiff/State made in the Notification in question, (Annexure 'A' to the notification) as well as, in the plaint. In this view of the matter, the evidence adduced by the plaintiff/ State remained unrebutted and there remained no reason why reliance should not be placed on the Plaintiff's evidence. In other words, the Plaintiff/State had proved its case and the result was that the Tribunal had held that the Association, 'People's League', was preaching, propagating and advocating the following feelings, theories, ideologies, cults and claims:

> The People's League stands for the right of self-determination for the right of Kashmiris.
>
> That the future of the Kashmir can only be decided by the people and none else.
>
> That the past assurances given by the political leaders of India from time to time regarding a fair and impartial Plebiscite have not been fulfilled and must be carried out.
>
> That the accession of Kashmir with India is only provisional and therefore, Kashmir cannot be said to be an integral part of India.
>
> The People's League had been carrying propaganda, which was spreading communal hatred in the State. Its activities and actions had an objective which was likely to threat or disrupt harmony between different religious groups of the State. Fear, alarm and feelings of insecurity amongst different religious groups and communities in the State were likely to be caused and in some cases may have been caused. Its aim is also to earn the odium of the people in general against the established government by levelling unsubstantiated charges of oppression and excesses, which adversely result in the interference with the public administration, administration of law and order and the maintenance of public order. Furthermore, by exhorting the public to observe frequent hartals and impose civil curfews, the Association had been interfering with the maintenance of supplies and services essential to the life of the people at large.

Conclusion

The aiding, undertaking and the propagating of the above stated feelings, cults, objects, claims etc; as stated above by the Association in question or by its office bearer or activists fall squarely within the ambit of Section (2)(b) and (c) of the Act as being the Commission of 'Unlawful Activities' by the Association in question."

sd/-	sd/-	sd/-
(Harbans Lal, Member)	(HS Bahri, Member)	(GD Sharma, Chairman)

SRO 151, dated April 16, 1990

Vide SRO 151 the government imposed ban on the Militant Association by the name Jammu Kashmir Liberation Front (JKLF).

This reference remained pending before the Tribunal for a period of more than one year. The Association had filed the reply to the accusations made by the State in the SRO plaint as well as the accompanying annexures. The Tribunal could not give its finding because the State Government under Governor's Rule took a policy decision to impose fresh ban on this Association under the Central Act known as Unlawful Association's activities (Prevention Act) of 1967. Under this very Act Sheikh Mohammed Abdullah's Secessionist Association by the name of All J&K Plebiscite Front had also been banned in 1971.

For the knowledge of the leaders a brief statement of facts is made hereunder to show the working of this Association (JKLF). In the reply filed before the Tribunal the Association had not taken any account of the history prior to 1586 because it did not suit to the 'Kashmiriat Cult' propounded by it. Thus, a historic fact was wilfully suppressed that Kashmir has always remained a part and parcel of the sub-continent's culture. Rather, the Association had taken a plea that after March 1586 when Kashmir's ruler Yusaf Shah was defeated by the Mughals and produced before the Emperor Akbar to accept the Mughal sovereignty Kashmir lost its Independence and its struggle for freedom started from that day. The Association had pleaded that the Instrument of Accession signed by the fleeing Maharaja Hari Singh is invalid document and State's accession is subject to Plebiscite. In the objections even the invasion made by Pakistan with the aid of tribals is denied and it is specifically pleaded that between 16 August 1947 and October 25, 1947, forces of Liberation had revolted against local king Maharaja Hari Singh and his defence forces could not offer any resistance to these forces of Liberation. The ruler was forced to flee from the Kashmir State but while fleeing, he stabbed the Kashmiri's in the back and entered into an alliance with India by executing Instrument of Accession. Maqbool Bhat was their greatest martyr who laid down his life for the struggle of freedom of the State. That Association wants to liberate the whole State of Jammu and Kashmir as it was during Maharaja Hari Singh's rule and want the freedom of self-rule. It is stated for readers knowledge that the ban imposed upon this Association under the Central Act was confirmed by Hon'ble Justice Saharia a sitting judge of the Delhi High Court much later in time and the Association was thereby declared an Unlawful Association. The Association is the first militant organisation which started killing of the innocent people in the State by resorting to gun culture.

SRO 169, dated 3 May 1990

Vide SRO 169; the Government of Jammu and Kashmir declared Dukhtaran-e-Millat as unlawful Association. In the Tribunal the State of Jammu and Kashmir through Additional Chief Secretary Home was arrayed as plaintiff and the Association Dukhtaran-e-Millat as defendant number 1. Mst. Asia Andrabi, D/o Shab-ud-Din Andrabi, R/o Kolipora Khanayar Srinagar who was the president of the Association was arrayed as defendant number 2. Mst. Tabassum Aziz, D/o Abdul Aziz Wani, R/o Ankigam, Anantnag was arrayed as defendant number 3.

Permod Kohli Advocate-General assisted by BS Salathia presenting counsel and LN Chadha presenting officer appeared for the State. Nobody appeared for the defendants as despite service they remained absent.

The case of the plaintiff/State before the Tribunal was as follows:

> The Association in question encourages or aids persons and its sympathisers to undertake unlawful activities within the meaning of the J&K Criminal Law Amendment Act of 1983.
>
> Such persons and sympathisers and members aforesaid have for their objects, activities and actions which interfere and aim at interference with the public administration, the administration and maintenance of law and order and which constitute a danger to the public peace;
>
> Such persons and sympathisers and members aforesaid have its objects and actions which intend to encourage and which encourages aids and incites the people to undertake such activities which are offences punishable under Section 153-A and 153-B of the State Ranbir Penal Code;

Such persons and sympathisers and members aforesaid have for its objects, activities and actions which are intended or which may form a part of the Scheme intend to cause threat or likely to threat or disrupt or likely to disrupt harmony between different religious groups of the State;

Such persons and sympathisers and members aforesaid have for its objects, activities and actions which are intended and which form part of the scheme intend to cause or likely to cause, fear, alarm and feelings of insecurity amongst members of different religious groups and communities in the State;

The Association in question printed several appeals in the press exhorting the ladies to join the struggle for liberation of Kashmir. A procession was also led to the UN Office at Srinagar and submitted memorandum seeking UNO intervention for Plebiscite.

The case was not contested by the defendants and they were proceeded ex-parte. Plaintiff/State in support of its case adduced ex-parte evidence. The Tribunal after discussing the legal aspects of the case on the basis of documentary as well as oral evidence held that plaintiff/State had proved that the Association in question (Dukhtaran-e-Millat) is preaching, propagating and advocating the following feelings, theories, ideologies, cults and claims:

"The aims and objects of the Association are to install Islamic rule in the State of J&K.

The Association lends support to the activities carried by different militant Associations in the State.

The activists of the Association believe in the Secession of the State of J&K from Indian Union.

The activists and sympathisers of the Association in question have for their objects, activities and actions which interfere and aim to interference with the public administration, the administration of maintenance of law and order and which constitute a danger to the public peace.

The activists and sympathisers of the Association in question have for their objects, activities and actions which are intended or which may form a part of the Scheme intended to threat or likely to threat or disrupt or likely to disrupt harmony between different religious groups of the State and intended to cause or likely to cause fear, alarm and feelings of insecurity amongst members of different religious groups and communities in the State.

Conclusion

The aiding, undertaking and the propagating of the above stated feelings, cults, objects, claims etc by the Association in question or by its office bearers or activists fall squarely within the ambit of Section 2(b) and (c) of the Act as being the Commission of 'unlawful activities' by the Association in question.

Result

For the reasons given above, the reference is accepted and the declaration that 'Dukhtaran-e-Millat' is an Unlawful Association made in the impugned notification Number 169 dated 3 May 1990 is hereby confirmed.

Let a copy of the judgement be sent to the Home Secretary, Government of J&K, Jammu for publication in the Government Gazette. Let the records of the case be also sent to the Home Ministry for safe custody."

sd/-	sd/-	sd/-
(Harbans Lal, Member)	(HS Bahri, Member)	(GD Sharma, Chairman)

The eighth banned militant Association was the Auxiliary Agency of the banned Jamaat-e-Islami Association. The name of this Association is Falah-e-Aam Trust. This Association had opened schools and Madrassas which numbered 157 in the State. There was also one college by the name of Islamic College which was being run by this Association. The funding of the Association was mostly from foreign fundamentalists Islamic countries and the Pakistan had the prominent hand in running these institutions by arranging the payments to the functionaries. These institutions were also at times managing to get government aids through their political and bureaucratic sympathisers.

The institutions were sowing the seeds of fundamentalism and fanaticism in the impressionable minds of the children who were mostly drawn from the poor and illiterate strata of the society. The indigenous Kashmiri Islam which is blended with Hindu Philosophy was being constantly weakened. In the mosques throughout the Kashmir Valley, the morning and evening recitations of prayers sound like Hindu prayers and this is a unique feature which is not found anywhere in any part of India and not to talk of Muslim world. For a layman it can be easily misunderstood that 'Shlokas' from Hindu scriptures are being recited. Kashmir has remained a nursery of Hindu culture/ Buddhist culture and a seat of Islamic sufism. There are many shrines which are equally revered by the Muslims and Hindus. The Jehadi fundamentalists are deadly opposed to this prevalent practice and other forms of worship on the principles of 'sufi-cult' of Kashmir. There is ample evidence that these Jehadi elements are always on the constant look to destroy such like holy places. At some places they have succeeded in their mission. The shining example is that of setting on fire the most famous shrine of Charar-e-Sharif by the notorious militants Abu Jindal (a Pakistani national from Dera Ismail Khan) and Gul Sher (a Pakistani national by profession a criminal). Abu Jindal was apprehended by the security forces and the writer of this book had the opportunity of personally hearing him as a Member of the Advisory Board for confirming his detention under the provisions of the J&K Public Safety Act when he was lodged in high security Sangrur Jail of Punjab State. The writer of this book had grilled him at length on the basis of known Islamic principles of brotherhood and mercy to mankind while his act was un-Islamic. He had no arguments to controvert these inquires and for the sake of arguments he pleaded that he had come to Kashmir as Muslims are denied to have four wives. He passed on the buck to the security forces for having themselves burnt the holy shrine in order to defame the ongoing struggle for freedom by the Muslims. The other notorious militant Gul Sher had succeeded in crossing over the border and going to his native country Pakistan where he received heroic welcome.

In these Madrassas, about 15,000 students had been admitted. After declaring this Association as Unlawful, the then Governor Jagmohan dismissed more than 700 teachers who were imparting the cults of violence and hatred. The writer of this book had the opportunity of going through the teaching curriculum of the Madrassas and was flabbergasted to know that Hindu's were being painted as cowards on the theory that one Muslim Mujahideen was capable to kill at least thirty out of them in one bout of straight fight. The Sikhs were being depicted in the primary books as brutes and murderers. In those books the students were being taught that Muslims are not supposed to obey the Indian Constitution when they owe a religious duty to obey Quran which declares that Muslims are born to rule over the world. That already in history, they had ruled India for more than one thousand years. That Hindus are born slaves and they have to remain so because it is the will of Allah. It is a matter of shock for every Patriotic Indian that 700 dismissed teachers from these madrassas after Governor Jagmohan's rule were slowly and steadily getting themselves absorbed in government run schools by backdoor entries after getting suitable orders in their favour from some judges of the Srinagar wing of the J&K High Court who were also the sympathisers of the ongoing Jehadi movement. Finally, a Division Bench ruling came from the

Srinagar wing of the High Court and the doors of unlawful entry into the government service were shut. Unfortunately, the matter did not end there but in a pre-planned clandestine manner all the remaining bulk of the dismissed teachers got absorbed into the Jammu and Kashmir Education Department during the popular rule of National Conference headed by Dr Farooq Abdullah from 1996 onwards. One can draw the inference that they might be again polluting the impressionable minds of the young students on communal lines. To add fuel to the fire, when the Tribunal had declared this Association as Unlawful the government should have attached their properties and not allowed their activities but again those Madrassas started functioning with hardened communal teaching staff drawn from Bihar State and from UP State. In the State Legislative Council during its session of March 2006, the Chief Minister Ghulam Nabi Azad has given a reply to a query made by Prof Bhim Singh MLC of National Panthers Party (NPP) that still more than one hundred unregistered madrassas are functioning in the State. How the militancy can be controlled when the education on the fundamental basis of hatred is being freely imparted to the young generation not only in J&K State but also in other parts of the country?

Note: Famous national newspaper *The Tribune* in its publication issue dated June 25, 2012 has reported the proceedings of a seminar sponsored by the Democracy Forum in London which was attended by eminent personalities of different countries. Nuclear physicist Dr Pervez Hoodbhoy, from Quaid-e-Azam University in Islamabad, was a key note speaker at the seminar titled, 'The Role of Education in Combating Terrorism'. In his views, the United States of America has played a major role in contributing to the radicalization that currently prevails in both Afghanistan and Pakistan. The function was chaired by Dr William Crawley of the Institute of Commonwealth Studies and addressed by the Democracy Forum head and British Conservative MP Stephen Hammond. In his speech Hoodbhoy started by commenting on the education curriculum in Pakistani schools, quoting from a 1995 primary document, published by Pakistan's Ministry of Education. The document states that after the completion of class V all children should be able to understand 'Hindu Muslim differences and the resultant need for Pakistan'. 'Children should be able to understand India's evil design against Pakistan'. Back in 1980, the US Government spent million of dollars to produce educational text books for Afghan refugee children that were filled with violent images and militant teachings from the Koran. These books were published in the University of Nebraska in USA and subsequently exported to the madrassas operating along the border of Pakistan Afghanistan. They distributed millions of

Korans to madrassas with the aim of fanning radicalism. Hoodbhoy explained, "It was viewed as the most efficient way of fighting the Soviet Union by putting this across as a Religious war. The policy was evolved between the USA and Pakistan and Saudi Arabia was the funder. But it was very close consultation between General Zia (Pakistan's late President) and the CIA which conducted the biggest covert war in history against the Soviet Union."

This type of madrassa virus for spreading hatred against non-Muslims was adopted by militant organizations working in our State and spoiled the tolerant and non-violent Kashmiri culture and ethos in the young generation's receiving education in madrassas.

CHAPTER 21

Subversion of Rule of Law

(A Great Step in the Aid of Militancy)

The subversion of rule of law is one of the major contributory factors for the rise and sustenancy of militancy in the State of Jammu and Kashmir. All the pillars of democracy that is the Executive, the Legislature, the Judiciary and the Press were infected by this virus. The main casualty has been the Legislature which mainly controls the Executive wing. The most glaring examples of this sad and shameful state of affairs is the sensational case of kidnapping of Dr Rubaiya Sayeed, the daughter of the then Home Minister of the Government of India Mufti Mohammad Sayeed (who later on became the Chief Minister of the coalition government in the State from 2002-2005) followed by the other case relating to the massacre of Air Force personnel. Dr Rubaiya was kidnapped by the militants in 1989 when her father was the Home Minister of the Government of India under VP Singh's rule. The CBI after investigating the case presented the Challan before the Presiding Officer Special Designated Court under TADA/ POTA Jammu. Militant Organisation by the name of JKLF which was declared as Unlawful Association in 1990 through its supremo Yasin Malik along with other top ranking militants are alleged to have kidnapped her. The State Government under the pressure of militants and at the direction of the Central Government had later released 5 hardcore militants of JKLF in lieu of Dr Rubaiya Sayeed's release and this illegal and unwarranted release emboldened the militants and the subdued movement of militancy was taken to its zenith. In other words, many people in the country have the opinion that this case was the turning point in the history of militancy to give the militants an upper hand in order to destabilise the duly elected government. The other case relates to the killing of Air Force Officials at Batmaloo and this incident had occurred in the month of January 1990. In this case also top ranking militants such as Yasin Malik and his associates were involved. It is horrifying to note that the accused stand bailed out in these two cases as well as in other such like cases where the punishments prescribed for the alleged heinous crimes are death sentence or life imprisonment. Such type of cases remained pending for decades even at the preliminary stages of framing the charges or recording the prosecution evidence. In most of the cases acquittal orders were passed as the prosecution witnesses were won over. The Presiding Officer of the Special Designated Court has taken a serious note of this deliberate delay which stands reported in the *Daily Excelsior* in its issue of 29 January 2006.

After the spurt of militancy and ouster of the rule of Dr Farooq Abdullah in 1990 till his coming to power again for the third time in the month of October 1996, the facts and figures of the militancy related incidents are given below:

During Governor's Rule (1990 to September 1996)

1. During the intervening night of August 13/14, 1993, at a place known by the name of Sarthal (in Doda district), seventeen Hindu pilgrims while on their way to the temple of Sarthal Devi from the town of Kishtwar were massacred in a passenger bus.
2. On January 5, 1996, sixteen Hindus were killed by the militants in a village known as Barshala of Doda district.
3. On January 12, 1996, seven Hindus were killed by the militants near the town of Bhaderwah in district Doda.
4. On May 6, 1996, seventeen Hindus were massacred by militants in broad-day-light in the village of Sumbar in tehsil Ramban of erstwhile district Doda and now district Ramban.
5. Between the intervening periods of June 7 and 8, 1996, in Kalmari village situated in district Doda seven Hindus were killed in broad day light.

Militancy Related Incidents During Dr Farooq Abdullah's Regime (October 1996 to July 13, 2002)

1. On March 20, 1997, in village Sangrampura (district Budgam) in Kashmir Valley seven Kashmiri Pandits were killed.
2. On June 15, 1997, three Kashmiri Pandit migrant teachers were butchered by making them to alight from a passenger bus

near the town of Gool of Mahore tehsil district Ramban in Jammu Division.

3. On September 24, 1997, eight Hindus were killed in village Swardi of district Rajouri.
4. Between the nights of 25/26, January 1998, in village Bandhama (teshil Gandharbal) in Kashmir Valley twenty-five Kashmiri Pandits were killed.
5. On January 30, 1998, nine Muslims who were not following the diktats of the militants were killed in village Navapachi of district Doda.
6. During the intervening night of 18/19 April 1998, in village Prankot of erstwhile district Udhampur (now district Reasi) twenty-seven Hindus were butchered by slitting their throats with sharp edged weapons.
7. On May 5, 1998, in the town of Swarankot of district Poonch, five Hindus of the same family were killed.
8. On May 6, 1998, eleven Hindu members of the Village Defence Committee were killed in village Dassa in district Doda.
9. On June 19, 1998, in village Chapnari of district Doda twenty-five Hindus of a marriage party including the bridegroom were killed.
10. Between the intervening nights of 27/28, 1998, in two villages of district Doda by the names of Sanna and Shravan twenty-five Hindus were killed.
11. On August 4, 1998, twenty-one patriotic Muslims were killed in village Buflayaz of district Poonch.
12. On August 8, 1998, in Kalaban Jungle of Himachal Pradesh falling near the boundary line of J&K State thirty-five Hindu labourers were killed.
13. On February 20, 1999, four Hindus in village Morapura in district Rajouri and seven Hindus in village Buriyara falling under Udhampur district and seven Hindus in village Belala of Rajouri district were massacred by gun fires.
14. On June 20, 1999, fifteen Hindu labourers of a brick-kiln were killed nearby the town of Anantnag in Kashmir Valley.
15. On July 19, 1999, fifteen Hindus were killed in village Layota of district Doda.
16. On February 28, 2000, five Hindu truck drivers were killed near the town of Qazigund on the National Highway in Kashmir Valley.

17. On March 20, 2000, in village Chattising Pura of district Anantnag forty Sikhs were killed and most of the victims were the family members of those persons whose male members were working in Intelligence Agencies.
18. On August 1, 2000, near the National Highway between Banihal and Qazigund nineteen Hindu labourers working in a brick-kiln were shot dead after making them to stand in a queue.
19. On August 2000, in village Pogal of district Doda fourteen Hindus were killed and in village Kung near Ramsoo of district Doda nine Hindus were killed.
20. On August 2000, in village Bayal Bashal near the town of Kishtwar of district Doda the militants while bearing the uniforms of army personnel killed eight Hindus who were the members of Village Defence Committee.
21. On November 24,2000, in village Patti Mahal of teshil Kishtwar in district Doda six Hindus were abducted from a bus who were taken to a jungle and five of them were killed but luckily one abducted person succeeded in running away from the place of massacre.
22. On August 7, 2001, in Railway Station of Jammu Tawi, five personnel of the para-military forces and seven civilians were killed while thirty-four were injured. One militant was also killed in retaliation by the forces.
23. On August 24, 2001, seven police jawans were killed in an attack made on the police station in the town of Poonch.
24. On 2 September 2001, one police jawan was killed and eleven were injured in an attack made on District Police Line, Poonch.
25. On October 25, 2001, in the town of Banihal of district Doda, two army jawans were killed while eight were injured.
26. On November 18, 2001, in the town of Ramban of erstwhile district Doda, ten army jawans and three civilians were killed while twenty-nine jawans were injured and four civilians were also injured.
27. On November 25, 2001, three army jawans were killed in an IED explosion.
28. On January 13, 2002, in village Khanetar of district Poonch, two army personnel were killed while three were injured.
29. On February 17, 2002, eight civilians were killed in village Banihal of district Rajouri.

30. On March 30, 2002, in the city of Jammu, nine civilians were killed and nineteen were injured. In this operation two militants were also killed.
31. On April 8, 2002, in the town of Udhampur, five civilians were killed and four were injured.
32. On May 14, 2002, in the military establishment known by the name of Kaluchak near the city of Jammu, thirty-four family members of the army personnel were killed whereas, forty-seven were injured.
33. On June 15, 2002, in village Khodakatwara of district Doda four Hindu pilgrims were killed.
34. Between the intervening night of 15/16 June 2002, in village Ind of erstwhile district Udhampur (now district Ramban), five persons were killed. After a gap of one year the Police-Post Ind was attacked and eleven police personnel were killed by the militants.
35. On July 13, 2002, in a colony known by the name of Sunjay Nagar/Qasim Nagar situated near the city of Jammu twenty-seven Hindus were killed and more than two dozen were injured.
36. The most revered Hindu temple known by the name of 'Raghunath Mandir' situated in the heart of the Jammu city was attacked on November 24, 2002 and in this attack 14 people including the security personnel were killed. Despite all the security arrangements, after a gap of few months the temple was again attacked for the second time and in this gory and fiendish act the militants had succeeded in defiling the deity of Lord Hanuman. One militant was also killed in one of these two attacks.

Besides the above stated incidents, there was also an attack on the military establishment known as 'Sunjawa Cantonment' which is situated in the outskirts of Jammu city. The militants had got the logistic support from the subversive elements settled in those illegal colonies part of Sidhra, Bathindi and Sunjawan. Besides the above stated incidents of militancy, an additional list of such incidents is reported hereunder from the publication made in the national newspaper *The Times of India* in its issue of Tuesday May 2, 2006 (Late City Edition). These incidents are: that on February 28, 2000, 5 Hindus were killed in Anantnag district; on August 1, 2000, 27 Hindu labourers were killed in Anantnag district and 31 Amarnath pilgrims were shot dead in Pahalgam. On August 2, 2000, 11 Hindus were killed in Doda district. The militants have not even spared the pilgrims of Baba Amarnath shrine and Shri Mata Vaishno Devi shrine. On August 6, 2002, nine of Amarnath pilgrims were shot dead at a base camp near Pahalgam. On February 11, 2001, 15 members of Gujjar families were killed in Rajouri district. On March 17, 2001, eight Hindus were killed in Doda district. On July 21, 2001, seven Amarnath pilgrims among thirteen were killed in Anantnag. On April 5, 2004, seven were killed in district Anantnag. On March 4, 2003, 24 Hindus were killed in Pulwama district. On January 7, 2002, seventeen Hindus were killed in Jammu district. On July 22, 2001, 15 Hindus were killed in Doda district. On August 4, 2001, 15 Hindus were killed in district Doda. In the local newspaper *Daily Excelsior*, veteran BJP leader Prof Chaman Lal Gupta ex-State Defence Minister Government of India of NDA regime gave his interview after visiting the sites of two massacres of Hindus carried on 31 April, and 1 May 2006 in the hilly areas of district Udhampur and Doda. He commented that government had made Village Defence Committees defunct defence bodies by not distributing them the salaries of Rs 1,500/- per month each as well as by not providing additional strength of three special police officials with each defence village committee. He said that the adoption of the policy of the previous government (National Conference) was keeping militancy alive in these areas. He also stated that 800 civilians had been killed in Doda district so far from the onset of militancy and during this long spell of 16 years till date the government had been able to provide relief to approximately only to 450 families who were the victims of the militancy.

When militancy raised its ugly head in Kashmir Valley in 1989-90, the Hindus and Sikhs were forced to become migrants and more than three lakhs became the migrants who took shelter in Jammu, Delhi and in other parts of the country. Along with them some migration of civilians hailing from majority community also took place who in the eyes of militants were hardcore nationalists or had not cooperated with them. After 1994-95, because of the spurt in militancy in the Jammu region, about fifty thousand Hindus became migrants from the hilly areas of district Doda, Rajouri, Poonch and tehsil Gool-Gulabgarh from erstwhile district Udhampur. The after effect of Kargil war was tension on the borders and because of heavy firing from Pakistani pickets on the civil population of the State, about one lakh people residing in the border areas of the Jammu region were forced to leave their hearths and homes. There is a long list of such incidents where the militants have eliminated even whole families belonging to the minority community of Hindus as well as majority community of Muslims who had refused to give them shelter, food, or did not render them logistic support or had become suspects in their eyes being the informers of the security forces.

In Kashmir region, the militants have killed more civilians in numbers belonging to majority community than belonging to minority community. On May 1, 2006, twenty-two Hindus were killed in village Kulhand of district Doda. This is the third biggest massacre in numbers done in district Doda after the onset of militancy beginning from 1990. Besides this, a heart wrenching incident had also taken place wherein thirteen Hindus were killed in a place known as Lolan Galla situated at the upper reaches of Basantgarh of tehsil Ramnagar, district Udhampur. These two incidents took place on the intervening night of April 31, and May 1, 2006 respectively. The above stated incidents establish the cavalier and casual mode of governance as well as lack of honesty in giving the fair administration. The existence of cogent and convincing evidence establishes the fact that not only the government led by Dr Farooq Abdullah but his successor coalition government of Mufti Mohammad Sayeed and Congress have also contributed towards the sustenance of the militancy by remaining soft towards the militants and in this manner indirectly helped them from being caught in the clutches of law. The above stated two incidents had taken place when Ghulam Nabi Azad was the Chief Minister of the coalition government with PDP support in the State.

CHAPTER 22

Coalition Government of Mufti Mohammad Sayeed with Congress

Mufti Mohammad Sayeed's government adopted 'Healing-Touch' policy and the main beneficiaries of this policy were the militants and their family members. The victims of the militancy remained at the receiving end. A militant was not only wages war against the State by violent means but also commits offence of sedition. The first one is punishable with death sentence or imprisonment for life under Sections 121-A, 122 of Ranbir Penal Code and the second offence under Section 124 of RPC for imprisonment for seven years and fine. The acts of militants and their family members who had acted as abettors or conspirators had also contravened the provisions of POTA. Family members of those militants who give shelter to the militants or indirectly encourage them to carry on the so called holy war are equally liable to be proceeded against as abettors or conspirators. Keeping of prohibited arms and ammunition is a cognizable offence under the Arms Act. It is not understandable how on the death of a hardcore militant such family members or relations are entitled to the benefits of the 'Healing-Touch' policy in providing them with government jobs in preference to the victims of the militancy or that of the dependants of martyred armed personnel? In this manner, the intentions of present day rulers become clear that militancy should remain in the State which is beneficial for them and for their followers at the cost of spilling of blood of the Armed Forces and innocent civilians causing serious drain to the exchequer of the Indian Tax Payers. However, it is an established fact that Karra, the then Finance Minister of PDP had been openly declaring that J&K State should have its own currency. This idea he might have drawn from the fact that second Dogra ruler Maharaja Ranbir Singh had his own currency. Presently it was only day dreaming as it is not possible to do so.

Mufti Mohammad Sayeed after becoming the Chief Minister was being repeatedly heard saying that, "there should be respectable solution of the State problem," but he never spelt out that problem. He intentionally had been avoiding saying something about the Azadi movement launched by the secessionists. He was never found to mourn the death of a single security personnel at his place of residence but was frequently found visiting the houses of slain militants and giving the benefits of 'healing touch policy' to the survivors of the family. A top ranking activist of militant organisation (JKLF) who was previously a junior engineer in the Government Rural Development Department had become PRO of a minister. A senior minister of his political party late Abdul Aziz Zargar was very much maligned in the press for having close links with a militant Chand Khan, resident of Uttar Pradesh who temporarily had settled in the constituency of Zargar. He was alleged to have attacked the famous temple of 'Akshar Dham' in the city of Ahmedabad Gujarat State and awarded death sentence by the trial court in Ahmedabad (Gujarat). However, the government had denied these allegations vide a news item published in local daily newspaper *Daily Excelsior* in its issue of 8 September 2003. This is a recorded fact that Zargar never took any security cover from the police while contesting the elections whereas, his rival Sakina Yattoo (present minister in Omar's government) who was a Minister of State of Tourism Department in Farooq's government had so many attacks on her life and many security guards of paramilitary forces had lost their lives. A few examples are set out here: one attack on 11 September 2002 in village Dahmal, on 15 September 2002 an IED blast nearby the vehicle of Miss Sakina followed by firing in which one Sub-Inspector of CRPF and a civilian died. On 21 September 2002 an IED blast near her vehicle in village Mirhama (Kulgam), wherein one Sub-Inspector of CRPF and a girl Naza of village Mirhama died. On the day of polling, i.e. on 1 October 2002 a grenade was blasted nearby a polling station and she had a narrow escape. She was attacked in Kulgam when she along with her supporters was celebrating the district headquarters status being conferred on the tehsil headquarters of Kulgam. In this attack she was injured and some casualties were caused to security personnel including innocent civilians. Dar, ex-MLA of Congress, was also killed in this attack. These incidents create a strong suspicion that Zargar might had a clandestine understanding with the militants. However, Sakina Yattoo had to brave the attacks by militants at every juncture. The then Central Government had no guts for asking the father and daughter duo to give the definition of their self-rule. Mufti himself in the past had ruled the State as a Minister in the Congress Party on different occasions. The Indian leadership had failed to elicit explanation from him to the effect that how he considers those governments whether personally ruled or ruled on the pattern of a democratically elected government by the people and for the people? All this shows that Kashmir Valley centric mainstream top politicians were abetting and conspiring the on going militancy in the State for their personal political gains and they did not allow the militancy to be rooted out because they had no will to do so. The then Governor SK Sinha had very sour relations with Mufti who openly had given vent to his feelings in a press release published in local newspaper *Daily Excelsior* under the heading, "Governor takes exception to Mufti's interference in Yatra affairs." In its issue of *Hindustan Times* of 26 September 2006, an Amalgam of 18 Kashmiri Pandit Organisations had exposed the misuse of temples and shrines left unclaimed by Kashmiri Pandits. Examples have been cited of setting up a poultry farm at Laboo Shah Temple at Tulmula, Ganderbal while a government run school has been established inside the Nand Kishore Temple at Sumbal Sonwari. There are several such other examples.

Shri Baba Amarnath Land Row Agitation

The holy cave of Shri Baba Amarnath is located in the southern part of Kashmir Valley at a height of 13,500 feet above the sea level and its pilgrimage at least once in a life span by a Hindu throughout the world is considered as a most pious and important spiritual act. There is natural formation of Ice Lingam of Lord Shiva along with Mata Parvati and Lord Ganesha inside the cave during a particular auspicious period of every year by the trickling of water from the cave roof and it is believed that it is a supernatural phenomenon. It is recorded in the history of Dogra rulers that they had been providing all logistical support and facilities to the pilgrims which during their time mostly consisted of Sadhus drawn from every nook and corner of India. In the uninhabited area of tehsil Pahalgam, Maharaja Pratap Singh had donated some state/forest land in the name of the shrine to provide facilities for staying and this place is known as, 'Sadhu Padao'. Simultaneously, Maharaja Pratap Singh had donated some forest land in favour of famous Muslim shrine known as, 'Baba Rishi', situated near the famous tourist resort of Gulmarg. After the end of Dogra rule, the democratic government was also providing some facilities at the level of district administration of Anantnag for regulating the yatra and providing medical facilities. The yatra period was limited coinciding with 'Shravan Purnima' numbering few thousands who were going only via Pahalgam route only. With the improvement of communication means and transportation facilities and the increase of population, the number of pilgrims also started swelling correspondingly. Dr Farooq Abdullah who was the Chief Minister during 2000 thought it appropriate to see that more number of pilgrims pour in the Kashmir Valley like the increase of numbers of pilgrims who pay obeisance to the holy shrine of Mata Vaishno Devi at Katra. The increase of pilgrims have brought economic boom in the State and in order to augment the economic conditions of the concerned areas of shrine Amarnath Yatra, he also thought of handing over the administration to a Board. Finally, on 14 November 2000, he got passed an Act which is known as, 'The Jammu and Kashmir Shri Amarnathji Shrine Act, 2000'. The aims and objects of the Act are for the constitution of a Board for the better management of Shri Amarnathji Yatra, upgradation of facilities for holy pilgrims and matters connected therewith or incidental thereto. Under Section 4 of the Act, the administration, management and governance of Shri Amarnathji Shrine and the Board Fund shall vest in a Board comprising a Chairman and not more than 10 members. The Governor of the State of J&K, if he is a Hindu, shall be ex-Officio Chairman of the Board and if, the Governor be not a Hindu, then he may nominate any eminent person of the State, professing the Hindu religion and otherwise qualified to be a member to function as Chairman of the Board. Section 4 of the Act, provides the qualifications of the members for their appointments by the Chairman for a term of three years which is extendable. The writer of this book was appointed as a member of the Shrine Board in 2002 by the then Governor Girish Chandra Saxena when for the first time the Board was constituted. Till date, he is being consecutively appointed as a member by successor Governors.

The present Governor NN Vohra took over the charge of Governor on 25 June 2008 after the expiry of term of the then Governor SK Sinha. Governor SK Sinha in order to cope with the increasing number of pilgrims and to provide them the facilities for having Darshans got extended the period of Yatra for two months and before handing over the robes of the office he had seen that some forest land at Baltal was diverted for providing facilities to the pilgrims during yatra period. This was not to the liking of the then coalition government of PDP and Congress. Ghulam Nabi Azad, who was the Chief Minister vide government order number 291-Fst of 2008 dated 1 July 2008 over-set the previous government order number 184-Fst of 2008 dated 26 May 2008. In terms of that order 39.88 hectares of forest land which vide above previous order was given to Shri Amarnathji Shrine Board at Baltal and Domail was cancelled. This order was passed after taking the consent of Governor NN Vohra in his individual capacity as

Chairman of the Board and not by the consent of all the other members of the Board. The Board as a whole with majority decision could give consent for such an act but this legal aspect was ignored by the Chairman (Governor). The Hindu public inside and outside the State took it as an insulting act and an agitation was started by an amalgamation of some socio-religious organisations in Jammu known as 'Shri Amarnath Yatra Sangharsh Samiti'. The agitation was so intense and severe that whole Jammu province was on agitation which extended for two months period. There was reaction in the Kashmir region and counter agitation was launched. The result was that coalition partner PDP withdrew the support of Congress(I) led government and Ghulam Nabi Azad's government fell due to minority status. The Governor's Rule was imposed and NN Vohra became the head of the administration and legislature. This hasty and illegal decision was taken by NN Vohra within a brief period of one month after taking over as Governor of the State. The writer of this book was prepared to tender resignation as a member of the Board, supported by another member hailing from Jammu region Dr Vishwa Murti who was the Principal of the Sanskrit Branch of Jammu of the Deemed Sanskrit University of India. The Chairman NN Vohra immediately appointed a committee to solve this tricky and sensitive issue amicably and appointed for the first time, two member committee of which the writer of this book was made as Chairman and the other member was his (Governor's) Principal Secretary BB Vyas (IAS officer) who is a man of integrity and competence. Meanwhile, a meeting was also held by the Governor in Jammu with eminent members of the civil society. The Jammu Bar Association was represented by DK Khajuria ex-President of the Bar. There was strong resentment about the action of NN Vohra in Jammu region. Meanwhile NN Vohra appointed his advisors and one of the advisors was Dr SS Bloeria, retired Chief Secretary of the State who hails from Jammu region. He was given the Home portfolio. On 6th August 2008, a four member committee comprising of Dr SS Bloeria (Advisor to Governor), the writer of this book, Prof Amitabh Mattoo (the then Vice-Chancellor, Jammu University) and BB Vyas (the then Principal Secretary to Governor and Chief Executive Officer, Shri Amarnathji Shrine Board) was constituted to "seek a peaceful resolution of the fundamental issues, to settle all existing doubts and clarify the continuing responsibility of the Shri Amarnathji Shrine Board." The above stated Sangharsh Samiti had also nominated their four member committee consisting of Tilak Raj Sharma (advocate), Brig Suchet Singh (Retd), Prof Narinder Singh and Pawan Kohli. After three rounds of discussions and deliberations it was agreed from both the sides:

(a) The State Government shall set aside for the use by Shri Amarnathji Shrine Board, exclusively, the land in Baltal and Domail (Compartment Number 63/S, Sindh Forest Division) comprising an area of 800 kanals, traditionally under use for the annual yatra purposes.
(b) The proprietary status/ownership/title of the land shall not undergo any change
(c) The Board shall use the aforesaid land for the duration of the yatra (including the period of making the required arrangements and winding up of the same) for the purpose of user by various service providers according to its needs and priorities.

The aforesaid land shall be used according to the Board's requirement, from time to time, including for the following:

(i) Raising of temporary prefabricated accommodation and toilet facilities by the Board;
(ii) Establishment of tented accommodation by private camping agencies (locals, permanent residents of the State);
(iii) Setting up of the shops by shopkeepers (locals, permanent residents of the State);
(iv) Facilities for Ponywallahs and Pithuwallahs;
(v) Provision of Health care and medical facilities;
(vi) Setting up of free langars by private persons and groups which are licensed by the Board;
(vii) Facilities for helicopter operations/parking of vehicles;
(viii) Arrangements of security by local police/paramilitary forces and other security agencies as per the arrangements in place heretofore; and
(ix) Undertaking measures relating to soil conservation, land protection and preservation of ecology.

2. It has further been agreed that the Board shall continue to remain responsible for the overall arrangements of the yatra on both the routes during the yatra period, including all arrangements as mandated under the provisions of the Shri Amarnathji Shrine Act, 2000.

3. Apart from the above, the committee set up by the Samiti had during the course of discussions, presented a 14 point 'Charter of Demands' for consideration by the State Government. The main demands related to withdrawal of criminal cases against various persons during the period of agitation, provision of

> compensation to the families of the deceased and the injured and working out of appropriate packages of financial assistance to compensate losses of the transport sector, trade and industry, horticulture sector, hoteliers and tourist operators. The State government had agreed to examine all these demands in an appropriate manner on time bound basis. There were other Clauses 4 to 8 in this signed agreement and they need not to be reproduced which to some extent were fulfilled later on.

The agreement was signed by Dr SS Bloeria and Leela Karan Sharma, Convener of the Samiti.

This agitation had paralysed the whole administration throughout the State. Some people had committed suicide in Jammu region and some lives were lost in violent police action. Unfortunately, more persons had died in violent actions started by the agitators of Kashmir Valley in retaliation who wanted opening of Muzaffarabad Road for free communication to Pakistan as the agitators in Jammu were putting blocks for the free flow of transport linking the Kashmir Valley from the rest of the country. The worst part of the agitation was that it was taking ugly communal turn and generating more hatred between the inhabitants of the two regions. A senior Congress leader and ex-minister of the coalition government hailing from Jammu was caught by the agitating mob but providence came to his rescue as some police personnel possessed of common-sense took him in their custody and in disguise as a police man he was rescued otherwise there was danger to his life. The famous agitation of 1953 launched by the then regional party Praja Parishad against the blatant discrimination had not generated so much communal hatred which was being generated by this agitation. Thank God! this black period in the history of the State has now been forgotten to some extent and the scars are healing. It is hoped that rulers of the State would not drag the inhabitants of any region to shake the foundations of communal harmony which is the hallmark of this State. Both regions are interdependent on each other but bad governance is responsible for such type of bitter experiences. The result was that Shri Amarnathji Yatra for subsequent years commencing from 2009 to 2014 have remained peaceful barring few irritant incidents which are created by the paid agents of anti-national elements. Inhabitants of the areas of Baltal and Pahalgam generally are direct beneficiaries of economic booms flowing from the Yatra. They are in favour of increase in the number of 'Yatris'. Similar is the case with the business community of J&K including hoteliers, transporters, shikarawalas, and shopkeepers etc who are benefited by the yatra. It is prayed that such type of agitation never starts in future in the State.

The people of Jammu region share a meagre portion of economic boon from this yatra.

Before we close this Chapter, it would be appropriate to mention here that in 2004, Mufti Mohammad Sayeed who was the Chief Minister had been trying his best to curtail the yatra period and the then Governor SK Sinha was opposing his move by tooth and nail. In the Board meting the Governor SK Sinha had revealed that they were not on talking terms on this issue. The Hindi daily newspaper *Navbharat Times* in its issue dated 30 May 2004, had reported the statement of Mufti Mohammad Sayeed in these words: "Yatra adversely affects the tourist traffic and his government would allow it from 1 August 2004." The Jammu newspaper *Daily Excelsior* in its issue of 23 June 2004, had reported that four Cabinet Ministers from Jammu Congress had submitted their resignations for curtailing the yatra period. On one occasion, some State Ministers hailing from Jammu who had used the State helicopter had to remain on the holy cave as on the direction of the Chief Minister they were not picked up for return journey. They had to spend the night at the holy cave. On another occasion, even the then Governor SK Sinha was refused to use the State helicopter and he had availed the services of Army helicopter. In the backdrop of political vote-bank game to win the sympathy of those elements in the Kashmir Valley who did not like the continuation of Amarnath Yatra, the support to the coalition government headed by Ghulam Nabi Azad of the Congress was withdrawn by the PDP and it resulted in the fall of the government.

CHAPTER 23

Rule of Omar Abdullah

Some people are born great and upon some greatness is thrusted. Omar Abdullah is one of such few privileged persons in the history of mankind upon whom greatness has been thrusted because of inheritance. His grandfather Sheikh Abdullah became the unchallenged ruler of the State because of invasion made by Pakistan after independence and caused the end of the Dogra dynastic autocratic rule. It has been recorded in detail in this book how Pandit Nehru at the cost of breach of terms and conditions of the Instrument of Accession made by the sole authority Maharaja Hari Singh appointed Sheikh Abdullah as the Prime Minister of the state from 1948 to 1953 and then his daughter Mrs Indira Gandhi for the second time in 1975 made him Chief Minister of the State at the cost of elected government of Congress. For the first time, Omar Abdullah fought the elections and for the first time lost the prestigious seat of Ganderbal constituency in 2002 which was constantly bringing back Sheikh Abdullah and his son Dr Farooq Abdullah as a successful National Conference elected member in the Legislative Assembly. This was the first occasion in the democratic history of the State when after his defeat Sheikh family lost the power. In the elections of 2008, Omar Abdullah had won this seat and became member of the Legislative Assembly. The elections were fought under the leadership of his father Dr Farooq Abdullah who had projected himself as future Chief Minister. The people in general and some elected Members of Legislature privately say that he has snatched away the chair of his father because of nearness with Rahul Gandhi through his brother-in-law, Sachin Pilot who is a Central Minister and one of the members of the coterie of Rahul Gandhi to project him as future Prime Minister of India in 2014 elections. In 2014 Dr Farooq Abdullah too, for the first time in his political career faced a defeat in the Parliamentary elections of Srinagar constituency.

Omar Abdullah only inducted two senior important ministers from the cabinet of his father Abdul Rahim Rather and Ali Mohammad

Sagar and the remaining ministers from National Conference quota are of his exclusive choice. Most of his Cabinet Ministers are semi-literates and of questionable ethics. Same is the case of his coalition partners from Congress party.

Omar Abdullah before becoming the Chief Minister of the State was elected member of Parliament and during the agitation of Baba Shri Amarnath Land Row had declared on the floor of the Parliament that not even an inch of land can be occupied by Amarnath Shrine Board when the fact of the matter is that yatra is ancient and sacred for every citizen of India from time immemorial. All the governments even prior to the present government of the time had been providing help to the yatris. It is now a constitutional duty of the government of Jammu and Kashmir to facilitate the yatra and provide security to the yatris.

Omar Abdullah is sometimes heard saying that the State has not merged with Union of India. The mastermind behind the attack on Indian Parliament, after exhausting all judicial processes, was hanged for death penalty and was addressed by Omar Abdullah as, 'Guru Sahib' and his dead body was demanded by him for burial in Kashmir though under the jail manual he could be buried in the premises of Tihar Jail, Delhi where ultimately he was buried. The uncalled for demand of Omar Abdullah was unheard by the concerned authorities because its result would have provided fuel to ignite the fading militancy. This demand was also against law of the land.

In reply to question number 178 in the Legislative Assembly he replied on 3 April 2013 that "no ex-militant has returned from Pakistan to the State through the identified routes under the policy and procedure for return of ex-militants to J&K State," notified by the State government vide Government order number Home/1376 (ISA) of 2010 dated 23 October 2010. When the fact of the matter is that during the past three years and the current year up to 15th February 2013, 241 ex-militants/terrorists have returned illegally via Nepal and other routes along with their family members.

1,089 applications are pending for return and out of these 191 cases have been recommended for return. The rest of the applications are being scrutinized and verified. Reportedly, around 3,974 ultras are still living in Pakistan Occupied Kashmir. He also admitted in the Assembly that the government is responsible for importing the terrorists to J&K via Nepal. This was exactly the case of Liaqat Ali Shah who recently was in NIA custody as Delhi Police had arrested him on the border of Nepal. He had his Pakistani wife and Pakistan born children. He and his colleagues had Pakistani passports. Chief Minister has admitted that 241 Pakistani nationals (terrorists) came with Pakistani Passports to Nepal. They were escorted by the Government of Jammu and Kashmir via Uttar Pradesh. From security point of view this policy can prove double edged weapon and more dangerous at any point of time. Opinion of security experts should be sought by Central Government and then this scheme should be allowed to be made operative.

There was headline news in the local newspaper *Daily Excelsior* in its issue of 21st November 2012, wherein it was reported, "Candidates approved for District Judges post have links with Pakistan-based militant outfit." Verification was done and it was found that one such candidate had close links with Pak-trained militants. His name was cancelled from the select list. There was another similar case regarding the elevation from Kashmir Bar Association to fulfil a vacancy in the High Court as a Judge. The State Government without proper verification on the recommendation of the High Court had sent the recommendation to the Centre but Central Government became aware of this fact and after verification his anti-national links were established. Later on, this recommendation became a matter of publication on the front page of national newspaper *The Times of India* and ultimately his name was withdrawn. In its issue of August 14, 2012, *Daily Excelsior* Jammu has reported that, "Political appointments in many departments cost crores of Rupees to exchequer." After this another list of four advocates (two each from Jammu and Kashmir bar) was sent for elevation as Judges of the J&K High Court. This proposal was outrightly criticised by some senior judges of the Supreme Court as one of the candidates had put external pressure on them to win the favour. There is hue and cry in the legal fraternity that many of the others are also not suitable. It was also the duty of the Governor NN Vohra being a constitutional head to get checked the antecedents of the recommendees to exclude the possibility for having any connection with anti-national elements. In the previous list which was sent earlier to this recommendation, one name was dropped for having links with anti-nationals. The Governor at that time also had not discharged his constitutional duties in a fair manner.

Most of the bureaucrats defy him and do not carry out his administrative directions or instructions and do not follow the rule of law as there is no accountability. There is a glaring personal experience of the writer of this book when in Public interest, he vide several letters DO number PS/2009/100 Srinagar dated May 18, 2009, followed by subsequent DO number J&K SCRDRC/2009/269 dated 4 August 2009 and lastly by DO letter dated 14 November 2011, had brought to the notice of Omar Abdullah for being Chairman of Katra Development Authority, how there is flagrant Vandalism of the Master Plan of the town of Katra, in connivance with official enforcing government agencies and they were bringing bad name to his (Chief Minister's) statutory authority, but unfortunately the Chief Minister failed to take any action thereon. Ultimately, some Public spirited people have taken the matter in PILs (Public Interest Litigation) in the High Court of J&K and the court has forced the authorities to check the future upcoming violations and make a report of the old existing violations.

The Times of India in its issue of 30 January 2013, has written about Misrule in Valley and according to this write-up it is stated that Chief Minister patted himself on the back for having transformed the State as he has completed his four years on January 5, 2013. At that time, most of the State was without power for prolonged periods when the mercury was below freezing point and in north Kashmir two infants died as the hospital incubator could not function. Earlier, five hundred babies had died in Srinagar's lone paediatric hospital for reasons ranging from lack of sanitation to negligence by untrained staff. There was serious LPG shortage and power cuts were growing day and night. The whole Jammu city was in the grip of water shortage. Similar was the situation in other urban and rural areas of the Jammu region.

Omar Abdullah was voted to power in 2008 after an unprecedented 68 per cent voter turn out in 2008. The number of jobless people since then has since mounted more than 60,000. At least 5 ministers face corruption charges making difficult to stem the rot from the top with a dubious distinction of being the second most corrupt State in the country. More than 50 bureaucrats too face graft charges. Chief Minister is satisfied that three tourist seasons have gone trouble free in the valley. He feels proud that his performance in Delhi is judged as very good but he does not know that issues that triggered protests from 2008 to 2010 have not melted away. There is unrest everywhere as there is no accountability in the State. The recent two communal incidents of Gool area of Ramban district and Kishtwar rioting are shining examples. His Home Minister Kichloo lost his berth as a State Minister Incharge Home Department because when the riots took place in Kishtwar he was camping there in his home town of Kishtwar but did not use police force or paramilitary forces which were present there to avert the riots. People of minority community are openly attributing mala fide motives to him behind those riots. It is widely reported in the press that Al-Qaida and other militant organizations are training some Kashmiri women in the valley itself to create women fidayeens. The number of trained militants is being quoted from 68 up to few hundreds. It is said that they are being locally trained. This is a very serious new trend for the security of the

State and the country and it can only happen when there is no hold over the administration. Recently the above-stated reports have appeared in the print media a few months back. It is feared that because of misgovernance or deficit governance militancy may again surface in more dangerous forms than it had happened in 1989-90 when his father was at the helm of the affairs. On the recent Parliamentary elections of 2014, he lost all the three Parliamentary seats to the opposition party (People's Democratic Party—PDP) from Kashmir Valley as well as lost two seats from Jammu region and one seat from Ladakh region to BJP.

Constitution-based Discrimination

In our Westminster Parliamentary form of Democracy, Constitution is the supreme authority to run the government but this principle is being observed in the State of Jammu and Kashmir in breach rather than in observance. This evil practice started immediately after the end of Dogra rule when the seat of power went into the hands of Kashmiri leadership, primarily in the hands of Sheikh Abdullah and his successors. The State of Jammu and Kashmir is composed of at least five different ethnic, linguistic and geographical areas—(1) the northern areas of Gilgit, Chitral and Baltistan comprising of Skardu etc and they are under the control of Pakistan; (2) POJK which is the western strip and is under the control of Pakistan; (3) Ladakh which is a huge area with Tibetan culture; (4) the Kashmir Valley which is the smallest of the five regions with two thousand square miles out of a total area of 84,000 sq miles and (5) Jammu region, which has also different culture. We must understand that it is not a single homogeneous ethnic problem but it is a problem of multiplicity of ethnic and linguistic causes. Thus, when one is talking of the State of Jammu and Kashmir we have to keep in mind that it is a subject of dispute with Pakistan on account of the aggression and forcible occupation of the northern areas of Gilgit, Chitral, etc and linguistically different inhabitants comprising of POJK area of district Muzaffarabad and part of district Baramulla in the Kashmir Valley and more than two third area of district Poonch and almost whole of the district area of Mirpur from Jammu region and majority area of erstwhile tehsil Rampur Rajouri of district Reasi. Under the Indian Constitution, the State has a distinct status because of accession made by the ruler under extraordinary special circumstances and that Instrument of Accession had Articles incorporated therein which preserved the sovereignty of the ruler, which he had not relinquished or surrendered. The ruler had made accession on specified matters mentioned therein. The Governor-General of India Lord Mountbatten on behalf of dominion of India had unilaterally inserted a clause that wishes of the people shall be ascertained after the aggression is vacated. All these legal aspects have been discussed earlier and there is no need for repetition. The above said redundant and unwarranted clause is the first seed sown in the dispute of Kashmir which gave a handle in the hands of Sheikh Abdullah to blackmail the dominion of India because at that relevant time he was the sole person to have won Plebiscite for India but his hidden intention was to carve out a 'Sheikhdom' for himself. It is thus, an admitted fact that under law the State has fully acceded with Union of India but technically a separate Agreement of merger was not allowed to be executed by Maharaja but illegally that power was vested in the Constituent Assembly of the State which was allowed to be constituted by Sheikh Abdullah as the sole authority against the provisions of the State Constitution of 1939 and in breach of loyalty to Maharaja and Government of India. This was done by Sheikh Abdullah because he knew his importance of winning Plebiscite in favour of India and Indian Government could neither restrain him nor harm him. Secretly he was hobnobbing with Anglo-American block to secure an Independent status for himself to rule the State. Later on, this type of conspiracy was unearthed and he lost the confidence of the Constituent Assembly constituted by him and the Cabinet Members of his government. They showed No-Confidence in his leadership and as a consequence he was dismissed and all the subsequent events have already been discussed in this book. Because of his initial unassailable position he had succeeded in engrafting Temporary Article of 370 in the Indian Constitution despite of great opposition in the Indian Parliament. Because of this special status which was acquired for temporary period of time, the State got a separate Constitution and a separate State flag. The State Subjects are the citizens of India while no Indian Citizen can become a resident of the State except a woman who is married to a State Subject. The women of the State married outside the State used to lose the status of being a resident of the State and inherit any property till the Full Bench Judgement in Dr Susheela Sawhny's case was delivered which has up to a limited extent settled the matter that a woman cannot lose the status either for inheritance purposes or losing the State Government job in the State. The decision has not been digested by the ruling political leadership who are in search of a finding a suitable opportunity to get undone the High Court verdict by an Act of Legislation. The women of the State till today are getting the State Subjects issued by the competent revenue authorities, with a rider imposed thereon, 'Valid up to Marriage'. In an attempt made during PDP and Congress coalition government headed by Mufti Mohammad Sayeed in the Legislative Assembly in order to make it a law, the bill was passed and then was referred to the Upper House to make it a law but the mischief was nipped in the bud. This topic has been discussed in detail in this book. Be that as it may, the inhabitants of Jammu region under the leadership of Maharaja Gulab Singh carved out the whole State partly from the debris of Sikh empire of Maharaja Ranjit Singh and partly by conquering vast adjoining areas from the independent local rulers. It is a matter of disgrace and regret that the offsprings of the founders and builders of Jammu region after 1947 till date are being treated as second class citizens in all respects of development, employment and to enter the portraits of State Legislature because they don't have equal right of franchise in voting process qua the natives of Kashmir region. Despite the availability of Fundamental Rights in the State guaranteed under the third part of the Indian Constitution as well as the extension of jurisdiction of the Election Commission of India they are suffering these humiliations of not being treated equally before law which is a constitutional guarantee to every citizen of India under Article 14 of the Indian Constitution. The genesis is found in the historical fact that the process of framing the Jammu and Kashmir Constitution, which started in early fifties as stands discussed fully in the foregoing relevant chapter is of unique type as it was the product of peculiar political circumstances of that time. On account of international and internal pressures, the State Constitution was framed to meet a particular emergency and, therefore, there was no time to visualise and provide safeguards for the regional tensions and conflicts which would generate in future in sharing the power on the basis of demographic, ethnical, cultural and historical factors.

The proposal of Autonomy for the entire State of Jammu and Kashmir (not for three regions, separately) was first mooted by Mirza Mohammad Afzal Beg, Chairman of the Basic Principles Committee, on March 20, 1952. In two articles published in the local newspaper *Kashmir Times* on 14 June 1992 and 15 June 1992, by late BP Sharma—a veteran media man from Jammu possessed of an experience of 65 years coupled with the special qualification that at the material time he was Director of the Jammu and Kashmir Radio Stations has recorded that Baig wanted internal Autonomy for the whole State and has reproduced his (Baig's) note thus:

> "The Jammu and Kashmir State would be an Autonomous Republic within the Indian Union. So far as the Constitution of the State is concerned we aim at making the frame work such that the State will be an Autonomous unit within the Indian Union."

In 1952, the spiritual-cum political leader of Ladakh, Kushak Bakula submitted a memorandum to Sheikh Mohammed Abdullah demanding statutory provision in the future constitution of the State under which Ladakh would become a Federating Unit of Jammu and Kashmir. He had urged that "a separate Ladakh Assembly of 15 Members with an Executive Council responsible to it should be set up for Ladakh to run the internal administration of the area." Prior to that, when Maharaja Hari Singh was not forced to leave State by Pandit Nehru at the behest of Sheikh Abdullah, Chhewang Rigzin President of Buddhist Association Ladakh had in 1949, written to the Prime Minister of India that on the eve of grant of responsible government to the people of Kashmir by the Maharaja they had presented to him (Maharaja) through their members in the 'Praja Sabha', (Legislative Assembly set up by the Maharaja under Constitution Act of 1939) that he himself should govern them directly through Legislative and Administrative machinery. That their homeland amalgamated with the Hindu majority parts of Jammu should form a separate province in which adequate safeguards should be provided for their distinctive rights and interests. They had spelled out that Maharaja's great grandfather (Maharaja Gulab Singh) in 1834 had conquered their homeland whileas, after 12 years the territory of Kashmir region came into his possession in 1846 because of Treaties of Lahore and Amritsar. That in the past, the administrators from Kashmir had governed them to their utter ruin. (Note: The full text of that memorandum is attached as Appendix 18.) So far as Jammu region is concerned, it is well known that the Praja Parishad—main political party of the State of that time had the thinking of its leadership that their interests identified with the interests of the Hindu ruler. They had openly declared that they would not rest till they would get rid of the Hindus of Jammu from what they described, "haunting fear of Muslim domination of the Kashmiris." A lonely voice raised by Balraj Puri—a freelance journalist at that time, mooted the idea of Regional Autonomy as the only via-media for keeping the three regions together and he had met Pandit Jawaharlal Nehru on April 14, 1952 and presented a memorandum to him. The Constituent Assembly of the State passed a resolution on June 7, 1952, adopting a flag for the State and Pandit Prem Nath Dogra, the President of the Praja Parishad condemned the decision as a, "provocative act which has caused resentment in Jammu." The Constituent Assembly on June 12, adopted the resolution by accepting the recommendation for the abolition of hereditary rule. After prolonged discussions in Delhi with leaders from Union of India and State, they reached on an understanding known as Delhi Agreement of 1952. This was not signed document but only an understanding as they were not legally competent to do so. Releasing the document at Press Conference in Delhi on July 26, 1952 Pandit Nehru had said, "that the State Government was considering Regional Autonomies within the larger State."

Simultaneously, Sheikh Abdullah who was in Delhi gave an assurance to the same effect. The Union Parliament discussed the Delhi Agreement on August 7, 1952 followed by motion of acceptance. The Jammu and Kashmir State Constituent Assembly ratified the agreement on August 21, 1952. The Praja Parishad had protested against the Delhi Agreement and they had opposed the grant of separate status to the State and demanded one Constitution, one Flag and one President.

On his return to Srinagar, Sheikh Abdullah had started giving serious thought to his commitment for providing constitutional guarantees to three cultural units of the State to ally fears of the people of Jammu and Ladakh against what they called 'Kashmiri Domination'. Broadcasting from the Srinagar station of Radio Kashmir, Srinagar (Simultaneously relayed by its Jammu counterpart) the Sheikh declared:

> "We have decided to give Autonomy to the different cultural units of the State as will be provided in the Constitution that is being drawn up. This will remove all the fears of domination of one unit over the other and will make for voluntary union and the consolidation of the people of the State."

Note: The above stated material in the form of some of the extracts from the article scribed by the above said one of the grand sires of journalism of the State of Jammu and Kashmir (late BP Sharma). He had the personal knowledge of the above stated statement of Sheikh Abdullah while discharging his official functions as Director of the Radio Station Kashmir in 1952. He has clearly recorded from his memory the following lines:

> "Unfortunately, the concerned file in the Information Department records which contained the full text of the draft proposals, as also the full text of Sheikh Sahib's Broadcast containing his summary prepared by me in English and its urdu translation by Hakim Ghulam Mohi-ud-Din (the then Station Director of Radio Kashmir) could not be traced in the Archives for lending more authenticity to this article. He has further recorded that, "the scheme envisaged a National Assembly for the State with three regional Assemblies for Jammu, Kashmir and Ladakh."

On the occasion of the end of Dogra rule in the State and the acceptance of the office of Sadar-i-Riyasat by Maharaja Hari Singh's son Dr Karan Singh the emotions of Dogras of Jammu flared up and they did not allow the State sponsored reception in Jammu to Dr Karan Singh on his first visit to Jammu, as elected head of the State called Sadar-i-Riyasat. On November 26, 1952, Pandit Prem Nath Dogra, Pandit Sham Lal Sharma, Lala Ram Nath Bhalgotra (advocate), Chatru Ram, Lala Shiv Charan, Lala Paras Ram, Pandit Bhikam Chand Magotra, Thakur Anant Singh, Thakur Baldev Singh and about a dozen other prominent activists of the Praja Parishad organisation were arrested and this sparked off a widespread agitation which spread like wild fire in other parts of the Jammu region. This agitation gained effective support from many quarters in India including a section of the Press and Dr Syama Prasad Mookerjee—President of the Bharatiya Jan Sangh raised a banner of protest. In this agitation more than twenty-five thousand people had been arrested and eighteen valuable lives were lost in police firing such as at Ramban, Hiranagar, Jourian etc. In his letter dated February 12, 1953, addressed to Pandit Jawaharlal Nehru, Prime Minister, Dr Syama Prasad Mookerjee sent a nine point formula for withdrawal of agitation started by Praja Parishad and one of the suggestions was: "Provincial Autonomy to Jammu and Ladakh without change of boundaries." Nehru gave reply of this letter on the same day to Dr Mookerjee and stated in his letter, "Even in States other than Jammu and Kashmir, we have to respect provincial Autonomy and, though we give advice to our colleagues there, we do not interfere." Again in his letter dated February 17, 1953, to Prime Minister Dr Mookerjee laid down the following as one of the conditions for withdrawal of the movement: "Both parties reiterate that the unity of the State of Jammu and Kashmir will be maintained and that the Principle of Autonomy will apply to the province of Jammu as a whole, and of course also to Ladakh and Kashmir Valley."

Dr Mookerjee in his letter dated February 11, 1953 to Sheikh Abdullah had criticised his stand on special status of the State by writing:

> "There cannot be a republic within republic. There can be one and only one sovereign Parliament and that is the Parliament of India. Consciously or unconsciously you are creating a new sovereignty for Jammu and Kashmir State. Stressing the desirability of giving Autonomy to Jammu as a whole and to Ladakh and Kashmir Valley, can be discussed in its merits at a later stage."

Subsequently, in his letter dated February 23, 1953 to Sheikh Abdullah, Dr Mookerjee even went to the extent of suggesting:

> "If the people of Jammu wanted full accession with India and the people of Kashmir Valley wanted a lose integration; clash and

> conflict are inevitable. One possible solution might be to form Kashmir Valley into a separate State and give it whatever it wants for its development. It would even then continue as one of the units of the Indian Union but would function according to special provisions of the Constitution."

Dr Mookerjee, however, added:

> "I had suggested this alternative with no pleasure. This I felt might become inevitable if no settlement could at all be reached. But let us drop this altogether and think in terms of united Jammu and Kashmir and find out how to consolidate it with the willing cooperation of the people."

Meanwhile, the leadership of Praja Parishad sensed a rat in the conduct of Sheikh Abdullah as he was wilfully delaying the implementation of the Delhi Agreement in toto. Dr Mookerjee also accused him to know the reasons for wilful delay. The writer of this book has fully discussed mens-rea of Sheikh Abdullah under the chapter 'Dreams of Independence of Kashmir' with the patronage of the Anglo-American block and he was scheming an Independent Kashmir as his personal Sheikhdom. Sheikh reacted in his letter dated February 4, 1953 and wrote to Dr Syama Prasad Mookerjee, "you support the Praja Parishad demand for complete integration of the State as a part of it with India. In that case, there can be no talk to these agreements as these agreements concretely confirm the special position which has been granted to the State by the Constitution. Praja Parishad has always opposed this and the present agitation has been started for the purpose of doing away with the special position which the State enjoys at present. I do not know what to make of this contradiction." The Veteran Jammu leader Pandit Prem Nath Dogra had also reacted on the utterances of Sheikh Abdullah and had said: "This is a fraud on the people of Jammu. The Sheikh wants to create a Sheikhdom for himself in the valley of Kashmir. We will never allow Kashmir to go out of our hands."

On May 1953, Dr Syama Prasad Mookerjee entered Jammu in defiance of the rules regarding entry and exit into and from the State without a valid permit. He was arrested at the entry point of the State, Lakhanpur in Kathua district and detained in a house near the famous Nishat Garden at Srinagar. Unfortunately, Dr Mookerjee died on June 23, 1953 within a period of one month and ten days when he was hardly fifty-two years old and not suffering from any serious ailment. His mysterious death raised a storm of indignation against Sheikh Abdullah throughout India. A large section of the people suspected foul play for the cause of his death. The martyrdom of Dr Syama Prasad Mookerjee for the national cause awakened Pandit Jawaharlal Nehru from his deep slumber who had always been blindly reposing faith in his old friend Sheikh Abdullah even at the annoyance of his Cabinet colleagues such as Sardar Patel, Maulana Abul Kalam Azad and Rafi Ahmed Kidwai etc. By this time, Pandit Nehru had come to know from the reports of different agencies that Sheikh Abdullah had been hobnobbing with Western powers to create an Independent State for himself. Till that time in his party there was a revolt due to his authoritarian attitude. There was vote of No Confidence which was supported by all his cabinet colleagues except Mirza Mohammad Afzal Beg. All of them were not tolerating his autocratic behaviour. With heavy heart, Pandit Jawaharlal Nehru agreed with his colleagues to remove Sheikh Abdullah from the scene and accordingly he was put under detention on August 9, 1953 and a new government with Bakshi Ghulam Mohammad (who was his Deputy Prime Minister) as Prime Minister was installed in the State. Sheikh Abdullah's arrest was celebrated as a 'Day of Deliverance' by the Praja Parishad's activists. They hoped that after the arrest of Sheikh Abdullah their demands would be accepted. But politically shrewd Bakshi Ghulam Mohammad started playing political games with the credulous leadership of Jammu by keeping them always in happy mood. He started fulfilling most of their local demands and was always alert not to give any opportunity to the inhabitants of the regions of Jammu and Ladakh that they are second class citizens. The scholarships for higher studies to the students belonging to all the three regions were equally distributed. At that time, there was no Medical, Engineering and Agricultural College in the State so they were being sent outside the State by bearing their expenses for studies on loan basis to be refunded in instalments after returning in the State and automatic reserved absorption into the government jobs. Road development activities, construction of 'Rest Houses' at important places and other developmental works were started in the State with the aid of Central Government funds and they were equally distributed. Education was made free in the State. Wheat flour, sugar and rice were distributed at subsidized rates to the inhabitants of the State through State controlled Ration Dealers on the basis of ration cards. Distribution of State licences for business and Route permits for transport business were equally distributed. Residential colonies were laid down to provide Houses to the people in all the regions. His political foresight can be judged from the single fact that he dissolved The Constituent Assembly without even seeking its opinion on Article 370. It has already been discussed that this Constituent Assembly had all the members from one political party National Conference and Bakshi Ghulam Mohammad after the arrest of Sheikh Abdullah had himself become the President of the regional political organisation. His infamous brother Bakshi Rashid had become the General Secretary of the Organisation. In other words, Bakshi's family rule was substituted for Sheikh Abdullah's family rule. In this manner, he ruled the State up to 1963 when Kamraj Plan of Pandit Nehru axed him and subsequently he faced an enquiry Commission. It deserves to be mentioned here that it was Ghulam Mohammad Sadiq who replaced Bakshi Ghulam Mohammad (after an interim rule of Bakshi Ghulam Mohammad's protege Khwaja Shamsuddin which lasted for about five months) as a Prime Minister. GM Sadiq became Prime Minister and got this nomenclature changed as Chief Minister. He did commendable work in bringing Jammu and Kashmir closer to India. He changed designation of the Sadar-i-Riyasat to that of Governor and changed the designation of Prime Minister of the State to that of the Chief Minister. It may also be mentioned here that in 1964, a resolution was moved in the Parliament seeking to repeal Article 370 of the Constitution and at that time there was no opposition. But Gulzarilal Nanda, the then Home Minister, told the Parliament on December 4, 1964, that, "it would be totally wrong to assume that with the repeal of the Article all constitutional provisions would automatically apply to Kashmir." (Refer Gulzarilal Nanda, Home Minister.)

It appears that on this principle neither the Janata Government nor the NDA Government at the centre could abrogate this Article when they were in power. After discussing the discrimination on the basis of facts and figures in the earlier relevant chapters in this book, it is mentioned here that with the return of Sheikh Abdullah to power in 1975 while remaining in wilderness for about 23 years, it was hoped that he would attempt to put the Autonomy scheme into action. OP Saraf (a Jammuite), who was a member of the State Legislative Council was told in reply to his question in the Legislative Assembly on August 2, 1975 that the government intended to setup a small Committee to asses the possibility of further decentralisation of constitutional and administrative powers consistent with the needs to preserve the integrity of the State. In those very days the National Conference published a pamphlet entitled, 'Why National Conference?' It contained a categorical statement that the party proposes to reorganise the internal set-up of the State on the basis of federal structure which would provide Regional Autonomy and further decentralisation of political power through appropriate constitutional arrangement at district, block and village levels.

The facts as discussed in earlier chapters have established how the National Conference rule proved to be worst in the history of the State in denying the equal treatment to the other two regions of the State Jammu and Ladakh. It stands already discussed how the National Conference rule has communalised the administration and given a handle to the militancy to grow and then it established its upper hand over the lawfully established government. Schemes were hatched to change the demographic composition of the Jammu region. Sheikh Abdullah by an ulterior design had diluted the recommendations of the Gajendragadkar Commission, the Wazir Commission as well as the recommendations of the Sikri Commission. The details have already been given under the relevant headings in the concerned chapters of this book. His son Dr Farooq Abdullah also seemed to work against the interests of Jammu region. The greatest harm is the change in the population composition which occurred on account of criminal trespass over State lands and forest lands. Dr Farooq Abdullah himself is a trespasser as his House in Bhatindi Colony which was discussed at great length in the Legislative Assembly when he was the Chief Minister but there was no conclusive outcome. The settlement of some nomads, Gujjars and Bakarwals was also allowed in the same manner in other parts of the Jammu region. For their settlement even forest land at some places was made available as well as even in the border belt dominated by Hindu population. Some of the unscrupulous inhabitants of these settlements are providing safe hideouts for the infiltration of militants coming across the border. Why some of them are not settled in Kashmir region where in fact they are traditionally going for summer season is a big question mark for the government. Mufti Mohammad Sayeed also did not fare better than his predecessors. During the rule of these Chief Ministers incompetent persons hailing from Jammu region were given Cabinet berths. Barring a few exceptions majority of them were under graduates when correspondingly, the Cabinet Ministers hailing from Kashmir Valley used to be mostly Law-Graduates. They had been dominating the proceedings in the Assembly. In order to bring home this point to the readers the writer of this book will cite two examples. The first one is how the State Constitution was amended when no single legislator from Jammu region could understand its adverse affect behind the amendment which is to the effect that equal right of voting was further denied by a constitutional bar beyond 2026 till the census could be held again and a Delimitation Commission is appointed.

The legal effects of the above stated amendment in detail have already been discussed at an early stage of this book.

The second mischief was done during the rule of Dr Farooq Abdullah by passing the Autonomy Resolution in the legislature which smacks of communalism, fundamentalism and regionalism. At this occasion also, no legislator from Jammu region belonging to any of the political party or print media effectively opposed this Resolution and they were only idle spectators when it was passed. Dr Farooq Abdullah, after totally forgetting the assurances given by his illustrious father late Sheikh Abdullah to grant Regional Autonomy to the regions of Jammu and Ladakh appointed State Autonomy Regional Committee which was headed by Mohi-ud-Din Shah (now dead) who divided the State into eight provinces on the basis of religion only. The shocking feature of the ignominious Autonomy Committee was that no person of any outstanding stature was appointed as a Member who could represent the aspirations of the people of Jammu and Ladakh. The recommendations of the Committee Report in brief were:

Number 1: Division carved out from the State was named as 'Kamraj Division' (having the areas from the districts of Anantnag and Pulwama).

Number 2: Division was named as 'Nandabad Division' (consisting of areas of the district of Srinagar and Budgam).

Number 3: Division was named as 'Maraj Division' (consisting of the areas from the district of Baramulla and Kupwara).

Number 4: Division was the 'Chenab Ghati Division' (consisting of the whole district of Doda and predominating Muslims inhabited areas of Mahore teshil of erstwhile district Udhampur and present district Ramban and partly of present district Reasi).

Number 5: Division was called as 'Pir Panjal Division' (consisting of the areas of districts Rajouri and Poonch).

Number 6: Division was called as 'Kargil Division' (consisting of the whole area of district Kargil).

Number 7: Division was called 'Ladakh Division' (consisting of the areas of district Ladakh).

Number 8: Division was called as 'Jammu Division' (having part of the Hindu-dominated areas of district Udhampur, whole Jammu district and whole of the area of Kathua district).

The Tribune newspaper in its issue of April 1, 2014 has written that: "In October 1994 National Conference President Dr Farooq Abdullah had declared, autonomy is our birth right and unless the greater autonomy is restored, the party would not participate in any election. This was a time when militancy was at its peak. The argument was that autonomy would help Kashmiris to revive their unique identity and would blunt the gun culture and peace would return to terror-torn Valley. This he had announced after National Conference Central Working Committee adopted a resolution in Jammu because Kashmir was too unsafe a place for National Conference. The party took plunge in 1996 Assembly elections on the assurance of Prime Minister HD Deve Gowda that J&K was a "Special State and deserves a Special Treatment." There was no commitment from him about critical feature of Autonomy. In 1996, National Conference took part in elections and won with two-third majority.

Coming to 1998, when NDA Government had come to power—the National Conference decided to align with political combination led by BJP. Farooq was the Chief Minister and he had already constituted an Autonomy panel headed by former Sadar-i-Riyasat Dr Karan Singh who had stepped down from the Chairmanship of the Autonomy panel in August 1997, citing personal reasons. (The personal reason was incurring the wrath from the people of his own community, i.e. Dogras of Jammu.) Then senior minister of National Conference Mohi-ud-Din Shah replaced Dr Karan Singh. When Dr. Farooq was asked, why he and his party had aligned with BJP? His answer was: "I was told by my father (Sheikh Abdullah) to always be friend with New Delhi even if it is ruled by RSS." This statement was published in newspapers including in some national dailies.

Today, again before the Parliamentary elections of April 2014, he had started talking of Autonomy, "Till my last breath." He is right as he picks up the issue at intervals when it suits him. People want consistency not the occasional emotional slogans. Let him give sufficient reasons why 1953 is relevant today? He should explain the emotional speech made by him on October 9, 1995 at SKICC Srinagar about his responsibilities after the Accord of 1975 between his father and late Mrs Indira Gandhi.

A careful analysis of this mischievous State Autonomy plan shows that there was only one Hindu majority division comprising the areas of two and half districts from Jammu region and one Buddhist-dominated division comprising the areas of Leh district. The remaining six so called Autonomous divisions were Muslim majority divisions. This scheme was the replica of the scheme of late Sheikh Abdullah and his trusted lieutenant Mirza Mohammad Afzal Beg, who had under Anglo-American influence thought out the division of the State and had even entered into a conspiracy to subvert the established government. They faced detention in 1953 and subsequently criminal trial known as 'Kashmir Conspiracy Case' for the violations of the laws of the land. This case has been discussed in detail in the previous chapters. The NDA Government at the centre outrightly rejected this Resolution of the State. Now, Dr Farooq Abdullah's son Omar Abdullah being the Chief Minister of the State sometimes is heard singing the song of his forefathers. On December 6, 2013 he uttered in a public meeting while giving a reply to the speech of Narendra Modi on December 1, 2013 that abrogation of Article 370 can affect the accession of the State with India. His other priority is to see that Armed Forces Special Powers Act (AFSPA) is withdrawn from some districts at once. This proposal is being opposed by tooth and nail by the Security forces on the plea that it would provide safe hideouts to the militants to augment the anti-national activities. Such types of subversive acts are only tolerated in the Indian democracy and no where else in the world. His latest song is that State has not merged with India. This statement was given in Srinagar and now in Jammu when Darbar opened in the winter capital on November 4, 2013, he in the Press Conference stated that State has acceded to India.

The third mischievous game plan was hatched by the Mufti Mohammad Sayeed's government when he was ruling the State with the support of Congress Party. Pandit Mangat Ram Sharma (the senior most Congress leader from Jammu region) at that time was the Deputy Chief Minister and the majority of the MLAs and Ministers were also from Jammu region belonging to the Congress Party. The then Law Minister MH Baig (of the PDP) introduced a Bill by the name of 'The Jammu and Kashmir Permanent Residents (Disqualification) Bill 2004'. In the Legislative Assembly this Bill was passed within few minutes. No elected member in the Legislative Assembly raised any voice against the aims and objects of this Bill which besides being unconstitutional was also communal in nature. In case the Bill had become the Act, it would have been used by the PDP as a handle in their hands to create vote banks on communal lines. The anti-national and secessionist elements would have been encouraged to whip up the hysteria of separatism and secession. When this Bill was referred to the Legislative Council (Upper House) for obtaining the consent of the Members, Sonia Gandhi (Chairperson UPA) got the wind of this nefarious design through different agencies. Before the Bill could become an Act she directed her partymen to resist its passing and becoming a law. Only at that time; the coalition partner Congress Party legislators for the first time raised a debate in the Upper House which lasted for a few hours and ultimately the Bill had to be deferred for future discussion. Meanwhile, the writer of this book wrote an Article on this Bill highlighting its unconstitutionality and the hidden communal agenda in its thick layers. This Article got wide publicity in the local as well as in the national press besides its publication in the important two national law reporters—*All India Law Reporter* and *Supreme Court Cases Reporter*. The last three paras of the Article from the original which as a whole was published in (2004) 6 SCC (Journal Section) page 23 are reproduced for readers interest:

> "The female members of the State shall not get social, economic and political justice. They will be deprived of the right to inherit ancestral property; they shall lose government jobs and shall stand disqualified to receive higher education and future government jobs and contest elections etc. Their status and dignity shall also be a casualty. Section 22 of the State Constitution deals with the directive principles of State policy and under Clause (d) it ensures,
>
> > "the right to full equality in all social, educational, political and legal matters."

Above all, their Fundamental Rights guaranteed under Articles 14, 15(1), 16(1) and 19(1)(e) of the Constitution of India shall stand whittled down. The authors of this proposed Act are deriving force from the mandate of Article 35(A) of the Indian Constitution to enact it. This Article States that:

> "35-A. Notwithstanding anything contained in this Constitution, no existing law in force in the State of Jammu and Kashmir, and no law hereafter enacted by the legislature of the State—
>
> (a) defining the classes of persons who are, or shall be, permanent residents of the State of Jammu and Kashmir: or
>
> (b) conferring on such permanent residents any special rights and privileges or imposing upon other persons any restrictions as respects—
>
> (i) employment under the State Government;
>
> (ii) acquisition of immovable property in the State;
>
> (iii) settlement in the State, or
>
> (iv) right to scholarships and such other forms of aid as the State Government may provide,
>
> shall be void on the ground that it is inconsistent with or takes away or abridges any rights conferred on the other citizens of India by any provision of this part."

The proposed Act is defining the classes of persons amongst the permanent residents of the State on the classification of genders. The female members from the category of genders marrying outside the State shall lose all the rights specified from heads (I) to (IV) of Clause (b) of the said Article. Clause (b) is an independent provision and not dependent on Clause (a) so far as its second limb is concerned. Clause (b) envisages the conferring on defined permanent classes of persons under Clause (a) any special rights and privileges, or imposing upon other persons any restrictions, as respects matters enumerated under heads (I) to (IV).

The female members who are classified under Clause (a) under the Act could only be conferred special rights and privileges under the first limb of Clause (b) of the Article. Their rights or privileges cannot be restricted under the second limb of Clause (b) of the Article and not to talk of extinguishing their vested rights. Under these provisions restrictions can be imposed as enumerated under heads (I) to (IV) upon other persons, i.e. persons who are not defined permanent residents of the State which means on non-residents or outsiders. In other words, the second limb of Clause (b) of the Article is not applicable to permanent residents of the State. A harmonious construction has only to be given to Clauses (a) and (b) of the Article, in order to arrive at the desired result contemplated by the Parliament. Parliament had never contemplated the growth and survival of fissiparous tendencies in this part of the country. The Act if comes into force shall breed hatred and conflict between males and female genders as well as between the inhabitants of the three regions of the State on the basis of communal and political lines. Educated and progressive female members from the majority community too have married outside the State and in future they shall also be getting married even if the Bill becomes an Act. The Act will advance mischief and create conflict in the society instead of resolving them. The Act lacks the legislative power of enactment as it falls outside the purview of Article 35(A). It is violative of the spirit of this Article.

Article 14 gives a fundamental right to equality before law but under the Bill in question males have been preferred because after marriage, females from outside will not lose the right of being permanent residents. A female from outside the State shall become a permanent resident on marrying a male permanent resident of the State but a daughter who is a born State Subject will lose the right on marrying an outsider. Unreasonable classification between males and females and between females and females is against the spirit of Article 14 of the Constitution. The discrimination against any citizen on the ground of sex is hit by Article 15(1). Clause (I) of Article 16 states that there shall be equality of opportunity for all citizens in matters relating to employment or appointment to any office under the State. The proposed Act is violating this provision of the Constitution too as a female marrying a non-State Subject shall lose employment and shall have no future right of employment in the State. Clause (e) of Article 19 provides that all citizens shall have the right to reside and settle in any part of the territory of India. Under the proposed Act, a daughter of the State may reside and settle in any part of the country at the cost of losing the acquired constitutional right of the State Constitution as well as the Indian Constitution of being a permanent resident of the State. The Act would have militated against the basic structure of the Constitution as the spirit of the Fundamental Rights cannot be taken away.

It is hoped that all the Hon'ble Members of the State Legislative Council and the State Legislative Assembly in their wisdom shall again think over their legal duty to bring this piece of legislation within the four corners and ambit of the State Constitution as well as Constitution of India.

Note: After the publication of this Article with wide publicity the ruling class lost its jaunty step and so far has not brought any fresh legislation on this sensible topic though Mufti Mohammad Sayeed's PDP (political party) sometimes raises the bogey of making it a law.

The fourth mischief was done through the organ of Legislature which already stands discussed in this book in the chapter, "Farooq Abdullah had got enacted the Jammu and Kashmir State Lands (vesting of ownership to the occupants) Act. With an ulterior motive to change the demographic composition of the Jammu region generally and particularly of the city of Jammu," Mufti Mohammad Sayeed got this Act amended by Act number XVI of 2004 making it more liberal for the unauthorised occupants/trespassers. In order to further perpetuate the desired mischief, the Revenue Minister Qayoom of PDP government, against the "provisions of the business rules for the conduct of Government" and against the provisions of relevant rules framed by the government prescribing the modes of transfer of the district level government employees himself in the capacity of a Minister transferred some pliable 'Girdawars and patwaris' mostly hailing from the districts of Doda, Poonch and Rajouri in order to make the State land and forest land available to the trespassers belonging to the majority community. This matter already has been discussed in the previous chapters. The transfer order is attached as Appendix 16.

CHAPTER 24

National Human Rights Commission

In the previous chapters, discussion has been made on the topic of how two Kashmir Valley based regional political parties National Conference and PDP are competing with each other in order to extend their respective sphere of influence amongst the Jehadi fundamentalist elements on the basis to increase their vote bank without realizing the long range ultimate result that this approach shall provide oxygen to keep the separatist cultural identity alive. In other words, this myopic, morbid and selfish approach, for the time being increases their respective vote bank in order to capture the political power. All the principles to govern the State in accordance with the mandates of the provisions of the State constitution and Indian constitution are given a go by. The Fundamental Rights enshrined in the Indian Constitution regarding equality before law, right to life and property and no discrimination on the basis of religion, race, caste and place of birth have become the main casualties. Not only that, long range national interest to get the State emotionally merged with national mainstream are also allowed to be kept on the back-burner.

Lackadaisical role of Election Commission of India in few cases where the Commission had failed to curb with a heavy hand electoral illegalities already have been highlighted in the previous chapter. One such glaring example of nauseating religious spectacle related to the Elections which were held in 1977, when National Conference was allowed freely to win the gullible electorates on the basis of religion by administering oaths to them in the name of Holy Quran and Pakistani salt to bring Sheikh Abdullah into power. In the book *My Frozen Turbulence in Kashmir* at page 135 Shri Jagmohan has recorded that during the elections of 1977, Sheikh Abdullah once again showed that he exploited Islam to the hilt. In April 1977, Sheikh Abdullah observed, "Kashmir Congress is a dirty gutter. Democracy will survive under Janata Party. We yearn to be its ally. Jan Sanghis are our Brothers." But as soon as the Janata Party decided to fight State Assembly elections on its own, he berated it on communal grounds. In June 1977, he said, "Janata Party is anti-Muslim, Jan Sanghi is new garb. The hands of Jan Sangh leaders are still soiled with Muslim blood." He sent his workers with Quran in one hand exhorting the Kashmiri Muslims not to vote for a party of the infidels." It has been observed on ground realities that after the Accord of 1975 between Mrs Indira Gandhi and Sheikh Abdullah, the application of relevant beneficial provisions of the Indian Constitution to the State as well as many Central laws of benevolent and socialistic public-oriented nature stand intentionally slowed down. Even some of them could have proved highly beneficial to the common masses for their betterment. On the contrary, the separatist segments in the society were being encouraged and the most glaring example is passing of the J&K Grant of Permit for Resettlement Act, 1982. At pages 150 and 151 Shri Jagmohan has exhibited in his above said book with details, the posters written in Urdu how Parliamentary elections of 1984 were fought by Dr Abdullah on the doctrine of communalism and freedom. In 1987, when Dr Farooq Abdullah was at the helm of affairs the elections were considered the worst rigged and notorious in the history for the murder of democratic process as it brought the gun culture in the State.

Be that as it may, in this chapter an attempt has been made to show how the National Human Rights Commission (NHRC) has not acted with same alacrity and alarm with which it acted in the rest of the country to uphold the basic Human Rights. Best Bakery case of Gujarat is the star example where the Commission suo motu had taken cognizance regarding the acquittal of the accused by the Trial Court of Gujarat. The NHRC registered the case to examine the above said acquittal under its Number 115016/2001-2002 and vide its order dated July 11, 2003, had instructed a team to proceed to Vadodara (Gujarat) to inspect the records of the case, examine the judgment and all other materials and submit a report to the commission within one week. At the request of the team, extension of time was granted for filing the report. Meanwhile, Sheikh Zahira Bibi approached the Commission and made a statement. She *inter-alia* stated that under threat to her life and the lives of the remaining members of her family, she had resiled in the Trial Court from the earlier statements made by her. She sought the help of the Commission to re-open the Best Bakery Case. Finally, the commission on consideration of the report of its own team filed a Special Leave Petition under Article 136 of the

Constitution of India in the Supreme Court with a prayer to set aside the impugned judgment of the Trial Court in Best Bakery Case and sought directions for further investigation by an independent agency and re-trial of the case in a competent court located outside the State of Gujarat. It was emphatically held by the Commission in its order while deciding the above said matter:

> "The right to fair trial is also explicitly recognized as a human right in terms of Article 14 of the International Covenant on Civil and Political Rights (ICCPR) which has been ratified by India and which now forms part of the statutory legal regime explicitly recognized as such under Section 2(i)(d) of the Protection of Human Rights Act 1993. Violation of a right to fair trial is not only a violation of fundamental right under our Constitution but also violative of the internationally recognized human rights as spelt out in the ICCPR to which India is a party. Whenever a criminal goes unpunished, it is society at large which suffers because the victims become demoralized and criminal encouraged. It therefore, becomes duty of the court to use all its powers to unearth the truth and render justice so that the crime is punished."

The Commission also filed a separate application under Section 406 CrPC before the Supreme Court for transfer of four other serious cases—the Godhra incident, Gulbarg Society incident, Naroda Patia incident and the Saddarpura case in Mehsana district—for their trial outside the State of Gujarat.

Ravindra Kumar, S/o late CL Gupta, R/o 43/41, Punjabi Bagh, Delhi presented petition in the National Human Rights Commission, Delhi on behalf of his relatives to initiate inquiry under Section 14 read with Section 17 of the Protection of Human Rights Act 1993, by invoking its jurisdiction for holding immediate inquiry and investigation against the alleged failure of administration according to the rule of law by the State Government of J&K and giving illegal patronage and protection to the highly dangerous terrorists even after registration of the cases against them. The State Government had so far not given sanction for their prosecution under Section 50 of the Prevention of Terrorists Act, 2002. Fourteen cases were annexed as Annexures 'A', 'B', 'C', 'D', 'E', 'F', 'G', 'H', 'I', 'J', 'K', 'L', 'M' and 'N' with that petition. It was also alleged in the petition that the accused of the cases under the 'Healing-Touch' policy of the State are still roaming at large after getting bail orders from the concerned TADA Court. The State had failed in its statutory duty to file the challans in all those cases within the prescribed statutory period and on account of withholding the required sanction to prosecute the accused they were favoured to enable themselves to get bailed out after the expiry of 6 months from the dates of their arrests. These were the main averments made in the application and the application was registered in the National Human Rights Commission under Case Number 91/09/2003-2004 (1626) dated October 3, 2003. The Commission issued notice to the State and in reply thereof the Director-General of Police, J&K State submitted explanation to the NHRC which is annexed as Appendix 19 in this book.

First case: Annexure 'F' to the application (which is at serial number 11 of Appendix 19) relates to the terrorist attack on 13 July 2002 made in the Hindu Basti at Rajiv Nagar, Narwal situated at the outskirts of Jammu city in which 29 civilians (Hindus) of minority community in J&K State were killed and serious injuries were caused to 22 others. The case was registered under FIR Number 134/2002, in Police Station Bahu Fort, Jammu Under/Section 3/4 POTA, 302/307/120-B, RPC, 4/5 ESA, 7/25 Arms Act. During investigation eight persons were named to have perpetuated the above stated crimes and the summary of the allegations reported in the TADA Court Jammu are reproduced from the court record as under:

> "These accused persons are the active members of LeT (Lashkar-e-Toiba) involved in a case in which 29 persons were killed and 22 persons have seriously been injured at Qasim Nagar/Rajiv Nagar, Jammu on 13th July 2002 by using bombs and prohibited arms and ammunition. Two police constables and Sub-Inspector Ranbir Singh were also killed by those militants/accused persons. One AK-47 (rifle) with 30 cartridges was also recovered from the place of occurrence. The accused who figured at Serial Number 8 Mehmood Ahmad had made this recovery. The accused figuring at Serial Number 5 Kabir-ul-Din was instrumental in organising the terrorist attack at Qasim Nagar as he had dumped the consignment of Arms and Ammunition in the house of Muneer Hussain Khan (accused at Serial Number 1). Accused Number 6 Mohammad Abdullah was a Pak national and he was kept in judicial custody and the remaining accused (numbering 7) stood bailed out on different dates for non-presentation of the challan by the prosecution wing of the State within the statutory period of six months." This incident, took place in the month of July 2002, when Dr Farooq Abdullah was the Chief Minister and he had to relinquish the office after three months on account of his defeat in the general elections. The coalition government headed by Mufti Mohammad Sayeed and Congress is mainly responsible for withholding the sanction for the

prosecution of the accused and report submitted by the Director-General of Police to the National Human Rights Commission under his Number T&I/INT/NHRC-49/2003-1979-80 dated 27 July 2004 regarding the annexures to the application (from 'A' to 'N') regarding 14 cases is a documentary proof of this lapse. The allegations contained in the above stated annexures to the application have not been denied in the report of Director-General of Police and the annexure of this case which is annexure 'F' to the application has been dealt with by the DG of J&K in his above stated report at serial number 11. For readers convenience the last few lines from the Director-General's report (Appendix 19) are reproduced in verbatim:

> "the case was later completed and challaned and sent for obtaining necessary government sanction for launching prosecution against the accused persons which is still awaited."

This report is an admission on the part of the State Government for withholding the sanction for more than two years. This indicates that in an indirect way, the State itself was providing fuel to the ongoing militancy by not dealing with the case earnestly in accordance with law.

The second case discussed hereunder is Annexure 'H' from the annexed record of the application and in the report of the DG Appendix 19 has been listed as case Number 6. It is a sensational case of suicidal attack on the famous Raghunath Temple of Jammu city. The incident took place on 30 March 2002, and is registered under FIR Number 20/2002 U/S 302, 307, 153-A, 120-B, 121 RPC, 3 POTA, 2/3 PSSA, in Police Station City. In this incident some security personnel and pilgrims were killed besides the Holy idol of Lord Hanuman was defiled in firing. During the course of investigation two persons Muneer Hussain, S/o Dilavar Khan and Sarfaraz, S/o Ataullah, residents of Surankot, district Poonch were arrested. The case is still under investigation. From the record of the TADA Court it is shown that accused Muneer Hussain on 17 March 2003 was detained for a period of 12 months under the provisions of the J&K Public Safety Act and the accused Sarfaraz Khan on 17 March 2003 was also detained by the government under the Preventive Detention (J&K Public Safety Act) for a period of six months. During this period Mufti Mohammad Sayeed was the Chief Minister and these accused persons were not even detained for a period of two years under the J&K Public Safety Act—which is the maximum prescribed detention period. Normally, most of the militants are detained under the said Act for a period of two years and this leniency was also a part of 'Healing-Touch' policy? However, the national newspaper *Hindustan Times* in its issue of October 31, 2006 has reported that the Principal Sessions Judge, Jammu acquitted the accused and in this case 11 people were killed. The court has taken the investigating officers to task by stating, "there were 84 witnesses in support of the charge-sheet, there was not an iota of evidence in their statements against the accused." Further more, the additional observations were made by the judge, "that there was sufficient material in the file, in the statements of Investigating Officers and the case diaries dated April 14, 2002 against Varinder Sharma from whom a huge quantity of arms and ammunition was recovered but it is astonishing to find that he had not at all been arrayed as accused in the present case. The judge had issued notice to the Investigating Officers to explain why Sharma was not made one of the accused."

The third case relates to Annexure 'E' in the application (before NHRC) and has been replied by the DG J&K in his report (Appendix 19) under serial Number 7. This case was registered under FIR Number 102/2002 in Police Station Pacca Danga, Jammu for the infractions of the provisions of Sections 3, 4, 5, 6 of POTA. There were six accused who were arrested by the police and accused number 1 was Zulfukar Ali Raina (code) Abu Zahad alias Mir Hussain alias Iqbal, S/o Mohd Yaseen, resident of Sansara Goraya Gujranwala, Pakistan. The remaining five accused are residents of the State of Jammu and Kashmir. Amongst them accused number 6 Sajjad Hussain is the son of a Senior Administrative Officer (of the rank of KAS in the Government of Jammu and Kashmir) and a resident of Mohalla Ustad in the city of Jammu. These accused had collected Arms and Ammunition/Explosives and raised terrorist funds to facilitate the terrorist acts particularly in the thickly populated areas of the Jammu city. They were arrested on 15 June 2002, and Mufti Mohammad **Sayeed** is responsible for not giving sanction for their prosecution. After the expiry of the period of six months the five accused who were the residents of the State of Jammu and Kashmir got themselves bailed out from TADA Court, Jammu.

The fourth case from Annexure 'C' of that application (before NHRC) stands replied by the DG J&K in his report under serial number 10 of Appendix 19. This case was registered on 23 December 2001 in Police Station Nowabad, Jammu city under FIR Number 222/2001 U/S 3/4/5 POTA, 4/5 ESA, 120-B RPC. The terrorists were travelling in a Gypsy towards Jammu city from Poonch area without displaying number plate of the vehicle because some of the accused travelling therein were police personnel. During search made by the police of that vehicle, five persons were found inside the vehicle and amongst them two were in police uniforms armed with one AK-47, one carbine and rest were civies. They were later on identified as (1) Mohd Latief Khan alias Qamar Ayoub, S/o Ghulam Rasool, R/o Sowgam, SPO of DPL, Kupwara; (2) Abdul Rahim Wani, S/o Amir-ud-Din, R/o Lolab Kupwara; (3) Bashir Ahmed Wani, SGCT DPL, Kupwara; (4) Malik Khan HC of 14 Battalion JKAP and (5) Mohd Tahir, S/o Sheikh Farman Ali, R/o Gujarat, Pakistan. From their search one hand grenade, one packet of RDX were recovered. Further investigation led to the recoveries at their instance of Rs 2,00,000 in Indian currency, two grenades, 3½ kg RDX and one electronic detonator from the bank of river Tawi. The record of the TADA Court reveals that accused number 1 Mohd Latief Khan alias Qamar Ayoob was shown as a resident of POJK area (district Mirpur) but the report of DG J&K shows him as a resident of Sowgam SPO of DPL Kupwara. The sanction for the prosecution of the accused was still awaited even after the expiry of a period of four years and eight months. After the expiry of the statutory period of six months all of them were granted bail by the TADA Court, Jammu. Accused number 2 Abdul Rahim Wani fought the elections to become a Member of the J&K Legislative Assembly on the ticket of PDP (political party) but was defeated. He is stated to be working as District President of PDP Kupwara (Kashmir). This is a matter of great concern as how some of these dangerous militants were allowed to work in the police force and remained as activists of PDP. Furthermore, it is also amazing how they were being shielded by the ruling masters for a period of about one decade. Both Dr Farooq Abdullah and Mufti Mohammad Sayeed are answerable for such type of subversion of law in favour of the terrorists.

The fifth case from Annexure 'K' of the application at Serial Number 14 of Appendix 19 relates to the abduction of the members of Village Defence Committee—Bishan Dass, Bishan Lal, Hoshiar Singh, Rattan Singh and Daya Ram. The case was registered under FIR number 41/2001 U/S 3/4 POTA Police Station Bani district Kathua. The militants had killed Daya Ram, one of the abducted persons. After the completion of the investigation offences falling U/S 364, 302, 120-B CrPC, read with Sections 7/25 Arms Act were added in the challan. In this case the accused had confessed their guilt and under the TADA Act it was sufficient evidence to convict them. The report of DG (J&K Police) reveals at serial number 14 that till date the sanction for the prosecution of the accused has not been granted even after the expiry of a period of more than four years and nine months at the material time when the record was scrutinized. Both Dr Farooq Abdullah and Mufti Mohammad Sayeed are answerable to the nation?

The sixth case mentioned herein is from Annexure 'G' to the application and relates to the recovery of arms and ammunition from the militant Surinder Singh alias Fouji, S/o Hardeet Singh, R/o Ward Number 1, Udhampur. Case was registered against him under FIR Number 111/02 U/S 4/5 ESA, 3/4/5 POTA, 7/25 Arms Act in Police Station Gandhi Nagar, Jammu. He was an activist of Khalistan Zindabad Force (a militant organisation). The Director-General of Police in his report in question has covered this case at serial number 12 and stated that challan has been completed against him but could not be filed in the court because of want of requisite sanction under law. He was arrested on 7 April 2002 and bail was granted to him by the TADA Court, Jammu on 7 October 2002. While remaining on bail he joined the PDP political party and became its District President.

Note: The remaining eight cases which also form the annexures of the application are equally important and the readers of this book can know about them from the perusal of Appendix 19. This report itself is an eye opener to establish that militants enjoy political patronage at the cost of national security. The spilling of blood of the victims of militancy and the gaping, moaning and wailing of their dependants are irrelevant considerations for the people who are at the helm of the affairs to rule the State. In the opinion of the writer of this book as a custodian and protector of the Human Rights violations, it was expected from the NHRC that speedy justice should also have been done in these fourteen cases in the same manner as it was done in the Best Bakery case and other four cases of Gujarat already discussed above. The Chairman of the Commission was Justice AS Anand who is a native of J&K State and remained a judge and then Chief Justice for 14 years in the State of J&K. After that, finally he retired as Chief Justice of India and previous NDA Government had appointed him the Chairman of National Human Rights Commission (NHRC). His tenure as a judge of the J&K High Court has been discussed in this book at pages 298-300. The writer of this book applied under RTI Act 2005 before the Public Information Officer of the National Human Rights Commission to elicit authentic information regarding the decision of above stated petition Number 91/09/2003-04. The application was registered under RC Number 16(1) EIO/2005 (RTI) 169 dated 17 December 2013 and accordingly replied by the Assistant Registrar (M-1) (by Mukesh) under his signatures dated 23 December 2013. The information provided is reproduced:

> "In this connection, it is submitted that as per record available with the Commission in its Complaint Management System, the

Commission took cognizance in case Number 91/9/2003-2004 on 24 September 2003. The case was closed on 17 November 2006. Since the case file has been weeded out as per procedure adopted by the Commission. Copies of orders sought for by the applicant cannot be provided."

The citizens of the country would draw necessary inference themselves from the above authentic record how terrorism is being combated in this country where the victims of local communal riots get preferential treatment over the human rights and Fundamental Rights of the victims of militancy both civilians as well as of para military forces. The writer of this book cannot understand why the principles of Best Bakery Case and other four cases laid down by the National Human Rights Commission were not made applicable in this unfortunate part of the country qua all the specified fourteen cases of Ravindra Kumar applicant mentioned in his petition. This falls within grey area to be studied but in the absence of relevant record of the Commission nothing more can be said.

It is known to every well meaning Indian Citizen that communal riots of 2002 of Gujarat State were blown out of proportions by the Congress Party and its allies on the basis of established British Colonial policy, 'divide and rule' least caring for long range national and international interests of the country. The BJP government of Gujarat headed by Shri Narendra Modi was made the target of allegations that the Chief Minister intentionally had become an idle spectator of all round destruction and mayhem. Those propagandists on the basis of vote-bank policy turned a blind eye to disclose the true genesis of those riots which purposely had been side tracked to let remain buried in the thick layers of mystery for the sake of religious and emotional black mailing and thereby increasing the number of vote bank for all times to come. To some extent, that policy yielded result in their favour but ultimately they have lost the ground as being exposed because truth has surfaced in the results of recent elections of 2014.

On 27 February 2002 Sabarmati Express train coming from Ayodhaya was brutally attacked by anti-nationals. Only those bogies of the train were attacked where Hindu pilgrims and religious workers were seated. They were returning to their homes after attending religious ceremonies at the site of demolished Babri Masjid at Ayodhaya. The manner in which the fire broke out rapidly is a telling circumstance for inferring that either highly combustible material had been already collected inside the bogies or it was stocked on the spot in such a huge quantity that when used instantly the chances of survival of the victims would be minimum. As a result of this pre-planned terrorist act, 25 women, 25 children and nine male members were burnt alive in those bogies. In reaction, there was retaliation from the side of members of the majority community as a result thereof 790 members of the minority community lost their lives in the whole State of Gujarat. In those riots 254 members of the majority community had also suffered casualties. Under those unprecedented pressing circumstances the newly established Government of Shri Narendra Modi succeeded in quelling the riots effectively and within 2-3 days the normal law and order position was restored. It is most noteworthy that in Gujarat there has not re-occurred any such unfortunate incident till date despite provocation after notorious terrorist attack on the world famous Akshardham Temple and other stray cases of terrorism. All the cases regarding rioting were registered in the concerned Police Stations and law was set in motion without any delay. The result was that some rioters have been convicted and sentenced by the concerned Courts including a lady who was then a minister in the Gujarat Government. All efforts were made by the political opponents belonging to UPA Government that Chief Minister must get implicated as an accused in some cases. All such fiendish intrigues fell flat like a house of cards at the anvil of judicial scrutiny made by the concerned Courts of law at different hierarchies in the country.

In contrast, the hapless and helpless patriot inhabitants of the State of Jammu and Kashmir belonging to both the communities have suffered more bloodshed and destruction of properties for decades together at the hands of anti-nationals than the victims of the communal riots of Gujarat State. The most unfortunate aspect of prevailing affairs in the country is that not even once anybody on behalf of UPA Government or other human rights activists or any such organization ever raised their voice of conscience to speak the truth in favour of the victims in the State of Jammu and Kashmir and resultant failure of the government to up-hold the rule of law. On the contrary, on some suitable occasions the concerned Chief Ministers of the State are found singing the songs of murder of democracy in the State of Gujarat for the alleged murders of the members of the minority community. In this book an honest attempt has been made to give true and possible account of some of the misdeeds on the part of the rulers of the State where they for their political benefits have extended a helping hand to save the known culprits of the crimes perpetuated against the innocent victims belonging to all segments of the society. List of above stated fourteen cases provides cogent and convincing proof. All the victims belonged to the minority Hindu community of the

State inclusive of slain members of the army and security forces as well as well as their family members. The attached record contains the names of the known culprits. Some of them are even police personnel. They had used police vehicle to carry the militants and arms and ammunition but in the concerned Court they could not be convicted because of legal infirmities purposely allowed to be crept in the record. These facts would send shock waves down to the spine of every citizen of the country who is concerned with human lives values, equality before law and upholding the constitutional duties by the State functionaries. The record itself tells a tale how two Chief Ministers, Dr. Farooq Abdullah and Syed Mohammad Mufti have failed to discharge their constitutional duties. It is a fact that they too have issued statements against Gujarat Chief Minister by making allegations that he had protected the rioters. Both of the above stated Chief Ministers have held the offices of Chief Minister respectively with the support of coalition partner Congress which too had also its representation in sufficient numbers in the respective Cabinets. It has appeared that for political gains or lack of courage in these cases the sanctions for the prosecution of accused were withheld for years together. The dominant purpose was to enable the accused to secure bails from the concerned courts and move freely in the civil society. Under these circumstances, how any witness could depose against accused in a court of law. It has also come out from the record that some accused were later on offered important posts in a particular political organization. This aspect has already been discussed hereinabove with full particulars. Not only that, the cases were also not properly pursued before the concerned Court/ Courts. At the cost of repetition it is stated that in FIR No. 41/2001 of Police Station Bani, District Kathua which has already been discussed above, the accused had been booked under the TADA Act also and they had made confession for the murder of victim Daya Ram. That confession was sufficient to award conviction and sentence. The concerned Chief Ministers are answerable to the citizens of the country how it has not happened. Likewise, how a dreaded militant by the name of Azhar-ul-Ameen could remain without trial in the Jail for sufficient long time and could secure his freedom in exchange of the release of hijacked passengers of the Indian Airlines plane in Kandhar (Afghanistan). For the security of the nation and good governance, the accused of militancy related cases require precedent for close watch and guidance from the side of State than the stray cases of riots. This does not mean that riots should not be taken seriously. Equally they require to be checked and guilty punished with heavy hands. Militancy has a direct relation with the ongoing proxy war which was started in 1990.

Let it be known to everybody that history is not a blind goddess and it also does not forgive the blindness of others. In the administration of criminal justice it is said that truth always adheres while falsehood falls apart. The crimes cannot be buried permanently as at proper stage it raises its head even from the grave. The history has given its verdict of innocence in favour of Shri Narendra Modi through the medium of Courts, a fact which has been fortified by the citizens of the country who really have the sovereign power under the Constitution in the verdict given by them in the Parliamentary elections of 2014. It is also embedded in the national emblem that, "Satyamev Jayate" and on this parable the edifice of this book is based.

Another false propaganda which has not yet died down fully requires attention of the public at large so that falsehood should not prevail over truth. The detractors of Shri Narendra Modi frequently were heard in the media that Chief Minister intentionally had shirked to appoint a Lokayukta in his State due to lurking fear of getting exposed. False allegations were made for years together regarding the alleged distribution of State largesses in favour of some big Corporate Houses. The writer of this book shall be failing in his moral duty in case from his personal knowledge he does not spill the beans in favour of truth without fear, favour or ill will through the medium of this Book. It is universally recognized that speaking lie is a sin. Equally suppressing the truth to counter it amounts to the commission of same sin. Unfortunately, the writer of this book could not get any proper platform to rebut this lie openly to the public because going directly to the press goes against the professional ethics of a Judge. The writer of this book has studied in Law College, Ahmadabad where his elder first cousin had a shop in the locality of Navrangpora. He obtained Law Degree from Gujarat University in 1961. Some of his acquaintances of the College days, from the civil society had developed friendship for having same mental wave length on social and political views concerning the country. Some class-mates have occupied high positions in Government services, Judiciary, Politics and business. One class fellow retired as Senior Judge of the Gujarat High Court. From some sources the Chief Minister Shri Narendra Modi may have got information about my reputation, integrity and judicial disposition while discharging the judicial functions in the most sensitive State of Jammu and Kashmir. He found the writer of this book suitable to be appointed as Lokayukta in his Gujarat State. Somewhere, in 2003 the process had started when the writer of this book already stood retired as a Judge of High Court in 2001. The Government of Gujarat through official channel had obtained the requisite information about service record of the writer of this book from the J&K High Court. Incidentally, the ex-Chief Justice of the J&K High Court Shri Bhawani Singh, who was firstly transferred as Chief Justice from J&K High Court to Madhya Pradesh High Court and after some time from that High Court to Gujarat High Court. During that time, he had taken over the charge as Chief Justice of Gujarat High Court. The Chief Justice Bhawani Singh's relations with the writer of this book had strained because he was always found adopting an approach to keep the State Government and the high ranking bureaucrats in good humour on his right side at the cost of dignity, honour and prestige of the institution, least caring for his own status as a Chief Justice. This assertion finds support from the documentary evidence recorded in Chapter 25 "Role of Judiciary" in this book, as well as discussion made in this book at pages 303 and 304 supported by Appendix 13.

Some professional sycophants may have succeeded in spoiling the relations of the writer of this book with Shri Bhawani Singh for their own advantage. They may have misled him that the writer of this book had been instrumental in getting him transferred from J&K High Court the fact which is totally wrong and divorced from truth. In the opinion of the writer of this book he may have nourished ill-will in his heart and in retribution did not allow the name of the writer of this book cleared for the proposed appointment as under law his opinion had primacy being one of the Members of the Selection Committee for the appointment of Lokayukta. The information had percolated to the writer of this book from a very important reliable source during 2004 on his visit to Gujarat Bhawan, New Delhi while accompanied by a politician friend on a social visit there. The controversy of appointment of Lokayukta remained alive for pretty long time because in the absence of cogent, reasonable and convincing cause; the Government still retains its power to get the matter verified. During this process, a new Governor of the Gujarat State was appointed. With the passage of time, it turned out that the Governor had her own private agenda and she directly started meddling in the appointment of Lokayukta of her choice. She excluded the role of Government and herself got appointed a Judge as Lokayukta, but the Government could not swallow such a move. The result was that there was a controversy which landed in litigation and all the rest is a matter of history. Thank God, now the matter has been set at rest after the appointment of new Lokayukta of course by following the proper procedure. Chief Justice Bhawani Singh after his retirement from Gujarat High Court immediately was appointed against the vacant post of the Chairman of the Human

Rights Commission in his native State of Himachal Pradesh, where the Congress Government was in Power. At the end I may state that I shall not be fair to my conscience to record my gratitude for Mr Bhawani Singh who had a magnanimous heart to help everybody. He had not created any hurdle in recommending my confirmation from Additional Judge to Permanent Judge at the initial stage. I have no ill-will or grudge against him.

CHAPTER 25

Role of Judiciary

(Sample Cases)

It has already been stated in this book that, "when a judge quails justice wails." In some cases, according to the view of the writer of this book some judges apparently seem to have failed in their duty to uphold the rule of law. This erosion may have happened either because of ideological affinity with jehadi elements or fear of gun or for some other reasons. The judgements given below speak for themselves.

Case Number 1

In the High Court of Jammu and Kashmir at Srinagar.

Name of the Judge: Hon'ble Justice GD Sharma

Civil Revision Numbers 51/1997 and 69/1997 decided on 10 August 2000

Title of the Case: MM Khajuria (Petitioner) *vs* Abdul Rashid Rather, constable, J&K Police (Respondent).

(The case is reported in the law journal (2001) 1 *J&K Law Reporter*, p. 342.)

The facts of this case are that petitioner MM Khajuria while posted as Director-General of J&K Police vide order number 1012 of 1985 dated 20 September 1985 transferred the respondent constable Abdul Rashid Rather Number 366/CID from CID range Srinagar to Jammu range with immediate effect. The transfer was made on the reports that respondent was an important activist of a militant organisation and was promoting the subversive activities. In the order of transfer the Deputy Inspector General of Police Jammu range was directed by the petitioner herein (MM Khajuria) that the constable, "be posted in the area where there is not a large Muslim population and watch his activities." When this Order was passed the respondent was on leave which expired on 26 September 1985 and after its expiry he did not join the duty and sent a telegram to his superior officer to extend the leave by two months as he was sick. After the expiry of two months period, he again telegraphically applied for the extension of leave by four months. His superior officer vide his Order Number 20 of 1986 dated February 20, 1986 placed him under suspension with effect from September 27, 1985. The order of suspension was challenged by the respondent by filing writ petition in the High Court at Srinagar. Vide Order dated March 18, 1986; the court directed the petitioner to pay him the subsistence allowance and a direction was also given to the DIG Range Jammu not to implement the direction given in the transfer order. After the passing of these interim orders by the court, the petitioner cancelled the transfer order of the respondent (herein) vide his Order Number 293 of 1986 dated 5 March 1986.

The respondent felt his pride hurt because of the direction in his transfer order which according to him was maliciously given by the petitioner herein. After giving notice under Section 80 CPC respondent herein filed the suit against his person (petitioner herein) claiming token damages to the tune of Rs 50,000 (Rupees fifty thousand). In the written statement the petitioner herein had mainly taken the pleas that the order of transfer was issued in the interest of administration and in the discharge of sovereign functions of the State and that the State was also a necessary party. Nine issues were framed in the case. The petitioner herein retired in 1989 and thereafter, there was a steep rise in militancy and militant related activities. The public prosecutor also stopped pursuing the case and on 7 February 1991 petitioner was proceeded ex-parte. The ex-parte arguments were heard by the presiding judge (third Additional District Judge, Srinagar) but he could not announce the judgement on account of his transfer. The respondent herein made an application before the Principal District Judge, Srinagar for the transfer of the case to some other court who without giving any notice to the petitioner (which was the requirement of law) in hot haste transferred the case from the file of third Additional District Judge, Srinagar to the court of Additional District Judge Srinagar who received the record of the case on the third day from the date of passing of the transfer order. This shows that the respondent who at that time was merely a constable could take the case of the record from one court to another within two days time. The Additional District Judge Srinagar even without hearing the arguments of the respondent (constable) straightaway adjourned the case for judgement on 29 May 1991 and it was announced on the same day.

A decree in the sum of Rs 50,000 along with costs was passed against the petitioner and when this decree was put to execution he (petitioner MM Khajuria) came to know when the number of his pension account was attached by the court. Thereafter, the petitioner filed the above stated civil revision petitions which were decided by the writer of this book after hearing the arguments of the counsel of the parties. The revision petitions were allowed and the order of the trial judge was set aside. The conduct of the judge was censured and because of the strictures passed in the judgement the judge was denied two years extension in service after attaining the age of 58 years by the full court in the administrative decision taken by it.

-sd-

Hon'ble Justice GD Sharma

Case Number 2

In the High Court of Jammu and Kashmir at Srinagar.

LPA NUMBER 08/9, Date of decision—30 July 1999

Title of the Case: State of Jammu and Kashmir *vs* HGC Abdul Rashid Rather

Name of the Judges: Bhawani Singh, Chief Justice and Syed Bashir-ud-Din, Judge

Constable Abdul Rashid Rather (respondent of above stated case number 1) had also filed the writ petition seeking from the court direction to the respondents therein (State and Others) to give him the same treatment which was given to his colleague constable Hamid Ullah Dar as his seniority was higher than him in the order of appointment as constables (government order number 689 of 1978 dated July 4, 1978). That government vide Order Number Home-202 Police dated April 1, 1987 appointed Hamid Ullah Dar as Sub-Inspector of police in relaxation of Recruitment Rules against direct quota vacancy. This order was passed with a rider that he (Dar) should have fulfilled educational, physical and age standards as laid down in the police rules for appointment of Sub-Inspectors. The petitioner had sought from the court the same treatment which was given to Hamid Ullah Dar. The learned single judge in the interim direction had directed the respondents therein to consider the case of the petitioner (Abdul Rashid Rather) and give him the same treatment. In the final order passed by the learned single judge the same relief was reiterated, i.e. to accord the same treatment to the petitioner also.

The State challenged the order of the single judge in this LPA and in the memorandum of appeal factual and legal pleas were taken to the effect that respondent herein (Abdul Rashid Rather) could not be given the same treatment because he did not fulfil the educational and other relevant requirements as laid down in the Police Rules for appointment of Sub-Inspectors. It was also pleaded that promotions cannot be given on humanitarian approach/grounds. There were some other objections which need not to be mentioned herein.

The Division Bench which was presided over by the Chief Justice himself without waiting or securing the presence of the government advocate decided the appeal on merits by recording the presence of the advocate of the respondent therein and performa respondent. The judgement appears to be not in consonance with law. The first patent legal infirmity is that in the absence of the counsel of the appellant (State) the LPA could not be decided on merits and under law the LPA could only be dismissed for non-prosecution. The second legal defect from which the judgement suffers is that an appeal cannot be decided without adjudicating upon the factual and legal points agitated in the memo of appeal. The judgement does not deal with any of the grounds which were taken in the memo of appeal. The respondent herein whose integrity was doubtful as being anti-national in the eyes of the DGP in 1985 succeeded in getting undue promotion up to the level of Sub-Inspector with the aid of High Court and at the end of 2000 he had become Inspector. It is not known why the State did not challenge this patent illegal judgement in the Hon'ble Supreme Court by filing SLP?

Case Number 3

In the High Court of Jammu and Kashmir at Srinagar

Present: Hon'ble Bhawani Singh J and Hon'ble MY Kawoosa J
LPA Nos: 72/87 and 68/95
Title: Rias Ahmed Gazi *vs* State of J&K and Ors
Syedan Shafi *vs* State of J&K and Ors
(Reported in SLJ, 1997, page 179)

The facts of these LPA's are that the appellants who were Public servants and serving in different departments were dismissed by the government because they were a threat to the security of the State and both the orders of termination are given below:

Governor of Jammu and Kashmir, Civil Secretariat, General Department.
Subject: Termination of the service of government servant in the interest of security of the State. Government Order Number 1586 of GD of 1985 Dated 15.10.1985.

Whereas the Governor is satisfied that in the interest of the security of the State, it is not expedient to hold an inquiry in the matter.

Now, therefore, in exercise of the powers conferred under Clause C of the proviso to Sub-Section (2) of Section 126 of the Constitution of J&K, the Governor dismiss Rayeez Ahmad Gazi, S/o Shamas-ud-Din, R/o Nawabazar, Srinagar working as Tracer/JA Civil Investigation and Design Wing, J&K Srinagar from the Civil Services of the State.

By order of the Governor.
Sd/-
Commissioner/Secretary to Government
General Department."

Similarly the order of termination passed against Syedan Shafi is quoted hereunder:

"Government of Jammu and Kashmir General Administration Department.

Subject: Dismissal from government service, Government Order Number 538-GAD of 1993 dated 25 June 1993.

Whereas the Governor is satisfied in terms of Proviso (c) of Sub-Section 2 of Section 126 of the J&K Constitution, that it is not expedient in the interest of security of the State to hold an enquiry against Syedan Shafi, Block Development Officer, Shahabad for various acts of commission and omission constituting misconduct in his capacity as Block Development Officer.

Now, therefore, in exercise of the powers under Section 126 of the J&K Constitution vested in the Governor, the said Syedan Shafi is dismissed from service.

By order of the Governor.
Sd/-
Secretary to Government
General Administration Department"

The appellant Riaz Ahmed of the above said (LPA Number 72/87) according to the CID reports had links with secessionist organisation, People's League and other unlawful associations whose aims and objects were to secede the State of Jammu and Kashmir from the Union of India and while indulging in these activities he was working as Junior Assistant/Tracer in the Designs Wing of the Power Development Department. He was also shown as a member of the secessionist organisation by the name of Islamic League and was alleged to have attended some meetings at Sopore. Then there were also allegations that he had participated in activities leading even to the use of explosives with a view to create disturbances and had been detained twice under the J&K Public Safety Act. Upon the commission of the above stated anti-national activities, the Chief Minister (Dr Farooq Abdullah) wrote a note that his actions were prejudicial to the security of the State and maintenance of public order. This recommendation was made to the Governor to take the legal action in accordance with law and the note accompanied a secret file which recited that he had attended some meetings of the secessionists and participated in anti-national activities. The Governor passed the above stated impugned order.

The allegations against the appellant Syedan Shafi of the above said LPA Number 68/95 are that he was working as a Block Development Officer in Rural Development Department in one of the blocks of the district Anantnag where huge amounts running into crores of rupees were embezzled by him along with other colleagues of the district and some other connected officers. There were also allegations that a portion of the embezzled amount was passed on to the terrorists to carry on the secessionist and violent activities. The services of the 14 officers including the appellant were terminated after the Governor was satisfied that their activities were anti-national and in the interest of the security of the State it was not expedient to hold an enquiry as contemplated by Article 311(2)(c) of the Indian Constitution and Section 126(2)(c) of the State Constitution. The appellant had challenged his order of dismissal in Writ Petition and the writ petition was dismissed by the single judge. Similarly, the dismissal order of his service which was challenged by above stated, Rias Ahmed in the writ petition was upheld and writ petition was dismissed. By this common judgement, both the LPA's (which were clubbed) were allowed and the orders of the learned single judge were set aside. The LPAs were heard by Chief Justice Bhawani Singh and Justice Mohammad Yasin Kawoosa. The learned judges have set aside the judgement of the learned single judge by appreciating the factual matrix of the cases and have found that the orders were passed on the basis of no material but on extraneous considerations. It appears very strange as it was not specifically mentioned in the impugned orders how the material was extraneous and not relevant to the security of the State. Furthermore, how it was not expedient to hold an enquiry in the interest of the security of the State. This judgement has been reported in Srinagar Law Journal 1997 at page 179. The decision of the Division Bench was challenged by the State in the Hon'ble Supreme Court by filing SLP but it is still a mystery why the cases were not contested and why SLP was allowed to be dismissed for non-prosecution. This judgement proved as a dose of panacea to cure all the sufferings of the anti-national public servants who were dismissed from service by the then Governor Jagmohan and his two successors General KV Krishna Rao and GC Saxena from the years 1990 to 1996 under Sub-Clause (2)(c) of Section 126 of the State Constitution read with Article 311(2)(c) of the Indian Constitution. According to a rough estimate anti-national public servants whose number had swelled up to hundreds got the benefit of this Division Bench Judgement. They got reinstatement in government jobs against their posts along with arrears of pay and attached perks.

The writer of this book personally is of the view that this was a very good case for the consideration of the Hon'ble Supreme Court in SLP in view of the law laid down by the Supreme Court in the Constitution Bench case of Union of India *vs* Tulsi Ram Patel (AIR 1985 SC 1416) and in the case of AK Koul *vs* Union of India (AIR 1995 SC, page 1403). In Tulsi Ram's case (Supra) the Supreme Court has held that in Clause (c) of Article 311 reasons are not to be recorded and that satisfaction has to be of the Governor. The courts have to see the existence of the material which could be a matter of satisfaction to the Governor to dispense with the enquiry. It has also been held that the satisfaction of the President or that of the Governor must therefore be with respect to the expediency or inexpediency of holding an enquiry in the interest of the security of the State. In AK Koul's case (Supra), the Supreme Court has again endorsed the view that the court can only review the order in case the satisfaction of the President or of the Governor is not based on circumstances which have a bearing on the security of the State. The Division Bench was under legal obligation to keep in mind the above stated legal parametres laid down by the Supreme Court and its findings had to be limited whether or not impugned orders of dismissal were vitiated by mala fides or were based on irrelevant considerations and that the material produced before the court by the State Government required the finding that prompt and urgent action was necessary and the holding of enquiry into the conduct of the each of the petitioners/appellants would not have been expedient in the interest of the security of the State. The requirement of natural justice in such a situation had to be tailored to safeguard public interest which must always outweigh every lessor interest. The learned Judge Mohammad Yaseen Kawsooa of the Division Bench who is the author of this judgement has admitted from the record produced by the State Government that it was found in the case of appellant Syedan Shafi, "funds have been misappropriated by the officers for their personal aggrandisement and for keeping up the militancy. Some officers, who are involved in the embezzlement, have nexus with the militancy which they want to keep up in view of the on going militancy in the district." The Constitution Bench ruling given in Tulsi Ram's case (Supra) clearly mandates, "that the Governor has not to record the reasons for his satisfaction and that the satisfaction has to be of the Governor." Justice Kawoosa in this judgement has stated, "merely, saying that the district is pro-militancy area and the misappropriation has been made for the personal aggrandisement and to keep up the militancy is not sufficient for the Governor to be satisfied for taking action under Section 126(2)(c) of the State Constitution." Chief Justice Bhawani Singh being the senior judge in the Division Bench concurred with him. This was a very good case for the consideration of the Hon'ble Supreme Court in SLP but the decision on merits was thwarted en route and this unusual course adopted by the concerned bureaucrats and politicians becomes a matter of concern for every patriot citizen of the country. A responsible and patriot government should again get the findings of this judgement tested on the legal touchstone by taking the appropriate matter in the Supreme Court because the militancy in the State was created and is being sustained mainly by some unscrupulous politicians and like-minded bureaucrats or other careerists.

Case Number 4

In the High Court of Jammu and Kashmir at Srinagar.

Cr. Acquittal Appeal Number 04/2000
State of J&K *vs* Niyaz Ahmed Sofi
Name of the Judges: 1. Hon'ble Justice GD Sharma
2. Hon'ble Justice Syed Bashir-ud-Din
Date of decision: 1 September 2000

Facts of the Case: The appellant in this case was a top ranking dreaded militant affiliated with secessionist organisation known as 'Ikhwan-ul-Muslimeen'. The deceased was a patriot police officer by the name of Ghulam Jeelani who in 1991 was posted as DySP in Police Station Nigeen (in the city of Srinagar). The prosecution case is that on 22 October 1991, the appellant/accused (Niyaz Ahmed Sofi) in the company of three dreaded militants Javid Ahmed Shalla @ Munna; Hilal Ahmed Baig (Chief Commander); and Israil Khan forced their entry in the office of the deceased located in the premises of the Police Station Nageen, Srinagar and attacked him with automatic weapons. Ghulam Geelani sustained fatal bullet injuries and breathed his last en route to the hospital. While fleeing from the scene of the occurrence the militants had taken away his service revolver. The crime and incident were registered as FIR Number 75/91 at Police Station Nageen. During the investigation, the police managed to apprehend only the appellant/

accused as his three above stated associates/accomplices were killed by the armed forces in different militancy related incidents.

The prosecution had listed twenty-two witnesses in the calendar of the witnesses and the challan (final report) was presented before the Learned Principal District and Sessions Judge, Srinagar who assigned the same for trial to the IVth Additional District and Sessions Judge, Srinagar. On 4 November 1999, the trial judge charged the accused for the Commission of offences falling under Sections 302, 307, 382 RPC read with Section 7/27 of the Arms Act. The concerned Prosecuting Officer (Addl Public Prosecutor) and the trial judge had entered into an unholy alliance of acquitting the appellant/accused which is evident from the fact that out of the twenty-two witnesses the trial judge fixed calendar for recording the evidence of only three witnesses figuring at serial number 2, 3 and 4 who belonged to lower strata of society and were cited only as chance witnesses of the occurrence. The trial of the case was concluded within fifty-seven days after the framing of the charges (charges were framed on 4 November 1999). The trial judge honourably acquitted the accused. It was also the legal duty of the prosecutor (Addl. Public Prosecutor) to get all the material witnesses examined but he also sided with the trial judge in closing the evidence. This was perhaps a first case of its peculiar nature in the judicial history of the State or it may be even in the whole country when the trial of a murder case was so speedily concluded after giving a go-by to the prescribed procedural law and the rules and the justice was buried. In the calendar of the witnesses Tanveer Jeelani who is the son of the deceased was also cited as an eye witness along with other six police personnel who were stated to be present on spot to have witnessed the occurrence while performing the duties but none of them was summoned to appear in the court either by the trial judge or by the Addl. Public Prosecutor to give evidence.

The appellant/State had filed the appeal against the order of acquittal which was pending for disposal. As luck would have it, during the intervening night of 11/12 April 2000, the accused was killed in an encounter within the territorial jurisdiction of Police Station Khanyar (Srinagar). After the death of the accused, the appeal stood abated and the result was that order of acquittal could not be interfered. Notwithstanding abatement of appeal, on examination of the record of the proceedings for the purpose of satisfying ourselves (the writer of this book and other bench judge Justice Syed Bashir-ud-Din) as to the correctness, legality or propriety of the order passed and the regularity of the proceedings, we (the court) found them illegal and perverse. The cause of justice had become casualty and the credibility of the judiciary was put at stake, therefore we (the court) treated and dealt with the matter in exercise of the superintendence/revisional powers of the court under Section 104 of the J&K State Constitution. After pointing out all the illegalities at page 7 of the judgement we (the court) had held: "the trial judge in charge of the trial of this case was required to conduct the proceedings in accordance with the mandates of the above referred provisions of law, rules made by this court as well as administrative instructions issued from time to time in the form of circulars that had to be adhered to. We (the court) notice with anguish that the trial judge, a District and Sessions Judge (Khwaja Mohammad Qasim) violated with immunity the prescribed Procedural Law (CrPC) and conveniently ignored the fundamentals of law. Statutory rules and orders were by-passed in this regard to the legal morality." Similarly at page 9 of the judgement we (the court) had observed as under, "In the instant case, justice has been buried at the altar of hurry, hurry and hurry least expected from a senior judge of the rank of District and Sessions Judge in a case where a police official—a DySP is killed in broad-day-light in a bizarre manner while sitting in his office. This is a premeditated murder of diabolical and fiendish nature. On a conspectus of the aforesaid discussion, we hold that the trial judge committed the illegalities and conducted grave irregularities and impropriety in these proceedings which are reprehensible leading to the miscarriage of justice. The object of revisional jurisdiction is to afford controlling and supervisory powers to correct illegal orders passed and set on course the trial and proceedings. In exercise of powers we set aside the proceedings taken by the court below. The trial judge is required to explain his conduct in the matter. The Registrar General is directed to call the explanation from the trial judge to be submitted within one month and place/the same along with a copy of this order on the personal file/Service record of this Judicial Officer for appropriate action. The Registrar General shall circulate copy of this order to all the Sessions Judges of the State for guidance."

Note: This judgement had some deterrent effect on those erring judges who were clandestinely helping the subversive elements in the State. The full court at the administrative side held the meeting and denied two years extension in service to the trial judge of this case when he had attained the age of 58 years.

Without any ill-will or rancour to anybody, and to uphold the dignity and honour of the Institution of this august High Court as an Institution where the writer of this book has discharged judicial functions for continuous forty years in different capacities right from the lowest rung, it would be a failure in discharging moral duty in case its erosion caused by some persons is not unfolded. From this case the conviction of the writer of this book is further fortified that virus of militancy had infected the judicial system from the roots up to the top. A strong sleeping cell seems to have been established in the Institution to render judicial help to the militants. The present case is one of the shining examples. When the judgement in the above said case was announced probably H Imtiyaz Hussain was the Registrar General of the High Court. The then concerned Registrar in the discharge of his judicial functions had circulated the judgment to all the District and Sessions Judges of the State to bring home the point that such type of judicial misconduct should not be repeated. The full court in its administrative meeting vide its decision number 527 dated 23 October 2002 denied the extension in service to the delinquent District Judge up to the age of 60 years. The aggrieved District and Sessions Judge (Mr Qasim) challenged the order of the High Court by filing SWP number 1315/2002. By the passage of time, H Imtiyaz Hussain was elevated as Judge of the J&K High Court. The petitioner was waiting for an opportune time for getting his writ petition decided in his favour from that judge because he is his close relation. He got the opportunity and ex-parte arguments were heard by Justice H Imtiyaz Hussain at a time when no body had appeared on behalf of the respondent High Court. The result was that writ petition was allowed and full courts administrative decision was quashed. The operative part of the judgment reads: "this petition is therefore allowed. The impugned order 527 dated 23 November 2002 denying benefit of two years to the petitioner is quashed and he shall be treated as having retired from service on attaining 60 years of age and shall be entitled to pay and allowances and also his pensionary benefits upon that basis." It is not understandable why the writ petition was allowed to be decided in an ex-parte manner. When the verdict was adverse why the order was not challenged in LPA? For the reasons best known to the then Registrar General and the Chief Justice although it was the duty of the then Registrar General of the High Court to contest the case in order to protect the dignity and honour of the High Court as an Institution.

Case Number 5

In the High Court of Jammu and Kashmir at Srinagar.

OWP Nos 221 to 224 and 227 of 1995; decided on 4 May 1996.
Reported in 1996 CR Law Journal 3006.
OWP Number 221/95
Title of the Case-Javid Ahmad Zargar and Ors, etc. Petitioners *vs* Attorney General of India and Ors Respondents.

OWP Number 222/95.

Showkat Ahmad Bakshi *vs* Attorney General of India and Ors.

OWP Number 223/95

Mohammad Salim Zargar *vs* Attorney General of India and Ors.

OWP Number 224/95

Mohammad Iqbal Gandroo *vs* Attorney General of India and Ors.

OWP Number 227/95

Rouf Rasool and Ors *vs* Attorney General of India and Ors.

Name of the Judges: 1. Hon'ble Justice VK Gupta
2. Hon'ble Justice GD Sharma

Facts of the case: The Central Government vide notification SO 551(E) dated 17th June 1995 issued by the Ministry of Home Affairs under Section 11(2) of the Terrorists and Disruptive Activities (Prevention) Act, 1987 (hereinafter to be referred as an Act) transferred pending cases stated therein from the Designated Court, Jammu (under the Act) to the Designated Court under the Act at Ajmer in the State of Rajasthan. All the accused were dreaded militants of top ranking category and were facing trials under POTA, Ranbir Penal Code, Arms Act etc. Some of the accused challenged the above stated notification through the medium of the above stated five writ petitions which were filed in the J&K High Court (Srinagar Wing) and the learned single judge (Justice Ali Mohd Mir) while entertaining them issued show cause notices to the respondents. Simultaneously, he by interim directions stayed the operation of the notification. Vide order dated 2nd August 1995. Also he referred the cases for disposal to a Division Bench in terms of rule 14(9) of the High Court rules. Some of the petitioners of those writ petitions were top ranking ideologues of on going militancy war including those who were exchanged for the release of the passengers of the hijacked Indian Airlines flight from Kathmandu to Kandhar (Afghanistan). The murderers of the Vice-Chancellor of the Kashmir University Mushir-ul-Haq and General Manager Harbans Lal Khera of the Hindustan Machine Tools, Srinagar, were also the petitioners. It shall be advantageous to reproduce the relevant text of the notification which reads as under:

New Delhi 17 June 1995.

SO 551(E): Whereas the Central Government is of the opinion that the situation prevailing in the State of Jammu and Kashmir is not conductive to a fair, impartial, or speedy trial, as there exists a grave risk to the safety of the accused, witnesses, public prosecutor and the judge of the Designated Court:

Whereas, the Attorney General of India moved motion for transfer of cases specified in the table below. The concurrence of the Chief Justice of India for such transfer, vide orders dated 4 January 1994 in motion numbers 305 and 307 of 1991 and order dated 6 January 1994 in motion numbers, 308, 309 and 310 of 1991. Now therefore, in exercise of the powers conferred by Sub-Section (2) of Section 11 of the Terrorist and Disruptive Activities (Prevention) Act, 1987 (28 of 1987) the Central Government with the concurrence of the Chief Justice of India hereby transfers the cases specified in the said table pending before the Designated Court at Jammu and Kashmir to the Designated Court at Ajmer in the State of Rajasthan."

The Chief Justice of the High Court had constituted the Division Bench comprising of Justice VK Gupta and the writer of the book. Justice Gupta had been elevated as Judge of the High Court from Jammu and Kashmir Lawyers' quota. On the basis of some grounds he was transferred from this High Court to Calcutta High Court and when this writ petition was at the hearing stage of the arguments, the rumours were floating thick and fast that he was under transfer. At this critical juncture Justice VK Gupta quashed the above stated notification of the Central Government while, the writer of this book gave a dissenting judgement, thereby, holding that the notification was valid in the eye of Law. The result of this conflicting judgment was that stay order granted by Justice Mir remained in operation and the trial of the cases as desired by the Central Government could not be held before Designated Court at Ajmer Rajasthan. The then Chief Justice Rama Krishna (of the State High Court) referred the matter to the third (1st Puisne) judge Justice Bhawani Singh who did not decide the matter and when he himself became the Chief Justice of the J&K High Court, he suo motu transferred the case to another judge who too delayed the decision. After considerable delay the Central Government itself withdrew the notification in question. The trial of the cases remained within the territorial jurisdiction of the TADA court Jammu. The result was that some of the prosecution witnesses were won over and the remaining out of fear to their lives turned hostile. It is a known fact that delay is always fatal to a prosecution case. After a time gap of about 23 years from the dates of commission of crimes not even one conviction could be secured. Some of the accused are found roaming free in the civil society. It is presumed that all the cases by now might have met their natural death. It is known to everybody that there was much electronic and print hype in the country about the Best Bakery

Case but not even a single feeble voice was ever heard regarding the trial and consequent acquittal of the accused of those cases. From this it stands proved that in this country militants are a special privileged class for the politicians, administration and media including the Legislature than the victims of militancy both civilians and personnel of armed forces. This can happen only in India and not elsewhere in any country.

The opinion of both the judges from the judgement is reproduced hereunder in brief: "**Per Gupta, J**—where the passing of Notification effecting transfer of pending cases from Jammu to Ajmer was based upon the situation of threat and perception prevailing at the relevant time and 5 years had lapsed from the date of initiation of motion to transfer the cases before the Chief Justice of India and the actual passing of Notification, the time-lag would give rise to a reasonable and bona fide belief in the minds of the accused petitioners, that the situation may have witnessed some changes where it might be possible to hold an impartial, fair and speedy trial at Jammu itself. The Central Government was therefore directed to re-examine the question with regard to the shifting of the trial as there was a possibility of emergence of some new facts which, on a fair assessment and equitable considerations, would bring a change in the entire perception of the Central Government. The concurrence of Chief Justice of India though imperative does not compel the government to pass any order if, for any other intervening causes, the Central Government even after obtaining the concurrence decides that there is no necessity of transferring any case. Therefore, the impugned notification would be liable to be quashed by reason of the time-lag of five years as aforesaid."

Per Sharma J: "Mere fact that the circumstances impelling the Central Government to transfer these cases to Ajmer having disappeared, the impugned notification does not perish. Whether or not those circumstances still exist and if exist to what extent, the High Court has no source or means to collect any evidence or material to justify the conclusion that such circumstances have ceased to exist. By striking down the notification on the ground of delay, the High Court would take away its right from the Central Government to re-assess the situation in the State and take a decision in regard to the trial of the cases in the State itself. Therefore, the impugned notification issued by the government with the concurrence of Hon'ble Chief Justice of India is still valid and cannot be quashed on any ground whatsoever."

Case Number 6

In the High Court of Jammu and Kashmir at Srinagar.

Criminal Revision Petition Number 21/98 Date of Decision: 10 September 1999.

Title of the Case

State of J&K, Through SP (Special Operations)	*vs*	1. Ab Majid Dar S/o Gh Rasool Dar R/o Majeed Bagh, Sanat Nagar, Srinagar. 2. Abdul Gani Lone. S/o Gh Ahmed Lone R/o Sanat Nagar, Srinagar.

Name of the Judge: Hon'ble Justice GD Sharma.

The facts of the case in brief are that Police Station Saddar Srinagar registered FIR Number 304/97 for the Commission of Offences falling Under Sections 121-A, 120-B and 212 RPC against above stated accused. Accused number 1 is a vegetable vendor and runs his shop in Sanat Nagar area of Srinagar city and is immediate neighbour of accused number 2 who was a senior leader of the secessionist organisation known as, 'J&K Hurriyat Conference', and that he had also close relations with Unlawful Secessionist Association known as 'Al-Barq'. (Note: Before the Assembly Elections of 2002 accused number 2 was liquidated by rival militants as according to them he had shunned the path of violence and wanted the return of peace in the State.) That in order to execute the secessional acts he (accused number 2) used to get secret monetary help from internal and external agencies who are hostile to the Union of India. He was also receiving the money through unlawful 'Hawala Transactions' and opened account number 191/2 in the name of accused number 1 in J&K Bank Limited Branch Sanat Nagar. At the diktates of accused number 2, accused number 1 used to frequently deposit and withdraw the money. The withdrawn money was being spent for the procurement of illegal arms, ammunition and explosive materials which were being distributed to concerned groups of militants for the purpose of committing the acts of violence and sabotage in the State and thus, threatening the integrity and security of the country. At the time of the seizure of the above stated account number by the police an amount of Rs 1 crore was found in it which was unaccounted money. The police after the investigation of the case presented the Challan before the Sessions Judge Budgam who on the basis of the prosecution evidence, at the initial stage vide his order dated 15 June 1998 discharged the accused on the basis that, "even the probability of existence of allegations prima facie justified by the material on record is not sufficient to charge the accused. He further held that there was no evidence to show that at any point of time any witness of the prosecution actually saw the accused number 1 Abdul Majid passing any money by cash or by cheque to the accused Abdul Gani Lone."

The State challenged the order of the Sessions Judge by filing this revision petition which was heard and decided by the writer of this book. The State had taken the plea that prosecution had seized a fixed deposit receipt from the possession of accused number 1 (Abdul Majid Dar) which had been given to him by accused Abdul Gani Lone. That there was direct evidence of three eye witnesses implicating the accused with the crimes and that the Sessions Judge had ignored that vital piece of evidence. The Sessions Judge had also ignored the legal aspects of the case that in order to constitute a conspiracy it is not necessary that any act or illegal omission shall take place in pursuance thereof. There was evidence that militants frequently used to visit the house of accused number 2 who had been harbouring them.

From the record and after hearing the submissions of MI Qadri, Senior Additional Advocate-General and SR Hussain, advocate of the accused it was found that prosecuting agency had not observed the legal requirement of getting the prior sanction for prosecution from the State Government as was mandated under Section 196 CrPC and a legal bar had been created even for the court to take cognizance of the alleged Commission of the Offences falling Under Sections 121 and 121-A RPC. The writer of this book had held in the order that: "the lapse which has been committed on its face does not appear to be honest and bona fide." After quashing the proceedings, the writer of this book had directed the Chief Secretary and the Director-General of Police to file a complaint against the accused as is required under law after obtaining the prior sanction for the prosecution in terms of Section 196 CrPC (in case the government decides so). An offence falling under Section 121-A RPC (waging war against the State) is of very serious nature and the prosecution in a ham handed manner has dealt with this case. All the concerned officials who under law were associated with the prosecution of this case were required to explain how they had been maladroiting by giving a go-by to the enabling provisions of Section 196 CrPC. The legal wrong could only be jettisoned by ordering an enquiry by top brass of administration and suitable follow up action, by them. After making the above stated, observations the writer of this book in the concluding para of the order had observed:

> "This court has a constitutional duty to uphold the rule of law and not to allow the trial of serious cases involving the security of the

State being scuttled or subverted en route. It is flabbergasting to note how the higher echelons in the concerned hierarchy had failed to give Nelson's touch to the trial of the case when in such like sensitive case supervision was required from the initial stage till the logical conclusion. In this view of the matter, the Chief Secretary of the State is required to constitute a committee consisting of himself, Additional Chief Secretary (Home) and Director-General of Police, to go into all the aspects of the case and submit their report in the registry within four months. The Registrar (Judicial) shall put up the report before this bench for perusal. The record of the trial court be returned."

Note: The Committee submitted its report under their Number PSH/HOME/99/370-ISA dated 28.12.1999 to the Registrar (Judicial), High Court of Jammu and Kashmir at Srinagar. The concluding para of the report is reproduced hereunder:

> "The Committee all the same regretted that such a serious lapse should have occurred in such an elementary matter of such an important case. The Committee, therefore, decided that the DGP would issue a stiff warning to each of the officers connected with investigation and prosecution of this case to be careful in future. DGP was also requested to issue instructions to the District Police and the Crime Branch to take notice of this lapse and the court's observations thereon and take such measures as may be necessary to prevent its recurrence.

Principle Secretary (Home)	Director-General of Police	Chief Secretary

Note: It is not known what subsequent action had been taken by the government in this case.

Case Number 7

In the High Court of Jammu and Kashmir at Srinagar.

Habeas Corpus Petition number 48/2000 Date of Decision: 5 September 2000.

Title of the Case.

Showkat Ahmed Bakshi *vs* State and Others.

Name of the Judge: Hon'ble Justice GD Sharma.

Facts: Showkat Ahmed Bakshi is a prominent leader and ideologue of secessionist association JKLF. On 17 January 2000, the Divisional

Commissioner Kashmir vide his order Number DMS/PSA/155 passed under Section 8 of the J&K Public Safety Act detained him for a period of 24 months. Besides other anti-national activities detailed in the record accompanying the detention order it was also attributed to him in his dossier that he being lodged in Central Jail Srinagar, was still carrying on anti-national activities and had hatched a criminal conspiracy to step up militant activities. He had been sending messages to different militant organisations and militants to step up anti-national activities. He had been facing trial before the Additional Designated TADA Court, Srinagar and there was likelihood of his being released on bail. The detaining authority (Divisional Commissioner, Kashmir) had filed their counter in the court on 14 June 2000 and he was ignorant about the representation made by the detenue to the government dated 16 March 2000, which stood sent through registered-post in the name of the Chief Secretary on 22 March 2000. In the counter, the detaining authority (Divisional Commissioner Kashmir) had taken the plea that detenue was asked to make a representation to the government but he had failed to do so which was a wrong statement of fact.

While quashing the detention order, the writer of this book had observed in the concluding para of the judgement:

> "The detenue is not an ordinary gun wielding militant but on the basis of the grounds of detention an ideologue of JKLF outlawed organisation. His alleged activities are of the nature of causing wider ramifications to threaten the security of the State. He has been in custody since 1990 facing trial for heinous crimes. It was required from the Chief Secretary to keep a close watch on his detention and the detaining authority should have acted in tandem under his instructions and guidance. The ignorance shown by Respondent number 2 (Divisional Commissioner, Kashmir) about the representation in question in the counter speaks volumes how the matters concerning the security of the State are dealt with casually from the top slot of the administration hierarchy down to the lowest concerned rung. Such a display of ostrich syndrome is reprehensible and it sends shivers down to the spine of every body who is concerned with the security of the State and upholding the rule of Law. A pragmatic and result oriented approach in dealing with such matters is the need of the hour."

While closing up this chapter the writer of this book deems it necessary to make a mention of the fact that the list of the above stated cases is only a tip of the iceberg. There are some cases of similar nature where a travesty of justice has also been done but because of the paucity of space they cannot be mentioned here. Undoubtedly, there are many black sheeps in every pillar of the government who for their personal monetary, political and ideological considerations or getting post-retiral plump employments have sold their conscience thereby allowing the subversive elements and inimical foreign forces to raise their ugly heads for endangering the security of the State. The Rule of Law has become the main casualty. As a last instance during Governor's rule hundreds of police personnel who had become stooges in the hands of subversive elements and were dismissed from service by invoking Section 126(2)(c) of the State Constitution read with Article 311 of the Constitution of India and as soon as Dr Farooq Abdullah became the Chief Minister in 1996 started winning their favours and succeeded to get many reinstated in the government job. The government at first instance had recommended the reinstatement of those dismissed police personnel numbering between 200 to 300 to be absorbed again in police force but the then Governor GC Saxena returned the file with some observations. But the second time, their file reached to the Governor with a renewed recommendation to get them absorbed in the J&K Fire Brigade Services and ultimately they have been absorbed in that service. The above discussed Syedan Shafi's Division Bench ruling has helped such elements a lot to find an entry again in the government services. About 700 dismissed teachers of the banned subversive association Falah-e-Aam Trust (which organization already has been discussed in details in this book) have been absorbed as teachers in government schools. The readers themselves can draw the requisite inference as how useful they might have proved in fanning the anti-national ideology of militancy at the cost of pay drawn from the Government treasury where the funds pour in by the Central aid which is collected from the innocent tax payers of the whole country.

CHAPTER 26

Causes for Spreading the Militancy

(1) Sheikh Abdullah's National Conference was the most powerful and organized political party in the State at the time of Pakistan's invasion in 1947 and it became an instrument to ratify the accession of the State with Union of India made by the sole authority Maharaja Hari Singh. Initially, Maharaja Hari Singh was indecisive to accede to the Union of India before Pakistan could make an armed aggression with the help of tribesmen of its own areas supported by regular army. The first opportunity which was available to the Maharaja Hari Singh was that he should have Acceded to Union of India when the Boundary Commission's Report was made public on August 17, 1947 as at that time, it was officially known that State had been connected with plane territory of India, touching the border of tehsil Pathankot. Maharaja Hari Singh had his own compulsions which have been discussed in details in this book as Pandit Nehru was outrightly in favour of giving the absolute power in the hands of Sheikh Abdullah. As a human being Maharaja had been resisting it by trying to protect his status to the extent of a model which had been guaranteed to the Maharaja of Mysore State. Had Government of India instead of following the political policy of Congress party strictly followed the relevant law of land Indian Independence Act of 1947 read with Government of India Act of 1935 there would have arisen no occasion to dilute the sovereign authority of the Maharaja. This topic already stands discussed in details in this book. National Conference as a regional party too had an inimical powerful political force led by Moulvi Yousuf Shah in the Kashmir Valley and many other splinter groups who were tooth and nail against the accession. Sheikh's National

Conference was known as, 'Sher (lion) Party' whereas; Moulvi Yousuf's party was known as 'Bakra (goat) Party'. There used to be often violent clashes between the activists of both these parties. In his book *Struggle for Freedom in Kashmir*, PN Bazaz, has stated that there were sixteen political parties on the day of accession, i.e. on October 26, 1947 espousing different political ideologies in the State. He further has stated that "from 1947 to 1953 more than ten thousand people belonging to different parties had been consigned to prisons in the Valley."

Sheikh's ambition at the behest of imperialist countries to create an Independent Sheikhdom for himself were thwarted by the leadership of Delhi and he was removed as Private Minister by his own Cabinet colleagues. His selected members who had won the election in 1951 of the Constituent Assembly of the State had disowned him as their leader. Thereafter, he started treating India as an enemy country and stuck to this position for 22 years. He preached for full 22 years to all his followers that Kashmiris have been deceived by India. He changed his stand in 1975 (after Indira-Sheikh Accord) and came back to the national mainstream but in the inner layers of his mind he dreamt to create the State as a hereditary fiefdom for himself and for his family and was opposed to democratic rule. This fact is borne out from the fact how mercilessly he clipped the wings of his life-long trusted lieutenant Mirza Afzal Beg to pave the way of smooth succession of Chief Minister's 'Gaddi' in favour of his inexperienced son Dr Farooq Abdullah. The subsequent events of his rule have already been discussed in this book and because of ineffective governance in the State as well as in the Centre, hostile neighbouring country took full advantage to step up external propaganda to poison the minds of the Kashmiri masses and giving them armed training because of rigged elections and other factors.

(2) In Kashmir, politics have remained always personalized. After the autocratic rule of Maharaja Hari Singh, Sheikh Abdullah stepped into shoes initially as head of the emergency administration and subsequently from March 4, 1948 as Prime Minister at the cost of Mehr Chand Mahajan, who stood duly appointed as Prime Minister of the State up to 1953 by Maharaja Hari Singh. Mehr Chand Mahajan was Maharaja's Prime Minister with Council of Ministers under the State Constitution of 1939. Under that Constitution Maharaja Hari Singh was the head of Executive, Legislature and Judiciary (because of the inherent absolute

powers as a fountain of State authority). This protection he had under that Constitution. Maharaja had reposed trust in Sheikh Abdullah to share power of governance as Emergency Administrator because Sheikh Abdullah had given a written assurance of loyalty to him and his family in view of his letter of September 26, 1947 (Supra) and subsequent request made to Maharaja Hari Singh by Pandit Jawaharlal Nehru as Prime Minister of India to trust Sheikh Abdullah as a true nationalist and loyal to the country. By betraying the trust of both of them, i.e. of Maharaja Hari Singh and Pandit Nehru, Sheikh Abdullah set out in motion his own agenda of dreaming an Independent State for his personal rule with the help of foreign powers.

To add fuel to the fire, after the unusual rigging of the elections which were held in 1987, there had remained no effective opposition in the legislature. At that time, Congress Party led by late Rajiv Gandhi and Dr Farooq Abdullah had entered into an unwritten Accord to rule the State. The affairs of the government were run by few selected bureaucrats who remained busy in making the hey while the sun of corruption was shinning. The rule of National Conference ended in 2002, after a gap commencing from 1990 to 1996 when Governor's Rule was imposed. He was succeeded by the coalition government of Congress party and PDP political party headed by Mufti Mohammad Sayeed. This new political party is also a family affair because his daughter Mehbooba Mufti was made its President. Though the period of Dr Farooq Abdullah's rule was being considered as a period of casual governance of the State affairs but the three-year period of Mufti Mohammad Sayeed could not avail the opportunity of curbing corruption. The educated unemployed youths were swelling in numbers and there was all around frustration amongst them. The militant activities were not curbed with iron hands. Rather, the administration became more soft and sympathetic towards them by adopting healing-touch policy in their favour. After losing the 'Gaddi' of Chief Ministership Mufti Mohammad Sayeed and his daughter Mehbooba Mufti are also singing the songs of self-rule which is a new theory on the pattern of original doctrine which was earlier propounded by General Musharraf of Pakistan.

(3) After the assassination of Mrs Indira Gandhi, the reins of leadership of the Central Government had gone into the hands of

her son Rajiv Gandhi who unwillingly had entered into politics because of special circumstances. Without much political experience and as a gentleman he was surrounded by a coterie of few childhood friends and some sycophants. Dr Farooq Abdullah exploited this situation to the maximum extent by reviving the old family ties of his father with the Nehru family. The result was that late Rajiv Gandhi having a magnanimous temperament started reposing full faith in the leadership of Dr Farooq Abdullah for running the affairs of the State. The result was that there was an unwritten Accord between the two as already stated above. The share to rule the State was fixed at the ratio of 40:60. This coalition period was most suited to the corrupt elements in the State administration including in the political apparatus of both the parties as there had remained no effective opposition in the State legislature. The anti-national elements got the best opportunity to exploit the situation. Local newspaper *Daily Excelsior* published one survey in its issue of January 23, 2003 by highligting the fact that 50 thousand employees of the State Government had remained in the past busy in extracurricular activities like politics, organized business, timber smuggling and drug trafficking. About 20 per cent of the militants who were killed or arrested during the last thirteen years of the turmoil were regular and ad hoc employees. Trade unions of the employees are still functioning as constituents of the separatist conglomerate Hurriyat Conference. Some undeserving bureaucrats found themselves in plump positions and they in turn became an instrument that caused losses to the State exchequer to the tune of crores of rupees as favours were showered on those who were in close proximity with the political leaders.

(4) The summary of the judgements given in the cases of John Peter and Others *vs* Mohan Lal Motial and Others (supra); Sukesh Khajuria *vs* Union of India (supra); Division Bench ruling of Syedan-e-Sufi (Supra), Dhanraj Bhargotra *vs* State of Jammu and Kashmir (supra) and Division Bench ruling given in Javid Ahmed Zargar and Others *vs* Union of India and others (Supra) throw sufficient light on the side of administration of justice. (Refer Chapter 25 'Role of Judiciary (Sample Cases)' of this book, as well as Appendix 12 and Appendix 15 of this book.)

(5) The genesis of the Kashmir problem lies initially in Maharaja's indecision, for sometime, about accession with Union of India within the prescribed time limit. In this venture he was encouraged by his unfaithful Prime Minister RC Kak and Stand

Still Agreement entered as a sovereign head of the State with a sovereign dominion of Pakistan. Prime Minister RC Kak later on proved to be an agent of Pakistan Muslim League and clandestinely was found developing hidden relations through his second wife who was a British national with Lord Mountbatten. The Britishers had also planted their officers in Maharaja's top administration such as Army and Police Chiefs. Both of them were more loyal to watch and protect British interest rather than that of the Maharaja Hari Singh. These factors also contributed to the delay. This has also been discussed in this book that Maharaja Hari Singh had developed an idea to go with India in last week of May 1947 when he allowed Maharani and Yuvraj Karan Singh to visit Lahore in order to persuade Justice Mehr Chand Mahajan to become the Prime Minister of the State. There was delay on the part of dominion of India for want of any Kashmir Policy to extend helping hand to Maharaja and appointment of Justice Mehr Chand Mahajan was delayed up to the month of September 1947 and practically up to October 10, 1947 (when he formally took over the charge as Prime Minister) when already situation had deteriorated to a great extent. Pandit Nehru's personal hatred for Maharaja Hari Singh, contributed a lot for the delay as he from the very beginning, wanted the transfer of power of governance in favour of his trusted friend Sheikh Abdullah to the exclusion of Maharaja even when accession had not been made. The dominion of Pakistan steadily and slowly committed the breach of Stand Still Agreement and with increased impatience made an attempt to swallow the Muslim-dominated State by committing an Aggression. The dominion of India also committed breach of Articles 7 and 8 read with other relevant Articles of the Instrument of Accession to diminish the sovereign status of Maharaja Hari Singh in the State and his subsequent forcible exit from the State to Bombay. In a nutshell, dominion of India headed by Pandit Nehru as Prime Minister has to be blamed more for the delayed accession and creation of Kashmir problem by abrogating the sovereign status of Maharaja against assurances given to him. Later on, uncalled for hesitations on the part of the Indian Union to annex the State fully aggravated Sheikh Abdullah's ambitions to carve out a fiefdom for himself.

(6) There were some elements occupying high political positions in the National Conference regime who had the similar mental orientations as that of the top ranking militants. Instead of checking the subversive elements, they encouraged them. One

concrete example is of late Attaullah Suhrawardy who had remained a Minister in Sheikh Abdullah's Cabinet and while Deputy Speaker of the J&K Legislative Council he made a speech in the Assembly: "I am first a Muslim and then an Indian. Islam does not need the support of anyone for its spread. It is spreading on its own. At the time of partition, there were only four and half crore Muslims in the country. However, in spite of bloody communal riots in Bhiwandi, Moradabad, Aligarh and other areas killing thousands of Muslims, the population of Muslims has increased to 14 crores. As for the question of conversion of all to Islam, it is the fundamental duty of a Muslim to strive for conversion and any Muslim, who does not remember this duty, does not deserve to be called a Muslim." (Reference: *My Frozen Turbulence in Kashmir* by Jagmohan.)

Sheikh Abdullah after winning the elections on communal card was sworn as Chief Minister on July 9, 1977 and he immediately withdrew criminal cases against 30 hardcore activists of Al-Fatah militant organisation. No reason was assigned for passing such an order. He passed the controversial Resettlement Bill and after his death his Son Dr Farooq Abdullah got it passed as an Act which is still under challenge in the Hon'ble Supreme Court of India. This Act on its face is discriminatory with Hindus of the State and has the tendentious effect of allowing the trained militants from POJK and Pakistan to settle in the State as State Subjects (permanent residents). Dr Farooq Abdullah in 1989 had let off 70 hardcore militants without any rhyme or reason which gave great impetus to the spread of militancy. Many of his deeds and utterances which fed fat to the militant movements have already been quoted in verbatim in this book and particularly under the chapter, 'Corruption in the Administration'.

(7) The Central Act known as Religious Institutions (Prevention of Misuse) Act, 1988 has not been made applicable in the State because some Mosques are being used as places of religious propaganda. The famous shrine of Hazratbal was being used by Sheikh Abdullah from the very beginning to spread the message of National Conference and his successors are following the suit. After National Conference came into power, government servants in large numbers started observing Friday prayers in the Mosques during office hours which practice was not in vogue during the earlier regimes from 1947 firstly headed by Sheikh Abdullah from 1948 to 1953 and then Bakshi Ghulam Mohammad, GM Sadiq and Syed Mir Qasim up to 1975. Even earlier to 1947, during

Maharaja's regime there was no such practice. At many times, militants take refuge in mosques where encounters with security forces take place and many of them are reported in the press. During the hey days of militancy, the exodus of Kashmiri Pandits was caused by using loudspeakers in many mosques in the Valley where terrorising speeches were given against the Kashmiri Pandits to leave the valley immediately or face complete annihilation.

(8) The J&K Jamaat-e-Islami has its educational wing known as 'Falah-e-Aam Trust' which had been spreading the message of establishing the rule of Islam (Nizam-e-Mustafa) in the world and particularly in the sub-continent of India. The State of Jammu and Kashmir has been chosen as a laboratory to carry on the experiments. The said Trust had opened Islamic Madrassas in large numbers with more concentrations in valley and Muslim populated areas of Jammu province including city of Jammu where fundamentalist education used to be imparted to the youths belonging mostly to the lower strata of society. These Madrassas were functioning in the valley in full swing even before Sheikh Abdullah came into power in 1975. During the earlier period of Congress regime (up to February 1975) they were also getting financial aid from the State Government (this fact was revealed to the writer of this book from the seized record of the Association and produced before him as Chairman of the Tribunal which was constituted in 1990 under the J&K Criminal Amendment Act). In addition to government aid, clandestine illegal petro dollars aid was also being given to the Trust by the subversive internal and external anti-nationals. Sheikh Abdullah had been expressing concern about the functioning of the Madrassas but he did not impose any ban on them as during his regime there was an impetus in their mushrooming growth. Finally, it was during Governor's Rule in 1990 when Jagmohan as the Governor of the State banned the Falah-e-Aam Trust along with its parental Organisation Jamaat-e-Islami and other six subversive Associations. (This fact has been discussed earlier under the heading "banning of subversive Organisation/Associations"). About seven hundred teachers were dismissed who were imparting education in these Madrassas run by the trust. The ban imposed was confirmed by the Tribunal headed by the writer of this book but no follow up action was taken which was a requirement of the relevant law. Under law the property of a judicially confirmed Unlawful Association has to be seized and the activists criminally

prosecuted. The only tangible result was that all the dismissed teachers of these Madrassas were subsequently absorbed in government schools as teachers. This was partly done during Governor's rule with the aid of the High Court after obtaining favourable orders from some judges. But when the Division Bench of the High Court refused to give any relief to these teachers in an appeal before it, then the bulk of the teachers succeeded in getting themselves absolved in government schools during the popular rule of National Conference (headed by Dr Farooq Abdullah from 1996 to 2002). The functioning of the Trust in question has already been discussed in detail under the chapter Banning of Subversive Associations. These Madrassas have proved as a breeding ground for the spread of hatred in the inter-religious tolerant culture in the country and particularly in the State of Jammu and Kashmir. They are full grown nurseries for providing recruitment of militant cadres available in the hands of anti-national elements. These teachers with their polluted mind set of hating other religious cultures can only teach hatred and not love to their pupils. In the session of the Legislative Council during the month of March 2006, the then Chief Minister Ghulam Nabi Azad replied to a question raised by Panthers Party MLC Bhim Singh that still more than one hundred unregistered 'madrassas' are functioning in the State. This shows that coalition government led by Mufti Mohammad Sayeed was also lukewarm toward these madrassas.

(9) The Indira-Sheikh Accord of 1975 proved as a foundation stone for raising the structure of the edifice of militancy in the State. After the death of Sheikh Abdullah this Accord ultimately proved as a weapon of discord to destabilise the duly established authority of the State. The suppressed and subdued anti-national elements who till date had been kept under control because of some fear of the rule of law started raising their ugly heads without any fear and accountability. The Hindu majority electorates had returned Congress MLAs in the Legislature but when they also joined sharing the crumbs of power at the rate of 40:60 there remained no opposition in the Legislature. Dr Farooq Abdullah started ruling the State like a real monarch of the medieval period and in the public he immediately was known as a 'Disco Chief Minister'. Many a times he used to dance in the private marriage parties of the influential people act which cannot be done by any well meaning Chief Minister to protect the dignity and honour of a high constitutional post. Moving with

heroes and heroines and playing golf even outside the States by misusing State aircraft became a routine affair of his way of life. When the affairs of the State were left uncared and unattended for most of the time, a golden opportunity came in the hands of some literate politically ambitious youths to accumulate political power in their hands after hobnobbing with subversive elements who were ready to provide them financial and material help. These elements with the aid of their sympathisers who were already in large numbers in the administration, in the legislature, in the press and in the judiciary convinced the common man in the public that their victory was certain to make Kashmir as an Independent State.

(10) Increase of corrupt practices in successive regimes and accumulation of wealth in few thousand Kashmiri families who were either politically near with the ruling families or were their blood-relations or were expert sycophants to act as their pimps made the conditions of the common man more miserable and they became the followers of subversive elements who projected their objects on puritanical basis.

(11) Through Hawala transactions and other illegal means the ISI of Pakistan had succeeded in keeping on their pay rolls the influential media persons in the valley. One English daily newspaper published from Jammu also had been trapped in the net by the subversives. Its publications in large numbers were smuggled to Pakistan as well as purchased in bulk in Kashmir Valley by the activists of the subversives. Like other purchased papers by the ISI agents in the valley, this paper had been also highlighting out of proportions the causes of the militants and at times giving clues to the militants to act on the advice of their master which advice was being published in guarded language in the newspaper/newspapers. Such category of purchased media carried false propaganda against armed forces for violating human rights and used to eulogise the militant's deeds. The slain militants were painted as heroes. The brutal acts of the militants against armed forces, their family members or innocent persons belonging to the minority community or sufferers from the majority community who represented nationalistic views or did not join with them were ignored. The ISI had been doling money by way of pay rolls to some influential members of the legal fraternity, bureaucracy, politicians and media etc. Some corrupt politicians in order to hide their misdeeds were/are abetting the actors of militancy.

(12) About 137 officials and bulk of them were highly placed IAS officers and even working in the Civil Secretariat had complained during 1989-90 to the 'World Forum', i.e. UNO against the excesses of the security forces. Instead of making specific complaints in the appropriate judicial fora of the State or before the constitutional head of the State Governor or Prime Minister or President of the country they had the guts to directly approach the UNO. This was a serious violation of public servants conduct rules entailing the punishment of dismissal and imprisonment. Neither the State Government nor the Central Government discharged their legal duty to take appropriate action against them. Late RK Takkar who was the Chief Secretary of the State during 1990-91 had tried to enforce discipline amongst the erring State employees but he was hounded and insulted by the employees during office hours in the Civil Secretariat. Even loud slogans were raised in the Civil Secretariat. The employees went on a long strike. Instead of taking stern action against those rowdy elements, the chief Secretary had to eat humble pie as the Central Government transferred him to Delhi. On his exit, the strike was called off. Some top ranking officers who had campaigned for obtaining signatures of other employees on the memorandum which was sent to the UNO, later on were given plum postings even in the Central Secretariat of the Union of India. Under the administrative control of many such delinquent officers their subordinates from the field services including police personnel had gone to Pakistan for receiving training in subversive activities but they were being marked present on duty and their salaries were distributed to their family members. Governor Jagmohan had identified some officials of this category and dismissed them summarily for being a threat to the security of the State (under Sub-Section 2(c) of Section 126 of the State Constitution read with Article 311(2)(c) of the Indian Constitution). Dr Farooq Abdullah's government had absorbed majority of them in the government services. A glaring example is that of the absorption of dismissed police personnel in hundreds from police cadre in the Fire Brigade Service cadre as already discussed in this book. The Governor Girish Chandra Saxena had initially shown some reluctance to sign the order but later on he did sign when he received the recommendation for the second time from the government.

(13) The Jammu region, Kashmir region, Gilgit, Baltistan and Ladakh region have strategic importance and there is international

intrigue hatched by the Western block from 1947 to have a foot hold in these areas in order to monitor the activities of other big powers like China and Russia and save the important cities of Pakistan from Indian domination such as Sialkot, Rawalpindi and Peshawar besides important Mangla Dam which is hardly few miles away from the original boundary of the State of Jammu and Kashmir from Mirpur district. The beautiful land of Kashmir is an ideal place for recreational activities. The population of Sunni Muslims dominates the Kashmir Valley and it is the largest homogeneous ethno-religious group. This group is the most articulate one and since 1947 till 2013 every Chief Minister in the State has come up from this ethno-religious group. Many influential politicians and top ranking bureaucrats also have the same common ancestry. The ISI (of Pakistan) has succeeded in penetrating mostly in this group of population, as on analysis, bulk of the militants are the recruits coming from this monolithic populace. Correspondingly they are the worst sufferers of the malice of militancy as large numbers of killings have taken place amongst them by the militants themselves because they in majority do not follow their path and are patriots. Article 370 even in its so-called 'eroded form' has successfully deprived such minorities in Kashmir Valley as Kashmiri Hindus, Shia Muslims, Gujjars and Bakarwals, Pahari-speaking people of Uri and Karnah areas, Pathans and Punjabi Hindus and Muslims, Dogras of Jammu region both Hindus and Muslims and Ladakhis who as a class in all constitute about 75 per cent of the population of the State, but their due shares in the Governance are constantly being denied to them. Even many meritorious students from Kashmir Valley from the group of Sunni Muslim population lose their due share as high and mighty people steal a march over them by corrupt means or being near to the seat of power. The recent scandal for distributing professional seats by the Chairman of the J&K Board of Professional Entrance Examination which got unearthed in December 2013 is a glaring example of favouritism. It was for the first time that during the month of November 2005, a Sunni Muslim hailing from Jammu region but of Kashmiri origin had succeeded in becoming the Chief Minister but he was not allowed to complete his full tenure of three years because of Kashmir-based regional coalition partner (PDP). The ethnic, religious and regional aspirations of all the inhabitants of the State are being ignored and the result is that majority of the people are disgruntled and frustrated. The internal and external enemies take undue benefit of such a discontentment. The history records that even before Dogra rule or during Dogra rule and particularly during Maharaja Ranbir Singh's time there used to be violent clashes in the valley between the Shia and Sunni-Muslim sects. Even recently in 2013 there occurred such a conflict in the valley. It is recorded in the history that some Sultans of Kashmir belonging to either of these groups had committed atrocities on the other ruled group and result was violent clashes. This lopsided way of ruling the State while ignoring the bulk of the other sects of population generates the vice of corruption in the administration. During the coalition rule of Mufti Mohammad Sayeed the State acquired the notorious status of second most corrupt administered State in the country when during Dr Farooq Abdullah's regime it was at number eighteen in the demerit list of corruption. The present Government of Omar Abdullah and coalition partner Congress has continued to retain second position or may be even has acquired first position for all around prevalent corruption and inefficiency.

(14) The Primary alienation is psychological one because of rise of Islamic Fundamentalism generally on the world scene and particularly in the neighbouring State. Some times Kashmiri Muslims perceive themselves as victims of history because they were constantly being told by their leaders to have been deceived in 1947 to join the Hindu-dominated Indian dominion on the eve of partition. They constantly feel that their particular identity will be eroded with national identity. International intrigue hatched by the western block and fundamentalist's Muslim block which exists in some Middle East countries are pouring in aid in petro dollars in millions and trillions to create a hegemonic State on religious basis. These funds are used to promote print media houses to spread radical ideas amongst the youth of Kashmir region. Many hawala transactions get surfaced at all times. This factor also keeps the part of militancy boiling.

(15) There is discrimination in the Right of Voting for the electorates of Jammu region as their value of vote has been decreased considerably as compared to the value of voters of Kashmir region. Factually and legally it is undemocratic and at length has been discussed in this book. Jammu region is legally entitled to more representation in the State Legislature.

(16) The leaders of the main regional parties, i.e. of National Conference and PDP are still singing the songs of Autonomy or of self-rule respectively. The idea of self-rule was in the past

propounded by General Musharraf when he was the President of Pakistan. Unfortunately, the top-ranking leadership of PDP has adopted this *mantra* as a panacea for every evil in the State. Both these terms are synonymous and mischievous in their nature to misguide the common people. The heads of both these regional parties have ruled the State on the guidelines of the J&K Constitution and Indian Constitution and they have to explain to the people as to whose rule it was. They remained the heads of the majority of the elected representatives of the Legislature. These slogans are even more dangerous than the original Dixon Plan of the UNO Commission which was set up in the early fifties. The above stated leaders of both the regional parties cannot rewrite the history ignoring the fact of accession made by the sole authority i.e., Maharaja Hari Singh in 1947 when Pakistan had made an aggression. Their predecessors were the leaders of the Legislature which constituted the Constituent Assembly and they had ratified the accession. Again when Pakistan committed two aggressions on the State to snatch it forcibly and consequently two wars were fought in which Pakistan was always a loser. Two sovereign countries, i.e. India and Pakistan had entered into two international treaties known as 'Tashkent Agreement' and 'Shimla Agreement'. Then there is Indira-Sheikh Accord of 1975. In this Accord Sheikh Abdullah had clearly admitted the accession of State with the dominion of India. Again, there exists an unwritten Accord between Dr Farooq Abdullah and late Rajiv Gandhi. There are two unanimous resolutions passed by the Indian Parliament declaring the whole State of J&K as was being ruled by Maharaja Hari Singh in 1947 as an integral part of India. There are constitutional provisions contained in the State Constitution and Indian Constitution which indubitably declare that the State of Jammu and Kashmir as a whole is a State in the Indian dominion. These turncoat leaders are forgetting all these historical and legal events which cannot be ignored. The anti-national voices of Self-Rule or Autonomy are being raised at the behest of some interested foreign powers who want to fish in the troubled waters of the river Jhelum. This is a repetition of an international intrigue which has been expounded by C Das Gupta in his book titled *War and Diplomacy in Kashmir (1947-1948)*. In this book it is clearly mentioned that Kashmir problem was created by the Western block who at that time controlled the military apparatus of both the newly created dominions that is of India and Pakistan. Indian head of the Army was also a British national and the same position was in Pakistan. Even Maharaja Hari Singh had an English Officer as the head of the Army establishment. The plan of committing an aggression was prepared by these officers even before the dawn of independence. These powers had dictated the ceasefire in the State. The Indian leaders should understand this international game plan which is being played by Kashmir-based politicians at their behest. These leaders should be firmly dealt with in accordance with law of the land because the majority of the people of the State as a whole are not with them. No-doubt some of their sympathisers are still with them for the above stated two theories but they have their share in the governance of the State. These types of doctrines, theories should not be allowed to be propounded or propagated as they go against the mandates of Indian Constitution as well as the Constitution of Jammu and Kashmir State.

Solution

The solution to violence is not violence but non-violence. The old age culture of the inhabitants of the State of Jammu and Kashmir had always been that of religious tolerance, brotherhood, co-existence and welfare of everybody and this spirit still survives but it has to be revived and strengthened and revived where it has been eroded by fundamentalistic doctrines let loose by the 'Jehadi Elements'. The people of Jammu region despite all sorts of provocations from the side of these Jehadi Elements had not shown any sign of change and collectively they frustrated their evil designs of spreading communal violence. Rather, with full determination the people of Jammu have accommodated the victims of militancy belonging to the majority and minority communities. Even some Jehadi militants under the guise of being the victims of the militancy have taken shelter in the benevolent land of Raja Jambu Lochan (the founder of Jammu city) where he had noticed a lion and a goat drinking water together on the bank of the Tawi river. This idea of co-existence worked in his mind for founding the present city of Jammu on the Bank of Tawi river. The causes of the spread of the monstrous menace of militancy have already been mentioned above. When the causes of a malady are diagnosed, the cure or the remedy thereof automatically surfaces. This formula applies with all force in the violence torn State of Jammu and Kashmir. In the past, the Valley of Kashmir has given to the world the philosophy of 'Shaivisim' (during the Hindu period) and then the philosophy of Buddhism got deep rooted in the Spiritually fertile soil of Kashmir Valley as from here Buddhism spread to Ladakh and some parts of Central Asia including Tibet. During the Islamic period Sufi saints made it as their abode of choice and Sufism also flourished here.

Ours is the most ancient nation, which had evolved and developed the oldest legal and judicial system in the world. Administration of justice was according to the Hindu Smritis, one of the most important and obligatory functions of a king and the following moral code of conduct which was prescribed for a king illustrates this idea:

दुष्टस्य दण्डः सुजस्य पूजा न्यायेन कोशस्य च सपृवृद्धिः।
अपक्ष पातोऽर्थिषु राष्ट्ररक्षा पञ्चेव यज्ञाः कार्यता नृपाणाम ॥

The English translation of the above stated Shloka is,

> "to punish the wicked, to honour and protect the good, to enrich the treasury (exchequer) by just methods, to be impartial towards the litigants (in the administration of justice) and to protect the kingdom (defence of the realm) these are the five Yajnas."

The concept of rule of law means that the society must be governed by law or Dharma and not according to the whims and fancies of a ruler or by powerful individuals. The necessity of scrupulous practice of Dharma is forcefully expressed by Manu:

धर्म एव हतो हन्ति धर्मो रक्षति रक्षितः
तस्माद्धर्मो न हन्तव्यो मा नो धर्मो हतोऽवधीत ॥

> "Dharma protects those who protect it. Those who destroyed get destroyed. Therefore, Dharma should not be destroyed, so that we may not be destroyed as consequence thereof."

The above said Shastric parables have applied in all fours in the State of Jammu and Kashmir because the majority of the Valley-based rulers have been violating the Raj Dharma for their personal happiness. Their misdeeds have been discussed in details in the foregoing chapters and they are responsible to have alienated the common people because of misgoverance. There has been no accountability for corrupt deeds of these rulers from the dawn of independence because Central Government has always failed to assert its authority in seeing the money of the Indian tax payers reaching to the masses. Only few thousand powerful families have usurped the Indian wealth meant for the development of common masses. Few glaring examples are given below: When the NDA Government was ruling in the Centre a sum of Rs 40 crore was given to the State (during Dr Farooq Abdullah's regime) which was meant to meet the security related expenditure but bulk of it was spent for furnishing the Bangalows of the Ministers, Legislators and top ranking bureaucrats. The First Law Officer of the State (Advocate-General) who had to advise the government to run the State administration according to the Rule of law could easily swindle a whopping amount of Rs 10,50,000 for the repairs of his private house (custodian property). These revelations were found in the audit report of the Comptroller Auditor General of India. One lakh and forty thousand government jobs in the Kashmir Valley and about fifteen thousands jobs in Jammu Division were distributed during the popular rule of National Conference during the years 1996 to 2002 as largesses to the blue-eyed favourites and not to the deserving people. The rulers should be taught by their mentors from the Central Government who rule the State at all the material times that old age Indian legal jurisprudence still holds good in the prevailing disturbed waters of river Jhelum in Kashmir Valley and that saying is:

प्रजोसुखे सुख राज्ञः प्रजाना च हिते हितम्।
नात्मप्रियं हितं राज्ञः प्रजानां तु प्रिय हितम् ॥

> "In the happiness of his subjects lies the happiness of the king. In their welfare his welfare, he shall not do what pleases him. He shall do what pleases his subjects."

We practise democracy of the majority. This suppresses the minority group. It has been fully explained in this book how the inhabitants of Jammu region irrespective of their caste, creed, colour and religion are being discriminated in the matters of developmental activities and sharing the political power. They don't even have equal voting rights a discrimination which is found nowhere in a democratic country and it was not in practice in the State even during autocratic Dogra rule. Two important Commissions were set up in the State to remove the imbalances and they are known as Gajendragadkar Commission and subsequently in order to sideline the report of that Commission which favoured the regions of Jammu and Ladakh for their discrimination, Sheikh Abdullah in order to divert the Public attention appointed another Commission known as Justice Sikri Commission and its report also corroborated the findings of the earlier above stated Commission. No implementations have been made of these reports except by changing the nomenclature of Deputy Chief minister hailing from Jammu region and establishing an Agricultural University. Same is the position with Ladakhis. The inhabitants of these two regions deserve the rights of self-rule or autonomy within the State as equal partners. Otherwise, the only way left to them would be to seek attention of the terrorist's activities as they are surging in other parts of the country. The elimination of the terrorists will not solve the problem but the grievances of all the inhabitants have to be solved.

What will take us beyond this conflict? The reply to this is that truth as we see it should be our religion which will enable us to live in peace with ourselves and everyone else. This is a noble way to accommodate everybody. It requires patience, but results in peace and harmony. Mere acquisition of wealth and power does not make a better individual. Selfishness creates problems. Growing in selflessness leads to solutions.

> "Happiness is spiritual, born of truth and love. It is unselfish;
> therefore it cannot exist alone, but requires all mankind
> to share it."

All over the world there are 140 minority groups wanting secession yet the fact is that claims of such groups for secession originating from representative democracies are not considered by the international community. In order to understand demand for secession in its proper perspective, two questions need to be asked.

First, what does self-determination in international law mean? Second, does it applies to the State of Jammu and Kashmir? It was first used by Woodrow Wilson and formally appeared in international landscape in 1945 and that too it was supported by Nation States under Colonial rule.

However, in 1970, the international community expanded the concept and the UN General Assembly said,

> "Emergence into any political status freely determined by a people constitutes a mode of implementation the right of self-determination." However, the UN added the caveat, "This shall not be construed as authorising any action which could dismember or unpair, totally or in part, the territorial integrity of sovereign States. Thus, the demands for secession or internal self-determination are not determined."

The State of Jammu and Kashmir is not a homogeneous territory but heterogeneous one. It was a conglomeration of territories brought under the political power of one Maharaja. There are three major religions practised in the State and three major languages are spoken. The ruler of the State has acceded to the Union of India which was ratified by the representatives chosen by the people which constituted the Constituent Assembly. Elections are being held from 1951 and it cannot be said that all were rigged. On the complaint of India, UNO has taken cognizance of the aggression. The Pakistan-occupied territory of Jammu and Kashmir is a distinct entity and its one towering leader Sardar Ibrahim Khan has stated on record that their territory was invaded by Pakistan. Due to constitutional abuse of Article 370 the separate status of the State is protected. The voice of secession is not the voice of all the people of all regions and majority of the people professing different religions. Not only that, it is not even the voice of the majority of the people of Kashmir region where people like late Maqbool Sherwani in 1947 and recently late Yusuf Halwai lived and they sacrificed their lives for the national cause. There are hundreds of such like patriots who are either unknown or unrecognized who too have attained martyrdom at the hands of jehadi elements because they were true to their hearts and faithful towards the national cause and did not side with militants. Being not hypocrites like the present day most of the people who are near the seat of power belonging to all the regions of the state, instead of enriching themselves, they sacrificed their lives. The militants have no religion and no mercy for human beings but they want to establish their own rule according to their whims. The writer of this book would be failing in his moral duty by not recording this fact that the inhabitants of Kashmir region have borne more brunt of violence and suffered more loss in losing human lives than the inhabitants of other two regions. From personal experience it can be said that in case those inhabitants are ruled by hearts rather than by heads they are more appreciative, responsive, cooperative and recognize the moral values of integrity, honesty and merit, the traits which remain ingrained in their hearts even when one is out of the seat of the power. The imbalances and irritations between the regions have been created by short sighted politicians who want to establish their family rule at the cost of justice, equity and fair play. What is causing even more anxiety with the passage of time is the sight of an ineffective and unpopular regime which is neither able to effectively meet the challenge of the secessionist groups nor is able to protect the lives and property of the peaceful citizens who are concerned with their day to day problems to earn livelihood with dignity, honour and peacefully. The monster of corruption has raised its ugly head and is eating the vitals of the society. The money and grants meant for developmental purposes are not mostly utilized for the people but go to the pockets of the high and mighty. People want selfless leaders of the old brand and calibre like late Bakshi Ghulam Mohammad, late GM Sadiq, late Pandit Prem Nath Dogra, late Girdhari Lal Dogra, late Pandit Trilochan Datt, late Ayub Khan, late Khwaja Mubaraq Shah, late Koushak Bukula, late Lala Ram Nath Bhalgotra, late Baldev Singh and others like-minded in the present set up who by their example can control the erring bureaucracy. Majority of the people from all the regions have expressed their views and desires for good and effective governance before the interlocutors which were appointed by the Central Government. The slogans of Autonomy and self-rule are vague and hallow and are permeated with personal agendas to create vote banks in order to rule the state by hook or crook.

The inhabitants of the areas which are under the illegal occupation of Pakistan do not want that they should remain under the rule of an aggressor. The international community has to ascertain their wishes. As far as the people of State of Jammu and Kashmir are concerned, they require eradication of corrupt rule to be substituted by self-rule of all the three regions within the parameters of the State Constitution and Indian Constitution. In other words, all the Fundamental Rights such as equality before law and no discrimination on the basis of religion, place of birth should be made available in practice to all the inhabitants. Through the medium of courts, the people have not been able to get this remedy because the wrongs are committed in such a clandestine manner that common people with meagre resources cannot get the knowledge of the wrongs committed and then fight it. The figures of regional imbalances which are given in the relevant chapters are sufficient to lend credence to this view. In a nutshell, good governance with the participation of all the people of the State on equal footing will minimise to a great extent the menace of militancy. Those mighty people who are responsible for the erosion of State authority should be identified by setting up commissions and exposed in the public. The people of Jammu and Kashmir crave for justice and fair play and not treachery, loot and falsehood.

At last it is reiterated that terrorism will have to be fought militarily while good governance by mature political leadership having sufficient academic qualification and good past record of rendering help to mankind at the helm of affairs, weeding out corruption, responsive administration and all around development will go a long way in tackling militancy. The old promises given by Sheikh Abdullah and Pandit Jawaharlal Nehru as reproduced in this book to safe guard the interest of other two regions, i.e. of Jammu and Ladakh should be fulfilled as soon as possible otherwise volcano of subdued injustice being perpetuated will erupt and a Telangana type of agitation may not start which would be difficult to tackle because of prevailing militancy in the State. The national interest of the inhabitants of all the regions should be given top priority rather than the interests of militants or so called surrendered militants.

Last of all, Article 370 which was engrafted in the Indian Constitution to meet a particular emergency situation and was of temporary nature, now requires to be abrogated after ascertaining the opinion of the inhabitants of all the three regions of the State in accordance with established law so that the State also acquires the equal status with the rest of the States of India and an era of industrialisation and social justice starts in the State at accelerated speed which whenever envisaged for the rest of the country.

CHAPTER 27

Unfinished Agenda of Pakistan

1. It was a long drawn plan of the Britishers before granting independence to the sub-continent of India that a soft State of Pakistan on the basis of religion should be established in order to watch their interest against the expansion of communism through Russia and China which was going to be a Communist country. The areas of Gilgit Agency and particularly that of Chitral was the most strategical area for keeping a watch on their activities. Already they had secured this area in their control from the Maharaja of J&K by way of lease executed in 1935 for sixty years and they had established their Military control through Gilgit Scouts and constructed an aerodrome. The Britishers were instigating mutiny in that area through *Amirs* to coerce Maharaja that he should accede to Pakistan and finally they had managed Military coup against him through Gilgit Scouts and got furled Pakistani flag in the month of November 1947 by arresting the Governor of Gilgit. Though this 1/6th area of the total area of the State had been taken by Pakistan yet the remaining area which could not be taken through invasion has remained unfinished agenda of Pakistan and constant help of Britishers was available at all times to Pakistan even after January 1, 1948, when India had gone to UNO against Pakistan aggression. Ceasefire was declared in January 1949. It is a matter of great mystery that Indian army wanted to free the entire Jammu and Kashmir State and it was capable to do so but why orders were not given to the Army to do so even after waiting for 13 months before declaring ceasefire? As a result thereof 84,000 sq kms areas continued to remain under the occupation of Pakistan and from that area Pakistan later on illegally ceded 500 sq kms area to China.
2. Pakistan tried to snatch Jammu and Kashmir through direct Wars of 1965 and 1971. After 1975 it had started proxy war by training terrorists, encouraging infiltration and Islamic fundamentalists

under 'Operation K-2'. During the last 20 years about one lac people (including about 5000 Security personnel) were killed and thousands became disabled permanently. During Kargil war in 1999 Pakistan tried to cut Ladakh from rest of India. About 500 Indian Army personnel were killed in this war.

Change in Strategy

The present unrest in the Kashmir Valley is also a part of the same strategy. Pakistan has understood the fact that it cannot defeat India in direct War and India cannot also be bowed down by terrorists. Pakistan has established a mechanism of former terrorists during the last three years and it wants to achieve its incomplete aim by resorting to violent mass agitations. Pakistan's aim is to bring down the morale of security forces by stone pelting, compel them to take action and also to compel all the parties in the valley in its favour under the pressure of public agitation. During the last 1 ½ year more than 3500 army personnel were injured. Pakistan has again succeeded to some extent in internationalizing the Kashmir issue through agitational terrorism. The successive weak governments in the State are providing Golden opportunities for these activities. Though America has been avoiding direct interference in Kashmir affairs, yet it has been extending silent support to the separatist's activities through Pakistan. Fact is that America either wants to keep the Kashmir dispute alive for ever or it wants to use it as a Buffer State. America had aroused Sheikh Abdullah's aspiration for an independent Kashmir in 1950. It wanted to maintain its influence in Central Asia through the permanent presence of its Army in Jammu and Kashmir. On the other hand, China also wants to keep Jammu and Kashmir dispute alive keeping in view its military interest in Gilgit (POJK Area). That is why it wants to keep the Jammu and Kashmir issue alive by violating the borders in Ladakh by its Army, stapled visa system for Jammu and Kashmir people and not showing Jammu and Kashmir as a part of India.

The country needs immediate answers to the following questions. Personal opinion of the writer of this book is also mentioned in the following paragraph.

(i) What is the policy of Congress with regard to Jammu and Kashmir?

The policy of Congress with regard to Jammu and Kashmir has been confusing from the very beginning.

(ii) Why did Sheikh Abdullah launch the Quit Kashmir Movement?

In 1946, the then leader of National Conference Sheikh Abdullah launched 'Quit Kashmir Movement' to remove popular Maharaja of Jammu and Kashmir and the end of Dogra rule. His slogans were 'Quit Kashmir', 'End of Dogra Rule', 'Independence of Kashmir' and 'Jehad'. Only few people from the valley were active in this agitation and it had no support of the remaining four major regions of the State Jammu, Ladakh, Baltistan and Gilgit. That was the time of Indian Independence Movement. In the rest of the country 'Quit India' movement had started in 1942 and it had ended long ago before 1946. There was no justification for such an agitation in any State at that time. Sheikh Abdullah wanted that Maharaja should transfer powers before announcement for country's independence is made. According to him, a Hindu ruler had no right to rule over Muslim majority of Jammu and Kashmir State.

(iii) Why did Pandit Jawaharlal Nehru insist to visit Jammu and Kashmir State in 1946?

It is a mystery as to why Pandit Nehru insisted on visiting Jammu and Kashmir to support this agitation which was based on communal disharmony and personal ambition. Whereas, Maharaja Hari Singh had personally requested Pandit Nehru not to visit Kashmir as also Congress Party had asked him not to do so. Pandit Nehru was bent upon to come to Kashmir and he was detained at Kohala Bridge and sent back from the State as a result of which Pandit Nehru became permanently anti-maharaja despite the fact that he was a great patriot. Maharaja had advocated for independence of India in Round-Table Conference of 1931. His speech also annoyed the Britishers. Lord Mountbatten by complicating the Kashmir issue took personal revenge from the Maharaja and the country is paying price for it even today.

(iv) Why Congress Party insisted for transfer of power to Sheikh Abdullah and his party National Conference before accession had been made by Maharaja?

Maharaja was ready for merger of the State before October 26, 1947 and possibly even before August 15, 1947, but Pandit Nehru had insisted for transfer of power to Sheikh Abdullah for internal administration for the best reasons known to him, for which Maharaja was never willing to do so.

(v) Why Pandit Nehru and his government made an unconditional and unilateral announcement for holding Plebiscite?

Maharaja was the sole authority under the Indian Independence Act of 1947 read with the relevant provisions of the Government of India Act 1935. He had made the accession perfectly in accordance with law. But as per the political decision of the Congress party, the wishes of the people were to be ascertained through their elected representatives and not through holding Plebiscite. In the rest of the country the wishes of the elected representatives were ascertained and that course was also adopted in case of Jammu and Kashmir as in 1954 the accession had been ratified by the Constituent Assembly which had been established by Sheikh Abdullah through holding elections.

(vi) Why Pandit Nehru had given an assurance about Plebiscite in the UNO?

Under the Indian Independence Act 1947, and Constitution Act of 1935 Maharaja was the sole authority to accede to any of the newly created two dominions and when he had exercised that power why holding of Plebiscite was insisted by UNO and why assurance was being given by Pandit Nehru remains a mystery. Probably it may be under the hope of winning plebiscite through the influence of Sheikh Abdullah.

(vii) Why did India give Chhamb area of Jammu and Kashmir State to Pakistan under Shimla Agreement of 1972?

India had won 1965 and 1971 wars but instead of getting back our areas, we had given Chhamb area to Pakistan under the 1972 Shimla Agreement, which was in our occupation from 1947 onwards. Shimla Agreement of 1972 was the result of total defeat of Pakistan when its Army personnel numbering about 91,000 were in our custody and we could dictate terms to Pakistan to our favour and could get the end of Kashmir dispute permanently. These are political blunders and the future generations have to find the answers themselves.

(viii) Why a motion was moved in Constituent Assembly in 1949 to give Right of Nomination to four members by Sheikh Abdullah?

There was a provision of four members from Jammu and Kashmir in Constituent Assembly of India. According to

Indian Independence Act 1947, that was to be filled by nomination from Maharaja. But a motion was moved in Constituent Assembly in May 1949 to give right of nomination to Sheikh Abdullah. There was uproar and resentment in Assembly against this unconstitutional act, but Pandit Nehru insisted on and ultimately prevailed. The result was that Sheikh Abdullah got an opportunity to put pressure for including Article 370 in the Indian Constitution.

(ix) Why did Central Government resort to remove Mehr Chand Mahajan and Maharaja Hari Singh from the administrative scene of the State in an unconstitutional manner?

After accession, under pressure from Pandit Nehru, Maharaja invited Sheikh Abdullah to assist his Prime Minister (Mehr Chand Mahajan) as Emergency Administrator for internal administration but he used to insult Maharaja Hari Singh and Prime Minister Mehr Chand Mahajan, again and again. Instead of advising him not to do so, the Central Government resorted to remove Mehr Chand Mahajan first and then Maharaja Hari Singh from the state administration and this was an unconstitutional act.

(x) Why did Indian Government yielded again and again before the anti-national demands of Sheikh Abdullah?

The ill-will of Sheikh Abdullah had started surfacing even in the beginning of 1949 and he had started building pressure on the Government of India. Instead of removing him from the State, Maharaja was removed in a very insulting manner. This act was done by the Central Government despite a severe opposition witnessed against him in the entire Ladakh and Jammu regions including famous agitation of Praja Parishad. This was an undue favour under the fear of holding a plebiscite.

(xi) Why Pandit Nehru insisted on inclusion of Article 306(A) (later on Article 370)?

Despite the fact that Dr Ambedkar and the entire Constituent Assembly and Congress Working Committee opposed it, Pandit Nehru in order to see that his close friend Sheikh Abdullah is given the power to govern the State, exercised his personal influence and got inserted Article 370 as a temporary measure with an idea to fully get the State merged with India regarding remaining certain provisions of the Indian Constitution.

(xii) Why did the Congress kept quite during the elections of 1951 to constitute Constituent Assembly in order to fulfil the concept of democracy in the State?

A drama was enacted in 1951 for elections to Constituent Assembly. The applications of all the candidates of the opposition parties were rejected. The candidates of National Conference were elected unopposed on 73 seats out of 75 seats. The Congress kept quiet about this type of murder of democracy, which could only be committed by setting aside the authority of Maharaja Hari Singh, as a ruler of the State who still at that time was the ruler and constitutionally speaking under the Constitution of the State of 1939 he was the sole authority to get convened the Constituent Assembly and keep Sheikh Abdullah under his Control. Why a great injustice was done to him despite the fact that the President of India Dr Rajendra Prasad had also raising objections by writing letters to Pandit Nehru as to how Maharaja Hari Singh who had been recognized by him as a Raj Pramukh has been removed from the same. Maharaja Hari Singh's letter to Dr Rajendra Prasad of 1952 written from Puna is an eye opener as to how the Government of India and Sheikh Abdullah had violated the legal and moral commitments and assurances and done a great injustice to him.

(xiii) Why Prime Minister Rajiv Gandhi ignored the intelligence reports in regard to existence of terrorist camps across the border and even in Kashmir Valley?

This had been ignored despite the schemes of Pakistan to spread terrorism in Kashmir in the coming years, increasing number of *Madrassas* as well as spreading fundamentalism by Jamaat-e-Islami.

(xiv) Why Congress kept quiet in regard to the frauds committed by the National Conference in the elections of 1983 and particularly of 1987?

Large scale frauds were committed in Jammu and Kashmir during elections again and again. There was a coalition government of Congress and National Conference to share the powers at the rate of 40:60 per cent, respectively. There was no accountability in the Central Government for the acts of corruption which were done at large scale in the State. Most of the aspiring youths from valley who wanted to enter in politics had won some seats in these elections but were prevented to do so and being disgruntled they crossed over to Pakistan and got arms and ammunition training.

(xv) Why is there permanent discrimination in the Right of Voting between the domiciles of Jammu region and that of Kashmir region?

After 1962, jurisdiction of the Election Commission of India (constitutional independent body) had been extended to Jammu and Kashmir, even then this discrimination was allowed to continue which is against the spirit of democracy. There is discrimination in the distribution of development funds providing job opportunities. These acts of discrimination had been judicially determined by high-powered Gajendragadkar Commission, Sikri Commission. On the contrary, on October 12, 1977 Sheikh Abdullah assailed the report of Gajendragadkar Commission, which gave rise to Poonch agitation in December 1978 and continued for 94 days. Sheikh Abdullah had agreed to concede the demands of the people of Jammu region but in order to side track the public attention and with utmost political cleverness appointed Justice Sikri Commission. This Commission gave its report on August 25, 1980 and had found regional imbalances in the same manner in which the Gajendragadkar Commission had found but both these reports had been kept under the carpet by the Ruling regional parties National Conference and PDP who always survived on the support of coalitions governments formed with the assistance of Congress party. Congress party is more responsible to explain its conduct than those regional political parties which have their base in Kashmir Valley, but the Congress party has to explain to whole of the country about their role for not providing democratic values and protecting the Fundamental Rights of the inhabitants of Jammu and Ladakh regions. Even Sheikh Abdullah had nullified the purpose of appointment of Wazir Commission whose report was given on January 3, 1984 and recommended three districts for Jammu, i.e. Kishtwar, Samba and Reasi and one district Bandipura for Kashmir but Sheikh Abdullah on his own on July 1, 1979 created three districts for Kashmir, i.e. Budgam, Pulwama and Kupwara. Besides that he upgraded the status of tehsil Kargil as a district.

(xvi) Why have all the governments of the State headed by

Abdullahs failed to fulfil the commitments made to Pandit Nehru, the Maharaja and the people of the State?

To establish his dynastic rule in the State, Sheikh Abdullah did not fulfil the commitments in his life-time. This policy is being followed by his son Dr Farooq Abdullah and now by his grandson Omar Abdullah. To continue their dynastic rule, Abdullah family from time to time has been raising the issue of Internal Autonomy and that the State has not fully merged with the dominion of India.

(xvii) Why should Article 370 of the Indian Constitution should not be abrogated?

The real cause of Jammu and Kashmir problem does not lie in the State but in the Central Government of New Delhi and its solution is to be found not only in Jammu and Kashmir but with the combined efforts of the nation. Now time has come that Article 370, which is only a temporary provision, should be abolished and encouraging separatist tendencies must be ended forever.

APPENDIX 1

Text of the Treaty

English translation of the Persian text of the treaty signed at Leh on second of Asuj 1899 Bikrami (September 1842) between the Government of Maharaja Gulab Singh and the Government of Tibet.

Whereas we the officers of the Lhasa country, viz, firstly, Kalon Surkhan, and secondly, Fepon Pishi, commander of the forces of the Empire of China, on the one hand and Dewan Hari chand and Wazir Ratanu, on behalf of Maharaja Gulab Singh, on the other, agree together and swear before God that the friendship between Maharaja Gulab Singh and the Emperor of China and the Lama Guru Sahib Lassawalla will be kept and observed till eternity; no disregard will be shown to anything agreed upon in the presence of God; and will respect the boundary of Ladakh and the countries bordering on it as fixed since olden times. We will carry on the trade in shawl, Pasham, and Tea before by way of Ladakh; and if anyone of the Shri Maharaja enemies comes to our territories and says anything against the Raja we will not listen to him, and will not allow him remain in our country, and whatever traders come from Ladakh shall experience no difficulty from our side. We will not act otherwise but in the same manner as it has been prescribed in this meeting regarding the fixing of the Ladakh frontier and the keeping open of the road for the traffic in shawl, Pasham, and Tea. We will observe our pledge to God, Gaitri and Pasi. Wazir Mian Khushal Chu is witness.

Written on the second day of Asuj 1899 (September 1842).

The Tibetan version of the treaty is as follows:

Kalon Surkhan and investigating officer Depon Pishi on behalf of his Holiness the Dalai Lama and his officials, and Khalsaji Absarani Shri Maharaja, Lala Golana, the representatives of Khashur Shag Golam Mohammed through an interpreter Amirshar (on behalf of Gulab Singh) have arrived at Ladakh and discussed the terms of the peace treaty. In the first place the two contracting parties have decided to sink all past differences and ill-feeling and to consider the friendship and unity between the two kings re-established forever. This peace treaty between Maharaja Gulab Singh and Guru Lama of Lhasa has been restored and there will be no cause for enmity in future in the two nations regarding their respective frontier. Maharaja Sahib has declared, invoking God as his witness that he will not deviate from the terms of this Agreement. It is agreed that the two brothers Kings of Ladakh and the Queen shall remain peacefully in Ladakh and shall not indulge in any intrigue, besides trying to promote the friendly relations between the two nations. The Ladakhis shall send the annual tribute to His Holiness the Dalai Lama and his ministers unfailingly as therefore and the Shri Maharaj Sahib will not interfere with this agreement. No restrictions shall be laid on the mutual export of commodities e.g., tea, piece goods, etc ... and trading shall be allowed according to the old-establishing custom. The Ladakhis shall supply the Tibetan Government traders with the usual transport animals and arrange for their accommodation as therefore, and the Tibetans will also do the same to the Ladakhis who come to Tibet with the annual tribute. It is agreed that no tribute that no trouble will be occasioned to the Tibetan Government by the Ladakhis. We invoke God to bear witness to this agreement whereby the friendly relations between the Maharajah Sahib and the Lhasa Government shall continue as between members of the same family. This is signed on the second day of the month of Assuj, year 1899.

APPENDIX 2

Treaty of Lahore

(March 9, 1846)

Treaty between the British Government and the State of Lahore, concluded at Lahore on March 9, 1846.

Whereas the treaty of amity and concord, which was concluded between the British Government and the late Maharaja Ranjit Singh, the ruler of Lahore in 1809, was broken by the unprovoked aggression on the British provinces by the Sikh Army, in December last; And whereas, on that occasion, by the proclamation dated 13th of December, the territories then in the occupation of the Maharaja of Lahore, on the left or British bank of the river Satluj, were confiscated and annexed to the British provinces; and since that time, hostile operations have been prosecuted by the two governments, the one against the other, which have resulted in the occupation of Lahore by the British troops: And whereas it has been determined that upon certain conditions, peace shall be re-established between the two governments, the following treaty of peace between the Honourable English East India Company, the Maharaja Dalip Singh Bahadur, and his children, heirs, and successors, has been concluded, on the part of the Honourable Company, by Frederick Currie, Esq; and Brevet-Major Henry Montgomery Lawrence, by virtue of full powers to that effect vested in them by the Right Honourable Sir Henry Hardinge, GCB, one of Her Britannic Majesty's most Honourable Privy Council, Governor-General appointed by the Honourable Company to direct and control all their affairs in the East Indies, and on the part of his Highness the Maharaja Dalip Singh, by Bhai Ram Singh, Raja Lal Singh, Sardar Tej Singh, Sardar Chattar Singh Attariwala, Sardar Ranjor Singh Majithia, Diwan Dinanath, and Fakir Nur-ud-Din vested with full powers and authority on the part of his highness.

Article 1

There shall be perpetual peace and friendship between the British Government, on the part, and Maharaja Dalip Singh, his heirs and successors on the other.

Article 2

The maharaja of Lahore renounces for himself, his heirs and successors all claim to or connection with, the territories lying to the south of the river Satluj, and engages never to have concern with those territories or the inhabitants thereof.

Article 3

The maharaja ceded to the Honourable Company in perpetual sovereignty, all his forts, territories, and rights in the Doab and country, hill and plain, situate between the rivers Beas and Satluj.

Article 4

The British Government having demanded from the Lahore State, an indemnification for the expenses of the war, in addition to the cession of territory described in Article 3, payment of a one and a half crores of rupees; and the Lahore Government being unable to pay the whole of this sum at this time, or to give security satisfactory to the British Government for its eventual payment; the Maharaja cedes to the Honourable Company, in perpetual sovereignty, as equivalent for one crore of rupees all his forts, territories, rights, and interests in the hill countries which are situate between the rivers Beas and Indus, including the provinces of Kashmir and Hazara.

Article 5

The Maharaja will pay to the British Government the sum of fifty lakhs of rupees, on or before the ratification of this treaty.

Article 6

The Maharaja engages to disband the mutinous troops of the Lahore army, taking from them their arms; and His Highness agrees to reorganize the regular, or Ain, regiments of infantry, upon the system, and according to the regulations as to pay and allowances, observed in the time of the late Maharaja Ranjit Singh. The Maharaja further engages to pay up all arrears to the soldiers that are discharged under the provisions of this Article.

Article 7

The regular army of Lahore State shall henceforth be limited to 25 battalions of infantry, consisting of 800 bayonets each with 12,000 cavalry: this number at no time to be exceeded with the concurrence of the British Government. Should it be necessary at any time for any special cause, that this force should be increased, the cause shall be fully explained to the British Government; and when the special necessity shall have passed, the regular troops shall be again reduced to the standard specified in the former clause of this Article.

Article 8

The Maharaja will surrender to the British Government all the guns, thirty-six in number, which have been pointed against the British troops, and which having been placed on right bank of the river Satluj, were not captured at the Battle of Sobraon.

Article 9

The control of the rivers Beas and Satluj, with the continuation of the latter river, commonly called the Ghara and Panjnad, to the confluence of the Indus from Mithankot, and the control of the Indus from Mithankot to the borders of Balochistan, shall in respect to tolls and ferries, rest with the British Government. The provisions of this Article shall not interfere with the passage of boats belonging to the Lahore Government on the said rivers, for the purpose of traffic or the conveyance of passengers up and down their course. Regarding the ferries between the countries respectively, at the several ghats of the said rivers, it is agreed that the British Government after defraying all the expenses of management and establishment, shall account to the Lahore Government for one half of the net profits of the ferry collections. The provisions of this Article have no reference to the ferries on that part of the river Satluj which forms the boundary of Bahawalpur and Lahore respectively.

Article 10

If the British Government should, at any time, desire to pass troops through the territories of his highness the Maharaja, for the protection of the British territories, or those of their allies, the British troops shall, on such special occasions, due notice being given, be allowed to pass through the Lahore territories. In such case the officers of the Lahore State will afford facilities in providing supplies and boats for the passage of rivers: and the British Government will pay the full price of all such provisions and boats, and will make fair compensation for all private property that may be undamaged. The British Government will, moreover, observe all due consideration to the religious feelings of the inhabitants of those tracts through which the army may pass.

Article 11

The Maharaja engages never to take, or retain in his service, any British subject of any European or American State, without the consent of the British Government.

Article 12

In consideration of the services rendered by Raja Gulab Singh of Jammu to the Lahore State, towards procuring the restoration of relations of amity between the Lahore and British Governments, the maharaja hereby agrees to recognise the independent sovereignty of Raja Gulab Singh, in such territories and districts in the hills as may be made over to the said Raja Gulab Singh by separate agreement between himself and the British Government, with the dependencies thereof, which may have been in the Raja's possession since the time of the late Maharaja Kharak Singh; and the British Government in consideration of the good conduct of Raja Gulab Singh, also agrees to recognize his independence in such territories, and to admit him to be privileges of a separate treaty with the British Government.

Article 13

In the event of any dispute or difference arising between the Lahore State and Raja Gulab Singh, the same shall be referred to the arbitration of the British Government; and by its decision the Maharaja engages to abide.

Article 14

The limits of the Lahore territories shall not be, at any time, changed without concurrence of the British Government.

Article 15

The British Government will not exercise any interference in the internal administration of the Lahore State; but in all cases or questions which may be referred to the British Government, the Governor-General will give the aid of his advice and good offices for the furtherance of the interests of the Lahore Government.

Article 16

The subjects of either State shall, on visiting the territories of the other, be on the footing of the subjects of the most favoured nation.

This treaty consisting of sixteen Articles has been this day settled by Frederick Currie, esq; and Brevet-Major Henry Montgomery Lawrence, acting under the directions of the Right Honourable Sir Henry Hardinge, GCB, Governor-General on the part of the British Government, and by Bhai Ram Singh, Raja Lal Singh, Sardar Tej Singh, Sardar Chattar Singh Attariwala, Sardar Ranjor Singh Majithia, Diwan Dina nath, and fakir Nur-ud-din, on the part of Maharaja dalip Singh; and the said treaty has been this day ratified by the seal of the Right Honourable Sir Henry Hardinge, GCB, Governor-General, and by that of his Highness Maharaja Dalip Singh.

Done at Lahore this 9th day of March in the year of our Lord 1846 corresponding with the 10th day of Rabi-ul-Awal 1262 Hijri and ratified the same day.

APPENDIX 3

Treaty of Amritsar

(March 16, 1846)

Treaty between the British Government on the one part and Maharaja Gulab Singh of Jammu on the other, concluded on the part of the British Government by Frederick Currie, Esquire, and Brevet-Major Henry Montgomery Lawrence acting under the order of the Right Honourable Sir Henry Hardinge, GCB, one of her Britannic Majesty's Most Honourable Privy Council, Governor-General of the possessions of the East India Company, to direct and control all their affairs in the East Indies and by Maharaja Gulab Singh in person in 1846.

Article 1

The British Government transfers and makes over, for ever, in independent possession, to Maharaja Gulab Singh and heirs male of his body, all the hilly or mountainous country, with its dependencies, situated to the eastward of the river Indus and westward of the river Ravi, including Chamba and excluding Lahaul, being part of the territories ceded to the British Government by the Lahore State, according to the provisions of Article IV of the Treaty of Lahore dated 9th March 1846.

Article 2

The eastern boundary of the tract transferred by the foregoing Article to Maharaja Gulab Singh will laid down by Commissioners appointed by the British Government and Maharaja Gulab Singh respectively for that purpose, and shall be defined in a separate engagement after survey.

Article 3

In consideration of the transfer made to him and his heirs by the provisions of the foregoing Articles, Maharaja Gulab Singh will pay to the British Government the sum of seventy-five lakhs of rupees (Nanakshahi). Fifty lakhs to be paid on ratification of this Treaty, and twenty-five lakhs on or before the 1st October of the current year, AD 1846.

Article 4

The limits of the territories of Maharaja Gulab Singh shall not be at any time changed without the concurrence of the British Government.

Article 5

Maharaja Gulab Singh will refer to the Arbitration of the British Government any disputes or questions that may arise between himself and the Government of Lahore or any other neighbouring State, and will b abide by the decision of the British Government.

Article 6

Maharaja Gulab Singh engages for himself and his heirs to join, with the whole of his Military Forces, the British troops, when employed within the hills, or in the territories adjoining his possessions.

Article 7

Maharaja Gulab Singh engages never to take or retain in his service, any British subject, nor the subject of any European or American State, without the consent of the British Government.

Article 8

Maharaja Gulab Singh engages to respect, in regard to the territory transferred to him, the provisions of Articles V, VI, and VII of the separate Engagement between the British Government and the Lahore Durbar, dated 11th March 1846.

Article 9

The British Government will give its aid to Maharaja Gulab Singh in protecting his territories from external enemies.

Article 10

Maharaja Gulab Singh acknowledge the Supremacy of British Government, and will in token of such Supremacy present annually to the British Government one horse, twelve perfect shawl goats of approved breed (six male and six female), and three pairs of Cashmere shawls.

This Treaty consisting of ten Articles, has been this day settled by Frederick Currie, Esquire, and Brevet-Major Henry Montgomery

Lawrence, acting under the directions of the Right Honourable Sir Henry Hardinge, GCB, Governor-General, on the part of the British Government, and by Maharaja Gulab Singh in person, and the said Treaty has been this day ratified by the seal of the Right Honourable Sir Henry Hardinge, GCB, Governor-General.

Done at Amritsar, the sixteenth day of March, in the year of our Lord one thousand eight hundred and forty six, (1846) corresponding with the seventeenth day of Rabi-ul-Awal 1262 Hijri.

APPENDIX 4

Stand Still Agreement

Between: Maharaja and the Government of Pakistan

Telegram from Prime Minister, Kashmir State, to Sardar Abdur Rob Nishtor, States Relations Department, Karachi, dated 12th August 1947.

Jammu and Kashmir Government would welcome Stand Still Agreement with Pakistan on all matters on which these exist at present moment with outgoing British Indian Government. It is suggested that existing arrangements should continue pending settlement of details and formal execution of fresh agreement.

Telegram from Foreign Secretary, Government of Pakistan, Karachi to Prime Minister of Jammu and Kashmir, Srinagar, dated 15th August 1947.

Your telegram of the 12th, the Government of Pakistan agrees to have a Stand Still Agreement of Jammu and Kashmir for the continuance of the existing arrangements pending settlement of details and formal execution of fresh agreements.

APPENDIX 4A

Instrument of Accession of Jammu and Kashmir

Whereas the Indian Independence Act, 1947, provides that as from the fifteen day of August 1947, there shall be set up as independent dominion, known as India and that the Government of India Act, 1935, shall, with such omission, additions, adaptations and modifications as the Governor-General may by order specify be applicable to the dominion of India;

AND WHEREAS the Government of India Act, 1935 as so adapted by the Governor-General provides that an Indian State may accede to the dominion of India by an Instrument of Accession executed by the ruler thereof:

Now Therefore

I, Shriman Inder Mahendra Rajrajeshwar Maharajadhiraj Hari Singh, ruler of Jammu and Kashmir in the exercise of my sovereignty in and over my said State Do hereby execute this my Instrument of Accession, and

1. I hereby declare that I accede to the dominion of India with the Intent that the Governor-General of India, the dominion Legislature, the Federal Court and any other dominion authority established for the purposes of the dominion shall, by virtue of this my Instrument of Accession, but subject always to the terms therefore and for the purpose only of the dominion, exercise in relation to the State of Jammu and Kashmir (hereinafter referred to as 'this State') such functions may be vested in them by or under the Government of India Act, 1935 as in force in the dominion of India on the 15th Day of August

1947 (which Act as so in force is hereinafter referred to as 'the Act').

2. I hereby assume the obligation of ensuring that due effect is given to the provision of the Act within this State as they are applicable therein by virtue of this my Instrument of Accession.
3. I accept the matters specified in the schedules here to as the matters with respect to which the dominion Legislature may make laws for this State.
4. I hereby declare that I accede to the dominion of India on the assurance that if an agreement is made between the Governor-General and the ruler of this State where by any functions in relations to the administration in this State of any law of the dominion Legislature shall be exercised by the ruler of this State, then any such agreement shall be deemed to form part of this Instrument and shall be construed and have effect accordingly.
5. The terms of this my Instrument of Accession shall not be varied by any amendment of the Act or of the Indian Independence Act, 1947, unless such amendment is accepted by me by an Instrument supplementary to this Instrument.
6. Nothing in this Instrument shall empower the dominion Legislature to make any law for this State authorizing the compulsory acquisition of land for any purpose, but I hereby undertake that should the dominion for the purpose of dominion law which applies in this State deem it necessary to acquire any land I will at their request acquire the land at their expense or if the land belongs to me transfer it to them on such terms as may be agreed or in d default of agreement determined by an arbitrator to be appointed by the Chief Justice of India.
7. Nothing in this Instrument shall be deemed to be a commitment in any way as to acceptance of any future Constitution of India or to fetter my discretion to enter into arrangement with the Governments of India under any such future Constitution.
8. Nothing in this Instrument affects the continuance of my sovereignty in and over this State, or save as provided by or under this Instrument the exercise of any powers, authority and rights now enjoyed by me as ruler of this State or the validity of any law at present in force in this State.
9. I hereby declare that I execute this Instrument on behalf of this State and that any reference in this Instrument to me or to the

ruler of this State is to be construed as including a reference to my heirs and successors.

Given under my hand this 26th day of October Nineteen Forty Seven.

Sd/- Hari Singh
Jammu Palace
Maharajadhiraj of Jammu and Kashmir

I do hereby accept this Instrument of Accession.

Dated this twenty seventh day of October,
Nineteen hundred and forty seven.

Sd/- Mountbatten of Burma
27th October 1947 Governor-General of India

APPENDIX 5

Resolution of the United Nations Security Council
(August 13, 1948)

Resolution of the Commission of August 13, 1948:

The United Nations Commission for India and Pakistan. Having given careful consideration to the points of view expressed by the representatives of India and Pakistan regarding the situation in the State of Jammu and Kashmir; and

Being of the opinion that the prompt cessation of hostilities and the correction of conditions the continuance of which is likely to endanger international peace and security are essential to implementation of its endeavours to assist the Governments of India and Pakistan in effecting a final settlement of the situation;

Resolves to submit simultaneously to the Governments of India and Pakistan the following proposal:

Part I—Ceasefire Order

The Governments of India and Pakistan agree that their respective High Commands will issue separately and simultaneously a ceasefire order to apply to all forces under their control in the State of Jammu and Kashmir as of the earliest practicable date or dates to be mutually agreed upon within four days after these proposals have been accepted by both governments.

The High Commands of the India and Pakistani forces agree to refrain from taking any measures that might augment the military potential of the forces under their control in the State of Jammu and Kashmir.

(For the purpose of these proposals forces under their control shall be considered to include all forces, organized and unorganized, fighting or participating in hostilities on their respective sides).

The Commanders-in-Chief of the forces of India and Pakistan shall promptly confer regarding any necessary local changes in present dispositions which may facilitate the ceasefire.

In its discretion and as the Commission may find practicable, the Commission will appoint military observers who, under the authority of the Commission and with the co-operation of both Commands, will supervise the observance of the ceasefire order.

The Government of India and the Government of Pakistan agree to appeal to their respective peoples to assist in creating and maintaining an atmosphere favourable to the promotion of further negotiations.

Part II: Truce Agreement

Simultaneously with the acceptance of the proposal for the immediate cessation of hostilities as outlined in Part I, both governments accept the following principles as a basis for the formulation of a truce agreement, the details of which shall be worked out in discussion between their representatives and the Commission.

A

As the presence of troops of Pakistan in the territory of the State of Jammu and Kashmir constitutes a material change in the situation since it was represented by the Government of Pakistan before the Security Council, the Government of Pakistan agrees to withdraw its troops from that State.

The Government of Pakistan will use its best endeavour to secure the withdrawal from the State of Jammu and Kashmir of tribesman and Pakistani nationals not normally resident therein who have entered the State for the purpose of fighting.

Pending a final solution, the territory evacuated by the Pakistani troops will be administered by the local authorities under the surveillance of the Commission.

B

When the Commission shall have notified the Government of India that the tribesmen and Pakistani nationals referred to in part II, A, 2 hereof have withdrawn, thereby terminating the situation which was represented by the Government of India to the Security Council as having occasioned the presence of Indian forces in the State of Jammu and Kashmir, and further, that the Pakistani forces are being withdrawn from the State of Jammu and Kashmir, the Government of India agrees to begin to withdraw the bulk of its forces from that State in stages to be agreed upon with the Commission.

Pending the acceptance of the conditions for a final settlement of the situation in the State of Jammu and Kashmir, the Indian Government will maintain within the lines existing at the moment of the ceasefire the minimum strength of its forces which in agreement with the Commission are considered necessary to assist local authorities in the observance of law and order. The Commission will have observers stationed where it deems necessary.

The Government of India will undertake to ensure that the Government of the State of Jammu and Kashmir will take all measures within its power to make it publicly known that peace, law and order will be safeguarded and that all human and political rights will be guaranteed.

C

Upon signature, the full text of the truce agreement or a communique containing the principles thereof as agreed upon between the two governments and the Commission will be made public.

Part III

The Government of India and the Government of Pakistan reaffirm their wish that the future status of the State of Jammu and Kashmir shall be determined in accordance with the will of the people and to that end, upon acceptance of the truce agreement, both governments agree to enter into consultations with the Commission to determine fair and equitable conditions whereby such free expression will be assured.

APPENDIX 5A

Proclamation of Regent

Proclaimation for the State of Jammu and Kashmir

Dated the 25th November 1949

Whereas with the inauguration of the new Constitution for the Whole of India now being framed by the Constituent Assembly of India, the Government of India Act, 1935, which now governs the constitutional relationship between this State and the dominion of Indian will stand repealed;

AND WHEREAS, in the best interest of this State, which is closely linked with the rest of India by a community of interests in the economic, political and other fields, it is desirable that the constitutional, relationship established between this State and the dominion of India, should be continued as between this State and the contemplated Union of India; and the Constitution of India, which includes duly appointed representatives of this State, provides a suitable basis for doing so;

I now hereby declare and direct—

That the Constitution of India shortly to be adopted by the Constituent Assembly of India shall in so far as it is applicable to the State of Jammu and Kashmir, govern the constitutional relationship between this State and the contemplated Union of India and shall be enforced in the State by me, my heirs and successors in accordance with the tenor of its provisions; that the provisions of the said Constitution shall, as from the date of its commencement, supersede and abrogate all other constitutional provisions inconsistent therewith which are at present in force in this State.

Yuvraj Karan Singh.
Regent of Jammu and Kashmir

APPENDIX 6

The Azad Jammu and Kashmir Interim Constitution Act, 1974

(Act Number VIII of 1974)

Despite lapse of 58 years and the claim of living in the so-called Azad Kashmir, the people of that area are unfortunate of not having adopted or enacted a Constitution for themselves. The Government of Pakistan prepared a Constitution and authorized the President of the administration of that area to introduce the same, "in the Legislative Assembly in the Azad Jammu and Kashmir for consideration and Passage." The so-called Constitution is in fact a command of Pakistan Government to the Legislature of the Pakistan Administrated Area of Kashmir (PAAK) to adopt the said Constitution and pass it. The people of the area have not accepted the said Constitution as their own. The Constitution Act of 1974 has been applied with certain amendments and changes made in the earlier similar Act of 1970. It has been termed as an insult to freedom and to the free nations. The Plebiscite Front had termed the 1970 Act as a document of serfdom and rejected it. The front has published a book called *Naya Dam Laya* condemning the enforcement of such a Constitution in that area of that State. No Constituent Assembly has so far been summoned for the people of the area living across the line of control. Abdul Khaliq Ansari in his book *Northern Areas in the Court's Dock* published from Mirpur, Azad Kashmir, has stated that the Government of Pakistan had no authority or power to enforce the enactment of such a Constitution and that the imposition of that Constitution is a conspiracy to deprive the people of the area of having their own Constitution. He has further alleged that there cannot be any worst joke with the people of Kashmir and their freedom struggle as has been perpetuated by imposing the 1974 Constitution on the people of the State.

For the interest of the readers and for comparative study of the J&K Constitution, and this so-called Interim Constitution of 1974 of POJK some salient features of the latter are discussed hereunder.

This Constitution has repealed with certain modifications the previous Azad Jammu and Kashmir Government Act, 1970. In the preamble it is provided that the future status of the State of Jammu and Kashmir is yet to be determined in accordance with the freely expressed will of the people of the State through the democratic method of free and fair plebiscite under the auspices of the United Nations as envisaged in the UNCIP Resolutions adopted from time to time.

In the definition part 'State Subject' has been defined and which means a person for the time being residing in Azad Jammu and Kashmir or Pakistan who is a 'State Subject' as defined in the late Government of the State of Jammu and Kashmir Notification Number I-l/84, dated 20 April 1927, as amended from time to time.

Under Section 3, Islam has been recognised to be the State religion of Azad Jammu and Kashmir. Under Section 4, 18 Fundamental Rights have been guaranteed in the form that no person shall be deprived of liberty save in accordance with law. No person who is arrested shall be detained in custody without informing the grounds for such arrest nor shall he be denied the right to consult and be defended by a legal practitioner of his choice. The arrested person has to be produced before the magistrate. Slavery and force labour are prohibited. Protection against retrospective punishment has been guaranteed. Subject to reasonable restrictions imposed by law in the public interest every State Subject shall have the right to move freely throughout Azad Jammu and Kashmir Territory and to reside and settle in any part thereof. There is freedom of Assembly subject to certain restrictions and on the same lines freedom of association is guaranteed. There is freedom of trade, business or profession and freedom of speech. Fundamental Right number 10 grants freedom of religion which is reproduced hereunder: Subject to law, public order and morality—

(a) every State Subject has the right to profess and practice his religion; and

(b) every religious denomination and every sect thereof has the right to establish, maintain and manage its places of worship:

Provided that nothing contained in sub-paragraphs (a) and (b) shall be so construed as to abridge the authority to promulgate law which may prescribe prohibition or penalty for conversion from Islam or the act of converting or the attempt of converting a Muslim to some other religion.

Fundamental Right number 11 provides safeguard against taxation for purposes of any particular religion. Fundamental Right number 12 provides safeguard as to educational institutions in respect of religion etc. Fundamental Right number 13 says that every State Subject shall have the right to acquire, hold and dispose of property. Fundamental Right number 14 provides protection to property by saying that no person shall be deprived of his property save in accordance with law. Fundamental Right number 15 provides equality of State Subjects. Fundamental Right number 16 says that there is no discrimination in respect of access to public places on the ground of only of race, religion, caste, sex or place of birth, but nothing herein shall be deemed to prevent the making of any special provision for women. Under Fundamental Right number 17 it is provided that there shall be no discrimination in respect of any appointment on the ground only of race, religion caste or sex. Fundamental Right number 18 abolishes the untouchability.

Note: These Fundamental Rights are not available to the members of the defence services or to the forces charged with the maintenance of public order.

Section 5 says that there shall be a President of Azad Jammu and Kashmir who shall be elected by the Members of the Joint Sitting by the votes of majority of the total membership of the Joint sitting in such manner as may be prescribed. Under Section 6 the President can be removed by a joint sitting by the votes of the Members of the Assembly. by not less then 2/3rd of the total number of members of the joint sitting. The President has to act on the advice of the Prime Minister. Under Section 11 the President may appoint a Plebiscite adviser to advise the government in relation to the holding of a Plebiscite in the State of Jammu and Kashmir in terms of the UNCIP Resolutions. Under Section 13 the Prime Minister is to be elected by the votes of the majority of the total membership of the Assembly. Under Section 14 the Prime Minister appoints the Ministers from amongst the members of the Assembly. Under Section 16 the President appoints a qualified person to be Advocate-General.

Under Section 21 there shall be an Azad Jammu and Kashmir Council consisting of:

The Prime Minister of Pakistan;

The President;

Five members to be nominated by the Prime Minister of Pakistan from time to time from amongst Federal Ministers and members of Parliament;

The Prime Minister of Azad Jammu and Kashmir or a person nominated by him; and

Six members to be elected by the Assembly from amongst State Subjects in accordance with the system of proportional representation by means of the single transferable vote.

Section 22 States about the Legislative Assembly which consists of 48 members and amongst them 40 shall be elected directly on the basis of adult franchise and five shall be women who shall be elected by the directly elected members. One member shall be from amongst the Ulema-e-Din or Mushaikh and well versed with the teachings of Islam who shall be elected by the directly elected members. One member shall be from amongst the Jammu and Kashmir State Subjects residing abroad and shall be elected directly by the elected members and one member shall be from amongst the technocrats and other professionals shall also be elected by the directly elected members.

Section 29 envisages for the appointment of the Speaker of the Assembly. Under Section 32 a council of Islamic Ideology is contemplated and in case one third of the total number of members of the Assembly require they can refer to this council which is constituted under the constitution of the Islamic Republic of Pakistan for its advice as to any question whether a proposed law is or is not repugnant to the injunctions of the Islam. The Assembly has to consider the advice of this Islamic Council.

Section 42 says that there shall be constituted a Supreme Court of Azad Jammu and Kashmir which has to be the highest court of appeal and it consist of a Chief Justice and two other judges. Appeals lie to the Supreme Court from the judgements decrees final orders or sentences of the High Court of Azad Jammu and Kashmir. The decisions of the Supreme Court are binding on all other courts in Azad Jammu and Kashmir and its seat of sitting is at Muzaffarabad. Under Section 46 the High Court has the superintending control over all courts subordinate to it. Section 48 contemplates of setting up a Public Service Commission. Section 50 says that there shall be Election Commissioner and Section 50(a) says that, there shall be Auditor General. There are total 59 Sections in this Constitution.

APPENDIX 7

Constitution Application Orders of 1950

Particulars of the orders regarding the extensions of the relevant provisions of Indian Constitution to the State of Jammu and Kashmir

1. CONSTITUTION APPLICATION ORDERS OF 1950

The Constitution (Application to Jammu and Kashmir)

Order, 1950.

CO 10, dated the 26th January 1950: In exercise of the powers conferred by Clause (1) of Article 370 of the Constitution of India, the President, in consultation with the Government of the State of Jammu and Kashmir, is pleased to make the following order:

(1) This order may be called the Constitution (Application to Jammu and Kashmir) Order, 1950.

(2) It shall come into force at once.

For the purpose of Sub-Clause (b)(i) of Clause (1) of Article 370 of the Constitution, the matters specified in the First Schedule to this Order being matters in the Union List, are hereby declared to correspond to matters specified in the Instrument of Accession governing the accession of the State of Jammu and Kashmir to the dominion of India as the matters with regard to which the dominion Legislature may make laws for that State, and accordingly, the powers of Parliament to make laws for the State shall be limited to the matters specified in the said First Schedule.

In addition to the provisions of Article 1 and Article 370 of the Constitution, the only other provisions of the Constitution which shall apply in relation to the States of Jammu and Kashmir shall be those specified in the Second Schedule to this order, and shall so apply subject to the exceptions and modifications specified in the said Schedule.

THE FIRST SCHEDULE

(See Paragraph 2)

Note: The number of each entry in the Schedule is the number of the corresponding entry in the Union List.

Defence of India and every part thereof including preparation for defence.

Naval, military and air forces work, and other armed forces of the Union.

Delimitation of cantonment areas, local self-government in such areas, the Constitution and powers within such areas of Constitution and powers within such areas of cantonment authorities and the regulations of house accommodation (including the control of rents) in such areas.

Naval, military and air force works.

Arms, firearms, ammunition and explosives.

Atomic energy for the purpose of defence and mineral resources necessary for its production.

Preventive detention for reasons connected with defence, Foreign affairs or the security of India.

Foreign Affairs; all matters which bring the Union into relation with any foreign country.

Diplomatic, consular and trade representation.

United Nations Organisation.

Participation in international conferences, associations and other bodies and implementing of decision made there at.

Entering into treaties and agreements with foreign countries and implementing of treaties, agreements and conventions with foreign countries.

War and Peace.

Foreign jurisdiction.

Naturalization and aliens.

Extradition.

Admission into, and emigration and expulsion from, India, passport and visas.

Pilgrimages to places outside India.

Piracies and crimes committed on the high seas or in the air offence against the law of nations committed on land or on the high seas or in the air.

Railways, but as respects any railway owned by the State of Jammu and Kashmir, and either operated by that State or operated on its behalf otherwise than in accordance with a contract with the State by the Government of India, limited to the regulation thereof in respect of safety, maximum and minimum rates and fares, station and service terminal charges, interchange of traffic and the responsibility of the railway administration as carriers of goods and passengers and as respects any railway which is wholly situate within the State and does not form a continuous line of communication with a railway owned by the Government of India, whether of the same gauge or not, limited to the regulation thereof in respect of safety and the responsibility of the railway administration as carriers of goods and passengers.

Maritime shipping and navigation, including shipping and navigation on tidal waters, provision of education and training for the mercantile marine and regulation of such education and training provided by States and other agencies.

Lighthouses, including Lightships, beacon and other provision for the safety of shipping and aircraft.

Ports declared by or under law made by Parliament or existing law to be major ports, including their delimitation, and the Constitution and powers of port authorities therein.

Port quarantine, including hospitals, connected there with, seaman's and marine hospitals.

Airways, aircraft and air navigation, provision of aerodromes, regulation and organization of air traffic and of aerodromes, provision for aeronautical education and training and regulation of such education and training provided by States and other agencies.

Carriage of passengers and goods by railway, sea or air.

Posts and telegraphs, telephones, wireless, broadcasting and other like forms of communication.

Trade and commerce with foreign countries.

Elections to Parliament, and the offices of President and Vice President, the Election Commission.

Salaries and allowances of members of Parliament, the Chairman and Deputy Chairman of the Council of States, and the speaker and Deputy Speaker of the House of the people.

Powers, privilege and immunities of each House of Parliament and of the members and the communities of each house, enforcement of attendance of persons for giving evidence or producing documents before committee of Parliament or commissions appointed by Parliament.

Salaries and allowances of the Ministers for the Union, the salaries, allowances and right in respect of leave of absence and other conditions of service of the Comptroller and Auditor General.

Audit of the accounts of the Union.

Constitution and organisation of the Supreme Court and the fees taken therein, persons entitled to practice before the Supreme Court.

Extension of the powers and jurisdiction of members of a police belonging to any State to railway areas outside the State.

Offences against laws with respect to any of the matters aforesaid.

Inquiries and statistics for the purpose of any of the matters aforesaid.

Jurisdiction and powers of all courts, except the Supreme Court with respect to any of the matter aforesaid but, except with the consent of the State Government nor so as to confer any jurisdiction or powers upon any courts other than courts ordinarily exercising jurisdiction in, or in relation to, the State, admiralty jurisdiction.

Fees in respect of any of the matters aforesaid but not including fees taken in any court.

THE SECOND SCHEDULE

Some Articles of the Constitution from part V with modifications were made applicable while leaving out some Articles having no application in the State. Similarly, some Articles from Part XI, Part XV, Part XVI, Part XVII, Part XIX, Part XX, Part XXI, were made applicable with certain modifications leaving out majority of the rest. For full particulars the readers can see Gazette of India, extraordinary, Part II Section 3, Number III, dated the 14th May 1954.

Note: For detailed study a reference can be made to the Commentary on the Constitution of Jammu and Kashmir by Justice RP Sethi, former judge, Supreme Court of India.

APPENDIX 8

Conquerors of Ladakh

Raja Gulab Singh
The Founder of Jammu and Kashmir

Gulab Singh started his career in the Sikh army as a petty cavalry officer in 1809. At this time, the Jammu kingdom had broken into a score of discordant and fragile principalities. Bhaderwah and Kishtwar had declared Independence while Basholi, Bhadu and Jasrota had fallen under Sikh control. Principalities West of Chenab had severed relations, and the State of Jammu had lost its pre-eminence as the nucleus of the Dogra State.

Gulab Singh as a military commander rendered meritorious services to the Sikh Army during their campaigns on the Attock Fort and Garh-Dhamala in 1812. Soon afterwards (1815) he conquered Reasi and subdued the rebellions in the area. Thereafter, in the frontier campaigns of Maharaja Ranjit Singh from 1815-1819, Gulab Singh again played a significant part. In 1819, he once again led successful expeditions to Rajouri and in the subsequent year to Kishtwar. In these expeditions Gulab Singh displayed amazing speed of operations, bold stratagem, great diplomacy and administrative abilities. For his invaluable services and the need to control a rebellious his state, Maharaja Ranjit Singh placed the hill territories under his supervision and made him a Raja with Rajtilak being done on 16th June 1822.

The task of liberation and unification of the Jammu and Kashmir under a compact political unit was left to the courage, sagacity, and political genius of Gulab Singh. By 1834 all the major principalities of the Jammu State to include Bhimber, Chibhal and Poonch were amalgamated into the Dogra Kingdom. Thus, was laid the foundation of the future State of Jammu and Kashmir in the third decade of the 19th century under the leadership of Gulab Singh whose diplomatic skills even outwitted the seasoned British politicians.

Having become de-facto Ruler of these territories, he now sought to extend his conquest still further into the northern mountains. After consolidating his position in Kishtwar, he launched expeditions for the capture of Zanskar, Padar, Purig, Ladakh and Baltistan. He also sought to annex Tibet in which endeavour he met with disaster. Ultimately, when the Sikhs were defeated in the Anglo-Sikh wars (1845-46), Gulab Singh played an important part in bringing about the honourable settlement with the Lahore Durbar. Not only was he able to save the hill State, but also obtained the dominion of Kashmir Valley by an agreement with the British on 16th March 1846. Gulab Singh was thus formally recognised as the Maharaja of the newly created Jammu and Kashmir State. The credit for this consolidation will ever remain a monument of his political and diplomatic skills along with his military genius and a visionary approach.

A remarkable statement, he was the very best of a soldier, bold and energetic, yet wise and prudent always relying on his subtle political talent than force of arms. In the battlefield he was always self composed, watchful and prudent to the last degree. Besides personal valour and perseverance, he was blessed with the sagacity of choosing the right man for the right job. Having selected his men he reposed complete confidence in them. His associates seldom betrayed his trust. During his service the Sikh Army, he was able to select and gather around him soldiers of proven calibre in whom he had unreserved confidence, trust and treated them as friends and associates in return won their unswerving loyalty, devotion and readiness to sacrifice. Some of his most able Generals were Diwan Jawala Sahai, Wazir Zorawar Singh, Diwan Hari Chand, Diwan Lakhpat Rai, Mehta Basti Ram, Sheikh Saudagar, Wazir Ratnu, Sheikh Mohi-ud-Din and General Hoshiara. His brother Raja Dhian Singh and Suchet Singh were also talented and gave him unflinching cooperation. While most of his military success and greatness was due to the martial genius of Zorawar Singh, this happy companionship brought the Dogras great honour and territorial gains.

Zorawar
The Genius General

Zorawar hailed from Kahlur (Bilaspur) a small Rajput State in the Shivaliks. He was born in 1786 in a Rajput family, probably the Raja of Kahlur. At the age of 16 he killed his cousin over a property dispute and escaped to Haridwar. Here he happened to meet Rana Jaswant Singh, a Jagirdar of Marmethi in Doda and accompanied him to Kishtwar as a private servant. While at Kishtwar, he learnt and developed the art of Archery and swordsmanship in the traditional manner of the Rajputs. Soon afterwards, he joined the service as a private soldier with the Kiladar of Reasi. Being well acquainted with the country and the people around, he soon rendered himself invaluable and won the favour of the Kiladar. Finding him intelligent and resourceful, he became a messenger of the Kiladar to Gulab Singh. During one of these meetings Zorawar rendered invaluable administrative advice to Gulab Singh who appreciated the merit and accepted the proposal. In addition, he asked Zorawar to implement the scheme and appointed him Inspector of Commissariat of Supplies in all the forts of Jammu Region.

In April/May 1814, Gulab Singh had taken over Reasi and ordered a construction of a new fort called Bhimgarh. Zorawar was deputed for completion of the task. The local rebels besieged the fort. However, Zorawar defended the fort and foiled all attempts towards its capture. The sedition was stamped out and Zorawar was made incharge of the administration of Reasi. His success as administrator led to his quick rise until he became Governor with absolute power over the territories of Khushal and Kishtwar in 1821. When Gulab Singh became Jagirdar of Jammu in 1820, he entrusted Zorawar with the title of Wazir. This period saw Zorawar wining a number of provinces and hoarding wealth for his patron. He however, exercised the most rigid self denial towards himself. He had never drawn pay from the time of his first interview with the Raja, he wore no clothes but those sent to him by his master, even his wife and children he left dependent on the Raja for their daily subsistence. For this, he was rewarded with the administration of his master and unlimited confidence that was placed on him. He had another conspicuous peculiarity. He seldom wrote to the Raja to tell him of his success. The tributes and revenue collected were sent post-haste to Jammu and the Raja had to discover from it what new country his General had conquered.

Zorawar was not only a spectacular conqueror, but a keen organizer of his conquests too, Conquest and consolidation went hand in hand. His experience of civil and military affairs, administration and organizational necessities learnt while at Reasi stood him a good stead later. As Governor of Kishtwar, he had the entire land measured and the State revenue fixed at 50 percent of the produce. He introduced the Judicial reforms giving proof of his hold over civil affairs as well. He perfected the military machine of Raja Gulab Singh. The lofty mountains of Kishtwar provided an excellent area for training the Dogra Army in the high altitude warfare. His relentless essays for subduing high mountains and snowy valleys situated above 14000 feet rendered him an object of dread among the people living below. The people regarded his progress in operations with alarm and considered him to be inexorably cruel and pitiless while in pursuance of his aims and objects. Boldness of design and fearless execution of plans amongst the unscanned high plateaus and desolate frozen plains made him one of the rare Generals with considerable success in high altitude warfare. He was undoubtedly the main character in Gulab Singh's kingdom around which was built the Dogra romance. His greatness will always shine through the pages of Indian history as a great and noble warrior.

Basti Ram Mehta
Tactician Par-Excellence

Basti Ram belonged to the famous Mehta family of Kishtwar. His grandfather Mehta Amru held charge of military affairs in Kishtwar under Raja Mohammad Tegh Singh in 1821. Following the occupation of Kishtwar by Gulab Singh, Basti Ram joined the service and became a protege of Zorawar Singh. He raised the famous Fateh Shibji battalion (now 4 JAK Rif) sometime in 1834. Though the official raising of the Battalion has been accepted as 1837, Basti Ram had already raised the forerunner of the battalion before embarking on the Ladakhi campaign. This companionship between Zorawar and Basti Ram lasting 19 years not only brought great honour to the Dogras, but created unparalleled dynamics in the history of high altitude warfare. They matched each other to perfection in their quest for conquest, trust and loyalty to each other. Imagination and initiative and above all complete loyalty to Raja Gulab Singh.

Basti Ram was a tactician par excellence. He participated in all battles and campaigns of Zorawar with great distinction; In fact he was instrumental in turning the tide on numerous occasions. Whether in the crossing of the Suru river in improvised boats made out of leather skins, or crossing the mighty semi frozen Indus by establishing a floating log bridge, Basti Ram displayed phenomenal reserves of energy, resourcefulness and intuition so necessary to a tactician. He discovered new routes and methods to destroy enemy fortifications. He epitomized the new breed of the emerging middle rung leaders that had so far been conspicuous by its absence in the annals of Indian history. He had a flair for technology and was willing to experiment with tactical procedures. Probably, he gained the maximum out of British teachings and their concepts of conducting battle. On numerous occasions he led night attacks completely surprising the enemy. His routines even when in fortified defences were dependent on aggressive actions. He never allowed any siege to take hold and always kept options for breaking out (Chltang). Despite severe casualties in battle, sometimes as high as 50 percent, Basti Ram could always reorganize and launch an attack to the complete amazement of his opponent. This capability allowed him to bring out his battalion (over 250 soldiers) after the disaster at Toyo to the safety of Almora.

While always aggressive in his intent, Basti Ram at all stages of battle displayed a rarity of cool courage. Besides the gift of intuition, he was always thinking ahead and planning his next move. It was because of his great strength and endurance that Basti Ram not only lasted the entire campaign from 1834-41. But also returned safely to take part in the re-conquest of Ladakh. He subsequently became the Thanedar of Zanskar and later on the Governor of Ladakh. During this period he constructed a fort at Zanskar and a large number of office buildings at Leh. He also built the Grand Place at Leh called Haveli Basti Ram. He introduced various administrative reforms to include reappraisal of fixation of land revenue. For all that happened in 1841, he could never forgive the British. Enraged by a slight from a British Officer, he slew him, for which he was sent into imprisonment in the Andamans. Later, Gulab Singh secured his release. He had no issues and he adopted a Kashmiri Pandit boy Narpat Rai. During his Governorship he wrote his memoirs, which are valuable source of information on the Zorawar campaigns.

Basti Ram emerges as an excellent military leader with genuine timbre of greatness. His organizational capabilities, inspiring tactical and operational leadership, capability to ensure combat cohesiveness and the sheer tactical brilliance borne out of unbelievable resourcefulness and initiative, allowed the Dogra armies a foothold in the strategic heartland of Asia. It was his skills and those of some others of his time that an amorphous and loose organization of armies in India graduated to semi-autonomous units with regimental type of bonding. The credit for the Ladakh, Baltistan and Tibetan campaigns while undoubtedly would go to Zorawar, such great success could not have been achieved without outstanding and loyal officers such as Mehta Basti Ram.

APPENDIX 9

Constitution (Application to Jammu and Kashmir)

2. CO 48 The Constitution (Application to Jammu and Kashmir) Order, 1954.

   On 14 May 1954 vide SRO 1610 the President of India in exercise of the powers conferred by Clause (1) of Article 370 of the Constitution and with the concurrence of the Government of the State of Jammu and Kashmir made the above said order which came into force on 14 May 1954 and it supersede the Constitution (Application to Jammu and Kashmir) Order, 1950. More provisions of the Indian Constitution were made applicable with certain modifications/omissions to the State including the Fundamental Rights and exhaustive list is given in the order itself. The most salient feature of this order is that to Article 3 of the Indian Constitution the following further proviso was added:

   "Provided further that no Bill providing for increasing or diminishing the area of the State of Jammu and Kashmir or altering the name or boundary of that State shall be introduced in parliament without the consent of the legislature of the State." In sum and substance the financial integration was effected through this order besides the operations of customs, central excise, civil aviation, posts and telegraph extended. Fundamental Rights with certain modifications/omissions were made available to the State Subjects. These constitutional provisions were made available from 14 May 1954 to the 'State Subjects' but Article 3 of the Indian Constitution as stated above along with Article 7 were made applicable from 26 January 1950. In Article 7 of the Indian Constitution the following further proviso was added:

"Provided further that nothing in this Article shall apply to a permanent resident of the State of Jammu and Kashmir who, after having so migrated to the territory now included in Pakistan, returns to the territory of the State under a permit for resettlement in that State or permanent return issued by or under the authority of any law made by the Legislature of that State, and every such person shall be deemed to be a citizen of India."

3. On 13th February 1956 the President under SRO 322 and Order CO 51 made certain amendments in the above stated Constitution Application Order of 1954.
4. The President in 1958 made two orders in exercise of the powers conferred by Clause (1) of Article 370 of the Constitution and with the concurrence of the Government of Jammu and Kashmir made applicable some provisions of the Indian Constitution and also made some amendments in the already operative Articles of the Indian Constitution in the State. The most salient features are that All India Services—IAS and IPS—were introduced. Functions of Comptroller and Auditor General were extended.
5. Vide CO 57 dated 9th February 1959 and vide CO 59 dated 23rd April 1959, The Constitution (Application of Jammu and Kashmir) Amendments were made and the legislative entry relating to census was applied as a result of which the census of 1961 could for the first time be conducted under the Central Law.
6. The President in exercise of the powers conferred by Clause 1 of Article 370 of the Constitution issued two orders. Under GSR 98, CO 60 was issued on 26 January 1960 and this order was made applicable in the State from 26 January 1960 while the other order was issued under GSR 721 dated 22 June 1960 and made that order applicable from 22 June 1960. One of the salient feature of these order was that the Supreme Court was given the powers to give special leave to appeal from the decisions of the High Court of Jammu and Kashmir. The elections to either House and the Resolution of doubts and disputes relating to them were placed under the supervision of the Election Commission of India, although they continued to be conducted according to the laws of the State Legislature. Both these orders deal exhaustively with the amendments in relation to the application or omissions or modifications of the Articles made applicable in the State of Jammu and Kashmir.
7. Under GSR 633 and CO 62 dated 2nd May 1961 the President made the Constitution (Application to Jammu and Kashmir)

Amendment Order, 1961 and the result was that the legislative entry relating to industries, the control of which by the Union is declared by law to be expedient in public interest was applied to the State and it enabled the extension of the Industries (Development and Regulation) Act, 1951, subsequently.

8. Under GSR 1567 and CO 66 dated 25th September 1963 the President made certain amendments in the Indian Constitution and made them applicable from 25 September 1963.
9. In 1964, the President in exercise of the powers conferred by Clause (1) of Article 370 issued three order i.e., CO 69 on March 6, 1964; CO 70 and CO 71 dated 21st of December 1964 effecting amendments in certain entries of the schedules of the Constitution and specifically making applicable Articles 356 and 357 of the Indian Constitution to the State. In view of the amendment under CO 71 the State now could be brought under President's Rule.
10. In 1965, vide CO 72 dated 17 May 1965 and CO 74 dated 24 November 1965 the President amended the Indian Constitution with the concurrence of the State of Jammu and Kashmir and a number of legislative entries relating to the welfare of labour, trade unions, social security and social insurance etc were applied. As a result of this a number of Central labour laws were extended.
11. In 1966 vide CO 75 dated 29 June 1966 for the purposes of Article 55, the population of the State of Jammu and Kashmir was deemed to be 44 lakhs and ten thousand. In Article 81 of the Constitution after inserting some clauses the State was allotted six seats in the House of the people (Lok Sabha). In this manner the provisions of the Constitution relating to the direct election of the representatives to Lok Sabha were applied.
12. Vide CO 76 dated 13 February 1967 amendment was made in paragraph 2 of the Constitution (Application to Jammu and Kashmir) Order, 1954 and vide CO 77 dated 5 May 1967 certain entries in the Seventh Schedule of the Indian Constitution were amended. Further, vide CO 79 dated 11th August 1967 an amendment was made in para 2 of the Constitution (Application to Jammu and Kashmir) order, 1954. Furthermore, vide CO 80 dated 26 September 1967 certain entries were amended in the Seventh Schedule.
13. Vide CO 83 dated 9th January 1968 entry 72 of the Union list was applied in a modified form in relation to the appeals to be filed in the Supreme Court from the decisions of the State High Court in Election Petitions.

14. Vide CO 85 dated 17 February 1969, Article 248 and entry 97 of the union list (relating to residuary powers of the legislature) of the Constitution were applied in a modified form and as a consequence, the Unlawful Activities (Prevention) Act, 1967, was extended subsequently.
15. Vide CO 86 dated 31st March 1969 sub-paragraph (4) of paragraph (2) of the Constitution (Application to Jammu and Kashmir) Order, 1954 was amended.
16. In 1971, the President made three amendments in the Constitution and with the concurrence of the Government of the State of Jammu and Kashmir made them applicable. The first amendment was effected vide CO 89 dated 24 August 1971 and certain additions and omissions were made for the application of the Articles of the Indian Constitution stated therein. The second amendment was made vide CO 90 dated 8th November 1971 and entries in the seventh schedule were amended for J&K State. Vide CO 91 dated 29th November 1971 certain amendments were made including an amendment in Article 38. Article 226 which relates to the powers of the High Court to issue certain writs was made applicable. It is noted that State High Court under the State Constitution has also the power to issue the writs under Section 103 of the State Constitution.
17. In 1972 vide CO 92 dated 24 February 1972, CO 93 dated 6th May 1972 CO 94 dated 1st August 1972 and CO 95 dated 10 August 1972 amendments stated therein in relations to the Articles and the entries mentioned relating to the State were effected and entry number 60 of the Union List (relating to the sanctioning of cinematograph films) was applied on 24th February 1972.
18. In 1974, vide CO 97 dated 1st May 1974 and CO 98 dated 26th June 1974, the President amended the Indian Constitution and with the concurrence of the Government of the State of the Jammu and Kashmir made those amendments applicable to the State with the additions and omissions stated therein regarding the Articles and the entries specified therein.
19. In 1975, vide CO 100 dated 29th June 1975, CO 101 dated 23rd July 1975, the President with the concurrence of the State Government made applicable to the State the amended Articles and entries of the Constitution stated therein.
20. In 1976, vide CO 103 dated 22nd March 1976, CO 104 dated 25th May 1976, CO 105 dated 12th October 1976, CO 106 dated 31st December 1976 in the same manner the president amended the Articles and the entries with addition and omissions

stated therein and made them applicable to the State of Jammu and Kashmir.

21. In 1977, vide CO 108 dated 31st December 1977 certain entries of the Constitution were amended and made applicable to the State of Jammu and Kashmir.
22. In 1985, vide CO 122 dated 4th June 1985, CO 124 dated 4th December 1985 the Articles and the entries of the Schedules stated therein were amended and made applicable by the President of India with the concurrence of the Government of the State of Jammu and Kashmir.
23. In 1986, vide CO 129 dated 30th July 1986 the provisions after amendments in Article 249 stated in the amendment were made applicable to the State by the President with the concurrence of the State Government.
24. In 1989, vide CO 142 dated 7th October 1989 an order was passed by the President after consultation with the Governor of the State of Jammu and Kashmir and this order was called the Constitution (Jammu and Kashmir) scheduled tribes order 1989. In the relevant schedule the residents of the State belonging to 8 groups stated therein were declared as Scheduled Tribes.
25. In 1993, vide CO 151 dated 24th February 1993 Clause (4) of Article 356 was amended by the President with the concurrence of the Government of the State of Jammu and Kashmir.
26. In 1994, vide CO 154 dated 19th February 1994 the President with the concurrence of the Governor (during Governor's rule) of the State of Jammu and Kashmir amended sub-paragraph (13) (relating to part XVIII) and for words "four years the words five years were substituted."

APPENDIX 10

Tashkent Declaration

The Prime Minister of India and the President of Pakistan, having met at Tashkent and having discussed the existing relations between India and Pakistan hereby declare their firm resolve to restore normal and peaceful relations between their countries and to promote understanding and friendly relations between their peoples. They consider the attainment of these objectives of vital importance for the welfare of the 600 million people of India and Pakistan.

(i) The Prime Minister of India and the President of Pakistan agree that both sides will exert all efforts to create good neighbourly relations between India and Pakistan in accordance with the United Nations Charter. They affirm their obligation under the charter not to have recourse to force and to settle their disputes through peaceful means. They considered that the interests of peace in their region and particularly in the Indo-Pakistan sub-continent and indeed, the interests of the peoples of India and Pakistan were not served by the continuance of tension between the two countries. It was against this background that Jammu and Kashmir was discussed, and each of the sides set forth its respective positions.

(ii) The Prime Minister of India and the President of Pakistan have agreed that all armed personnel of the two countries shall be withdrawn not later than 25th February 1966 to the positions they held prior to 5th August 1965, and both sides shall observe the case-fire terms on the ceasefire line.

(iii) The Prime Minister of India and the President of Pakistan have agreed that relations between India and Pakistan shall be based on the principle of non-interference in the internal affairs of each other.

(iv) The Prime Minister of India and the President of Pakistan have agreed that both sides will discourage any propaganda directed against the other country and will encourage propaganda which promotes the development of friendly relations between the two countries.

(v) The Prime Minister of India and the President of Pakistan have agreed that the High Commissioner of India to Pakistan and the High Commissioner of Pakistan to India will return to their posts and that the normal functioning of diplomatic missions of both countries will be restored. Both governments shall observe the Vienna Convention of 1961 on Diplomatic Intercourse.

(vi) The Prime Minister of India and the President of Pakistan have agreed to consider measures towards the restoration of economic and trade relations, communications as well as cultural exchanges between India and Pakistan, and to take measures to implement the existing agreements between India and Pakistan.

(vii) The Prime Minister of India and the President of Pakistan have agreed that they will give instructions to their respective authorities to carry out the repatriation of the prisoners of war.

(viii) The Prime Minister of India and the President of Pakistan have agreed that the two sides will continue the discussions of questions relating to the problems of refugees and evictions/illegal immigrations. They also agreed that both sides will create conditions which will prevent the exodus of people. They further agree to discuss the return of the property and assets taken over by either side in connection with the conflict.

(ix) The Prime Minister of India and the President of Pakistan have agreed that the two sides will continue meetings both at highest and at other levels of matters of direct concern to both countries. Both sides have recognised the need to set up joint India-Pakistani bodies which will report to their governments in order to decide what further steps should be taken.

(x) The Prime Minister of India and the President of Pakistan record their feelings, deep appreciation and gratitude to the leaders of the Soviet Union, the Soviet Government and personally to the Chairman of the Council of Ministers of the USSR for their constructive, friendly and noble part in bringing about the present meeting which has resulted in mutually satisfactory results. They also express to the government and friendly people of Uzbekistan their sincere thankfulness for their overwhelming reception and generous hospitality.

They invite the Chairman of the Council of Ministers of the USSR to witness this declaration.

Prime Minister of India	President of Pakistan
Lal Bahadur Shastri	Mohammed Ayub Khan

Tashkent, 10 January 1966

APPENDIX 11

Kashmir Accord
(February 1975)

Agreed conclusions which led to Sheikh Mohammed Abdullah's accord with Mrs Indira Gandhi, Prime Minister, and his subsequent assumption of office as Chief Minister in February 1975.

1. The State of Jammu and Kashmir which is a constituent unit of the Union of India, shall, in its relation with the Union, continue to be governed by Article 370 of the Constitution of India.
2. The residuary powers of legislation shall remain with the State; however, Parliament will continue to have power to make laws relating to the prevention of activities directed towards disclaiming, questioning or disrupting the sovereignty and territorial integrity of India or bringing about secession of a part of the territory of India or secession of a part of the territory of India from the Union or causing insult to the Indian National Flag, the Indian National Anthem and the Constitution.
3. Where any provision of the Constitution of India had been applied to the State of Jammu and Kashmir with adaptations and modifications, such adaptations and modifications can be altered or repealed by an order of the President under Article 370, each individual proposal in this behalf being considered on its merits; but provisions of the Constitution of India already applied to the State of Jammu and Kashmir without adaptation or modification are unalterable.
4. With a view to assuring freedom to the State of Jammu and Kashmir to have its own legislation on matters like welfare measures, cultural matters, social security, personal law and procedural laws, in a manner suited to the special conditions in

the State, it is agreed that the State Government can review the laws made by Parliament or extended to the State after 1953 on any matter relatable to the concurrent list and may decide which of them, in its opinion, needs amendment or repeal. Thereafter, appropriate steps may be taken under Article 254 of the Constitution of India, the grant of Presidents's assent to such legislation would be sympathetically considered. The same approach would be adopted in regard to laws to be made by parliament in future under the Proviso to Clause 2 of the Article. The State Government shall be consulted regarding the application of any such law to the State and the views of the State Government shall receive the fullest consideration.

5. As an arrangement reciprocal to what has been provided under Article 368, a suitable modification of that Article as applied to the State should be made by Presidential order to the effect that no law made by the Legislature of the State of Jammu and Kashmir, seeking to make any change in or in the effect of any provision of Constitution of the State of Jammu and Kashmir relating to any of the undermentioned matters, shall take effect unless the Bill, having been reserved for the consideration of the President, receives his assent; the matters are:
   (a) the appointment, powers, functions, duties, privileges and immunities of the Governor and
   (b) the following matters relating to elections: the superintendence, direction and control of elections by the Election Commission of India, eligibility for inclusion in the electoral rolls without discrimination, adult suffrage and composition of the Legislative Council, being matters specified in Sections 138,139, 140 and 50 of the Constitution of the State of Jammu and Kashmir.

6. No agreement was possible on the question of nomenclature of the Governor and the Chief Minister and the matter is thereof remitted to the Principals.

Mirza Mohammad Afzal Beg — G Parthasarathi

New Delhi, November 13, 1974

APPENDIX 12

Judgement of the Supreme Court

IN THE SUPREME COURT OF INDIA
CIVIL APPELLATE JURISDICTION
CIVIL APPEAL NUMBER 3024 OF 1990

John Peter and others ...... Appellants

Versus

Mohan Lal Motial and others ...... Respondents

ORDER

This appeal is directed against the judgment and order of the High Court of Jammu and Kashmir dated December 21, 1989 dismissing the appellants revision made under Section 115 of the Code of Civil Procedure against the judgment and order of the District Judge, dated May 29, 1989.

The appellants filed a suit for declaration that the decree obtained by the respondents in the earlier suit was nullity. During the pendency of the suit an application for grant of interim injunction was made by the appellants, and the Trial Court issued an interim injunction restraining the respondents from executing the decree obtained by them. On appeal the District Judge held that the Trial Court was not justified in issuing interim injunction as the appellants had failed to make out a prima facie case and further the balance of convenience was also against them. The appellants filed revision against the District Judge's order before the High Court but that too was dismissed. The High Court instead of going into the facts held that the execution of a decree cannot constitute an injury within Rule 2, Sub-Rule 1 of Order 39 of the Code of Civil Procedure. On behalf of the appellants it is contended that the question whether execution of a decree constitute a legal injury within Rule 2 of Order 39 of the CPC should be considered and decided by this court as there is conflict of decisions on this question in the various High Courts. We do not consider it necessary to express any opinion on the question, as, in our opinion, the appellants are not entitled to interim injunction on facts.

The learned District Judge has recorded elaborate findings in holding that the appellants had failed to establish a prima facie case and the balance of convenience was also against them. The findings recorded by District Judge are findings of fact which could not be interfered with by the High Court. In this view, we uphold the order of the High Court although on facts and not on the question of law.

Under the decree which is disputed in the Suit, the respondents are entitled to realise and collect a sum of Rs 38,971.20 from the State through Collector, Jammu. The respondents are now free to collect the same but we direct that the respondents shall furnish security before the Trial Court that in the event of success of the appellants in the Suit, the respondents shall refund the said amount together with interest thereon at the rate of 12 per cent.

The appeal fails and is accordingly dismissed but there will be no order as to costs.

New Delhi — Sd/- ... CJI

November 28, 1991 — Sd/- ... (NM Kasliwal)

APPENDIX 13

Order for Shifting the Headquarters

HIGH COURT OF JAMMU AND KASHMIR AT JAMMU
ORDER NO: CJ/JB/02 OF 1999

Dated: 28/04/1999

The Headquarters of Justice GD Sharma is shifted to Srinagar. His Lordship shall sit at Srinagar with effect from 3rd May 1999 till further order.

Sd/-
(BHAWANI SINGH)
CHIEF JUSTICE

No: 2684-2701/RS
Dt: 29-4-1999

Copy of the above forwarded to the:

1-2. Registrar Judicial High Court Wing, Jammu/Srinagar.
3. Registrar Vigilance, High Court of J&K, Jammu.
4. Principal Secretary to Hon'ble the Chief Justice.
5-14. Private Secretary to Hon'ble Justice.
15-16. Court Officer High Court Wing, Jammu/Srinagar.
17-18. Section officers, Gazetted/Non-Gazetted Section

High Court Main Wing Jammu—for information and necessary action.

(MS Arshad)
Deputy Registrar (Adm)

APPENDIX 14

Interim Order Passed by the Author

HIGH COURT OF JAMMU AND KASHMIR AT JAMMU
PRESENT
THE HON'BLE JUSTICE GD SHARMA-J

OWP Number 101/1991

Sukesh Khajuria S/o late NN Khajuria R/o 190 Mohalla Gujjran, Jammu ... Petitioner.

vs

1. Union of India through Home Secretary New Delhi.
2. State of J&K through Home Secretary, Civil Secretariat, Jammu.
3. District Magistrate (DC) district Jammu.
4. Editor and Publisher, *The Times of India*, Bahadur Shah Zafar Marg, New Delhi - 2.
5. Dr Farooq Abdullah, former Chief Minister of J&K, Sher-i-Kashmir Bhawan, Jammu/New Delhi.

Respondents

Mr KL Sharma for the petitioner.

Mr Subash Bhat, Sr CGSC for respondent number 1.

Mrs Shahista Hakim, GA for respondents number 2 and 3.

Mr R Pant for respondent number 5.

Interim Order

Bhat prays that time may be granted to him for filing the application on behalf of respondent number 1. Mrs Hakim states that she had filed application for setting aside the ex parte proceedings initiated against respondent number 2 and 3 on 12 February 1999, but that application is not on the record of this petition. However, application filed on behalf of respondent number 5 (CMP Number 12/99) is on the record and counsel for the petitioner States that he has received its copy. As all the respondents except respondent number 4 are seeking adjournment for making submissions for setting aside the ex parte proceedings, it becomes necessary that respondent number 4 is also given a chance for appearance. Counsel for the petitioner is directed to provide fresh copy of the writ petition and office shall issue Registered Notice accompanied by that copy of the petition to respondent number 4. The registered cover be provided during the course of this week. Also notice shall go in ordinary mode. The Registry is directed to place on record the application filed by Mrs S Hakim, GA. In case the application is not traceable, then fresh application be filed in the office with advance copy to the counsel to the petitioner during the course of this week who shall file the objections.

Subash Bhat shall also provide copy of the application to KL Sharma, advocate who shall file the objections. List in the court on April 16, 1999 higher-up in the column.

Jammu — Sd/-

March 15, 1999 — Hon'ble (GD Sharma, J)

APPENDIX 15

Full Text of the Judgement

HIGH COURT OF JAMMU AND KASHMIR AT JAMMU
PRESENT
THE HON'BLE JUSTICE OP SHARMA-J

OWP Number 101/1991

Sukesh Khajuria S/o late NN Khajuria R/o 190 Mohalla Gujjran, Jammu ... Petitioner

vs

1. Union of India through Home Secretary New Delhi.
2. State of J&K through Home Secretary, Civil Secretariat, Jammu.
3. District Magistrate (DC) district Jammu.
4. Editor and Publisher *The Times of India*, Bahadur Shah Zafar Marg, New Delhi - 2.
5. Dr Farooq Abdullah, former Chief Minister of J&K, Sher-i-Kashmir Bhawan, Jammu/New Delhi.

Respondents

Petitioner(s) Mr KL Sharma, advocate.
M/s S Bhat Sr CGSC, S Hakim, GA, R Pant.

This writ petition came to be filed by a public spirited person questioning the bona fides of the statement attributed to Dr Farooq Abdullah after he had demitted the office of the Chief Minister of the State. The case of the petitioner is that the statement constituted commission of offence because by making this statement the respondent 5 had incited his partymen to take up arms against the State which is a cognizable offence.

The stand of the respondent—Dr Farooq Abdullah is that he never made such a statement as has been attributed to him. He has also alleged that the reporting has been made out of context and does not convey the real meaning.

Be that as it may, the short question is whether the statement as reported in the *The Times of India* dated 6th February 1990 reads as under:

> "Perhaps the most remarkable thing he said was that I directed my partymen to lie low, go across the border, get training in arms handling, do anything but do not get caught by Jagmohan. For the former Governor was out to wipe out the National Conference and the Congress from the State so that he could prop up other political parties and hand them over the power."

The statement as a whole has not been reproduced by the paper but even if it is admitted to be correct, the question is whether it constitutes a cognizable offence. The contention of Mr Sharma, appearing for the petitioner is that it constitutes an offence within the meaning of Section 121 of the Penal Code because of taking up the arms against the Government of India and waging war. I am afraid such an inference is not permissible or cannot be read into the statement. At best the statement amounts to asking the partymen to cross the border and get training in arms handling. A person who goes abroad commits an offence if he returns and is caught not otherwise. But if the statement as a whole is read then perhaps it was a defensive measure against the alleged threat and elimination of National Conference workers. The statement may be slanderous and may be malicious against the erstwhile Governor Jagmohan. However, it was for him to react and not for a public spirited person to come to his rescue. The portion of the statement reproduced above certainly does not disclose any commission of offence much less commission of cognizable offence. There is absolutely no substance in the petition which is dismissed.

05/10/1999 Sd/-

Hon'ble (OP Sharma) J

Narinder.

APPENDIX 16

List of Girdawaras and Patwaris of other districts posted in Jammu district

Sl No	*Name*	*Post*	*Distt*	*Place of posting*
1.	Prabu Lal Parihar	Girdawar	Doda	Gole
2.	Mohd Abbas Khan	do	Doda	Gole
3.	Amar Singh	do	Doda	Jammu
4.	Mohd Sahni	do	Doda	Nagrota
5.	Subhash Chander	Patwari	Poonch	Ploura-III
6.	Roshan Lal	do	Rajouri	Ambala
7	Rajinder Singh	do	Doda	Ploura-III
8.	Mkohd. Bashir	do	Poonch	Channi Himmat
9.	Shabir Ahmed	do	Poonch	Muthi
10	Tanvir Ahmed	do	Doda	Seri Pandita
11.	Riaz Ahmed	do	Doda	Dansal
12.	Mohd Taslem	do	Doda	Jammu
13.	Ghulam Rasool	do	Udhampur	Gangyal
14.	Karam D Khan	do	Poonch	Bahu Number 1
15.	Mohd Iqbal	do	Doda	Channi Rama
16.	Farooq Iqbal	do	Doda	Doli
17.	Shakeel Ahmed	do	Kathua	Jammu
18.	Suresh Kumar	do	Kathua	Jammu

19.	Mohd Aslam	do	Poonch	Kaink
20.	Ram Peshin	do	Kupwara	Khomansa
21.	Mushtaq	do	Doda	Thathar
22.	Mohd Shafi	do	Doda	Thanger
23	Mohd Salim	do	Udhampur	Palura Nagbani
24.	Mustaq Ahmed	do	Poonch	Palora, Jammu
25.	Shakti Kumar	do	Doda	Sunjwan (Addition)

Appendix 17

List of Terrorist Organisations Operating in the Kashmir Valley on or before January 19, 1990

1. J&K Liberation Front.
2. Hizb-ul-Mujahideen
3. Allah Tigers
4. Zia Tigers
5. Islamic Jamiat Tulba
6. Dukhtaraan-e-Millat (Women Wing)
7. Al Bader
8. Operation Balakote
9. Kashmir Freedom Army Guerilla Commando
10. Student Liberation Front.
11. Al-Khomeni
12. Hizbi Islami
13. Hizbullah
14. Kashmir Freedom Movement
15. Kashmir Liberation Front
16. J&K Liberation Organization
17. Peoples League
18. Islamic Students League
19. Al-Mehmoodi Mijahdin
20. Inquilabi Council

21. J&K Mahaji Azadi
22. Victory Commando Force
23. Islamic Jamurie Kashmir
24. J&K Inquilabi Front.
25. Kashmir Students Force
26. Peoples Liberation Organization
27. Tehrike-Jahad
28. All J&K Soldiers Field Front
29. Hizab-Ullah-Islamic-Jammohuria J&K
30. Free Army
31. Ikhwan-ul-Musalmaan
32. Kashmir Liberation Tiger
33. Peoples Front
34. Hiz-ul-Zaheed
35. National Muslim United Front
36. Al Hamzah
37. Ansor-ul-Islam
38. Muslim Student Front
39. Tehriqe Azadi
40. Jinnah Liberation Tiger
41. Kashmir Freedom KLF Wing
42. KVC
43. TF
44. Al Qarblaie Group

APPENDIX 18

Excerpts from the Memorandum of Buddhist Association

Excerpts from the Memorandum Submitted by Chhewang Rigzin, President Buddhist Association Ladakh to the Prime Minister of India on behalf of the people of Ladakh in 1949.

Sir,

On the eve of the grant of responsible government to the people of Kashmir by the Maharaja, we the Buddhists of Ladakh and adjoining areas presented to him through our representatives in the Praja Sabha a memorial, a copy of which was submitted to you for your information and consideration. This memorial, which was prompted by our apprehensions for our future, based on our bitter experience of nearly a century and a quarter, embodied the following proposals;

1. That he should govern us directly through legislative and administrative machinery, proposals for which would be submitted by us at his command.
2. That our homeland amalgamated with the Hindu majority parts of Jammu should form a separate province in which adequate safeguards should be provided for our distinctive rights and interests.
3. That we should be permitted to join east Punjab.

Proposals (1) originated in our respect for the obligation we owed to the ruler in view of the relation which bound us to him from the day of the conquest of our land by his great grandfather.

Proposals (2) emanated from the fact that we desire to see nothing more of the administrators from Kashmir, who had mostly governed us during the past to our utter ruin, that our cultural kinship with the Hindus encouraged us to expert a sympathetic regard for our interests and an assured future in a Hindu majority province, and finally that historically causes bound us to the people of Jammu and not to those Kashmir, for it was the Jammu Dogras who conquered Ladakh for Maharaja Gulab Singh in 1834, while Kashmir came into his possession in 1846, twelve years later.

All things considered, however, proposals number 1 and 2 were concessions to treaty obligations imposed on us by the Dogras conquest while proposal number 3 which would come into force on the failure of (1) and (2) was put forward because it is the only panacea for all our ills, the only guarantee for our future progress and development.

The Maharajadhiraj has so far vouchsafed to us no reply and we have taken this silence of his Highness to imply the relinquishment by him of his position as a party in respect of proposals (1) and (2) a tacit recognition of our right to choose our path independent of him. We have given most anxious thought to this grave problem and after mature deliberation arrived at the decision that we should straightaway merge with India.

That we have the right to determine our own future apart from other communities and people inhabiting the State and that we cannot be affected by the result of the forthcoming plebiscite in the event of its being favourable to Pakistan is evident from the following facts.

(1) We are a separate nation by all the tests—race, language, religion, culture—determining nationality. The only link connecting us with the other people of the State being the bond of common ruler. If the Indian National Congress could persuade itself to recognise the Muslims of India as a separate nation although they had so much in common with the other elements of the Indian population the Government of India should have no hesitation in recognising what is patent and incontrovertible fact in our case.

(2) Sheikh Mohammed Abdullah built up his case on the validity of the Treaty of Amritsar. This treaty bears upon the territory of Kashmir only. So while the ruler has consented to the transfer of his sovereign power in favour of all his people. Mohammad Abdullah and the people of Kashmir can, through this transference manage the affairs

of their country as they will. But they have not the power to appropriate against their will, a people, a separate nation, whom a separate treaty—the result of the war of 1834 twelve years anterior to the Treaty of Amritsar—bound to the ruler in a special relationship, in which, the people of Kashmir, who came into the picture later, naturally, did not figure at all.

(3) The right of self-determination claimed by us cannot be claimed with equal force by the people of Baltistan including Skardu and parts of Kargil tehsils predominantly peopled by Muslims as they are connected by ties of religion with the majority community in Jammu and Kashmir nor by the people of Gilgit who came under Dogra rule through conquest after the annexation of Kashmir and whom not only identity of religion but of race as well binds to the majority community of Jammu and Kashmir. It may be added that at the time of the conquest of Ladakh by Zorawar Singh, the entire area compromised under the tehsils of Leh and Kargil acknowledged the suzerainty of our Raja, while Baltistan had several Rajas of its own.

In case the result of the plebiscite is favourable to India, we simply go a step further than other people of State in seeking a closer union with that great country and in case it is otherwise, our verdict stands clear and unchallengeable. When we have decided to cut ourselves asunder from the State itself, the question of our forming part of Pakistan cannot arise at all.

We have indeed made up our minds to join India; but what is our decision worth until India is prepared to accept it? We certainly make the offer for our won advantage; we see in our merger with India the only hope of our salvation. But India, too, will not be loser by this arrangement. The tehsils of Leh alone covers 23,000 sq miles and, if we add to it the other areas predominantly inhabited by Boudhs viz, Zanskar, Bodhkharbo, Mulbek, Fukar, Darcik, Garcon, in Kargil tehsil and Padar in Kishtwar, the total acquisition territory to India will not probably measure less tan 33,000 sq miles. It is true that the whole of this area is undeveloped and most of it at present barren. But it must also be remembered that its economic potentialities are tremendous and in the hands of a great country like India is bound to be transformed into a smiling garden and a source of immense wealth and power. Its strategic and commercial importance too cannot be underrated. The teshil of Leh has Tibet and China among its neighbours land the town of Leh is the nerve centre of Central Asia trade.

There is nothing in our offer which is in any way incompatible with the high idealism which characteristics India international policy. We might even say in positive terms that it is perfectly consistent with it, for has not India repeatedly declared that it stands for the right of self-determination for all nations, and we are not a nation whose right of self-determination it should uphold and to whom it should extend the protection it seeks.

Tibet is a cultural daughter of India and we seek the bosom of that gracious mother to receive more nutriment for growth to our full stature in every way. She has given us what we prize above all other things. Our religion and culture and it is the experience of having been recipients of such precious gifts which encourage us to ask for more. The Ashoka wheel on her flag symbol of goodwill for all humanity and her concern for her culture. Will the great mother refuse to take to her arms one of her weakest and most forlorn land distressed children—child whom filial love impels to respond to the call.

Sir, the absence of a reply to our previous references on the subject of our future has depressed us greatly. We beseech you with all earnestness to be so kind as to vouchsafe a line in reply to this our last prayer on the subject.

APPENDIX 19

Report of Director-General of Police, J&K to National Human Rights Commission

Reference: Police Headquarters J&K Srinagar

Number: T&I/INT/NHRC—49/2003-1979-80

Dated: 27-7-2004

The Sr Supdt of Police
Fact Finding Cell, Investigation Division
National Human Rights Commission
Sardar Patel Bhawan, Sansad Marg
New-Delhi - 110001

Subject: Initiating inquiry under Section 14 R/W 17 of the protection of Human Rights Act, 1993.

Sir,

This has reference to case Number 91/9/2003-2004(1626) dated 3 October 2003 with regard to the subject cited above.

In this regard report obtained from concerned in 14 cases which have been registered in different districts of Jammu Zone are as under:

1. On a specific information police arrested 3 persons (1) Gh Hassan, S/o Rajab Sheikh, R/o Qudrena, (2) Gh Hassan, S/o Bahadur Chopan, R/o Chnager Marwah, and (3) Gh Mohd, S/o Abdul Gani Rather, R/o Teller Marwah. During their sustained interrogation they admitted their association with LeT and JeM outfit. At their instance, three radio sets, and a Chinese grenade were recovered, consequent upon their

involvement and recovery of weapons etc a case under FIR Number 6/02 U/S 121-A 212-B RPC 3/4/5/6 POTA was registered at P/S Marwah. Statements of confession were recorded U/S 32 POTA and accused were produced before CJM Doda along with their statements. The case was later completed as challenged and submitted for accord of sanction.

2. On 4 January 2002; CRPF personnel of 7th Bn posted at Pranoo Camp while conducting frisking/checking of a passenger bus bound for Bhaderwah from Doda recovered one plastic bag containing RDX which was taken into possession. In the meantime, CRPF Nafri posted at Police Post Bhalla launched search operation in Shahpur area and recovered one more bag containing RDX concealed near a bridge. Consequent upon this recovery, a case FIR Number 1/2002 U/S 216/120-B RPC, 3/4/5/POTA was registered at Police Station Bhaderwah. The case was completed as challenged against three accused persons (1) Farooq Ahmed, S/o Mohd Maqbool, R/o Gangatha; (2) Mohd Shafi, S/o Qutab Din, R/o Kahila Paranoo; and (3) Mohd Sharief, S/o Gh Mohd, R/o Shahpur, Paranoo, Distt. Doda.

The case is presently under process for rectifying some observations.

3. On 2 March 2002 information about presence of militants in the area of P/S Bhaderwah was received. Accordingly, a raid was conducted in the House of Ishtiaq Ali R/o Bhadroot, Bhaderwah and some photographs of militants were seized. Statements of witnesses were recorded U/S 161 CrPC and said Ishtiaq Ali was arrested. During his sustained interrogation, he admitted to be an Under Ground Worker (UGW) of HM outfit who used to motivate youths to join the ranks besides providing food and shelter to the militants. It was also established during investigation that militants Liaqat Bloch, Farooq Ahmed, Mohd Ashraf, Mohd Sadiq and Mohd Irshad also used to visit his house. The case was finally completed as challenged.
4. On 25 May 2002, a joint search operation was conducted in village Chhawa and Gurdanbala during which there was an exchange of fire resulting on spot death of constable Mohd Shakoor and one army Jawan, besides injuries to 4 others including 3 militants killed. During search operations one foreign militant Anjum Sohail @ Amir-ul-Islam S/o Younis Sohail R/o Kotli Pakistan Occupied Kashmir was arrested.

During his interrogation Mohd Hussain S/o Mohd Din R/o Gurdanbala was found associated with the arrested militants. Upon this a case FIR Number 178/2002 U/S 302, 307, 120-B, 121, 124-A RPC 7/25 AA, 4 POTA was registered at P/S Rajouri and said Mohd din was arrested on whose instance recovery of 20 kg explosives, 19 detonators, 6 remote control, 15 mtrs RDX wire was made. On the interrogation of Anjum Sohail search operation for recovery of Arms/Ammunition in Alla Thanamandi area was carried out. The militants who were hiding in the area fired upon the searching party resulting in death of Anjum Sohail. The investigation of the case was completed as challaned against accused Mohd Hussain only as the other three militants involved in the above killings had already died in the encounter. The case is under process for want of DM sanction.

5. On 29 January 2002; the Army (3rd Sikh) lodged a written report in P/S Rajouri that on specific information search operation was carried in the house of Gh Hussain @ Gani S/o Lal Din R/o Trala Jagir, Rajouri and recovery of 4 hand grenades, 3 rifle grenades, PE 3 A (Explosive) 10 bricks pieces 175 grams, each, HE-1,100 rounds of AK-47 rifle one poach combat was made which were concealed in a wooden box, Upon this a case FIR Number 32/02 U/S 4/27 AA, 4/5 ESA, 120-B 124-A RPC, 3 POTA was registered and the accused arrested. The statements of witnesses were recorded U/S 161 CrPC. However, during further investigation offence U/S 3 POTA and 4/5 ESA was not established against accused therefore same was deleted and on 17 January 2004, challan was produced in the Court of Law against accused Ghulam Hussain @ Gami, S/o Lal Din R/o Trala Jagir tehsil and district Rajouri where it is still sub-judice.

6. On 30 March 2002, PSI Vishal Sharma who was on duty near Raghunath Temple reported in P/S City about attack by terrorists on said temple. Police swung into action and an encounter took place, during which few civilians and security force jawans died on spot and some got injured. Upon this a case FIR Number 20/02 U/S 302, 307, 153-A, 120-B, 121 RPC, 3 POTA 2/3 PSA has been registered in Police Station City. During the course of investigation two persons Muneer Hussain S/o Dilavar Khan and Sarfaraz S/o Ataullah resident of Surankot, Poonch were arrested. The case is still under investigation.

7. On 15 June 2002; local police received information about hiding of militants in Mohalla Ustad Jammu. A raid was conducted resulting into the arrest of Zulfiqar Ali @ Abu Jihar, S/o Mohd Yaseen, R/o Gujranwala, Pakistan and Zakir Hussain, S/o Abu Jabar, R/o Mathori Doda. Arms/Ammunition were recovered from their possession. Upon this a case FIR Number 102/02 U/S 3/4/5 POTA was registered in P/S Pacca Danga, Jammu. During investigation four more terrorists Sajad Hussain, S/o Ab Gani, R/o Mohalla Ustad; Mohd Zamir, S/o Mohd Ashraf, R/o Fazalabad, Poonch; Shaowkat Ali, S/o Habid Joo, R/o Masalandara, Surankot and Masrat Hayat, S/o Mohd Hamid, R/o Fazalabad Poonch were arrested. The case was later completed as challaned and is pending for accord of government sanction.
8. On 20 January 2002; police party from Police Station, Pacca Danga, Jammu was on patrol duty when near Ramnagar More Manda, they observed two boys who on seeing the police party tried to escape from the spot, but the police party chased them and arrested. They were identified as Mohd Shafi Dar, S/o Mohd Akbar and Bashir Ahmed Sheikh, S/o Mohd Ramzam residents of Ahungam, Budgam. During their search one pistol, with 6 cartridges and 1 kg RDX was recovered. Upon this a case FIR Number 11/02 U/S 3/4/5 POTA, 4/5 ESA 7/25 IAA was registered in P/S Pacca Danga, Jammu. The case is still under investigation.
9. On 4 May 2002; SHO P/S Domana, tehsil Jammu along with his men during patrolling noticed movement of two persons in suspicious circumstances near Punnu-Di-Hati on Gajansoo Road. Both were arrested and identified as Bashir Ahmed Bhat, S/o Ab Ahad, R/o Panjwan, Kupwara and Basharat Majid Mir, S/o Ab Majid, R/o Kupwara. During their questioning they lead the recovery of one AK-56 rifle, 3 magazine containing 90 rounds one pistol along with magazines containing 14 rounds and 8 grenades. A case FIR Number 104/2002 U/S 3/4/5 POTA was registered at P/S Domana. The case was completed as challaned against the two accused persons and sent to government for accord of sanction. However, the same has been returned back with the directions to substitute the POTA offence by relevant provision of law which has been done now and same is being challaned in the Court of Law.
10. On 23 December 2001, SHO P/S Nowabad came to know that some terrorists are travelling in a Gypsy towards Jammu city

from Poonch along with Arms/Ammunition. Accordingly, a naka was organised and one Gypsy without displaying number plate was intercepted near Poonch House. During search five persons were found travelling in the Gypsy among them two were in police uniform armed with one AK-47 and one carbine and rest were in civies. These were later on identified as Mohd Latief Khan @ Qamer Ayoub S/o Gh, Rasool R/o Sowgam SPO of DPL Kupwara (2) Abdul Rahim Wani S/o Amir-ud-Din R/o Lolab Kupwara (3) Bashir Ahmed Wani SGCT DPL Kupwara (4) Malik Khan HC of 14 Bn JKAP and (5) Mohd Tahir S/o Sheikh Farman Ali R/o Surat Gujarat, Pakistan. All the accused persons were arrested and a case FIR Number 222/2001 U/S 3/4/5 POTA 4/5 ESA, 120-B RPC was registered at P/S Nowabad. From the search of vehicle, one hand grenade one packet of RDX were recovered. Further investigation revealed the recovery of Rs 2 lakh Indian currency, 2 grenades, 3½ kg RDX and one electronic detonator from the river Tawi. The case was later completed as challaned U/S 3/4/5 POTA 4/5 ESA 120-B RPC 2/3 E&IMCO and sent to government for accord of necessary sanction but subsequently the CD file of the case has been received back with some observations and the concerned supervisory officer has been directed to do the needful.

11. On 13 July 2002; terrorists attacked a Hindu Basti at Rajiv Nagar, Narwal and killed 29 civilians and also inflicted injuries to 29 others. A case FIR Number 134/02 U/S 302,307, 120-B, RPC, 3/4 POTA, 4/5 ESA 7/25 AA has been registered in Police Station Bahu Fort. During investigation eight accused persons (1) Mohd Abdullah code Abu Talha S/o Hassan Bakash R/o Multan, Pakistan; (2) Altaf Shah S/o Jamat Ali R/o Kellar Kotal, Poonch; (3) Maroof Khan S/o Ataullah Khan R/o Mohra Bachi, Surankot; (4) Muneer Hussain S/o Dilawar Hussain R/o Mohra Bachi; (5) Shabir Ahmed S/o Khadim Hussian R/o Sanai Surankot; (6) Sarfaraz Khan S/o Ataullah R/o Mohra Bachi, Surankot; (7) Mehmood Ahmed S/o Gh Mohd R/o Lathung, Surankot and (8) Kabir Din S/o Aziz-ud-Din R/o Lathmung have been arrested. The case was later completed as challaned and sent for obtaining necessary government sanction for launching prosecution against the accused persons which is still awaited.

12. During investigation of the case FIR Number 75/02 U/S 4/5 ESA of P/S Gandhinagar accused Surinder Singh @ Fouji,

S/o Hardeet Singh, R/o WN 1 Udhampur disclosed before ASI Amolik Singh the concealing of some Arms/Ammunitions near Sher-e-Kashmir Bridge. Accordingly on 7 April 2002 one AK-47 rifle with 2 magazines, two pistol with 3 magazines, 6 feet fuse wire, one detonator, 2 hand grenade, 2 PDD switch, 5 kg RDX were recovered at his disclosure. A case FIR Number 111/02 U/S 4/5 ESA 3/4/5 POTA, 7/25 AA has been registered in Police Station Gandhi Nagar. The subject admitted to be activists of KZF. The case was completed as challaned and submitted for sanction. However, the offence of POTA was not fully established against the accused person and finally the same was completed as challaned U/S 4/5 ESA, 7/24 AA and sent to DM Jammu for accord of sanction which is awaited.

13. On 31 January 2002; an explosion took place in Bus Stand Reasi resulting in death of some civilians and injuries to few. A case FIR Number 11/2002 U/S 302, 307, 121-A RPC, 3 PSSA, 3(2) 1 POTA was registered at P/S Reasi. Investigation of the case was finalized and sent to government for accord of sanction under POTA. However, the same has been returned back with the directions to substitute the POTA offence by relevant provisions of law. After doing the needful the case will be processed for sanction from District Magistrate before challan.

14. On 29 November 2001; information was received in P/S Bani that the militants have kidnapped Daya Ram, S/o Balia, R/o Badyal, Sham Lal, S/o Tej Ram, R/o Mangia and Rattan Chand, S/o Hari Om, R/o Badh Bhat and also snatched .303 rifles from the VDC member Bishan Dass, Bishan Lal, Hoshiar Singh and Rattan Singh. Upon this a case FIR Number 41/2001 U/S 3/4 POTA was registered. During investigation the dead body of one Daya Ram was recovered in presence of witnesses whose statements were recorded U/S 161 CrPC. On specific information about presence of the militants responsible for said kidnapping/killing another operation was launched in village Challoge. An encounter took place in which 2 militants got killed and 5 others arrested. They were identified as—1) Gias-ud-Din, S/o Shamas Din, R/o Khadwah; 2) Munwar Din, S/o Nissar Din, R/o Lawang; 3) Mohd Shafi, S/o Ab Qayoom, R/o Lawang Morah; 4) Mohd Yasin, S/o Sebu; 5) Mohd Ayaz, S/o Ab Qayoom, R/o Lawang Morh. During their sustained interrogation Mohd Yasin, S/o Bashir has not been found involved and accordingly he was released U/S 169 CrPC

whereas the case was prima facie proved against Shabir Ahmed; 2) Mohd Ashraf, S/o Munawar Din. Shah Nawaz, S/o Ab Jabar; Mohd Ayaz, S/o Din Mohd; Munawar Din, S/o Nassar Din; Gias Din, Mohd Ayaz U/S 364, 302, 120-B RPC, 7/25 AA, 3, 4 POTA and case completed as challaned which has been sent to DM for sanction.

Yours faithfully,
For Director-General of Police,
Jammu and Kashmir, Srinagar.

Copy to:

The Financial Commissioner, Head Department, J&K Srinagar for information with reference to Home Department letter Number Home/NHRC—01/2004 dated 14 January 2004.

Index